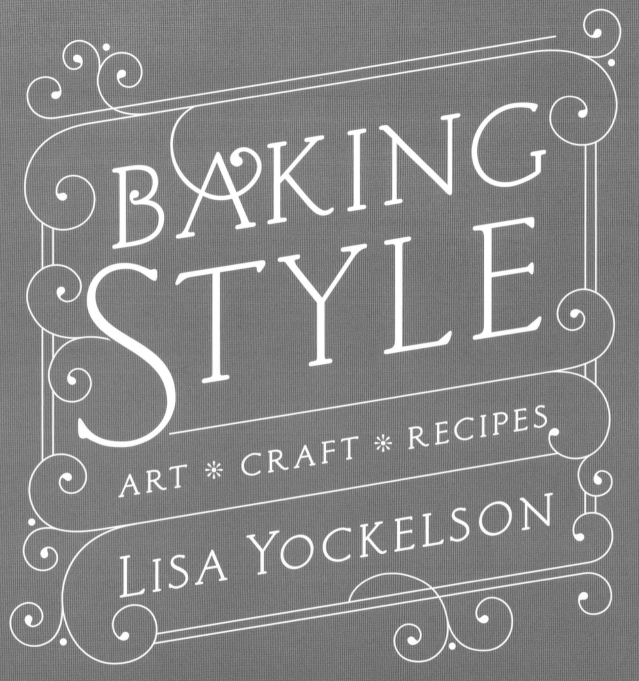

BAKING STYLE

ART ✳ CRAFT ✳ RECIPES

LISA YOCKELSON

WILEY

John Wiley & Sons, Inc.

*this baking diary is dedicated to
the life and times of my mother*

**Irene Ida Understine Yockelson
January 1, 1917—June 13, 1980**

*for the remarkable buttermilk chocolate cake
recipe, the memory of the meringue gâteau of
many layers cemented to the baking pans, and
the babka that broke the garbage disposal*

Contents

plain*old-fashioned* 112

very*naughty* 148

dreamy*regal* 186

texture*exquisite*   228

contour*fanciful*   266

intense*bold*   300

baking*Storybook*Epilogue   493

❋ ❋ ❋

Baking is one of the most engaging and animated of all of the kitchen arts. And the *style* of baking–the visual experience, the lure of the hands-on, the literary expression of it all–is as essential as what you whip in a mixing bowl, compose on a baking sheet, and relay into the oven.

Imagine: Velvety cake layers, covered with graceful swaths of frosting, and presented on a serene white platter. Mounds of cookie dough posing on a baking sheet, waiting to be turned into something chewy, crispy, or tenderly submissive. The heft of a pure butter cake presented on

an antique footed plate. Monster meringues, looming in big, crunchy shapes stacked like sweet oversized clouds.

This is baking style.

Combining 100 culinary essays and their accompanying recipes with more than 150 brilliant full-color photographs, Lisa Yockelson's *Baking Style* is her uniquely personal expression of the craft of baking. On each page of this beautiful and thoughtfully written volume, Lisa reveals her lifetime commitment to exacting but simple recipes for transforming a recipe into a luscious art.

A graduate of the London Cordon Bleu, Lisa Yockelson is an award-winning cookbook author whose articles, essays, and recipes have appeared in national publications such as *The Boston Globe*, *The Washington Post*, and *Gastronomica: The Journal of Food and Culture*. As a baking journalist who concentrates on classic and contemporary American as well as European regional baking specialties, Lisa has spent many professional years establishing techniques for flavor-building and texture-polishing baked goods–two compelling areas that form the groundwork for two previous books, *Baking by Flavor* and *ChocolateChocolate*.

Lisa welcomes your observations about *Baking Style* at www.bakingstylediary.com. In her diary-style blog, you will find recipes and essays, in addition to cookbook reports, notes on bakeware and ingredients, and reflections on all manner of in-vogue baking.

with*Gratitude*

For a baking cookbook to grow up, it needs significant feeding, not to mention steady and uncompromising attention. The recipes and prose that make up the book you now hold in your hands and take into the kitchen were pampered by my first-rate literary agent, Mickey Choate of The Choate Agency in Pelham, New York, and my wondrous editor, Pamela Chirls, executive editor, culinary arts, at John Wiley & Sons, Inc. This is our third book together. Thank you, Mickey and Pam, for your sensitivity and skill, and recognition of the exacting and sometimes complicated combination of meshing the how-tos of baking with a heady mix of art, storytelling, and diary entries.

For the visuals and expression of text, both the poetic camera-eye of Ben Fink and the creative expertise of Mucca Design are responsible for furnishing "the look" to my fine-tuned pages of notes, recipes, essays, collections, baking for the visuals, and memorabilia, culminating in a published work by vividly capturing my baking personality. Ben, your camera is merely an extension of the remarkable level of fine art brought to your work. At Mucca Design, Erica Heitman-Ford and Melissa Chang are praiseworthy for their collective imagination and ability to translate my baking philosophy into a particularly gorgeous volume; it was a great professional moment of mine to be present at the design launch for this book. Matteo Bologna, the guiding spirit of Mucca Design, brought his own sense of style and artistic sensibility to this project. Ava Wilder, my former production editor, contributed a kind of laser-like vision to the material in this book, a trait carried on—beautifully—by Jacqueline Beach, my new production editor. Jackie is both a caring professional and a detail-oriented editor—two admirable qualities. Deborah Weiss Geline, the sharp-penciled whiz of a copyeditor who insightfully worked her way through *Baking Style,* should be inducted into the copyeditor hall of fame for her understanding and exceptional skill. Lisa Story, the typesetter and updater, made sure that the production transition from stage to stage was accomplished seamlessly (a daunting task if there ever was one). The work of Polly

Cone and Rochelle Palermo, my proofreaders, is admirable for their keen reading of the text and recipes. Marilyn Flaig, my indexer, created a detailed overview of this book's sizeable contents.

My life is enriched with colleagues who edit, review, write, and create, and I have depended on their camaraderie for years: food and travel editor Joe Yonan of *The Washington Post,* deputy food editor Bonnie Benwick of *The Washington Post,* multiplatform editor Jane Touzalin of *The Washington Post,* food editor Sheryl Julian of *The Boston Globe,* and founding editor Darra Goldstein of *Gastronomica: The Journal of Food and Culture.* The exceptional works of baking and dessert authors Rose Levy Beranbaum (author of *The Cake Bible* and *Rose's Heavenly Cakes,* among other works) and Flo Braker (author of *The Simple Art of Perfect Baking* and *Baking for All Occasions,* among other works) continue to inspire and delight both home and professional bakers on a daily basis, and each shares my enthusiasm for every large and small detail relating to batters and doughs: you are thoughtful, supportive, and spirited friends. The two of you, unknowingly, were my mentors long before our paths crossed, friendships developed, and bonds that great bakers make took place. Our publishing and baking lives have interlocked in the most openhearted of ways. Greg Patent's historical research (in his cookbook *A Baker's Odyssey*) has become a new model for bakers and, Greg, it is divine to have you in the fold. Equipment and ingredient specialist Nancy Pollard of La Cuisine—The Cook's Resource in Alexandria, Virginia, refines and hand-selects the to-the-brim stock in the charming space that is her store as tightly as I do my recipes.

More than thirty years ago, Marcella Hazan, the esteemed author who, through words and recipes, so eloquently brought the Italian art and culture of food to the American table, generously offered advice on cookbook writing, in addition to pointing me to a literary agent for representation in the field. Years later, thinking back on that week in Italy that galvanized my career, I cherish—even more—the support. Marcella, your kindness and your work have long been an inspiration to me.

For unraveling the hows and whys of the chemistry of baking, I turn to the peerless scientific minds of Robert Wolke and Shirley Corriher. Your help and research have unlocked many kitchen mysteries for me. Robert Wolke, author of *What Einstein Told His Cook: Kitchen Science Explained,* helped me understand the effects of the potency of leavening agents relative to filling baking pans with batters and doughs, and reviewed an important paragraph that explains the cycle of time-lapse changes through which a batter or reasonably soft dough travels. Shirley Corriher, author of *CookWise* and *BakeWise,* offered her usual—and enviable!—razor-sharp insight on cake flour, all-purpose flour, and baker's ammonia so that I, in turn, could communicate the essentials to you.

John George, my gifted and patient computer professional (whose "real" work is in the realm of health care technology as director at CGI) and his talented life partner Peter Maye (director of print and interactive production at Discovery Communications) are esteemed neighbors as well as bake-off experts for almost every confection in this book. John and Peter, the two of you are a genuine delight. And Isaac (the newest member of the George-Maye household), you and I have had such fun baking and decorating chocolate chip cookies together and, of course, eating them while they're warm and gooey.

On a personal note, it is important for me to tell you about the people under eighteen years of age who touch my work and life. Alexander Choate, Clara Choate, Isabelle Chirls, Julia Chirls, and Allix Chirls, the offspring—respectively—of my literary agent and editor, are great taste-testers of the goodies emanating from my cookbooks, having taught me such things as not to put nutmeg in the vanilla cupcake batter, to add lots of chocolate candy decorations to the tops of cookies, to make the frosting for sheet cakes really fluffy (that is, load it on), and to delete the "funny" spices in the banana cake. (Isabelle: I know how much you love butter, and think that you'll agree with me that this is the buttery-est book ever. Clara: the cupcake iced with pink frosting—my *blushing birthday girl*—is in your honor. Allix: thank you for really loving my *a very*

vanilla bread, which you ate in thirty-six hours—in its entirety. Alexander: I am happy to know that my *favorite chocolate sheet cake* is your favorite, too. And Julia: it's wonderful that you are turning your creative interests to baking and decorating cookies, and learning all about presentation and plating.)

Of no less importance, these longtime friends and associates have been there at diverse life moments and, in ways too complex to describe, conform to the dictionary definition of "friend": Sanford Ain, Larissa Avendano, Laurie Bell, baking-sister-in-pearls Rose Levy Beranbaum (again) and Elliot Beranbaum, Colleen Birmingham, Flo Braker (again), Peter Brett, Joan Burka, Ellen Ficklen, Mindy Galke Fletcher, Yvonne Fyan, Alexandra Greeley, Sarah Hanks, Marcella Hazan (again) and Victor Hazan, Alice Louise Horn, Michèle Jacobs, Gregory Johnson, Susan Lampton and David Michael Lampton, everyone at Landscape Projects, Inc., Daniel Magruder, Brian McBride, Sallee McCarthy, Laurent Merdy, Milite Ogbit, Elizabeth Parvu, Dorothy Patent and Greg Patent (again), Merle Postal, Frank Babb Randolph, Marie Romejko, Renee Schettler Rossi, Anna Saint John, Lorna Sass, Lisa Stark, Judith Sutton, Alan Walding, Kenneth Wirsching, and Woody Wolston.

As well, my admiration goes to a certain person of rare skill and exceptional kindness, for your gift of friendship and overarching intelligence over the years. (You know who you are, sir.)

The transit of time snatched away—abruptly and in what seems like several lifetimes ago—my parents, Irene and Bernard Yockelson; great-grandmother Rebecca Levy; grandmother Lillian Levy Yockelson; and uncle Wilbert Yockelson too soon in their respective life spans and so many years before they had the opportunity to know me or my baking studies on any significant level—if at all. My mother's and grandmother's recipes—even those that seem so peculiar (this is lovingly written)—continue to have an impact on my present-day work. Though departed long ago, each left his or her own bookmark in and on my life, and so this volume honors the historical pages of their lives.

✳ ✳ ✳

bakingStylePrelude

an introduction to cultivating your own baking style

A ball of yeast-risen dough is responsive to the touch. Cake layers, velvety and moist, are ready for covering with simple but graceful swaths of frosting. Mounds of cookie dough pose on a baking sheet, their creamy essence and uniquely individual figures waiting to be transformed into something chewy, crispy, or tenderly submissive. The modest but pure heft of a butter cake beams from a footed antique cake plate. Monster meringues, looming in big, crunchy shapes are stacked like sweet oversize clouds on a platter.

Baking is, perhaps, one of the most engaging and animated of all of the kitchen arts. And the aesthetic of baking—the visual experience, the lure of the hands-on, the literary expression of it all—is as important as what you actually stir, whip, or beat in a mixing bowl, pour into a pan or compose on a baking sheet, and relay into the oven. The best of it promotes a natural kind of exquisiteness, moving from all kinds of batters and doughs to the parade of frostings, toppings, fillings, and flavor compounds that comprise them.

Baking Style captures, in one hundred essays, a rich assortment of partnering recipes that underscore the craft and scent of baking at home. (The essays are detailed, and because of this, a recipe is presented without a head note; the nuances of each recipe can be found in the context of the companion essay.) This volume is my personal storybook, a kind of how-to scrapbook that invites you to take in the art of baking as the evocative, gorgeous, and creative lifestyle that it is—a delicious kind of pursuit for feeding every one of the senses.

The architecture of *Baking Style* is built on essays that offer a magnifying-glass look at a particular baking recipe—its design, reasons for interest, and composition—embracing the quirks along the way. Each essay is accompanied by one or more primary recipes and appropriate supplementary recipes as needed. An essay, essentially its own package that evolves into a narrative of how something came to be in my hands, is one of my favorite ways of enlightening and teaching. Through it, I can tell you what has inspired, astonished, or utterly badgered me as I bake. The stirrings, backstage baking stories, and all-encompassing love of the process shape the groundwork for my choice of recipes passed along in this diary format.

In my baking life (and in the flow of life that surrounds it), I continue to follow a certain wisdom: that you have to decide which pieces of the past you want to bring with you—to share and to teach to readers and fellow bakers. These "pieces" are my favorite doughs and batters that spring to life again and again. I want to dish out the recipes for the most delicious things I bake frequently—those bar, hand-formed, and drop cookies; casual tarts; yeast-raised breads, large and small; puffs, muffins, and scones; waffles and crêpes; tea cakes, breakfast slices, and buttery squares; as well as big cakes and those smaller playful darlings of the baking world, cupcakes. The recipes—in addition to their accompanying observations—that make up this work have been hard-won objects of desire. Certainly, the formulas have changed over the years as different ingredients have become available, my past recipes have been enlivened, and studies into the various subject areas were affected by ongoing research into building flavor and texture. In essence, a good part of my baking life is represented in the recipes that compose this book, an edible sweet-and-savory trip for you to read and enjoy.

baking*Elements*

The ingredients of baking are classic: fundamental to their particular place in a recipe is their function and quantity, both of which work in concert to develop flavor, texture, structure, and, ultimately, design.

A slice of feathery, nearly fluffy butter cake, the tender crunch of a shortbread cookie, the craggy flakiness of a scone—these qualities inherent in each sweet are the direct result of the interplay of ingredients and the method used to accomplish their baked form, inside and out.

The principal staples—butter, sugar, flour, eggs, liquid and soft dairy, leavening, and flavorings—are the working cornerstones of the baking kitchen. The integrity of the basic components relates directly to quality and, with regard to taste, is—very simply—the difference between just-average and absolutely luscious.

Consider the following listings—including their applications and my preferences—a basic reference tool to the ingredients used in the recipes that make up this volume.

Flour provides structure to a batter or dough and works with the fat and liquid to develop and achieve a textural "crumb." Bleached all-purpose flour (preferably Gold Medal) is stronger than cake flour and weaker than bread flour as it contains about 12 grams of protein in 1 cup. Cake flour (preferably Swans Down or Softasilk) is designated as a "soft" flour due to a lower percentage of gluten and contains about 8 grams of protein in 1 cup; it creates a tender-textured batter or dough, a silky crumb, and can be combined with flour of a higher protein content for use in some batters and doughs. With an elevated protein content of 16 grams of protein in 1 cup, unbleached all-purpose flour (preferably King Arthur) excels when used in sweet and savory yeast-risen doughs and can be mixed with flour of a slightly lower protein content for use in some sweet yeast-based recipes. Whole wheat flour (preferably King Arthur 100% Organic Whole Wheat Flour), with 16 grams of protein in 1 cup, contributes great grainy, wheaty flavor to batters

and doughs; it can be mixed with unbleached all-purpose flour for use in yeast-risen doughs and with all-purpose flour for use in quick breads, such as for biscuits, scones, soda bread, and muffins.

Cornstarch (preferably Argo or Bob's Red Mill) is a white, finely milled starch used to thicken stove top–cooked puddings, pastry creams and other custard fillings, and some cooked toppings and glazes. Also, it can appear as an occasional ingredient (replacing a portion of the all-purpose or cake flour) in a tender butter cookie dough.

Rolled oats (such as Quaker Old Fashioned Oats, Quaker Quick Cooking Oats, or Bob's Red Mill Extra Thick Rolled Oats) are used as an ingredient in cookie doughs, sweet and savory yeast-raised breads (sometimes with a presoak in a warm or hot liquid, such as water, milk, or buttermilk), and in cake batters (usually with a presoak in hot or boiling water).

Corn meal (such as Arrowhead Mills Organic Yellow Corn Meal or Quaker Yellow Corn Meal) is used in quick-bread batters, in some cake batters and cookie doughs, and in some yeast doughs, along with a certain quantity of all-purpose flour. It contributes to the overall texture (while playing a smaller role in building volume) and conveys an earthy corn flavor. Stone-ground corn meal yields denser, grittier, more intensely fragrant breads, whereas fine corn meal produces lighter breads and more delicately textured cakes and cookies.

Rising agents—baking powder, baking soda, and yeast—are responsible for establishing volume and developing structure in a batter or dough, affecting its overall density and finished height. Double-acting baking powder (preferably Rumford) discharges gas both prior to and during the baking process; this leavening agent is composed of monocalcium phosphate, bicarbonate of soda, and cornstarch. Baking soda (preferably Arm & Hammer) is composed of sodium bicarbonate and, in the presence of an acid-based ingredient (such as an acid-based liquid, acid-based soft dairy ingredient, or acid-based sweetener or flavoring agent), discharges carbon dioxide, creating that all-important "lift" of a batter or dough prior to and during the baking process. Active dry yeast (preferably Fleischmann's or Hodgson Mill) can be defined as a microscopic organism that generates fermentation, a process whereby the enzymes produced convert sugar into carbon dioxide (and alcohol, which dissipates during the baking process). Yeast establishes volume in a batter or dough, initiates the fermentation process, builds flavor, establishes the overall height of a risen batter or dough, and contributes to establishing its fully baked crumb. It's a good idea to be respectful of the nature and capacity of a rising agent by using fresh baking powder not more than three months old (once opened) and active dry yeast a month or two before the suggested pull date on the packet or jar. Baking soda should be stored in an airtight container, where it will keep for six months. None of these agents lasts forever, and old, past-their-prime leavening agents definitely compromise the quality and construction of the finished product.

Salt, preferably ultra-fine or extra-fine sea salt, is both a flavoring agent and flavor accentuator. It develops flavor in a batter, dough, filling, or frosting in the presence of granulated sugar or other sweetening agents, such as molasses, balances out the sweet quotient, and regulates the process of fermentation in a yeast dough. (A few favorite salts are: Masserie diSant'eramo Sale Marino Fino, Lima Atlantic Sea Salt, Tidman's Sea Salt Fine, and Cerulean Seas Fine Sea Salt.) The absence of salt creates flat-tasting baked goods. Unless dietary restrictions demand otherwise, add the recommended amount of salt listed in a recipe.

Butter acts as the primary (or secondary) fat component of a dough or batter, filling, sauce, icing, glaze, or frosting. Technically, butter is called a "shortening" because it abbreviates, or reduces, the length of the gluten chain (the filaments or strands), and so reduces textural firmness in a batter or dough. It is composed mostly of fat (about 80 percent) and contains a certain amount of water (about 15 percent), along with stray milk solids, proteins, and minerals (constituting a total of about 5 percent). Butter creates tenderness, contributes flavor, enriches the crumb, imparts moisture, and encourages leavening action in a batter when creamed on its own or with nearly any type of sugar. (A few favorite butters are: Organic Valley European Style Cultured Unsalted Butter, Cabot Natural Creamery Unsalted Butter, Celles sur Belle, Isigny Ste. Mère Beurre Cru de Normandie, Kate's Homemade Butter Unsalted, Kate's Homemade Butter Sea Salted, Beurre Président Unsalted Butter from France, Plugrá European Style Unsalted Butter, and Lurpak Danish Butter Unsalted.)

Clarified butter, melted and brushed on the interior surface of bakeware, is a peerless preparatory ingredient. I wish all bakers would use it instead of softened butter. It is ideal for filming a crêpe pan before swirling in the batter and for brushing on unbaked and baked yeast rolls, as it adds pure, unblemished flavor. Be advised: if you use melted butter that has not been treated to the clarifying process, the attendant milk solids usually darken or burn, creating nasty little blotches.

To make clarified butter, cut ¾ pound (3 sticks) unsalted butter into chunks. Place the chunks in a heavy, medium-size saucepan (preferably enameled cast iron) and set over moderate heat to melt them. Raise the heat to moderately high. When the melted butter begins to bubble, let it gurgle (a low, only slightly enthusiastic bubble) for 30 seconds, then remove the saucepan from the heat and place it on a heatproof surface. Using an impeccably dry metal spoon, skim off and discard the white surface foam. The entire surface should be clean enough so that you can readily see the upper-level golden butter and the milky solids at the bottom of the saucepan. If necessary, use a folded paper towel to pick up any stray bits or patches of foam. Wash and dry the spoon. Angle the saucepan slightly to one side and spoon out only the clear, liquefied butter into a clean, dry, heatproof storage container. The milky residue at the bottom of the pan should be discarded. Cool the butter, then cover tightly and refrigerate. When thoroughly chilled, it will solidify. To use it, portion some out with a palette knife, then gently melt it in a small, heavy saucepan (preferably enameled cast iron). Clarified butter will keep for up to 4 weeks, refrigerated in a covered container.

Sugar develops and cultivates texture when creamed with butter; imparts moisture; contributes to the coloration of the baked crust/surface of cakes, cookies, quick breads and yeast-risen breads; and becomes an important nutrient in the presence of yeast. Its primary use is for sweetening batters and doughs, toppings, and some frostings or glazes; its secondary use is for sprinkling on the top of unbaked batters or over the top of a baked confection, such as shortbread. Free-flowing granulated sugar should be sifted before measuring to hold back any small hardened pellets of sugar; this may seem like a conceit, but the resulting batter or dough is truly superior if the little bits are strained out. Superfine sugar, with its ultra-fine granulation, is perfect for using in cake batters, some cookie doughs, and loaf cakes, for it creates a lighter batter or dough than the granulated variety. When superfine sugar is present in a baking formula as the sweetening agent, a higher percentage of fat in the form of egg yolks, butter, or sour cream can be used. Confectioners' sugar (10-X is preferable, yielding a polished texture in frostings, icings, and glazes) is used as a primary or secondary sweetening agent—with or without granulated sugar—in batters and doughs (for cakes, cookies, sweet biscuits, scones, and tarts) and in some frostings or icings. When used simply sifted, it becomes an effortlessly sweet coating for the tops of bar cookies, tortes, coffee cakes, pound cakes, and Bundt cakes. Light or dark brown sugar (typically, cane sugar [that is, primarily sucrose] with added molasses, caramel, or cane caramel color) must be moist and strained before measuring to dispel any hardened lumps of sugar; it is used as a sole or partial sweetening agent in a batter or dough, contributing moistness and textural density. Specialty sugars (such as 365 Organic Evaporated Cane Juice Sugar, Alter Eco Organic Ground Cane Sugar, Hain Natural Turbinado Sugar, 365 Organic Evaporated Cane Juice Turbinado Raw Sugar, India Tree Demerara Sugar from Mauritius, India Tree Golden Bakers Sugar from Mauritius, India Tree Light Muscovado Sugar from Mauritius, India Tree Dark Muscovado Sugar from Mauritius, and India Tree Maple Sugar from Vermont) work as a flavoring agent, a highlighting and intensifying agent, and as a finishing sugar to top cookies, sweet quick breads, and yeast-raised breads.

A vanilla-scented sugar adds a plane of flavor, building and enlarging the overall taste of a batter or dough. While the magnification may be subtle, this fast-to-create flavoring is made from a simple formula that returns memorable results.

To make vanilla-scented granulated or confectioners' sugar, pour 2 pounds of either sugar into a clean, dry glass storage container. Split 2 plump vanilla beans down the center to expose the tiny seeds, cut the beans in half, and bury them in the sugar. Cover the container and let the sugar stand for at least 3 days before using (it will keep for at least 3 months). Over time, the sugar will clump due to the moisture exuded from the vanilla beans during storage; simply sift a quantity of sugar—minus the beans—before measuring (or press a smaller amount through a medium- or fine-mesh sieve).

Light or dark corn syrup is a thick sweetener made from the base ingredient of starch. It is used frequently in sugar syrups and candy making to prevent crystallization, and in some icing and glaze formulas. Corn syrup weakens or modifies the texture of a batter or candy mixture, as it adds a certain degree of moisture. Golden syrup (preferably Lyle's Golden Syrup)—cane sugar syrup—can be used in place of light corn syrup and, in small quantities ($\frac{1}{3}$ cup and under), in place of honey; it adds moisture, acts as a sweetening agent, and creates density in cake batters and cookie doughs. Blue agave nectar, both amber and light, is a syrupy, concentrated sweetener made from the juice of the agave plant (the plant is a succulent) and is lighter in weight/texture than honey; either variety can be used as a sweetening agent for fruit sauces and syrups or as a liquid sweetener in a glaze or icing (especially with lemon and lime accenting flavors, where it would lend a bright, slightly acidic tang). Honey is a thick, sticky, and reasonably fluid sweetening agent, generally ranging from golden to amber and scented by the provenance of the nectar; no matter the source, it is hygroscopic (having the ability to pull in and retain moisture) and contributes a sweet level of flavor (depending on its origin) while delivering light to moderate density in a dough or batter. Cane syrup (preferably Steen's 100% Pure Cane Syrup), made from pure sugarcane juice, is used as a sweetening/flavoring agent; it is wonderful for highlighting flavor in a spice cake batter, gingerbread batter, and a gingerbread or molasses cookie dough. Molasses (preferably Grandma's Original Unsulphured Molasses) is a treacle-y syrup made from the natural (that is, "unprocessed") concentrated juices of sugarcane, and is used primarily as a sweetening/flavoring agent.

Eggs contribute moisture to batters and doughs. Whole eggs or a combination of whole eggs and egg yolks work during the emulsion phase of a batter or dough, affecting and creating the desired baked texture while enriching its internal composition and coloring the crumb. An egg yolk is a combination of both protein and fat; an egg white is principally protein, and understood to be "albumin" protein. For use in batters and doughs, organic eggs are preferable for their overall quality—of flavor, texture, and body.

✳ When preparing any dough, batter, or mixture for refrigeration or freezing, use organic eggs only. Never consume any uncooked batter, dough, or other mixture containing eggs. Cook, griddle, or bake all batters, doughs, or other mixtures containing eggs to the proper temperature. Any sauces, fillings, or toppings made with cooked eggs should be refrigerated within 30 minutes of cooking (use an ice-water bath to hasten cooling, if necessary). Use pasteurized eggs as directed. Wash eggs prior to cracking them or in advance of all food preparation. Thoroughly clean and disinfect your hands, containers, mixing bowls, and all work surfaces that come in contact with eggs.

Embraced under the umbrella of liquid dairy ingredients, whole milk, half-and-half, light (table) cream, heavy (whipping) cream, and buttermilk are essential ingredients for adding moisture, developing the crumb, and contributing volume to baked batters and doughs. Whole milk contains between 3.5 and 4 percent fat; half-and-half contains between 10 and 11 percent fat; light (table) cream contains between 18 and 19 percent fat; and heavy cream contains between 36 and 40 percent fat. Buttermilk, usually skim milk treated with a bacteria or "cultured" with lactic acid, adds a gentle tang to a batter or dough.

Soft dairy ingredients, namely sour cream and yogurt, add moisture, contribute to the texture, develop the crumb, and soften/relax the internal texture of batters and doughs. Typically, sour cream—cream that has been cultured by lactic acid, rendering it thickened and slightly tart—contains between 18 and 19 percent fat; yogurt is bacteria-cultured milk, generating a gently tart mixture ranging from moderately thick to thickly dense.

Vanilla extract, used primarily as a flavoring agent, is a classic for scenting batters and doughs. It adds a distinguished highlighting layer of flavor, counterbalances the sweetness factor in a batter or dough, and lends significant aroma and flavor to a syrup or glaze. It's easy to intensify a bottle of vanilla extract by adding a vanilla bean to it and allowing it to steep for a little while. My preference is for a fairly intense vanilla flavor in baked goods, so I usually use the same amount of intensified vanilla—teaspoon for teaspoon—unless the quantity of vanilla extract called for in a recipe is 1½ teaspoons or more, when the amount of intensified extract should be reduced by one-third.

To make intensified vanilla extract, pour 4 ounces vanilla extract into a clean, dry glass jar. Split a vanilla bean down the center to expose the tiny seeds and halve it width-wise. Open up the split halves so that the seeds reveal themselves. Bend the halves in half and push them gently into the extract. Close the jar tightly and swish the extract around and about the sections of the split bean. Place the extract on a pantry shelf well away from heat and light. Let the extract strengthen for a few days before using it in a batter, dough, frosting, filling, or sauce. The extract will keep for at least 3 months.

Intense essences, used primarily as flavoring agents, flavor batters and doughs in a complex, but understated way and scent a syrup, icing, glaze, or frosting without compromising its consistency. Depending upon the pastry essence flavor you have chosen, use one-half, one-third, or one-quarter the amount of any one of these essences in place of a similarly flavored commercial extract. Among my favorite essences, available at La Cuisine—The Cook's Resource in 2-ounce stoppered bottles, are: orange, blood orange, lemon, almond, lavender, coconut, violet, peppermint, rose flower, orange flower, *fiori di sicilia*, vanilla, caramel, pistachio, and apricot.

Choosing ingredients should be a thoughtful act rather than a unmindful one, for there are so many exceptional items available to the baker that produce doughs and batters full of character. Choices abound, even for the very basic staples, and the exploration is part of the fun. One of my favorite rainy-day weekend activities is to bake three versions of one recipe, each one, for example, with a different type of butter, level of spice, or variable flavoring essence. The results are always delicious, yet the contrast of the different versions turns out to be intriguing. If you are a daredevil, inquisitive baker (like me), you can have a field day with the many varieties of baking ingredients available at the market.

baking*Craft*

baking*Process*

The process of baking is based on measured, clearly articulated steps that depend on the kind of dough, batter, frosting, filling, or sauce that you are creating. Both the way the ingredients are cared for and the procedure for combining them are essential in order to arrive at just the right textural and shape-specific outcome—a downy cake, moist biscuit, chewy cookie, plump sweet roll, or gossamer coffee cake.

A batter or reasonably soft dough (with the exception of a yeast dough, which proceeds on a somewhat different course) travels through seven important phases once it is mixed, and those levels present themselves—when heat is applied—in a flowing cycle of time-lapse changes: 1. The solid fats melt, releasing their trapped water and air, creating steam and air bubbles. 2. Carbon dioxide discharged by the leavening agents present (baking powder and baking soda, alone or in combination, along with or without cream of tartar), air created in a creamed batter, and vapor (steam) cause the dough or batter to rise in the presence of heat (some gas expansion may begin before baking); as the bubbles of gas(es) expand, they are snared within the cell walls made of proteins in the dough or batter. 3. Any undissolved sugar (in a relatively dry batter) dissolves, forming a syrup that thins out the batter. 4. The proteins in the egg(s) and gluten from the flour become much tighter (coagulate), creating the overall structure appropriate to each type of baked item; coagulation is important because, along with the gelatinized starch, it ultimately contributes to the finished, end product's volume and texture. 5. The starches present gelatinize, or draw in the moisture present, and firm up. 6. Moisture continues to evaporate. And 7. The exterior of the item (bottom, sides, and—especially—the top) browns and the top forms a crust; the level—or intensity—of browning as residual moisture

evaporates is directly related to the type and amount of ingredients such as sugar, dairy, and whole eggs or egg yolks present *in* the batter or dough, or a finishing glaze or egg wash brushed *over* a dough just before baking.

The overview of techniques that follows is outlined to provide a touchstone-like view of the methods encountered in this book and to instruct beginning bakers, as well as to provide a useful tip or two to those who have logged in many baking years. The method for each type of technique is offered in the procedure of the particular recipe in a somewhat stylized version—that is, the most important elements are spotlighted and set forth, leaving the more comprehensive elements to be discussed below.

For a "creamed" cake batter, measurements of flour and leavening (baking powder, baking soda, or a combination of the two) are sifted with salt and any other additional ingredients, such as ground spices, cream of tartar, or cocoa powder. Butter, the key fat, is used in its softened form and beaten until smooth. The butter, light and mayonnaise-like in consistency, is now ready to take in the sugar (granulated, light brown, dark brown, confectioners', or any of those in combination) in several additions. At this point, the process of beating is accomplished by degree, or specific amounts, meaning that portions of sugar are added and incorporated thoroughly; this is crucial to establishing volume and, later, during baking, texture. Any leavening that is part

of the ingredient list in the recipe acts only to build the volume created by beating the sugar and fat together, for it does not expand the crumb of the baked cake beyond what is already initiated by the creaming process. Unless the recipe indicates otherwise, use the whip or flat paddle mixer attachment for creaming the butter and sugar. Whole eggs, a combination of whole eggs and egg yolks, or egg yolks alone are incorporated next, followed by ingredients such as a flavoring extract, melted chocolate, or molasses. The flour mixture is usually added alternately with the liquid, beginning and ending with the sifted ingredients. At each stage, the mixer should be stopped and the sides and bottom of the bowl scraped thoroughly, using a sturdy rubber spatula. Scraping the bowl is necessary in order to prepare and maintain a batter of even, gossamer consistency. Any additions to the batter not incorporated at an earlier stage, such as chocolate chips or chunks, chopped candy, dried fruits, sweetened shredded coconut, or chopped nuts, are integrated at this point, either by machine or by hand (using a sturdy wooden spoon or flat wooden paddle). A light, beautifully mixed creamed batter and the resulting perfectly textured cake are achieved by using a freestanding electric mixer. The strength of the mixer beats the requisite amount of air into the butter and sugar mixture, ultimately building volume and guarding against dense cakes (with a tighter, chewier, more compact crumb).
✳ Never consume raw batter.

For a "creamed" cookie dough, dry ingredients (flour, leavening[s], spices, salt, cocoa powder, and such) are either whisked together in a bowl to blend them or sifted to aerate. Softened butter is creamed until pearly and yielding before the sugar is added, frequently in several additions, though not for the length of time that takes place in cake batters. Unless the recipe indicates otherwise, use the whip or flat paddle mixer attachment for creaming the butter and sugar. Eggs and a flavoring extract follow, with the mixing-in time kept at a minimum, as volume is usually not on the procedural agenda here. The flour mixture is then integrated, along with any other substantial ingredients, such as rolled oats. Other items, such as raisins, nuts, chocolate chips or chunks, sweetened shredded coconut, chopped candy, or dried fruits, are added by machine or by hand (using a sturdy wooden spoon or flat wooden paddle). Cookie doughs are typically creamy-textured and range

as follows: soft, moderately dense, dense-heavy. Many cookie doughs in this book refrigerate or freeze well, and this will be noted in the recipe.
✳ When preparing cookie dough for refrigeration or freezing, use organic eggs only and never consume raw cookie dough.

For a "melt, whisk, and combine" batter (typically a brownie or dense, chocolate-laden bar cookie batter), flour and leavening (baking powder or baking soda) are sifted, whisked, or stirred with salt and any additional ingredients, such as cocoa powder or freshly grated or ground spices. Chocolate and butter are melted and combined (frequently with a whisk) until smooth. The eggs are whisked until just combined and blended with the sugar, followed by the melted butter-chocolate mixture and vanilla extract. For most brownie batters, the melted butter and chocolate are used in the tepid (not cooled) state, the flour mixture is sifted over the whisked ingredients, and the contents of the mixing bowl is combined to form a dense batter, using a whisk, wooden spoon, or flat wooden paddle. This decidedly low-tech approach to mixing ingredients makes for the best-textured brownies. At this point, it is important to mix just until the particles of flour are absorbed. For dense, golden batters (the mixtures that result in characteristically traditional blondies), whole eggs or egg yolks are blended together with brown sugar, melted butter, and a flavoring extract; the combined flour mixture is resifted over it all and a thick batter is formed. Occasionally, a blond batter is so thick that it resembles a moist and heavy dough. Enrichments, such as chocolate chips, chocolate chunks, candy bar nuggets, or chopped nuts are worked into the batter at the end, usually by hand.
✳ Never consume raw batter.

For a "cut-in" dough (for sweet and savory biscuits, most scones, and some tea cakes), the flour, sugar, and leavening are whisked or sifted with salt and any additional ingredients, such as cocoa powder or spices. Occasionally, a type of sugar is whisked into, as opposed to sifted with, the dry ingredients. Butter is strewn over the leavened flour mixture in chunks and "cut-in" using a pastry blender or two round-bladed table knives. Sometimes the butter is crumbled lightly between the fingertips to further reduce the fat into smaller flaky bits. A whisked mixture—usually cream (or buttermilk), sometimes whole eggs or egg yolks, and occasionally a flavoring extract—is poured over the

flour mixture. Additions such as chocolate chips, chocolate chunks, candy bar nuggets, chunks of dried fruit or pieces/shreds of fresh fruit or berries, shredded or cubed cheese, or chopped nuts are then scattered over, and everything is mixed to form a cohesive dough. For biscuits and scones, the resulting dough, usually dense and gently moist, is lightly kneaded in the bowl or on a floured work surface. The brief kneading time, just a few turns, helps to establish texture as the dough rises in the oven. For soda breads and some free-form tea cakes made with a "cut-in" dough, the dough is mixed to shape and form into a "well-domed ball," as even a short, light kneading can result in a dense-textured, somewhat greasy crumb. Depending on the recipe, the formed dough may be refrigerated to rest and firm up before shaping and cutting, or it may be cut into wedges, rounds, or squares immediately, or left whole, its surface crosscut in an X; the X cut allows the dough to expand properly as the quick bread bakes. In any case, "cut-in" doughs should be handled as lightly as possible to secure a tender, rather airy texture on baking. Overhandling the dough during mixing or kneading can produce a leathery, dense quick bread. Dividing baking powder– or baking soda–leavened doughs into decorative shapes with a dull knife or a blunt cookie cutter will result in misshapen baked goods that are unable to rise fully or bake evenly. Actually twisting a cookie cutter or angling a knife while cutting a biscuit or scone dough will cause either batch to slump or rise with one high side and one slouched side.
✳ Never consume raw dough.

For a sweet or savory yeast dough, active dry yeast, sugar, and warm water are combined and set to proof until swollen. A dough is created by combining the expanded yeast mixture with, in addition to flour, ingredients such as sugar, spices, a liquid (frequently milk or a combination of milk and water, or buttermilk), a flavoring extract or a concentrated highlighting essence, melted or softened butter, whole eggs or egg yolks, and salt. Salt, which acts as a flavoring agent as well as an ingredient that balances and controls fermentation, should never come in direct contact with the swollen yeast mixture; rather, salt is always combined with all or a significant portion of the flour (or flour mixture) in order to introduce it properly, otherwise the rising capability and resulting leavening power of the yeast may be compromised. Note that active dry yeast is used. Classically, active dry yeast contains a

certain proportion of inactive yeast cells and, as such, more yeast is used to achieve a proper rise (and, in some cases, to match successfully with the amount of sugar, eggs, or butter present in a dough); the presence of inactive cells, does, however, contribute great flavor to the dough and resulting bread or batch of sweet rolls, buns, or coffee cake.

Occasionally, a dough is made by incorporating a sponge mixture into the remaining ingredients (this gives the finished dough a measure of depth and complexity); other times, a partial dough is prepared to the stage of a "thick batter," left to rest for a few minutes, then finished with the remainder of the dry ingredients (this technique yields a more tractable dough with a finer finished texture).

The resulting dough is kneaded (by hand or in the mixing bowl of a heavy-duty freestanding electric mixer), turned into a large buttered mixing bowl, and set to rise, either at cool room temperature or by a combination of room temperature and refrigerator. At a point in the mixing and kneading process, if a sweet yeast dough is prepared in a heavy-duty freestanding electric mixer, the partially kneaded dough may be covered with a sheet of food-safe plastic wrap and put aside for ten minutes to rest before the machine-kneading resumes. The purpose of this rest is to allow the flour to absorb the liquid and fat, to prevent overworking the dough, to retain the dough's flavor, and to keep the dough supple (review this technique as it works in the recipe for *rich, richer, richest sticky buns,* page 231). The method of most yeast-raised recipes in this book proceeds without this step, but you can employ it with most doughs by halting the beating, covering the bowl, then resuming the beating. The technique works best with the rich doughs destined for forming into sweet rolls, sticky buns, and coffee cakes.

Many doughs rich in butter, eggs, and sugar are slashed or cut ¾ to 1 inch deep with a pair of kitchen scissors right before the first long rise; the deep cuts in the dough encourage a good and supportive rise. The top of the dough, with its gashes, initially looks like a flower with wide, semicircular petals.

The yeast dough is then set to rise (to doubled in bulk or tripled in bulk, generally at room temperature or cool room temperature (about 68 degrees F) in a heavily buttered bowl. The term "doubled in bulk" refers to dough having risen twofold, and "tripled in bulk" refers to the dough having risen threefold.

The resulting risen dough, significantly lighter and gently voluminous, is compressed slightly and set to rest for a short while. I prefer to compress the dough with my fingertips or a flexible rubber spatula. Compressing, rather than punching down, the dough keeps the risen framework intact and contributes to a fine baked texture. (See *compress,* page 13, in *Baking Style* terminology for further explanation of the process.) At this point, additions such as chopped or diced dried fruits, shredded cheese, bits of chocolate, and such are integrated within the dough's mass. (Some refrigerated doughs may not need a rest period just before shaping.) The dough is then formed into individual breads, buns, or rolls; transferred to one single-unit fancy tube pan or deep fluted tart pan, or one large loaf pan; and set aside to rise again before baking. Sometimes, and just prior to the last rise, the yeast dough will be rolled into a large sheet, spread with a filling, then formed into small coffee cake–like sweets. Formed coffee cakes or sweet rolls may be covered with a streusel topping before baking.

Within the recipes in this book, the phrase "almost doubled in bulk" means that the fully shaped dough for the final rise should be about 90 percent risen (not quite 100 percent doubled in bulk), leaving the remaining 10 percent to rise in the initial baking minutes when "oven-spring" takes place. ("Oven-spring" is defined as a final burst of rise or expansion when the panned and risen yeast dough is placed in the oven to be baked. This lift to a dough's final form takes place during the first 5 minutes or so of baking.) In *some* of the yeast-risen dough recipes, this rising stage will be noted as "until almost doubled in bulk (see page 6 to reference this stage)." Some recipes, however, such as *rich, richer, richest sticky buns* (page 231), *a 14-year-old's rolls still tasty after all these years* (page 105), *the cinnamon-raisin buns of my childhood, #1* (page 445), and *craggy-top sour cream buns* (page 173) call for a complete doubling in bulk for the final rise. This is necessary to maintain and establish shape and texture, as a certain oven-spring will still take place within the confines of the fully risen dough.

✳ Any and all yeast doughs prepared in an electric mixer must be made in a heavy-duty freestanding model. While mixing and beating a yeast dough in a heavy-duty freestanding electric mixer, always stand by the mixer to ensure that it is stable on the work surface, be constantly available to adjust the speed and position on the work surface, and never, ever leave it unattended. Never consume raw dough.

Remember that the recipes call for active dry yeast, as it is preferred for ease of availability, overall flavor, and consistency. As well, the amount of active dry yeast in a particular recipe is determined by the weight of rich ingredients, such as eggs and butter, and by the amount of sugar or a sugar-based ingredient (such as honey). The recipes in this baking cookbook were developed to use enough—and only enough—yeast to sustain rise and develop texture, without incurring off-flavors and misshapen textures. (Note: other types of yeast, specifically made to tolerate doughs rich in sugar or fat, or with significant amounts of textural whole grains or whole grain flours, can be used, but they generally require a reconfiguration of the ingredient amounts to accommodate their use; specialty yeasts can also be difficult to purchase during certain seasons of the calendar year.)

For a buttery tart dough (as called for in the *rustic fig tart,* page 274), flour, salt, and baking powder are whisked together in a bowl. Chunks of butter are dropped onto the surface and cut into the flour mixture, using a pastry blender or two round-bladed table knives, until pea-size bits are formed. Sugar is sprinkled over and blended in. The fat is dispersed further by crumbling it lightly with your fingertips. A whisked mixture consisting of a whole egg, milk, and vanilla extract is poured over the buttered flour mixture and mixed to form a lightly moist dough, cohesive in clusters. The dough is then turned onto a work surface to blend into a mass, using the heel of your hand and short pushing motions. This dough, used for a free-form fruit tart, is sweet, butter-rich, and very lightly leavened with baking powder. The presence of the baking powder makes the dough a little more fragile as it gently expands the texture; the sugar also contributes to its delicacy and tenderness.

✳ Never consume raw dough.

For a stove top–prepared *pâte à choux* dough (puffy dough for profiteroles, *gougères,* éclairs, beignets, soufflés, and the like), flour is sifted with salt and sugar (if destined to become a sweet) or aromatic ground spices (if it is to become a savory). A liquid (milk or a combination of water and milk), a flavoring extract (if a sweet), minced fresh herbs (if savory), and chunks of butter are placed in a heavy (usually medium-size) saucepan (preferably enameled cast iron). The saucepan is placed over high heat and its contents brought to a boil. As soon as the mixture has reached the boil, the saucepan is removed from the heat, the sifted mixture is added, and the contents mixed to form a dough. The dough base should be smooth (and reasonably soft) and will have pulled away from the sides of the saucepan. The saucepan of dough is then returned to the heat for a brief time to dry out the dough a bit. After the dough steadies in the pan (off the heat) for a minute, whisked eggs are mixed in, a little at a time. Adding and beating in the eggs in stages is what creates the texture and fulsome puff of the dough during baking. My favorite tool for the beating process of the procedure is a flat wooden paddle. When enough of the beaten eggs is incorporated, the dough should be thick and hold its shape, but not obviously stiff; usually, a portion of the beaten egg mixture is reserved to achieve proper density. Both the humidity (or lack of it) of the day and absorption quality of the flour determine how much of the remaining egg mixture needs to be added. Remember that if the dough is too moist, or slack, the baked *choux* will be misshapen—that is, saggy and droopy. Conversely, if the dough is too firm, the pastries will be too dry and less fulsome, with a compromised rise. Once the dough has been egg-enriched, it is beaten further for about 2 minutes, or until quite smooth. The finished dough, which you should form by spooning or piping immediately, will be quite lustrous.

✳ Never consume raw dough.

For a confectioners' sugar frosting, confectioners' sugar, butter, salt, vanilla extract, and a liquid or soft dairy ingredient (and, now and then, melted chocolate) are combined in stages, usually in a freestanding electric mixer fitted with the flat paddle attachment. (A hand-held electric mixer can be used in some recipes if the frosting is not too thick or ample, and *only* if the equipment is heavy-duty.) With the mixer fully stopped, the sides of the bowl are scraped down with a rubber spatula to maintain an even consistency to the frosting. At this point, you can adjust the consistency of the frosting by adding tablespoons of milk, cream, or more confectioners' sugar to arrive at a mixture that spreads easily or can be piped smoothly and efficiently for decorative work. In a hot kitchen or on a humid day, it may be necessary to increase the amount of confectioners' sugar; on a dry and cold day, you may need to add more liquid. The core amount of liquid is frequently heated to tepid—slightly warm—before it is added to the other ingredients so that it creates a smooth suspension; if the recipe does not call for it to be warmed first, then use it at room temperature or at another temperature specified in the recipe.

For frosting that is to be put through a pastry bag and piped decoratively, beat the frosting on low to moderately low speed in the bowl of a freestanding electric mixer until all the ingredients are combined at each stage, using the flat paddle attachment; beating the mixture until fluffy will produce lots of air bubbles that will interrupt the flow of the frosting as it is piped. If necessary, press the frosting against the sides of a mixing bowl with a spatula to expel any air bubbles. If the frosting is fluffy, you can usually restore the texture by blending in several additional tablespoons of confectioners' sugar and an extra tablespoon or two of softened butter on low speed.

For frosting that is designed to be billowy and fluffy, use the mixing speed specified in that particular recipe.

To use the frosting for spreading on sheet cakes, place spaced dollops of the frosting on top of the cake, then smooth them over the surface; finally, dip and swirl the frosting with the back of a large spoon, flexible palette knife, or long and slender icing spatula before it firms up. For cupcakes, mound the frosting in the center of each cupcake, smooth down the sides just to the ruffle of the ovenproof paper baking cup liner. For the nicest presentation, the frosting should completely conceal the surface of the cake and meet the paper liner but not droop over it, then swirl on a top coat of frosting. For layer cakes, after the layers are spread with frosting and assembled, spread frosting on the top of the cake, then on the sides, and, finally, touch up the entire rounded edge where the sides meet the uppermost surface layer of frosting.

To make high, thickly frosted cupcakes, use a fairly firm confectioners' sugar frosting and load it onto the surface of the cupcake in the shape of an inverted cone or a tepee with the top squared off—that is, thickly at the base and narrower toward the top—then smooth the sides and top. At this point you can swirl on additional frosting for a fanciful finish, but beware of "frosting overload"—top-heavy cupcakes that are overwhelmed by the sheer weight of all that sweet goodness. When the frosting is still moist, decorate the surface with sprinkles or other edible decorations, if you wish. Cupcakes can also be garnished with cupcake picks—nonedible decorations that should be removed before enjoying the cakes—and all cupcakes decorated with picks must be served responsibly with an adult present.

✳ As a general rule, any frosted cake or cupcake not consumed after two hours of assembling should be refrigerated, though the time frame is based on the temperature or atmospheric conditions of the room in which the particular sweet is held—that is, a warmer environment may necessitate refrigerating the composed cake or cupcake immediately after frosting or glazing.

To embellish the top of bar and drop cookies, scones, and muffins, sprinkle extra or reserved chips, chunks, nuts, or chopped candy (mated to an ingredient in the recipe) onto the surface of cookie dough mounds, sweet rolls, or the whole block of bar cookies either just before baking or 5 to 10 minutes before the baking time is up. For bar cookies, scatter the chips, chunks, nuts, or chopped candy here and there on the surface (avoiding the edges). If the particular bar cookie batter is only moderately thick, add the topping before the final 5 minutes of baking because topping the sweet any sooner will lose the definition of the ingredient. Cookies made from a dense dough (such as one containing rolled oats) can be topped prior to baking; cookies made from a softer dough that spreads more than one-half inch during baking should be topped 3 to 4 minutes before the baking time is up (most chocolate chip cookie doughs fall in this category). For scones, a topping of extra chips or chunks of candy can be gamely pressed onto the top of the scones just before baking; the shape of the scones usually flattens after this application, so just plump up the sides with two flexible palette knives. Sturdy muffin batters, divided and turned into the prepared cups, can be topped with extra nuts or chips prior to baking; the tops of freshly baked plain muffins can be dipped in melted butter and a scented sugar after baking.

To dramatize and heighten the surface of plain-topped (that is, without streusel or any other specialized topping or finish) yeast-raised coffee cake, bread, or rolls with a glaze, you can choose among a number of formulas, depending on the look desired and the type of sweet or savory bread to be glazed. The introduction of a pinch of sugar ties in nicely with a sweet bread, but salt is necessary to break up, and slightly liquefy, the whole egg(s), egg yolk(s), or egg whites. Always apply the glaze on cakes, breads, or rolls risen up to the point of 20 minutes before baking, using a soft pastry brush and light-handed strokes, leaving whatever has been coated uncovered for the remainder of the rise. Immediately before baking, you can reglaze the bread for a deeper finish.

For a plain, lustrous top, beat 2 large egg whites until frothy with a pinch of salt and 2½ teaspoons water. Use this glaze on home-style rolls (with a high egg and butter content) or on egg- and butter-rich fruit- or nut-filled coffee cakes.

For a deeply golden glaze, beat 2 large egg yolks with a pinch of salt and 3 teaspoons cold milk. Use this glaze on buttermilk-based yeast breads, rolls, and coffee cakes or American-style pan rolls. As a sweet roll finish, add ¼ teaspoon granulated sugar to the egg yolks, salt, and milk.

For a moderately golden glaze that is both rich and a little shiny, beat 1 large egg and 1 large egg white with a pinch of salt and 3 teaspoons cold water. As a pan-bread finish of rolls baked nestled against one another (such as for rich butter and egg breads or potato bread), replace the water with cold heavy cream. This is a luxurious finish.

The amount of liquid—water or milk—depends on the age of the whole eggs or egg yolks. On occasion, a little more liquid, usually no more than a teaspoon or two, may need to be added in order to form a glaze that is paintable.

For an egg yolk–enriched custard or pastry cream, it is important that the sauce or cream filling is completely cooked through, supple, smooth, and thickened. There are several important technical notes to remember: a pastry cream that is enriched with egg yolks and thickened with cornstarch is cooked at a reasonably low boil; it should reach between 199 degrees F and 201 degrees F, averaging out at 200 degrees F. A properly cooked pastry cream will coat a wooden spoon thickly and continue to firm up as it cools. An egg yolk–enriched custard sauce (the *custard to pour* on page 222 is a good example) must be cooked until thickened so that it reaches and maintains a temperature of 160 degrees F; this sauce, lightly thickened with arrowroot, is still fragile (be sure to use a heavy saucepan, preferably enameled cast iron). To test the temperature of the custard sauce, remove the saucepan from the heat for a moment and, protecting your hands with oven mitts, tip the pan slightly so that the sauce pools to one side, then test with a heatproof instant-read thermometer. For safety, technical precision, and accuracy, always use a thermometer to verify the temperature of the completed sauce or pastry cream.

In this volume, a *custard sauce* is defined as the result of combining warmed liquid dairy ingredients with a pinch of salt into a sugar, arrowroot (or another light thickener, if used), and egg yolk mixture, then cooking it slowly in a heavy saucepan until it reaches the correct temperature and lightly coats the back of a wooden spoon. The custard is strained through a fine-mesh sieve before being seasoned with an extract. Some custard sauces are thickened gently with arrowroot, while others rely on the thickening power of egg yolks alone to arrive at a sauce that is slightly dense, but with a good flow. A *pastry cream* is made by combining liquid dairy ingredients and a sifted mixture of salt, sugar, and cornstarch in a heavy saucepan. The mixture is brought to the boil over moderately high heat and cooked until thickened, stirring slowly all the while with a wooden spoon or flat wooden paddle. Lightly beaten egg yolks are introduced into the mixture off the heat after the yolks have been "tempered" by mixing them with a small amount of the hot mixture. The tempering process moderates the temperature at which the yolks are introduced into the hot cream. By mixing some of the yolks with a little of the hot mixture, and so acclimating them to the heat, they can be added to the thickened cream without risking an inappropriate change in texture, like curdling. The saucepan is returned to the heat and the mixture is cooked to complete the thickening process. The filling should reach a temperature of 200 degrees F (or within a degree or two of this) to achieve a thickness resembling soft pudding. Depending on the recipe, the filling may be strained into a heatproof bowl or simply turned into the bowl. A flavoring extract is added at this time, and a little softened butter may be incorporated as a final enhancement. (For a brief but detailed explanation of working with cornstarch, refer to the second paragraph in *For a cornstarch-thickened fresh berry compote,* below.)

To confirm the temperature of an egg yolk–enriched custard sauce or pastry cream, use an instant-read temperature probe. Mine is a Thermapen Digital Thermometer (model: Thermapen 5). It operates on a 12-volt battery, with a range of between –50 degrees F and +572 degrees F. It is used by unfolding the needle-like probe and inserting it into the sauce or filling; the temperature is displayed digitally on a window inset on one flat side.

✱ Never consume raw or undercooked pastry cream or custard sauce; always refrigerate pastry cream or custard sauce in a tightly sealed container and refrain from storing beyond the suggested time limits.

For a cornstarch-thickened fresh berry compote, such as the *blueberry compote* (page 455), a sieved and whisked mixture of cornstarch, sugar, and salt is combined with a quantity of fruit juice in a heavy saucepan. The mixture is brought to the boil over moderately high heat and cooked until thickened, clear, and glossy, stirring slowly all the while with a wooden spoon or flat wooden paddle, then cooked at a gentle bubble to establish the thickened texture (this will take about 1 minute for a mixture that uses a 1-cup quantity of fruit juice). Off the heat, fresh berries are added and incorporated, and the saucepan is returned to the heat to warm the berries and gently ease them out of their firm state. At this point, it is important to carefully warm, but not cook, the berries or they will collapse and lose their structure. Once removed from the heat and turned into a heatproof bowl, the sauce is highlighted with a little flavoring extract and is then ready for serving warm or at room temperature. The best berries to use in this type of sauce are blackberries, blueberries, or pitted cherries—with a juice that corresponds to and highlights the flavor, rather than contrasts to it; if you are using fresh cherries, increase the warming phase to about 2 minutes. The juice should be as pure as possible. If you are using softer, more fragile berries (such as red or golden raspberries), simply turn the hot, thickened mixture into the bowl and fold through the fruit, thus avoiding the final warming phase (which would break down the fruit too much).

Cornstarch can be a tricky ingredient to master, but as long as you understand a few concepts and techniques for working with this carbohydrate as it responds to heat, a sweetening agent, and liquid, you'll avoid any unfortunate experiences. As a thickening agent, cornstarch loses its power in the presence of an excessive amount of sugar; in an unchecked amount of acid; in a low percentage of liquid (such as water or fruit juice); if treated to excessive beating or using a whisk during the mixing process while the mixture is heating or boiling; or if exposed to extended mixing. The idea is to keep any utensil from shearing through the granules of starch and thus rupturing them. When the swollen starch granules have been battered, by either excessive or prolonged mixing, the resulting mixture thins out. It should also be noted that cornstarch-thickened sauces cannot be frozen because, on defrosting, the mixture usually turns thin and watery.

For a moist and craggy streusel (used for topping sweet biscuits, scones, and some coffee cakes), flour and salt (and sometimes a ground spice) are sifted into a mixing bowl. Sugar (light brown sugar, dark brown sugar, or granulated sugar, or a combination of brown sugar and granulated sugar) is incorporated. Chunks of butter are scattered over and, using a pastry blender or two round-bladed table knives, reduced to small bits. Frequently, a flavoring extract is drizzled over before the mixture is crumbled between your fingertips to create large and small lumps. Overworking the mixture is not a problem. The lumps will be moist and of varying size. This type of streusel is made with cold butter. Another version, a *flaky streusel,* is made with melted butter and produces a lighter, less chunky streusel: flour, sugar, and salt are whisked together in a mixing bowl. A melted butter-vanilla mixture is scattered over and the components are crumbled together to make a light, but somewhat sandy and bulky mixture. This is further fragmented into smaller crumbs. This streusel is wonderful sprinkled over individual buns and sweet rolls or big yeasted coffee cakes before baking.

✳ Never consume a raw streusel mixture.

For a butter candy mixture for coating popcorn or nuts (such as the one in the recipe for *golden popcorn croquant,* on page 312), sugar is sifted into a deep, heavy casserole (preferably enameled cast iron). Sifting the sugar is not a conceit: this frees it of all hardened pellets that would skew—and ultimately spoil—the texture of the finished syrup. I caution you not to skip this step. Light corn syrup, water, and chunks of butter are added. The pot is covered and placed over moderately low heat. When the sugar has dissolved, the casserole is uncovered and the mixture is cooked at a medium boil until it turns a light golden color and registers about 277 degrees F to 278 degrees F on a heatproof candy thermometer or instant-read thermometer. Now it will be thick and bubbly, and look somewhat viscous. Off the heat, and without delay, salt, baking soda, and vanilla extract are added—in that order. The syrup will bubble up wildly when both the baking soda and vanilla extract are added. When the baking soda is added, it will darken the syrup slightly (this is to be expected). At this point, you can pour it over the ingredients to be coated (such as popped corn), or stir ingredients (such as whole roasted nuts) into it. When preparing and handling the buttery sugar syrup, always use a heatproof utensil for stirring, wear sturdy oven mitts to protect your hands and forearms, and have a heatproof trivet for placing under the hot pot.

For washing up, I rely on thorough but gentle means. I use a good antibacterial soup and fresh sponges to clean off all surfaces, and refrain from scouring the insides of any type of bakeware. Appropriate seasoning and pan preparation usually assure an easy cleanup. The interiors of my bakeware have developed a sort of nonstick patina over time because they have been treated to a proper and thorough washing and good advance preparation before batters and doughs are placed in them. In fact, I generally keep a set of natural sponges to use to clean the insides of bakeware. I also use linen towels for drying the internal and external surfaces. There are many good and natural antibacterial soaps for washing up. In addition, I am quite particular about cleaning agents that are both luxurious, aroma-intense, and as natural as possible. I especially love Mrs. Meyer's Clean Day, a scented liquid dish soap (available in 16-ounce squeeze bottles); One with Nature Lavender Restorative Hand Wash with Dead Sea Salts & Shea Butter (available in 12-ounce pump bottles); and Caldrea Lavender Pine Countertop Cleanser (available in 16-ounce spray bottles). Of course, the choice of cleaning products is dependent on the materials to be cleaned in your kitchen, but I firmly believe that soaps should be both safe and restorative, as well as effective. (Many of the soaps and cleaners come in various scents, but I am partial to lavender.)

One memorable cleanup footnote: I cannot help but relate this personal experience to you—the time when my late mother, ever impatient, devised her own urgent but effective way to deal with extremely sticky bakeware. After a baking episode that left her with a number of encrusted baking pans (pretreatment or lining with parchment paper not in effect here), my mother tossed the pans, sugary implements, and all other seemingly irredeemable items relevant to the recipe in the trash. A few years later, release-surface bakeware began to appear, along with my mother's more respectful attitude toward equipment and the baking process.

the language of *Baking Style*

The baking process—the real how-tos—can be communicated by words or short phrases, and the subtleties of their meanings can vary from baker to baker and cook to cook. For this reason, and because I am particular about conveying exactly what I do, it is important that the following collective list of definitions be at your fingertips for reference.

Baking Style terminology

Each recipe in *Baking Style* was written in a way that allows you to prepare it by reading and working through the method without sifting through lots of explanatory material, so when your eye alights on something delectable, it is immediately accessible. The information that follows, though, is for the time when you want a booster dose of baking advice, and can enjoy sitting back at leisure to learn how I approach the hows and whys of baking.

These are the words of baking, the carefully chosen, small phrases that mean so much, found neatly in phrases that create a passage from one part of the method to another and, in the end, compose the how-to of a recipe. Many are repeated often, and some appear only in a specific context. A nimble baker will absorb them over time and circumstance, then readily use the instructions instinctually. It is my goal to have you understand how the words apply intellectually, in the context of my recipes, and practically, when ingredients and equipment encounter each other in your hands.

ahead Storage information for the beautifully appealing treats baked from this book appears following the word "ahead" and under "serving" in each recipe. Some baked goods are best served on baking day, for then they are at their flavorful and textural best. Randomly, there are options for freezing and reheating if an item is not served within the baking day time frame. Even if you are serving the item on baking day, storage in an airtight container or cake keeper is recommended.

bake The act of baking as designated in the procedure of each recipe should be understood as placing the item on the oven rack. In general, I bake everything on the lower-middle-level rack (in some ovens, this is the bottom third). For the best results, consider baking cookies in relays of one baking pan at a time; if you are pressed, two pans can be baked on the lower- and upper-third-level racks, if you shift and reverse the baking pans from top to bottom and bottom to top midway through the baking time.

beat The act of beating combines ingredients, whether by hand or by machine, using varying speeds—low, moderate, high, or in between. Butter, for example, is beaten on low or moderate speed until lightened and creamy. Butter and sugar are mixed to build the internal structure of a batter or dough, creating a certain amount of volume by lightening the mixture. Cool or softened butter is beaten into a yeast dough for enrichment. Whole eggs or egg yolks are beaten into a creamed butter and sugar mixture, carefully and usually for a short span of time, to establish texture and enrich. Beating is a balanced and orderly process. For general creaming of butter alone or butter and sugar, use the flat paddle or whip mixer attachment, unless the recipe indicates otherwise.

blend When two or more ingredients are combined by hand or in a freestanding electric mixer on low or moderately low speed to combine them without generating too much change in the consistency of a batter or dough, the operative word for this function is "blending." In essence, blending is the correct, time-honored method for mixing ingredients without creating or losing volume.

blossoming When finely grated fruit peel and a flavoring extract are combined and left to marinate for a short period of time, this technique is called blossoming. As an example, look at the recipe for *orange and bourbon: cake,* *saturated* (page 59): orange peel and orange extract are mixed and set aside while you are preparing the batter. This method brings out the best flavor from the peel.

compress To compress means to lightly push down upon a batch of puffy, once-risen yeast dough with your fingertips, the palms of your hands, or a flexible rubber spatula. I have found that punching down the dough, a livelier act, actually blemishes the wonderful structure and network of the dough developed during the rising time.

cream or **creaming** The act of creaming butter centers around beating the fat until smooth and, depending on the degree necessary, pearly to mayonnaise-like. Creaming butter properly is necessary to achieve a fine-grained and evenly textured cake or cookie dough with a tender melting quality. To cream generally refers to beating a fat (shortening, butter, cream cheese) on the low, moderately low, or moderate speed of a freestanding electric mixer. Further, to cream occasionally can refer to beating a softened fat with a quantity of sugar until the mixture is lightened. For the record, a creamed mixture of butter and sugar never quite achieves the state of "fluffy," despite the fact that it is referred to in this way in some baking textbooks; a test of that theory was confirmed in my kitchen—butter and sugar is lightened in texture (and becomes almost white if beaten for a long enough time), though I would not characterize it as "fluffy." In my experience, "fluffy" has an expanded, almost inflated look to it, like whipped cream or whipped cream–enriched riced potatoes.

crumb The crumb of a slice of cake or tea bread, bar or drop cookie, scone, muffin, or sweet roll refers to its internal texture. Depending on the baked good, the crumb of a cake made from a "creamed" batter can range from close-textured, to lightly fine-grained, to moderately fine-grained.

dip When the tops of baked muffins are not treated to a glaze or icing, they can be dipped in melted butter, followed by scented sugar. (A scented sugar is sugar—usually granulated or superfine—that is seasoned with a ground spice, such as cinnamon or nutmeg, or steeped with lengths of dried fruit peel, such as orange or lemon.) The act of dipping should be rather quick, with just

enough time dedicated to give the muffin a light veneer of butter, not a soaking. Make sure that the dipping materials are in smallish, deep bowls to keep the ingredients centered, rather than scattered over a large surface area. Hold the muffin by the base and douse the top lightly, first dipping it into the melted mixture, then into the perfumed sugar. Return the muffin to the cooling rack once it receives this coated treatment.

dredge To dredge is to enrobe a baked item, such as a cookie, in sugar—of either the granulated or confectioners' variety. The cookie is not only completed in this manner, but it is sweetened further; a shortbread-style cookie is usually treated to this finish. Some bar cookies are also swept through sugar, creating sweet, snowy exteriors. When dredging cookies, use a light hand; some patches of the cookie may show through, and that is just fine.

dust Dusting a work surface with flour or covering the top of a cake with a light dusting of confectioners' sugar means using the lightest cloak of the ingredient. It is always preferable to dust a surface or baked good by putting the flour or sugar in a sieve or strainer, thereby avoiding the formation of small and large clumpy areas that would mar the end result. Dusting also refers to the act of lightly coating the entire interior surface of a greased baking pan with flour (or, occasionally, unsweetened cocoa powder) before filling it with a batter or dough; any excess flour (or cocoa powder) should be removed by inverting the pan and tapping it lightly over the kitchen sink.

enrobe Thoroughly covering an item in an ingredient defines the act of enrobing. As an example, small shortbread-like butter cookies are sometimes rolled in confectioners' sugar as a sweet finish. Unbaked mounds of firm cookie dough can be rolled in chopped nuts or chocolate chips, for flavor and texture. Solid balls of ganache are dressed in a covering of unsweetened cocoa powder. When enrobing an item, be sure to do so evenly.

film When the interior of a baking pan (bottom, sides, and, if appropriate, a central tube) is coated with nonstick flour-and-oil spray or nonstick oil spray, it is said to be filmed. Filming the pan means that a sheer, but thorough, application of the spray is used to prevent the baked cake, bread, pan of buns, or loaf from sticking. A baking pan may also be filmed with softened unsalted butter, softened unsalted butter and flour, or clarified butter and flour, depending on the type of batter or dough that will rest within it. When a pan is treated with a combination that includes fat and flour, the flour is present for the batter or dough to cling to as it rises. This helps to provide height and structure to the finished product. Always use unsalted butter when preparing a baking pan, as the salt present in salted butter will likely cause sticking, making unmolding difficult.

fold When two (or more) elements are combined in the lightest but most thorough way possible, the folding process is enacted. Folding whipped egg whites into a lightly dense or moderately dense batter is a good example of this procedure: the most efficient way to merge the two components is to stir about one-quarter (or up to one-third) of the whipped whites into the prepared batter to lighten it, spoon the remaining whites over the mixture, then dip and sweep the whites into, around, and through the batter to arrive at a buoyant mixture. This is best accomplished by using a very large flexible rubber spatula or mixing spoon (metal, not wooden). Folding should be done rapidly, with as few strokes as possible to keep the batter from becoming heavy. Unless the procedure in a particular recipe indicates otherwise, any irregular, small patches of whipped whites will probably survive the folding process and not harm the mixture during baking.

form Sections of dough, cut into biscuit, scones, sweet rolls, and other individual breads, are formed into equal pieces, whether they are wedges, rounds, spirals, or logs. The shape is usually formed by dividing the dough with a long-bladed chef's knife. Perfectly formed shapes bake evenly.

frost To frost is to cover one or more layers of cake with a creamy frosting (not to be confused with a sheer, light, and sometimes spoonable or pourable icing or glaze). Using the "crumb coat" method is especially helpful when frosting tender, freshly baked butter cake layers: brush off any crumbs from the top of a sheet cake, or the tops and sides of multiple layers. For a sheet cake, spread a thin layer of frosting on top and let it firm up

at room temperature for 20 minutes or refrigerate it for 15 minutes, then apply the remaining frosting in sweeps and swirls. For a layer cake, spread the entire surface with a thin coating of frosting, and let stand for 30 minutes or refrigerate for 20 minutes, then frost the cake with whirls of frosting. In warm weather, or in a hot kitchen, simply set up the crumb coat in the refrigerator, rather than at room temperature. This method works with creamy, billowy, buttercream-style frostings. When frosting a cake, use a flexible icing spatula. Although not essential, frosting a cake on a revolving decorating stand is remarkably easy; assemble the cake on a cardboard circle first for easy removal. Typically, cake circles are corrugated, with a shiny side (assemble the layers on this side) and a matte side.

mash To mash is to reduce an ingredient to a soft state. Ripe bananas are mashed to break down their structure. The soft, nearly pulpy mixture can then be added to a cake, muffin, or tea bread batter. It is important to crush the bananas with a potato masher or wide-tined fork, rather than pureeing the chunks in a food processor, which inevitably liquefies the fruit; runny pureed bananas will impair the texture and stability of the baked sweet.

measure *To measure flour* for the recipes in this book, aerate the flour with a table fork to relieve it of any heavy, compacted settling, then dip the appropriate-size dry measuring cup into the flour and level off with the straight edge of a palette knife. *To measure leavening,* first make sure that it is free of lumps, sink the appropriate-size measuring spoon (not a spoon taken from your dinnerware service) into the leavening, then level the surface with the straight edge of a palette knife. *To measure soft, clumpy sugar,* such as light brown, dark brown, or muscovado, pack the sugar into the appropriate-size dry measuring cup, then smooth off the top with a flexible rubber spatula. *To measure granulated or superfine sugar,* first make sure that it is free of lumps, then dip the appropriate-size dry measuring cup into the sugar and level off with the straight edge of a palette knife.

melt To melt is to apply heat (of varying strengths) to an ingredient, such as butter or chocolate, so that the texture changes from semisolid or solid to a flowing, or thickly fluid, state.

mix Strictly speaking, the act of mixing is one of combining two or more ingredients carefully by whisking, stirring, or beating without overworking the components. Usually, mixing takes place on low or moderately low speed in a freestanding electric mixer, or by hand, using a wooden spoon, flat wooden paddle, large metal spoon, or flexible rubber spatula.

pipe To pipe is to force a mixture (a soft creamed dough, a stove top–cooked pastry dough such as *pâte à choux,* frosting, or firmly whipped cream) through a pastry bag fitted with a tip. The tip can be plain (round), decorative, or simply functional (such as an éclair or Bismarck tip). The act of piping both requires and allows the baker to be precise and neat.

rice When an ingredient (such as thoroughly cooked potatoes) is riced, it is put through a device (a ricer) that breaks it down into a soft, evenly textured mass. The ricer that I use for hot, freshly cooked potatoes is a single unit, with a fine-hole disk that's one with the container, without any other interchangeable disks.

rising oven or **baking in a rising oven** When you are directed to increase the preheated oven temperature at any point in a recipe (either initially or toward the end of the baking time), the technique of baking in a rising oven is applied. The reason the oven temperature is increased at the beginning of the baking time is to encourage a good rise, or lift, at the outset; increasing the temperature toward the end of the baking time finishes the baking without compromising the texture by extending the baking time unnecessarily.

scatter To scatter is to sprinkle or strew a mixture, such as a streusel, over an unbaked batter or dough. It is important to scatter an ingredient in a balanced way. Nubbins of handmade streusel should be applied in an even layer or some small sections of the sweet will bake unevenly and encourage buttery pools to form—not a tragedy if this happens, though, as the pools will blend into the topping as the sweet cools. However, the texture of larger, unbalanced sections may become pasty on cooling.

scrape down As a batter or dough is formed, the sides of the mixing bowl need to be scraped down to effect a thorough incorporation of the ingredients. Scrape down the sides of the bowl cleanly with a rubber spatula, sweeping down the batter that clings to the sides. In the course of mixing a batter, I do this during all of the stages to maintain an even consistency—creaming butter, creaming butter and sugar, incorporating the eggs and flavoring extract, alternately mixing in dry and liquid ingredients, and adding any flavoring components (such as nuts, flaked coconut, chips, or chunks of candy).

serving When the word "serving," followed by an amount, appears as information under the list of ingredients in the recipe, it refers to the yield. Note that depending on how you cut a cake, bread, or torte, or how you portion drop cookie dough, and so on, will have an impact on the actual amount that the recipe makes.

short The word "short" used to describe the baked texture of a cookie generally means that the item is tender, buttery, melt-in-the-mouth exquisite, and sometimes softly crumbly.

sift To sift is to process one dry ingredient or a collection of dry ingredients through the fine mesh of a sieve or a rotary sifter. The purpose of sifting is to aerate the dry ingredients and rid them of any pebble-like bits or clumps, rather than actually to mix them. While a flour mixture or sugar-cornstarch mixture is lightened somewhat by this act, it is not well mixed. If the recipe requires it, the ingredients will be mixed further by whisking them together in a bowl.

smooth over To smooth over is to grade the surface of a batter or dough with a flexible rubber spatula, thin flat wooden spatula, or thin-bladed palette knife (standard or offset) so that it is relatively smooth and even. The step of smoothing over a surface should be done with short, quick motions.

spoon To spoon is to move a batter, filling, topping, or soft dough from the mixing bowl to a baking pan with a spoon. A large stainless steel spoon with a wide-surfaced bowl is ideal for filling a baking pan with batter, as is a flexible rubber spatula with a spoon-like depression (sometimes referred to as a "spoonula"). In the ingredient preparation stage, some items may be spooned into dry measuring cups, then leveled off with a flexible palette knife or other straight-edged knife.

sprinkle To sprinkle is to dust a work surface with flour or sugar, an unbaked batter or dough with a flavoring mixture (such as a streusel, cheese topping, or sugar and spice filling), a baked cake with confectioners' sugar (or a blend of confectioners' sugar and cocoa powder or ground spice), or a block of bar cookies with confectioners', superfine, or granulated sugar.

stir To stir is to slowly combine two or more ingredients or keep a mixture in motion in a saucepan or bowl. Stirring is usually a low-speed act. A variety of utensils can be used for this purpose, such as a flat wooden paddle, wooden spoon, flexible or rigid rubber spatula, whisk, or stainless steel mixing spoon. The idea is to blend the mixture rather than to agitate it.

strain To strain is to pass a mixture through a mesh sieve to refine it, separating out and freeing it from impurities (such as lumps or coagulated egg protein) in order to render it smooth. Occasionally, a mixture is strained simply to make it silky and shiny.

swirl To swirl is to create arcs and curls in a frosting; in a cake batter with a center filling of chopped nuts, sugar, or spice; in a cake batter composed of two or more flavors or textures; or in a mixture that tops a bar cookie batter or dough. When a filling is swirled within a cake batter, part of the batter is turned into the cake pan, a trench is formed, and the filling is covered with the remaining batter; a round-edged table knife or flexible palette knife is drawn through the mixture to create loopy curves. When swirling, avoid scraping the bottom and sides of the baking pan with the knife and remember that overswirling smudges (and eventually would homogenize) the batter. It is frequently better to underswirl because a leavened batter will actually create some additional curves as it bakes. To swirl a topping, such as a cream cheese–based batter that tops an unbaked brownie base, I use a wooden pick or a slim wooden or metal skewer; the resulting marbleizing effect is delicate, clear, and defined.

toss To toss is to mix two or more elements—usually flavored baking chips, fresh berries, or bits of dried fruits or nuts—with a little of the sifted flour mixture in a bowl. Tossing chips with a spoonful of the dry ingredients coats them enough to prevent their sinking to the bottom of a batter during baking; it is generally unnecessary to flour ingredients that are stirred through a dense bar cookie batter or drop cookie dough. Use a sturdy metal spoon or spatula for tossing ingredients.

tent To tent is to lay a sheet of aluminum foil over the top of a cake or bread as it bakes in order to keep the surface from overbrowning during the baking process (usually toward the middle or during the final 10 or 15 minutes of the baking time). When tenting, I usually place the foil shiny side up (dull side down) for reduced heat absorption. It is important to avoid folding down the sides of the foil. Keep the foil relatively loose.

turn To turn is to transfer a dough, such as a yeast dough, into a bowl (usually coated with softened unsalted butter) in order to contain it for rising. An ancillary meaning of "turn" is to roll the yeast dough around in the greased bowl to film it in a haze of butter. The former meaning refers to the act of placing a dough or batter into a bowl, the latter to the act of coating the dough in fat and so preventing a crust from forming.

whip To whip is to beat an ingredient, such as egg whites or heavy cream, in a brisk and lively way in order to create volume and develop texture. The act of whipping generates volume by incorporating air. While equipment (such as a rotary beater, hand-held electric mixer, or freestanding electric mixer fitted with the whip attachment) can be used and is commonly specified within the procedures of this cookbook, it should be noted that the silkiest results are achieved with a bowl and a whisk. As an example, for whipping heavy cream I am a great fan of using a well-chilled bowl and a well-chilled balloon whisk, for this duo will deliver the lightest, texturally creamiest accompaniment. Egg whites should always be whipped in a grease-free bowl made of relatively lightweight stainless steel (the most accessible material) with the widest diameter whisk—a balloon shape—possible. No matter the stage of firmness required by a recipe, whipped egg whites should remain lustrous, glossy, and creamy-looking, not dry or grainy, and heavy cream should be smooth and puffy in a cloud-like way.

whisk To whisk is to merge two or more ingredients in an active way or to mix an ingredient in order to homogenize it. The concept of whisking is often thought of as a snappy and animated act, but it can also be slow and carefully business-like. I use a whisk to mix a brownie batter because it takes care of the task easily and seamlessly, leaving no unsightly pockets of flour lurking at the bottom of the mixing bowl that would, eventually, mar the baked texture of the finished bar cookie.

work in To work in is to integrate one or more ingredients into a baking powder– or baking soda–leavened or yeast-raised batter or dough; this usually takes place at the end of the procedure, before baking or the final rise. The ingredients are likely such goodies as chocolate in the form of chips, shards, or chunks; nuts; flaked coconut; large or small pieces of dried fruits; and shredded cheese. To work an ingredient into a relatively dense (and small-quantity) batter or dough, use a firm rubber spatula or wooden spoon and mix by hand; for a creamy batter, use a flexible rubber spatula and mix by hand; for a big batch of dense or heavy and creamy-thick dough, rich in ingredients, use a heavy-duty freestanding electric mixer fitted with the flat paddle and set on low speed (keeping the mixing time as short as possible). To incorporate one or more ingredients into a once- or twice-risen yeast dough, pat out the dough on a work surface dusted with flour. Sprinkle over the ingredient(s), fold the dough into thirds (as you would a business letter), then form into a loose jellyroll. The resulting form does not need to be exact or perfect. Knead the dough lightly until the addition is integrated; this will take 3 to 4 minutes. At first, the dough will tear around the ingredient(s) and possibly break up into smaller sections, but this is to be expected. Just continue on, even though it will look as if the texture is spoiled—it isn't. After a few minutes of kneading, the dough will accommodate the ingredient(s).

baking*Shape* *StructureForm*

Form and function merge when batter or dough is spooned, pressed, smoothed, or spread into all kinds of bakeware—fanciful or plain—and the shape of what you bake becomes its own art form.

The following catalog of equipment casts light on the basics and beyond: cooks dedicated to the baking process are usually charmed into amassing all the baking pans, molds, cutters, and tools appropriate to the process.

I continue to add to my own ever-growing wealth of bakeware, most notably to my specialty collection of small individual baking molds (from the tiniest half-bite-size to a maximum of three-big-bites-size); it began more than thirty years ago and I continue to find new miniatures to add.

With regard to equipment, a recipe can flow into seven stages and, by their very nature, those phases call for a different set of baking materials. It is important to note that any and all baking supplies or materials (including pans, utensils, and decorating supplies) that come into contact with unbaked or baked batter or dough should be designated as food-safe. When searching for specific equipment, it is wise to seek out an item, whether it is an important piece of electrical equipment or a simple spatula, by its name and manufacturer, rather than its code or item number. Though designed to be thorough, the codes listed in the material that follows are based only on information tallied at a certain time and at a certain place, and sites or catalogs tend to shift, alter, or otherwise change information from time to time. As well, product availability is sometimes inconsistent and, for this reason, the specifics of an item must be checked prior to purchase.

To achieve the proper results, equipment needs to be prepared (by lining with ovenproof parchment paper or release-surface aluminum foil, or filming with nonstick spray), and the creations emanating from the recipes need to be stored or enclosed in them in various stages of preparation. Ingredients must be measured and combined correctly, necessitating accurate liquid and dry measuring cups, measuring spoons, a dependable scale, and sifter. See *basics for preparation, finishing, and establishing quantity* (page 19), which will offer you guidelines for gathering those items.

Moving from measurement directly into the method for putting together a batter, dough, filling, frosting, icing, or sauce involves using, at one time or another, a freestanding electric mixer, heavy-duty freestanding electric mixer, hand-held electric mixer, range of bowls, spatulas, spoons, whisks, and strainers. *art of mixing* (page 20) will reveal those quality pieces that I have come to rely on over the years and value for overall construction, efficiency, and classic style.

shaping tools (page 22) outlines the best rolling pins, knives, and scrapers that take care of managing the size and form of a dough.

bakeware that creates form (page 24) reveals all of the baking pans that are wonderful to collect and to use, including layer cake, sheet cake, square and rectangular pans; false-bottomed cake pans; plain and fluted tube pans; shallow and deep false-bottomed tart pans; cookie sheets and rimmed sheet pans; waffle irons and a crêpe pan; springform pans; tea cake-size muffin cups, standard muffin/cupcake cups, jumbo muffin/cupcake cups, and king-size muffin cups; fluted panettone molds; popover cups; small fluted brioche molds; individual straight-sided metal baking pans; rectangular *financier* molds and *barquette* molds; a savarin mold; and madeleine molds, among them.

In between phases, a dough or batter is frequently spread out or brushed, and, of course, there exist process-specific items to accomplish both. For a description of the pastry brushes and offset spreading knives that I find invaluable, look at *distributing and sweeping* (page 28).

At the end, when that confection of yours radiates from the baking pan, all just-baked and breathtaking, expressing in its fragrance a buttery gust of homemade goodness, it's time to have at hand cooling racks and lifting spatulas. The former allow air to circulate beneath while stabilizing the bakeware during the designated cooling time and the latter ease certain items out of the pan at the appropriate time to assure that both the composition and internal structure retain their integrity. *a good rest and a thoughtful lift* (page 29) offers equipment recommendations for completing the recipe.

Why not adorn a tender, frosted cupcake with big and beautiful swirls, a baby bouquet of flowers and a leafy rambling vine, or a bundle of stars? What about piping meringues into colossal squiggles or rosettes? Or gracing a miniature torte with a topknot of swirls? *craft of decorating* (page 30) lists the supplies needed to color, tint, pipe, and otherwise turn your kitchen into a sweet warehouse for embellishing all kinds of things. Once you think of a cupcake (of any size), layer cake, or butter cookie as a surface waiting to be adorned, you will uncover a seemingly unlimited expanse of food paste colors and sparkling sugars to keep you going until three o'clock in the morning, playing with—I mean, beautifying—your newest creation.

basics for preparation, finishing, and establishing quantity

Ovenproof parchment paper, release-surface aluminum foil, and waxed paper are a baker's best friends. Lining a baking pan with food-safe parchment paper or a particular kind of foil liberates baked goods in a sleek and tidy way. A sheet of waxed paper becomes a simple surface onto which ingredients can be sifted and picked up with ease to transfer the contents into a mixing bowl. Rolls of food-safe plastic wrap and freezer paper are essential to the process of storing doughs and enclosing sweet and savory baked items.

The basics for preparation and finishing

ovenproof parchment paper Paper Maid Kitchen Parchment (20-square-foot roll); Reynolds Parchment Paper (30-square-foot roll); Beyond Gourmet Unbleached Parchment Paper, chlorine-free (71-square-foot roll); and *Papier Sulfurisé*, cellulose-fiber, chlorine-free (71-square-foot roll) allow easy removal of baked goods. Parchment paper is also useful for rolling sheets of pie, pastry, and yeast dough.

release-surface aluminum foil Both Reynolds Wrap Release Non-Stick Heavy Duty Aluminum Foil (35-square-foot roll; 11⅔ yards by 12 inches) and Reynolds Wrap Release Non-Stick Heavy Duty Aluminum Foil (45-square-foot roll; 10 yards by 18 inches) are effective for lining baking pans that receive sticky batters or doughs.

waxed paper Reynolds Cut-Rite Wax Paper (75-square-foot roll; 75.7 feet by 11.9 inches) is a fine all-purpose waxed paper to keep on hand.

plastic wrap Glad Press'n Seal (70-square-foot roll; 25.4 yards by 11.8 inches); Glad Press'n Seal (140-square-foot roll; 47.4 yards by 11.8 inches); Saran Cling Plus Junior (75-square-foot roll; 177 feet by 7¾ inches); and Saran Cling Plus (200-square-foot roll; 205 feet by 11¾ inches) provide good protection for unbaked and baked items. All plastic wrap intended to touch unbaked doughs and batters, and finished baked goods, should be designated as food-safe.

✳ Regarding plastic food-packaging materials, and in response to ongoing awareness of the components related to their manufacture, it is preferable to use those that do not contain bisphenol-A, phthalates, or styrene.

freezer paper Reynolds Freezer Paper (75-square-foot roll; 16⅔ yards by 18 inches) is substantial and prevents the dreaded freezer burn. Freezer paper, however, should be the final wrapper for doughs or baked goods that first should be tightly enclosed in food-safe plastic wrap and aluminum foil.

The basics for establishing quantity

Measuring spoons accurately quantify ingredients such as salt, ground spices, baking powder, baking soda, cream of tartar, and small amounts of sugar. As with dry measuring cups, a spoon should be filled to the brim, then leveled off flat to its surface with a flexible palette knife or the firm, straight edge of a spatula. Dry ingredients such as flour, sugar (superfine, granulated, or light or dark brown), cornstarch, rolled oats, and cocoa powder are routinely measured in dry measuring cups. Most ingredients are spooned into the cups (flour, sugar, cocoa powder, and the like) and a few others are packed into them (such as light or dark brown sugar), and in both cases, the top of each cup is leveled off with the straight edge of a palette knife. Liquid measuring cups are made of clear glass or semitransparent, heavy-weight plastic. Of the two, I prefer heatproof glass. Regardless of the materials, either type should have clear and accurate line indicators that mark ounces and cups. Use them for measuring liquid and soft dairy products, such as milk, buttermilk, heavy cream, light cream, half-and-half, sour cream, yogurt, and sweetened condensed milk.

ring of measuring spoons Spoons set in a ring, available in gradations of ⅛ teaspoon, ¼ teaspoon, ½ teaspoon, 1 teaspoon, and 1 tablespoon, are best purchased in stainless steel for durability and cleaning ease.

dry measuring cups Nested stainless steel cups in gradations of ⅛ cup, ¼ cup, ⅓ cup, ½ cup, ⅔ cup, and 1 cup are standard, though it is wise to invest in a 2-cup dry measuring cup as well.

liquid measuring cups One-, 2-, and 4-cup measuring cups are the handiest to own.

scale The Edlund digital scale (Model E-80) is used on an ongoing basis in my kitchen for weighing numerous ingredients. By virtue of its tare function, the scale is able to weigh ingredients in consecutive stages. The tare function allows you to add ingredients consecutively when the tare function pad (or button) is pushed, by subtracting the weight of the last ingredient added to the bowl or platform and resetting the weight at "0" (at which point it is ready to receive the next ingredient). Ingredients can be weighed in ounces and grams, ranging from 0.1 ounce to 80 ounces or 1 gram to 2,000 grams. The scale works either by battery (it takes one 9 volt) or with the power adapter, furnished with the scale, for plugging into an electrical outlet.

art of mixing

The act of combining measured and prepared ingredients, generically known as mixing, is a straightforward one, though the process can be short and simple, or longer and a little bit more detailed. No matter the length of the procedure, a dough or batter is made in natural, rhythmic steps, and each stage is designed to use specific equipment to bring it to the precise point of becoming baking-ready.

The basics for mixing

sifter The primary function of a sifter is to aerate flour and other dry ingredients, such as leavening (baking powder or baking soda), salt, finely ground spices, and cocoa powder, just prior to the mixing process. Occasionally, granulated or superfine sugar is included among the ingredients to be sifted with a flour mixture. Granulated or superfine sugar is sometimes sifted alone to rid it of any hardened pellets, or sifted with cornstarch to begin the process of creating a base for a thickened pastry cream or pudding mixture. The act of sifting dry ingredients lightens them considerably before they are incorporated into a dough or batter. Sifting differs from mixing, as the latter acts to combine the elements, not aerate them. Sifting also causes the dry ingredients to be more absorptive. To mix the ingredients after sifting, turn them into a bowl and agitate with a whisk. Sometimes a mixture will be sifted two times before being added to a batter in progress; at other times, a flour mixture will be sifted once to aerate, then sifted again directly over a batter or dough mixture (when making brownies, for example).

mixing bowls I reach for a nested set of stainless steel mixing bowls, balanced but reasonably lightweight, when putting together most baking recipes. Any batter or dough that is assembled by hand, or without the intervention of a freestanding electric mixer in a particular stage, gets assembled—in one way or another—in a separate mixing bowl.

A set of four graduated bowls in the following sizes will serve you well: small (8 inches in diameter, with a capacity of 6 to 7 cups); small-medium (9 inches in diameter, with a capacity of 10 cups); medium (10 inches in diameter, with a capacity of 16 cups); and large (11½ inches in diameter, with a capacity of 22 cups).

freestanding electric mixer A powerful freestanding electric mixer is an invaluable tool for a baker. With it, you will be able to spoon out gossamer batters and see the silky pull of a yeast dough come into being. The following mixers handle baking recipes beautifully: KitchenAid Professional 600 Mixer (10 speeds, 575-watt motor, 6-quart capacity, Model KP26M1XLC, with a stationary bowl, whip, spiral hook, and flat paddle attachment), KitchenAid Professional 610 Mixer (10 speeds, 590-watt motor, 6-quart capacity, Model KP26N9XNP), Cuisinart 7.0-quart Stand Mixer (1,000-watt motor, Model SM-70, with auto shutoff), and Viking Professional Stand Mixer with Blender Attachment (stainless steel, 1,000-watt motor, 7-quart capacity, Model VSM). Never leave any piece of equipment, electric or otherwise, including a freestanding electric mixer or a hand-held electric mixer, unattended when preparing a mixture—be it a dough, batter, filling, icing, or frosting.

hand-held electric mixer Smaller mixing tasks (such as light icings and small-quantity soft frostings) can be handled by a hand mixer, such as the KitchenAid Ultra Power Hand Mixer (5 speeds, Model KHM5DH).

mixing spoons, flat paddles, and heat-resistant spatulas Mixing and scraping utensils execute a procedure (beating, whisking, smoothing, folding) while acting as an extension of a baker's hands. Any one of them should feel comfortable in your hands while it is moved around in a bowl or saucepan, or when grazing the top or sides of a baking pan. Spoons make light work of combining liquidy mixtures. Flat paddles are good for working ingredients into a dense (but creamy) cookie dough, or mixing some yeast doughs and quick-bread batters. Flat paddles (as opposed to paddles that have slightly curved sides that touch a batter or dough) are composed of a single piece of wood that crests in the shape of an elongated teardrop. Rubber spatulas are invaluable for folding together two disparate mixtures to create a batter, for scraping batter from mixing bowls into prepared baking pans, and for pressing a dessert sauce or pastry cream through a fine-mesh strainer to silken its texture.

Spoons, made of boxwood or olive wood and measuring 11½ inches, 12 inches, and 12½ inches (measurement is taken from the base of the handle to the top of the rounded bowl), are convenient to own. Flat paddles in overall lengths of 11¾ inches, 12 inches, and 12½ inches should feel steady in the hand, firm, and smooth to the touch.

A heat-resistant mixing spoon and flat paddle, made of Exoglass, are effective for creating stove top–cooked sauces, pastry creams, and puddings. My mixing spoon measures 11¾ inches in length (made by Matfer Bourgeat of France #300) and flat paddles measure 9¾ inches in length (made by Matfer Bourgeat #250) and 11¾ inches in length (made by Matfer Bourgeat #300). The high-heat–resistant spatula I depend on is made by Rubbermaid and measures 10 inches in length, with a 3½-inch blade.

whisks Using a whisk is an efficient way to combine elements for a preliminary commingling—different stages of a recipe call for two or more ingredients (such as whole eggs or egg yolks and granulated sugar) to be merged; a medley of dry ingredients (after sifting); two or more liquids (such as milk and heavy cream); or a heavy cream-eggs-flavoring extract mixture (when composing a sweet biscuit or scone dough). My preference is for whisks to be made of 18-8 stainless steel.

The following whisks can handle most baking tasks quite skillfully: 11¾ inches in length, with rounded wires measuring 7¾ inches long (a good, all-purpose whisk); 12

inches in length, with 8-inch rounded wires; 13 inches in length, with 8½-inch rounded wires; and 14 inches in length, with 9-inch rounded wires.

sieves (or strainers) Straining can be described as a processing act used to achieve a certain textural refinement for pastry creams, custard and other sweet dessert sauces, stove top–cooked puddings, crêpe batters, and the like, as well as the action of sieving (or sifting) confectioners' sugar over a completed cake or batch of cookies, or flour over a work surface for kneading a yeast dough.

For straining mixtures, a nest of fine-mesh stainless steel sieves, measuring 4¾ inches, 5½ inches, and 6¼ inches in diameter, have the best utilitarian value. A fine-mesh miniature strainer, measuring 2¾ inches in diameter across the top, functions nicely for small sifting/straining needs. A fine-mesh miniature conical strainer, measuring 3 inches in diameter across the top, is fun to have on hand for angle-specific sifting/straining needs (it is also endearing).

My Ateco 4-ounce stainless steel shaker (which some bakers—including myself—usually refer to as a dredger) is 3 inches deep and measures 2¼ inches in diameter across the top mesh (Code 1347). It is perfect for sifting over confectioners' sugar, granulated sugar, superfine sugar, spiced sugar, cocoa powder, and flour. A mesh surface (rather than tiny holes) produces an evenly fine dredging on any surface, and beautifully distributes the goods onto the edges of baked tarts and tortes, and over the tops of cookies (baked and unbaked).

shaping tools

Aside from the obvious use of a rolling pin to extend a dough by flattening it out to a specifically desired thickness on a work surface, it can also be used to press a mixture (such as nut-spiced sugar, chocolate chunks or chips, chopped dried fruits or nuts) onto the dough's surface or to create a smooth plane for decorating at a later point in the recipe. Knives create overall shape, cutting unbaked doughs and baked cakes, bar cookies, and the like. Pastry scrapers cut (and clean off surfaces as well) and otherwise manage dough, and pastry blenders reduce chunks of fat into a leavened or unleavened flour mixture.

The basics for rolling

french rolling pin My pin is made of oak, measures 19½ inches in overall length (with a rolling surface of about 18½ inches), and weighs 1 pound 2 ounces. It is a level length of wood (as opposed to tapered) that can manage most doughs. The pin has been in use for more than thirty years and is kept in shape by my caring for it in the following way: it is cleaned thoroughly after each use with a thoughtful (and quick) rinsing and drying and never left to soak in water, and it is followed by an occasional massage with a light coat of food-safe neutral oil. (It should be noted that all debris of dough should be cleaned off the pin before washing; to do this, use the rounded edge of a nylon pastry scraper, rather than the sharp blade of a knife or even the rounded blade of a palette knife.) Initially, and so very long ago, I gave the pin several good coats of oil to preserve its surface. It now carries with it a beautiful, aged patina, and I would not exchange it for the fanciest rolling pin available to man- or womankind.

ball-bearing rolling pin A maple ball-bearing rolling pin made by Thorpe (in Hamden, CT) really does the work for you, rolling out any kind of dough to a desired thickness. Weighing in at a hefty 4 pounds, and with an 18-inch rolling surface, it is wonderful to use for all kinds of laminated pastry doughs and sweet yeast-raised doughs.

nylon rolling pin This pin, measuring 20 inches in overall length (with a rolling surface of 19 inches) and weighing a little more than 1 pound, provides a great nonstick surface for rolling, as does a *silicone rolling pin*. I own and use two silicone pins, a Sil-pin and Sil-pin Jr (Fiesta Products, Clark, NJ). The larger Sil-pin weighs a generous 3 pounds and measures 12 by 3 inches, with an 11-inch rolling surface, and has stainless steel ball bearings; the petite pin has a 4-inch rolling surface and weighs 5.5 ounces.

The basics for cutting, scraping, and blending

Knives are fundamental to the sweet kitchen, for chopping nuts, dried fruits, and chocolate; fashioning clean, size-specific lengths and widths to rolled or pressed doughs; tidying up the border of a tart dough or edges of a bar cookie dough; slicing through spiral-y rolls of yeast dough; trimming cake layers; and cutting through big tube cakes. Pastry cutters and dough scrapers trim and section both soft and firm doughs, in addition to removing bits and fragments of dough from a work surface with a few quick swipes. A pastry blender breaks down large chunks of butter into smaller pieces within a flour mixture destined to become a pie or pastry dough or a flavorful streusel topping.

paring knife A small paring knife, measuring 7 inches in total length (with a blade length of 3 inches) is ideal for light trimming and cutting. I rely on a carbon-steel paring knife made by Sabatier.

chef's knife A good, all-purpose knife for light-to-medium chopping and slicing measures in at a generous 12½ inches total length (with a blade length of 7¾ inches). Mine is made by Sabatier and has a carbon-steel blade that requires frequent sharpening, but the quality of slicing and chopping is unparalleled, so I think it to be worth the extra attention. A larger chef's knife, measuring 14½ inches total length (with a blade length of 9¾ inches) takes care of larger batches of ingredients, such as nuts or dried fruits.

beef slicer The long and slender blade of a beef slicer is just right for cutting through some loaf cakes, homemade marshmallows, fudgy and cakey bar cookies, or tender tarts. Mine is made by Sabatier, with a total length of 14¼ inches and a blade length of 9¾ inches.

serrated knife With its finely serrated 8-inch stainless steel blade, my Victorinox knife can slice through the most texturally challenged biscotti loaf, slice up a dainty pound cake or quick bread, and shear through a rolled and filled yeast-risen log to form individual rolls.

cake knives The Ateco 10-inch cake knife (Code 1315) or 14-inch cake knife (Code 1316) makes light work of slicing through cake to compose multiple layers. A cake knife/server made by Friedrick Dick (#1105-16), with its high-carbon no-stain 7-inch triangular blade, moves through the crumb of a cake with ease, as does the tart/cake knife made by Wüsthof (#4821), with its 6¾-inch triangular blade.

plain pastry cutters Ateco makes two pastry cutters that cut through all kinds of dough beautifully: the 2½-inch pastry cutter (Code 1392) has a stainless steel blade and a wooden handle; the 4-inch pastry cutter (Code 1394) also has a stainless steel blade and a wooden handle.

pastry cutter with fluted wheel This fancier version of a pastry cutter, made by Ateco (Code 1397), has a stainless steel blade and wooden handle. The pretty edging created by running the wheel across a dough makes attractive lattice strips for weaving on the top of a tart or pie. It is also useful for cutting through rolled cookie dough.

pastry scrapers The Racle Tout by Matfer Bourgeat (#82231) is a nylon pastry scraper/dough cutter that easily lifts and cuts dough, levels the surface of thick batter or dough, and cleans a pastry board. A pastry scraper made by Ateco (Code 1319), with its 4-inch-wide blade, functions similarly, as does the stainless steel scraper with a plastic handle made by Ateco (Code 1318) and the stainless steel–bladed bench scraper made by Ateco (Code 1300).

pastry blender The chief purpose for this humble but highly efficient tool, nothing more than six rounded stainless steel wires converging into a wooden or metal handle, is to break down fat into flour. The resulting mixture, with its small bits, pieces, and shards of butter, becomes the base for a leavened dough (biscuit or scone, for example) or streusel mixture.

bakeware that creates form

The design of baking pans spans the basic forms (layers, loaves, and such) to the specialty shapes that introduce whimsy and novelty for baking traditional doughs and batters.

The basics for bakeware

The basics (and beyond) for bakeware follow, and it is important to note that you may find very subtle differences in size measurement and capacities in random pans listed below, as their manufacture may change over time. However, there is some flexibility in the recipes within *Baking Style* that will accommodate those changes.

layer cake pans Layer cake pans made of medium-weight aluminum, 9 inches in diameter and 1¾ inches deep, are the classic workhorses of the traditional two- and three-layer cakes. Nine- and 10-inch layer cake pans that are 2 inches deep can be substituted for fluted false-bottomed tart pans and some extra-deep cake pans. When appropriate, each recipe will offer a substitution suggestion in the notes section.

deep single-layer cake pans A round 8-inch cake pan (3 inches deep), round 9-inch cake pan (3 inches deep), and round 10-inch cake pan (3 inches deep) are great for coffee cake and dessert cake batters, as are their relatives, a false-bottomed round 8-inch cake pan (3 inches deep), false-bottomed round 9-inch cake pan (3 inches deep), and false-bottomed round 10-inch cake pan (3 inches deep). The pans, made of medium-weight aluminum, produce tall, beautifully textured single layers.

specialty single-layer cake pan A pan somewhere in height between a standard layer cake pan and a deep (3 inches) pan, a 9¼ to 9½-inch plain or fluted cake pan (2½ inches deep), makes a fine single-layer torte.

springform pans This type of single-layer pan has the advantage of allowing the baker an easy time of unmolding (and serving): the side hinge, clasped into place before filling and baking, unlocks handily, leaving the contents on its round base. Pans with the following dimensions will accommodate most batters nicely: 8½ inches in diameter (2½ inches deep), 9 inches in diameter (2¾ inches deep), and 10 inches in diameter (2¼ inches deep).

specialty heart cake pan The Wilton Decorator Preferred Heart Pan (#2105-600), measuring 6 by 2 inches, makes a lovely looking quick bread to serve four. I use it for cornbread and banana bread, and even spoon craggy dollops of drop biscuit dough into it, creating what I described to a baker friend as "The Great Biscuit."

Bundt pans Who can exist without a Bundt pan? Or two? One pan in my collection measures 10 inches in diameter and is a generous 3¾ inches deep, with a capacity of 14 cups. The other Bundt pan, which measures 10 inches in diameter, is 4½ inches deep, with a capacity of 15 cups, and is known as the 60th Anniversary Bundt Pan. I love both pans, but the 60th Anniversary pan is a particular favorite. The resulting swirls form natural divisions for cutting, and the rounded top of the baked and inverted cake is tailor-made for glazing. (Bundt is a registered trademark of Northland Aluminum Products, Inc.)

plain tube pans For pound cakes and big, flavored butter cakes, a one-piece (not false-bottomed), straight-sided tube pan houses the batter in a magnificent way. Two of the best examples are a plain, one-piece 9¾-inch tube pan (6 inches deep, with a capacity of 18 cups) and a plain, one-piece 10-inch tube pan (4¼ to 4½ inches deep, with a capacity of 18 cups).

fluted tube pans Three deep pans—a fluted 9-inch tube pan (4¼ inches deep, with a capacity of 11 cups), fluted 10-inch tube pan (4¾ inches deep, with a capacity of 13 to 13½ cups), and deeply swirled 10-inch tube pan (4¼ inches deep, with a capacity of 12 to 13 cups)—make pretty cakes and striking yeast-risen breads.

deeply swirled tube pan This pan, also known as a *kugelhopf pan*, measures 10 inches in diameter (4¼ inches deep, with a capacity of 12 to 13 cups). It is the time-honored form for baking kugelhopf, a classic yeast-risen raisin bread. Though pricey, the pan can also be used for yeast-risen coffee cakes and batter breads, some large-quantity quick breads, and many types of butter cakes.

muffin and cupcake pans Miniature muffin pans (12 cups to a pan, each cup measuring 1¾ inches in diameter and ¾ inch deep, with a capacity of 1 tablespoon plus 2 teaspoons); tea cake–size muffin cups (24 cups to a pan, each cup measuring 2 inches in diameter and 1³⁄₁₆ inches deep, with a capacity of 3 tablespoons); muffin/cupcake cups (12 cups to a pan, each cup measuring 2¾ inches in diameter and 1⅜ inches deep, with a capacity of ½ cup); fluted Bundt cupcake pan cups (12 fluted cups to a pan, each fluted cup measuring 2½ inches in diameter and 1¼ inches deep, with a capacity of ⅓ cup); jumbo muffin/cupcake cups (6 cups to a pan, each cup measuring 4 inches in diameter and 1¾ inches deep, with a capacity of 1⅛ cups); and king-size muffin cups (6 cups to a pan, each cup measuring 3½ inches in diameter and 3 inches deep, with a capacity of 1¼ cups) make terrific small-to-large treats. Depending on the type of batter used, and (obviously) except for the fluted Bundt cupcake pan cups, you will get a better rise and peak if the pans are first lined with ovenproof baking cup liners; this is generally the case with creamed batters and less important with many quick-bread batters (such as for corn muffins).

popover cups Even though a popover batter can be baked in individual muffin cups of all sizes, small popover cups (12 cups to a pan, each cup measuring 2¼ inches in diameter [interior diameter, minus the lip; 3 inches in diameter if including the lip] and 2 inches deep, with a capacity of ⅓ cup plus 1 tablespoon) and large popover cups (two 6-cup pans, each cup measuring 3 inches in diameter [interior diameter, minus the lip; 3¾ inches in diameter if including the lip] and 2½ inches deep, with a capacity of ⅔ cup) are designed for creating prettier, and texturally creamier, results. And the crown on each bread baked in either of the traditional pans is generously puffy.

straight-sided baking pans This type of pan satisfies numerous baking needs, from baking bar cookies and coffee cakes to housing yeast-risen pull-apart rolls and buns, both savory and sweet. In addition to collecting the pans with a more-or-less standard height of 2 inches, give serious thought to acquiring those measuring 3 inches in height. Remember that a deeper pan can contain a batter or dough that rises only to fill the pan halfway, for example, but a pan of lesser depth is not made to hold a more voluminous batter or yeast dough that has the capability—and the need—to expand to greater heights, especially if a flavorful and textural filling or topping is a part of the recipe.

For 2-inch-deep pans, consider the following sizes: 8 by 8 by 2 inches, 9 by 9 by 2 inches, 13 by 9 by 2 inches, and 12 by 15 by 2 inches. For 3-inch-deep pans, consider the following sizes: 5 by 5 by 3 inches (it is a good idea to own three of these), 12 by 8 by 3 inches, and 13 by 9 by 3 inches.

cookie sheets Medium- and heavy-weight aluminum cookie sheets, with a raised rim or ledge on the two shorter sides, measuring 14 by 17¾ inches, should be a baking kitchen staple. It is wise to invest in at least two (or three) sheets, which make relaying cookies (and more) into the oven without delay. Insulated cookie sheets, with one raised rim on one of the shorter sides, measuring 14 by 16¼ inches, should be reserved for baking delicately tender cookies, like shortbread cut-outs, sandies, and *sablés*.

rimmed sheet pans Imagine a cookie sheet with four 1-inch raised (and slightly outwardly angled) rims and you have a rimmed sheet pan. The basic sheet pans that I own, and use regularly, are made of medium-weight aluminum and measure 13 by 18 by 1 inch and 10 by 15 by 1 inch. The pans are ideal for baking drop cookies, plain rolled and intricately stamped cookies, biscuits, scones, soda bread, and anything else that requires a stable, flat surface that is capable of even heat distribution.

jellyroll pan A jellyroll pan that measures 10½ by 15½ by 1¾ inches does double duty for baking light cake roll batters and thin cookie doughs that are spread into the pan, baked until firm, and texturally resemble crunchy brittle, like my *riot-of-ingredients breakup* (page 235). A jellyroll pan is best made of medium-weight aluminum to prevent warping.

shallow fluted false-bottomed tart pans and deep fluted false-bottomed tart pans Made of tinned steel, these tart pans are ideal for the obvious (tarts and tart-like single-layer sweets), but also function magnificently for a range of sweet and savory yeast doughs, press-in-the-pan cookie doughs, and moderately dense or dense cake batters. Of the shallow pans (1 to 1¼ inches deep), the following diameter sizes are useful to collect: 8 inches (1 inch deep), 8½ to 9 inches (1 inch deep), 11 inches (1 inch deep), and 4 inches (1¼ inches deep). It would be helpful to own eight 4-inch pans. Of the deep pans (2 inches deep), these are the two diameter sizes to collect: 8½ to 9 inches and 10 inches.

individual baba (dariole or timbale) and small, individual tart molds Baba molds, made of tinned steel (each mold measuring a scant 2¼ inches high and 2½ inches in diameter [measured across the top], with a capacity of ⅔ cup), are the classic containers for individually assembled and baked *babas au rhum,* made from a buttery and eggy savarin dough. The mold is small, cylindrical, and flares outward slightly toward the rolled rim. Sometimes a baba mold is referred to as a dariole or timbale mold, though the former generally contains a custard mixture (usually savory) or a sweet cake batter and the latter a custard, pasta, or rice mixture. Baba, dariole, and timbale molds narrow slightly toward the bottom. The timbale molds that I own measure a generous 2¼ inches high and 2½ inches in diameter (measured across the top), with a capacity of ⅔ cup; they are almost identical to the baba molds. Round tart molds (each mold measuring 2½ inches in diameter and ¾ inch deep, with a capacity of a scant 2 tablespoons plus 1½ teaspoons) and slightly larger round tart molds (each mold measuring 2¼ inches in diameter and ½ inch deep, with a capacity of 2 tablespoons) are wonderful to collect for baking sweet batters, whether crusted or crustless.

individual brioche molds Small fluted molds (each mold measuring 3¼ inches in diameter across the top, from end of flute to end of flute, and 1⅝ inches deep, with a capacity of ⅓ cup plus 1 tablespoon plus 2½ teaspoons) and baby fluted brioche molds (each mold measuring 2¼ inches in diameter across the top, from end of flute to end of flute, and 1 inch deep, with a capacity of 2 tablespoons), made of tinned steel, are structurally necessary to bake

classic brioche, that egg and butter-saturated yeast-risen dough, but the molds can also be used to house muffin and "creamed" cake batters.

individual straight-sided metal baking pans Small, moderately heavy aluminum pans with rolled edges (each measuring 3 inches in diameter and 2 inches deep, with a capacity of scant ¾ cup) are just perfect for filling with a muffin or creamed cake batter. In them, the batter bakes into high, moist sweets—wonderful for topping with an icing, frosting, or glaze.

madeleine *plaques* The tender, ephemeral little cakes known as madeleines should be baked in the classic pans called *plaques à coques* (each *plaque* contains 8 shells measuring 2½ inches long, 2½ inches at the widest point, with a capacity of 1 tablespoon plus 2¾ teaspoons each) or the *plaques à madeleine* (each *plaque* contains twelve 3-inch shells, with a capacity of 2 tablespoons each). The *plaques* should be cared for properly: avoid using a blunt or sharp metal instrument to dislodge the cakes (if the pans are treated correctly before use, the cakes will release when each pan is inverted onto a cooling rack) and wipe the ridges clean before washing to head off any seriously abrasive scrubbing.

loaf pans Miniature loaf pans (each pan measuring 3¼ by 2 inches and 1¼ inches deep, with a capacity of a scant ½ cup), made of aluminum, look like baking toys for toddlers, but in actuality neatly hold mounds of moist biscuit or muffin batter, yeast dough for tidy little rolls, and firm but buttery cake batters. A 9 by 5 by 3-inch pan, also made of aluminum, makes a fine-looking loaf, big and bold; the loaf pan of this size that I regularly use has outwardly sloping, rather than straight, sides and, in it, a sweet bread or tea cake crests appealingly.

panettone molds Fluted molds made of tinned steel (measuring 6 inches in diameter and 5½ inches deep, with a capacity of about 8 cups) bake tall breads with an impressive build to them. Though a typical panettone cuts into long and lanky pieces, the overall structure is tight, due to the shape and steadiness of the mold.

savarin mold This mold looks similar to a ring mold, but is low-set and squat; it measures 9¼ to 9½ inches in diameter and 1⅞ to 2 inches deep, with a capacity of 5 to 5½ cups. The 9¼ to 9½-inch-diameter surface area is necessary to contain the expansion of a very sticky and buttery-soft dough.

ring mold This round, aluminum mold, 10 inches in diameter and 3 inches deep, has been around for years. Mine is made by Mirro, and it has a capacity of 12 cups. It is a classic, and so fine to use for making a sweet yeast bread ring, such as *the cinnamon-raisin buns of my childhood, #2* (page 447).

financier **molds** Rectangular tinned-steel molds (measuring 1⅞ by 2¾ inches, with a capacity of about 3 tablespoons) are made especially for baking an almondy batter that usually corresponds to the mold itself. Though other flavors can be made to suit the size and shape of the mold, the word *financier* is classically associated with a dense and somewhat chewy almond butter pastry. A *financier* batter can be baked in miniature muffin pans with acceptable results.

barquette **molds** Boat-shaped molds (measuring 1⅞ by 3¾ inches, with a capacity of 2 tablespoons), made of tinned steel, make elegantly elongated pastries. Spoonfuls of *financier* batter can be baked in these molds, as can almost any flavored macaroon mixture, sponge cake, madeleine, or other lightened butter cake batter.

crêpe pan A carbon-steel crêpe pan measuring 6¾ inches in diameter across the top, with a base of 4¾ inches, will turn out beautiful "handkerchief" pancakes. A crêpe pan needs to be scrubbed and seasoned before use (see page 398, in *thin and jam-packed*). Small, folded crêpes of this size look pretty on the plate, though larger crêpes are equally delicious and can be used for filling with sautéed fruit.

cast-iron skillet Though not strictly bakeware, a well-seasoned, well-used cast-iron skillet is as fine a baking pan for a cornbread batter as any other piece of equipment, such as a square pan or a multisectioned muffin pan. The preseasoned Lodge 9-inch skillet (about 1¾ inches deep) would be a good size to own, as it can accept most batters built on 1 cup all-purpose flour and 1½ cups corn meal to 2 eggs and 1 cup milk or buttermilk (as in my *pan cornbread* on page 134); for a lesser quantity of dry ingredients, you may wish to use a smaller pan, such as a 7- or 8-inch pan. Though the current cast-iron pans are preseasoned, I like to get that earthy darkness going early in the game and, having washed and dried the new pan thoroughly, coat the *inside* to ¼ inch of the rim with a good smear (about ¹⁄₁₆-inch thickness) of solid shortening, and "bake" the pan on the lower-third-level rack of a preheated 275 degrees F oven for at least 1½ hours (2 hours is preferable), then turn off the heat and let the pan stand in the oven (undisturbed) for 1 hour. After the oven sojourn, cool the pan on a heatproof rack for 2 hours, then completely mop up the shortening from the inside of the pan with paper towels. Store the pan in a humidity-free spot.

waffle irons A 2-grid, deep-dish (Belgian-style) waffle iron (each grid measuring about 4½ by 4½ inches) will provide breakfast-hungry guests with luxuriously thick waffles. A 6-stick waffler (each grid measuring 5 by 1½ inches) is a kick to use, as 3 double-sided rounded sticks (or 6 individual sticks) emerge hot from the griddle ready to be crisscrossed onto plates. The 6-stick waffler is the first iron I have ever owned that inspired me to make savory waffles and serve those as "bread" with my Official Sunday-Best Fried Chicken Dinner. The Vitantonio Danish waffler, composed of 5 interconnected hearts (the diameter of the grid is 7 inches), makes a large, very pretty single-serving waffle, though this piece of equipment makes thinner, more delicate-looking waffles.

Some advice on pan substitutions

A range of recipes can be baked in alternative pans, and suggestions for swapping sizes are reflected in individual recipes where the switch will not have a large impact on the end result (though baking times will be affected slightly and are accounted for). It is important to use the suggested bakeware for accuracy. Here is a general list of bakeware exchanges that work out within the context of the recipes in this book:

For a round 9-inch cake pan (3 inches deep) or false-bottomed round 9-inch cake pan (3 inches deep), use a round 10-inch cake pan (2 inches deep), reducing the baking time by about 5 minutes.

For a deeply swirled 10-inch tube pan (4¼ inches deep, with a capacity of 12 to 13 cups), use a 10-inch Bundt pan (a generous 3¾ inches deep, with a capacity of 14 cups), reducing the baking time by 5 to 7 minutes.

For a plain, one-piece 9¾-inch tube pan (6 inches deep, with a capacity of 18 cups), use a plain, one-piece 10-inch tube pan (4¼ to 4½ inches deep, with a capacity of 18 cups), reducing the baking time by 5 to 6 minutes.

For a fluted 8½ to 9-inch false-bottomed tart pan (2 inches deep), use a round 9-inch layer cake pan (2 inches deep).

For a fluted 10-inch false-bottomed tart pan (2 inches deep), use a round 10-inch layer cake pan (2 inches deep).

For three 5 by 5 by 3-inch baking pans, use two 8 by 8 by 2-inch baking pans, reducing the baking time by 4 to 5 minutes.

For a 12 by 8 by 3-inch baking pan, use a 13 by 9 by 2-inch baking pan, reducing the baking time by 5 minutes.

For a 12 by 15 by 2-inch baking pan, use two 8 by 8 by 2-inch baking pans.

For a 13 by 9 by 3-inch baking pan, use two 9 by 9 by 2-inch baking pans, reducing the baking time by about 5 minutes.

For a 10-inch springform pan (2¼ inches deep), use a false-bottomed round 10-inch cake pan (3 inches deep), reducing the baking time by 2 to 3 minutes.

For 16 round tart molds (each mold measuring 2¼ inches in diameter and ½ inch deep, with a capacity of 2 tablespoons), use two miniature muffin pans (12 cups to a pan, each cup measuring 1¾ inches in diameter and ¾ inch deep, with a capacity of 1 tablespoon plus 2 teaspoons), reducing baking time by about 5 minutes.

distributing and sweeping

Spatulas and pastry brushes are designed to extend, spread, coat, or otherwise disperse a mixture (batter, dough, frosting, icing, glaze, liquidy-sugary wash) over and about a baked or unbaked sweet.

The basics for smoothing, spreading, and brushing

icing spatula An icing spatula smooths icing, glazes, and frostings, but also takes care of leveling the surface of batters and doughs. Look for stainless steel–bladed icing spatulas that are firmly flexible, with just a little give. Both of these spatulas perform well: Ateco Ultra (Code 1304), with its stainless steel blade and polypropylene handle, measures 8½ inches in overall length (4¼-inch-long blade), and Ateco Ultra (Code 1308), with its stainless steel blade and polypropylene handle, measures 13 inches in overall length (8-inch-long blade).

offset icing spatula An offset version of an icing spatula offers excellent control for working over the surface of a frosted or glazed cake and polishing the surface (including inside those tight little corners) of a batter- or dough-filled cake or sheet pan. Simply described, a bend in the blade differentiates this type of spatula from the one above. Two estimable versions of the offset spatula are the Ateco Ultra (Code 1307), with its stainless steel blade and polypropylene handle (12 inches overall length and 6¼-inch blade angled about 1¾ inches from the handle), and the Ateco Ultra (Code 1309), with its stainless steel blade and polypropylene handle (14¾ inches overall length and 7¾-inch blade angled about 2¼ inches from the handle).

pastry brushes Food-safe pastry brushes are used for applying glaze, a sugary wash, preserves, or jelly as a glaze topping for tarts, cookies, and cakes; for brushing off flour from a yeast dough; for brushing melted butter on a formed or unformed dough or batter; for basting the tops and sides of a cake or bread; and for painting dry, royal icing–covered surfaces of baked cookies with food-safe food color powder. Separate pastry brushes should be reserved for sweet and savory baking.

The following brushes are dependable: Sparta brush (#432-1"), 8½ inches in overall length, with the bristle width at 2 inches and length at 2 inches, is a good all-purpose brush for applying glaze, wash, and jelly topping; Carlisle croissant basting brush (#40377), 11¾ inches in overall length, with the bristle width at 1½ inches and length at 3¼ inches, is perfect for glazing delicate yeast pastries, tender loaf and tube cakes, and tarts; Carlisle brush (#40375), 9½ inches in overall length, with the bristle width at 2¾ inches and length at 2¼ inches, takes care of covering extensive areas of pastry and yeast doughs with liquid mixtures, and glazing the tops and sides of Bundt cakes and pound cakes; and Ateco pastry brush with rounded bristles (Code 61000), 10¼ inches in overall length, with the bristle width at 1⅛ inches and length at 2¼ inches, gets easily into the flutes of cakes and the surface crevices of sweet rolls or tarts when finishing with a glaze.

a good rest and a thoughtful lift

A baking pan filled with crispy-chewy cookies or crusty-on-the-outside-and-tender-within scones, a tube pan cradling a good-looking cake, or a square pan holding golden yeast rolls or a spice-scented coffee cake all have two pivotal procedures in common: the need to cool the contents and the requirement to remove the contents. A gridded cooling rack is essential, as it provides a heatproof surface for raising up the hot baking pan to allow air to circulate; a wide offset spatula (which differentiates itself from the narrower versions on page 28) elevates the goods carefully without crushing them; and a boxwood crêpe spatula is an item specifically designed to pick up the delicate pancake from a hot pan to turn or remove it.

The basics for cooling and lifting

cooling racks Cooling racks, sometimes simply called racks in the method of a recipe, are available in round and rectangular shapes, and in a nonstick version as well. These merit owning: round racks measuring 8 and 9 inches in diameter; a rectangular rack measuring 13 by 22 inches; and nonstick racks, made by Wilton, measuring 13 inches in diameter (#2305-230); 10 by 16 inches (#2305-228); 14½ by 20 inches (#2305-229).

wide offset spatula A stainless steel spatula with a broad offset blade (or lifting surface area) is a necessity for removing cookies, pancakes, squares or rectangles of sheet cake, squares or rectangles of bar cookies, and individual or sections of yeast rolls and buns from a baking pan. The overall length of the offset spatulas I find most helpful are: 7½ inches (with a total blade area, including offset, of 3½ inches), 9½ inches (with a total blade area, including offset, of 5¼ inches), and 14¼ inches (with a total blade area, including offset, of 10 inches).

crêpe spatula This type of boxwood spatula looks like a slender, elongated paddle—ideal for lifting crêpes from the pan (10¼ inches in overall length, with a blade length of 6¼ inches and blade width of 1½ inches). Initially, you may think that this is a trivial item, but as the slim sheath of wood flawlessly slips under a lacy crêpe so elegantly and effortlessly, you'll never go back to using any other implement when making these lovely pancakes.

craft of decorating

A range of items is available to take a cake, bread, batch of cookies, or pastries to the next level, ornamenting them with icing, frosting, colored sugar, sprinkles, and more. Boards (rounds and rectangles) function as sturdy bases for assembling and decorating single- and multiple-layered cakes; revolving turntables (both round and rectangular) allow you to add embellishments to the top and sides of a sweet with ease; and frostings or other toppings can be put through tip-attached pastry bags to add dressy touches.

The basics for decorating

corrugated cake boards Cake boards provide a surface area for assembling (that is, for frosting and decorating) a cake or other baked goods. Both Ateco and Wilton offer a range of sizes.

In the Ateco line, 6-, 7-, 8-, 9-, 10-, 12-, 14-, 16-, and 18-inch round boards will meet most baking needs; and 13 by 18½-inch half-sheet-size boards and 9½ by 13½-inch quarter-sheet-size boards are ideal to use for specialty sheet and other larger single layer cakes.

In the Wilton line, 6-, 8-, 10-, 12-, 14-, and 16-inch round boards will satisfy many cake-baking needs, as will 10 by 14-inch and 13 by 19-inch boards.

round and rectangular cake decorating turntables
Placing an item to be decorated on a turntable allows you to move it (and with one version, angle it), rather than yourself, around and around, to smooth a frosting and apply embellishing touches to the surface. The following round turntables are substantial in form and function: the Ateco Professional Cake Decorating Turntable (Code 612), made of heavy-duty aluminum, measures 12 inches in diameter and 4⅝ inches high (this one may be used with a cake up to 16 inches in diameter); the Wilton Professional Turntable (#307-2501), made of heavy-duty aluminum, measures 12 inches in diameter and 4½ inches high; and the Wilton Titling Cake Turntable (#307-894) measures 12 inches in diameter and angles to 12 degrees, 24 degrees, and level (the angled-degree positions lock in place). A rectangular cake decorating turntable is suitable for decorating rectangular cakes,

and also a run of cookies or scones, and this is a respectable one: Ateco Revolving Cake Stand with Rectangular Top (Code 614), measuring 12 by 16 inches.

doilies A doily, slipped under a stack of cookies, biscuits, or scones, or beneath a tea loaf or layer cake, adds a clean, frilly touch for presentation. Wilton Grease-Proof White Cake Doilies are useful to have on hand in the following sizes: 8-, 10-, 12-, and 14-inch rounds, and a special dimension, 10 by 14 inches, appropriate for long loaves of yeast bread and slices of coffee cake, shingled for serving.

pastry bags Pastry bags are available in a reasonably wide variety of sizes, though 8-inch, 10-inch, and 12-inch bags are the most effective when using standard tips and smaller quantities of material to be piped, and 14- and 18-inch bags can accommodate larger tips and contain larger amounts of filling or dough. Of all the bags available, these are timeless with regard to construction and style: Ateco Plastic Coated Decorating Bag, made of polyethylene-lined cloth (8, 10, 12, 14, 16, and 18 inches in size); Ateco Wunderbag Decorating Bag, made of heavy-weight polyurethane (10, 12, 14, 16, and 18 inches in size); Ateco Flex Decorating Bags, made of nylon-coated polyurethane (8, 10, 12, 14, 16, and 18 inches in size); and Wilton Featherweight Decorating Bags, made of flexible polyester (8, 10, 12, 14, 16, and 18 inches in size).

couplers A coupler is a two-piece accessory that allows you to exchange tips without emptying the bag of its contents, a small (but necessary) item, whether you change tips frequently or sporadically during the decorating process. The larger of the two couplers is vital to use in tandem with large tips and some of the larger specialty tips. Both sizes are available (at the Ultimate Baker Web site) from Ateco (Large Coupler [Code A404] and Standard Pastry Bag Coupler [Code A400]) and Wilton (Standard Coupler [#411-1987] and Large Coupler [#411-1006]).

tip brushes and covers A tip brush effectively cleans both large- and standard-size tips; tip covers cover filled, pastry tip–attached pastry bags to keep the contents moist and to avoid leakage when traveling or between decorating phases. Both are available from Wilton.

sets of decorating tips While an enormous range of decorating tips for outfitting pastry bags exists, I find the following, from Ateco and Wilton, at the top end of usefulness and quality:

From Ateco: 7 Piece Fancy Cake and Pastry Decorating Set (Code 701), 12 Piece Large Tube Set (Code 786), 29 Piece Decorating Tube Set (Code 782), Closed Star Tube Set (Code 850), French Star Tube Set (Code 870), Plain Tube Set (Code 810) Star Tube Set (Code 830), and Pastry Tube Set (Code 787).

From Wilton: Deluxe Tip Set (#2104-6666), Master Tip Set (#2104-7778), 50 Piece Tool Caddy Decorating Set (#2109-859), 25 Piece Cake Decorating Set (#2104-2536), and 18 Piece Cake Decorating Set (#2104-2530).

food-safe paste colors Paste food colors are used for tinting batters (or any kind of mixture), doughs, icings, frostings, and glazes, and only those designated as edible, food-safe colors should be mixed into recipes for baked goods. The following food-safe paste colors are only a sampling of those available for baking and cake decorating enthusiasts:

Ateco: Soft Paste Gel Food Color 6 Pack of assorted food colors (Code 1106) and Soft Paste Gel Food Color 12 Pack of assorted food colors (Code 1112), in addition to a complete range of colors available in .75-ounce jars.

Cake Craft Food Color Kits: Junior 4 Color Kit, Basic 8 Color Kit, Student 9 Color Kit, and Professional Icing Colors Kit of eight 1-ounce bottles and twelve 1-ounce bottles. Cake Craft also sells a sensational line of pastel colors including Buttercup, Apricot, Peach, Mello Melon, Wild Rose, Miami Mauve, Wedgwood Blue, and Meadow Green, in addition to other concentrated paste colors.

AmeriColor Soft Gel Paste is available in forty first-rate colors in .75-ounce dispensers.

piping gel This product, which is generally used—tinted—in the preparation of writing or other piped design work, is also effective for adding luster and stability to buttercream-based and confectioners' sugar–based frostings: Wilton Piping Gel is available in a 10-ounce container (#704-105). For each 1½ cups of prepared frosting, you can safely blend in 1½ teaspoons of piping gel.

Baking Storybook

In my kitchen, a recipe developed, perfected, and sent on its way, journeying into the hands of those who love to bake or simply to read about baking, has a sense of evolution and of history.

A formula may be the result of my emotional attachment to a flavor or a tasty response to something encountered in the distant past or in the here and now. The dogged pursuit of a set of components and an accompanying method for a cake, scone, bar cookie, or sweet roll oftentimes presents itself as a challenge, not unlike putting together a puzzle. There is always that moment in time when I remove the item from the oven, deposit it on a cooling rack, and wait—sometimes impatiently—to study its contents and then to taste it, and at this time I see that all the elements have come together beautifully and the challenge no longer exists. Temporarily. It is then that a fountainhead of memories, collected over a life span of baking years, breaks loose and whips around, provoking me to recall each and every aspect of its core goodness. How did the sweet or savory baked good come to be? Where is it going? Can it survive another shift of flavor or tilt of texture? And even thinking about the recipe draws out another incarnation of it. Sometimes it's that inevitable, and the whole process begins once again.

The life of a recipe begins in my mixing bowl. In addition to ingredients, that bowl houses a backlog of tastes, thoughts, tweaks, and triumphs. Plus an occasional nuisance. For me, a recipe is never merely a fixed combination of ingredients and procedure, it is a tale…a point of interest…a vexation…something of a chronicle…and, once in a while, a revelation.

Revelations are hard to come by, but when one happens, it places everything at a temporary standstill. But there is always a reason for it, as the search usually has some kind of narrative associated with its existence. A recipe, then, springs from a kind of baking event. It is in that all-embracing context that the following stories exist. A recipe plumps up the narration, but the companion tale is the grounding for its existence.

My baking accounts or concepts do not live independent of the content of the recipes. There is context. The recipes may have a certain spirit on their own, but they are enriched, punctuated, and enlarged by circumstances that attend them. The roots of the recipes in this book have taken form, in one way or the other, over more than thirty years, and the refinement of each appears now, finally, in its written form. In fact, I could fill up another book by chronicling the history of each. I encourage you to do what I have done in this book. Begin a baking diary, add your own anecdotes, and note your personal changes in the recipes that I offer–go right ahead and add more chocolate chips to the cookie dough, pile the frosting extra-high on each rise of a batch of cupcakes, flavor your lofty meringue with a colorful swath of pink peppermint. Annotate recipes. Revise them. Add atmosphere. And of course, take time to enjoy the art, the scent, and the taste of great home baking along the way.

a baking life

One of the first recipes slipped into my baking file (begun at age seven) was for brownies. You could very well say that the placement of that recipe sealed my professional fate then and there—unknowingly.

An earnest passion for the art and craft of a recipe whose critical components include flour, butter, sugar, and eggs has captivated me since that point in time. While others my age were playing in a sandbox, I was busy spinning my fingers through a powdery sifted mound of flour. The flour captivated me and playing with it annoyed my late mother to no end.

The act of baking—and I think those with whom I share this profession would agree—is an organic process. A baking recipe, and how it behaves, can change from time to time and even morph into something completely different when you least expect it to. Ingredients are mutable, including the rock-steady ones like flour and butter; their inherent changes are, on occasion, sometimes woeful and mostly glorious. Equipment, and the quality of it, vary. Flavors come in and out of vogue, but, thankfully, the basic ones, like chocolate and vanilla, endure. And then there is the renaissance of forgotten flavors that enjoy a homecoming, like caramel, almond, lemon, and apricot.

And so it seems brownies always reign. I am never far away from anyone who doesn't love a brownie. In any form. I'm personally in the fudgy-chewy camp, but would not turn down a moist-cakey one either. The brownie recipe that has undergone the most modification over the last thirty years (it is not the one referenced above in the file box of my childhood) is presented here. Is a recipe of mine ever definitive? Not in my kitchen. I diddle with ingredients mercilessly. I play with a method or two, or three. I toy with baking times and temperatures. I flirt with all shapes of baking pans. I shamelessly reconfigure brownie recipes. In my hands, no amount of butter or chocolate is safe. What's worse, just when the outside world thinks that my latest confection is *the one,* I offer another—a slight variation on the previous model. The drama continues.

Besides the big-batch brownies represented elsewhere in this volume, let me present the newest configuration of one of my oldest formulas, the *forever brownies.* The "forever" part of the title means that the recipe is continually (understand that this means *forever*) in progress and eternally beloved as well. In this book, it is frozen in time and space, but who knows, you might well read about it months or years from now when it takes a different form. In all, it has been a gratifying road to travel, perfecting recipes that find a loving place in the baking pans of others. It is in this selfsame spirit that this baking diary begins, with brownies.

Hold on to your whisk—it's a sweet ride ahead.

Preheat the oven to 325 degrees F.

Lengthwise and width-wise, line the inside of a 9 by 9 by 2-inch baking pan with sheets of release-surface aluminum foil, pressing in the foil release side up and leaving 2 to 3 inches of foil to extend on all four sides; film the inside of the pan with nonstick oil spray. Or, line the inside of the pan with sheets of ovenproof parchment paper, leaving about 2 inches of paper to end on all four sides.

For the batter, sift the all-purpose flour, cake flour, baking powder, salt, and cocoa powder onto a sheet of waxed paper.

Whisk the melted butter, melted unsweetened chocolate, and melted bittersweet chocolate in a medium-size mixing bowl until smooth. In a large mixing bowl, beat the eggs just to mix thoroughly. Add the superfine sugar and beat for 45 seconds, just to combine. Blend in the butter-melted chocolate mixture, vanilla extract, and corn syrup. Resift the flour mixture over the chocolate mixture. Whisk slowly to form a batter, scraping down the sides of the mixing bowl with a rubber spatula to keep the batter even-textured.

Pour and scrape the batter into the prepared pan. Smooth the top with a flexible palette knife.

Bake the sweet in the preheated oven for 30 to 33 minutes, or until just set. There may be a few very slender surface cracks on top of the sweet.

Cool the sweet in the pan on a cooling rack for 30 minutes. Refrigerate for 4 hours. Gently lift out the large block, using the aluminum foil or parchment paper sides to remove it from the pan. Cut the sweet into squares, using a chef's knife. Detach the squares from the aluminum foil or parchment paper. Store in an airtight tin with parchment paper separating the layers. Sift confectioners' sugar over the tops of the bars just before serving.

notes
- using good-quality chocolate-based ingredients, plus high-fat butter, makes an exceptional brownie batter
- in the image, the brownie blocks were stamped out with heart-shaped cutters, just for fun (I love heart-shaped baking implements)

dark chocolate batter

⅔ cup plus 1 tablespoon unsifted bleached all-purpose flour

⅔ cup unsifted bleached cake flour

¼ teaspoon baking powder

¼ teaspoon salt

⅓ cup unsweetened alkalized cocoa powder

½ pound plus 2 tablespoons (18 tablespoons or 2 sticks plus 2 tablespoons) unsalted butter, melted and cooled to tepid

5 ounces unsweetened chocolate, melted and cooled to tepid

4 ounces bittersweet chocolate, melted and cooled to tepid

5 large eggs

2 cups superfine sugar

2½ teaspoons vanilla extract

2 tablespoons light corn syrup

confectioners' sugar, for sifting over the baked bars

serving: 16 squares
ahead: up to 5 days at room temperature; for longer storage, refrigerate for 2 weeks or freeze for 6 weeks

Pure

the vibrancy of fruit—ripe, crisp, and sparkling ✳ the depth that cinnamon brings ✳ a blast of bourbon ✳ orange sticky ✳ the richness of almond ✳ big-on-butter rolls ✳ hooray for lemon ✳ chocolate cookie history ✳ molasses/delicious

Flavor

almond essence

I've traded in my favorite amaretti cake for this buttery, remarkably almond-y cake fashioned with marzipan, a few tablespoons of slivered almonds, almond extract, vanilla extract, and a notable ingredient, called *fiori di sicilia*.

That exchange was neither simple nor sweetly efficient, as the recipe, born and raised in my kitchen, kept swerving in the wrong direction.

The narration goes like this: almond is such a luscious flavor that I wanted to incorporate it into a cake to develop something expressly moist, a little dense, and resounding with deep, aromatic savor. It would be guaranteed to please as an informal dessert, sliced and served alone or with poached fruit, and it could find its easy way onto a plate at breakfast to accompany strong coffee. Not a fancy cake by any means, but, as it is rather big on intensity, the batter would be baked as a single layer and cut into thick wedges. Well, sometimes the fantasy of the baker, armed with enough organic marzipan and premium butter to make the budget wilt, can get her into trouble.

All of the ingredients, synchronized as such, created a moist and heavenly scented cake all right, and it *looked* great right out of the oven, but then misbehaved on cooling. The cake kind of sank in the middle, in a small but irritating afterthought of deflation. The taste, however, was stunning.

I returned to my mental mixing bowl, then slid and pulled the cake into and out of the oven nine more times every three or four days. I fed the tester cakes to the neighborhood and dropped off parcels of it to friends. Everyone seemed unsuspecting of the fact that I was tormented by this cake and probably viewed this serial baking situation as normal—for me. A little time progressed, and the results turned more bizarre than ever—the top of the cake turned into crusty meringue, the crumb overexpanded, the taste was alternately too sweet or not sweet enough, and, yes, it slumped in the center. Still.

Then I did something uncharacteristic of my personality: I abandoned the recipe. But the private admission of having been clobbered by a cake got me back into the grittiness of it all. Fortified with another serious replenishment of marzipan, I increased the amount of cake flour, fiddled with the leavening, subtracted one egg, modified the amount of butter, returned to my original two types and quantities of sugar, and sent that pan into the oven. By the way, I baked it at two different temperatures.

As the recipe appears here, you already know the result: ravishing. At the market, I noticed in passing that the shelf has been doubly restocked with marzipan. Perhaps I should tell them that my pilgrimage to deliciousness is over.

Two almond-y footnotes: the journey was not officially over. Nine months later (how appropriate) came the "birth" of little almond tart-like things, without the underlying pastry crust base, made of a vivid, thoroughly saturated-in-almond batter. The recipe for *little almond cakes* follows the cake. You will love to have these small, sweet nibbles on hand. Shortly after that came the *marzipan scones*, luscious tea or coffee breads that enfold marzipan within their sweet, biscuity network of dough. The scones vie for my attention and, sometimes, win out over the cake for their great almond flavor and quickly-put-together nature. I love any one of them freshly baked, when I am immediately greeted by the fragrance of almond in a cakey, tender, or buttery form.

a noble marzipan cake

Preheat the oven to 350 degrees F.

Film the inside of a false-bottomed round 9-inch cake pan (3 inches deep) with nonstick flour-and-oil spray. Line the bottom with a round of ovenproof parchment paper and film the surface with the spray.

For the batter, sift the flour, baking powder, salt, and nutmeg onto a sheet of waxed paper.

Break up the marzipan into the work bowl of a food processor fitted with the steel blade. Sprinkle the slivered almonds and confectioners' sugar over the marzipan; cover and process for 2 minutes, using quick on-off pulses, or until the mixture looks like coarse, damp sand. Set aside.

Cream the butter in the large bowl of a freestanding electric mixer on moderate speed for 3 minutes. Add the granulated sugar in 2 additions, beating for 1 minute after each portion is added. Beat in the eggs, one at a time, blending for just 10 seconds after each addition. Blend in the vanilla extract, almond extract, and *fiori di sicilia*. On low speed, add the marzipan mixture and blend it in. Add the sifted mixture in 2 additions, beating only until the particles of flour are absorbed. Scrape down the sides of the mixing bowl 2 or 3 times with a rubber spatula during this time to keep the batter even-textured.

Spoon the batter into the prepared baking pan. Smooth the top with a rubber spatula.

Bake the cake in the preheated oven for 50 minutes. Increase the temperature to 375 degrees F and continue baking for 10 minutes longer, or until the cake is set and a wooden pick withdraws clean when tested 1 inch from the center or with a few moist crumbs attached. The baked cake will dome in a slightly rounded crown, the surface will be golden brown, and the rounded edge of the cake will just begin to pull away from the sides of the baking pan.

Cool the cake in the pan on a cooling rack for 10 to 15 minutes. Gently and carefully lift the cake by the bottom, pushing it up and out to unmold. Cool completely. When completely cooled, invert the cake onto another rack, remove the base, peel away the parchment paper, and invert again to stand right side up. Slice into wedges. Store in an airtight cake keeper.

(continued on the next page)

almond-deluxe batter

1¾ cups plus 2 tablespoons unsifted bleached cake flour

¼ teaspoon baking powder

½ teaspoon salt

¼ teaspoon freshly grated nutmeg

12 ounces marzipan

4 tablespoons slivered almonds

⅓ cup confectioners' sugar

½ pound (16 tablespoons or 2 sticks) unsalted butter, softened

1 cup granulated sugar

5 large eggs

2 teaspoons vanilla extract

1 teaspoon almond extract

¾ teaspoon *fiori di sicilia*

serving: one 9-inch cake, creating about 16 slices

ahead: 2 days; the cake is irresistibly soft on baking day (within the first 12 hours), but over the next 3 days deepens in flavor and moisture

notes

• resist the temptation to add more *fiori di sicilia* (the essence of Sicilian flowers), that extremely potent and refined flavoring of citrus (notably orange and lemon) and vanilla, as it will make the batter taste far too pungent

• the best marzipan to use for this cake is Bia Organic Marzipan (from BIA Stramondo, produced and packed by Stramondo srl, Sicily; imported exclusively by Purely Organic, Ltd., Fairfield, IA)

• overbeating the mixture when mixing in the eggs will skew the texture of the finished cake, increasing more volume than needed and risking the destabilization of the batter

• the technique of increasing the oven temperature by 25 degrees F for the last 10 to 15 minutes of baking fully bakes the cake without drying out the crumb

• the false-bottomed round 9-inch cake pan (3 inches deep) I use for this cake is made by Magic Line (Parrish bakeware); a 10-inch layer cake pan (2 inches deep) may be substituted, reducing the baking time at 375 degrees F by about 5 minutes

• for a lavish presentation, lightly toast two big handfuls (about 2/3 cup) of sliced or slivered almonds, cool the nuts, scatter them over the surface of the baked cake, and dredge the top with confectioners' sugar

• use a finely serrated knife to cut the cake

little almond cakes

marzipan batter

8 ounces marzipan

2/3 cup superfine sugar

1/2 cup confectioners' sugar

large pinch of salt

3 tablespoons almond flour or almond meal

4 large egg whites

2 teaspoons vanilla extract

1 teaspoon almond extract

almond finish

about 1/3 cup sliced or slivered almonds

confectioners' sugar, for sifting over the cakes (optional)

serving: 27 small cakes
ahead: 2 days

Break up the marzipan into the work bowl of a food processor fitted with the steel blade. Add the superfine sugar, cover, and process, using quick on-off pulses, until the mixture looks like moderately fine, damp sand.

For the batter, place the marzipan-sugar mixture in a medium-size mixing bowl. Add the confectioners' sugar, salt, almond flour or almond meal, and egg whites. Combine all of the ingredients, using a hand-held electric mixer on low speed. Add the vanilla extract and almond extract and mix to blend.

Refrigerate the batter for 20 minutes (uncovered is fine).

Preheat the oven to 375 degrees F in advance of baking.

Film the inside of 27 round tart molds (each mold measuring 2½ inches in diameter and ¾ inch deep, with a capacity of 2 tablespoons plus 1½ teaspoons) with nonstick flour-and-oil spray. Have a large rimmed sheet pan at hand.

Fill each mold with 1 tablespoon of batter (the pans will be about half full), using a teaspoon. Overfilling the molds will cause the batter to swell over the sides, bake unevenly, and, ultimately, stick. Arrange the molds on the rimmed sheet pan. Sprinkle some sliced or slivered almonds on top of the batter in each mold.

Bake the cakes in the preheated oven for about 13 minutes, or until risen and golden around the edges. Cool the cakes in the molds on a cooling rack for 5 minutes, then unmold them carefully onto a sheet of ovenproof parchment paper. Store, in single layers, in airtight tins. Just before serving, sift a little confectioners' sugar over the cakes, if you wish.

marzipan scones

Preheat the oven to 400 degrees F.

Line a heavy rimmed sheet pan or cookie sheet with a length of ovenproof parchment paper.

For the dough, cut the block of marzipan into small cubes and set aside.

Sift the flour, baking powder, salt, and nutmeg onto a sheet of waxed paper.

Cream the butter in the large bowl of a freestanding electric mixer on moderate speed until smooth, about 1 minute. Add the granulated sugar and beat for 1 minute on moderate speed. Whisk the eggs, milk, almond extract, and vanilla extract in a small mixing bowl. On low speed, blend in a little less than half of the sifted mixture, all of the whisked eggs and milk mixture, then the balance of the sifted mixture. Scrape down the sides of the mixing bowl thoroughly with a rubber spatula after each addition. The dough will be firmly moist. By hand, work in the chunks of marzipan, using a sturdy rubber spatula.

On a lightly floured work surface, form the dough into a plump 5½- to 6-inch disk. Cut the disk into 6 wedges. Place the scones on the prepared baking pan, spacing them 3 inches apart.

Bake the scones in the preheated oven for 20 minutes, or until risen, set, and golden on top. Cool the baked scones on the pan for 1 minute, then remove them to a cooling rack, using a wide offset metal spatula. Serve the scones warm or at room temperature, their tops sprinkled with confectioners' sugar, if you wish. Store in an airtight container.

notes
• the method for making the dough differs from the classic "cut-in" or "rub-in" of the fat (butter) into a lightly sweetened and leavened flour mixture; this technique produces a stable framework for enclosing chunks of marzipan in a baked scone with a slightly fluffy, rather than break-apart-crumbly, texture
• the recipe doubles successfully; use two rimmed sheet pans or cookie sheets, assembling 6 scones on each baking pan

almond-y dough

7 ounces marzipan

2 cups plus 2 tablespoons unsifted bleached all-purpose flour

2¼ teaspoons baking powder

¼ teaspoon salt

¼ teaspoon freshly grated nutmeg

6 tablespoons (¾ stick) unsalted butter, softened

5 tablespoons granulated sugar

2 large eggs

⅓ cup plus 2 tablespoons milk

1 teaspoon almond extract

¾ teaspoon vanilla extract

confectioners' sugar, for sifting over the baked scones (optional)

serving: 6 scones
ahead: best on baking day; or freeze for 1 month, defrost, bundle in aluminum foil, and reheat in a preheated 300 degrees F oven for 10 minutes

blueberries, melding and melting

When fleshy, silver-hued blueberries appear each summer for an all-too-brief period of time, my biggest challenge is to see exactly how many berries one can actually fold through a cake or muffin batter, gingerly cram into a scone dough, or heap precipitously into a pie dish and cover with a sheath of pastry dough or moist, biscuity topping.

It is a contest of sorts, every berry season, to get this bounty to form as many melting pools of fruitiness as possible. In a succulent way, overloaded results are delicious—even if a little too bubbly. But, in the end, when blueberries are deep within, who cares?

The sheer, delicious extravagance of it all encourages me to gather cartons of berries in quantity and dump them directly into a well-orchestrated recipe—or two, or three. Creamed muffin, cake, and buckle batters, so simple in form and style, display the berries beautifully.

In each of the recipes, the batter trapping the berries is undeniably cakey and velvety, not that pebbly, coarse-textured batter that is synonymous with certain kinds of fruit-enhanced baked goods. The berries—floured to keep them from settling to the bottom of the individual cakes, the round breakfast cake, or the square coffee cake—compose definite puddles here and there in a not-too-sweet setting. Served fresh and warm, all are pure joy. An unhurried late weekend morning or afternoon would be graced by any one of these sweets tumbling from a basket, heaped onto an old-fashioned compote dish, or sliced and arranged on a pristine plate, accompanied by hot coffee or sparkly iced tea.

a gentle blueberry buckle

Preheat the oven to 350 degrees F.

Film the inside of an 8 by 8 by 2-inch baking pan with nonstick flour-and-oil spray.

For the topping, blend together the granulated sugar, cinnamon, and walnuts in a small mixing bowl. Scatter over the bits of butter. Crumble the mixture between your fingertips until sandy-textured nuggets and flecks are formed. Set aside.

For the batter, sift the flour, baking powder, salt, cinnamon, and nutmeg onto a sheet of waxed paper.

In a small mixing bowl, toss the blueberries with 1½ teaspoons of the sifted mixture.

Cream the butter in the large bowl of a freestanding electric mixer on moderate speed for 2 minutes. Add the granulated sugar in 2 additions, beating for 1 minute after each portion is added. Beat in the eggs, one at a time, mixing for 45 seconds after each addition. Blend in the vanilla extract. On low speed, alternately add the sifted mixture in 3 additions with the milk in 2 additions, beginning and ending with the sifted mixture. Scrape down the sides of the mixing bowl with a rubber spatula to keep the batter even-textured. Stir in the blueberries along with any flour not clinging to the berries.

Spoon the batter into the prepared baking pan. Smooth the top with a rubber spatula. Scatter the topping evenly over the surface of the batter.

Bake the cake in the preheated oven for 45 minutes, or until risen, set, and a wooden pick withdraws clean or with a few crumbs attached. Cool the cake completely in the pan on a cooling rack. Sift confectioners' sugar over the top of the cake just before cutting into squares for serving. Store in an airtight cake keeper.

notes
• simple and direct, a buttery and milky batter is the best textural contrast for highlighting the berries

scented nut topping

3 tablespoons granulated sugar

½ teaspoon ground cinnamon

¼ cup finely chopped walnuts

3 tablespoons cold unsalted butter, cut into small bits

sweet milk–blueberry batter

1¾ cups unsifted bleached all-purpose flour

2 teaspoons baking powder

¼ teaspoon salt

¼ teaspoon ground cinnamon

¼ teaspoon freshly grated nutmeg

1 cup plump blueberries, picked over

8 tablespoons (1 stick) unsalted butter, softened

½ cup granulated sugar

2 large eggs

2 teaspoons vanilla extract

1 cup milk

confectioners' sugar, for sprinkling on top of the baked cake

serving: one 8-inch cake, creating 9 or 16 squares (depending on size)
ahead: best on baking day

special blueberry cakes

sour cream batter

2¼ cups unsifted bleached cake flour

½ teaspoon baking powder

½ teaspoon baking soda

¼ teaspoon salt

¼ teaspoon freshly grated nutmeg

1¼ cups plump blueberries, picked over

8 tablespoons (1 stick) unsalted butter, softened

⅔ cup plus 2 tablespoons superfine sugar

2 large eggs

2½ teaspoons vanilla extract

¾ cup sour cream

about 3 tablespoons granulated sugar or superfine sugar, for sprinkling on the tops of the baked cakes

serving: 7 jumbo cakes
ahead: best on baking day

Preheat the oven to 375 degrees F.

Line the inside of 7 jumbo muffin/cupcake cups (6 cups to a pan, each cup measuring 4 inches in diameter and 1¾ inches deep, with a capacity of 1⅛ cups) with ovenproof paper baking cup liners. (Note that you will need 2 pans, using the second pan for a single cake, and so leaving the 5 remaining cups in the second pan empty.)

For the batter, sift the flour, baking powder, baking soda, salt, and nutmeg onto a sheet of waxed paper.

Toss the blueberries with 1 tablespoon of the sifted mixture in a medium-size mixing bowl.

Cream the butter in the large bowl of a freestanding electric mixer on moderate speed for 3 minutes. Add the superfine sugar in 2 additions, beating for 1 minute after each portion is added. Beat in the eggs, one at a time, mixing for 45 seconds after each addition. Blend in the vanilla extract. On low speed, alternately add the sifted mixture in 3 additions with the sour cream in 2 additions, beginning and ending with the sifted mixture. Scrape down the sides of the mixing bowl with a rubber spatula to keep the batter even-textured. The batter will be moderately dense, but creamy. Using a rubber spatula, blend in the blueberries, including any residual flour that may have drifted to the bottom of the bowl.

Spoon the batter into the lined muffin cups, dividing it evenly among them. Mound the batter lightly in the center of each cup.

Bake the cakes in the preheated oven for 30 minutes, or until risen, set, and a wooden pick withdraws clean or with a few crumbs attached. The tops of the baked cakes will be a medium golden color. Immediately sprinkle the tops with the granulated sugar or superfine sugar. Cool the cakes in the pans on racks for 10 minutes, then remove them to other cooling racks. Cool for 20 minutes and serve gently warm, or cool completely and serve at room temperature. Store in an airtight container.

notes
• it is preferable to use a good, thick organic sour cream in this batter for the purest flavor and best-textured cakes
• the cakes are generously sized, but not too sweet, and ideal for serving at breakfast

blueberry breakfast cake

buttery vanilla batter

2 cups unsifted bleached all-purpose flour

1 teaspoon baking powder

½ teaspoon baking soda

⅛ teaspoon cream of tartar

¼ teaspoon salt

¼ teaspoon freshly grated nutmeg

8 tablespoons (1 stick) unsalted butter, softened

¾ cup plus 1 tablespoon granulated sugar

3 large eggs

2¾ teaspoons vanilla extract

¾ cup sour cream

1¼ cups blueberries, frozen for 1 hour

confectioners' sugar, for dredging the top of the baked cake

serving: one 9-inch cake, creating 10 slices
ahead: best on baking day

Preheat the oven to 375 degrees F.

Film the inside of a false-bottomed round 9-inch cake pan (3 inches deep) or a 9-inch springform pan (2¾ inches deep) with nonstick flour-and-oil spray. Line the bottom of the pan with a circle of waxed paper or ovenproof parchment paper cut to fit and film its surface with the spray.

For the batter, sift the flour, baking powder, baking soda, cream of tartar, salt, and nutmeg onto a sheet of waxed paper. Reserve 1 tablespoon of the sifted mixture for tossing with the frozen blueberries.

Cream the butter in the large bowl of a freestanding electric mixer on moderate speed for 2 minutes. Continuing on moderate speed, add the granulated sugar in 2 additions, beating for 1 minute after each portion is added. Beat in the eggs, one at a time, mixing for 30 seconds after each addition. Blend in the vanilla extract. On low speed, alternately add the sifted mixture in 3 additions with the sour cream in 2 additions, mixing just until the particles of flour are absorbed. Scrape down the sides of the mixing bowl with a rubber spatula to keep the mixture even-textured. The mixture will be dense, but creamy.

In a medium-size mixing bowl, toss the frozen blueberries with the reserved 1 tablespoon of the sifted mixture.

Gently stir the blueberries into the batter, using a rubber spatula. As the frozen blueberries are added, the dough will stiffen slightly.

Scrape the dough into the prepared baking pan. Spread it evenly in the pan, using a flexible palette knife.

Bake the cake in the preheated oven for 40 to 45 minutes, or until set and golden on top. Cool the cake in the pan on a cooling rack for 10 minutes. If you are using the false-bottomed 9-inch cake pan, carefully lift the cake by the bottom, pushing it up and out to unmold, removing the outer side. If you are using the springform pan, open the hinge and remove the outer ring, allowing the cake to stand on the circular metal base. Serve the cake at room temperature, its top dredged with confectioners' sugar, and sliced into wedges. Store in an airtight cake keeper.

notes
• freezing the berries for 1 hour allows them to remain intact while being stirred into the buttery batter and allows a larger quantity to be used

butter*luscious*

When butter and eggs meet in yeast-risen bread, defining its crumb and adding a distinguishing amount of golden richness, you know that the result is bound to be majestic.

If any bread could magically appear on a cooling rack each week in my kitchen, this one would be it: regal dinner rolls, and perfect for spreading with salted butter or almost any kind of sweet condiment. The recipe, one which I developed twenty years ago and revise yearly, is one of my prized formulas. The relentless pursuit of roll-perfection is responsible for the set of ingredients and method offered here.

"Dinner rolls." The phrase sounds so antebellum, but I always find the slender silver tray empty when these are presented at my table—and so the stodgy reputation of the phrase is banished after one bite. When golden-yolk eggs and good butter are used in the dough, I am once again reminded how those deliciously pure elements reveal themselves, front and center, in these light, feathery, aristocratic rolls.

For the sponge, stir together the yeast, the ½ teaspoon sugar, and the warm water in a heatproof measuring cup. Allow the mixture to stand until swollen, 6 to 7 minutes.

Turn the yeast mixture into a small-to-medium-size heatproof mixing bowl. Stir in the warm milk, the 2 tablespoons sugar, and the flour. Mix well (a few very small, floury lumps may remain, but larger lumps should be mixed to disperse). Cover the bowl with a sheet of food-safe plastic wrap and set aside at room temperature for 30 minutes, or until doubled in bulk and the surface is animated with large and small bubbles. The mixture will be moderately thick and fairly pourable.

For the foundation dough, scrape the sponge mixture into a large mixing bowl. Stir in the whole eggs-egg yolk-vanilla extract mixture, using a wooden spoon. Add 2¾ cups of the flour-salt mixture in 2 additions, mixing well with a flat wooden paddle. The dough will be shaggy. Turn the dough mixture (and all bits and fragments of unabsorbed flour) into the bowl of a heavy-duty freestanding electric mixer. Set the bowl in place and attach the flat paddle. Beat on moderate speed for 3 minutes. Add the remaining ¼ cup flour-salt mixture and beat for 4 minutes longer. At this point, the dough will be smooth.

For the finishing enrichment, add the butter to the dough base, 2 tablespoons at a time, beating for a full minute after each portion is added. When all of the butter has been added, beat the dough on moderate speed for 4 minutes. The dough will be very smooth and slightly tacky to the touch. Resist the urge to add more flour. From time to time in the beating process, stop the mixer and scrape down the sides of the mixing bowl and paddle, using a firm rubber spatula. The finished dough will leave a streaky film on the sides of the bowl; do not expect the sides to be clean.

Scrape the dough into a bowl filmed with softened unsalted butter, lightly turn to coat all sides in a film of butter, make several cuts in the dough with a pair of kitchen scissors, cover tightly with a sheet of food-safe plastic wrap, and let rise in a cool place (ideally, 67 degrees F to 68 degrees F) for 1 hour and 45 minutes to 2 hours, or until doubled in bulk.

Uncover the dough and discard the plastic wrap. Compress the dough by folding it over on itself from the edge to the center 4 or 5 times, using your fingertips.

(continued on the next page)

luxury yeast dough

sponge

2¾ teaspoons active dry yeast

½ teaspoon granulated sugar

⅓ cup warm (105 to 110 degrees F) water

3 tablespoons warm (105 to 110 degrees F) milk

2 tablespoons granulated sugar

⅓ cup plus 2 tablespoons unsifted unbleached all-purpose flour

egg and egg yolk foundation dough

4 large eggs plus 1 large egg yolk, lightly beaten with ¼ teaspoon vanilla extract

3 cups unsifted unbleached all-purpose flour blended with 1 teaspoon salt

butter finishing enrichment

½ pound (16 tablespoons or 2 sticks) cool unsalted butter, cut into tablespoon-size chunks

glaze

1 large egg

1 teaspoon water

pinch of salt

(continued on the next page)

(continued from the previous page)

butter and salt finish

about 3 tablespoons butter (preferably clarified butter, page 1), melted and still warm

coarse salt, for sprinkling

serving: three 5-inch breads (each bread is composed of 4 interlocking rolls), creating 4 servings each
ahead: best on baking day; or freeze for 3 weeks, bundle in aluminum foil, and reheat in a preheated 325 degrees F oven for 10 minutes, then brush with melted butter and sprinkle with coarse salt

Transfer the compressed dough to a very lightly oiled double sheet of plastic wrap, enclose to wrap securely, and refrigerate the dough for 3 hours. Remove the dough from the refrigerator, unwrap the package, and gently compress by patting down the top with your fingertips. Rewrap the dough in lightly oiled sheets of plastic wrap, slip into a jumbo, food-safe freezer-weight plastic bag, seal leaving ample headspace, and refrigerate overnight.

On baking day, film the inside of three 5 by 5 by 3-inch baking pans with nonstick flour-and-oil spray.

To form the rolls, remove the dough from the refrigerator. Remove and discard the plastic wrap. Divide the dough into 12 even-size pieces (a generous 3 ounces each). Smooth each piece into a plump ball. Place 4 balls of dough in each of the prepared baking pans, assembling the balls in two rows of 2 each.

Cover each pan of dough loosely with a sheet of food-safe plastic wrap. Let the balls of dough rise in a cool place (again, around 68 degrees F) for 3 hours to 3 hours and 30 minutes, until a little more than doubled in bulk. The sections will merge as they rise, forming one 4-part square bread in each pan.

For the glaze, whisk the egg, water, and salt in a small mixing bowl. After about 2¾ hours, uncover the breads, lightly sweep the glaze over the top of each bread, using a soft pastry brush and a light hand. Cover the breads once again and continue to let them rise.

Preheat the oven to 375 degrees F in advance of baking.

Remove and discard the sheets of plastic wrap covering the breads.

Bake the breads in the preheated oven for 30 to 35 minutes, or until set and a golden color on top. Place the pans on cooling racks and let stand for 10 minutes. Carefully invert the breads onto other cooling racks, lift off the pans, then invert again to stand right side up. Brush the tops of the breads with the melted butter and sprinkle with coarse salt. Serve the bread warm or at room temperature, by pulling the sections apart at their natural seams. Store in an airtight container.

notes
• stand by the mixer for each beating time referenced in the procedure
• the food-safe freezer-weight plastic bag must be jumbo size or the dough will not have room to breathe during the overnight refrigeration
• the rolls are arranged and baked in three 5 by 5 by 3-inch baking pans; two 8 by 8 by 2-inch baking pans may be substituted, creating smaller rolls and a larger yield (divide the dough into 24 balls and assemble 12 balls in three rows of 4 in each pan), reducing the baking time by 5 to 6 minutes

mellow

Apple threads that weave their way through a spice-scented batter become tart-sweet filaments that melt lusciously within its very textural composition. The oil keeps everything moist and dewy, and a final fillip of glaze, made primarily of maple syrup and butter, sinks into the warm cake for a mellow touch.

Such a cake batter, dense with fruit, is usually baked in a rectangular pan or in a tube pan with a larger diameter (and lesser depth) than the one called for in the recipe that follows. For this cake batter, I use a deep 9-inch tube pan. Using a deeper pan, with a *slightly* less extensive diameter, keeps the baked cake a little more compact (in a good way) and so alleviates overall dryness. It also encourages the apples to bind, fitting closely inside. This is so appealing to the baker in me because I usually aim for moistness in a cake as a dominant characteristic. The warm glaze seals the surface of the cake. Stroke it on while oven-fresh and just released from the baking pan. This flavor topping becomes a sweet finishing "varnish." A ruffle of lightly whipped cream, sweetened with maple syrup, or not, would complete a thick slice of cake, and create a wonderfully autumnal dessert plate.

apple cake, maple butter glaze

Preheat the oven to 350 degrees F.

Film the inside of a fluted 9-inch tube pan (4¼ inches deep, with a capacity of 11 cups) with nonstick flour-and-oil spray.

For the batter, sift the flour, baking powder, baking soda, salt, cinnamon, nutmeg, allspice, and ginger onto a sheet of waxed paper.

Place the granulated sugar, dark brown sugar, and eggs in the large bowl of a freestanding electric mixer and beat on moderate speed for 2 minutes. With the mixer running, add the oil in a thin, steady stream. Beat on moderate speed for 2 minutes. Blend in the vanilla extract and the apples. On low speed, add the sifted mixture in 2 additions, scraping down the sides of the mixing bowl thoroughly with a rubber spatula after each addition.

Pour and scrape the batter into the prepared baking pan. The batter will appear somewhat soupy.

Bake the cake in the preheated oven for 1 hour, or until risen, set, and a wooden pick inserted into the cake withdraws clean or with a few particles attached. The baked cake will pull away slightly from the sides of the baking pan.

Cool the cake in the pan on a rack for 10 minutes. Invert onto another cooling rack. Lift off the pan. Paint the warm glaze over the top and sides of the cake, using a soft pastry brush. Cool completely. Store in an airtight cake keeper.

notes
- Empire, Paula Red, Jonathan, or Granny Smith apples make a flavorsome cake; for the best texture, be sure to grate the apples on the coarse holes of a 4-sided box grater
- nuts (either walnuts or pecans) would add a crunchy, autumnal counterpoint to the apples; 1 cup coarsely chopped nuts (ideally, lightly toasted before chopping) can be stirred into the batter after the apples are added
- granulated sugar is used as the primary sweetening agent, along with ½ cup dark brown sugar for a light, caramel-flavored undertone
- a fluted tube pan that is 4¼ inches deep must be used in order to contain all of the batter and to bake properly
- use a finely serrated knife to cut the cake

spiced apple batter

3 cups unsifted bleached all-purpose flour

1 teaspoon baking powder

1 teaspoon baking soda

¾ teaspoon salt

1¾ teaspoons ground cinnamon

1 teaspoon freshly grated nutmeg

½ teaspoon ground allspice

¼ teaspoon ground ginger

1½ cups granulated sugar

½ cup firmly packed dark brown sugar

3 large eggs

1 cup neutral vegetable oil (such as soybean or canola)

2 teaspoons vanilla extract

3½ cups peeled, cored, and coarsely shredded apples

maple butter glaze (page 56)

serving: one 9-inch cake, creating about 12 slices
ahead: 2 days

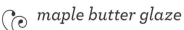 *maple butter glaze*

sweet buttery maple coat

⅔ cup pure maple syrup

4 tablespoons (½ stick) unsalted butter, cut into chunks

pinch of salt

1 tablespoon apple brandy (such as Calvados, optional)

½ teaspoon vanilla extract

serving: about ¾ cup

Place the maple syrup, butter, and salt in a small, heavy saucepan (preferably enameled cast iron). Set over moderately low heat and bring to the simmer, stirring occasionally. Simmer for 1 minute. Remove from the heat and stir in the apple brandy (if you are using it), return the saucepan to the heat, bring to the simmer, simmer for 1 minute, then remove from the heat. Pour the glaze into a heatproof bowl. Stir in the vanilla extract.

Use the glaze immediately to brush lavishly over the surface of the warm cake.

notes

• this simple glaze is a good one to remember for applying to the surface of fresh apple or pear butter cakes, or to cakes composed of dried fruit, especially those containing dates or raisins

bright, not perky

"Saturated" is a tip-top word to describe the state of the cake—its batter and glaze, which is liberally brushed on the baked cake moments after unmolding it. Drenched in butter, orange flavor, and bourbon, this is a cake for the dark days of winter when citrus abounds and we all need to be consoled with something rich and sweet. The sweet rolls, however, are illuminated with orange in a more serene, but likewise radiant way.

For the cake, the patchwork of ingredients in the glaze—butter, sugar, bourbon, orange juice concentrate—repeats the flavoring (and its inherent spirit) present in the batter in an energetic way. As the mixture sinks in, it not only expands the overall taste, but dampens the crumb in a style that an icing cannot. All that butter in it rounds out the bourbon, balances the acidity of the orange, and plays along with the sugar to give the brushing mixture depth and substance. Orange wedges—bright, sparkling, and relaxing in a caramel syrup—would make a fine accompaniment to this sweet, but a slice of cake, on its own with simply a cup of hot tea, would be every bit as swell.

For the rolls, a yeast dough flavored with grated orange peel, blood orange essence, and orange juice concentrate enfolds a spiral of butter, light brown sugar, and honey. As the rolls bake, the filling moistens the creases while forming a luscious caramel-like coating on their undersides. Soon after baking, the raft of rolls is covered in a soft orange glaze.

Imagine this: having your glass of orange juice turned into a tapestry of cake batter or sweet yeast dough....

orange and bourbon: cake, saturated

Preheat the oven to 350 degrees F.

Film the inside of a 10-inch Bundt pan (generous 3¾ inches deep, with a capacity of 14 cups) with nonstick flour-and-oil spray.

Place the orange peel in a small nonreactive ramekin. Sprinkle over the orange extract and spoon through lightly. Let the peel blossom while you prepare the batter, at least 5 to 8 minutes.

For the batter, sift the all-purpose flour, cake flour, baking powder, and salt onto a sheet of waxed paper.

Cream the butter in the large bowl of a freestanding electric mixer on moderate speed for 3 minutes. Add the sugar in 3 additions, beating for 1 minute after each portion is added. Beat in the eggs, one at a time, mixing for about 20 seconds after each addition. Scrape down the sides of the mixing bowl with a rubber spatula to keep the batter even-textured. Blend in the orange peel–orange extract mixture. On low speed, alternately add the sifted mixture in 3 additions with the orange juice concentrate-water-bourbon blend in 2 additions, beginning and ending with the sifted mixture. Scrape down the sides of the mixing bowl thoroughly with a rubber spatula to keep the batter even-textured.

Spoon the batter into the prepared baking pan. Smooth the top with a rubber spatula.

Bake the cake in the preheated oven for 55 minutes, or until risen, set, and a wooden pick inserted into the cake withdraws clean. The baked cake will begin to pull away from the sides of the baking pan.

While the cake is baking, make the glaze by placing the chunks of butter, the sugar, bourbon, and orange juice concentrate in a heavy, medium-size nonreactive saucepan (preferably enameled cast iron). Set over low heat to melt the butter and dissolve the sugar, stirring now and again. Remove the saucepan from the heat and set aside.

Cool the cake in the pan on a rack for 10 minutes. Invert onto another cooling rack. Lift off the pan. Place a sheet of waxed paper underneath the cooling rack to catch any drips of glaze. Rewarm the glaze and brush the mixture over the top and sides of the cake. Serve the cake warm or cool completely. Store in an airtight cake keeper.

orange batter

2 tablespoons finely grated orange peel

2 teaspoons orange extract

2¾ cups unsifted bleached all-purpose flour

¼ cup unsifted bleached cake flour

3 teaspoons baking powder

½ teaspoon salt

½ pound (16 tablespoons or 2 sticks) unsalted butter, softened

2 cups superfine sugar

5 large eggs

½ cup best-quality orange juice concentrate blended with 2 tablespoons water and 2 tablespoons bourbon

butter, orange, and bourbon glaze

12 tablespoons (1½ sticks) unsalted butter, cut into chunks

½ cup plus 3 tablespoons superfine sugar

¼ cup bourbon

¼ cup best-quality orange juice concentrate

serving: one 10-inch cake, creating about 16 slices
ahead: best on baking day

orange and honey: sunshine rolls, orange glaze

orange-scented buttermilk yeast dough

4¼ teaspoons active dry yeast

½ teaspoon granulated sugar

¼ cup warm (105 to 110 degrees F) water

1 cup buttermilk

5 tablespoons granulated sugar

7 tablespoons (1 stick less 1 tablespoon) unsalted butter, cut into chunks

3 tablespoons plus 2 teaspoons best-quality orange juice concentrate

4 teaspoons finely grated orange peel

1 teaspoon vanilla extract

¾ teaspoon blood orange essence (see notes)

2 large eggs, lightly beaten

½ teaspoon baking soda

5 cups unsifted bleached all-purpose flour, plus an additional ¼ cup, as needed for kneading

1 teaspoon salt

For the dough, stir together the yeast, the ½ teaspoon granulated sugar, and the warm water in a heatproof measuring cup. Allow the mixture to stand until swollen, 6 to 7 minutes.

In the meantime, place the buttermilk, the 5 tablespoons granulated sugar, and the chunks of butter in a small saucepan, set over low heat, and warm until the butter has melted. Remove from the heat and whisk in the orange juice concentrate, orange peel, vanilla extract, and blood orange essence. Scrape into a medium-size heatproof mixing bowl. Let the mixture stand for 5 to 6 minutes to cool to tepid, stirring once or twice, then blend in the eggs, baking soda, and yeast mixture. Whisk 4 cups of the flour and the salt in a large mixing bowl. Add the yeast mixture and stir to mix well. Let the mixture stand, uncovered, for 5 minutes. Add the remaining 1 cup flour and blend well, using a wooden spoon or flat wooden paddle. The dough will be soft in sections and slightly shaggy in other sections, with drier patches. Let the dough stand, uncovered, for 3 minutes. Turn the dough out onto a work surface sprinkled with the additional flour. Knead the dough for 8 to 9 minutes, or until supple and bouncy, using as much of the flour as needed to keep the dough moving.

Turn the dough into a bowl heavily coated with softened unsalted butter, lightly turn to coat all sides in a film of butter, make several cuts in the dough with a pair of kitchen scissors, cover tightly with a sheet of food-safe plastic wrap, and let rise at room temperature for 1 hour and 45 minutes, or until doubled in bulk.

For the filling, place the butter, light brown sugar, nutmeg, honey, orange juice concentrate, and blood orange essence in a medium-size mixing bowl. Using a hand-held electric mixer, beat the ingredients on moderate speed until smooth, stopping to scrape down the sides of the mixing bowl with a rubber spatula once or twice. Cover the bowl with a sheet of food-safe plastic wrap and let stand until needed, or up to 2 hours in advance of baking.

Remove and discard the plastic wrap covering the dough.

Film the inside of a 13 by 9 by 3-inch baking pan with nonstick flour-and-oil spray or softened unsalted butter.

To form the rolls, roll out the dough into a sheet measuring 14 by 16 inches. Spread the filling on the surface of the dough. Fold in the sides, press them down firmly, and roll the dough tightly into a log. Pinch the long edge to seal. Twist the dough several turns and elongate the roll to measure about 21 inches. Cut the dough into 15 even-size slices. Place the spirals of dough in the prepared baking pan, assembling them in three rows of 5 each.

Cover the pan of rolls loosely with a sheet of food-safe plastic wrap. Let the rolls rise at room temperature for 1 hour and 30 minutes to 1 hour and 45 minutes, or until a little more than doubled in bulk.

Preheat the oven to 375 degrees F in advance of baking.

Remove and discard the sheet of plastic wrap covering the rolls.

Bake the rolls in the preheated oven for 35 to 40 minutes, or until set and golden. The surface of the rolls will be irregular, with peaks and valleys on and about the spirals.

Place the pan on a cooling rack and let stand for 10 minutes. Spoon and sweep the glaze over the surface of the warm rolls, spreading it carefully as it melts down over the irregular surface. Cool completely. Detach the rolls from one another and lift out of the pan for serving, using a small or medium-width offset metal spatula. Store in an airtight container.

notes
• blood orange essence is available in stoppered bottles at La Cuisine—The Cook's Resource (see page 501, baking*SelectedSources*); if blood orange essence is unavailable, substitute 1¼ teaspoons orange extract in the dough and ½ teaspoon orange extract in the filling
• use pulp-free orange juice concentrate

honey, brown sugar, and butter filling

6 tablespoons (¾ stick) unsalted butter, softened

¾ cup firmly packed light brown sugar

¼ teaspoon freshly grated nutmeg

⅓ cup honey

1 tablespoon best-quality orange juice concentrate

¼ teaspoon blood orange essence (or substitute ½ teaspoon orange extract, if blood orange essence is unavailable)

orange glaze (below)

serving: 15 sweet rolls
ahead: best on baking day; or freeze for 1 month, defrost, bundle in aluminum foil, and reheat in a preheated 300 degrees F oven for 15 minutes, then glaze

orange glaze

Sift the confectioners' sugar and salt into a medium-size mixing bowl. Add the butter, orange juice concentrate, and blood orange essence. Using a hand-held electric mixer, beat the ingredients on low speed only until smooth, stopping to scrape down the sides of the mixing bowl with a rubber spatula 2 or 3 times.

Use the glaze on warm, freshly baked rolls.

notes
• use pulp-free orange juice concentrate
• this is a soft glaze that, when applied, forms a creamy coating as it melts down on the surface of the warm sweet rolls

soft orange glaze

2¼ cups confectioners' sugar

pinch of salt

2 tablespoons unsalted butter, softened

5 tablespoons best-quality orange juice concentrate

⅛ teaspoon blood orange essence (or substitute ¼ teaspoon orange extract)

serving: about 1 cup
ahead: 2 hours (covered with a sheet of food-safe plastic wrap and held at room temperature)

revisiting a cookie

The depth of flavor in this buttery cookie dough is developed by unsweetened cocoa powder. And that item is a perfect "delivery system" ingredient. A small amount of baking powder is used to open the crumb and relieve its density; a bit of salt accentuates the chocolate taste.

It has taken me some time to construct a simple but deluxe butter cookie dough, one that conveys, with a minimal amount of ingredients, a rounded essence.

The rolled-out cookies need to be baked until firm throughout; for that stage, you'll need to bake them at a moderately low temperature until set, following the time frame represented in the recipe. Blond butter cookies, which turn golden as they bake and send forth a lightly caramelized aroma, broadcast their finish; chocolate cookies do so in a slightly different way. A gentle waft of chocolate can be detected, but you should also look out for a slight puff and firmness to the center.

The cookies are an exceptional accompaniment to ice cream, pudding, or mousse. In addition, consider them a natural for serving with espresso or cappuccino.

butter dough, personalized in chocolate

cocoa butter dough

3 cups unsifted bleached all-purpose flour

¾ cup unsweetened alkalized cocoa powder

¼ teaspoon baking powder

⅛ teaspoon baking soda

¼ teaspoon salt

¾ pound (3 sticks) unsalted butter, softened

1½ cups confectioners' sugar

2¼ teaspoons vanilla extract

granulated sugar or sanding sugar (plain or a color), for sprinkling on the cookies before and just after baking (optional)

serving: about 3 dozen cookies (using a 1¾ to 2-inch cutter) or about 2 dozen cookies (using a 2¼ by 2-inch cutter)
ahead: 1 week

For the dough, sift the flour, cocoa powder, baking powder, baking soda, and salt onto a sheet of waxed paper.

Cream the butter in the large bowl of a freestanding electric mixer on moderately low speed for 3 minutes. Add the confectioners' sugar in 2 additions, beating on moderate speed for 1 minute after each portion is added. Blend in the vanilla extract. On low speed, blend in the sifted ingredients in 3 additions, beating just until the flour particles are absorbed. Scrape down the sides of the mixing bowl frequently with a rubber spatula to keep the dough even-textured.

Divide the dough into 2 portions. Roll each portion of dough between two sheets of waxed paper to a thickness of a generous ¼ inch. Carefully stack the two sheets of dough on a cookie sheet and refrigerate for 6 hours, or until quite firm (or overnight).

Preheat the oven to 325 degrees F in advance of baking.

Line several cookie sheets with lengths of ovenproof parchment paper.

Remove one sheet of dough at a time from the refrigerator. Carefully peel off both sheets of waxed paper and place the dough on a sheet of ovenproof parchment paper. Stamp out cookies with a decorative 1¾ to 2-inch cutter or a 2¼ by 2-inch cutter. Place the cookies, 1 inch apart, on the prepared baking pans. Sprinkle the tops with granulated sugar or sanding sugar, if you wish. For a decorative flourish, the center tops of the cookies stamped out with a 2¼ by 2-inch cutter can be pierced in three rows with the tines of a dinner fork.

Bake the cookies in the preheated oven for 22 to 25 minutes, or until set. Let the cookies stand on the baking pans for 1 minute, sprinkle with additional sugar, if you wish, then transfer them to cooling racks, using a wide offset metal spatula. Cool completely. Store in an airtight tin.

notes
• a favorite cocoa powder to use in this recipe is Droste
• if you are using a small decorative cutter, choose one that is not too intricate (such as a round, heart, or square) for the best definition of the dough on baking
• never consume raw cookie dough

sweetly tart

The merging of sweet and sharp, of sugar and acid, makes a plainspoken butter cake sing.

The substructure of the recipe for *lemon cake, sublime and divine, lemony sugar wash with glazed lemon threads* includes all the usual but high-end elements (butter, eggs, heavy cream), but the burst of lemon and the way it toys with the batter and the finished cake are what really matter, flavor-wise. Lemon peel combined with lemon extract is set aside for a short while to blossom before it is introduced into a genial batter. Its tart presence is reiterated—sweetly—in the dewy topping of glazed lemon peel and a sugar-tart coating that gets swept across the top of the baked cake. The finish is brash. The tender crumb of the cake within and beneath its crackly surface embraces it handily. In all, this confection is a real keeper.

But wait, there's more.

The recipe for *the lemon cake that won't go away (updated), lemon soaking glaze, lemon pour* is a different species of cake, and it has its own history. This recipe, in somewhat different form, appeared in *Baking by Flavor*, my cookbook that recorded a decade's worth of research in establishing and pyramiding flavors in doughs and batters. Caterers, avocational bakers, and nearly everyone who opened the book and baked from it have been turning their collective mixers on to prepare this cake. The communal enthusiasm for it encouraged me to offer a new version. Don't worry, the changes are subtle—at best—but the new incarnation will give you every reason to add lemons to your weekly shopping list.

lemon cake, sublime and divine, lemony sugar wash with glazed lemon threads

Preheat the oven to 325 degrees F.

Combine the lemon peel, lemon extract, and lemon juice in a small nonreactive mixing bowl. Set aside to blossom.

Film the inside of a 10-inch Bundt pan (generous 3¾ inches deep, with a capacity of 14 cups) or a 10-inch Bundt pan (4½ inches deep, with a capacity of 15 cups) with nonstick flour-and-oil spray.

For the batter, sift the all-purpose flour, cake flour, baking powder, and salt onto a sheet of waxed paper.

Cream the butter in the large bowl of a freestanding electric mixer on moderate speed for 4 minutes. Add the superfine sugar in 4 additions, beating for 1 minute after each portion is added. Add the confectioners' sugar and beat for 45 seconds. Beat in the whole eggs, one at a time, mixing for about 20 seconds after each addition to combine. Add the egg yolks and beat for 30 seconds longer. Scrape down the sides of the mixing bowl with a rubber spatula to keep the batter even-textured. Blend in the lemon peel and extract mixture. On low speed, alternately add the sifted mixture in 3 additions with the heavy cream in 2 additions, beginning and ending with the sifted mixture. Scrape down the sides of the mixing bowl thoroughly with a rubber spatula after each addition. Beat the batter on moderately high speed for 1 minute.

Pour and scrape the batter into the prepared baking pan. Smooth the top with a rubber spatula.

Bake the cake in the preheated oven for 1 hour and 15 minutes, if you are using the 10-inch Bundt pan (generous 3¾ inches deep, with a capacity of 14 cups), or 1 hour and 20 minutes, if you are using the 10-inch Bundt pan (4½ inches deep, with a capacity of 15 cups), or until risen, set, and a wooden pick inserted into the cake withdraws clean. The baked cake will retract slightly from the sides of the baking pan. Cool the cake in the pan on a rack for 10 minutes. Invert onto another cooling rack. Lift off the pan. Place a sheet of waxed paper underneath the cooling rack holding the cake.

Spoon the lemony topping over the rounded edges of the cake, letting the glazed threads settle on the uppermost rounded surfaces. Make sure to brush the wash on the sides of the cake as well. Cool completely. Just before

(continued on the next page)

lemon butter batter

2 tablespoons finely grated lemon peel

2½ teaspoons lemon extract

1 tablespoon freshly squeezed lemon juice

2 cups unsifted bleached all-purpose flour

1 cup unsifted bleached cake flour

¼ teaspoon baking powder

¾ teaspoon salt

½ pound plus 2 tablespoons (18 tablespoons or 2¼ sticks) unsalted butter, softened

2½ cups superfine sugar

⅓ cup plus 3 tablespoons confectioners' sugar, sifted

6 large eggs

2 large egg yolks

1 cup heavy cream

lemon topping

lemony sugar wash with glazed lemon threads (page 68)

non-melting confectioners' sugar, for sifting over the lemon-washed cake slices (optional)

serving: one 10-inch cake, creating about 16 slices
ahead: best on baking day

serving, and after slicing, you can curl a few glazed lemon threads against the surface nap of the cakes' slices, then dust the top and edges with non-melting confectioners' sugar, if you wish. Store in an airtight cake keeper.

notes
• it is important to note that generous bits of the marinated lemon peel will cause paler dots to appear on the rounded (inverted) surface of the baked cake—to be expected and certainly not a flaw
• Snow White Topping Sugar is available from King Arthur Flour, The Baker's Catalogue (page 501, baking*SelectedSources*); this is non-melting sugar
• use a finely serrated knife to cut the cake

lemony sugar wash with glazed lemon threads

glazed lemon threads

julienne of lemon peel from 2 lemons (preferably organic)

⅓ cup freshly squeezed lemon juice

6 tablespoons granulated sugar

lemon sugar wash

½ cup granulated sugar

⅓ cup freshly squeezed lemon juice

serving: about ⅔ cup

For the glazed lemon threads, blanch the lemon peels in boiling water for 1 minute, drain, and refresh in cold water; repeat this process. Place the lemon juice and sugar in a small nonreactive saucepan, cover, and set over low heat to dissolve the sugar. Uncover the pan, raise the heat to moderately high, and bring to the boil. Stir in the lemon peels and simmer for 3 to 4 minutes; the peels should curl and look lustrous. Remove the saucepan from the heat. Cool for 10 minutes. Pour into a heatproof bowl. Cool completely.

Use the glazed lemon threads in the lemon sugar wash. Or, turn the glazed lemon threads and all of the accompanying syrup into a small nonreactive container, cover tightly, and refrigerate. As the threads chill in the syrup, they will curl. The glazed threads can be stored in the refrigerator for up to 1 week.

For the lemon sugar wash, combine the sugar and lemon juice in a small nonreactive bowl. Stir in the cooled lemon threads along with 2 tablespoons of the syrup that clings to them.

Use the syrup for spooning over a warm cake or batch of muffins.

notes
• thin, delicate threads of lemon peel make the prettiest presentation

the lemon cake that won't go away (updated), lemon soaking glaze, lemon pour

Preheat the oven to 350 degrees F.

Combine the lemon peel, lemon extract, and lemon juice in a small nonreactive mixing bowl. Set aside to blossom.

Film the inside of a 10-inch Bundt pan (generous 3¾ inches deep, with a capacity of 14 cups) with nonstick flour-and-oil spray.

Sift the all-purpose flour, cake flour, baking soda, and salt onto a sheet of waxed paper.

Cream the butter in the large bowl of a freestanding electric mixer on moderate speed for 3 minutes. Add the 2 cups superfine sugar in 3 additions, beating for 1 minute after each portion is added. Beat in the egg yolks, 2 at a time, mixing for about 20 seconds after each addition to combine. Scrape down the sides of the mixing bowl with a rubber spatula to keep the batter even-textured. Blend in the lemon peel and extract mixture. On low speed, alternately add the sifted mixture in 3 additions with the buttermilk in 2 additions, beginning and ending with the sifted mixture. Scrape down the sides of the mixing bowl thoroughly with a rubber spatula after each addition.

In a clean, dry medium-size mixing bowl, whip the egg whites until just beginning to mound, add the cream of tartar, and continue whipping until soft peaks are formed. Sprinkle over the 2 tablespoons superfine sugar and continue whipping until firm (but not stiff) peaks are formed. The whipped egg whites will look glossy. Stir one-quarter of the whipped egg whites into the batter, then fold in the remaining whites, taking care to be thorough while keeping the batter buoyant.

Spoon the batter into the prepared baking pan. Smooth the top with a rubber spatula.

Bake the cake in the preheated oven for 55 minutes, or until risen, set, and a wooden pick inserted into the cake withdraws clean or with a few moist crumbs attached. The baked cake will retract slightly from the sides of the baking pan. Cool the cake in the pan on a rack for 10 minutes. Invert onto another cooling rack. Lift off the pan. Place a sheet of waxed paper underneath the cooling rack holding the cake.

(continued on the next page)

lemon butter batter

5 teaspoons finely grated lemon peel

1½ teaspoons lemon extract

2 tablespoons freshly squeezed lemon juice

2¾ cups unsifted bleached all-purpose flour

⅓ cup unsifted bleached cake flour

¼ teaspoon baking soda

½ teaspoon salt

½ pound (16 tablespoons or 2 sticks) unsalted butter, softened

2 cups superfine sugar

4 large eggs, separated

1 cup buttermilk

¼ teaspoon cream of tartar

2 tablespoons superfine sugar

lemon soaking glaze (page 70)

lemon pour (page 70)

serving: one 10-inch cake, creating about 16 slices
ahead: best on baking day

Coat the surface of the cake with the *lemon soaking glaze,* taking care to moisten the sides of the cake as well as the top, using a soft pastry brush. After 25 to 35 minutes, or when the top of the cake is no longer wet to the touch, spoon over the *lemon pour,* allowing it to cascade over the rounded edges of the cake's surface. Let the cake stand for at least 1 hour before slicing and serving. Store in an airtight cake keeper.

notes
• use a finely serrated knife to cut the cake

 ## *lemon soaking glaze*

lemony brushing wash

½ cup freshly squeezed lemon juice

½ cup granulated sugar

¼ teaspoon lemon extract

serving: about ⅔ cup

Combine the lemon juice and sugar in a small nonreactive saucepan (preferably enameled cast iron). Cover and set over moderately low heat. When every last granule of sugar has dissolved (in 5 to 8 minutes), uncover the pan, bring to the simmer, and simmer for 1 minute. Off the heat, stir in the lemon extract.

Use the warm or hot glaze over a warm or cool cake. Or, use the cool glaze over a warm or hot cake. For the best results, avoid using the cool glaze over a cool cake.

notes
• be sure to use a small saucepan or the glaze will overly reduce

 ## *lemon pour*

lemony icing

2 cups plus 3 tablespoons plus
2 teaspoons unsifted confectioners' sugar

5 tablespoons freshly squeezed
lemon juice

2 tablespoons unsalted butter, softened

serving: about 1¼ cups

Place the confectioners' sugar, lemon juice, and butter in a medium-size nonreactive mixing bowl. Using a hand-held electric mixer, blend the ingredients on low speed for 30 seconds, or until just combined. Scrape down the sides of the mixing bowl once or twice with a rubber spatula to keep the topping smooth-textured. Do not overbeat or the topping will be spongy instead of smooth. The topping should be slightly thick, but still pourable.

Use the topping immediately, before it has the opportunity to firm up.

notes
• the density of the glaze will depend on the atmospheric conditions of the day and your kitchen (whether arid or humid)
• the density of the mixture can be adjusted to achieve its thick-but-pourable consistency by adding up to 2 tablespoons confectioners' sugar (1 to 2 teaspoons at a time) or up to 2 teaspoons freshly squeezed lemon juice (½ teaspoon at a time)

the morning belongs to cinnamon

In addition to a jaunty piece of pastry knitted with some form of chocolate (OK, so I'm chocolate-obsessed), a breakfast cake perfumed with cinnamon is a soothing way to start the day.

Plain old-fashioned, this warm sweet spice is displayed so well in the presence of two other ingredients—butter (first and foremost) and eggs. Frequently, the traditional baker in me gets all weak for a perfect union of butter and cinnamon.

My friendly chocolate bias aside, cinnamon simply blossoms at breakfast in cakey squares or fingers—moist, tender, and rich—and in cakey muffins. Butter and cinnamon get together naturally and mannerly in baked goods, each reinforcing the flavor of the other.

About the cake: the composition of the thick and silky batter is the result of an uncomplicated match of ingredients baked in a basic square pan. Cinnamon appears inside and out, and its pungency is, in an overall sense, relieved by a sweetener in the form of sugar. For years now I have worked on reconfiguring a classic butter cake (someplace in the domain of the iconic 1-2-3-4 cake) into a coffee cake because I wanted to confer onto it the wonderful texture of a creamed batter. This cake does not disappoint on any level. Its structure is stable enough to include a ripple of filling, but I love it undecorated on the inside and generously topped with cinnamon sugar on top. Despite the absence of chocolate (forgive the repetition, chocolate is forever on my mind), the cake is high on my list of baking pleasures.

About the muffins: when there is only so much seasoning a batter or dough can take in its basic form, you have to look for a secondary path to assist its flavor complexion. For this, I like to lean on a douse of butter, sugar, and the tasty (and earthy) scent of spice. A tender muffin is a perfect base for that treatment. What could be better than something warm and cinnamon-y and nutmeg-y inside and out? As the topping is generously sweet, the batter is built with just enough sugar to develop its structure and crumb. Two of the warm spices that shade the fine batter (cinnamon and nutmeg) are repeated in the topping, reinforcing each other with an easygoing but full-toned degree of depth (a touch of ground cardamom is a third—and optional—spice to add to the butter, sugar, and spice dip finish). The batter is brought together by buttermilk, a liquid ingredient that tenderizes and, with its light acidic edge and inherent tanginess, acts as a beneficial contrast to the butter. Size is adjustable: for the brunch basket, make these mini; for a hearty breakfast, use the bakeware as recommended; or, for a sweetly frivolous look, turn the batter into infant brioche molds.

Chocolate is eternal, but the morning belongs to cinnamon....

butter+cinnamon+sugar=cake

Preheat the oven to 350 degrees F.

Film the inside of a 9 by 9 by 2-inch pan with nonstick flour-and-oil spray.

For the batter, sift the flour, baking powder, salt, and cinnamon onto a sheet of waxed paper.

Cream the butter in the large bowl of a freestanding electric mixer on moderate speed for 3 minutes. Add the sugar in 2 additions, beating for 2 minutes after each portion is added. Beat in the eggs, one at a time, mixing only until incorporated. Blend in the vanilla extract. On low speed, alternately add the sifted mixture in 3 additions with the half-and-half in 2 additions, beginning and ending with the sifted mixture. Scrape down the sides of the mixing bowl with a rubber spatula to keep the batter even-textured. Beat the batter on moderately high speed for 30 seconds. The batter will be very creamy and moderately dense.

Spoon and scrape the batter into the prepared baking pan. Smooth the top with a rubber spatula.

Bake the cake in the preheated oven for 40 to 45 minutes, or until risen, set, and a wooden pick withdraws clean when inserted 1 to 2 inches from the center. Cool the cake in the pan on a cooling rack for 5 minutes. Sprinkle half of the cinnamon-sugar topping evenly over the surface of the cake. The first sprinkling will cause the surface to darken as it absorbs the mixture because the cake is emitting warmth. Let the cake rest for 30 minutes, then sprinkle the remaining cinnamon-sugar topping on the surface of the cake. The dual sprinklings at different cake temperatures will result in an interesting definition of taste and color. Serve the cake cut into squares or fingers directly from the pan. Lift out the pieces of cake, using a small offset metal spatula. Store in an airtight cake keeper.

notes
• overbeating the mixture when the eggs are added may destabilize the cake as it bakes (risking an uneven rise), so be sure to beat the mixture just to incorporate each egg
• the fine, close-textured (some would call it "compact") crumb of the cake is ultra-buttery and creamy

cinnamon butter batter

2¾ cups unsifted bleached all-purpose flour

1¾ teaspoons baking powder

½ teaspoon salt

1 tablespoon ground cinnamon

½ pound (16 tablespoons or 2 sticks) unsalted butter, softened

1 cup plus 3 tablespoons granulated sugar

3 large eggs

2 teaspoons vanilla extract

1 cup plus 2 tablespoons half-and-half

cinnamon-sugar topping

½ cup granulated sugar blended with 1 tablespoon ground cinnamon

serving: one 9-inch cake, creating 16 squares or 12 ample fingers
ahead: 2 days

cinnamon buttermilk butter dips

cinnamon buttermilk batter

2¼ cups unsifted bleached
all-purpose flour

1¾ teaspoons baking powder

½ teaspoon baking soda

½ teaspoon salt

3 teaspoons ground cinnamon

½ teaspoon freshly grated nutmeg

9 tablespoons (1 stick plus 1 tablespoon)
unsalted butter, softened

¾ cup granulated sugar

2 large eggs

2 teaspoons vanilla extract

¾ cup buttermilk

butter, sugar, and spice dip

1 cup granulated sugar

3 teaspoons ground cinnamon

¼ teaspoon freshly grated nutmeg

⅛ teaspoon ground cardamom (optional)

6 tablespoons (¾ stick) unsalted butter,
melted and cooled but still warm

serving: 1 dozen muffins
ahead: best on baking day

Preheat the oven to 375 degrees F.

Film the inside of 12 muffin/cupcake cups (12 cups to a pan, each cup measuring 2¾ inches in diameter and 1⅜ inches deep, with a capacity of ½ cup) with nonstick flour-and-oil spray. Or, place ovenproof paper baking cup liners in the individual cups.

For the batter, sift the flour, baking powder, baking soda, salt, cinnamon, and nutmeg onto a sheet of waxed paper.

Cream the butter in the large bowl of a freestanding electric mixer on moderate speed for 3 minutes. Add the sugar in 2 additions, beating for 1 minute after each portion is added. Beat in the eggs, one at a time, mixing for 30 seconds after each addition. The mixture may look a little loose at this point, which is fine. Blend in the vanilla extract. On low speed, alternately add the sifted ingredients in 3 additions with the buttermilk in 2 additions, beginning and ending with the sifted mixture. Scrape down the sides of the mixing bowl with a rubber spatula to keep the batter even-textured. The batter will be thick and creamy.

Spoon the batter into the prepared muffin cups, dividing it evenly among them.

Bake the muffins in the preheated oven for 18 to 20 minutes, or until nicely risen, set, and a wooden pick withdraws clean. The rims of the baked muffins will be a light to medium golden in color, and the tops spotty golden-colored.

While the muffins are baking, prepare the butter, sugar, and spice dip by thoroughly whisking the sugar, cinnamon, nutmeg, and cardamom (if you are using it) in a small, deep mixing bowl. Place the melted butter in a small, deep bowl.

Cool the muffins in the pans on racks for 5 minutes. Remove the muffins to other cooling racks. Carefully, using sturdy, heatproof gloves to protect your hands, dip and twirl the tops of the muffins into the butter to coat well, then into the topping to enrobe them in the sugar and spice mixture. (If you like, the tops can be dipped again into the spiced sugar.) Place the coated muffins on cooling racks. Serve warm or at room temperature. Store in an airtight container.

notes
- the muffin batter can also be divided among 9 individual straight-sided metal baking pans (each measuring 3 inches in diameter and 2 inches deep, with a capacity of a scant ¾ cup); bake the larger muffins for 25 minutes
- for a spicier topping, whisk ⅛ teaspoon ground allspice and ⅛ teaspoon ground cloves along with the cinnamon, nutmeg, and optional cardamom into the granulated sugar

zesty, spicy, sweet

The earthiness of fall baking is what categorically sets it apart from spring or summer's fling of sweetness and light. Fall is a season built on deeply bittersweet chocolate, molasses and spice, nuts and dried fruits, sturdy apples and pears.

Gingerbread men and women are cute and pudgy, of course, but there is another classic that should not be overlooked in the rush to stamp out and decorate a pack of all those cookie people: molasses crinkles. The cookies are made from a well-chilled dough, with enough sugar to sweeten and release the aroma of the four "sweet" spices (ginger, cinnamon, cloves, and allspice) and light molasses, in addition to other baking staples. The dough is made by the creamed method, and this technique refines the overall baked texture and contributes to its tender-crunchy snap. As soon as the dough is put together, it must rest for several hours (or overnight) in the refrigerator to make it sturdy enough for hand-rolling first into balls, then into granulated sugar sparked with just a little more ground ginger and a dash of ground cloves; this sugary cloak gives the surface of the baked cookies a soft glimmering look.

To spotlight the ginger flavor and advance it in a pungently assertive way, it is important to add ¾ cup chopped crystallized ginger to the dough after the last addition of flour. Using the crystallized variety of the root, rather than stem ginger in syrup, maintains the texture and stability of the dough. This final enrichment brightens the taste in a sunshiny, very adult way.

For the dough, sift the flour, baking soda, baking powder, salt, ginger, cinnamon, cloves, and allspice onto a sheet of waxed paper.

Cream the shortening and butter in the large bowl of a freestanding electric mixer on moderately low speed for 4 minutes. Add the sugar in 3 additions, beating on moderately low speed for 1 minute after each portion is added. Blend in the whole egg and egg yolk. Blend in the molasses and vanilla extract. On low speed, mix in the sifted ingredients in 3 additions, beating just until the flour particles are absorbed and blending in the crystallized ginger along with the last third of the sifted mixture. Scrape down the sides of the mixing bowl frequently with a rubber spatula to keep the dough even-textured.

Refrigerate the dough, covered with a sheet of food-safe plastic wrap, for 3 hours, or until moldable and rollable into balls. (The dough can be refrigerated overnight in the covered mixing bowl.)

Preheat the oven to 375 degrees F.

Line several cookie sheets or rimmed sheet pans with lengths of ovenproof parchment paper.

Place the sugar and spice rolling mixture in a shallow bowl handy at your work surface.

Scoop up heaping 2-tablespoon-size mounds of dough and roll into balls. Roll each ball in the sugar mixture and place on the prepared baking pans, spacing them about 3 inches apart and arranging 9 mounds to a pan. Lightly press a chunk or two of crystallized ginger into the center of each ball, if you wish.

Bake the cookies in the preheated oven for 14 minutes, or until set. Let the cookies stand on the baking pans for 1 minute, then transfer them to cooling racks, using a wide offset metal spatula. Cool completely. Store in an airtight tin.

notes
• an all-butter dough can replace the butter/shortening mix; use ½ pound plus 2 tablespoons (2 sticks plus 2 tablespoons) unsalted butter, softened
• for the *sugar and spice rolling mixture*, make sure you blend the mixture well so that the ground ginger and cloves are well distributed within it (to dispel tiny clumps of ginger or cloves, sift, then whisk, the sugar and spices)
• roll the balls of dough in the sugar mixture to coat the surfaces lightly, but evenly
• never consume raw cookie dough

molasses crinkles

molasses and spice dough

3 cups unsifted bleached all-purpose flour

2½ teaspoons baking soda

½ teaspoon baking powder

½ teaspoon salt

1 tablespoon ground ginger

¾ teaspoon ground cinnamon

½ teaspoon ground cloves

¼ teaspoon ground allspice

½ cup plus 2 tablespoons solid shortening

8 tablespoons (1 stick) unsalted butter, softened

1½ cups granulated sugar

1 large egg

1 large egg yolk

6 tablespoons light unsulphured molasses

2½ teaspoons vanilla extract

¾ cup coarsely chopped crystallized ginger

sugar and spice rolling mixture

¾ cup granulated sugar blended with ¼ teaspoon ground ginger and ⅛ teaspoon ground cloves

ginger finish (optional)

about ⅓ cup small crystallized ginger chunks

serving: about 3 dozen cookies
ahead: 2 days

Past

buttery cookies, crafted over time ✳ sweetly and heavenly pink ✳ coconut *dreamy* ✳ a milky, sentimental cake and a bread inspired by it ✳ rolls in the hands of a young (and now older) baker ✳ a mother's way with chocolate, times two ✳ dipping cookies: my baking past and present

Perfect

a baking memento

Looking back at the sheer variety of cookies that formed my childhood memories, perhaps no cookie was adored by so many and so scorned by me (as a child) as the "california" almond rusks.

We defined rusks as a crisp-tender kind of dipping cookie, and these cookies always appeared on the kitchen countertop.

Now, the nifty twice-baked almond and cinnamon sugar delights are loaded into my cookie tins—regularly. I love them. They are a genteel pick-up with morning or afternoon coffee and sturdy enough to tie up in a pretty package for rounding out a picnic dessert. In the method of my mother's recipe, the batter was divided into two plain 11 by 4 by 1½-inch metal ice cube trays (with the dividers removed). I still use those trays, but baking pans nearly the same size are available as a specialty item. It seems that metal ice cube trays are such a sought-after domestic relic that they show up with some regularity at tag sales and flea markets that focus on American kitchen collectibles.

My mother's version of the cookie used orange juice and orange peel, but, in mine, both the citrus juice and peel are excluded in favor of adding ground cinnamon plus vanilla and almond extracts to the batter to complement the nuts and the sugary dusting. Occasionally, Mom would enclose a layer of apricot or ginger preserves (the latter, her favorite), sandwiching the spread between two layers of batter. The sticky, flavorful center is, admittedly, awfully good.

Following are interpretations of my mother's mandel breit, *"california" mandel breit*, so named to identify her having received the recipe from a friendly neighborhood recipe swap with a West Coast friend, and *lisa's mandel breit*, my turned-inside-out configuration of that recipe. In a departure from those carefully formed cookies, I sometimes turn to an almond mixture that bakes into free-form panels (really wide ovals); these slightly puffy baked mounds are then sliced into long or stubby dipping sweets—full of almond flavor, one batch is tender, the other crunchy/brash. Both recipes are included here, as their core philosophy is pulled from the first two. Since I can never choose which one to bake, I'll leave the dilemma for you to resolve. (Let me know which one is your favorite.)

"california" mandel breit

Preheat the oven to 350 degrees F.

Film two plain 11 by 4 by 1½-inch metal ice cube trays (dividers removed) with nonstick flour-and-oil spray.

For the batter, sift the flour, baking powder, and salt onto a sheet of waxed paper.

Beat the eggs in the large bowl of a freestanding electric mixer on moderate speed for 1 minute. Add the sugar and beat for 1 minute on moderately high speed. Continuing on moderately high speed, add the oil in a steady stream. Blend in the orange juice and orange peel. Scrape down the sides of the mixing bowl with a rubber spatula to keep the batter even-textured. Blend in the almonds. On low speed, beat in the sifted mixture in 2 additions, mixing just until combined. The batter will be only softly thick and spoonable/pourable.

Pour and scrape the batter into the prepared baking pans, dividing it evenly between them.

Bake the loaves in the preheated oven for 30 minutes, or until risen, set, and a wooden pick withdraws clean from the center of each. Reduce the oven temperature to 275 degrees F. Cool the loaves in the pans on racks for 10 minutes, then carefully invert onto other cooling racks to stand right side up. Cool for 10 minutes.

For the topping, combine the sugar and cinnamon in a small mixing bowl.

Have two cookie sheets or rimmed sheet pans at hand.

Transfer the cooled loaves to a cutting board. Slice each loaf on the diagonal into 12 thick slices (each slice will be ¾ inch thick). Arrange the slices on the baking pans. Let stand for 15 minutes. Sprinkle the exposed cut surfaces with some of the cinnamon sugar.

Bake the slices for 15 minutes. Turn the slices over, sprinkle the cut surfaces with the remaining cinnamon sugar, and bake for 15 minutes longer, or until firm. Transfer the cookies to cooling racks, using a wide offset metal spatula. Cool completely. Store in an airtight tin.

citrus and almond batter

2¼ cups unsifted bleached all-purpose flour

1 teaspoon baking powder

¼ teaspoon salt

3 large eggs

1 cup granulated sugar

1 cup neutral vegetable oil (such as soybean or canola)

¼ cup freshly squeezed orange juice

2 teaspoons finely grated orange peel

1 cup finely chopped skinless almonds

cinnamon-sugar topping

⅔ cup granulated sugar

1½ teaspoons ground cinnamon

serving: about 2 dozen cookies
ahead: 2 weeks

lisa's mandel breit

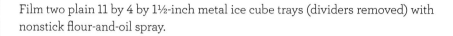

thoroughly almond batter

2¼ cups unsifted bleached
all-purpose flour

1 teaspoon baking powder

½ teaspoon salt

1½ teaspoons ground cinnamon

3 large eggs

1 cup granulated sugar

1 cup neutral vegetable oil
(such as soybean or canola)

2 teaspoons vanilla extract

1 teaspoon almond extract

⅔ cup ground almonds or almond meal

cinnamon-sugar topping

⅔ cup granulated sugar

1½ teaspoons ground cinnamon

serving: about 2 dozen cookies
ahead: 2 weeks

Preheat the oven to 350 degrees F.

Film two plain 11 by 4 by 1½-inch metal ice cube trays (dividers removed) with nonstick flour-and-oil spray.

For the batter, sift the flour, baking powder, salt, and cinnamon onto a sheet of waxed paper.

Beat the eggs in the large bowl of a freestanding electric mixer on moderate speed for 1 minute. Add the sugar and beat for 1 minute on moderately high speed. Continuing on moderately high speed, add the oil in a steady stream. Blend in the vanilla extract and almond extract. Scrape down the sides of the mixing bowl with a rubber spatula to keep the batter even-textured. Blend in the ground almonds or almond meal. On low speed, beat in the sifted mixture in 2 additions, mixing just until combined. The batter will be only softly thick and spoonable/pourable.

Pour and scrape the batter into the prepared baking pans, dividing it evenly between them.

Bake the loaves in the preheated oven for 30 minutes, or until risen, set, and a wooden pick withdraws clean from the center of each. Reduce the oven temperature to 275 degrees F. Cool the loaves in the pans on racks for 10 minutes, then carefully invert onto other cooling racks to stand right side up. Cool for 10 minutes.

For the topping, combine the sugar and cinnamon in a small mixing bowl.

Have two cookie sheets or rimmed sheet pans at hand.

Transfer the cooled loaves to a cutting board. Slice each loaf on the diagonal into 12 thick slices (each slice will be ¾ inch thick). Arrange the slices on the baking pans. Let stand for 15 minutes. Sprinkle the exposed cut surfaces with some of the cinnamon sugar.

Bake the slices for 15 minutes. Turn the slices over, sprinkle the cut surfaces with the remaining cinnamon sugar, and bake for 15 minutes longer, or until firm. Transfer the cookies to cooling racks, using a wide offset metal spatula. Cool completely. Store in an airtight tin.

notes

• this recipes creates a light and tender cookie, perfect for serving with coffee or tea (hot or iced)

biscotti²: languorous afternoon almond cookies for dipping and its going-boldly-into-almond cousin

biscotti #1

Preheat the oven to 350 degrees F.

Line a large, heavy cookie sheet or rimmed sheet pan with a length of ovenproof parchment paper.

For the batter, sift the flour, baking powder, baking soda, cream of tartar, and salt onto a sheet of waxed paper.

Beat the eggs in the large bowl of a freestanding electric mixer on moderate speed for 1 minute. Add the granulated sugar and beat for 1 minute on moderately high speed. Continuing on moderately high speed, add the oil in a steady stream. Blend in the almond extract and vanilla extract. Scrape down the sides of the mixing bowl with a rubber spatula to keep the batter even-textured. On low speed, beat in the sifted mixture in 2 additions, mixing just until combined. Blend in the slivered almonds. The batter-like dough will be moderately dense.

Spoon the batter-dough onto the prepared baking pan, forming two 4¾ by 12-inch panels and placing the panels at least 3½ inches apart. With water-moistened fingertips, smooth the edges of each panel to neaten them, keeping the shape in a somewhat elongated oval. Sprinkle the tops of the panels with the turbinado or sparkling sugar, dividing the sugar evenly between them.

Bake the panels in the preheated oven for 35 to 40 minutes, or until set and a wooden pick withdraws clean. Reduce the oven temperature to 300 degrees F. Cool the solid panels on the baking pan on a rack for 10 minutes.

Have two cookie sheets or rimmed sheet pans at hand.

Slip an offset spatula underneath the baked panels to loosen them from the parchment paper. Carefully transfer one panel to a cutting board. Using a serrated knife, slice the panel on a slight angle into ½ to ¾-inch cookies. Repeat with the remaining panel. Arrange the cookies cut side down on the baking pans.

Bake the cookies for 20 to 25 minutes, or until they are firm and dry, turning them halfway through the baking time. Let the cookies stand on the baking pans for 10 minutes, then carefully transfer them to cooling racks, using a pair of sturdy tongs. Cool completely. Store in an airtight tin.

almond batter

3 cups unsifted bleached all-purpose flour

1¾ teaspoons baking powder

¼ teaspoon baking soda

⅛ teaspoon cream of tartar

½ teaspoon salt

4 large eggs

1 cup granulated sugar

½ cup neutral vegetable oil (such as soybean or canola)

1¼ teaspoons almond extract

1 teaspoon vanilla extract

1 cup slivered almonds, lightly toasted and cooled completely

about ¼ cup turbinado sugar or sparkling sugar (plain or a color), for sprinkling on the unbaked lengths of batter

serving: about 3 dozen cookies
ahead: 3 weeks

biscotti #2

ultra-crunchy almond batter/dough

3 cups unsifted bleached all-purpose flour

1½ teaspoons baking powder
(or substitute baker's ammonia; see notes)

½ teaspoon salt

4 large eggs

1 large egg yolk

1 cup plus 2 tablespoons granulated sugar

2 tablespoons neutral vegetable oil
(such as soybean or canola)

1 tablespoon almond liqueur
(such as amaretto, optional)

2 teaspoons almond extract

1½ teaspoons vanilla extract

1¼ cups slivered almonds, lightly toasted
and cooled completely

about ⅓ cup sparkling sugar
(plain or a color), for sprinkling on the
unbaked lengths of batter

serving: about 33 cookies
ahead: 3 weeks

Preheat the oven to 350 degrees F.

Line two large, heavy cookie sheets or rimmed sheet pans with lengths of ovenproof parchment paper.

For the batter, sift the flour, baking powder, and salt onto a sheet of waxed paper.

Beat the whole eggs and egg yolk in the large bowl of a freestanding electric mixer on moderate speed for 1 minute. Add the granulated sugar and beat for 1 minute on moderate speed. Blend in the oil, almond liqueur (if you are using it), almond extract, and vanilla extract. Scrape down the sides of the mixing bowl with a rubber spatula to keep the batter even-textured. On low speed, beat in the sifted mixture in 2 additions, mixing just until combined. Blend in the slivered almonds. The batter-like dough will be only moderately dense.

Spoon the batter-dough onto the baking pans, forming three 3 by 13-inch panels, placing two panels on one baking sheet (4 inches apart), and the third panel on the second baking sheet. With water-moistened fingertips or a rubber spatula, smooth the edges of each panel to neaten them. Sprinkle the tops of the panels with the sparkling sugar, dividing it evenly among them.

Bake the panels in the preheated oven for 35 minutes, or until set and a wooden pick withdraws clean. Reduce the oven temperature to 300 degrees F. Cool the solid panels on the baking pans on cooling racks for 10 minutes.

Slip an offset spatula underneath the baked panels to loosen them from the parchment paper. Carefully transfer one panel to a cutting board. Using a serrated knife, slice the panel on a slight angle into 1-inch cookies. Repeat with the two remaining panels. Arrange the cookies cut side down on the baking pans. (The temperature of the pans will not affect the texture of the cookies during the second bake.)

Bake the cookies for 20 to 25 minutes, or until they are firm and dry, turning them over after 10 to 12 minutes of baking time. The rebaked cookies should be light golden on both cut sides. Let them stand on the baking pans for 10 minutes, then carefully transfer them to cooling racks, using a pair of sturdy tongs. Cool completely. Store in an airtight tin.

notes
• ¾ teaspoon baker's ammonia can be substituted for the 1½ teaspoons baking powder (in substitution, half the amount specified for baking powder can be replaced with baker's ammonia);

baker's ammonia, also called hartshorn and technically known as ammonium carbonate, is an old-time yet classic (and now fashionable) leavening agent that renders the biscotti very crisp and slightly porous; as the ammonium carbonate–raised biscotti dough sections bake, a light ammonia-type vapor is usually emitted during baking (avoid opening the oven and breathing it in), but is completely clean-smelling when baking is complete; aside from texture, an advantage to using baker's ammonia is the purity of its leavening capability; that is, any alkaline edge present in other leaveners is completely absent when ammonium carbonate is used; if ammonium carbonate is unavailable, or does not dovetail with your comfort level in any way, use baking powder, as the biscotti are delicious either way; baker's ammonia should be stored in an airtight container on a cool cupboard shelf and never inhaled directly

• the slivered almonds create a pretty mosaic on the cut surface of each cookie and keep the texture of the cookies intact as they are sliced with the serrated knife (whole almonds, while attractive, can sometimes challenge the even, clean slice of a serrated knife)

• granulated sugar can replace the sparkling sugar for topping the unbaked panels of dough; if you are in a festive mood, the Hot Pink sparkling sugar, available bottled by India Tree, makes for a dazzling finish

• be sure to use *toasted* almonds in the batter/dough or the nuts will be chewy, rather than crunchy, in the baked cookies

• the small amount of vegetable oil serves to refine the crumb of the baked cookies

• if the cookies are not baked until firm and dry, their crunchy texture will be compromised

a holiday ritual, dozen upon dozen

After years of fashioning—in form and substance—a slew of ornate Christmas cookies (a notable one being batches of *a cookie dough with history,* page 329), my baking psyche and hands continually revert to, by instinct perhaps, some permutation of a plain sugar cookie.

This one, in particular, has been on my "cookie menu" for thirty years, and has survived more changes than my wardrobe.

But not just any sugar cookie. My notion of plain is this: unvarnished, unpatterned, point-blank honest—in flavor and texture. It is buttery and vanilla-y that I crave in this kind of cookie. The aroma of butter must knock you in the face as soon as the tin is opened. "Dainty and fragile" would not be operative descriptive words; "tender but crisp-crunchy" fairly explains their wonderfulness.

It took some time to turn up such a good, butter-magnified dough, one that behaved in a stable way but yielded a fine, nuanced cookie. The subtlety of this dough, made by the creamed method, is carried out by a combination of cream of tartar, baking soda, and baking powder (as conjunctive leavening agents); whole eggs (for richness and stability); and a walloping one pound of butter. There is enough granulated sugar present to sweeten and soften the crumb, but not to an excessive degree. The vanilla extract polishes and connects all of the other ingredients.

As with many butter-based doughs, which can have a rather unruly personality if not treated properly, this one achieves the best results on baking if allowed to rest overnight in the refrigerator. Further, the structure of the baked cookie is reinforced if the dough is sent into the freezer for a brief period of time before being stamped out with a cutter. Important to its handling is the way the dough goes into storage: the technique I established—way back when—was to roll out portions of dough between sheets of waxed paper or parchment paper as soon as the dough was composed in the mixing bowl, for I never really understood the reason for working with hard, chilled lumps of dough. The point of this is two-fold: to streamline the process and to create the best baked duo of crumb and flavor possible. Cookie doughs (and most pastry doughs for that matter) benefit from unwinding (or, technically, "relaxing") in a cold environment in the rolled-out state.

Once the sheet of dough is cut—a scalloped cutter would be a good choice, as the dough is somewhat expansive on baking—the individual cookies are topped with sugar. This can be your nod to holiday frivolity: use shimmery sparkling sugar (a wild color is perfectly acceptable, but clear is pretty, too) or plain granulated sugar. Sanding sugar would also be an agreeable option. "Sweetness" and "light" are, of course, two constituents of a holiday baking rendezvous in the kitchen.

roll out those cookies

mega-butter dough

5 cups unsifted bleached all-purpose flour

1¾ teaspoons cream of tartar

1 teaspoon baking soda

¼ teaspoon baking powder

1 teaspoon salt

1 pound (4 sticks) unsalted butter, softened

1⅔ cups plus 2 tablespoons granulated sugar

4 large eggs

4 teaspoons vanilla extract

granulated sugar, sparkling sugar, or sanding sugar (fine or coarse, and plain or a color), for sprinkling on the cookies before baking

serving: about 5 dozen 2½ to 3-inch cookies or about 3½ dozen 4-inch cookies
ahead: 1 week

For the dough, sift the flour, cream of tartar, baking soda, baking powder, and salt onto a sheet of waxed paper.

Cream the butter in the large bowl of a freestanding electric mixer on moderately low speed for 4 minutes. Add the granulated sugar in 3 additions, beating on moderate speed for 1 minute after each portion is added. Add the eggs, one at a time, beating on low speed until incorporated, about 45 seconds. Blend in the vanilla extract. On low speed, mix in the sifted ingredients in 3 additions, beating only until the flour particles are absorbed. Scrape down the sides of the mixing bowl frequently with a rubber spatula to keep the dough even-textured. At this point, the dough will be quite moist and sticky, but be patient and continue with conviction into the next step.

Divide the dough into 4 portions. Roll each chunk of dough between two sheets of waxed paper to a thickness of ¼ inch. As the dough is so soft, it will be very easy to roll. Stack the sheets of dough on a large cookie sheet. Refrigerate the dough overnight on the cookie sheet, covered with food-safe plastic wrap.

On baking day, place the sheets of dough in the freezer for 20 minutes before cutting out the cookies and baking them.

Preheat the oven to 375 degrees F in advance of baking.

Line several cookie sheets with lengths of ovenproof parchment paper.

Remove one sheet of dough at a time from the freezer. Carefully peel off both sheets of waxed paper. Place the length of rolled-out dough on one of the sheets of waxed paper or on a sheet of ovenproof parchment paper. Stamp out cookies with a 2½ to 3-inch cutter or a 4-inch cutter. Place the cookies, 2½ to 3 inches apart, on the prepared baking pans. Sprinkle the tops liberally with plain granulated sugar, clear sparkling sugar, or any shade of sanding sugar desired.

Bake the 2½ to 3-inch cookies in the preheated oven for about 10 minutes, and the 4-inch cookies for about 12 minutes, or until set, baked through, and golden in color on the edges. Let the cookies stand on the baking pans for 1 minute, then transfer them to cooling racks, using a wide offset metal spatula. Cool completely. Store in an airtight tin.

notes
• for a richer cookie, 3 large whole eggs and 2 large egg yolks can replace the 4 large whole eggs
• the cookies in the photograph were stamped out with a 4-inch fluted oval cutter

blushing birthday girl

Pink is an inviting color—it has such a fun, sugar-coated spirit. Birthday cupcakes are so adorable in pink: I say pile on the frosting and let the sprinkles be plentiful.

My "pink birthday" began young with the ever-present bubble gum–colored roses of shortening-based frosting that took over the top of a cake from the neighborhood bakery. The flowers of butter-free frosting enthralled me then, as they were so antithetical to anything my mother would have (or could have) made. I remember the cake well: two colossal, malformed corsages sat on the upper left and upper right corners of a rectangular cake, causing both to sag just like a down pillow does when you elbow it. At home, there was a coconut cake in the shape of a lamb and a chocolate layer cake. A box of cupcakes was carried off to school. There was an unabashed amount of cake.

And so, even now, as the calendar years progress, a pink-hued treat seems quite right in the dreary and at times foreboding week of very late February when my birthday occurs (for the record, the twenty-seventh), acting as a sugary announcement that the next regenerative, pastel-colored season—springtime—is only weeks away.

vanilla cupcakes, pink frosting

Preheat the oven to 350 degrees F.

Line the inside of 17 muffin/cupcake cups (12 cups to a pan, each cup measuring 2¾ inches in diameter and 1⅜ inches deep, with a capacity of ½ cup) with decorative ovenproof paper baking cup liners.

For the batter, sift the flour, baking powder, and salt onto a sheet of waxed paper.

Cream the butter in the large bowl of a freestanding electric mixer on moderate speed for 3 minutes. Add the sugar in 3 additions, beating for 1 minute after each portion is added. Beat in the eggs, one at a time, mixing for about 20 seconds after each addition to combine. Blend in the vanilla extract. On low speed, beat in half of the sifted mixture and mix just until the particles of flour have been absorbed. Add the milk, mix to combine, then blend in the balance of the sifted mixture. Scrape down the sides of the mixing bowl thoroughly with a rubber spatula after each addition. The batter will be moderately dense and creamy.

Spoon the batter into the lined muffin cups, dividing it evenly among them.

Bake the cupcakes in the preheated oven for 18 minutes, or until risen, set, and a wooden pick withdraws clean. Cool the cupcakes in the pans on racks for 10 minutes, then remove them to other cooling racks. Cool completely.

Apply the frosting generously to the tops of the cooled cupcakes in peaks and swirls, or pipe stars, rosettes, or drop flowers, using a pastry bag and tip appropriate to the chosen design. For decorating cupcakes, it is most helpful to use 12-inch piping bags.

notes
• decorative ovenproof paper baking cup liners must be food-safe; the cup liners used in this image are Wilton Bridal Shower baking cups (75 per package, 2½-inch-diameter base)
• the frosting in the image was tinted with dabs of Cake Craft Standard Pink paste food color
• the swirls created from the cupcake frosting (depending on size) were made using a combination of the Ateco #820 open-star tip and the Ateco #823 open-star tip; the Wilton #16 open-star tip can also be used
• the small rose "corsage" adorning the cupcake was made with extra-firm royal icing and painted with Crystal Colors, from Sugarpaste (see page 502, baking*SelectedSources*), certified powdered food color (moistened with a neutral spirit, such as gin or vodka) in the following combination of hues: Fuschia, Baby Pink, and Azalea

(continued on the next page)

vanilla batter

1⅔ cups unsifted bleached cake flour

1¼ teaspoons baking powder

¼ teaspoon salt

8 tablespoons (1 stick) unsalted butter, softened

1 cup granulated sugar

2 large eggs

1½ teaspoons vanilla extract

⅔ cup milk

pink frosting (page 92)

serving: 17 cupcakes (as the capacity of muffin cups can be inconsistent from manufacturer to manufacturer, the exact yield may vary)
ahead: best on baking day

- the ballet tutu embellishment on the cake stand is made by Jolee's by You (EK Success, Ltd., Clifton, NJ; www.eksuccess.com); it is for decorative use only
- the pink rocking horse cupcake pick is available packaged from Fran's Cake and Candy Supplies (see page 500, baking*SelectedSources*); it is for decorative use only and must be removed before the cupcake is consumed
- high-quality tips are available in two decorating systems, Wilton and Ateco: in the Wilton cake decorating system, the closed-star tips (for stars, rosettes, and shells) appear as #26, #29, #30, and #35; the open-star tips (for stars, drop flowers, and rosettes) appear as #15, #18, #21, #172, #199, #364, and #2110 (#1M for piping out one very large swirl); and the drop flower tips (for drop flowers) appear as #107, #109, #129, #191, #225, #2C, and #2F; in the Ateco system, seamless 10-piece sets of pastry tubes are available in the 10 Piece Closed Star Pastry Set and the 10 Piece Star Pastry Tube Set
- any and all ornaments and nonedible embellishments or decorations, including "jewelry" and decorative picks, fastened to the paper baking cup liners or enhancing serving platters, are for decorative use only; only *décoratifs* safe for consumption should be eaten
- any ornamental decorations (including chains, golden ropes, strings of pearls, or ribbons) are for decorative use only; decorations should be fastened to the sides of the baking cup liners or tucked in between the middle of double- or triple-layered baking cup liners
- frosted cupcakes are perishable and should be consumed within 2 hours of composing them

pink frosting

pink butter and cream frosting

6 tablespoons (¾ stick) unsalted butter, softened

4¾ cups confectioners' sugar, sifted with a large pinch of salt

1 teaspoon vanilla extract

½ cup plus 1 tablespoon heavy cream

pink food-safe paste food color, as needed (choose from Salmon Pink by Cake Craft, Fuchsia Pink by Cake Craft, Standard Pink by Cake Craft, Rose Petal Pink or Deep Pink soft gel paste by AmeriColor)

serving: about 3½ cups

Place the butter in the large bowl of a freestanding electric mixer fitted with the flat paddle and beat on moderately low speed for 2 minutes, or until smooth (not fluffy). Add 3 cups of the confectioners' sugar-salt mixture, the vanilla extract, and heavy cream. Combine the mixture on low speed, beating for about 2 minutes. Add the balance of the confectioners' sugar-salt mixture and beat until incorporated. Beat on moderately low speed until creamy, scraping down the sides of the mixing bowl to create a dense, but smooth frosting. Adjust the consistency, if necessary, by incorporating additional confectioners' sugar (1 tablespoon at a time) or heavy cream (1 teaspoon at a time) to build a frosting that can be spread or piped, as need be, for either decorating procedure.

As soon as the frosting is completed, tint it with the paste food coloring: dip a clean wooden pick into the paste, then sink the pick into the frosting. Remove the pick and beat the frosting slowly to disperse the color throughout, scraping down the sides of the mixing bowl to color the frosting evenly. Continue to tint the frosting, as necessary, to achieve the depth of pink you desire: dip a clean wooden pick into the paste color and repeat its immersion and mixing into the frosting. Paste color intensifies as it stands, so begin slowly by introducing careful amounts into the frosting. Use the frosting immediately.

notes
- the paste color used to tint the frosting must be designated as food-safe
- mixing the frosting on low speed until smooth prevents air bubbles from forming

coconut queen

The unvarnished truth: I love sweetened flaked coconut—in most any kind of batter or dough, as the ingredient adds its own kind of splendor to a layer cake, sheet cake, or stack of cookies.

Far from venturesome, but long-cherished all the same, the recipes for the three-layer coconut cake and the cookies start out from my paternal grandmother's recipe file. In her day, the cake would appear in either of two forms: in coconut-saturated layers connected by a billowy stove top–cooked frosting, or in the shape of a lamb (baked in one of those two-piece metal pans) and cloaked in piped stars of vanilla buttercream, with the exterior receiving lots of fleecy shredded coconut. I am presenting her recipe for the cake in both layer cake pans and in a sheet pan. I am partial to baking the batter in a sheet pan, topping it lavishly with the full amount of frosting (this is no time to cut back) and dividing the sweet-scented treat into attention-getting untidy squares—a case where messy equals delicious.

In an instant, I am channeled back to my grandma Lilly's kitchen: a tall stainless steel cake keeper flashes in my mind's eye and, in it, the cake sits comfortably fresh and soft, just waiting to be sliced. While others are delighting in some kind of newfangled conceptual dessert, I am craving this sweet. Its best attribute—and time-wise, the most challenging—is its ephemeral quality. It's not as good the next day. Gather everyone about and serve it within hours of its composition. The cookies are another matter: while I remember that they were served freshly baked with premium vanilla ice cream, the few dozen of them can be stored in the cookie jar. On cookie-baking day, Grandma's container—really a Depression glass lidded box—made it out onto the countertop to replace the cake keeper, with its attendant black knob.

Nostalgia prevails. And, in the instance of these two recipes, rules.

an indulgent coconut cake

buttery coconut batter

2½ cups sifted bleached cake flour

½ cup sifted bleached all-purpose flour

2¼ teaspoons baking powder

½ teaspoon salt

½ pound (16 tablespoons or 2 sticks) unsalted butter, softened

one 1-pound box confectioners' sugar, sifted

4 large eggs, separated

2½ teaspoons vanilla extract

1 cup milk (or ⅓ cup coconut milk and ⅔ cup whole milk—see notes)

1¼ cups firmly packed sweetened flaked coconut

¼ teaspoon cream of tartar

fluffy frosting

4 large pasteurized egg whites (see notes)

large pinch of salt

1 cup granulated sugar

½ cup light corn syrup

1½ teaspoons vanilla extract

~ or ~

creamy vanilla frosting (see notes, below, page 95)

about 3¾ cups firmly packed sweetened flaked coconut, for sprinkling between the cake layers and covering the frosted, assembled cake, or covering the top of the sheet cake

Preheat the oven to 350 degrees F.

Film the inside of three round 9-inch layer cake pans (1¾ inches deep) with nonstick flour-and-oil spray. Line the bottom of each pan with a circle of waxed paper or ovenproof parchment paper cut to fit and film each surface with the spray. Or, film the inside of a 13 by 9 by 2-inch baking pan with nonstick flour-and-oil spray.

For the batter, resift the cake flour and the all-purpose flour with the baking powder and salt onto a sheet of waxed paper.

Cream the butter in the large bowl of a freestanding electric mixer on moderate speed for 3 minutes. Add the confectioners' sugar in 3 additions, beating for 1 minute after each portion is added. Beat in the egg yolks, 2 at a time, mixing for 30 seconds after each addition. Scrape down the sides of the mixing bowl with a rubber spatula to keep the batter even-textured. Blend in the vanilla extract. On low speed, alternately add the sifted mixture in 3 additions with the milk in 2 additions, beginning and ending with the sifted mixture. Scrape down the sides of the mixing bowl thoroughly with a rubber spatula after each addition. Blend in the coconut.

In a clean, medium-size mixing bowl, whip the egg whites until foamy, add the cream of tartar, and continue beating until firm (but not stiff) peaks are formed. Stir about one-quarter of the whipped egg whites into the coconut batter, then fold through the remaining whites, mixing until every large patch is absorbed but avoid overfolding the mixture.

Spoon the batter into the prepared layer cake baking pans, dividing it evenly among them. Or, spoon the batter into the prepared 13 by 9 by 2-inch baking pan. Smooth the top(s) with a rubber spatula.

Bake the cake layers in the preheated oven for 30 minutes, or until risen, set, and a wooden pick inserted about 2 inches from the center of each layer withdraws clean. Bake the single-layer sheet cake for 40 minutes, or until risen, set, and a wooden pick inserted about 1 inch from the center of the cake withdraws clean. No matter the shape of the pan, the baked cake will pull away slightly from the sides.

Cool the cake layers in the pans on racks for 10 to 12 minutes. Invert the cake layers onto other cooling racks and peel away the paper rounds, if they are adhering to the layers. Cool the sheet cake on a rack, leaving it in the pan. Cool completely.

For the fluffy frosting, place the egg whites, salt, granulated sugar, and corn syrup in the upper pan of a double boiler. Mix to combine, using a hand-held electric mixer. Bring about 1½ inches of water to the simmer in the bottom pan of the double boiler. Set the top pan in place (it should not touch the water, but if it does, pour off enough water to clear the bottom of the top pan) and beat the frosting mixture continually for 7 minutes, or until voluminous and fluffy. Remove the entire assembly from the heat, lift off the top pan, dry the outside, and beat in the vanilla extract.

To assemble the layer cake, tear off four 3-inch-wide strips of waxed paper. Place the strips in the shape of a square around the outer 3 inches of a serving plate. Center a cake layer on the plate (part of each strip should be visible). Spread a little of the frosting on the cake layer and sprinkle with some of the coconut. Carefully place the second layer on top, spread with a little frosting, and top with some coconut. Carefully place the third layer on top. Frost the top and sides of the cake and generously coat the freshly frosted surface with the remaining coconut.

To finish the sheet cake, spread the frosting on the cooled layer and top its surface with the coconut.

Let the frosted layer cake stand for 1 hour, then slip away the strips of waxed paper. Cut the cake into thick slices for serving, using a long-bladed serrated knife. Let the sheet cake stand for 1 hour before cutting it into squares for serving directly from the pan, using a medium-width offset metal spatula to remove the squares.

notes
- for the batter, sifting the confectioners' sugar before beating with the butter returns a batter with a lightened, creamy-smooth texture
- to create a batter with greater stability, I now use a combination of cake flour and all-purpose flour, and while Grandma used whole milk, I sometimes replace one-third of the whole milk with unsweetened coconut milk (especially in the sheet cake version)
- if pasteurized egg whites are unavailable, make a creamy vanilla frosting by beating 11 table-spoons (1 stick plus 3 tablespoons) unsalted butter, softened, for 4 minutes in a heavy-duty freestanding electric mixer; beat in 2 cups confectioners' sugar, a pinch of salt, and ½ cup heavy cream, and continue beating on moderate speed for 2 minutes; add 2 teaspoons vanilla extract and 2 cups confectioners' sugar and continue beating for 3 minutes, adjusting the tex-ture of the frosting to spreading consistency by adding heavy cream (1 teaspoon or 2 at a time) or confectioners' sugar (1 tablespoon or 2 at a time)
- use a long, finely serrated knife to cut the layer cake and a shorter serrated knife to cut squares from the single frosted layer; inevitably, as the cake is so moist, each cut will generate lots of crumbs
- any frosted cake not consumed after 2 hours of assembling must be refrigerated in an airtight container

serving: one three-layer, 9-inch layer cake, creating 12 to 14 slices, or one 13 by 9-inch sheet cake, creating 20 squares
ahead: best on baking day

brown sugar-coconut cookies

For the dough, sift the flour, baking powder, baking soda, salt, and nutmeg onto a sheet of waxed paper.

Cream the butter in the large bowl of a freestanding electric mixer on moderate speed for 2 minutes. Add the light brown sugar and beat on moderate speed for 1 minute. Add the granulated sugar and beat for 1 minute longer. Blend in the egg, vanilla extract, and milk. On low speed, blend in the sifted ingredients in 2 additions, beating just until the flour particles are absorbed. Scrape down the sides of the mixing bowl frequently with a rubber spatula to keep the dough even-textured. Work in the coconut. The dough will be moderately firm. Form the dough into a slab about 1½ inches in height and enclose it in a sheet of food-safe plastic wrap. Refrigerate the dough for 2 hours.

Preheat the oven to 375 degrees F in advance of baking.

Line several heavy cookie sheets or rimmed sheet pans with lengths of ovenproof parchment paper.

Take up rounded 2-tablespoon-size mounds of dough, roll into chubby oblongs, and place them on the prepared baking pans, spacing them about 3 inches apart and arranging 12 oblongs to a pan. Lightly flatten the oblongs of dough using the bottom of an offset spatula (the smooth bottom of a juice glass works just as well); the oblongs should be about ½ inch thick. If need be, film the underside of the spatula (or the bottom of the juice glass) with nonstick oil spray to make the process manageable; this is especially helpful on a humid day or if your kitchen is warm. With the tines of a lightly floured fork, striate the tops of the cookies by pressing down on the surface of each to form lengthwise corrugated-like markings.

Bake the cookies in the preheated oven for 12 to 14 minutes, or until set and with golden edges. The perimeters of the cookies will look delightfully craggy, and the striated markings will bake up slightly muted. Let the cookies stand on the baking pans for 1 minute, then transfer them to cooling racks, using a wide offset metal spatula. Cool completely. Store in an airtight tin.

notes
• the recipe for the dough is an extension of a family—and childhood—favorite; brown sugar (as the only sweetening agent) figured in one of the early models, but I much prefer the taste and texture of the baked cookie when a combination of granulated sugar and light brown sugar is used

brown sugar-coconut cookie dough

2 cups unsifted bleached all-purpose flour

½ teaspoon baking powder

¼ teaspoon baking soda

¼ teaspoon salt

¼ teaspoon freshly grated nutmeg

8 tablespoons (1 stick) unsalted butter, softened

½ cup firmly packed light brown sugar

½ cup granulated sugar

1 large egg

2 teaspoons vanilla extract

1 tablespoon milk

1½ cups firmly packed sweetened flaked coconut

serving: about 26 cookies
ahead: 2 days

granddaughter's bread, grandmother's cake

Wouldn't it be interesting if cake and bread could converge, exchanging traits with each other, broadcasting characteristics such as light, buttery, milky? Luckily, in my mixing bowls, my grandmother's cake, delicate, with a gentle vanilla and butter flavor, is mirrored in a cakelike bread, with its own smooth and elastic batter. The two recipes overlap, if only from the standpoint of ingredients.

The cake has a long family history attached to it, for it was the favorite cake Grandma Lilly baked and served with scoops of premium vanilla ice cream bought at a local catering and pastry shop to friends who congregated at her home on Saturday night. There were a few variations of the cake, recipe-wise, floating around her files and surfacing over time, but this one is my favorite because it is the one that includes the seed scrapings of a vanilla bean in addition to the vanilla extract; it is also the last interpretation of the batter, prepared a year or two before her death, a clear but far-off memory of mine.

The bread has its own story: this very soft and cozy dough bakes up light and tender. The bread is best within an hour of pulling from the oven (sorry, but this does go against the dictate of the experts who insist that bread cool down for a few hours before diving in), when its cushiony softness grabs you, and is a longtime favorite of those who bunch around my kitchen island on the weekend. The recipe has been shaped (really cobbled together) over the last twenty-five years, and is based on my flavor-and-texture memory of a milky bread I baked in a tube pan as a teenager. With a big block of softened salted French butter at hand, it's easy to tear apart sections of the bread and smear on the premium spread with the kind of exquisite abandon that only takes place when something freshly baked presents itself at its very moment of completion. If the cake (with its nearly Twinkie-like texture—minus the cream filling) was a fixture of my childhood, then this bread is a staple of my grown-up kitchen. Both are simple, and simply delicious.

hot milk bread

dairy-deluxe yeast dough

2¼ teaspoons active dry yeast

¼ teaspoon granulated sugar

¼ cup warm (105 to 110 degrees F) water

¾ cup milk

⅓ cup plus 1 tablespoon granulated sugar

8 tablespoons (1 stick) unsalted butter, cut into chunks

1 large egg and 2 large egg yolks, lightly beaten

2¾ teaspoons vanilla extract

4 cups unsifted bleached all-purpose flour

½ teaspoon salt

serving: one 9-inch fluted bread, creating about 14 slices
ahead: best on baking day; or freeze for 1 month, defrost, bundle in aluminum foil, and reheat in a preheated 325 degrees F oven for 10 to 15 minutes

For the dough, stir together the yeast, the ¼ teaspoon sugar, and the warm water in a heatproof measuring cup. Allow the mixture to stand until swollen, 6 to 7 minutes.

In the meantime, place the milk, the ⅓ cup plus 1 tablespoon sugar, and the chunks of butter in a small saucepan and set over moderate heat. When the butter has melted, remove from the heat, pour into a medium-size heatproof mixing bowl, and cool to tepid. Quickly blend the beaten whole egg and egg yolks and the vanilla extract into the butter mixture. Mix in the yeast mixture.

Place 3 cups of the flour and the salt in a large mixing bowl. Whisk to integrate the salt. Blend in the milk-butter-egg-yeast mixture. Mix well to form a dense batter. Beat vigorously for 2 minutes, using a wooden spoon or flat wooden paddle. Add the remaining 1 cup flour, ⅓ cup at a time. The final ⅓ cup will not integrate into the dough fully by hand.

Turn the dough and all of the unincorporated flour into the bowl of a heavy-duty freestanding electric mixer. Set the bowl in place and attach the dough hook. Mix on moderate speed until the mixture is combined, about 1 minute. Beat on moderately low speed for 7 full minutes, or until quite smooth and elastic, stopping the machine midway to scrape down the sides of the mixing bowl and dough hook; refrain from stinting on the beating time, as this stage develops the texture of the baked bread. The dough will leave a slight film on the sides of the bowl and stick to the bottom.

Scrape the dough into a bowl heavily coated with softened unsalted butter, make several cuts in the dough with a pair of kitchen scissors, cover tightly with a sheet of food-safe plastic wrap, and let rise at cool room temperature for 1½ hours, or until doubled in bulk.

Remove and discard the plastic wrap. Gently compress the dough, using a buttered rubber spatula. Let stand for 3 minutes. Turn the dough out onto a work surface and form into a log-like cylinder 10 to 11 inches long and about 3½ inches in diameter. Let stand for 2 minutes.

Film the inside of a fluted 9-inch tube pan (4¼ inches deep, with a capacity of 11 cups) with nonstick flour-and-oil spray.

To form the bread, join the two ends of the cylinder of dough into a ring, pinching the ends together with your fingertips. Smooth out the seam with your fingertips as best as you can (the seam will still show at one side after baking, but the purpose of sealing is to effect an even rise of the bread). Set the ring of dough into the prepared baking pan.

Cover the pan loosely with a buttered sheet of food-safe plastic wrap. Let the bread rise at cool room temperature for 45 minutes to 1 hour, or until almost doubled in bulk (see page 6 to reference this stage). The bread should rise to about ¼ inch of the rim of the baking pan and crest in a rounded center crown that is slightly higher than the sides.

Preheat the oven to 350 degrees F in advance of baking.

Remove and discard the sheet of plastic wrap covering the bread.

Bake the bread in the preheated oven for 45 minutes, or until a deep golden brown color on top and set. The baked bread will pull away slightly from the sides of the baking pan. Place the pan on a cooling rack and let stand for 10 minutes. Invert the bread onto another cooling rack to stand fluted side up. Lift off the pan. Serve the bread cut into thick slices. Store in an airtight container.

notes
• 2 large eggs can be used in place of the whole egg and 2 egg yolks, though the interior of the bread will be a little less golden in color
• in a perfectly temperate rising atmosphere (such as on a 70 degrees F day), the surface of the bread will balloon beautifully during the initial oven-spring
• use a finely serrated knife to cut the bread or just break it apart with your hands

vanilla milk cake

vanilla milk batter

1¾ cups unsifted bleached cake flour

¼ cup unsifted bleached all-purpose flour

½ teaspoon salt

8 tablespoons (1 stick) unsalted butter, cut into chunks

1 cup milk

4 large eggs

2 cups superfine sugar (see notes)

2 teaspoons vanilla extract

seeds from 1 small vanilla bean, scraped clean

1 teaspoon baking powder

confectioners' sugar, for sifting over the baked cake

serving: one 9-inch cake, creating about 12 slices
ahead: best on baking day

Preheat the oven to 350 degrees F.

Film the inside of a fluted 9-inch tube pan (4¼ inches deep, with a capacity of 11 cups) with nonstick flour-and-oil spray.

For the batter, sift the cake flour, all-purpose flour, and salt onto a sheet of waxed paper.

Place the chunks of butter and the milk in a heavy medium-size saucepan. Set over moderate heat and bring to the boil.

In the meantime, beat the eggs in the large bowl of a freestanding electric mixer on moderate speed for 2 minutes. Add the superfine sugar in 3 additions, beating for 1 minute after each portion is added. Blend in the vanilla extract and vanilla bean seeds. On low speed, add the sifted mixture in 2 additions, beating just until the flour particles are absorbed. With the mixer on low speed, very slowly pour in the hot butter and milk mixture; beat until thoroughly combined, scraping down the sides of the mixing bowl now and again to keep the batter even-textured. Immediately add the baking powder and mix it in. The batter will be relatively thin and pourable.

Pour and scrape the batter into the prepared baking pan.

Bake the cake in the preheated oven for 1 hour, or until risen, set, and a wooden pick inserted into the cake withdraws clean. The baked cake will begin to pull away from the sides of the baking pan.

Cool the cake in the pan on a rack for 10 minutes. Invert onto another cooling rack. Lift off the pan. Cool completely. Store in an airtight cake keeper. Just before slicing and serving, sift confectioners' sugar over the top of the cake.

notes
• do not use a false-bottomed pan for this cake batter as the batter is too thin
• my grandma most certainly used granulated sugar, but I prefer the texture of the cake when superfine sugar is swapped for it; she also used cake flour entirely in the batter, but the overall texture is improved by replacing some of the cake flour with a small amount of all-purpose flour
• avoid lingering once the butter and milk are bubbly/hot, and add them to the batter-in-progress exactly at that very point; likewise, get the batter into the pan and into the oven promptly
• once the cake is in the oven, refrain from opening the door for the first 40 minutes of baking, as this is a tender and fragile batter that easily deflates

learning to knead

Butter, sugar, eggs, and milk. These are the distinguishing ingredients that appear in my yeast dough formula that goes back many years—several decades, in fact.

The recipe for the rolls appeared in my baking file when I was fourteen, although the little metal box holding a reasonably large collection of index cards for this yeasty delight and other baked goods began in earnest at age seven. Working with yeast was at times a challenge because my late mother, whose very cakes and cookies were sought after—if not envied—by others (by today's standards her range was small but noteworthy), never did seem to connect with yeast baking. Her impatient personality did her in. The proofing, the waiting! The rising, the waiting! The forming, the waiting! The baking! All of this seemed to have eluded her. Her agitation probably killed off any potentially thriving organisms of yeast. Irrespective of this or perhaps in spite of it, I managed to convince her to add fresh yeast cakes to the shopping cart one Saturday at the market, just for me, and so my odyssey began.

It was, as memory serves up, a jerky start.

Intermittent intervals of reading about yeast in whatever form I could, rushing into the kitchen to make a batch of dough, checking its swollen progress, viewing the state of a prepared and enlarging loaf, and finally baking whatever resulted was like playing culinary ping-pong. Back and forth, hit and miss. I made all the classic blunders: giving the dough too much or too little liquid; using those same liquids at the wrong temperature; misjudging the amount of flour; adding salt at an ill-timed juncture; or, worst of all, overfilling the individual baking cups in such a way that the tops of the rolls interlinked to form one gloriously solid shelf of bread (hilarious, but only in retrospect). And then there was the time that I doubled the yeast—or was it tripled?—only to walk into our tiny kitchen to see an overspill of dough exiting the top of the bowl, past its sides, over the countertop, and straight down the cabinet into the vented grill at the base of the dishwasher. Somehow the dough crept into the sides of the dishwasher itself and gummed up the rubber seals, and then, you guessed it, the unit was reduced to, in a word, junk.

Months passed, and I convinced my mother to buy more yeast. (By that time, she had gotten over the equipment fiasco—barely—and besides, we had a new dishwasher.) This was after my baking foray into shortbread. The return to bread baking probably seemed like a good and relieving shift from my insistence on buying butter in three-pound lots every few days and cranking out cookie dough after cookie dough. After all, how much shortbread can one really consume in a week? I became a recipe sleuth and, finally, learned to predict errors and inconsistencies. And then I learned how to knead a dough properly—by hand. This was key. Years later, I cannily thought that the whole process could be adapted to using a heavy-duty mixer fitted with the correct attachment and, with the formula in hand, I discovered how *not* to create a responsively refined dough. This is not a recipe for an electric mixing device, a notion that many contemporary bread bakers have concluded in their writings on far more complicated offerings than what you have below. You can be sure that the dough hook tortured this genteel and submissive dough. (Don't get me wrong: while a heavy-duty electric mixer does come in handy, I find that this dough is ever-so-better and more responsive when made by hand.)

Here are the rolls that are a personal nod to both my own baking chronicles and thoroughly American style. They are especially and wonderfully light, buttery, a little eggy, and sweet in the demure, simple way that some dinner rolls are, historically. And the dough unquestionably flourishes in the hands of a baker. Of any age.

a 14-year-old's rolls still tasty after all these years

For the dough, stir together the yeast, the ¼ teaspoon sugar, and the warm water in a heatproof measuring cup. Allow the mixture to stand until swollen, 6 to 7 minutes.

Place the milk, the chunks of butter, and the ¼ cup sugar in a medium-size saucepan and set over low heat. When the sugar has dissolved, remove the saucepan from the heat; pour and scrape the mixture into a medium-size heatproof mixing bowl. Cool to warm, about 105 degrees F. Quickly blend in the eggs and yeast mixture.

Place 3 cups of the flour in a large mixing bowl and blend in the salt. Add the yeast mixture and mix to combine, using a wooden spoon or flat wooden paddle. Let stand for 5 minutes. Add 1 cup more of the flour, mix well, and let stand for 1 minute. Place the remaining ½ cup flour on a work surface, and knead the dough on it, incorporating all of the flour. The dough should be moderately soft. Continue kneading the dough for 6 minutes longer, adding the additional 2 tablespoons flour only if the dough begins to seriously adhere to the work surface.

Turn the dough into a bowl heavily coated with softened unsalted butter, lightly turn to coat all sides in a film of butter, make several cuts in the dough with a pair of kitchen scissors, cover tightly with a sheet of food-safe plastic wrap, and let rise at cool room temperature for 1 hour and 30 minutes (in humid weather or on a rainy day) to 2 hours, or until quite puffy and doubled in bulk.

Remove the plastic wrap. Lightly compress the dough with a rubber spatula, cover loosely with the plastic wrap, and let stand for 10 minutes. Remove and discard the plastic wrap.

In the meantime, film the inside of 24 muffin/cupcake cups (12 cups to a pan, each cup measuring 2¾ inches in diameter and 1⅜ inches deep, with a capacity of ½ cup) with nonstick flour-and-oil spray.

To form the rolls, divide the dough in half. Cut each half into 12 even-size pieces. Cut each of the 12 pieces into 2 even-size pieces. Roll the pieces into a smooth, slightly elongated, somewhat oval ball. Place 2 ovals in the bottom of each prepared muffin cup.

(continued on the next page)

lightly sweetened yeast dough

2¼ teaspoons active dry yeast

¼ teaspoon granulated sugar

¼ cup warm (105 to 110 degrees F) water

1 cup milk

8 tablespoons (1 stick) unsalted butter, cut into tablespoon-size chunks

¼ cup granulated sugar

2 large eggs, lightly beaten

4½ cups unsifted bleached all-purpose flour, plus an additional 2 tablespoons, as needed for kneading and shaping

1 teaspoon salt

butter mop (optional)

3 tablespoons unsalted butter (preferably clarified butter, page 1), melted and warm

serving: 2 dozen rolls
ahead: best on baking day; or freeze for 3 weeks, defrost, bundle in aluminum foil, and reheat in a preheated 300 degrees F oven for 10 minutes

Cover each pan of rolls loosely with a sheet of food-safe plastic wrap. Let the rolls rise at room temperature for 45 minutes to 1 hour, or until doubled in bulk. They should look puffy but stable.

Preheat the oven to 375 degrees F in advance of baking.

Remove and discard the sheets of plastic wrap covering the rolls.

Bake the rolls in the preheated oven for 15 to 18 minutes, or until set and a golden color on top. Cool the rolls in the pans on cooling racks for 5 minutes.

For the butter mop (if you are using it), brush the warm melted butter on top of the rolls. After 5 minutes, carefully remove the rolls, using the tip of a round-edged flexible palette knife to nudge them out, if necessary, for they are fragile when freshly baked. Serve warm or at room temperature. Store in an airtight container.

notes
• mixing and kneading the dough by hand creates the finest, airiest rolls
• the slow first rise at cool room temperature, taking up to 2 hours, makes the lightest rolls
• using clarified butter for brushing on the tops of the baked rolls gives them a finish with the pure taste of butter; the final swipe with butter is an optional, but flavorful, finish
• upon seeing a basket of these rolls, a friend offered this assessment: "These look like the brown-and-serve rolls my mother served when I was a kid." (A compliment, I presume?)

mother*love*

You can be "mothered" by a mother or, if time and circumstance detach you from your birth mother, a substitute mother. Linked by genes or not, male (as in "mothering") or female, a person who touches your life is sure to leave an imprint. For me, that embossment was chocolate-based. And it has happened twice.

#1 Mother: According to Irene Yockelson, my late genetically-related mother, her chocolate buttermilk cake reigned supreme. It beat out the so-called "fancy cakes" (her words, uttered in a disparaging tone of voice) I turned out while baking during my "imperious" youth, when I turned my back on this structure of two layers and its attendant runny, flowy icing/glaze that sets up beautifully into a soft, fudgy mantle. As a child, that topping delighted me to no end, and there was simply never enough of it. The layers, good as they were—buttermilk-moist, wonderfully chocolaty, undeniably cushiony—were just an excuse to eat more of the icing.

Now, the cake and the icing/glaze, in a very sweet and emotional union, entice me back. Right now, my mother, in some apparitional state, is likely giving me that "I told you so" look as I glorify its virtues and claim the cake's formula as my own. Since I'm in charge, I make a lot more glaze and use the extra to double-coat the dessert plates as well. Finally, without a quarrel and unable to dispute my mom, I cave to say: this is one terrific cake. So good, in fact, that now I love to double the recipe, bake it in a deep tube pan, and let the glaze run in a deviant way over monster-thick slices in a kind of chocolate torrent. It's not just a chocolate cake. It's *the don't-dispute-your-mother cake.*

#1 Substitute Mother: Alice Moberley Romejko was born on November 21, 1915, and raised in a small town in north central Texas called Albany. Along with Alice's eldest daughter and husband, she and I "adopted" each other around the time of the death of my own mother. Alice loved to bake, and in 1997 I encouraged her to "write" her own cookbook. I agreed to "publish" it for her, by photocopying her handwritten and clipped recipes and assembling them in binders. Our first (and only) "print run" totaled a grand twelve copies. This "book" was given to each of her four children and to me. A year later, Alice passed away.

One of the first recipes she gave me, and one that was prominent in her file, is this chocolate sheet cake. Alice loved the cake, accented with big handfuls of pecans locked in the frosting. Just before her death, I "remade" the cake with Alice, and we upgraded it with more vanilla extract, superfine sugar in place of plain granulated, and lots of pecans (as well as a pinch of salt) in the frosting. My own mother made a similar cake, using walnuts. (The Coca-Cola cake of my childhood eerily mimics this recipe.) The cake never failed to please, and has even survived being made incorrectly at times due to an inadvertent mismeasuring of the liquid, sugar, or leavening agent. What can I say? Life can be imprecise at times. When the telephone rings or someone cries out for attention, the recipe somehow changes—despite any attempt by the baker to account for everything within it.

When I think of chocolate cake, my mind always sways to the two recipes that follow, and, before I know it, an endearing chunk of the past is sitting right on my marble-topped island in the center of the kitchen. All memories should be this sweet, don't you think?

the don't-dispute-your-mother cake

buttermilk chocolate batter

2 cups unsifted bleached cake flour

1½ teaspoons baking soda

¼ teaspoon salt

8 tablespoons (1 stick) unsalted butter, softened

1½ cups superfine sugar

2 large eggs

3 ounces unsweetened chocolate, melted and cooled

1½ teaspoons vanilla extract

1½ cups buttermilk

~ or ~

buttermilk chocolate batter,
above ingredients doubled (see notes)

chocolate glaze (icing)

4½ ounces unsweetened chocolate, chopped

9 tablespoons (1 stick plus 1 tablespoon) unsalted butter, cut into chunks

¾ cup superfine sugar

1 tablespoon plus 1½ teaspoons cornstarch

pinch of salt

¾ cup milk

1¼ teaspoons vanilla extract

serving: one two-layer, 8 or 9-inch layer cake, creating 10 or 12 slices respectively
ahead: best on baking day

Preheat the oven to 350 degrees F.

Film the inside of two round 9-inch layer cake pans (1¾ inches deep) or two round 8-inch cake pans (3 inches deep) with nonstick oil spray. Line the bottom of each pan with a circle of waxed paper or ovenproof parchment paper cut to fit and film each surface with the spray. If you are baking a double recipe of the cake batter in a big tube pan, refer to the directions that follow this recipe (see notes).

For the batter, sift the flour, baking soda, and salt onto a sheet of waxed paper.

Cream the butter in the large bowl of a freestanding electric mixer on moderate speed for 3 minutes. Add the sugar in 3 additions, beating for 1 minute after each portion is added. Beat in the eggs, one at a time, mixing for 45 seconds after each addition. Scrape down the sides of the mixing bowl with a rubber spatula to keep the batter even-textured. Blend in the melted chocolate and vanilla extract. On low speed, alternately add the sifted mixture in 3 additions with the buttermilk in 2 additions, beginning and ending with the sifted mixture. Scrape down the sides of the mixing bowl thoroughly with a rubber spatula after each addition.

Spoon the batter into either set of the prepared baking pans, dividing it evenly between them. Smooth the tops with a rubber spatula.

Bake the cake layers in the preheated oven for 25 to 30 minutes, if you are using the 9-inch pans, and for 30 to 35 minutes, if you are using the deeper 8-inch pans, or until risen, set, and a wooden pick inserted about 2 inches from the center of each cake layer withdraws clean.

Cool the cake layers in the pans on racks for 10 to 12 minutes. Invert onto other cooling racks, lift off each pan, and peel away the paper rounds if adhering to the layers. Cool completely.

For the glaze (icing), place the chocolate and butter in a heavy medium-size saucepan (preferably enameled cast iron), and set over low heat to melt both. Sift the sugar, cornstarch, and salt into a small mixing bowl. Slowly blend in the milk and vanilla extract; mix well. Off the heat, stir the sugar-cornstarch-milk mixture into the melted chocolate-butter mixture. Return the saucepan to moderate heat, bring the mixture to a low boil, then simmer until lightly thickened, 1 to 2 minutes, stirring slowly all the while with a wooden spoon or flat wooden paddle. Avoid rapidly mixing or whisking the glaze or it may thin out. The glaze should coat a spoon and thicken further as it cools. Cool the glaze for 10 minutes, stirring once or twice during that time.

To assemble the cake, tear off four 3-inch-wide strips of waxed paper. Place the strips in the shape of a square around the outer 3 inches of a serving plate. Center one cake layer on the plate (part of each strip should be visible). Spoon and spread some of the glaze (icing) onto the cake layer and carefully place the second layer on top. Spoon or spoon-and-spread the glaze over the top and sides of the cake. The glaze (icing) will flow readily, coating the layers as it is spooned over. You can keep the cake rustic-looking by letting the glaze (icing) cover the cake in patches rather than in one solid cloak. Glide the strips of waxed paper away from the surface of the cake plate after 1 hour. Cut the cake into slices for serving. If you wish, at this point the individual slices can be coated with a double layer of glaze (icing) (see notes).

notes

- for a dramatic version of this cake, double the recipe for the buttermilk chocolate batter and pour it into a plain, one-piece 9¾-inch tube pan (6 inches deep, with a capacity of 18 cups) filmed with nonstick flour-and-oil spray; bake the cake for 1 hour and 10 minutes, or until set; cool for 10 to 15 minutes, unmold and carefully invert again to cool right side up on a rack, and cool completely; pour the warm glaze (icing) over the top and sides of the cake or, alternately, simply assemble hefty slices of the cake and spoon the glaze over and about each portion, letting it puddle on the plate and around the base; this cake will create 16 to 18 slices
- use the glaze (icing) warm, not hot; if it cools too much, it will set up like very soft fudge before you have the opportunity to spread it, but if the glaze (icing) seems to be too runny and pools excessively, just wait a moment or two until the heat subsides a little more
- a further coating of the glaze (icing) can be napped over individual slices at serving time, just after plating the cake; to do this, you'll need to prepare an additional recipe of the glaze and use it freshly made and very warm to spoon over each portion, letting it flow down the sides and pool on the plate
- a crystallized rose petal (must be designated as food-safe) can be used to top a glazed piece of cake, if you wish
- use a finely serrated knife to cut the cake
- frosted cake not consumed after 2 hours of assembling should be refrigerated

favorite chocolate sheet cake, to the memory of alice

cocoa buttermilk batter

2 cups unsifted bleached cake flour

2 cups granulated sugar

½ teaspoon salt

½ cup buttermilk

1 teaspoon baking soda

½ pound (16 tablespoons or 2 sticks) unsalted butter, cut into chunks

¼ cup unsweetened alkalized cocoa powder

1 cup water

2 large eggs

2 teaspoons vanilla extract

chocolate frosting

3¾ cups plus 2 tablespoons confectioners' sugar

large pinch of salt

8 tablespoons (1 stick) unsalted butter, melted and cooled

2 ounces unsweetened chocolate, melted and cooled

1½ teaspoons vanilla extract

6 tablespoons milk

1 cup chopped pecans

serving: one 13 by 9-inch cake, creating 20 squares (or 40 small rectangles)
ahead: best on baking day

Preheat the oven to 400 degrees F.

Film the inside of a 13 by 9 by 2-inch baking pan with nonstick flour-and-oil spray.

For the batter, sift the flour, granulated sugar, and salt into the large bowl of a freestanding electric mixer.

In a small nonreactive mixing bowl, combine the buttermilk and baking soda. Let stand while you continue with the recipe. As the buttermilk and baking soda mixture stands, it will swell and expand somewhat.

Place the chunks of butter, the cocoa powder, and water in a medium-size saucepan. Set over moderate heat and bring to the boil, whisking once or twice as the mixture approaches the boil. Pour the boiling mixture over the flour and granulated sugar mixture and beat on low speed to combine. At this point, the mixture will be soupy. Add the swollen buttermilk-baking soda mixture, the eggs, and vanilla extract. Blend well, scraping down the sides of the mixing bowl with a rubber spatula to keep the batter even-textured. The batter will be quite thin.

Pour and scrape the batter into the prepared baking pan.

Bake the cake in the preheated oven for 20 minutes, or until risen, set, and a wooden pick withdraws clean.

While the cake is baking, prepare the frosting: sift the confectioners' sugar and salt into a large mixing bowl. In a small bowl, whisk the melted butter and chocolate until smooth. Blend in the vanilla extract. Pour the chocolate mixture over the confectioners' sugar, add the milk, and beat on low speed for 1 to 2 minutes, or until just combined and smooth, using a hand-held electric mixer. Blend in the pecans by hand, stirring them in with a rubber spatula. Press a sheet of food-safe plastic wrap directly onto the surface. The prepared frosting can be made up to 20 minutes in advance.

Place the baking pan holding the cake on a cooling rack. Cool for 2 minutes. Dollop the frosting onto the surface of the hot cake and smooth over, using a small offset palette knife. Cool completely. Cut the cake into squares for serving. Store in an airtight container.

notes
• I like to sift a little cocoa powder on top of the cake squares

Plain

cornbread*forms* ❋ I'll take my cake loaded with chips, thank you ❋ good stuff in cookies ❋ banana baking ❋ two butter cakes for all seasons ❋ tempt me with chocolate—downy, soft, and creamy ❋ peanut butter cookie construction ❋ a deliciously littered cake ❋ rolls like soft pillows: one plain, one cardamom-perfumed

Old-Fashioned

a chocolate blanket

Wrapped in chocolate. For ultimate security and well-being, few things are better than a deep, single-layer chocolate cake, moist and capped with oceanic waves of frosting.

This is no discreet blanket, as butter and not a gentle amount of unsweetened chocolate animate both elements. How can you bake with any less chocolate when the flavor needs to resonate so vividly?

Unsweetened chocolate flavors and colors both the cake batter and frosting. The taste of each is supported by butter (a full half-pound in the batter, and ten tablespoons in the frosting), by buttermilk to extend its suppleness (in the cake batter), by heavy cream to add luxury (in the frosting), and by vanilla extract to equalize the boldness. The batter bakes into a reasonably light-textured cake, soft of crumb and feathery-textured. The frosting is a fudgy contrast to what it covers, creating a thick dividing line of chocolate intensity.

A cake such as the one before you is dessert-perfect for serving to a happy bunch of guests at a holiday gathering, over a long weekend of fun and friendship, or at a casual potluck supper. Cut it into brawny squares—the bigger the better—and see how many people appreciate your baking talent.

chocolate comfort cake, creamy chocolate frosting

Preheat the oven to 350 degrees F.

Film the inside of a 13 by 9 by 2-inch baking pan with nonstick flour-and-oil spray.

For the batter, thoroughly stir together the melted chocolate and boiling water in a small heatproof mixing bowl until very smooth. Set aside to cool to slightly warm, when it should be the consistency of a moderately thick pudding.

Sift the flour with the baking soda, baking powder, and salt onto a sheet of waxed paper.

Cream the butter in the large bowl of a freestanding electric mixer on moderate speed for 3 minutes. Add the sugar in 3 additions, beating for 1 minute after each portion is added. Beat in the eggs, one at a time, mixing only to blend. Blend in the chocolate mixture and vanilla extract. On low speed, alternately add the sifted mixture in 3 additions with the buttermilk in 2 additions, beginning and ending with the sifted mixture. Scrape down the sides of the mixing bowl with a rubber spatula to keep the batter even-textured. The consistency of the batter will be creamy.

Scrape the batter into the prepared baking pan. Smooth the top with a rubber spatula.

Bake the cake in the preheated oven for 40 minutes, or until risen, set, and a wooden pick withdraws clean or with a few moist crumbs attached when tested about 2 inches from the center of the cake. The baked cake will pull away slightly from the sides of the baking pan. Cool the cake completely in the pan on a cooling rack.

Spread and swirl the freshly made frosting on top of the cake. Let the frosting set for 1 hour before cutting the cake into squares for serving, using a medium-width offset metal spatula to remove the squares.

notes
• overbeating the batter at the stage when the eggs are added will cause the batter to dry out as it bakes, so be sure to incorporate each egg only until combined
• a tiny crystallized violet (must be designated as food-safe), set on the corner of a piece of cake, would make an understated finishing touch
• any frosted cake not consumed after 2 hours of assembling should be refrigerated

chocolate cake batter

4 ounces unsweetened chocolate, melted

⅓ cup plus 3 tablespoons boiling water

2 cups unsifted bleached cake flour

¾ teaspoon baking soda

¼ teaspoon baking powder

½ teaspoon salt

½ pound (16 tablespoons or 2 sticks) unsalted butter, softened

1⅔ cups plus 1 tablespoon superfine sugar

4 large eggs

2 teaspoons vanilla extract

⅔ cup plus 2 tablespoons buttermilk

creamy chocolate frosting (page 116)

serving: one 13 by 9-inch cake, creating 20 squares
ahead: best on baking day

creamy chocolate frosting

butter and chocolate frosting

5¾ cups confectioners' sugar,
sifted with a large pinch of salt

6 ounces unsweetened chocolate,
melted and cooled to tepid

10 tablespoons (1 stick plus 2 tablespoons)
unsalted butter, cut into chunks, softened

2 teaspoons vanilla extract

⅔ cup plus 1 tablespoon heavy cream,
warmed to tepid

serving: about 5 cups
ahead: spread the frosting as soon
as it is made, while it is still suave
and creamy-smooth

Place 5 cups of the confectioners' sugar-salt mixture, the melted chocolate, the chunks of butter, the vanilla extract, and the heavy cream in the large bowl of a freestanding electric mixer. Set the bowl in place and attach the flat paddle. Mix on low speed to blend, about 2 minutes. Scrape down the sides of the mixing bowl with a rubber spatula twice, stopping the mixer to do so. Beat on moderate speed for 1 minute. Add the remaining ¾ cup confectioners' sugar-salt mixture and beat for 1 minute to blend, then increase the speed to moderately high and continue beating for 2 minutes longer, or until very smooth and creamy-textured. Once or twice, stop the mixer and scrape down the sides of the mixing bowl to keep the frosting even-textured. Adjust the consistency, if necessary, by incorporating additional confectioners' sugar (1 tablespoon at a time) or heavy cream (1 to 2 teaspoons at a time) to arrive at a frosting that is easy to spread. Use the frosting immediately.

notes
• the heavy cream builds a luxuriously smooth and rich frosting
• the reason that the heavy cream (and in other cases, milk or half-and-half) is warmed before blending into a melted chocolate batter is to keep the frosting smooth and free of suspended flecks of cocoa solids; by comparison, this is not a critical step in a vanilla- or cream cheese–flavored batter, unless the batter contains a measure of melted white chocolate

bananarama

Two expanses of cake and a tidy, cushy loaf: as casual treats, all three are sweet-scented with the moistening, tropical allure of plain-old mashed bananas.

The setting for the swath of sheet cake, baked comfortably in a large but cozy 13 by 9 by 2-inch pan, is a buttermilk-based batter, made richer with butter and sweetened with sugar. The absence of spices allows the full banana flavor to dominate. The moist cake is covered with a sexy cream cheese frosting. Exactly what makes a cream cheese frosting so tempting? The way that it sweeps across the top of a freshly baked cake? The soft tang set against its buttery sweetness? The contrast of its inherent creaminess and dewy cake? All of these things make the partnership so fantastic.

Overly ripe, slippery, sludgy bananas, in my experience, make for a perfume-y cake or tea bread. I use ripe—but not gooey—bananas broken down well with a potato masher or the tines of a fork (not a food processor, by the way, which would liquefy the fruit) until creamy in a very lightly chunky way; the resulting texture of the fruit creates a cake with a downy, soft crumb. The buttermilk in the sheet cake batter virtually guarantees a texture that says "homemade cake." Vanilla extract ties the taste of the fruit to the creaminess of the butter.

The banana cake baked in the deep Bundt pan is tall and, for all of its girth, quite tender. A combination of all-purpose flour and cake flour builds its structure, one that is expanded by a generous amount of the fruit, butter, and enough buttermilk to bind the ingredients. This is the banana cake that I bake for brunch and to have on hand for slicing during the weekend—it is also the cake that has been configured to accept any number of additions (such as miniature semisweet chocolate chips, coconut, chopped nuts), though I am just as happy to have it plain and unpatterned but for the filaments of the fruit that enlace the batter.

As for the loaf, I have depended on this recipe for years, and have never gone too far beyond its simple and basic formula. The sweetness of the fruit comes through clearly, and enough granulated sugar builds the banana flavor; either chopped walnuts or macadamia nuts adds a nice crackle and crunch, and a sweet snarl of coconut imparts a tropical edge (you can go with nuts or coconut alone, or mix the two). The interior is naturally fine-crumbed and tightly textured, and for that reason, toasts well; for fun, you could sprinkle a generous crumble (½ cup) of banana chips on the top of the batter just before baking, creating a crunchy, textured surface.

Following is my panorama—or bananarama—of recipes that play up the flavor of the fruit.

a gentle banana cake

buttermilk banana batter

2⅔ cups plus 1 tablespoon unsifted bleached cake flour

½ cup unsifted bleached all-purpose flour

1½ teaspoons baking powder

½ teaspoon baking soda

½ teaspoon salt

½ pound (16 tablespoons or 2 sticks) unsalted butter, softened

2 cups granulated sugar

2 large eggs

2 large egg yolks

2½ teaspoons vanilla extract

1½ cups coarsely mashed ripe bananas (about 3 large bananas)

⅔ cup plus 4 tablespoons buttermilk

perfect cream cheese frosting

one 8-ounce package cream cheese, softened

8 tablespoons (1 stick) cool unsalted butter, cut into tablespoon-size chunks

4¾ cups confectioners' sugar sifted with ⅛ teaspoon salt

2½ teaspoons vanilla extract

serving: one 13 by 9-inch cake, creating 20 squares
ahead: best on baking day

Preheat the oven to 350 degrees F.

Film the inside of a 13 by 9 by 2-inch baking pan with nonstick flour-and-oil spray.

For the batter, sift the cake flour, all-purpose flour, baking powder, baking soda, and salt onto a sheet of waxed paper.

Cream the butter in the large bowl of a freestanding electric mixer on moderate speed for 4 minutes. Add the granulated sugar in 3 additions, beating for 1 minute after each portion is added. Beat in the whole eggs, one at a time. Blend in the egg yolks and vanilla extract. Blend in the mashed bananas. On low speed, alternately add the sifted mixture in 3 additions with the buttermilk in 2 additions, beginning and ending with the sifted mixture. Scrape down the sides of the mixing bowl with a rubber spatula to keep the batter even-textured.

Spoon and scrape the batter into the prepared baking pan. Smooth the top with a rubber spatula.

Bake the cake in the preheated oven for 40 minutes, or until risen, set, and a wooden pick withdraws clean when tested about 2 inches from the center of the cake. Cool the cake completely in the pan on a cooling rack.

For the frosting, beat the cream cheese and butter in the large bowl of a freestanding electric mixer on moderately low speed for 3 minutes, or until very smooth but not lightened. Beat in half of the confectioners' sugar-salt mixture and the vanilla extract. Add the remaining confectioners' sugar-salt mixture in 2 additions, beating until incorporated. Beat on moderate speed for 1 minute, raise the speed to high, and beat for 2 minutes longer, or until quite creamy. From time to time, stop the mixer and scrape down the sides of the mixing bowl to create a smooth, evenly blended frosting.

Spread the freshly made frosting on top of the cake. Let the frosting set for 1 hour before cutting the cake into squares for serving, using a medium-width offset metal spatula to remove the squares.

notes

• the combination of cake flour and all-purpose flour creates a tender, but gently substantial batter
• refrigerate any frosted cake not consumed after 2 hours of assembling

banana tea loaf

Preheat the oven to 350 degrees F.

Film the inside of a 9 by 5 by 3-inch loaf pan with nonstick flour-and-oil spray.

Sift the flour, baking soda, baking powder, and salt onto a sheet of waxed paper.

Cream the butter in the large bowl of a freestanding electric mixer on moderate speed for 3 minutes. Add the sugar in 2 additions, beating for 1 minute after each portion is added. Beat in the eggs, one at a time, mixing for 30 seconds after each addition. Blend in the vanilla extract. On low speed, blend in half of the sifted ingredients, the mashed bananas, and milk, then the balance of the sifted ingredients, beating just until the particles of flour have been absorbed. Scrape down the sides of the mixing bowl frequently with a rubber spatula to keep the batter even-textured. Stir in the walnuts, macadamia nuts, or coconut, or a combination of nuts and coconut.

Spoon the batter into the prepared baking pan, lightly mounding it down the center of the pan in a 2- to 2½-inch panel.

Bake the tea loaf in the preheated oven for 1 hour, or until risen, set, and a wooden pick withdraws clean. The baked loaf will just begin to pull away from the sides of the baking pan.

Cool the loaf in the pan on a rack for 10 to 12 minutes. Invert the tea cake onto another cooling rack, lift off the pan, then invert again to stand right side up. Cool completely. Store in an airtight cake keeper.

notes
• for the best flavor and texture, use ripe, rather than overripe, bananas
• use a finely serrated knife to cut the loaf

---

simple banana batter

2 cups unsifted bleached all-purpose flour

¾ teaspoon baking soda

¼ teaspoon baking powder

¼ teaspoon salt

8 tablespoons (1 stick) unsalted butter, softened

1 cup granulated sugar

2 large eggs

2 teaspoons vanilla extract

1⅛ cups coarsely mashed ripe bananas (2 large or 3 small bananas)

3 tablespoons milk

¾ cup coarsely chopped walnuts or macadamia nuts, or firmly packed sweetened flaked coconut, or a combination of nuts and coconut

serving: one 9-inch loaf, creating 8 to 10 slices
ahead: 3 days

a big banana cake

banana-deluxe batter

3 cups unsifted bleached all-purpose flour

1 cup unsifted bleached cake flour

2 teaspoons baking soda

1½ teaspoons baking powder

1¼ teaspoons salt

½ pound (16 tablespoons or 2 sticks)
unsalted butter, softened

2 cups granulated sugar

4 large eggs

4 teaspoons vanilla extract

2½ cups mashed ripe bananas
(about 5 medium-size bananas)

¾ cup buttermilk

confectioners' sugar,
for sifting over the baked cake

serving: one 10-inch cake,
creating 16 slices
ahead: best on baking day

Preheat the oven to 350 degrees F.

Film the inside of a 10-inch Bundt pan (4½ inches deep, with a capacity of 15 cups) with nonstick flour-and-oil spray.

Sift the all-purpose flour, cake flour, baking soda, baking powder, and salt onto a sheet of waxed paper.

Cream the butter in the large bowl of a freestanding electric mixer on moderate speed for 5 minutes. Add the granulated sugar in 3 additions, beating for 1 minute after each portion is added. Beat in the eggs, one at a time, mixing for 30 seconds after each addition. Blend in the vanilla extract and mashed bananas. The mixture will look slightly curdled at this point, but it will smooth out at the end of the next step. On low speed, alternately add the sifted mixture in 3 additions with the buttermilk in 2 additions, beginning and ending with the sifted mixture. Scrape down the sides of the mixing bowl with a rubber spatula to keep the batter even-textured.

Pour and scrape the batter into the prepared baking pan. The batter should settle lightly into an even layer.

Bake the cake in the preheated oven for 1 hour, or until risen, set, and a wooden pick withdraws clean. The baked cake will just begin to pull away from the sides of the baking pan and the top will be golden brown.

Cool the cake in the pan on a rack for 10 minutes. Invert the cake onto another cooling rack. Lift off the pan. Cool completely. Store in an airtight cake keeper. Just before slicing and serving, sift confectioners' sugar over the top of the cake.

notes
• use ripe, rather than overripe, bananas
• use a finely serrated knife to cut the cake

freckled

This is my desperation cake. I bake it when everyone wants something chocolaty (and vanilla-y) in a cakey, buttery setting. When everyone is tired of eating anything fussy and overwrought. When I need something that's easy to top with a rainstorm of confectioners' sugar and just call it dessert.

A vanilla-flavored batter splattered with so many chocolate chips, a batter that rises tall and tender, has bailed me out of countless situations—sweetly. This is a plain and simple cake, and a sweet that, when freshly baked, is easy to serve and devour. The formula is embarrassingly elementary, ½ pound of butter and 2 cups of sugar enrich a sifted combination of leavening, salt, and two types of flour. Milk and whole eggs round out a mixture that awaits a rush of miniature chocolate chips. It is a cake for all seasons and times of day.

I compose a great platter of thick slices to offer with tumblers of crystal-clear iced tea in summer, with cups of hot strong coffee in winter.

The *chocolate chip cake* is the kind of cake that I fall back on, again and again. It reminds me of another cake I crave and bake on a regular basis: my grandmother's butter cake, also straightforward and very delicious. Put the recipe in your baking file and tag it so the next generation of cooks knows where to find it. This is one good-taste heirloom that will never go out of fashion.

chocolate chip cake

buttery chocolate chip batter

2¼ cups unsifted bleached all-purpose flour

¾ cup unsifted bleached cake flour

1½ teaspoons baking powder

1 teaspoon salt

2 cups miniature semisweet chocolate chips

½ pound (16 tablespoons or 2 sticks) unsalted butter, softened

2 cups granulated sugar

4 large eggs

2½ teaspoons vanilla extract

1 cup plus 1 tablespoon half-and-half

confectioners' sugar, for sifting over the baked cake

serving: one 10-inch cake, creating about 16 slices
ahead: best on baking day

Preheat the oven to 350 degrees F.

Film the inside of a 10-inch Bundt pan (generous 3¾ inches deep, with a capacity of 14 cups) or a fluted 10-inch tube pan (4¾ inches deep, with a capacity of 13 to 13½ cups) with nonstick flour-and-oil spray.

For the batter, sift the all-purpose flour, cake flour, baking powder, and salt onto a sheet of waxed paper.

Toss the chocolate chips with 1 tablespoon of the sifted mixture in a medium-size mixing bowl.

Cream the butter in the large bowl of a freestanding electric mixer on moderate speed until creamy, 3 to 4 minutes. Add the granulated sugar in 3 additions, beating for 1 minute after each portion is added. Beat in the eggs, one at a time, mixing for about 15 seconds after each addition to blend. Scrape down the sides of the mixing bowl with a rubber spatula to keep the batter even-textured. Blend in the vanilla extract.

On low speed, alternately add the sifted mixture in 3 additions with the half-and-half in 2 additions, beginning and ending with the sifted mixture. Scrape down the sides of the mixing bowl thoroughly with a rubber spatula after each addition. Blend in the chocolate chips, using a wooden spoon or flat wooden paddle.

Spoon the batter into the prepared baking pan. Smooth the top with a rubber spatula.

Bake the cake in the preheated oven for about 55 minutes (if you are using the 10-inch Bundt pan) or about 1 hour (if you are using the fluted 10-inch tube pan), or until risen, set, and a wooden pick inserted into the cake withdraws clean. The baked cake will pull away slightly from the sides of the baking pan.

Cool the cake in the pan on a rack for 10 minutes. Invert the cake onto another cooling rack. Lift off the pan. Cool completely. Store in an airtight cake keeper. Just before slicing and serving, sift confectioners' sugar over the top of the cake.

notes
• whole milk may be substituted for the half-and-half, if you wish, but the cake will be a shade less moist
• baking the cake in a deep fluted tube pan makes the prettiest slices
• use a finely serrated knife to cut the cake

more-than-the-kitchen-sink

Stockpile the fruit and nuts, buy the toffee and chocolate, measure out the rolled oats, get out the mixing bowls, and gather around the countertop: friendship cookies are ready to be made.

This expansive, big-batch treat is great to fix with an armload of sweet-loving friends, as these cookies are big, ample, and stuffed to the brim with chewy, dense, mellow, and crunchy things that congregate wondrously in a drop cookie dough: about three dozen of them, full-grown and moist. Can you stand it?

This first-class cookie is a prized recipe: the mix-in ingredients can be juggled and rejuggled; here I *would* say "tweaked," but it can be so much more than that because you cannot possibly wreck the dough with a bold exchange of ingredients. The gold mine of what you stir into the dough at the end defines it. My standards are bittersweet or semisweet chocolate chips, chopped toffee, sweetened flaked coconut, raisins, dried cherries, and walnuts. Cashews, macadamia nuts, or pecans can replace the walnuts; dried cranberries are easily swapped for the dried cherries; and a combination of white chocolate chips and bittersweet chocolate chips can sub for the all-bittersweet or all-semisweet variety (use 1 cup of each). In all, a terrific—and terrifically flexible—recipe, and bountiful, indeed.

lady bountiful cookies

Preheat the oven to 375 degrees F.

Line several heavy cookie sheets or rimmed sheet pans with lengths of ovenproof parchment paper.

For the dough, sift the flour, baking powder, baking soda, and salt onto a sheet of waxed paper.

Cream the butter in the large bowl of a freestanding electric mixer on moderately low speed for 3 minutes. Add the light brown sugar in 2 additions, beating on moderate speed for 2 minutes after each portion is added. Add the granulated sugar and beat for 1 minute longer. Add the eggs, one at a time, beating on low speed until incorporated. Blend in the vanilla extract and rolled oats. On low speed, blend in the sifted ingredients in 2 additions, beating just until the flour particles are absorbed. Scrape down the sides of the mixing bowl frequently with a rubber spatula to keep the dough even-textured. Work in the chocolate chips, toffee, coconut, walnuts, cherries, and raisins, using a sturdy wooden spoon or flat wooden paddle. The dough will be dense but creamy and, of course, thick-set with oats, fruits, nuts, and chocolate.

Place heaping 3-tablespoon-size mounds of dough onto the prepared baking pans, spacing the mounds about 3 inches apart, and arranging 9 mounds to a pan. Keep the edges of the mounds rough-textured.

Bake the cookies in the preheated oven for 15 minutes, or until just set. Let the cookies stand on the baking pans for 2 minutes, then transfer them to cooling racks, using a wide offset metal spatula. Cool completely. Store in an airtight tin.

notes
• the cookie dough will be both chunky and creamy-textured
• when preparing cookie dough for refrigeration or freezing, use organic eggs only
• never consume raw cookie dough

"everything" dough

1½ cups unsifted bleached all-purpose flour

½ teaspoon baking powder

½ teaspoon baking soda

½ teaspoon salt

½ pound (16 tablespoons or 2 sticks) unsalted butter, softened

1 cup firmly packed light brown sugar

½ cup granulated sugar

2 large eggs

4 teaspoons vanilla extract

2 cups "quick-cooking" (not instant) rolled oats

1¾ cups bittersweet or semisweet chocolate chips

¾ cup coarsely chopped toffee (such as Heath bars)

1 cup firmly packed sweetened flaked coconut

1 cup walnuts, preferably halves and pieces

¾ cup tart (Montmorency) dried cherries

¾ cup dark seedless raisins

serving: about 3 dozen cookies
ahead: 2 days; refrigerate cookie dough for 2 days or freeze for 1 month

peanuts reign

Hurrah for peanut butter cookies! In all their permutations—plain old-fashioned, or with crunchy whole roasted peanuts or chocolate chips lollygagging in the dough—they are forthright and rustic, the essence of the nut packaged in a sweet hand-formed parcel.

If you love peanut butter, the cookie interpretation of the flavor can go in multiple textural directions: chewy, tender, crispy, or a combination of any two. If you maintain butter as the creaming fat, the baked cookies will be full of peanut "spirit" and have a discernible snap, as butter forwards the taste of the nut. If you swap out half of the butter for good-quality shortening, the cookies will be puffier, and crisp around the edges with a chewy center. The dough keeps nicely in the freezer, compacted into logs, and that fact leads me to the following confession: I want to eat my peanut butter cookie slightly warm, in a twenty-minutes-or-so-out-of-the-oven state. (That preference, of course, cancels out its cookie jar status—see next sentence—but I don't mind contradicting myself occasionally.)

This version is a cookie jar darling, a front-runner sweet that brings together nostalgia and flavor in several bites. The dough is carefree, yet sturdy and substantial. Baked to perfection until set, with their identifiable fragrance floating in the air, the oven-fresh saucers are marvelous for having in the summertime with icy lemon tea or in windswept fall with hot cider.

navigating the peanut butter cookie

all-butter peanut butter dough

3 cups unsifted bleached all-purpose flour

1¾ teaspoons baking soda

¼ teaspoon baking powder

¾ teaspoon salt

¼ teaspoon freshly grated nutmeg

¼ teaspoon ground allspice (optional)

½ pound (2 sticks or 16 tablespoons) unsalted butter, softened

1¼ cups firmly packed light brown sugar

¾ cup granulated sugar

2 large eggs

2½ teaspoons vanilla extract

1 cup smooth (creamy) peanut butter

serving: about 3 dozen cookies
ahead: 3 days

For the dough, sift the flour, baking soda, baking powder, salt, nutmeg, and allspice (if you are using it) onto a sheet of waxed paper.

Cream the butter in the large bowl of a freestanding electric mixer on moderate speed for 3 minutes. Add the light brown sugar in 2 additions, beating for 1 minute after each portion is added. Add the granulated sugar and beat for 2 minutes longer. Add the eggs, one at a time, beating for 30 seconds after each addition. Blend in the vanilla extract. Add the peanut butter and blend until the mixture is smooth, about 1 minute. Scrape down the sides of the mixing bowl frequently with a rubber spatula to keep the dough even-textured. On low speed, beat in half of the sifted mixture, then the balance of the sifted mixture. The dough will be moderately dense, creamy-textured, and sticky. Divide the dough into thirds and enclose each portion, patted into a flat slab about 1 inch thick (more or less), in a sheet of food-safe plastic wrap. Chill the dough, covered, for 3 hours (or overnight, if you wish).

Preheat the oven to 350 degrees F in advance of baking.

Line several heavy cookie sheets or rimmed sheet pans with lengths of ovenproof parchment paper.

Scoop up heaping 2-tablespoon-size mounds of dough, roll into balls, and place on the prepared baking pans, spacing the balls about 3 inches apart, and arranging 9 to a pan. Gently flatten the cookies in a crisscross fashion with the tines of a lightly floured table fork.

Bake the cookies in the preheated oven for 15 minutes, or until set. Let the cookies stand on the baking pans for 1 minute, then transfer them to cooling racks, using a wide offset metal spatula. Cool completely. Store in an airtight tin.

notes
• a deeply flavored and creamy peanut butter, MaraNatha Organic No Stir Peanut Butter (available in 16-ounce jars at Whole Foods and other markets), is the perfect choice for using in this cookie dough; or, Jif or Skippy peanut butter also make delectable cookies
• coarsely chopped roasted peanuts, 1 cup lightly salted or unsalted, can be added to the dough *after* the first half of the sifted ingredients are incorporated; using lightly salted peanuts creates a cookie with a salty-sweet contrast, unsalted peanuts a gentler flavor (if using lightly salted peanuts, reduce the amount of salt to ¼ teaspoon)
• for bonanza-of-chocolate-chips peanut butter cookies, add 2 cups bittersweet chocolate chips to the dough after half of the sifted flour mixture has been added
• when preparing cookie dough for overnight refrigeration or freezing, use organic eggs only
• never consume raw cookie dough

quite golden

The differences between my childhood and adult breadbaskets are stark. Growing up, dinner bread was either an afterthought or a lifeless decoration.

Sweet breads and coffee cakes were another matter altogether, for those were worshipped in all their buttery glory. Bread on my grown-up table is a treasure—and a given—at any time of the day or night. Whether of the quick bread or yeasted variety, bread always makes the meal, and some of my meals are even created around the bread, not the reverse. That calls for keeping a good supply of corn meal, because cornbread (in the pan, or as muffins or sticks), hot from the oven, is the baking equivalent of a cashmere blanket. It sustains. It consoles. It warms. It's a classic.

Associated by virtue of similar ingredients, the two versions of cornbread that follow are, at once, luminous and earthy. The muffins, stout and grainy, use stone-ground corn meal, but the pan bread recipe calls for fine corn meal. Both of the breads contain a good amount of butter, eggs, and milk. This collusion of elements envelops the corn flavor, making the surface and the crumb of each bread a warm and inviting place for honey in drizzles or butter (sweet or salted) in softened pats.

Preheat the oven to 400 degrees F.

Film the inside of 13 tea cake-size muffin cups (24 cups to a pan, each cup measuring 2 inches in diameter and 1³/₁₆ inches deep, with a capacity of 3 tablespoons) with nonstick flour-and-oil spray.

For the batter, sift the flour, sugar, baking powder, and salt into a large mixing bowl. Whisk in the corn meal.

Whisk the butter, eggs, and half-and-half in a medium-size mixing bowl, pour over the sifted ingredients, and stir to form a batter (it will be slightly lumpy). Make sure that all particles of flour and corn meal are dispersed in the batter while you are combining the ingredients, but avoid overmixing. The lumps will dispel as the muffin batter bakes.

Spoon the batter into the prepared muffin cups, dividing it evenly among them.

Bake the muffins in the preheated oven for 15 to 17 minutes, or until risen, set, and a wooden pick withdraws clean or with a few crumbs attached.

Cool the muffins in the pans on a rack for 5 minutes, then remove them to other cooling racks. Serve the muffins warm.

notes
• three wonderful meals to use for both this muffin batter and the pan cornbread batter (see page 134) are Bob's Red Mill Fine Grind or Medium Grind Cornmeal (both are available in 24-ounce packages) and Arrowhead Mills Organic Yellow Corn Meal (available in a 32-ounce bag)
• when fully baked, the edges of the muffins will be golden; the tea cake-size muffin cups encourage the formation of beautiful plump "crowns"
• for *muffins, with blueberries*, toss 1¼ cups blueberries, picked over, with 1 tablespoon of the flour and corn meal mixture, proceed with the recipe, then carefully stir the blueberries into the batter and bake as directed above
• this recipe can also be baked in a 5 to 6-inch decorative heart-shaped baking pan (2 inches deep) in a preheated 400 degrees F oven for 15 to 18 minutes
• the tea cake-size muffin cups bake up into two-bite gems
• the recipe doubles beautifully

rich egg and butter corn meal batter

1 cup unsifted bleached all-purpose flour

¼ cup granulated sugar

1½ teaspoons baking powder

¼ teaspoon salt

½ cup stone-ground yellow corn meal

8 tablespoons (1 stick) unsalted butter, melted and cooled to tepid

2 large eggs

¼ cup half-and-half

serving: 13 petite (tea cake-size) muffins
ahead: best on baking day

pan

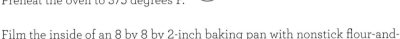

golden milk batter

1 cup unsifted bleached all-purpose flour

2¾ teaspoons baking powder

½ teaspoon salt

1½ cups fine yellow corn meal

2 large eggs

5 tablespoons granulated sugar

7 tablespoons (1 stick less 1 tablespoon) unsalted butter, melted and cooled to tepid

7 tablespoons solid shortening, melted and cooled to tepid

1⅓ cups plus 2 tablespoons milk

serving: one 8-inch cornbread, creating 16 squares
ahead: best on baking day

Preheat the oven to 375 degrees F.

Film the inside of an 8 by 8 by 2-inch baking pan with nonstick flour-and-oil spray.

For the batter, sift the flour, baking powder, and salt into a medium-size mixing bowl. Whisk in the corn meal.

Beat the eggs and sugar in the large bowl of a freestanding electric mixer on moderate speed for 1 minute. Add the melted butter and melted shortening and beat for 1 minute longer. On low speed, add about one-third of the flour and corn meal mixture and about one-third of the milk at once; mix for 15 seconds or until just combined. Add half of the remaining flour and corn meal mixture and half of the remaining milk; mix for 10 seconds. Add the balance of the flour and corn meal mixture and the milk; mix for 10 seconds. Scrape down the sides of the mixing bowl thoroughly with a rubber spatula after each addition. The batter will be moderately thick, and should be turned into the pan immediately. The batter is somewhat pourable at this stage, but will thicken considerably as it stands.

Scrape the batter into the prepared baking pan. Smooth the top with a rubber spatula, making sure that it settles into the corners completely.

Bake the cornbread in the preheated oven for 35 minutes, or until risen, set, and a wooden pick withdraws clean or with a few crumbs attached. The baked cornbread will pull away slightly from the sides of the pan, and there may be a few cracks and golden surface bubbles on top (which is to be expected in this recipe).

Cool the cornbread in the pan on a cooling rack for 10 minutes. Cut the cornbread into squares directly from the pan, lifting them out with a small offset metal spatula. Serve warm.

notes

• the cornbread can be made entirely with melted unsalted butter; use 1 stick plus 6 tablespoons (1¾ sticks)
• this is a rich, somewhat densely substantial and reasonably close-textured cornbread
• the batter can also be baked in a well-seasoned 9-inch cast-iron skillet (1¾ inches deep) for 25 minutes; mine is a Lodge Logic skillet (numerical reference for identification on the bottom of the skillet is 6 SK); preheat the skillet for 10 minutes in the oven, then plop 1 tablespoon unsalted butter into the pan, return the pan to the oven for 3 to 5 minutes (or until sizzling), then carefully remove from the oven, pour in the batter, and bake; always use ovenproof mitts when handling a hot skillet

streaky, moist, and messy

A messy cake can be a tasty pleasure.

Throughout my baking life, I have always been transfixed by coffee cakes: fruit-substantial, spiced, copiously streuseled, brown sugar-swirled, overflowing with chips, well-moistened with sour cream or buttermilk, and, in every case, supported by unsalted butter. Sometimes, it seems, the more littered or cluttered the cake, the better it is.

If a coffee cake could be called "rambunctious," this one would fit that description. It is centered on cinnamon, treated to a brown sugar and cinnamon filling, and amply plumped out with butter and sour cream. The cake has both a mellow and hearty forward taste. The filling spirals this way and that way throughout, disturbing the interior nicely.

Baked in a rectangular pan, the cake can serve a weekend of guests who will undoubtedly take delight in cutting away pieces now and then throughout their stay. But remember to enjoy the cake once the flush of the oven's heat has subsided, lifting out the warm slices to accompany coffee or tea.

dirty cake

Preheat the oven to 350 degrees F.

Film the inside of a 13 by 9 by 2-inch baking pan with nonstick flour-and-oil spray.

For the filling, combine the light brown sugar, granulated sugar, and cinnamon in a small mixing bowl. Set aside.

For the batter, sift the flour, baking powder, baking soda, salt, and cinnamon onto a sheet of waxed paper. Cream the butter in the large bowl of a freestanding electric mixer on moderate speed until quite smooth and creamy, about 4 minutes. Add the granulated sugar in 2 additions, beating for 1 minute after each portion is added. Beat in the whole eggs, one at a time, mixing for about 30 seconds after each addition. Beat in the egg yolk. Scrape down the sides of the mixing bowl with a rubber spatula to keep the batter even-textured. Blend in the vanilla extract. On low speed, alternately add the sifted mixture in 3 additions with the sour cream in 2 additions, beginning and ending with the sifted mixture. Scrape down the sides of the mixing bowl thoroughly with a rubber spatula after each addition.

Spoon two-thirds of the batter into the prepared baking pan. Spoon over the cinnamon and brown sugar filling, leaving about ½ inch of the batter exposed on all sides, and press down lightly with the back of the spoon. (The reason for this is to prevent the filling from fusing into sugar patches at the sides of the pan.) Dollop on the remaining batter. Gently smooth over the top with a medium-width offset metal spatula; the top layer may pull away slightly as it is smoothed over, and this is to be expected (just keep going). Using a palette knife or a round-bladed table knife, swirl the batter in wide, sweeping strokes, taking care to avoid scraping the bottom and sides of the baking pan. Smooth over the top once again.

Bake the cake in the preheated oven for 1 hour to 1 hour and 5 minutes, or until risen, set, and a wooden pick inserted into the cake withdraws clean or with a few moist crumbs attached. The baked cake will pull away gently from the sides of the baking pan.

Cool the cake in the pan on a cooling rack for at least 20 minutes before cutting into squares or fingers for serving. Or, cool completely, cut, and store in an airtight cake keeper. Just before serving, sift confectioners' sugar over the tops of the squares or fingers.

cinnamon and brown sugar filling

⅔ cup firmly packed light brown sugar

¼ cup granulated sugar

2 tablespoons ground cinnamon

cinnamon butter batter

3 cups unsifted bleached all-purpose flour

1½ teaspoons baking powder

1 teaspoon baking soda

1 teaspoon salt

2 tablespoons ground cinnamon

¾ pound (3 sticks) unsalted butter, softened

1⅔ cups granulated sugar

3 large eggs

1 large egg yolk

2½ teaspoons vanilla extract

1⅔ cups sour cream

confectioners' sugar, for sifting on top of the baked cake

serving: one 13 by 9-inch cake, creating 20 squares or 27 fingers
ahead: 2 days

dirty cake   plainold-fashioned **137**

the aroma of plain

Plain is good. Plain can even be fascinating. And if it's cake, its texture and flavor are probably (and typically) unvarnished—certainly not overwrought by too many authoritative ingredients vying for attention.

The structure of *exquisite cake*, a tall and buttery treat, is developed with whole eggs and just enough baking powder (a mere ½ teaspoon is used with a total of 4 cups flour) to reinforce its height and elaborate its internal structure. The scents of vanilla, lemon, and orange combine to create a softened sweetness, the lightest suggestion of scent: the trio of extracts also helps to banish the sense of "egginess" occasionally present in butter cakes with a significant dairy presence.

A well-rounded view of a slice of cake has the polish of golden on the outside and is softly flaxen within, its texture built on the intersection of heft and moistness. Three-quarters cup of heavy cream helps out. The cake is good enough to act as the foundation for another dessert, such as a layered composition of fruit, custard, and cream, but, day-old and sliced, can be relegated to a two-sided toasting and slathering with apricot jam and softened salted butter. Did I say "relegated"? The

latter would be no less sublime—and reason enough to bake with "leftovers" (such a tragic word) in mind.

In a kind of flavor coda, working the scent of nutmeg into a butter-concentrated batter seemed like an idea worth the hunt. Nutmeg, with its certain old-timey appeal and specific taste, is a kind of spice talisman for me. I remember nutmeg, along with mace (nutmeg's own enveloping cover), as prominent spices in my grandmother's pound cake and in one of my mother's sugar cookie recipes. Many bakers sniff out its aroma and add it lovingly, while others banish it. I am in the former camp and have built a cake batter to include it. The effect is the tender, both in texture and feeling, result of two baking memories.

Though in the same category, the two cakes that follow have enough individuality to be identified as different. Those of you who are emotional about the baking process know just what I mean.

exquisite cake

buttery scented batter

3 cups unsifted bleached all-purpose flour

1 cup unsifted bleached cake flour

½ teaspoon baking powder

1 teaspoon salt

1 pound (4 sticks) unsalted butter, softened

3 cups superfine sugar

6 large eggs

2 teaspoons vanilla extract

1 teaspoon lemon extract

1 teaspoon orange extract

¾ cup heavy cream

2 teaspoons freshly squeezed lemon juice

confectioners' sugar,
for sifting on top of the baked cake

serving: one 9¾-inch cake,
creating about 16 slices
ahead: 2 days

Preheat the oven to 325 degrees F.

Film the inside of a plain, one-piece 9¾-inch tube pan (6 inches deep, with a capacity of 18 cups) with nonstick flour-and-oil spray.

For the batter, sift the all-purpose flour, cake flour, baking powder, and salt onto a sheet of waxed paper.

Cream the butter in the large bowl of a freestanding electric mixer on moderate speed for 5 minutes. Add the superfine sugar in 3 additions, beating for 1 minute after each portion is added. Beat in the eggs, one at a time, mixing for about 30 seconds after each addition. Scrape down the sides of the mixing bowl with a rubber spatula to keep the batter even-textured. Blend in the vanilla extract, lemon extract, and orange extract. On low speed, alternately add the sifted mixture in 3 additions with the heavy cream in 2 additions, beginning and ending with the sifted mixture. Scrape down the sides of the mixing bowl thoroughly with a rubber spatula after each addition. Add the lemon juice and beat for 1 minute longer.

Spoon the batter into the prepared baking pan. Smooth the top with a rubber spatula.

Bake the cake in the preheated oven for 1 hour and 25 minutes to 1 hour and 30 minutes, or until risen, a deep golden color on top, set, and a wooden pick inserted into the cake withdraws clean. The baked cake will pull away slightly from the sides of the pan.

Cool the cake in the pan on a rack for 12 to 15 minutes. Invert the cake onto another cooling rack, lift off the pan, then invert again to stand right side up. Cool completely. Store in an airtight cake keeper. Just before slicing and serving, sift confectioners' sugar over the top of the cake.

notes
• the presence of lemon juice helps to tenderize the cake batter
• the cake is baked in a plain, one-piece 9¾-inch tube pan (6 inches deep, with a capacity of 18 cups); a plain, one-piece 10-inch tube pan (4¼ to 4½ inches deep, with a capacity of 18 cups) may be substituted, reducing the baking time by 5 to 6 minutes
• use a finely serrated knife to cut the cake

nutmeg nostalgia: a sentimental butter cake

Preheat the oven to 350 degrees F.

Film the inside of a 10-inch Bundt pan (generous 3¾ inches deep, with a capacity of 14 cups) with nonstick flour-and-oil spray.

For the batter, sift the flour, baking powder, baking soda, salt, and nutmeg onto a sheet of waxed paper.

Cream the butter in the large bowl of a freestanding electric mixer on moderately high speed for 3 minutes. Add the sugar in 4 additions, beating thoroughly after each portion is added. Beat in the eggs, one at a time, mixing for 45 seconds after each addition. Blend in the vanilla extract. On low speed, alternately add the sifted mixture in 3 additions with the buttermilk in 2 additions, beginning and ending with the sifted mixture. Scrape down the sides of the mixing bowl thoroughly with a rubber spatula after each addition.

Spoon the batter into the prepared baking pan. Smooth the top with a rubber spatula.

Bake the cake in the preheated oven for 55 minutes to 1 hour, or until risen, set, and a wooden pick withdraws clean or with a few moist crumbs attached.

Prepare the glaze while the cake is baking: place the chunks of butter, the sugar, and nutmeg in a small, heavy saucepan (preferably enameled cast iron). Partially cover the pan and place over low heat to dissolve the sugar, stirring once or twice. Remove from the heat, uncover, and set aside.

Cool the cake in the pan on a rack for 10 minutes. Invert the cake onto another cooling rack. Lift off the pan. Place a sheet of waxed paper underneath the cooling rack to catch any drips of glaze. Rewarm the glaze, uncovered, and brush the mixture over the top and sides of the cake. Let the glazed cake stand for 30 minutes, slice, and serve, or cool completely. Store in an airtight cake keeper.

notes
• in general, and especially for this cake, the whole nutmeg should be reduced as fine as possible, using a nutmeg grater
• use a finely serrated knife to cut the cake

nutmeg buttermilk batter

3 cups unsifted bleached all-purpose flour

1 teaspoon baking powder

½ teaspoon baking soda

1 teaspoon salt

2 teaspoons freshly grated nutmeg

½ pound (16 tablespoons or 2 sticks) unsalted butter, softened

2 cups superfine sugar

4 large eggs

3 teaspoons vanilla extract

1 cup buttermilk

nutmeg butter glaze

6 tablespoons (¾ stick) unsalted butter, cut into chunks

⅔ cup plus 2 tablespoons superfine sugar

½ teaspoon freshly grated nutmeg

serving: one 10-inch cake, creating about 16 slices
ahead: 2 days

sunday bread

Soft, plushy rolls with a smear of honey butter lavished over their broken segments take me way back to the remote country inn where, even as a ten-year-old child, I recognized the deliciousness of homemade rolls served with fried chicken and country ham.

The rolls, flecked with corn meal, were substantial but fluffy, and brushed with melted butter. The film of butter was the real thing and made my fingertips slick and glossy. The memory of the rolls, still haunting, inspires their creation at home, as well as a meal around them: chicken (deep-fried, preferably), burnished slices of ham, macaroni salad, stewed okra, creamed yellow crookneck squash (seasoned with lots of freshly ground pepper and baked in a casserole), sweet-and-sour slaw, and that must-have slice of coconut layer cake or square of chocolate fudge cake to end it all.

But back to the rolls. Little balls of enriched dough arranged in muffin cups, comfy and snug, merge as they rise to plumpness as ample cloverleaf rolls. While the dough is easily baked in a loaf pan, the real appeal is in the individual breads, for they look so captivating piled into a woven basket or toppled onto an oval silver bread tray. The rolls are light morsels and become the perfect surface for thin slices of something cured or smoked when they are not accompanying the big, highly nuanced Sunday lunch or supper. Or to revive the luncheon plate of my mother's generation, consider pairing the rolls with a fine chicken or shrimp salad presented in a nest of soft butter lettuce leaves.

Speaking of demure and exquisite, rolls served at the other end of the day—morning time—are usually well-seasoned and sweet, but there is another culture of rolls,

only lightly sweetened and scented with just a single spice, alluring for their delicacy and stylistic comfort. This type of sweet roll is sometimes called a "coffee roll" and, my oh my, how satisfyingly appropriate it is with this beverage. My coffee rolls, in contrast to my cloverleaf rolls, are not a childhood memory—these, shaded with crushed cardamom seeds or ground cardamom (either makes a compelling bread), are the essence of lightness and the result of a very adult baking foray. Borrowing from a cake-making method, the butter, sugar, whole eggs, and egg yolks that make up the yeast dough are treated to a creaming before those soft and svelte ingredients are introduced into the swollen yeast mixture, flour, and spice. The dough turns remarkably floaty on rising and bakes into a soft, fine-grained but airy bread. (An optional sprinkling of turbinado sugar on the surface of the high-rise rolls just after applying the egg white and sugar wash and before baking, creates crackly, sweeter tops.)

If bread could be characterized as serene, then these two doughs and their accompanying outpouring of rolls would measure up to that description. You will find them a welcome change from some of the more rugged, boldly flavored, intensely crusted, and wildly burnished of-the-moment offerings. Gentle bread—this is another name I like to give to the very ladylike, diaphanous rolls that follow.

soft cloverleaf rolls, cozy and warm

corn meal and butter dough

2½ teaspoons active dry yeast

¼ teaspoon granulated sugar

¼ cup warm (105 to 110 degrees F) water

1¼ cups milk

½ cup water

8 tablespoons (1 stick) unsalted butter, cut into chunks

5 tablespoons granulated sugar

2 large eggs

5½ cups unsifted bleached all-purpose flour, plus an additional 3 to 4 tablespoons, as needed for kneading

¾ cup fine yellow corn meal

1¼ teaspoons salt

butter brush

5 tablespoons unsalted butter (preferably clarified butter, page 1), melted and cooled to tepid

serving: 30 rolls

ahead: best on baking day; or freeze for 3 weeks, defrost, bundle in aluminum foil, and reheat in a preheated 325 degrees F oven for 10 minutes, then brush with butter

For the dough, stir together the yeast, the ¼ teaspoon sugar, and the ¼ cup warm water in a heatproof measuring cup. Allow the mixture to stand until swollen, 6 to 7 minutes.

Place the milk, the ½ cup water, the chunks of butter, and the 5 tablespoons sugar in a medium-size saucepan and set over low heat. When the sugar has dissolved, remove the saucepan from the heat. Pour and scrape the mixture into a medium-size heatproof mixing bowl. Cool to tepid, whisking now and then to hasten the process, then quickly whisk in the eggs and yeast mixture.

Place 3 cups of the flour, the corn meal, and salt in a large mixing bowl. Whisk to combine. Add the yeast-milk-egg mixture and mix to combine, using a wooden spoon or flat wooden paddle. Let stand for 1 minute. Mix in 2 cups of the remaining flour, 1 cup at a time, letting the dough rest for 1 minute after each addition. Blend in the remaining ½ cup flour.

Turn the dough out onto a work surface sprinkled with a little of the additional flour. Knead the dough for 7 to 8 minutes, or until it is resilient and supple. The dough will feel somewhat gritty to the touch—the corn meal makes it so and this is as it should be. Knead in as much of the additional flour as necessary to keep the dough from sticking too much, but realize that the dough should not be too stiff or its lovely, tender quality will be compromised.

Turn the dough into a bowl heavily coated with softened unsalted butter, lightly turn to coat all sides in a film of butter, make several cuts in the dough with a pair of kitchen scissors, cover tightly with a sheet of food-safe plastic wrap, and let rise at room temperature for 1 hour and 15 minutes to 1 hour and 25 minutes, or until doubled in bulk.

Remove the plastic wrap. Lightly compress the dough with a rubber spatula, cover loosely with the sheet of plastic wrap, and let stand for 10 minutes.

In the meantime, film the inside of 30 muffin/cupcake cups (each cup measuring 2¾ inches in diameter and 1⅜ inches deep, with a capacity of ½ cup) with nonstick flour-and-oil spray.

To form the rolls, remove and discard the sheet of plastic wrap covering the dough. Divide the dough in half. Cut each half into 15 even-size pieces. Cut each of the 15 pieces into 3 even-size pieces. Roll the pieces into smooth balls by rolling each piece on a work surface briskly under the palm of your hand. Place 3 in the bottom of each prepared muffin/cupcake cup. The fit will be snug.

Cover each pan of rolls loosely with a sheet of lightly buttered food-safe plastic wrap. Let the rolls rise at room temperature for 1 hour, or until doubled in bulk and puffy.

Preheat the oven to 375 degrees F in advance of baking.

Remove and discard the sheets of plastic wrap covering the rolls about 15 minutes before the rolls are completely risen.

Using the butter brush ingredient, carefully paint the melted butter onto the surface of the risen rolls, using a soft pastry brush. Continue to let the rolls finish rising (uncovered).

Bake the rolls in the preheated oven for 15 to 16 minutes, or until set and a golden color on top. Cool the rolls in the pans on cooling racks for 10 minutes. Carefully remove the rolls, using the tip of a round-bladed flexible palette knife (as necessary); the rolls are quite tender at this point. Serve warm.

notes
• fine corn meal gives the dough a wonderfully nubby-grainy texture, though it does not overwhelm
• the total amount of flour is subject to atmospheric conditions—on a cool, dry day less flour is needed to form a dough, and on a warm or humid day a little more flour may be needed
• mixing and kneading the dough by hand is critical to the dough's pleasingly soft and gentle structure, so put aside the stand mixer for this recipe
• using clarified butter for brushing on the tops of nearly risen rolls gives them a smoothly even color when baked and a fresh butter taste

cardamom buns that (almost) levitate

light cardamom yeast dough

4½ teaspoons active dry yeast

¼ teaspoon granulated sugar

⅓ cup warm (105 to 110 degrees F) water

½ cup warm (105 to 110 degrees F) milk

2 teaspoons granulated sugar

1 cup unsifted unbleached all-purpose flour

8 tablespoons (1 stick) unsalted butter, softened

½ cup granulated sugar

2 large eggs

4 large egg yolks

2 teaspoons vanilla extract

3 cups unsifted bleached all-purpose flour, plus an additional ⅓ cup, as needed for kneading

finely crushed seeds from 1 rounded teaspoon cardamom pods (or 1½ teaspoons ground cardamom)

1 teaspoon salt

egg white and sugar wash

1 large egg white

½ teaspoon granulated sugar

1 teaspoon water

serving: 18 rolls
ahead: freshly baked, or up to 3 days later, revived in a preheated 300 degrees F oven for 10 minutes

For the dough, stir together the yeast, the ¼ teaspoon sugar, and the warm water in a heatproof measuring cup. Allow the mixture to stand until swollen, 6 to 7 minutes.

Scrape the yeast mixture into a medium-size mixing bowl. Stir in the warm milk, the 2 teaspoons sugar, and the unbleached flour. Mix well. Cover the bowl with a sheet of food-safe plastic wrap and let stand for 30 minutes—the mixture will be bubbly, thickened, and swollen.

In the meantime, place the softened butter in a medium-size mixing bowl and cream for 1 minute, using a wooden spoon or flat wooden paddle. Add the ½ cup sugar and continue creaming for 2 minutes longer. The mixture should be smooth, but don't worry if it looks grainy. Blend in the whole eggs. Blend in the egg yolks, one at a time, adding the vanilla extract along with the last yolk. Blend the yeast mixture into the creamed mixture, using a rubber spatula. Whisk the bleached flour, the cardamom, and salt in a large mixing bowl. Add the eggs-yeast mixture and stir to mix well, using a flat wooden paddle. At this point, the dough will be soft, slightly sticky, and a little shaggy. Let the dough stand, uncovered, for 5 minutes. Turn the dough out onto a work surface dusted with the additional ⅓ cup bleached flour. Knead the dough for 7 minutes, incorporating all of the ⅓ cup flour as necessary to make the dough resilient and supple, smooth, and just barely sticky.

Turn the dough into a bowl heavily coated with softened unsalted butter, lightly turn to coat all sides in a film of butter, make several cuts in the dough with a pair of kitchen scissors, cover tightly with a sheet of food-safe plastic wrap, and let rise at room temperature for 1 hour and 45 minutes, or until doubled in bulk.

Remove and discard the plastic wrap. Avoid compressing the dough at this point.

Film the inside of two 8 by 8 by 3-inch baking pans with nonstick flour-and-oil spray.

To form the rolls, place the dough on a lightly floured work surface. Divide it in half, then cut each half into 9 even-size pieces. Smooth each piece into a plump ball by rolling it on a work surface briskly under the palm of your hand. Place the balls of dough in the prepared baking pans, assembling them in three rows of 3 each.

Cover the pans of buns loosely with buttered sheets of food-safe plastic wrap. Let the rolls rise at room temperature for 2 hours, or until almost tripled in bulk. Remove and discard the sheets of plastic wrap covering the buns about 1 hour and 45 minutes into the rising time (about 15 minutes before completely risen).

Preheat the oven to 350 degrees F in advance of baking.

For the egg white and sugar wash, whisk the egg white with the sugar and water in a small mixing bowl. Carefully brush the wash over the tops of the buns, using a soft pastry brush. Continue to let the buns finish rising, uncovered, about 15 minutes.

Bake the buns in the preheated oven for 35 minutes, or until set and a golden brown color on top. The baked buns will pull away slightly from the sides of the baking pan. Place the pans on cooling racks and let stand for 15 minutes. Carefully (the buns are so very tender at this point) invert each pan of buns onto other cooling racks, then invert them again to stand right side up. Serve the buns warm or at room temperature, by detaching them at their natural creases. Store in an airtight container.

notes
- the amount of *crushed* cardamom seeds is about ½ teaspoon (very lightly packed measurement)
- the dough for these buns is *just* firm enough to hold its shape, though slightly tacky to the touch, especially as it is divided and formed into buns; its tenderness at this stage keeps the lightness intact when fully baked
- about ¼ cup turbinado sugar can be sprinkled on the top of the unbaked buns right after the egg white and sugar wash is applied
- the buns are delicious with butter and streaks of wildflower honey
- this recipe is loosely based on the formula for *majestic*bread: luxury rolls (page 51), but focuses on a different method and reduced amount of sugar

Very

falling in love—all over again—with dates ✳ crumb buns, the passionate version ✳ not your everyday waffles ✳ frosted little muffins ✳ blissful bars and squares—chocolate, of course ✳ a dough overflowing with ingredients ✳ racy chocolate tortes ✳ lighthearted sweetness out of the fryer

Naughty

chocolate, and a lot of it, in the right place

When it comes to the flavor and ingredient called chocolate, there are a lot of options (read: batters and doughs) for putting this flavor in "the right place."

In no particular order, it can go:
1. into a brownie
2. into a layer cake
3. into a sheet cake
4. into a muffin
5. into a scone
6. into a coffee cake
7. into a drop cookie
8. into a waffle
9. into a pancake
10. and on…and on…and on

Clearly, by reviewing this list, you have figured out that chocolate is in "the right place" if the flavor is highlighted in a recipe that features a batter or dough. When excess is a great choice, I vote for localizing 12 ounces of bittersweet chocolate in a one-layer cake batter, along with a benevolent 14 tablespoons of unsalted butter. So there. And then, in another recipe, I vote for using 1 pound of chocolate and ½ pound of butter, with a little heavy cream thrown in. While some would find these types and amounts unchecked, they seem entirely reasonable to me as someone who deeply admires the overall intensity of low-on-flour chocolate cakes.

As looks go, both tortes are homely but distinguished in a rustic way—the word "untidy" comes to mind, meaning that the tops and sides are imprecise—craggy here, with fault lines, cracks, and fissures there; slightly sunken in places; and dramatically one color, which can be redeemed by a stream of vanilla custard sauce. Yet the inherent spirit of each will sweep you away.

a nice, untidy torte, #1

Preheat the oven to 350 degrees F.

Film the inside of an 8½-inch springform pan (2½ inches deep) with softened unsalted butter.

For the batter, sift the flour, cocoa powder, and salt onto a sheet of waxed paper.

Place the chopped chocolate in a heavy, medium-size saucepan (preferably enameled cast iron) and set over low heat to melt it. Remove the saucepan from the heat to a heatproof surface and cool for 3 minutes. In the meantime, whisk the egg yolks in a small mixing bowl and add the sugar and vanilla extract; whisk slowly for 2 minutes. At first the mixture will be thick and resemble wet sand, but it will begin to relax in a minute or so. Blend the egg yolk and sugar mixture into the melted chocolate, mixing quickly but thoroughly. The mixture will begin to stiffen when the egg yolk mixture is introduced, so you must work speedily at this point. Whisk in the softened butter, a few chunks at a time. Resift the flour-cocoa powder-salt blend over the chocolate mixture and combine well.

Whip the egg whites until frothy in a large mixing bowl. Continue whipping until quite foamy, then add the cream of tartar and continue whipping until creamy, firm (but not stiff) peaks are formed.

Stir one-third of the whipped egg whites into the chocolate mixture to lighten it, then gently whisk in the remaining whites to create an evenly colored batter. Make sure to dispel any cottony strands of whipped whites. The batter will be moderately dense.

Scrape the batter into the prepared baking pan. Smooth the top with a rubber spatula. Bake the torte in the preheated oven for 30 minutes, lower the oven temperature to 325 degrees F, and bake for 5 minutes longer. The torte will rise as it bakes, form surface cracks, and settle as it cools. The center of the torte will be soft and the outer band firmer.

Cool the torte in the pan on a rack for 1 hour. It will sink further as it cools, forming deeper cracks, a significantly depressed center that makes the outer band higher, and it will look, as I say in the name of the recipe, "untidy." Untidy *and* delicious. Refrigerate the torte for 4 hours, or until firm. Open the hinge on the side of the springform pan and remove the outer ring, allowing the torte to stand on the circular metal base. Store the torte in an airtight container. Just before serving, sift cocoa powder on top of the cooled torte. Serve the torte, cut into triangular slices, napped with a little of the custard sauce.

(continued on the next page)

cocoa and bittersweet chocolate batter

¼ cup unsifted bleached cake flour

1 tablespoon unsweetened alkalized cocoa powder

⅛ teaspoon salt

12 ounces bittersweet chocolate, chopped

5 large eggs, separated

¾ cup superfine sugar

2½ teaspoons vanilla extract

14 tablespoons (1¾ sticks) unsalted butter, cut into small chunks, softened

¼ teaspoon cream of tartar

unsweetened alkalized cocoa powder, for sifting over the baked torte

stirred custard (page 153)

serving: one 8½-inch torte, creating 8 slices
ahead: 3 days, without the cocoa powder topping

notes
• select a bittersweet chocolate in the cacao range of 60% to 66%
• it is important to use superfine sugar in the batter or the texture of the baked torte may be
  slightly gritty
• use a long, thin-bladed knife to cut the torte

a nice, untidy torte, #2

**plenty-of-chocolate-
and-butter batter**

2 tablespoons bleached cake flour

2 tablespoons unsweetened alkalized
cocoa powder

⅛ teaspoon salt

5 large eggs

2 large egg yolks

5 tablespoons superfine sugar

½ cup heavy cream

1 tablespoon vanilla extract

1 pound bittersweet chocolate,
melted and cooled to tepid

½ pound (16 tablespoons or 2 sticks)
unsalted butter, cut into small chunks,
softened

unsweetened alkalized cocoa powder, for
sifting over the baked torte

stirred custard (page 153)

serving: one 9-inch torte, creating 12 slices
ahead: 3 days, without the cocoa powder
topping

Preheat the oven to 325 degrees F.

Film the inside of a 9-inch springform pan (2¾ inches deep) with softened
unsalted butter.

For the batter, sift the flour, cocoa powder, and salt onto a sheet of waxed paper.

Whisk the whole eggs and egg yolks in a medium-size mixing bowl to
combine. Add the sugar and whisk slowly for 1 minute. Blend in the heavy
cream and vanilla extract. Place the melted chocolate in a large mixing bowl.
Whisk in the butter, a few chunks at a time, blending well after each addition.
Pour over the egg and cream mixture and blend well to combine, making
sure that the batter is a uniform color.

Scrape the batter into the prepared baking pan. Smooth the top with a
rubber spatula. Bake the torte in the preheated oven for 40 minutes, or
until just set. The edges of the torte will rise above the center portion as
the torte bakes. The center will be slightly glossy-looking and a few cracks
usually surface. Cool the torte in the pan on a cooling rack for 1 hour and 30
minutes. The sides may have slumped and the top may have cracked a little
more in a few places.

Refrigerate the torte for 3 hours, or until firm. Open the hinge on the side of
the springform pan and remove the outer ring, allowing the torte to stand on
the circular metal base. Store the torte in an airtight container. Just before
serving, sift cocoa powder on top of the cooled torte. Serve the torte cut into
triangular slices, napped with a little of the custard sauce.

notes
• use a good 65% to 66% cacao bittersweet chocolate in the batter
• use a long, thin-bladed knife to cut the torte

stirred custard

Warm the half-and-half, heavy cream, sugar, and salt in a heavy, medium-size saucepan (preferably wide-bottomed enameled cast iron) over low heat (to 110 to 115 degrees F), whisking occasionally. The goal is to heat the liquid and dissolve the sugar. Remove the saucepan from the heat.

In the meantime, place the egg yolks and vanilla bean seeds (if you are using them) in a large nonreactive mixing bowl. Add ½ cup of the warm creamy mixture through a medium-size fine-mesh sieve in a slow, steady stream, stopping from time to time to blend the mixture as the creamy mixture is added. Strain over the remaining liquid in 3 or 4 additions, thoroughly whisking in each batch. Wash and dry the saucepan, then pour the custard sauce mixture into it.

Set the saucepan over low heat and cook the sauce, stirring with a wooden spoon or flat wooden paddle, until lightly thickened, 6 to 10 minutes, stirring slowly but constantly. In the beginning, the top may be slightly foamy (depending on how vigorously you have whisked the mixture), but the lighter-colored foam will dissipate as the custard cooks. The completed sauce will very lightly coat the back of the spoon or paddle; once chilled, the sauce will thicken further. The cream must be cooked until thickened, reaching and maintaining a temperature of 160 degrees F. (To test the temperature of the sauce, remove the saucepan from the heat for a moment and, protecting your hands with oven mitts, tip the pan slightly so that the sauce *just* pools to one side, then test with a clean, dry food-appropriate thermometer.) The sauce should never simmer—or even verge on this stage—or the yolks will begin to scramble in little light yellow pellets and the mixture will begin to smell eggy.

Place the vanilla extract in a medium-size heatproof bowl. Strain the custard sauce through a medium-size fine-mesh sieve into the bowl. Immediately press a sheet of food-safe plastic wrap directly over the surface of the sauce to prevent a surface skin from forming. Cool for 20 minutes.

When cooled, pour the sauce into a storage container, cover tightly, and refrigerate. Chill for 3 hours before serving as an accompaniment.

notes
- using ½ cup sugar creates a custard sauce with just the right sweetness; using a lesser amount of sugar would produce a sauce that tastes too eggy, as sugar rounds out the flavor as well as increases what I like to call the "luscious-quotient" by balancing and enhancing the half-and-half and heavy cream
- using a wide-bottomed saucepan speeds up the time it takes to thicken the sauce
- if the sauce seems very thick after several hours of chilling (depending on the richness—that is, percentage of fat—of the heavy cream you have used), thin it out with a little milk or half-and-half, 1 tablespoon at a time

creamy vanilla custard

1½ cups half-and-half

1 cup heavy cream

½ cup granulated sugar

large pinch of salt

6 large egg yolks

seeds from ½ small vanilla bean, scraped clean (optional)

2½ teaspoons vanilla extract

serving: about 2 cups
ahead: 1 day

cookies, untamed

On the wild side of baking, when a profusion of ingredients is not questioned and for the time when butter can be used in an unrestrained but no less thoughtful way, this recipe will suit you just fine—as it would anyone whose devotion to chocolate and nuts overrules anything else. I say this in a confident manner. Read on.

These big, bold cookies are compelling in flavor and simplicity: the brown sugar targets and builds on the taste of the butter, and the butter, in turn, forms a creamy canvas for the heap (and I do mean *heap*) of bittersweet chocolate chunks. The amount of chocolate called for seems like a daunting amount, and it is. That the chocolate crowds the dough, jumbling itself here and there and all over the place, asking for attention among the pecans, makes it all the more worthwhile. I don't think there's anything wrong with that. Because it is a breathtakingly handsome amount, this mass of chocolate, it would be wise to chop up a stack of bars in the 60% to 64% cacao category, in an effort to keep it interesting all the way around.

Cooks beware: if you are shaky about the flavor of chocolate or about using a really big block of butter, look elsewhere for a gentler, more unassuming recipe. Those, however, who rejoice in the depth, strength, and suave creaminess of both will really go for this cookie, with its casual undertone of caramel and its eye-catching measure of chocolate. In all, the cookie tastes like a wedge of brown sugar shortbread, texturally crisp and sandy, disrupted with bold blots of chocolate.

larger-than-life, chunky-bulky bittersweet chocolate praline cookies

larger-than-life, chunky-bulky bittersweet chocolate praline cookies

chocolate and nut butter dough

4 cups unsifted bleached all-purpose flour

¼ teaspoon baking soda

1 teaspoon salt

1 pound (4 sticks) unsalted butter, softened

1 cup firmly packed light brown sugar

1 cup granulated sugar

5 teaspoons vanilla extract

24 ounces bittersweet chocolate, cut into rough ½-inch chunks

2 cups pecan halves and pieces, lightly toasted and cooled completely (for adding directly to the dough) or untoasted (for pressing onto the mounds of dough just before baking)

serving: about 3½ dozen oversize (meaning *extremely* and deliciously large) cookies
ahead: 2 days; refrigerate cookie dough for 2 days or freeze for 1 month

Preheat the oven to 350 degrees F.

Line several heavy cookie sheets or rimmed sheet pans with lengths of ovenproof parchment paper.

For the dough, sift the flour, baking soda, and salt onto a sheet of waxed paper.

Cream the butter in the large bowl of a freestanding electric mixer on moderate speed for 3 minutes. Add the light brown sugar and beat on moderate speed for 1 minute. Add the granulated sugar and beat for 1 minute longer. Blend in the vanilla extract.

On low speed, mix in the sifted ingredients in 2 additions, beating just until the flour particles are absorbed. Scrape down the sides of the mixing bowl frequently with a rubber spatula to keep the dough even-textured. Work in the bittersweet chocolate chunks and lightly toasted pecans. Or, work in the chocolate chunks and reserve the untoasted pecans for topping the mounds of dough. The dough will be moderately firm and dense, but malleable.

Place scant ⅓-cup mounds of dough on the prepared baking pans, spacing the mounds about 3 inches apart and arranging 8 mounds to a pan. If you are pressing the untoasted pecans into the surface of the dough mounds, do so now.

Bake the cookies in the preheated oven for 16 to 18 minutes, or until set and light golden (the edges will be a slightly deeper golden color). The cookies must be baked through to establish their exquisite shortbread-like texture. Let the cookies stand on the baking pans for 1 minute, then transfer them to cooling racks, using a wide offset metal spatula. Cool completely. Store in an airtight tin.

notes
• for a smaller batch of cookies, the recipe can be halved
• this cookie dough freezes beautifully (assemble ⅓-cup portions on baking pans, freeze until firm, then enclose in plastic wrap and self-sealing food-safe freezer-weight plastic bags or sturdy airtight containers); defrost the dough in the refrigerator and bake, adding about 2 minutes to the total baking time
• when preparing cookie dough for refrigeration or freezing, use organic eggs only
• never consume raw cookie dough

fudge griddled

Not a morning waffle by any means, this griddled treat is designed for serving on a languorous weekend evening, well after dinner has settled in, when its richness can be relished.

I don't know anyone who would brush off a warm and fudgy waffle featuring tiny semisweet chocolate chips romping through a cocoa-intensified batter. These are a shoo-in on the dessert plate, accompanied by whipped cream or premium vanilla ice cream and an underseal of *chocolate darkness* (page 424). Or, ignore the whipped or frozen creamy component and the sauce in favor of a little smear of *very bittersweet chocolate cream spread* (page 160). This is as intense and dramatic as you can get. And chocolate-rich. Do I have your attention now?

cocoa waffles, very bittersweet chocolate cream spread

Preheat a 2-grid deep-dish (Belgian-style) waffle iron (each grid measuring about 4½ by 4½ inches).

For the batter, sift the flour, cocoa powder, baking powder, baking soda, salt, and superfine sugar into a large mixing bowl. In a medium-size mixing bowl, whisk the melted butter, melted unsweetened chocolate, eggs, buttermilk, heavy cream, and vanilla extract. Pour the buttermilk mixture over the sifted ingredients and stir to form a batter, using a wooden spoon or flat wooden paddle. Mix in the chocolate chips. The batter will be moderately thick.

Spoon a generous ⅓ cup batter into each grid, cover the iron, and cook until baked though (at the medium heat setting, if your waffler has one), following the directions supplied by the manufacturer of the appliance. Lift up the waffle squares onto individual plates, dredge with confectioners' sugar, and serve immediately, accompanied by a bowl of the bittersweet chocolate cream spread.

notes
- using a moderate setting for griddling the waffles cooks them through in an even way without drying out the squares
- enjoy the waffles freshly griddled, but wait a moment or two for the chocolate chips to cool

chip-tangled cocoa and buttermilk batter

2 cups unsifted bleached all-purpose flour

1 cup unsweetened alkalized cocoa powder

1¼ teaspoons baking powder

¾ teaspoon baking soda

¼ teaspoon salt

1⅓ cups plus 3 tablespoons superfine sugar

10 tablespoons (1 stick plus 2 tablespoons) unsalted butter, melted and cooled to tepid

1 ounce unsweetened chocolate, melted and cooled to tepid

4 large eggs

2 cups buttermilk

⅓ cup heavy cream

4 teaspoons vanilla extract

1¼ cups miniature semisweet chocolate chips

confectioners' sugar, for sprinkling on the finished waffles

very bittersweet chocolate cream spread (page 160), to accompany the waffles

serving: 8 pairs (16 individual) Belgian-style waffles

very bittersweet chocolate cream spread

dense chocolate "butter"

1 cup heavy cream

pinch of salt

3 tablespoons light corn syrup

1 teaspoon vanilla extract

8 ounces bittersweet chocolate
(65% to 70% cacao content), chopped

serving: about 1¼ cups
ahead: 3 days

Place the heavy cream, salt, and corn syrup in a small saucepan. Set the saucepan over moderate heat and let the mixture come to a low boil (prominent bubbles will appear at the edges of the pan), stirring once or twice to disperse the corn syrup throughout it as the mixture heats up. In the meantime, place the chopped chocolate in the work bowl of a food processor fitted with the steel blade. Cover and process the chocolate until very finely chopped.

Turn the chopped chocolate into a medium-size stainless steel bowl. Blend the vanilla extract into the hot cream mixture, then pour it through a fine-mesh strainer over the chopped chocolate. Let the mixture stand for 2 minutes. Begin stirring the chocolate into a smooth, well-amalgamated mixture by beginning in the center and slowly moving outward, using a wooden spoon or heatproof flat paddle. Do not use a whisk as the mixture will aerate and bubbles will be produced, rather than result in creamy, dense smoothness. Pour the chocolate mixture through a clean fine-mesh strainer into a wide bowl. The mixture should be smooth, dark, and lightly glossy. Cool, undisturbed, at room temperature for 30 minutes, then stir lightly with a flexible rubber spatula and turn into a small bowl. Cool at room temperature until set, about 3 hours.

Use the spread immediately, or cover tightly and refrigerate, bringing the spread to cool room temperature before using.

notes
• this is an "adults-only" spread, as it is intensely bittersweet

lacking restraint

When it comes to "chew" (now that's an unfortunate term for such a fine characteristic), one of the most sought-after attributes of a bar cookie and some breads, the sweet that follows has it. In spades.

Dates and coconut clog up a simple batter that is tinged with nutmeg and leavened lightly to elevate its crumb and free it from somber density. The resulting bars have a deep, mellow liveliness—thanks to the dates and brown sugar. And there's more to recommend it, for the batter easily is mixed in a bowl, and the fruit, tangled within, adds its own particular moistness—simple and unassuming. The finish for the bars, hand-cut to reveal their rugged sides, is a light wrapping in snowy confectioners' sugar. Have these around in a tin during the December holiday season or pack them up for an autumnal picnic. As well, the same batter, modified slightly and baked in pretty fluted pans, creates a half dozen first-class tart-cakes. In a date trifecta of sorts, the third recipe is for a sultry torte baked in a fluted tart pan and completed with an overrun of toffee spooning sauce.

Whether the sweet is in bar or cake form, you will fall in love with the deep, resonating flavors of brown sugar and fruit at first, then with the richness of texture with the first bite.

date bars deluxe, big and crazy chewy

Preheat the oven to 375 degrees F.

Lengthwise and width-wise, line the inside of two 8 by 8 by 2-inch baking pans with release-surface aluminum foil, pressing in the foil release side up and leaving 2 to 3 inches of foil to extend on all four sides by about 1 inch. Film the inside of the pans with nonstick oil spray.

For the batter, sift the flour, baking powder, baking soda, salt, and nutmeg onto a sheet of waxed paper.

Whisk the melted butter, light brown sugar, eggs, and vanilla extract in a large mixing bowl to blend. Blend in the sifted mixture. Stir in the dates and coconut. The batter will be dense and heavy.

Scrape the batter into the prepared pans, dividing it evenly between them. Spread and press the batter into an even layer, using a flexible palette knife.

Bake the sweet in the preheated oven for 30 to 35 minutes, or until a medium golden color on top and just set.

Cool the sweet in the pans on cooling racks. Gently lift out each block, using the aluminum foil sides to remove it from the pan. Cut each block in half horizontally, then cut each section vertically into 5 long bars. Detach the bars from the foil.

Place the confectioners' sugar in a shallow bowl. Carefully and lightly, dredge each bar in confectioners' sugar, coating all sides. Cool completely. Store in an airtight tin.

notes
• the bars must be thoroughly cooled before enrobing in confectioners' sugar or their surfaces will be gummy

buttery brown sugar–date batter

1 cup unsifted bleached all-purpose flour

1¼ teaspoons baking powder

¼ teaspoon baking soda

½ teaspoon salt

1¼ teaspoons freshly grated nutmeg

½ pound (16 tablespoons or 2 sticks) unsalted butter, melted and cooled

1⅓ cups firmly packed light brown sugar

4 large eggs

4 teaspoons vanilla extract

3¾ cups firmly packed pitted dates, coarsely chopped

2 cups firmly packed sweetened flaked coconut

about 2 cups confectioners' sugar, for dredging the baked bars

serving: 20 big bars
ahead: 5 days

date tart-cakes

**bar cookie batter especially
for tart-cakes**

½ cup unsifted bleached all-purpose flour

½ teaspoon baking powder

¼ teaspoon baking soda

¼ teaspoon salt

¾ teaspoon freshly grated nutmeg

9 tablespoons (1 stick plus 1 tablespoon)
unsalted butter, melted and cooled

⅔ cup firmly packed light brown sugar

2 large eggs

2 teaspoons vanilla extract

2¼ cups firmly packed pitted dates,
coarsely chopped

1¼ cups firmly packed sweetened
flaked coconut

spooning sauce

6 tablespoons firmly packed
dark brown sugar

3 tablespoons unsalted butter,
cut into chunks

¼ cup heavy cream

½ teaspoon vanilla extract

serving: 6 tart-cakes
ahead: freshly baked,
or up to 12 hours in advance

Preheat the oven to 375 degrees F.

Film the inside of six fluted 4-inch false-bottomed tart pans (1¼ inches deep) with nonstick flour-and-oil spray.

For the batter, prepare the bar cookie mixture as described in the method on page 163. Divide the mixture evenly among the pans. Smooth and spread the mixture evenly, using a flexible palette knife. Assemble the filled pans on a cookie sheet, spacing them at least 3 inches apart.

Bake the tart-cakes in the preheated oven for 20 minutes, or until just set.

Cool the tart-cakes in the pans on racks for 3 minutes. Carefully release the tart-cakes from the outer rings, leaving them on their bases. Return the tart-cakes to the cooling racks. Cool completely. Remove the bases from the tart-cakes, slipping a small offset metal spatula between each cake and the round metal base.

For the spooning sauce, place the dark brown sugar, butter, and heavy cream in a small, heavy saucepan (preferably enameled cast iron). Cover, set over low heat, and cook until the sugar has melted down, stirring 2 or 3 times. Uncover the pan, raise the heat to moderate, and bring to the simmer. Simmer for 2 minutes. Off the heat, stir in the vanilla extract.

To assemble the dessert, place a freshly baked tart-cake on a plate and spoon a little of the sauce over and about the sweet.

notes
• it is important to unmold the tart-cakes soon after they are pulled from the oven or they may stick to the sides, occasionally causing some of the edges to pull away
• as well, a dollop of whipped cream would be a luscious contrast to each plate of sauced cake

Preheat the oven to 350 degrees F.

Film the inside of a fluted 10-inch false-bottomed tart pan (2 inches deep) with nonstick flour-and-oil spray. Have a rimmed sheet pan at hand.

Place the water in a small saucepan and bring to the boil. Place the chopped dates in a medium-size nonreactive heatproof mixing bowl. Stir the baking soda into the boiling water (it will foam up a bit, then subside) and pour this over the dates. Mix lightly with a spoon and set aside to cool to tepid (uncovered).

For the batter, sift the flour, baking powder, salt, nutmeg, allspice, and cardamom onto a sheet of waxed paper.

Cream the butter in the large bowl of a freestanding electric mixer on moderate speed for 45 seconds, and no longer. Add the dark brown sugar in 2 additions, beating for 45 seconds after each portion is added. Add the granulated sugar and beat for 45 seconds longer. Blend in the egg and vanilla extract. On low speed, blend in the liquidy date mixture. At this point, the mixture will be a bit soupy. Add the sifted ingredients in 3 additions, mixing on low speed to combine. Scrape down the sides of the mixing bowl with a rubber spatula to keep the mixture even-textured. The batter will be creamy, chunky with dates, and moderately thick.

Place the rimmed sheet pan in the preheated oven.

Scrape the batter into the prepared baking pan. Spread it evenly in the pan, using a flexible palette knife. Place the filled baking pan on the rimmed sheet pan.

Bake the torte in the preheated oven for 45 to 50 minutes, or until set. The baked torte will begin to pull away from the sides of the baking pan. Avoid inserting a wooden pick into the center of the torte as the torte may deflate. Cool the torte in the pan (still on the rimmed sheet pan) on a cooling rack for 15 minutes.

While the torte is cooling, make the toffee spooning sauce: place the dark brown sugar, butter, heavy cream, and salt in a heavy, medium-size saucepan (preferably enameled cast iron) and set over low heat. When the sugar has melted down, raise the heat to moderately high and bring the

(continued on the next page)

spiced batter

¾ cup water

1¾ cups firmly packed pitted dates, coarsely chopped

¼ teaspoon baking soda

2 cups unsifted bleached all-purpose flour

1 teaspoon baking powder

½ teaspoon salt

½ teaspoon freshly grated nutmeg

¼ teaspoon ground allspice

¼ teaspoon ground cardamom

8 tablespoons (1 stick) unsalted butter, softened

⅔ cup firmly packed dark brown sugar

⅓ cup granulated sugar

1 large egg

2 teaspoons vanilla extract

toffee spooning sauce

½ cup firmly packed dark brown sugar

4 tablespoons (½ stick) unsalted butter, cut into chunks

½ cup plus 1 tablespoon heavy cream

pinch of salt

½ teaspoon vanilla extract

serving: one 10-inch torte, creating 10 slices
ahead: freshly baked

contents of the saucepan to a moderate boil. Cook the sauce at a low boil for 2 minutes. Remove the saucepan from the heat and stir in the vanilla extract. Set a fine-mesh sieve over a medium-size heatproof bowl, pour the sauce into the sieve, and strain it, pushing it through with a heatproof spatula. There should be about ¾ cup. Cool for 15 minutes.

Glaze the top of the torte with the warm sauce, spooning it over in 3 portions. Let the sauce run down the sides between the edges of the torte and the pan, but try not to concentrate it in the center or the pooling may cause the tender torte to slump. Use a soft pastry brush to brush it around. Use all of the sauce. (This takes some patience to get the torte to absorb the sauce fully; another option is to brush about one-third of the sauce on the torte, then completely unmold the torte onto a serving plate and spoon the remaining sauce over and about it. It will be delicious either way.) Cool for 45 minutes. Carefully lift the torte by the bottom, pushing it up and out to unmold and remove the fluted ring. Serve the torte sliced into wedges.

notes
• overcreaming the butter, and then the butter-sugar mixture, will destabilize the batter during baking and cause the baked torte to dip in the center
• use a finely serrated knife to cut the torte

little muffins, sauced

Good muffins get star-quality treatment when trimmed with a chocolate glaze. By design, this overlay of choice is a smooth, nearly satiny chocolate mixture that cascades over freshly baked little fluted muffins, heightening the moist and cakey goodness beneath.

Anyone can have a muffin modest and unvarnished, but I'll have mine doubled up on the chocolate, and buttery inside and out, top to bottom.

Three-bite muffins are sweet, cherubic things—so tempting with their plump, rounded tops partially concealed by casual, glossy coats of glaze.

And treats are always needed in life, because homemade goodies never fail to raise your spirit, especially the "sauced" kind. Just for an hour or two, your focus centers on two bowls, one of batter and one of glaze, and everything seems so sweet, so perfect, so chocolaty.

chocolate chip muffinettes, satiny chocolate overlay

Preheat the oven to 375 degrees F.

Film the inside of 20 fluted Bundt cupcake pan cups (12 fluted cups to a pan, each fluted cup measuring 2½ inches in diameter and 1¼ inches deep, with a capacity of ⅓ cup) with nonstick flour-and-oil spray.

For the batter, sift the all-purpose flour, cake flour, baking powder, baking soda, and salt onto a sheet of waxed paper.

Toss the chocolate chips with 2 teaspoons of the sifted mixture in a medium-size mixing bowl.

Cream the butter in the large bowl of a freestanding electric mixer on moderately high speed for 2 minutes. Add the granulated sugar and beat for 1 minute. Add the light brown sugar and beat for 1 minute longer. Beat in the eggs, one at a time, mixing for 45 seconds after each addition. Blend in the vanilla extract. On low speed, alternately add the sifted mixture in 3 additions with the half-and-half in 2 additions, beginning and ending with the sifted mixture. Scrape down the sides of the mixing bowl with a rubber spatula to keep the batter even-textured. The batter will be creamy, but moderately dense. Stir in the chocolate chips.

Spoon the batter into the cups, dividing it evenly among them. Mound the batter lightly in the center of each cup.

Bake the muffinettes in the preheated oven for 15 minutes, or until risen, set, light golden on top, and a wooden pick withdraws clean (if you bump into a chip, the pick will be chocolate-stained). Cool the muffinettes in the pans on racks for 7 to 10 minutes, then remove them to other cooling racks. Cool completely. Place sheets of waxed paper underneath the cooling racks to catch any drips of the overlay.

For the overlay, sift the granulated sugar, cornstarch, and salt into a small mixing bowl, then whisk to combine. Add the milk in a slow, steady stream, mixing with a wooden spoon or flat wooden paddle. Melt the chocolate and butter in a heavy, medium-size saucepan (preferably enameled cast iron) over low heat, stirring occasionally. Remove the saucepan from the

(continued on the next page)

chocolate chip batter

1¾ cups unsifted bleached all-purpose flour

¼ cup unsifted bleached cake flour

1½ teaspoons baking powder

½ teaspoon baking soda

¼ teaspoon salt

1¼ cups miniature semisweet chocolate chips

8 tablespoons (1 stick) unsalted butter, softened

6 tablespoons granulated sugar

6 tablespoons firmly packed light brown sugar

2 large eggs

1½ teaspoons vanilla extract

¾ cup half-and-half

satiny chocolate overlay

½ cup granulated sugar

3 teaspoons cornstarch

pinch of salt

½ cup milk

3 ounces unsweetened chocolate, chopped

6 tablespoons (¾ stick) unsalted butter, cut into chunks

1 teaspoon vanilla extract

serving: 20 muffinettes
ahead: best on baking day

heat. Blend in the milk-sugar-cornstarch mixture. Return the saucepan to the heat. Bring the mixture to the boil over moderately high heat, stirring slowly, using a wooden spoon or flat wooden paddle. When the mixture has thickened, lower the heat and simmer for 1 minute. Remove the saucepan from the heat and stir in the vanilla extract. Pour and scrape the icing into a heatproof bowl and cool, stirring slowly now and again, until the rush of heat subsides and the glaze begins to thicken and cool slightly, but use it slightly warm for good flow and coverage.

Spoon the warm glaze on top of the muffinettes, letting it flow across the tops and sides in an irregular fashion. Let the muffinettes stand until the glaze firms up, at least 45 minutes, then enjoy.

notes
- the combination of all-purpose flour and cake flour makes a tender-textured batter that holds its shape nicely during baking
- for a deeper caramel-like tone to the muffin batter, omit the granulated sugar and use a total of ¾ cup firmly packed light brown sugar
- it is important to use whole milk in the *satiny chocolate overlay*
- any glazed muffinettes not consumed after 2 hours of assembling should be refrigerated in a covered container for serving later on baking day

rough and tumble, moist and sensual

Yeast-raised streusel buns really sizzle—in a sumptuous way, of course. A dough that is sturdy yet tender, dense and rich with sour cream, egg yolks, and butter, makes a stirring sweet roll.

Surprisingly, the involvement of the cook is not excessively demanding: the dough is mixed into silky submission in the bowl of a heavy-duty mixer equipped with the dough hook, given a first rise on the countertop, and then an overnight rest in the refrigerator. What ensues is a beautifully developed coffee cake–like bread that is reasonably schedule-accommodating. Its time line is a good fit for those who want to create a dough and have the freedom to form and bake the buns the next day. The chilled dough is easy to handle and, once formed, risen, and baked into buns, becomes a stellar package of flavor and texture. Emanating from the buns warm from the oven, the buttery perfume really ensnares you, and there you are tearing apart the buns willy-nilly, diving into the crumbly tops and buttery interiors with deeply rich notes of vanilla and sour cream. Surely this is the dictionary definition of "cloud-nine."

craggy-top sour cream buns, vanilla streusel

For the dough, stir together the yeast, the ¼ teaspoon granulated sugar, and the warm water in a heatproof measuring cup. Allow the mixture to stand until swollen, 6 to 7 minutes.

In the meantime, whisk the sour cream, egg yolks, vanilla bean paste, vanilla extract, and the ⅓ cup granulated sugar in a medium-size mixing bowl. Blend in the yeast mixture. Whisk 4 cups of the flour and the salt in a large mixing bowl. Drop in the butter chunks and, using a pastry blender or two round-bladed table knives, cut the fat into the flour mixture until reduced to large, irregularly sized flakes. Add the sour cream and yeast mixture and stir to combine. The dough will not come together at this point; there will be dry patches and moist sections.

Scrape the dough mixture, including all of the unincorporated flour, into the bowl of a heavy-duty freestanding electric mixer. Set the bowl in place and attach the dough hook. Beat on low speed for 2 minutes; the dough will be quite sticky. Stop the mixer and scrape down the sides of the mixing bowl and the dough hook. Beat the dough on moderate speed for 3 minutes. Add the remaining ¼ cup flour and beat for 6 minutes longer. Once or twice in the beating process, stop the mixer and scrape down the sides of the mixing bowl and the dough hook. At this point, the dough will be exceptionally smooth, silky, pull-y, but still somewhat moist—it will not clean the bottom or sides of the mixing bowl.

Turn the dough into a bowl heavily coated with softened unsalted butter, lightly turn to coat all sides in a film of butter, make several cuts in the dough with a pair of kitchen scissors, cover tightly with a sheet of food-safe plastic wrap, and let rise at room temperature for 1 hour and 45 minutes to 2 hours. During this time frame, the dough should just double in bulk. During this rise, make sure that the dough reaches, but does not exceed, the doubled-in-bulk stage.

Remove and discard the plastic wrap. Lightly compress the dough with your fingertips.

Transfer the compressed dough to a very lightly oiled double sheet of food-safe plastic wrap, enclose to wrap securely, and refrigerate the dough overnight, or for at least 12 hours. As the dough rises in the refrigerator, it will look like a fat, inflated pillow. After 4 hours of refrigeration, compress the dough lightly, rewrap it in lightly oiled plastic wrap, and return it to the refrigerator.

Film the inside of two 8 by 8 by 2-inch baking pans with softened unsalted butter. Dust the bottom of each pan with all-purpose flour, leaving the sides simply buttered.

(continued on the next page)

sour cream yeast dough

4½ teaspoons active dry yeast

¼ teaspoon granulated sugar

⅓ cup warm (105 to 110 degrees F) water

1 cup sour cream

5 large egg yolks

1 tablespoon vanilla bean paste

1½ teaspoons vanilla extract

⅓ cup granulated sugar

4¼ cups unsifted bleached all-purpose flour

¾ teaspoon salt

½ pound (16 tablespoons or 2 sticks) cool unsalted butter, cut into teaspoon-size chunks

vanilla streusel (page 174)

confectioners' sugar, for sprinkling over the baked buns

serving: 16 buns
ahead: best on baking day; or freeze for 3 weeks, defrost, bundle in aluminum foil, and reheat in a preheated 300 degrees F oven for 10 to 12 minutes

To form the buns, remove the dough from the refrigerator. Remove and discard the plastic wrap. The cold dough will be pliable and moldable. Divide the dough in half, then cut each half into 8 even-size pieces. Flatten each piece into a patty measuring about 2 by 3½ inches. Arrange the sections of dough in the pans, spacing them in two rows of 4 patties each.

Cover each pan of buns with a sheet of lightly buttered food-safe plastic wrap and let rise at room temperature for 2 hours and 30 minutes. Remove the sheets of plastic wrap. Sprinkle the streusel mixture over the tops of the buns, dividing it evenly between the two pans. Lightly cover with plastic wrap. Let the pans of buns stand for 1 hour and 10 minutes to 1 hour and 20 minutes longer, or until quite puffy and a little more than doubled in bulk. The buns should rise to almost fill the pan, leaving about ¼ inch headspace.

Preheat the oven to 350 degrees F in advance of baking.

Bake the buns in the preheated oven for 40 minutes, or until set and a medium golden color on top. The fully baked buns will pull away slightly from the edges of the baking pans. Let the buns cool in the pans on cooling racks. Carefully detach the buns with two small offset metal spatulas, taking care not to compress them, then remove them from the pan. Serve the buns freshly baked, their tops dusted with confectioners' sugar.

notes
• three leisurely rises (after mixing, during an overnight refrigeration, and once again after forming and topping) greatly enhance the flavor of the dough and stabilize its texture

 vanilla streusel

butter crumble

1 cup unsifted bleached all-purpose flour

large pinch of salt

⅔ cup granulated sugar

⅓ cup firmly packed light brown sugar

8 tablespoons (1 stick) cool unsalted butter, cut into tablespoon-size chunks

1¼ teaspoons vanilla extract

serving: about 2 cups
ahead: 2 days

Combine the flour, salt, granulated sugar, and light brown sugar in a medium-size mixing bowl. Scatter over the chunks of butter and, using a pastry blender or two round-bladed table knives, cut the fat into the flour until it is reduced to pieces about the size of large pearls. Sprinkle over the vanilla extract. Using your fingertips, crumble the mixture together until it clings in nuggets, large, small, and in between. The clumps will be moist and sandy-textured.

Use the streusel immediately, or turn it into a food-safe container, cover, and refrigerate.

seductive times two

Here are two top-notch bar cookies: ounce for ounce, both sweets are authoritative. In the first bar cookie, the batter is dense, very dark, weighty. Unsweetened chocolate, bittersweet chocolate, and cocoa powder combine to develop an attractive and generous portrait of the flavor.

The bars have an undeniable feeling of plenty and the taste conveyed in one bite immediately reinforces a sense of richness. The second bar cookie, a vague mix of the *edge-of-darkness bars* (page 176) and *dark shadows* (page 342), is the chewiest version of all, with light corn syrup replacing a portion of the sugar, and a reduction in the number of eggs.

What makes the *edge-of-darkness bars* so magnetic is the combination of ingredients and method for preparing the batter, the handling of the butter and chocolate, the baking pan of choice, and the oven temperature: all of these elements and factors, engagingly linked, create a sweet that is at once chewy-creamy-mellow. That these traits have spiraled together in one sweet place is not a coincidence, for I have been plotting this get-together for some time—years, in fact. With regard to brownie-style batters, I have long campaigned for reducing the baking temperature, adjusting and subsequently limiting the amount of leavening, using two types of flour (usually all-purpose and cake) for establishing texture and double-sifting that merged set of dry ingredients, combining two or more types of chocolate for a prominent flavor boost, replacing granulated sugar with the superfine variety, and mixing the batter thoughtfully by hand. Whew. The result? A confection that announces *chocolate* (and, by extension, *butter*) over and over again.

The *confection brownies* (page 178) have a permanent place in my baking repertoire. I would definitely label them a "staple," for there are always a few uncut blocks on a freezer shelf waiting to be cut and, in truth, eaten directly in their frozen form. Especially late-night. Up to now, this admission was private. The batter is somewhat thick and heavy, and with a ropy, shiny pull that is evident when you scrape it into the baking pan. At first, it may seem as if the batter is fighting you, but that is just the stretch of eggs, corn syrup, melted chocolate, and butter creating thick, elongated, ribbony extensions.

The potency of each bar is not to be missed. If you are swift in the kitchen, the batter can be prepared in the time it takes to preheat the oven, but the wait to cut the big block of fudginess into neat sections seems like forever. In the end, the boundaries of presentation can be turned topsy-turvy, and instead of clean lines, dish out rambunctious, untidy sections. Messy. Gooey. Fun.

edge-of-darkness bars

dark, damp, and buttery batter

2 cups unsifted bleached all-purpose flour

2/3 cup unsifted bleached cake flour

½ teaspoon baking powder

½ teaspoon salt

½ cup plus 2 tablespoons unsweetened alkalized cocoa powder

1 pound (4 sticks) unsalted butter, melted and cooled to tepid

10 ounces unsweetened chocolate, melted and cooled to tepid

6 ounces bittersweet chocolate, melted and cooled to tepid

10 large eggs

4 cups superfine sugar

4 teaspoons vanilla extract

confectioners' sugar,
for sifting over the baked bars

serving: 40 bars
ahead: 5 days

Preheat the oven to 325 degrees F.

Lengthwise and width-wise, line the inside of a 13 by 9 by 2-inch baking pan with sheets of release-surface aluminum foil, pressing in the foil release side up and leaving 2 to 3 inches of foil to extend on all four sides; film the inside of the pan with nonstick oil spray. Or, line the inside of the pan with sheets of ovenproof parchment paper, extending the lengths slightly to create four short side flaps.

For the batter, sift the all-purpose flour, cake flour, baking powder, salt, and cocoa powder onto a sheet of waxed paper.

Whisk the melted butter, melted unsweetened chocolate, and melted bittersweet chocolate in a medium-size mixing bowl until smooth. In a large mixing bowl, whisk the eggs just to mix. Add the superfine sugar and beat for 1 minute. Blend in the butter-melted chocolate mixture and the vanilla extract. Resift the flour mixture over the chocolate mixture. Whisk slowly to form a batter, scraping down the sides of the mixing bowl with a rubber spatula to keep the batter even-textured.

Pour and scrape the batter into the prepared pan. Smooth the top with a flexible palette knife.

Bake the sweet in the preheated oven for 36 to 39 minutes, or until just set. There will be a few hairline cracks on the surface of the large block close to the edges of the baking pan.

Cool the sweet in the pan on a cooling rack for 30 minutes. Refrigerate for 4 hours. Gently lift out the large block, using the aluminum foil or parchment paper sides to remove it from the pan. Cut into 20 squares, then cut each square in half, using a long, heavy chef's knife. Detach the bars from the aluminum foil or parchment paper. Store in an airtight tin with parchment paper separating the layers. Sift confectioners' sugar over the tops of the bars just before serving.

notes
- be sure to sift out any lumps present in the superfine sugar before adding to the beaten eggs
- tepid, not cooled, melted butter and melted chocolate return the fudgiest bar cookie
- refrigerating the baked confection in the pan (after a 30-minute cooldown) for a period of 4 hours defines its texture, but for ultimate ooze the chilling time can be reduced to—gasp!—1 hour
- a few bars can be reserved and used in the filling for my *"brownie" babka* (page 196)

confection brownies

chocolate-times-four batter

1½ cups unsifted bleached all-purpose flour

¼ cup unsweetened alkalized cocoa powder

¼ cup unsweetened alkalized black cocoa powder (see notes)

½ teaspoon baking powder

½ teaspoon salt

½ pound plus 4 tablespoons (2½ sticks) unsalted butter, melted and cooled to tepid

6 ounces unsweetened chocolate, melted and cooled to tepid

2 ounces bittersweet chocolate, melted and cooled to tepid

6 large eggs

1½ cups plus 1 tablespoon superfine sugar

1¼ cups firmly packed light brown sugar

⅔ cup plus 2 tablespoons light corn syrup

3 teaspoons vanilla extract

confectioners' sugar, for sifting over the baked squares

serving: 20 generously sized squares
ahead: 5 days

Preheat the oven to 325 degrees F.

Lengthwise and width-wise, line the inside of a 13 by 9 by 2-inch baking pan with sheets of release-surface aluminum foil, pressing in the foil release side up and leaving 2 to 3 inches of foil to extend on all four sides; film the inside of the pan with nonstick oil spray. Or, line the inside of the pan with lengths of ovenproof parchment paper, extending them slightly to create four short side flaps.

Sift the flour, cocoa powder, black cocoa powder, baking powder, and salt onto a sheet of waxed paper.

Whisk the melted butter, melted unsweetened chocolate, and melted bittersweet chocolate in a medium-size mixing bowl until smooth. In a large mixing bowl, beat the eggs just to mix. Add the superfine sugar and beat for 1 minute, using a whisk. Add the light brown sugar and beat for 1 minute to combine. Blend in the butter-melted chocolate mixture, mixing just until incorporated. Blend in the corn syrup and vanilla extract. Resift the flour mixture over the chocolate mixture. Whisk slowly to form a batter, scraping down the sides of the mixing bowl with a rubber spatula to keep the batter even-textured. The batter will be moderately thick and glossy.

Pour and scrape the batter into the prepared pan. Smooth the top with a flexible palette knife.

Bake the sweet in the preheated oven for 35 to 40 minutes, or until just set. The top will puff slightly.

Cool the sweet in the pan on a cooling rack for 2 hours. Refrigerate for 4 hours, or until firm enough to cut. Gently lift out the large block, using the aluminum foil or parchment paper sides to remove it from the pan. Cut into squares, using a chef's knife. Detach the squares from the aluminum foil or parchment paper. Store in an airtight tin with parchment paper separating the layers. Sift confectioners' sugar over the tops of the bars just before serving.

notes
• dutch-process black cocoa is available in 1-pound bags from King Arthur Flour (page 501, baking*SelectedSources*); it's much darker, somewhat richer, and more intense than alkalized cocoa powder

fry happy

These cakey strips, yeasty doughnut pillows, and featherweight puffs have long been a tradition—if not a passion—of mine.

My French assembly for deep-frying, a large two-handled carbon-steel pan with its wire basket made of tinned steel residing inside (the basket of the newer version is made of nickel steel), turns the actual preparation of these golden morsels into an art form.

Doughnut art. Now there's a concept. In a baker's reality, doughnuts are a sweet, graphically interesting, of-the-moment item. Doughnut dough is controllable only up to a point. The ultimate form a doughnut takes bobbing about in the hot oil is the result of its own spirited force, despite attempts to rein it in (and I have certainly tried to rein in a few doughs in my time). A limited shelf life makes a doughnut even more urgently interesting, as the treat peaks into some kind of sublime sweet tenderness, then nosedives within the fastest span known to a cook. Its tasty window is a short, but happy, one.

I love to watch the inflation of every one of the doughs, the first leavened with baking powder, the second one with yeast, and the third with beaten whole eggs. Lifting a batch out of the rippling oil offers lots of delicious texture—crunchy, smooth, buttery, tender, moist—from a simple set of ingredients. The method for each differs, but the result is something worth the need to fry and eat them on the spot, and this is not quite an imposition on any count.

cake doughnut strips

Pour enough oil to rise to a depth of 2 inches into a heavy casserole measuring 9½ to 10 inches in diameter. Have a length of ovenproof parchment paper, measuring 8 by 8 inches, at hand; film the paper with nonstick oil spray and set aside. Have a cookie sheet at hand lined with several thicknesses of paper towels.

Outfit a pastry bag with an Ateco #825 or Ateco #823 open-star tip.

Heat the oil to 370 degrees F.

For the dough, sift the flour, baking powder, salt, and nutmeg onto a sheet of waxed paper.

Cream the butter in the large bowl of a freestanding electric mixer on moderate speed for 2 minutes. Add the ⅓ cup plus 3 tablespoons sugar in 2 additions, beating for 1 minute after each portion is added. Beat in the eggs, one at a time, mixing for about 20 seconds after each addition to combine. Blend in the vanilla extract. On low speed, add half of the sifted mixture, the heavy cream, then the balance of the sifted mixture. Scrape down the sides of the mixing bowl thoroughly with a rubber spatula to keep the dough even-textured. The dough will be only moderately firm.

Fold back a wide cuff on the pastry bag and fill with the dough. Flip up the cuff, smooth down the dough, and twist the top closed.

For each strip, pipe a 4 or 5-inch length of dough onto the lightly oiled piece of parchment paper. Use the side of a palette knife or the blunt edge of a paring knife to cut the end of the dough away from the top of the tip. Using sturdy, heatproof gloves to protect your hands and forearms, carefully release the strip of dough from the paper into the hot oil by turning the paper slightly so that the strip slips into the oil. The dough strip will sizzle. Continue adding 2 more strips to the hot oil in this way. Turn the strips to deep-fry until golden on all sides. Lift the strips as they are cooked (2 to 3 minutes total frying time) to the paper towel–lined cookie sheet, using a large slotted spoon or slotted spatula: the exteriors will be very crispy and the insides tender and cakey.

When all of the strips have been piped and deep-fried, carefully transfer them while they are still warm to a paper towel–covered clean length of ovenproof parchment paper and sprinkle with the ⅓ cup finishing sugar. Serve immediately.

(continued on the next page)

pure soybean oil, for deep-frying

vanilla and cream dough

1¾ cups plus 1 tablespoon unsifted bleached all-purpose flour

1¾ teaspoons baking powder

¼ teaspoon salt

½ teaspoon freshly grated nutmeg

5 tablespoons unsalted butter, softened

⅓ cup plus 3 tablespoons granulated sugar

2 large eggs

1½ teaspoons vanilla extract

5 tablespoons heavy cream

about ⅓ cup granulated sugar, for sugaring the fried strips

serving: 14 to 15 strips (using Ateco tip #825) or 18 to 20 strips (using Ateco tip #823)

notes
• the presence of frying oil, deep and hot, requires constant and careful attention; never leave the oil unattended, either while it is heating up or at frying temperature
• for heating frying oil, always use a pot that is heavy, stable, deep, and wide enough to accommodate the contents as the *cake doughnut strips*, *glazed risers* (below), and *beignets soufflés* (page 184) fry to a golden conclusion; protect your hands and forearms at all times while deep-frying

glazed risers, vanilla-maple glaze

buttermilk yeast dough

2½ teaspoons active dry yeast

¼ teaspoon granulated sugar

¼ cup warm (105 to 110 degrees F) water

¾ cup buttermilk

3 tablespoons unsalted butter, cut into chunks

3 tablespoons granulated sugar

2 teaspoons vanilla extract

2 large egg yolks

¼ teaspoon baking soda

3 cups unsifted bleached all-purpose flour, plus an additional 2 tablespoons, as needed for rolling

¼ teaspoon salt

pure soybean oil, for deep-frying

vanilla-maple glaze (page 184)

serving: about 1 dozen doughnuts
ahead: 6 hours

For the dough, stir together the yeast, the ¼ teaspoon sugar, and the warm water in a heatproof measuring cup. Allow the mixture to stand until swollen, 6 to 7 minutes.

Place the buttermilk, the chunks of butter, and the 3 tablespoons sugar in a small saucepan and set over low heat. When the butter has melted, remove the saucepan from the heat. Pour and scrape the mixture into a medium-size heatproof mixing bowl. Cool to tepid, then whisk in the vanilla extract, egg yolks, and baking soda. Blend in the yeast mixture.

Place 2 cups of the flour in a large mixing bowl and mix in the salt. Add the yeast-buttermilk mixture and mix to combine, using a wooden spoon or flat wooden paddle. The consistency of the mixture will resemble a thick, sticky batter-like dough. Let stand, uncovered, for 5 minutes. Add ¾ cup of the remaining flour and mix to form a scraggly dough. Turn the dough out onto a work surface and knead for 7 minutes, using as much of the remaining ¼ cup flour as needed to produce a dough that is firm but resilient. When kneaded for the full time given, the dough should be smooth.

Turn the dough into a bowl heavily coated with softened unsalted butter, turn to coat all sides in a film of butter, cover tightly with a sheet of food-safe plastic wrap, and let rise at room temperature for 1 hour and 30 minutes, or until doubled in bulk.

Remove the plastic wrap. Lightly compress the dough with a rubber spatula, cover loosely with the plastic wrap, and let stand for 5 minutes. Remove and discard the plastic wrap.

Line a heavy cookie sheet with a length of ovenproof parchment paper.

Lightly flour a work surface with the additional 2 tablespoons flour. Roll out the dough to a thickness of a generous ½ inch. Cut into sections, using a 2¼ by 2¼-inch cutter. Press together the scraps, reroll the dough, and cut out additional sections. There will be about 12 pieces in total. Arrange the sections 2½ to 3 inches apart on the parchment paper–lined cookie sheet.

Cover the pan of doughnut sections loosely with a sheet of food-safe plastic wrap. Let the doughnuts rise at room temperature for 1 hour, or until doubled in bulk.

In anticipation of frying the doughnuts, line a cookie sheet with several thicknesses of paper towels. Pour enough oil to rise to a depth of 2 inches into a heavy casserole measuring 9½ to 10 inches in diameter.

Heat the oil to 370 degrees to 375 degrees F.

Remove and discard the sheet of plastic wrap covering the risen doughnut sections. Protect your hands with sturdy heatproof gloves to guard against any spits of hot oil. Fry the doughnuts, a few at a time (and no more than 3 at once), in the hot oil, lowering each in slowly with a long-handled spatula, and taking care to avoid spattering the oil. When the sections are deep golden on one side (about 1 minute), carefully nudge them over to fry the other side until deep golden, using a slotted spoon or slotted spatula. Remove the fried doughnuts with a slotted spoon or slotted spatula to the paper towel–lined baking pan.

Place the fried and drained doughnuts on cooling racks. Let stand for 2 minutes.

Spread the vanilla-maple glaze over the top of the warm doughnuts, letting it cascade gently here and there. Let the doughnuts cool and the glaze set, 20 to 30 minutes, before serving.

notes

- the sections of dough must be puffy after the second rise and the oil at the correct temperature, or the fried doughnuts will be heavy rather than tender-textured
- the amount of vanilla-maple glaze is enough to create a light coating for the doughnuts; the recipe can be doubled successfully to double-glaze the doughnuts and so create a thicker, sweeter finish
- for oil and frying watch points, see notes, page 182

vanilla-maple glaze

sweet doughnut glaze

1½ cups confectioners' sugar

pinch of salt

6 tablespoons maple syrup

½ teaspoon vanilla extract

serving: about ¾ cup
ahead: 30 minutes

Sift the confectioners' sugar and salt into a medium-size mixing bowl. Add the maple syrup and vanilla extract. Using a hand-held electric mixer on low speed, blend together the ingredients until a smooth glaze is formed, scraping down the sides of the mixing bowl several times with a rubber spatula. The icing will be creamy-textured and moderately firm. Place a sheet of food-safe plastic wrap directly on the surface of the glaze.

Use the glaze for spooning on top of the warm fried doughnuts.

notes
• sifting the confectioners' sugar and salt together before adding the maple syrup and vanilla extract creates a smooth-textured glaze
• a special confectioners' sugar known as glazing sugar produces the glossiest icing

beignets soufflés

eggy vanilla orange dough

⅔ cup unsifted bleached all-purpose flour

⅛ teaspoon salt

⅔ cup water, preferably bottled

1 teaspoon granulated sugar

5 tablespoons plus 1 teaspoon
unsalted butter, cut into chunks

1½ teaspoons vanilla extract

½ teaspoon orange flower water

¾ teaspoon finely grated orange peel

4 large eggs

pure soybean oil, for deep-frying

confectioners' sugar, for
sifting over the fried puffs

serving: about 30 puffs, if made from rounded teaspoons of dough, or about 20 puffs, if made by level tablespoon-size portions of dough

Have two cookie sheets at hand. Line a cookie sheet with several thicknesses of paper towels and set aside.

For the dough, sift the flour and salt onto a sheet of waxed paper.

Place the water, granulated sugar, and chunks of butter in a heavy, medium-size saucepan (preferably enameled cast iron or tin-lined copper). Place over high heat and bring to the boil. As soon as the contents of the saucepan reach the boil, immediately remove the saucepan from the heat, add the vanilla extract, orange flower water, orange peel, and sifted mixture (all at once), and mix to form a dough, using a flat wooden paddle. Reduce the heat to low, return the saucepan holding the dough base to the heat, and let the dough "dry out" for 30 seconds to 1 minute, stirring once or twice during this time. Remove the saucepan from the heat. Let the dough stand in the saucepan (still off the heat) for 1 minute. Whisk 3 of the eggs in a small mixing bowl to combine. Continuing off the heat, beat in the whisked eggs in 5 additions, beating until thoroughly incorporated before adding the next portion. (Using a flat wooden paddle for beating in the eggs returns the smoothest mixture.) Scrape down the flat paddle with a rubber spatula after each addition of beaten egg. Beat the remaining egg in a small mixing bowl. Add the remaining egg, a little at a time, to create a dough that is smooth, shiny, and somewhat sticky; it should hold its shape softly in a spoon. On most occasions, the dough will take at least half of the last egg, and sometimes all but a teaspoon or two; this depends on the absorption quality of the flour and atmospheric conditions in your kitchen.

Pour enough oil to rise to a depth of 2 inches into a heavy casserole measuring 9½ to 10 inches in diameter.

Heat the oil to 375 degrees F.

Drop rounded teaspoons or level tablespoons of the dough into the hot oil, about 5 at a time, and fry until golden, gently turning the puffs over carefully. This will take about 3 minutes total frying time for each batch, but the exact time depends on the type of pan you are using and its weight, which affect its ability to maintain a steady temperature. Crowding the pan with too many portions of dough will impede their ability to fry and float easily, possibly creating undercooked beignets.

Transfer the fried puffs to the paper towel–lined baking pan, using a slotted spoon or skimmer, then continue to fry more puffs, a batch at a time. When the puffs have drained, move them to a serving dish and cap the tops with generous siftings of confectioners' sugar. Serve the puffs as soon as they are fried and sugared.

notes

- a little granulated sugar has—forever—been an addition to my beignet dough, for it contributes to the caramelization of the dough's surface on frying
- for beignets soufflés that are exceptionally light, with fragile-crisp exteriors, maximum puff, and moist-airy, tender centers, the egg-enriched paste must be used freshly beaten
- crowding the pot with too many spoonfuls of dough will prevent the puffs from frying correctly (by taking up too much surface area, lowering the temperature of the oil, and creating overly thick, greasy surfaces)
- my 7-inch-diameter FryDaddy Junior makes it easy work to fry a batch of beignets soufflés as it maintains an even 375 degrees F temperature; in this appliance, fry only 4 spoonfuls of dough at a time—perfect for four guests with an appetite for golden, tempting puffs
- a warm sauce made of best-quality apricot preserves is delicious served alongside the puffs (1 cup apricot preserves simmered with ⅓ cup unsweetened apple juice until bubbly, then seasoned with ¼ teaspoon vanilla extract and ¼ teaspoon freshly grated orange peel)
- for oil and frying watch points, see notes, page 182

Dreamy

cakelike bread ✳ sweet powder puffs ✳ like a big sandwich cookie (and proper sandwich cookies, the project version) ✳ chocolate coffee cake deluxe, cinnamon coffee cake deluxe ✳ cheesecake that will make you weak in the knees ✳ cake, fruit, and custard in the relaxed mode ✳ bugged out, blossomed, and pouf-y ✳ yeasty cake in-the-round

Regal

a golden ring of cake

Resplendent. That's an apt description for this savarin, a lustrous and plump band of yeasty cake: buttery, lightly spongy (the better to absorb a syrupy concoction later on), and eggy, with just enough of everything else to make a soft dough that rises impressively and bakes into a winsome ring.

The ring mold typically used for cradling a savarin dough is not excessively deep and comes in a range of capacities, including, for those who just are not satisfied with making one big proper cake, miniature size. Truly die-hard bakers have a secret stash of small savarin molds lurking about their kitchens. I have painstakingly filled mine with the satiny, tacky dough, mold by mold, and this somewhat insane act takes me right back to a point in time in my childhood when I made tiny chocolate cakes for my family of dolls. (Always the baker.) Baby savarins are endearing, and a near-perfect vehicle for highlighting whatever summer fruit is in season—raspberries, peaches, cherries, blackberries, and such—or wintery poached dried fruit. But endurance must rule on that baking day.

The creation of this yeast dough hangs only on the ability to follow a recipe and possess a certain amount of patience while the dough develops. Impatience will tank the recipe. Compassion for the dough will not. This rather loose dough is made by combining a yeast mixture with a whole egg, extra egg yolks (three of them), vanilla (in the form of paste and extract), some sugar, flour, and salt. Softened butter is added by degrees to form a sleek and silky mass. The dough rises at room temperature in a bowl, then again once it is transferred to the mold. The baked savarin—burnished outside, flaxen inside, and so very tender—is treated to brushings of syrup and, later on, to an overlay of apricot glaze. Finally, after all this primping, the savarin is transferred to a serving plate and, somewhere on it, heaps of sweetened cream and fruit take up sweet space as well.

Sigh. Whimper. Moan.

savarin, well-nourished: imbibing syrup, apricot glaze, sweetened cream

For the dough, stir together the yeast, the ¼ teaspoon sugar, and the warm water in a heatproof measuring cup. Allow the mixture to stand until swollen, 6 to 7 minutes.

Whisk 1½ cups of the flour and the salt in a medium-size mixing bowl. In a small mixing bowl, whisk the whole egg, the egg yolks, the 3 tablespoons sugar, the vanilla bean paste (if you are using it), and vanilla extract. Stir in the yeast mixture, then add this to the whisked flour and salt. Combine the ingredients to a firm, shaggy dough stage, leaving any unincorporated flour. Add the softened butter, 2 tablespoons at a time. The dough will look quite rough at this point, and the butter will not be completely dispersed within it. Turn the dough mixture into the bowl of a heavy-duty freestanding electric mixer. Set the bowl in place and attach the flat paddle. Beat on moderately low speed for 2 minutes. Add the remaining ¼ cup flour and continue beating for 5 minutes longer, stopping the machine once or twice to scrape down the mixing bowl and flat paddle. At this point, the dough will be smooth, elastic, glossy, ropy, and very soft. The dough will leave a very streaky film on the sides of the mixing bowl and most of it will ball up on the paddle.

Scrape the dough into a bowl heavily coated with softened unsalted butter, cover tightly with a sheet of food-safe plastic wrap, and let rise at room temperature for 2 hours to 2 hours and 30 minutes, or until doubled in bulk.

Remove and discard the plastic wrap. Compress the dough very lightly with your fingertips. Cover loosely with plastic wrap and let stand for 5 minutes.

In the meantime, film the inside of a 9¼ to 9½-inch savarin mold (1⅞ to 2 inches deep, with a capacity of 5 to 5½ cups) with softened unsalted butter. Lift up the dough, pull it gently to extend it to a long band, then place it in the prepared mold, filling the mold evenly. The mold should be about one-half filled. Gently pat the dough to even it; if the dough is not leveled at this stage, the savarin may rise and bake lopsided. Cover the mold loosely with a buttered sheet of food-safe plastic wrap. Let rise at room temperature for 50 minutes to 1 hour, or until doubled in bulk. The doubled-in-bulk risen dough should fill the pan up to about ¼ inch of the rim (take care to watch for this, for if the dough extends past the rim, it will have over-risen, taste yeasty or overfermented, and may bake out of shape).

(continued on the next page)

eggy vanilla yeast dough

2¼ teaspoons active dry yeast

¼ teaspoon granulated sugar

¼ cup warm (105 to 110 degrees F) water

1¾ cups unsifted bleached all-purpose flour

⅛ teaspoon salt

1 large egg

2 large egg yolks

3 tablespoons granulated sugar

¼ teaspoon vanilla bean paste (optional)

1½ teaspoons vanilla extract

6 tablespoons (¾ stick) unsalted butter, softened

imbibing syrup (page 190)

apricot glaze (page 191)

sweetened cream (page 191)

serving: one 9-inch savarin, creating 10 slices
ahead: best on baking day; or freeze for 2 weeks, defrost, bundle in aluminum foil, and reheat in a preheated 325 degrees F oven for 10 to 15 minutes, then imbibe it with syrup and glaze

Preheat the oven to 350 degrees F in advance of baking.

Remove and discard the sheet of plastic wrap covering the savarin.

Bake the savarin in the preheated oven for 30 minutes, or until set and a golden color on top. The fully baked savarin will show significant oven-spring, between ½ and 1 inch, and pull away slightly from the sides of the mold. Let the savarin stand in the pan on a rack for 5 minutes, then invert onto another cooling rack. Lift off the pan. Cool for 15 minutes.

Set the savarin, still on its cooling rack, on a jellyroll pan or other rimmed sheet pan. Apply the imbibing syrup to the top and sides of the warm savarin, using a wide, soft pastry brush. For the best-tasting cake, use all of the syrup and be patient, waiting for it to soak in before brushing on another layer. Eventually, the savarin will take in all of the syrup. Let the savarin stand for about 1 hour before glazing.

To finish the savarin, warm the prepared apricot glaze. Lightly brush the glaze over the surface, creating a sparkly veneer, using a soft pastry brush.

To serve, carefully transfer the savarin to a serving plate (it will be so beautifully light) and fill the center with the sweetened cream, piling it in oh-so-casually. Or, slice the savarin and accompany each section with a generous spoonful or two of the sweetened cream. Serve the savarin with sliced fresh or poached fruit, or berries, if you wish (see notes).

notes
- a scattering of raspberries, blackberries, or blueberries would add a fruity note to the yeast cake
- once the savarin is glazed, you can decorate the rounded edge with angelica, cut into small diamonds; crystallized violets; or dried, sweetened hibiscus flowers (available packaged from Trader Joe's); all must be made from non-chemically treated, food-safe-genus flowers and/or stems

imbibing syrup

rummy syrup

1 cup granulated sugar

1 cup water, preferably bottled

⅓ cup dark rum

1 teaspoon vanilla extract

serving: about 1 cup
ahead: 3 days

Place the sugar and water in a medium-size saucepan, cover, set over low heat, and warm to dissolve the sugar. Uncover the saucepan, raise the heat to high, bring to the boil, and boil for 3 minutes. Add the rum, stir, and cook at a low boil for 1 to 2 minutes, or until the syrup is lightly condensed to about 1 cup. Remove the syrup from the heat. Immediately stir in the vanilla extract. Tip out the syrup into a heatproof bowl and cool to lukewarm.

Use the syrup on the warm savarin.

notes
- kirschwasser, a clear, cherry-flavored brandy, is a traditional addition to the sugar syrup, but I prefer rum; here, the rum is added after the sugar syrup solution has condensed (once the requisite boiling is completed) and the mixture is allowed to bubble further for 1 to 2 minutes, thus concentrating the flavor
- a lightly condensed syrup, rather than a watery one, is preferable for the way that it maintains the integrity of the crumb of the baked savarin as it soaks into the yeast cake
- if the syrup is made in advance and refrigerated (in an airtight container), reheat it in a heavy saucepan before applying it to the surface of the baked savarin

apricot glaze

Place the jam and water in a small, heavy saucepan. Stir, set over moderate heat, and bring to the simmer. Simmer the jam mixture for 2 minutes, then remove from the heat.

Turn the jam mixture into a stainless steel strainer set over a heatproof nonreactive bowl, and smooth it through, using a heatproof spatula, leaving the solids in the strainer.

To use the glaze now, return it to a clean, dry saucepan. Bring to the simmer. Simmer for 30 seconds, then use immediately. Or, refrigerate the cooled glaze in an airtight container.

notes
- to use the prepared, refrigerated glaze, scrape it into a small, heavy saucepan, bring to the simmer over moderate heat, simmer for 30 seconds, then apply it to the syrup-enhanced savarin

shimmery glaze

1⅓ cups best-quality apricot jam

1 tablespoon water

serving: about ⅞ cup
ahead: 2 weeks

sweetened cream

Chill a set of beaters and a medium-size mixing bowl for at least 45 minutes.

Pour the heavy cream into the bowl and whip until just beginning to mound.

Sprinkle over the sugar and continue whipping for 2 minutes longer, or until the cream forms soft, gently firm drifts. By hand, blend in the vanilla extract. Serve the cream immediately in large dollops.

notes
- using superfine sugar, rather than confectioners' sugar (which contains a small percentage of cornstarch), gives the whipped cream a smoother, less chalky, sensation on the tongue

soft and floaty vanilla cream

1½ cups cold heavy cream

3 tablespoons superfine sugar

1¼ teaspoons vanilla extract

serving: about 3 cups
ahead: freshly whipped

all tucked in

You could say that I am babka-obsessed, haunted by the moist denseness of a buttery yeast dough bundling in dips and folds around a filling of chocolate or cinnamon sugar. This statement is confirmed by the fact that I have at least one type, cut into giant slices, in my freezer and another one about to be assembled—any time now—in a mixing bowl.

Babka, the chocolate-pumped version: hidden in a buttery yeast dough, within its eggy, gathered and spiraled wrinkles, is a surprise of bittersweet chocolate. In other versions, some have had the babka baked in a loaf pan, bulked up with nuts and spices, and touched with cinnamon. I love babka plaited and entwined with cinnamon, but I also love to pull apart those big spirals and taste chocolate. Allowing chocolate to have sovereign power over all other tastes in a yeast dough is a powerful act. Caught up in the coil of dough is a full six ounces of good bittersweet chocolate, chopped and drawn into the expanse. A brownie filling variation follows: it makes good use of a few bar cookies (stash five or six of them in the freezer) by breaking them into large crumbly pieces and tossing those with the chopped chocolate.

The dough is at the same time moist, butter-packed, and light, providing a gripping surface for the filling. While the coffee cake can be baked free-form or in loaves (a delight, no matter the shape), it is best and easiest to assemble the individual sections in deep, round baking pans. If you are concealing the surface with the vanilla butter crumb topping, a wider rather than narrower sweep is preferable. Anyone found hanging about the kitchen while the sweet bakes and cools will find it hard not to break into it once it is unmolded from the baking pan, before it cools down. Admittedly, the babka does not cut cleanly at that time, making an utter mess of the knife and surrounding bread, but it lures nonetheless. The only resolution to this is to make two babkas (this recipe obliges nicely)—one for demolishing and another to admire and eat in a respectable way.

Babka, the defiantly cinnamon versions: while the chocolate babka is the sweet bread I have loved for years, two much older coffee cakes, chronologically speaking, draw my attention whenever my breakfast bread supplies become depleted. It is then that I go for either interpretation: the whirly twists baked in two round pans; the morning cake baked in a grand tube pan. Both are wonderfully appealing, but the latter, with its meandering eddies and veins of spice meshed in moist yeasty cake and baked in one big pan, is my idea of a great "birthday breakfast cake." Why should a birthday cake appear only at dessert time?

"All tucked in"—this refers to both the chocolate or the expanse of cinnamon sugar enclosed in a rich yeast bread, and to the best way to enjoy the sweet: pull away a fresh hunk, place on a big napkin, climb into bed, perch yourself upright on several pillows, pull up the blanket, and nibble away. Day or night. And watch those crumbs.

chocolate babka

butter and egg yeast dough

sponge

3 teaspoons active dry yeast

½ teaspoon granulated sugar

½ cup warm (105 to 110 degrees F) water

⅓ cup plus 3 tablespoons unsifted
unbleached all-purpose flour

2 tablespoons granulated sugar

finishing dough

4 large eggs

2 tablespoons granulated sugar

2 teaspoons vanilla extract

1 teaspoon salt

1¾ cups unsifted bleached
all-purpose flour

1½ cups unsifted unbleached
all-purpose flour

½ pound (16 tablespoons or 2 sticks)
cool unsalted butter, cut into
tablespoon-size chunks

chocolate butter filling

6 tablespoons (¾ stick) unsalted butter,
softened

pinch of salt

½ cup confectioners' sugar

6 ounces bittersweet chocolate,
finely chopped

(continued on the next page)

For the sponge, stir together the yeast, the ½ teaspoon granulated sugar, and the warm water in a heatproof measuring cup. Allow the mixture to stand until swollen, 6 to 7 minutes.

Place the ⅓ cup plus 3 tablespoons unbleached flour and the 2 tablespoons granulated sugar in a medium-size mixing bowl and stir in the yeast mixture. Mix well. Cover with a sheet of food-safe plastic wrap and let stand for 40 minutes, or until the sponge is bubbly and doubled in bulk.

For the finishing dough, whisk the eggs, 2 tablespoons granulated sugar, vanilla extract, and salt in a medium-size mixing bowl. Place 1½ cups of the bleached flour and all of the unbleached flour in the bowl of a heavy-duty freestanding electric mixer. Add the egg mixture. Pour and scrape the yeasty sponge mixture over and stir to form a shaggy dough. Set the bowl in place and attach the flat paddle. Mix the dough on moderately low speed for 2 minutes, or until well-blended, stopping the mixer once or twice to scrape down the sides of the mixing bowl and paddle. Remove the flat paddle and replace with the dough hook. Beat in the butter, 2 tablespoons at a time, doing so by stopping the machine first before adding the butter. Stop the machine from time to time to scrape down the sides of the mixing bowl and the dough hook, using a sturdy rubber spatula. Beat the dough on moderate speed for 2 minutes. Sprinkle over the remaining ¼ cup bleached flour and beat for 2 to 3 minutes longer. The dough should be smooth, satiny, and pull-y at this point. The finished dough will almost clean the sides of the mixing bowl, leaving a streaky film.

Scrape the dough into a bowl heavily coated with softened unsalted butter, lightly turn to coat all sides in a film of butter, cover tightly with a sheet of food-safe plastic wrap, and let rise at cool room temperature for 2 hours and 30 minutes, or until doubled in bulk.

Remove and discard the sheet of plastic wrap. Lightly compress the dough by folding it over itself while compressing it at the same time; this will take three fold-over motions. Enclose the dough with a buttered sheet of food-safe plastic wrap (all areas of dough exposed to the plastic wrap must touch a buttered surface or the dough will stick to it and not lift off cleanly), set on a cookie sheet, and refrigerate for 1 hour and 45 minutes to 2 hours. The dough should be lightly chilled, but not cold-rock-hard.

For the filling, place the butter, salt, and confectioners' sugar in a small bowl and beat for 1 to 2 minutes, using a hand-held electric mixer. Have the chopped chocolate at hand.

To form the babkas, remove the dough from its plastic wrapping. Roll out the dough on a lightly floured work surface to a sheet measuring about 15 by 17 inches. Using the filling ingredients, spread the sweetened butter on the surface of the rolled-out dough and sprinkle on the chocolate in an even layer. Press down lightly on the chocolate. Fold in ¾ inch of each edge, pressing down on the folded-over edges. Roll the dough into a tight jellyroll and seal the long seam end by pinching it lightly between your thumb and forefinger. Plump up the roll of dough by patting it with your hands so that it measures 17 inches in length. Carefully transfer the roll to a cookie sheet and refrigerate for 30 minutes (it is unnecessary to cover it at this point).

Coat the inside of two round 9-inch cake pans (3 inches deep) with softened unsalted butter.

Cut the roll in half, then cut each half into 7 even-size pieces, using a large chef's knife. (Avoid using a serrated knife for this procedure.) Plump up the cut spirals. Place a spiral of dough in the center of each pan, then circle each spiral with a ring of 6 spirals. Cover each pan with a buttered sheet of food-safe plastic wrap and let stand at cool room temperature for 2 hours and 45 minutes (if you are finishing the coffee cakes with the optional vanilla butter crumbs) or for 3 hours (if you are omitting the topping, noting that the plainer babka finishes the last 30 minutes of the rise without the plastic wrap covering).

For the crumb topping (if you are using it), whisk the flour, sugar, and salt in a medium-size mixing bowl. Drizzle over the melted butter-vanilla mixture and, using your fingertips, crumble the mixture firmly to create a moist and sandy mass. Break up the mixture into small crumbs. Remove and discard the sheets of plastic wrap covering the babkas, and sprinkle the crumbs on top (without mashing down the surface of the spirals), dividing them evenly between the pans. Let the crumb-topped babkas stand, uncovered, for 15 minutes to complete the final rise.

If you are not using the topping, remove and discard the plastic wrap covering the babkas after 2½ hours, leaving them uncovered for the final 30 minutes of rising time.

Preheat the oven to 350 degrees F in advance of baking.

Bake the babkas in the preheated oven for 50 minutes to 1 hour, or until nicely risen, set, and golden. Cool the babkas in the pans on racks for 10 minutes. Carefully invert each babka onto another cooling rack. Lift off the pans, and invert the babkas again to stand right side up. Serve the babkas very fresh, at room temperature.

(continued on the next page)

vanilla butter crumb topping (optional)

⅔ cup unsifted bleached all-purpose flour

⅔ cup granulated sugar

large pinch of salt

6 tablespoons (¾ stick) unsalted butter, melted but still warm, and blended with 1 teaspoon vanilla extract

serving: two 9-inch coffee cakes, creating about 8 slices each
ahead: best on baking day; or freeze for 1 month, defrost, bundle in aluminum foil, and reheat in a preheated 300 degrees F oven for 12 minutes

notes

- the pure tastes of the chocolate and butter reign in the filling, unadulterated by spices or chopped nuts: use a good bittersweet chocolate in the 65% cacao range
- confectioners' sugar is used in the filling for creaming with the butter, making for a lighter, less gritty counterpoint to the chocolate
- the optional topping gives the finished babkas an uneven, pebbly surface as it weighs down the dough here and there (part of the charm of a very moist streusel), so be sure to sprinkle most of the crumbs on the top of the dough spirals, rather than in borders between them; without the topping, the spirals bake into plumper hillocks
- be sure not to underbake the babkas or the interiors will be pasty
- use a finely serrated knife to cut the coffee cakes

"brownie" babka

butter and egg yeast dough, prepared through sponge and finishing dough, taken through the complete refrigeration after the first rise (see page 194)

brownie chocolate butter filling

6 tablespoons (¾ stick) unsalted butter, softened

pinch of salt

⅓ cup confectioners' sugar

6 ounces bittersweet chocolate, finely chopped

1 cup small (½ inch) hand-crumbled pieces of moist chocolate fudge brownies (such as my *edge-of-darkness bars*, page 176, or my *dark shadows*, page 342)

(continued on the next page)

For the filling, beat the butter, salt, and confectioners' sugar in a small mixing bowl until smooth, 1 to 2 minutes. Blend in the bittersweet chocolate. Have the brownie crumbles at hand.

To form the babkas, remove the refrigerated dough from its plastic wrapping. Roll out the dough on a lightly floured work surface to a sheet measuring about 15 by 17 inches. Using the filling ingredients, spread the sweetened butter on the surface of the rolled-out dough and sprinkle on the chocolate and brownie crumbles in an even layer. Press down lightly on the chocolate-brownie pieces. Fold in ¾ inch of each edge, pressing down on the folded-over edges. Roll the dough into a tight jellyroll and seal the long seam end by pinching it lightly between your thumb and forefinger. Plump up the roll of dough by patting it with your hands so that it measures 17 inches in length. Carefully transfer the roll to a cookie sheet and refrigerate for 30 minutes (it is unnecessary to cover it at this point).

Coat the inside of two round 9-inch cake pans (3 inches deep) with softened unsalted butter.

Cut the roll in half, then cut each half into 7 even-size pieces, using a large chef's knife. (Avoid using a serrated knife for this procedure.) Plump up the cut spirals. Place a spiral of dough in the center of each pan, then circle each spiral with a ring of 6 spirals. Cover each pan with a buttered sheet of food-safe plastic wrap and let stand at cool room temperature for 2 hours and 45 minutes (if you are finishing the coffee cakes with the optional vanilla butter crumb topping) or for 3 hours (if you are omitting the topping, noting that the plainer babka finishes the last 30 minutes of the rise without the plastic wrap covering).

For the crumb topping (if you are using it), whisk the flour, sugar, and salt in a medium-size mixing bowl. Drizzle over the melted butter-vanilla mixture and, using your fingertips, crumble the mixture firmly to create a moist and sandy mass. Break up the mixture into small crumbs. Remove and discard the sheets of plastic wrap covering the babkas, and sprinkle the crumbs on top (without mashing down the surface of the spirals), dividing them evenly between the pans. Let the crumb-topped babkas stand, uncovered, for 15 minutes to complete the final rise.

If you are not using the topping, remove and discard the plastic wrap covering the babkas after 2½ hours, leaving them uncovered for the final 30 minutes of rising time.

Preheat the oven to 350 degrees F in advance of baking.

Bake the babkas in the preheated oven for 50 minutes to 1 hour, or until nicely risen, set, and golden. Cool the babkas in the pans on racks for 10 minutes. Carefully invert each babka onto another cooling rack. Lift off the pans, and invert the babkas again to stand right side up. Serve the babkas very fresh, at room temperature.

notes
- make the brownie crumbles by trimming away any firmer, crusty edges from good fudge brownies and crumble them roughly with your fingertips; or, reduce bars or squares to small, irregular pieces on a chopping surface, using a large chef's knife, turning the brownies into ½-inch-long irregular crumbles
- be sure not to underbake the babkas or the interiors will be pasty and the sides may collapse
- refrigerating the brownie squares or bars before reducing them to crumbles is the easiest way to work with the bar cookies

vanilla butter crumb topping (optional)

⅔ cup unsifted bleached all-purpose flour

⅔ cup granulated sugar

large pinch of salt

6 tablespoons (¾ stick) unsalted butter, melted but still warm, and blended with 1 teaspoon vanilla extract

serving: two 9-inch coffee cakes, creating about 8 slices each
ahead: best on baking day; or freeze for 1 month, defrost, bundle in aluminum foil, and reheat in a preheated 300 degrees F oven for 12 minutes

babka pan twist

For the dough, stir together the yeast, the ½ teaspoon sugar, and the warm water in a heatproof measuring cup. Allow the mixture to stand until swollen, 6 to 7 minutes.

In the meantime, place the milk and the ¾ cup sugar in a small saucepan, set over moderately low heat, and warm for 5 minutes; the sugar will not have dissolved completely. Remove from the heat, whisk well, scrape into a medium-size heatproof mixing bowl, and whisk in the vanilla extract. Add the chunks of butter and stir, now and again, until the mixture cools to tepid; the butter need not melt entirely. Blend in the beaten egg yolks and the yeast mixture.

In a large mixing bowl, whisk 3 cups of the flour and the salt. Pour the butter-egg yolk-yeast mixture over the flour and salt, and stir to combine, using a wooden spoon or flat wooden paddle. The mixture will resemble a thick batter. Let the mixture stand, uncovered, for 7 minutes. Add the remaining 3 cups flour in 2 additions, mixing after each addition; after the second addition, the dough will be moist in some sections and shaggy in other sections, and patches of unincorporated flour will remain—normal at this point in the development of the dough.

Turn the dough mixture (including all patchy pieces and any remaining unincorporated flour) out onto a work surface. Bring the dough together by kneading lightly for about 2 minutes. It will be sticky in the beginning, but use a pastry scraper to move the dough as you are kneading it. Knead the dough for 5 minutes longer, at which point it will be smooth, with a buttery feel. The properly kneaded dough will be somewhat firm to the touch.

Turn the dough into a bowl heavily coated with softened unsalted butter, lightly turn to coat all sides in a film of butter, make several cuts in the dough with a pair of kitchen scissors, cover tightly with a sheet of food-safe plastic wrap, and let rise at cool room temperature for 2 hours and 30 minutes, or until doubled in bulk.

Uncover the dough and discard the plastic wrap. Compress the dough lightly, using your fingertips. Enclose the dough in lightly buttered sheets of food-safe plastic wrap and refrigerate for 12 hours, or up to 24 hours. During this time, the dough will expand to a puffy, inflated pillow—allow enough clearance space above it on the refrigerator shelf to accommodate this rise.

Film the inside of two round 9-inch cake pans (3 inches deep) with nonstick oil spray.

Roll out the dough on a lightly floured work surface to a sheet measuring about 15 by 17 inches. Using the filling ingredients, spread the softened butter on the surface of the rolled-out dough and sprinkle on the cinnamon sugar. Fold in ¾ inch of each edge, pressing down lightly on the folded-over edges, and roll the dough tightly into a fat log. Pinch the long seam end to seal, using your fingertips. Extend the log to a length of 20 inches by rolling carefully with the palms of your hands on the work surface. Cut the roll in half. Pinch the two cut edges to seal. Extend each log to a length measuring 13 inches, again rolling it lightly on the work surface with the palms of your hands. Twist each log into a corkscrew shape (about 6 twists), then form into a tight knotty round. The diameter of the round will measure about 6 inches.

Using the coating ingredients, one at a time place the knotted round in the bowl of melted butter and turn to coat it; carefully transfer the coated twist to the bowl of cinnamon sugar and turn to enrobe it. Place each coated twist in the center of the prepared baking pan. There should be about 1½ inches of space between the round of dough and the sides of the pan at this point.

Cover each pan of coffee cake loosely with a sheet of food-safe plastic wrap. Let the coffee cakes rise at cool room temperature for 2 hours to 2 hours and 30 minutes, or until almost doubled in bulk (see page 6 to reference this stage).

Preheat the oven to 350 degrees F in advance of baking.

Remove and discard the sheets of plastic wrap covering the coffee cakes.

Bake the coffee cakes in the preheated oven for 50 minutes to 1 hour, or until baked through and set. Place the pans on racks and let stand for 10 minutes. Carefully invert the coffee cakes onto other cooling racks. Lift off each pan, then invert the coffee cakes again to stand right side up. Store in airtight cake keepers.

notes
• if this type of dough (so rich in butter and egg yolks) is allowed to over-rise (that is, beyond almost doubled in bulk), the coffee cakes may collapse slightly during baking
• be sure not to underbake the babkas or the interiors will be pasty and the sides may collapse
• use a finely serrated knife to cut the coffee cakes

cinnamon babka morning cake

egg yolk and butter yeast dough

4 teaspoons active dry yeast

¼ teaspoon granulated sugar

¼ cup warm (105 to 110 degrees F) water

½ cup half-and-half

¼ cup milk

½ cup granulated sugar

2½ teaspoons vanilla extract

12 tablespoons (1½ sticks) unsalted butter, cut into chunks, softened

6 large egg yolks, lightly beaten

5 cups unsifted bleached all-purpose flour

1¼ teaspoons salt

butter and cinnamon-sugar filling

8 tablespoons (1 stick) unsalted butter, softened

1 cup granulated sugar blended with 3 tablespoons ground cinnamon

butter and cinnamon-sugar coating

6 tablespoons (¾ stick) unsalted butter, melted, cooled to tepid, and placed in a mixing bowl

¾ cup plus 1 tablespoon granulated sugar blended with 2 tablespoons ground cinnamon, and placed in a mixing bowl

serving: one 10-inch coffee cake, creating 16 slices
ahead: best on baking day; or freeze for 1 month, defrost, bundle in aluminum foil, and reheat in a preheated 325 degrees F oven for 15 minutes

For the dough, stir together the yeast, the ¼ teaspoon sugar, and the warm water in a heatproof measuring cup. Allow the mixture to stand until swollen, 6 to 7 minutes.

In the meantime, place the half-and-half, milk, and the ½ cup sugar in a small saucepan, set over moderately low heat, and warm until the sugar has dissolved. Remove from the heat, whisk well, scrape into a medium-size heatproof mixing bowl, and whisk in the vanilla extract. Add the chunks of butter and stir, now and again, until the mixture cools to tepid; the butter need not melt entirely. Blend in the beaten egg yolks and the yeast mixture.

In a large mixing bowl, whisk 3 cups of the flour and the salt. Pour the yeast-liquid-butter-egg yolk mixture over the flour and salt, and stir to combine, using a wooden spoon or flat wooden paddle. The mixture will resemble a thick batter. Let the mixture stand, uncovered, for 5 minutes. Add the remaining 2 cups flour, one-third at a time, mixing after each addition. The dough will be shaggy in parts, and somewhat moist in patchy sections.

Turn the dough mixture (including all unincorporated flour and patchy pieces) out onto a work surface. Bring the dough together by kneading lightly for about 2 minutes, using a pastry scraper to move the dough along. In the beginning, the dough will be sticky. Continue kneading for 3 minutes longer; at this point the dough will come together and begin to smooth out. Let the dough rest for 4 minutes, then knead for 5 minutes longer. Now the dough should be smooth, with a satiny feel to it.

Turn the dough into a bowl heavily coated with softened unsalted butter, lightly turn to coat all sides in a film of butter, make several cuts in the dough with a pair of kitchen scissors, cover tightly with a sheet of food-safe plastic wrap, and let rise at cool room temperature for 2 hours and 30 minutes, or until doubled in bulk.

Uncover the dough and discard the plastic wrap. Turn the dough onto a work surface and let stand for 2 minutes.

Film the inside of a 10-inch Bundt pan (4½ inches deep, with a capacity of 15 cups) with nonstick oil spray.

Roll out the dough on a lightly floured work surface to a sheet measuring 16 by 16 inches. Using the filling ingredients, spread the softened butter on the surface of the sheet of dough and sprinkle on the cinnamon sugar.

Fold in ¾ inch of each edge, press the edges down lightly, and roll the dough tightly into a fat log. Pinch the long seam to seal, using your fingertips. Twist the log into a corkscrew shape 6 times, by twisting half of the dough 3 times on one end and the other half 3 times on the other end.

Using the coating ingredients, place the twist in the bowl of melted butter, tucking it in here and there just to situate it, and turn to coat it in the butter. Carefully transfer the coated twist to the bowl of cinnamon sugar and turn it to enrobe it thoroughly. Place the coated twist in the prepared baking pan, circling it around to fit. Gently pat down the top of the twist to form an even top layer. If the top layer is irregular, the babka will rise unevenly—this is not a tragedy, but be as careful as possible to avoid creating a hilly mound or section. Crumble any of the remaining moist and sandy coating mixture lurking in the mixing bowl over the top of the coffee cake.

Cover the coffee cake loosely with a sheet of food-safe plastic wrap. Let the coffee cake rise at cool room temperature for 1 hour and 30 minutes, or until almost doubled in bulk (see page 6 to reference this stage).

Preheat the oven to 350 degrees F in advance of baking.

About 5 minutes before baking the coffee cake, place a large rimmed baking sheet on the oven rack. The purpose of placing the pan on a baking sheet is two-fold: to moderate the heat and catch any butter driplets that might cascade over the sides of the baking pan.

Remove and discard the sheet of plastic wrap covering the coffee cake.

Bake the coffee cake on the baking sheet in the preheated oven for 55 minutes to 1 hour, or until baked through and set. The baked coffee cake will pull away slightly from the sides of the baking pan. Place the pan on a cooling rack and let stand for 10 minutes. Carefully invert the coffee cake onto another cooling rack. Lift off the pan. Cool the coffee cake for at least 45 minutes before slicing and serving. Store in an airtight cake keeper.

notes
• if this dough (so rich in egg yolks) is allowed to rise beyond the "almost doubled in bulk" stage, the top of the coffee cake may compress slightly during baking
• use a finely serrated knife to cut the coffee cake

bouffant

It is always so much fun to have a batter take off (when it should)—skyrocket in a pan, rise to a lofty dome, and break into pretty tufted poufs. An uncomplicated popover batter, whisked with a smack of freshly grated Parmesan and Gruyère cheeses or a sweet flash of spice, does just that, reaching to great crusty-eggy heights in individual baking cups.

The basic components—flour, whole eggs, melted butter, and milk—form a simple backdrop for a selection of sweet or savory flavorings. It's easy to come up with a laundry list of possible additions: sweetened shredded coconut; a mingling of chopped fresh herbs; or bits of smoked protein, such as crispy shards of bacon or moist flecks of ham. Popovers in the realm of the zesty are just made for serving with roasted meats or poultry. Those that are confectionlike and amply topped with confectioners' sugar or glazed would make a fine breakfast or brunch bread, and I have been making both kinds for more than twenty years, giving the recipes to everyone who has tasted them.

To bring a batch of popovers—sweet and savory alike—to the next level, I think it's fun to dramatize the flavor. For savory popovers, such as my *parmesan and gruyère popovers,* you can sprinkle a little extra finely-grated Parmesan on the top of the hot breads just as they are pulled from the oven for a lush finish. My favorite deluxe treatment for the *cinnamon breakfast popovers* is to omit the confectioners' sugar and cinnamon sifting mixture and, instead, paint on a confectioners' sugar glaze. To do this, sift ½ cup confectioners' sugar and ¼ teaspoon ground cinnamon into a small mixing bowl, then whisk in 1 tablespoon cold water or milk and add a few drops of vanilla extract (if you like); the mixture should be loosely fluid enough to paint on the top of the warm popovers, using a pastry brush. (The exact texture of the painting glaze may fluctuate due to the amount of cornstarch present in the confectioners' sugar and the atmospheric conditions of the day, and you can make a small adjustment easily by blending in additional confectioners' sugar or liquid. Remember, though, that this is a rustic, naturally simple topping.)

Full credit goes to the late Michael Field, whose words and methods instruct that it is just fine—if not preferable—to let the batter stand for 30 minutes (I refrigerate the batter at this stage) and to preheat the pans before baking, all with a view toward establishing a big rise and accompanying crusty-on-the-outside, custardy-on-the-inside texture. If you need bread on the table in a reasonably short window of time, simply memorize a sweet or savory popover formula.

parmesan and gruyère popovers

cheese batter

1 cup unsifted bleached all-purpose flour

¼ teaspoon salt

½ teaspoon smoked sweet paprika

⅛ teaspoon cayenne pepper

1 cup milk

2 large eggs

3 tablespoons unsalted butter, melted and cooled to tepid

3 tablespoons freshly grated Parmesan cheese

2 tablespoons freshly grated Gruyère cheese

serving: 6 popovers
ahead: best on baking day

For the batter, whisk the flour, salt, paprika, and cayenne pepper in a medium-size mixing bowl. Whisk the milk, eggs, and melted butter in a small mixing bowl. Pour the milk and egg mixture over the dry ingredients and combine to form a batter, using a whisk (this will be accomplished in about 15 strokes). The batter will be slightly lumpy. Refrigerate the batter, covered with a sheet of food-safe plastic wrap, for 30 minutes (or up to 3 hours).

Preheat the oven to 400 degrees F in advance of baking.

Film the bottom only of 6 large popover cups (6 cups to a pan, each cup measuring 3 inches in diameter [interior diameter, minus the lip; 3¾ inches in diameter if including the lip] and 2½ inches deep, with a capacity of ⅔ cup) with nonstick oil spray made for high-heat cooking. Ten minutes before baking, place the prepared popover cups in the preheated oven.

To assemble the popovers, sprinkle the Parmesan and Gruyère over the batter and mix to combine, using a flexible rubber spatula.

Quickly and carefully, remove the pan from the oven. Divide the batter evenly among the prepared popover cups.

Place the popovers in the preheated oven, immediately raise the oven temperature to 425 degrees F, and bake for 30 minutes, or until risen, set, and deeply golden. The centers will remain slightly custardy. Resist the temptation to open the oven before 20 minutes, or the rise of the popovers will be compromised. Let the popovers stand in the pan on a cooling rack for 1 minute, remove them to a breadbasket or platter, and serve.

notes

- this batter doubles beautifully, creating 12 "small" popovers; the use of the word "small" is somewhat deceiving, as even the batter divided among 12 cups makes generously sized popovers; small popover cups are available interconnected as one "tray" (12 cups to a pan, each cup measuring 2¼ inches in diameter [interior diameter, minus the lip; 3 inches in diameter if including the lip] and 2 inches deep, with a capacity of ⅓ cup plus 1 tablespoon)
- for larger, very dramatic popovers, double the recipe and divide the batter among 10 large popover cups (two pans, 6 cups to a pan, each cup measuring 3 inches in diameter [interior diameter, minus the lip; 3¾ inches in diameter if including the lip] and 2½ inches deep, with a capacity of ⅔ cup); bake the popovers as directed for 20 minutes, at 425 degrees F, then at 400 degrees F for 12 minutes longer
- remember that the small-cup popover cup pan houses 12 popovers in total, whereas the large-cup popover cup pan houses 6 popovers in total

cinnamon breakfast popovers

For the batter, whisk the flour, salt, and cinnamon in a medium-size mixing bowl. Whisk the milk, eggs, melted butter, superfine sugar, and vanilla extract in a small mixing bowl. Pour the milk and egg mixture over the dry ingredients and combine to form a batter, using a whisk (this will be accomplished in about 15 strokes). The batter will be slightly lumpy. Refrigerate the batter, covered with a sheet of food-safe plastic wrap, for 30 minutes (or up to 3 hours).

Preheat the oven to 400 degrees F in advance of baking.

Film the bottom only of 6 large popover cups (6 cups to a pan, each cup measuring 3 inches in diameter [interior diameter, minus the lip; 3¾ inches in diameter if including the lip] and 2½ inches deep, with a capacity of ⅔ cup) with nonstick oil spray made for high-heat cooking. Ten minutes before baking, place the prepared popover cups in the preheated oven.

Quickly and carefully, remove the pan from the oven. Divide the batter evenly among the prepared popover cups.

Place the popovers in the preheated oven, immediately raise the oven temperature to 425 degrees F, and bake for 25 to 30 minutes, or until risen, set, and deeply golden. The centers will remain slightly custardy. Resist the temptation to open the oven before 20 minutes, or the rise of the popovers will be compromised. Let the popovers stand in the pan on a cooling rack for 1 minute, then dust the tops of the popovers with the cinnamon-seasoned confectioners' sugar (it is easiest to do this by placing the mixture in a sifter or small strainer), remove them to a breadbasket or platter, and serve.

notes
- superfine sugar is used in the popover batter for its ability to dissolve quickly and evenly
- this batter doubles beautifully, creating 12 "small" popovers; the use of the word "small" is somewhat deceiving, as even the batter divided among 12 cups makes generously sized popovers; small popover cups are available interconnected as one "tray" (12 cups to a pan, each cup measuring 2¼ inches in diameter [interior diameter, minus the lip; 3 inches in diameter if including the lip] and 2 inches deep, with a capacity of ⅓ cup plus 1 tablespoon)
- for larger, very dramatic popovers, double the recipe and divide the batter among 10 large popover cups (two pans, 6 cups to a pan, each cup measuring 3 inches in diameter [interior diameter, minus the lip; 3¾ inches in diameter if including the lip] and 2½ inches deep, with a capacity of ⅔ cup); bake the popovers as directed for 20 minutes, at 425 degrees F, then at 400 degrees F for 12 minutes longer

cinnamon batter

1 cup unsifted bleached all-purpose flour

¼ teaspoon salt

1 teaspoon ground cinnamon

1 cup milk

2 large eggs

3 tablespoons unsalted butter, melted and cooled to tepid

2 tablespoons plus 1 teaspoon superfine sugar

1 teaspoon vanilla extract

½ cup confectioners' sugar sifted with ¼ teaspoon ground cinnamon and whisked to combine, for sifting over the tops of the baked popovers

serving: 6 popovers
ahead: best on baking day

egg whites to the nth degree

Egg whites whipped until amply swollen, given sweetness and structure with granulated sugar, and baked until firm and crisp on the outside and marshmallow-like and chewy on the inside, are a simple delight.

The whole affair—whipping and forming—is sensibly easy and you can get as elemental or frivolous as you like. Wild and irregular shapes—why not? Big, evenly matched twirls and swirls? Beautiful.

Meringues can act as the substructure for a relaxed dessert—spoon over whipped cream and a cascade of fresh berries, especially blackberries, which act as a tart foil. Pretend each is a raft and top with a generous scoop of ice cream and a bold pour of fudge or caramel sauce. Pile them on a big round plate and have them with coffee. Adults will find a certain childlike delight in them and children, well, they will be mesmerized by the fun of the crispy-chewy packages.

monster vanilla meringues

cloud-like vanilla meringue mixture

6 large egg whites

¼ teaspoon cream of tartar

1½ cups granulated sugar

1¼ teaspoons vanilla extract

food-safe paste food color (optional)

granulated sugar, for sprinkling over the unbaked meringues (optional)

confectioners' sugar, for sprinkling over the baked meringues (optional)

serving: about 10 meringues
ahead: 2 days

Preheat the oven to 250 degrees F.

Outfit a 12-inch pastry bag with an open-star tip, either Ateco #823 or Wilton #1M. Or, have two large metal spoons at hand.

Line two heavy cookie sheets or rimmed sheet pans with lengths of ovenproof parchment paper.

For the meringue mixture, place the egg whites in the bowl of a heavy-duty freestanding electric mixer. Set the bowl in place and attach the whip. Whip the egg whites until soft peaks are formed, add the cream of tartar, and continue whipping until firm peaks are formed. Sprinkle over 6 teaspoons of the granulated sugar (taken from the 1½ cups) and whip until stiff peaks are formed. Add the vanilla extract and whip for 1 minute longer on high speed. (If you are tinting the meringue, add a generous fleck of food-safe paste food color by dipping the end of a wooden pick in the color and sinking it into the meringue, then continue whipping for 30 seconds longer.) After 2 minutes of whipping, the meringue mixture will ball up on the whip—this is as it should be. Carefully detach the whip and scrape all of the meringue into the mixing bowl. Sprinkle over all of the remaining sugar and fold it through the whipped egg whites, using a large metal spoon.

If you are using the pastry bag to form the meringues, drop the pastry tip into the bag, twist a little of the bottom part of the bag into the tip, turn back a wide cuff on the pastry bag, and fill about half full with the meringue mixture. Undo the twisted base of the bag, flip up the cuff, lightly smooth down the meringue mixture until it approaches the tip, crimp the remaining part of the bag to close, and twist the top. Pipe out random forms with the meringue—abstract squiggles, curlicues, double-decker S shapes, or large and high turban-like rosettes—onto the prepared baking pans. Leave at least 3 inches around each meringue form. Meringues about 3 inches in diameter and 2 inches high will yield about 10 individual pieces. Refill the bag and continue to pipe out meringues. Or, scoop up large ovals and deposit them on the prepared baking pans, leaving at least 3 inches between each meringue form; you can keep them as is or spread out the meringue in irregular directions to create whirly, spiky forms.

If you want the meringues to have a slightly shiny-glossy surface, sprinkle a little granulated sugar over the surface of each meringue, then let the meringues stand for 4 to 5 minutes to absorb the sugar. However, if you wish to sprinkle the baked meringues with a little confectioners' sugar just before serving, omit this step, as the glossy surface will be generally obscured.

Bake the meringues in the preheated oven for 1 hour and 20 minutes or until set, firm, and a light cream color (if not tinted). If the meringues have been tinted with paste food color, a few areas on the surface will be tawny-colored. Turn off the oven and set the door ajar about 3 inches. Let the meringues stand in the oven for 10 minutes, then remove the baking pans to cooling racks. Cool for 15 minutes. Lift off the meringues to other cooling racks, using a wide offset metal spatula. Cool completely. Store in an airtight tin. Just before serving, sprinkle a little confectioners' sugar over the tops of the meringues, if you wish.

notes

• this is a typical *meringue Suisse* (which is also defined as "ordinary" meringue) and uses granulated sugar alone: a small amount (1 teaspoon for each egg white) is whipped into the egg whites and the remainder is folded through the stiffly beaten whites; note that a slightly different meringue mixture made by stiffly whipping a quantity of granulated sugar into each egg white (2 tablespoons for each large egg white), then folding through confectioners' sugar (¼ cup for each egg white), produces a sweet that bakes lighter (in weight), but can leave a slightly chalky sensation on the tongue, depending on the cornstarch level present in the confectioners' sugar used, so I prefer the style of the mixture in the above recipe; as well, the piped double-decker S shape of the meringue mixture is much more stable when granulated sugar alone is used in creating the sweet

• leaving the meringues to stand for 4 to 5 minutes after sprinkling with the granulated sugar gives their surfaces a certain glimmer

• along with the final fold-through of granulated sugar, the meringue base can be enriched with ⅓ cup almond meal (for this, use almond extract in place of the vanilla); these meringues will be a shade denser and chewier

• the meringue mixture can be flavored with rose water, lavender essence, or *fiori di sicilia* instead of the vanilla extract (use ½ teaspoon rose water, or ¼ teaspoon lavender essence, or ¼ teaspoon *fiori di sicilia*)

• it is unwise to bake meringues on a humid or rainy day because the ambient air will be too moist and cause the meringues to be tacky, rather than crisp and airy

• somewhat smaller versions of these meringues can be sandwiched with firmly whipped heavy cream scented with a few droplets of vanilla extract

• the meringue mixture in the image was tinted with a combination of equal dabs of Cake Craft Standard Lavender and Cake Craft Standard Fuchsia Pink food-safe paste food colors

• a final sprinkling of confectioners' sugar, which should be elfin-light, highlights the surface pattern of the baked meringues nicely

finally, after all these years

My life with cheesecake: flawless cheesecake issued from my mixing bowl, into a baking pan, and sent into the oven was always touch and go on a number of levels. A fissure here, a hairline break there (no sweat?), but usually slices of cake were full of creaminess, suave, and tangy.

Until such time as I was challenged (in the friendliest way possible) by more than one colleague who presented me with a cheesecake recipe that, on baking, produced some strange things: sinking, then breaking open on cooling or lifting, and separating into sections during and after baking; cracking on baking or cracking on cooling; splitting at the edges; baking with dry edges and a wet middle; and curiously enough, baking with wet edges and a dry wide center core. Oh dear. The cheesecake issue was never-ending, thoroughly occupied my waking hours, and so became one of the most significant brainteasers of my baking life. I even had a nightmare or two about wayward cheesecakes (a baker's life continues into sleep and rearranges one's existence, no doubt about it). I even tried to ignore the whole thing.

But…I eventually took on the challenge presented, and finally came up with a way to assure creaminess and guard against the dreaded cracking, odd fissures, random dryness, and so on. I wasn't as upended with the "cracking problem," as others were, as I was with texture and flavor—but I learned that the annoying cracks ultimately pointed to a certain texture malfunction. Pounds and pounds of cream cheese later, I assessed irregularities and ultimately gave up buying those shrimpy eight-ounce packages (like normal people do) in exchange for lugging home

rectangular, I'm-a-big-girl-now, commercial-size three-pound blocks. Six or eight blocks at a time.

Armed with one of my dearest formulas, and a slew more, I took on the components of a cheesecake recipe: ingredients, method, and baking. In the final analysis, it seemed like the cracks—and the problems caused by and attendant to them—are a legitimate source of unending frustration. In an effort to fix the overall "problem" of cracking, the procedure was clear, but the overall baking panorama of this type of cake demanded my time. A cheesecake mixture likes to be mixed until just combined, pockets of air being the enemy if what you are sleuthing for is a densely creamy slice; the main component, the cream cheese, must be softened at room temperature and prebeaten slowly and thoroughly (but not overbeaten or whipped) to ultimate smoothness before any other ingredients are added or little pellets of it will fleck the baked cake. The sugar and eggs must be incorporated only until taken in by the cream cheese. The selection of the pan and the actual, physical act of baking the cake are two intertwined and complex matters. Ruling out a direct water bath—where the pan is submerged in hot water to coddle it, dispersing and modifying the heat in an attempt to shield it from overbaking—allowed me to consider pouring the batter into either a springform pan or plain round cake pan. A prepared springform pan (first buttered then filmed with nonstick oil spray) seemed the best and most direct route, for the cake could be removed without any accompanying gymnastics. No hand-wringing over inverting a luxurious, custardy cream cheese–based cake. Yet the concept of steamy, protective water still lodged in my mind, as did the appropriate oven temperature.

After significant temperature manipulation, it seemed best to bake a 10-inch cheesecake at 300 degrees F. This oven heat was dependent on placing a 13 by 9 by 2-inch baking pan, a little more than halfway filled with boiling water, on the lowest-level rack. The moist internal atmosphere enveloped the custardy mixture (after all, eggs, cream cheese, and sugar make the most decadent custard of all) and allowed it to set correctly.

The idea for using the steamy water bath on the rack under the cake, rather than submerging the pan of batter in it, came to me as a result of working out my favorite recipe for baklava many years ago, when I decided that the prolonged baking of this sweet needed some oven moisture to create just the right texture. The baking pan filled with the cheesecake mixture is then set on a sheet pan. Prior to baking, any bubbles that found their way to the surface after the batter was slowly poured in were pricked with a thin metal skewer or wooden pick to dissipate them. While this may seem an obsessive act, it is, in fact, not: the bubbles—large or minute—can burst during the concluding ten minutes of baking, then form small spiderlike breaks on cooling—at last, one contentious culprit of cracking was driven out. Finally, it was imperative to let the cake cool slowly and purposefully, as sudden changes in temperature could also give rise to cracks during the time that the cheesecake steadied after baking.

After all this, it was on to baking the cheesecake batter in small, one-person-size ovenproof containers to make a kind of cheesecake/pudding arrangement: this is ideal for serving to a crowd and for those who whimper at managing one big hulking cheesecake. In fact, I am so enamored of this treatment that I may forgo baking the batter as a single cheesecake in the future. This way is *so easy*. The mixture sets (and cools) more quickly in ramekins, and is less fiddly to work with. As well, you can top the little devils with a kind of warm chocolate ganache (wo*weee*), and for that treatment, I recommend using the recipe for *very bittersweet chocolate cream spread* (page 160); once the chocolate mixture has been strained and cooled for 30 minutes, carefully pour it over the cooled, cheesecake-filled ramekins. Other embellishments for the individual cheesecakes: warm apricot glaze, spooned over the tops, would create a sweet-tart veneer and a few floaty rosettes of whipped cream piped on the surface would add a texturally creamy top note. Or, offer them straight-out plain, save for a dusting of confectioners' sugar on the edges. The batter remains the same, but the vessel changes in order to yield one diaphanous spoon dessert.

Beware: this is a purist's cheesecake—lightly flavored, stripped of crust, just the immaculate taste of sweetened cream cheese and eggs bolstered by a little heavy cream and vanilla extract. The small amount of lemon juice is a teaser, and is precisely enough to balance out the sugar in the most delicate way possible. This cheesecake is, really, my (delicious) pride and joy.

Preheat the oven to 300 degrees F.

Film the inside of a 10-inch springform pan (2¼ inches deep) with softened unsalted butter, then spray the inside with nonstick oil spray. Or, have 12 ovenproof ramekins (with a capacity of 1 cup or slightly less) at hand; there is no need to treat them prior to filling. Have a 13 by 9 by 2-inch baking pan and large rimmed sheet pan at hand.

For the batter, place the cream cheese in the large bowl of a freestanding electric mixer and beat on low speed until very smooth, about 2 minutes. Add the superfine sugar in 2 additions, beating until just incorporated and no longer than 45 seconds after each portion is added. Blend in the cornstarch (if you are using it). Add 2 of the eggs and beat just until integrated, about 20 seconds. Add 2 more eggs and beat for 20 seconds. Add 2 more eggs and beat for 15 seconds. Add the remaining egg along with the salt, heavy cream, lemon juice, and vanilla extract. Before each new ingredient is added, it is critical to scrape down the sides of the mixing bowl with a rubber spatula to keep the batter as smooth as possible. It should be entirely free of small lumps.

Strain the batter, a little at a time, through a fine-mesh sieve into a large mixing bowl. This is tedious. You can skip this step if you are *absolutely certain* that your batter is perfectly smooth, but I would recommend proceeding with this step in any case, for the smoothest, silkiest texture.

Pour (slowly!) and scrape the batter into the prepared springform pan. Or, if you are using the ramekins, carefully (and slowly!) ladle the batter into the smaller dishes, filling each to ½ inch of the top. In either case, do this at a steady rate, creating as few air bubbles as possible. Inevitably, a few bubbles will lurk on the surface, so dispel them with a wooden pick, to avoid surface breaks or small fissures on the top later on.

Fill the 13 by 9 by 2-inch baking pan a little more than halfway with boiling water and set it on the lowest-level rack of the oven. Set the filled baking pan or the little filled ramekins on the rimmed sheet pan and place on the rack above the pan filled with water.

For the larger single cheesecake, bake it in the preheated oven for 1 hour and 35 minutes. Note what happens to the cheesecake as it bakes at the following points in the baking time: at 50 minutes, a wide center portion

(continued on the next page)

gorgeous and elegant cream cheese batter

3 pounds cream cheese, softened

2¼ cups superfine sugar

1 tablespoon cornstarch (optional, see notes)

7 large eggs

⅛ teaspoon salt

2 tablespoons heavy cream

2 teaspoons freshly squeezed lemon juice

4 teaspoons vanilla extract

confectioners' sugar, for sifting over the cheesecake (optional)

serving: one 10-inch cake, creating about 18 slices, or 10 to 12 individual-serving-size cakes (depending on the capacity of the ramekins)
ahead: 3 days

will still be wobbly; at 1 hour and 5 minutes, a wide circular outer band will have puffed and risen slightly and a 4-inch center portion will be wobbly; at 1 hour and 20 minutes, the cake will have puffed/risen, but a 3-inch center will remain wobbly; at 1 hour and 35 minutes, a 1¼-inch circular band around the edge of the pan will be golden and the center 3 inches will have only the mere suggestion of a wobble. After 1 hour and 35 minutes, turn off the oven, leaving the cheesecake in it for 5 minutes. After 5 minutes, open the oven door and prop it open 2 inches, using a heatproof implement, such as a stainless steel kitchen spoon (not a dinnerware spoon). Cool the cake in the oven with the door ajar for 20 minutes. Remove the cake from the oven and cool in the pan on a cooling rack (removed from the sheet pan) for 1 hour. The edges will be slightly raised and the top flat. Carefully open the hinge on the side of the pan, then close it. Refrigerate the cake in the pan for at least 6 hours (after 6 hours, transfer the cheesecake to an airtight container). Note that prematurely opening the hinge of the pan may cause the top to crack.

For slicing the larger cheesecake, release the hinge of the pan and remove the outer ring, allowing the cake to stand on its circular metal base. Run a long thin knife under hot water, dry thoroughly, and spray lightly with nonstick oil spray. Clean off the knife, leaving only a suggestion of the spray. Slice the cheesecake into triangular wedges for serving.

For the single-serving ramekins, bake them in the preheated oven for 35 minutes, or until set. The baked cheesecakes will puff lightly, then settle slightly on cooling. Turn off the oven, open the oven door, and prop it open 2 inches, using a heatproof implement, such as a large stainless steel kitchen spoon (not a dinnerware spoon). Cool the little cakes in the oven with the door ajar for 5 minutes. Remove the cakes from the oven, transfer the ramekins to cooling racks, and cool to room temperature. Refrigerate the little cakes for 2 hours (after 2 hours, cover the cakes with food-safe plastic wrap or assemble them in a large storage container and cover with a tight-fitting lid). When the cakes are thoroughly chilled, you can spoon warm *apricot glaze* (page 191) or warm *chocolate darkness* on top (page 424). Sift confectioners' sugar over the edges of the large or small cheesecake(s) just before serving, if you wish.

notes
• the texture of the baked cheesecake is extra-satiny and quite creamy when organic eggs are used
• the cornstarch adds a touch of stability to the batter, and is especially useful when baking the larger cheesecake; when included, as a tradeoff, the baked cheesecake is slightly less creamy
• adding and beating the eggs on low speed allows the batter to remain smooth and dense, thus eliminating any enthusiastic inflation during the baking process; this tactic keeps the finished cake moister and creamier, and the texture consistently creamy from the very center core to the outer edge

in the round, fluted

With its golden and open crumb, this bread is nurturing and dramatic, and impossible to resist. The curvaceous turban is light, with a kind of floaty feel to it.

The bread rises impressively (and dramatically) to form a plump crown. The yeasty mixture, built on half-and-half, butter, and eggs—a favorite ingredient threesome of mine—is so simple to put together that you can think about making it, then have it fresh and hot within several hours, for the bread requires only two reasonably short rises and a forty-minute bake. Rough tears or tall and stately slices of freshly baked bread truly captivate when the surfaces are concealed with softened salted butter.

Slices of the bread, a yeasty version of a butter cake, also offer a fine platform for—what else?—my *very bittersweet chocolate cream spread* (page 160). This "bread and butter" arrangement is my idea of morning food.* And don't bother pointing a nutritional finger at me, or think about lecturing me in a letter, because I secretly know that, in good time, you'll be doing the same.

✳ Footnote on healthy eating: I believe in treats, a bowl of steel-cut oats, cooked to porridge-status, or clumps of homemade granola with organic yogurt notwithstanding. But I do love my chocolate and bread+chocolate.

For the dough, stir together the yeast, the ¼ teaspoon granulated sugar, and the warm water in a heatproof measuring cup. Allow the mixture to stand until swollen, 6 to 7 minutes.

In the meantime, place the half-and-half and the ¼ cup granulated sugar in a small, heavy saucepan and set over moderately low heat. When the sugar has dissolved, remove the saucepan from the heat, pour into a medium-size heatproof mixing bowl, and cool to tepid. Blend in the chunks of butter, beaten eggs, vanilla extract, and the yeast mixture. The butter will still be in small pieces at this point.

Place 3 cups of the flour and the salt in a large mixing bowl. Whisk well to integrate the salt. Blend in the butter, half-and-half, egg, and yeast mixture. Mix well to form a soft dough, using a wooden spoon or flat wooden paddle. Add the remaining 1 cup flour and mix until most of the flour is moistened. Turn the dough mixture (and all patches of unabsorbed flour) into the bowl of a heavy-duty freestanding electric mixer. Set the bowl in place and attach the flat paddle. Beat on moderate speed for 7 minutes. At this point, the dough will be exceptionally moist, smooth, and elastic.

Scrape the dough into a bowl heavily coated with softened unsalted butter, cover tightly with a sheet of food-safe plastic wrap, and let rise at room temperature for 1 hour, or until doubled in bulk.

Remove and discard the plastic wrap. Lightly compress the dough and let stand for 5 minutes.

Film the inside of a fluted 9-inch tube pan (4¼ inches deep, with a capacity of 11 cups) with nonstick flour-and-oil spray.

Turn the dough into the prepared baking pan, creating as even a layer as possible and smoothing over the top as best as possible (avoid compressing the dough too much at this point, as it is fine if the top looks rustic, but the surface should be reasonably even).

Cover the pan loosely with a buttered sheet of food-safe plastic wrap. Let the bread rise at room temperature for 40 minutes, or until it almost reaches the top of the pan.

Preheat the oven to 375 degrees F in advance of baking.

(continued on the next page)

butter, egg, and milk yeast dough

2½ teaspoons active dry yeast

¼ teaspoon granulated sugar

¼ cup warm (105 to 110 degrees F) water

¾ cup half-and-half

¼ cup granulated sugar

8 tablespoons (1 stick) unsalted butter, cut into tablespoon-size chunks, softened

3 large eggs, lightly beaten

1 tablespoon vanilla extract

4 cups unsifted bleached all-purpose flour

½ teaspoon salt

butter and sparkling sugar finish (optional)

about 3 tablespoons butter (preferably clarified butter, page 1), melted and still warm

sparkling sugar (plain or a color), for sprinkling on the baked bread

serving: one 9-inch fluted bread, creating about 14 slices
ahead: best on baking day; or freeze for 2 weeks, defrost, bundle in aluminum foil, and reheat in a preheated 300 degrees F oven for 10 minutes

Remove and discard the sheet of plastic wrap covering the bread.

Bake the bread in the preheated oven for 40 minutes, or until a deep golden brown color on top and a hollow sound is emitted from the bread when the top is tapped (do so gently!) with the handle of a wooden spoon. The baked bread will have crested impressively—stunning. Place the pan on a cooling rack and let stand for 10 minutes. Invert the bread onto another cooling rack to stand fluted side up. Lift off the pan. If you wish, brush the top of the bread with the melted butter and top with sprinklings of sparkling sugar. Serve the bread very fresh, warm or at room temperature.

notes
• stand by the mixer for the entire beating times referenced in the procedure
• use a finely serrated knife to cut the bread, or tear the freshly baked bread apart with two big forks

undone

I have always wanted to undo a trifle—to deconstruct it and so preserve the individuality of the ingredients, to release the texture from the thrall of sogginess, reconfigure and highlight the custardy component, and pattern the sweet to embrace a range of sliced fruit and berries.

In the end, the remodeling seems to have made the entire dessert easier to do in stages and, in the main, a lot looser. Relaxed is good. And less tightly contrived is certainly as delicious as any layered concoction.

The cake, once baked and sliced—that forms the support for the fruit and cream and soaks up the pouring custard so deliciously—is made from a fine buttermilk batter. There is a little more cake than you need for composing the dessert for eight guests, so the extra can be enjoyed sliced, lightly toasted, and strategically positioned in the breakfast breadbasket or on the teatime plate.

The floaty custard, less fulsome than a pastry cream, but just as rich in its streamy state, adds moisture to the dessert in a way that the whipped cream accompaniment alone could not. The choice of fruit means that this is definitely a summertime delicacy. I adore the sweet clutter of cake, fruit, custard, and whipped cream happily mingling on one plate. If you are a cagey cook, you'll prepare more custard than needed and really pool it around the fruit and cake. (Serving alert: use wide soup bowls for this and make sure that all guests bring a big appetite for dessert.)

a relaxed trifle, no construction necessary: cake, custard to pour, fruit and cream

To assemble the dessert, sift the confectioners' sugar called for in the cake recipe over the top of the cake. Cut the cake into slices. Have the chilled custard, the fruit, and the cream ready and at hand. For each guest, place a thick slice (or two thinner slices) of cake on a plate or in a shallow bowl, spoon some fruit to the side, pool a little of the custard around the edges, and finish with a hillock of cream. Serve immediately.

cake (below)

custard to pour (page 222)

fruit and cream (page 222)

cake

Preheat the oven to 350 degrees F.

Film the inside of a fluted 10-inch tube pan (4¾ inches deep, with a capacity of 13 to 13½ cups) with nonstick flour-and-oil spray.

For the batter, sift the flour, baking soda, baking powder, and salt onto a sheet of waxed paper.

Cream the butter in the large bowl of a freestanding electric mixer on moderately high speed for 3 minutes. Add the superfine sugar in 3 additions, beating for 1 minute after each portion is added. On moderately low speed, beat in the eggs, one at a time, mixing for 30 seconds after each addition. Blend in the vanilla extract, orange extract, and lemon extract. On low speed, alternately add the sifted ingredients in 3 additions with the buttermilk in 2 additions, beginning and ending with the sifted mixture, and beating just until the particles of flour have been absorbed. Scrape down the sides of the mixing bowl thoroughly with a rubber spatula after each addition.

Spoon the batter into the prepared baking pan. Smooth the top with a rubber spatula.

Bake the cake in the preheated oven for 1 hour, or until risen, set, golden on top, and a wooden pick withdraws clean. The baked cake will pull away slightly from the sides of the pan. If the cake seems to be browning too fast after 45 minutes, lightly tent a sheet of aluminum foil over the top (but avoid pressing down the sides of the foil).

Cool the cake in the pan on a rack for 10 minutes. Invert the cake onto another cooling rack. Lift off the pan. Cool completely. Store in an airtight cake keeper.

buttery buttermilk batter

3 cups unsifted bleached all-purpose flour

½ teaspoon baking soda

¼ teaspoon baking powder

1 teaspoon salt

½ pound (16 tablespoons or 2 sticks) unsalted butter, softened

2 cups superfine sugar

4 large eggs

1½ teaspoons vanilla extract

½ teaspoon orange extract

½ teaspoon lemon extract

1 cup buttermilk

confectioners' sugar, for sifting on top of the baked cake

serving: one 10-inch cake, creating 12 to 14 ample slices
ahead: 2 days

custard to pour

creamy custard sauce

⅓ cup superfine sugar

½ teaspoon arrowroot

pinch of salt

5 large egg yolks, lightly beaten

1½ cups heavy cream, warmed

1 teaspoon vanilla extract

serving: about 1½ cups
ahead: 1 day

Sift the sugar, arrowroot, and salt into a heavy, medium-size saucepan (preferably enameled cast iron). Whisk the sifted mixture to combine thoroughly. Blend in the beaten egg yolks. In small batches, slowly stir in the warmed cream, mixing with a wooden spoon or flat wooden paddle.

Place the saucepan over low heat and cook until the mixture is lightly thickened and coats the back of a spoon, taking care to baby the sauce. The sauce should not even approach the simmer, yet the sauce must be cooked until thickened so that it reaches and maintains a temperature of 160 degrees F. Adjust the heat accordingly. (To test the temperature of the sauce, remove the saucepan from the heat for a moment and, protecting your hands with sturdy, heatproof gloves, tip the pan slightly so that the sauce collects to one side, then quickly test with an instant-read thermometer designed for using with food.)

Strain the sauce through a fine-mesh sieve into a heatproof bowl. Stir in the vanilla extract. Immediately press a sheet of food-safe plastic wrap onto the surface of the sauce. Cool for 20 minutes. Turn the sauce into a clean storage container, cover, and refrigerate until cold, at least 4 hours.

notes
• the sauce can be stored in the refrigerator overnight (up to 1 day), but it usually needs to be restored to pouring consistency by stirring in about 2 tablespoons cold milk

fruit and cream

glossy fruit

¼ cup best-quality apricot or peach preserves (for golden-colored-flesh stone fruits) or best-quality red currant jelly (for blackberries, blueberries, plums, or pluots)

2 tablespoons superfine sugar, or to taste

4 cups berries (red raspberries, golden raspberries, blueberries, or blackberries) or pitted and sliced stone fruits (peaches, nectarines, or pluots)

sweet cream

1½ cups cold heavy cream

3 tablespoons superfine sugar

1 teaspoon vanilla extract

serving: 4 cups sweetened fruit and about 3 cups cream

For all fruits other than the raspberries, combine the preserves or jelly and the sugar in a small, heavy saucepan, set over low heat, and warm the contents just until the sugar has dissolved, stirring briefly once or twice. Turn the mixture into a large nonreactive mixing bowl, cool for 5 minutes, add the fruit, and toss gently. Let the fruit stand for 3 minutes, then adjust the sweetness, lightly mixing in additional sprinkles of superfine sugar as necessary (blackberries, especially, may need extra sweetening). If you have selected the red raspberries or golden raspberries, use them fresh and stellar, as neither needs the enhancement of preserves or sugar.

For the cream, chill a set of beaters and a medium-size mixing bowl for at least 45 minutes. Pour the cream into the bowl and whip until just beginning to mound. Sprinkle over the sugar and vanilla extract, and continue whipping for 2 minutes longer, or until the cream forms soft mounds when a spoon is dipped into and lifted from the cream.

jammy

As a child, I always loved a particular butter cookie my mother brought home for me as a present when I was home sick from school—a little beribboned box of miniature tiered wedding cakes from a caterer's bakery.

These were nutty, tiny, scalloped shortbread cookies with apricot jam between each of three miniature cookie levels. My adult translation of this treat: two recipes, one for a tart and the other for sandwich cookies.

For the tart, a moist and buttery almond-speckled dough that holds a center layer of bubbly apricot preserves bakes into one large and jammy cookie. Even though most bakers would think of it as an in-between-the-seasons tart and a good recipe to know when fresh berries and stone fruits are not available, I bake this one year-round, and especially during summer's picnic season, as it transports neatly in the pan and does not ooze or wither on a humid day. In fact, it just gets better.

A trio of my favorite baking ingredients—butter, almonds, and apricots—is represented in the tart, and in the sandwich cookies as well. Of the two, the cookie recipe is more of an undertaking, but one that can be accomplished over two or three days (make the dough one day, bake the cookies on the next, and fill them on the third day, or bake and assemble on day two) and produces a beautiful tin of baking handiwork. Hint: the tart is less of a project than the cookies, can be made ahead, and is so good that you might consider making two.

Buttery. Jammy. Nutty.

sweet sandwiches: apricot-filled nut cookies

almond cookie dough

3½ cups unsifted bleached all-purpose flour

1½ teaspoons baking powder

1 teaspoon salt

½ teaspoon ground allspice

½ teaspoon ground cinnamon

1 cup almond flour or finely ground almonds

½ pound (16 tablespoons or 2 sticks) unsalted butter, softened

1 cup granulated sugar

2 large eggs

1 teaspoon vanilla extract

1 teaspoon almond extract

apricot cookie filling

2½ cups best-quality apricot preserves

2½ teaspoons water

¼ teaspoon vanilla extract

confectioners' sugar, for sprinkling on the edges of the baked and filled cookies (optional)

serving: about 26 sandwich cookies
ahead: 3 days

For the dough, sift the flour, baking powder, salt, allspice, and cinnamon into a large mixing bowl. Whisk in the almond flour or ground almonds.

Cream the butter in the large bowl of a freestanding electric mixer on moderate speed for 2 minutes. Add the granulated sugar in 3 additions, beating on moderate speed for 30 seconds after each portion is added. Add the eggs, one at a time, beating on low speed until incorporated, about 45 seconds. Blend in the vanilla extract and almond extract. On low speed, mix in the sifted ingredients in 3 additions, beating just until the flour particles are absorbed. Scrape down the sides of the mixing bowl frequently with a rubber spatula to keep the dough even-textured.

Divide the dough into 3 portions. Roll each chunk of dough between two sheets of waxed paper to a thickness of about ⅛ inch. Stack the waxed paper–wrapped sheets of dough on a cookie sheet. Refrigerate the dough overnight (or for up to 2 days in advance).

For the filling, place the preserves and water in a heavy, medium-size nonreactive saucepan (preferably enameled cast iron) and stir to combine. Bring the contents of the pan to a low boil, reduce the heat, and simmer for 1 minute. Strain the preserves through a fine-mesh stainless steel sieve into a heatproof bowl, pressing the preserves through with a heatproof spatula. Stir in the vanilla extract. Cool completely. Scrape the filling into a clean, dry storage container, cover, and refrigerate. (The filling can be prepared up to 5 days in advance.)

On baking day, place the sheets of dough in the freezer for 1 hour before stamping out the cookies and baking them.

Preheat the oven to 350 degrees F in advance of baking.

Line several cookie sheets with lengths of ovenproof parchment paper.

Remove one sheet of dough at a time from the freezer. Carefully peel off both sheets of waxed paper. Place the length of rolled-out dough on a clean length of parchment paper. Stamp out the cookies with a decorative 3-inch cookie cutter; in half of that batch of cookies, stamp out a smaller shape from the centers. Place all the cookies, 2 inches apart, on the prepared baking pans.

Bake the cookies in the preheated oven for 10 to 12 minutes, or until just set. Let the cookies stand on the baking pans for 5 minutes, then transfer them to cooling racks, using a wide offset metal spatula. Cool completely.

To sandwich the cookies with the filling, place the prepared filling in a heavy, medium-size saucepan and bring to the simmer. Simmer gently for 1 minute. Carefully spread a little of the warm filling over the surface of each solid cookie to about ¼ inch from the edges. (The filling should be used warm or the cookies will soften on standing.) Set a cut-out cookie on top, evenly lining up the borders. Place the filled cookies on cooling racks to set.

Store the cookies, in single layers, in airtight tins. Just before serving, sift a little confectioners' sugar around the edges, if you wish.

notes
• finely ground almonds, as long as the ingredient is powdery and loose (not clumpy), can replace the almond flour; almond meal, usually a little coarser in texture, would be too rough, texturally speaking, to use in this cookie dough

jam tart

For the dough, sift the flour, baking powder, salt, cinnamon, and nutmeg into a medium-size mixing bowl. Sprinkle over the ground almonds and whisk to combine.

Cream the butter in the large bowl of a freestanding electric mixer on moderate speed for 1 minute. Add the granulated sugar and beat for 1 minute. Blend in the egg, vanilla extract, and almond extract. Scrape down the sides of the bowl with a rubber spatula to keep the mixture even-textured. On low speed, add the sifted mixture in 2 additions, beating only until the dough comes together in large and small lumps. Remove the bowl from the mixer stand. With a rubber spatula, work the mixture until it comes together into a dough, kneading it lightly with your fingertips to merge the lumps. The dough should be buttery, but firm.

Divide the dough in half and form each portion into a rounded cake. Roll each portion of dough between two sheets of waxed paper to a round about 9 inches in diameter. Place one round of dough on a cookie sheet and refrigerate for 30 minutes. Place the second round of dough on another cookie sheet and freeze for 30 to 45 minutes.

Preheat the oven to 375 degrees F.

Have a rimmed sheet pan at hand. About 5 minutes before baking the tart, place the sheet pan on the oven rack.

(continued on the next page)

almond tart dough

1½ cups unsifted bleached all-purpose flour

¾ teaspoon baking powder

¼ teaspoon salt

½ teaspoon ground cinnamon

¼ teaspoon freshly grated nutmeg

½ cup ground almonds (or substitute almond meal or almond flour)

8 tablespoons (1 stick) unsalted butter, softened

¾ cup granulated sugar

1 large egg

1¼ teaspoons pure vanilla extract

½ teaspoon almond extract

(continued on the next page)

(continued from the previous page)

apricot preserves layer

1 cup best-quality apricot preserves blended with ¼ teaspoon vanilla extract and ¼ teaspoon almond extract

confectioners' sugar, for sifting on the edges of the baked tart (optional)

serving: one 9-inch tart, creating 8 to 10 slices
ahead: 5 days

Film the inside of a fluted 8½ to 9-inch false-bottomed tart pan (1 inch deep) with nonstick flour-and-oil spray.

After 30 minutes, remove the first sheet of dough from the refrigerator. Peel off one sheet of waxed paper and invert the dough into the prepared tart pan. Peel off the remaining sheet of waxed paper. Lightly press the dough onto the bottom of the tart pan and up the sides just shy of the rim. The sides may not be covered with enough dough at this time, but will when you have the scraps from the next step at hand. Set the dough-lined tart pan aside while you cut the second sheet of frozen dough into decorative shapes.

To create the top of the tart, remove the sheet of dough from the freezer, peel off both sheets of waxed paper, and place the dough on a length of ovenproof parchment paper. Using a 1¼-inch cookie cutter (use a heart, half-moon, round, or other relatively plain shape and avoid a too-detailed or intricate shape, as the dough will expand somewhat on baking), stamp out 18 to 20 pieces of dough as close as possible to one another. Or, use a 2¾-inch cutter to stamp out 10 to 11 pieces of dough (this will depend on the exact shape of the cutter you are using and how close together the dough can be stamped).

Press the remaining scraps evenly onto the surface and sides of the dough-lined tart pan, using all of them; you can even thicken up the bottom layer of dough if one or another section seems too thin. Spoon the apricot preserves mixture over the bottom of the dough-lined pan. Spread the preserves in an even layer, using a small offset palette knife.

Place the cutouts on the surface of the filling, beginning at the perimeter, then follow with subsequent rings, ending up toward the middle of the tart and, finally, filling in the center with one or more cutouts.

Bake the tart on the preheated rimmed sheet pan for 35 minutes, or until the apricot preserves are bubbly and the cutouts are set and a light golden color. The edges of the tart will be a deeper golden color. As the tart bakes, the dough will rise to fill the tart pan. The tart must be fully baked or it will be pasty-textured in the center. Cool the tart on a cooling rack for 30 minutes.

Carefully release the tart from the outer ring, leaving it on its base, then return it to the cooling rack. Cool completely. Place the tart in an airtight container and let it "cure" for 6 hours, or overnight, at room temperature. Serve the tart cut into pie-shape slices. Sift confectioners' sugar lightly on the edges of the tart (or on the edges of the cut slices), if you wish. Store in an airtight container.

notes
• overbeating the dough will spoil its texture
• various almond ingredients will color the dough differently

Texture

fundamentally sticky ❋ don't tell Mom: it's cake for breakfast ❋ all broken up ❋ what corn meal can do ❋ surprise ingredient: vinegar in a cookie dough ❋ almond chewy, almond puffy, almond ethereal ❋ butter bread, feathery and light, times two ❋ cultivating the icebox cookie ❋ daydreaming of butter: hand-formed cookie doughs model beautifully

Exquisite

awfully sticky

In my pantheon of sticky buns, there is one recipe that rules for a top-notch clutch of yeasty, buttery buns—despite years of manipulating ingredients and tampering with so many different techniques.

The dough is quite basic, but the filling and sticky undercoating are what distinguish it: in both, cinnamon, butter, and brown sugar dominate, and an undercurrent of vanilla extract plays into the substance of it all.

My mania is clearly for buns with structure and substance and, may I say, a little heft to them. Why be concerned with vaporous sweet rolls when the strapping sort, full of flavor, are so much better? The kind that you can really sink your teeth into—not the dissolving, fragile variety. The adherent sticky mixture, a base of butter and brown sugar beefed up by honey and applied to the bottom of individual muffin cups, is pure and chaste; thankfully, it lacks corn syrup, which adds a false and flavorless sense of "sticky" to the buns. Currently, I want a sticky mixture uncomplicated by nuts, though a wild tease can be had if you use handfuls of pecans or walnuts. Nutless or nut-decadent and, size-wise, made just right for eating two at a time, they will capture your attention and then, your affection.

rich, richer, richest sticky buns

For the dough, stir together the yeast, the ½ teaspoon granulated sugar, and the warm water in a heatproof measuring cup. Allow the mixture to stand until swollen, 6 to 7 minutes.

Place the milk and the 5 tablespoons granulated sugar in a small saucepan and set over low heat. When the sugar has dissolved, remove the saucepan from the heat. Pour and scrape the mixture into a medium-size heatproof mixing bowl. Cool to warm, about 110 degrees F, then blend in the vanilla extract.

Scrape the yeast mixture into the bowl of a heavy-duty freestanding electric mixer fitted with the flat paddle. Add the milk mixture; beat on low speed until combined, about 1 minute. Blend in the eggs and the chunks of butter. Blend the 4 cups of flour with the salt. Add half of the flour-salt mixture to the mixing bowl. Mix on low speed to combine. Add the remaining flour mixture and beat slowly to combine. Stop the machine now and then to scrape down the sides of the mixing bowl and the paddle. Beat for 3 minutes. Remove the flat paddle and scrape down the dough that clings to it. Cover the bowl with a sheet of food-safe plastic wrap and let it rest at room temperature for 10 minutes. Set the bowl in place. Replace the flat paddle with the dough hook. Beat the dough for 4 minutes on moderate speed, adding up to ½ cup additional flour to create a supple, but moderately firm dough. Stand by the mixer for the entire beating times.

Turn the dough into a bowl heavily coated with softened unsalted butter, lightly turn to coat all sides in a film of butter, make several cuts in the dough with a pair of kitchen scissors, cover tightly with a sheet of food-safe plastic wrap, and let rise at room temperature for 1 hour and 45 minutes to 2 hours, or until doubled in bulk.

Remove the plastic wrap. Lightly compress the dough with a rubber spatula, cover loosely with the plastic wrap, and let stand for 10 minutes.

In the meantime, film the inside of 24 muffin/cupcake cups (12 cups to a pan, each cup measuring 2¾ inches in diameter and 1⅜ inches deep, with a capacity of ½ cup) with softened unsalted butter.

For the filling, combine the granulated sugar and cinnamon mixture and the dark brown sugar in a small mixing bowl. Have the 7 tablespoons softened butter at hand.

(continued on the next page)

cushy yeast dough

3 teaspoons active dry yeast

½ teaspoon granulated sugar

¼ cup warm (105 to 110 degrees F) water

⅔ cup plus 3 tablespoons milk

5 tablespoons granulated sugar

2 teaspoons vanilla extract

2 large eggs

7 tablespoons (1 stick less 1 tablespoon) unsalted butter, cut into tablespoon-size chunks, softened

4 cups unsifted bleached all-purpose flour, plus an additional ½ cup flour, as needed for kneading

¾ teaspoon salt

cinnamon butter filling

½ cup granulated sugar blended with 5 teaspoons ground cinnamon

⅓ cup firmly packed dark brown sugar

7 tablespoons (1 stick less 1 tablespoon) unsalted butter, softened

(continued on the next page)

(continued from the previous page)

cinnamon sticky

8 tablespoons (1 stick)
unsalted butter, softened

⅔ cup plus 3 tablespoons firmly packed
dark brown sugar

¼ cup honey

1½ teaspoons ground cinnamon

large pinch of salt

2½ teaspoons vanilla extract

serving: 2 dozen buns
ahead: best on baking day; or freeze for
1 month, defrost, bundle in aluminum foil,
and reheat in a preheated 300 degrees F
oven for 10 to 12 minutes (the reheating is
for refreshing the buns, but remember to
eat them only after they have cooled)

For the cinnamon sticky, cream the 8 tablespoons softened butter in a medium-size mixing bowl, using a wooden spoon or flat wooden paddle. Add the dark brown sugar, honey, cinnamon, salt, and vanilla extract. Continuing by hand, blend the mixture thoroughly to combine, about 2 minutes. In order for the sticky mixture to coat the bottom of the buns in a dewy, glossy way, the mixture must be completely amalgamated. Do not hesitate to mix it well by hand, but refrain from beating it until too fluffy as it should remain smooth and not too airy.

To form the buns, roll out the dough on a lightly floured work surface to a sheet measuring about 15 by 15 inches. Using the filling ingredients, spread the 7 tablespoons softened butter on the surface of the rolled-out dough and sprinkle over the cinnamon and sugar mixture. Tamp down lightly on the sugary filling with the bottom of a juice glass or wide offset metal spatula. Roll the dough into a thick jellyroll and seal the long seam end by pinching it lightly between your thumb and forefinger. Pull the roll lengthwise to elongate it to a length of 24 inches. Cut the roll into 24 even-size slices, using a sharp chef's knife. Let the slices stand for 5 minutes.

Place dollops of the cinnamon sticky in the bottom of each muffin/cupcake cup, dividing them evenly among the cups. Form each slice into a casual, but tight, little knot by twisting the slice into a spiral and tucking the end into the center, forming a plump ball. If the knot is too loose, the buns may unravel a bit—not a calamity, as they will still taste delicious, but look just a little more rustic. Place each knot in a prepared muffin/cupcake cup.

Cover each pan of buns loosely with a sheet of food-safe plastic wrap. Let the buns rise for 1 hour, or until the individual buns have risen by about half their total volume.

Preheat the oven to 375 degrees F in advance of baking.

Have two rimmed sheet pans at hand.

Remove and discard the sheets of plastic wrap covering the buns. Place the pans of buns on the rimmed sheet pans (to catch any drips of the cinnamon sticky that bubble over here and there during baking).

Bake the buns in the preheated oven for 25 minutes, or until set and golden brown on top. The fully baked buns will bake up quite moist.

Place the pans on cooling racks and let stand for 5 minutes. Carefully invert the buns onto clean baking sheets. Lift off the pans. Quickly dip out any cinnamon sticky that remains on the bottom of the muffin/cupcake pans with a small spoon and scrape it onto the glazed top of each bun while it is still warm and manageable. Serve the buns at room temperature, not hot or warm, as the cinnamon sticky retains significant heat.

crispycrunchycookie

The recipe that follows allows one mass of flamboyant cookie dough to merge into a sheet of sugary connectedness. The operative word here is "allows," as the style mark of the dough is its nature to spread out formlessly in the pan as it bakes.

Baking alert: this is not a mistake.

Here you are given license not to drop the dough into perfect-figure rounds, but, instead, to smooth, press, and pat it into a large-scale sheet onto the bottom of a jellyroll pan. Baked as a unit—one single cookie of sorts—it firms up as it cools and gets crispy all over. The proportion of butter to flour, with an attention-getting amount of add-ins, such as semisweet chocolate chips, chocolate baking candies, and chopped toffee, develops the structure and personality of the dough. Shredded coconut, plus nuts, if you like them, may also be added to the buttery, nearly brittlelike concoction. This big piece of sweetness and crunch, broken into odd fragments, lurks somewhere between candy (like a sweetmeat) and cookie (a hand-held crispy cookie, that is). This I love: it is unstudied, great fun to put together, and dessert itself when delivered on one really big plate. Note: you might become hooked on this.

riot-of-ingredients breakup

Preheat the oven to 375 degrees F.

Film the inside of a 10½ by 15½ by 1¾-inch jellyroll pan with nonstick oil spray.

For the dough, sift the flour, baking soda, and salt onto a sheet of waxed paper.

Cream the butter in the large bowl of a freestanding electric mixer on moderate speed for 2 minutes. Add the granulated sugar and beat on moderately low speed for 1 minute. Add the light brown sugar and beat for 1 minute longer. Blend in the vanilla extract. On low speed, beat in the sifted ingredients in 2 additions, mixing just until the flour particles are absorbed. Scrape down the sides of the mixing bowl frequently with a rubber spatula to keep the dough even-textured. Beat in the coconut. By hand, work in the M&M's, Kissables, or chopped toffee, and chocolate chips.

Scrape the dough onto the prepared baking pan. Press the dough in an even layer, using a combination of your fingertips and the bottom of a small offset metal spatula. The dough should be spread evenly, but it does not need to be pressed perfectly into the corners.

Bake the sweet in the preheated oven for 15 minutes. After 15 minutes, carefully, and with fully protected, oven-mitted hands, quickly remove the pan from the oven, rap it several times on a heatproof surface, and return it to the oven to bake for 10 to 13 minutes longer, or until set and evenly golden brown on top. Transfer the pan to a cooling rack. Cool completely. Lift the sheet of cookie off the baking pan, using a palette knife to elevate it. Break the cookie into irregular pieces. Store in an airtight tin.

notes
- unsalted pecans, walnuts, peanuts, or cashews (½ cup) and firmly packed sweetened flaked coconut (⅓ cup) can be added to the dough along with the chocolate chips, M&M's Minis, Kissables, or toffee
- bittersweet chocolate chips (regulation-size or baby ones, if you can find them) can replace the semisweet variety
- as noted in the image that accompanies this recipe, an extra ¾ cup of any of the chocolate-based items (the chips or candies) can be pressed onto the surface of the dough just before baking
- never consume raw cookie dough

all-the-goodies dough

2 cups unsifted bleached all-purpose flour

⅛ teaspoon baking soda

¼ teaspoon salt

½ pound (16 tablespoons or 2 sticks) unsalted butter, softened

½ cup granulated sugar

½ cup firmly packed light brown sugar

2½ teaspoons vanilla extract

½ cup natural unsweetened short- or medium-flake coconut

1¼ cups milk chocolate M&M's Minis, Kissables, or coarsely chopped toffee (such as Heath bars), or a combination

1 cup semisweet chocolate chips

serving: about 30 irregular pieces
ahead: 5 days

gritty but good

Corn meal, a spunky and "sweet" cereal grass, is a tantalizing ingredient in a tea cake and twice-baked cookie. Depending on how gritty you like your so-good-with-coffee dipping cookies and cake, either fine or stone-ground corn meal can be used.

The latter, the result of a whole-kernel grind, has a deeper flavor and offers a more rustic, naturally coarse texture; the former makes for a more delicately structured sweet. Both please me, though I do lean toward working with the finer pulverization for the cake and the coarser, earthier type for the rusk-styled cookies.

The corn meal butter dough, which contains jagged pieces of almonds and tart dried cherries, is made by the creamed method, a process that tenderizes, develops texture, and builds volume. It also has the added bonus of improving the look of the cookies, giving the baked oval—and subsequently, the slices—a certain depth. The tea cake batter, also prepared by the creamed method, bakes into a close-textured cake, golden and not-too-sweet; what makes this cake so impressive and gently slips it away from other typical quick-bread batters made with mashed bananas or perfumed with winter citrus peel and juice, is the pleasantly grainy texture of corn meal. Just baked, triangles of cake will remind you of lightly sweetened cornbread, though more delicate and much richer,

thanks to the heavy cream and butter. To enhance the overall flavor of the cake (and differentiate it from the concept of dinner bread), granulated sugar and a combination of vanilla extract and *fiori di sicilia* allows it to flourish on the dessert plate or teatime tray. (*Fiori di sicilia* is a citrusy essence for flavoring batters and doughs; it is a fragrant scent that gives the cake its soft-spoken complexity.) Together, the combination of vanilla extract, a circumspect amount of *fiori di sicilia,* and the grated orange peel, cultivates an aroma that distinguishes, rather than overwhelms, giving the cake its soft-spoken complexity.

Having a tea cake or tin of cookies on hand is a luxury, and the following formulas produce two deluxe sweets to enjoy at any time of the day. Pair the cake or cookies with a summery salad of sliced stone fruit (peaches, plums, or nectarines), a bowl of cherries with their stems still attached, or with a poached fruit compote—dried prunes or figs, or fresh velvety pears—come wintertime.

corn meal and cherry dipping cookies

corn meal butter dough

2 cups unsifted bleached all-purpose flour

1½ teaspoons baking powder

¼ teaspoon salt

½ cup stone-ground yellow corn meal

8 tablespoons (1 stick)
unsalted butter, softened

1 cup granulated sugar

2 large eggs

1¼ teaspoons almond extract

1 teaspoon vanilla extract

2 tablespoons almond liqueur
(such as amaretto)

¾ cup skinless slivered almonds

¾ cup moist tart (Montmorency)
dried cherries

about ¼ cup granulated sugar, for
sprinkling on the sliced cookies

serving: about 2 dozen cookies
ahead: 3 weeks

Preheat the oven to 350 degrees F.

Line the bottom of a heavy cookie sheet or rimmed sheet pan with a length of ovenproof parchment paper.

For the dough, sift the flour, baking powder, and salt into a medium-size mixing bowl. Add the corn meal and whisk well to combine.

Cream the butter in the large bowl of a freestanding electric mixer on moderate speed for 3 minutes. Add the sugar in 2 additions, beating for 1 minute after each portion is added. Beat in the eggs, one at a time, mixing for 45 seconds after each addition. Blend in the almond extract, vanilla extract, and almond liqueur.

On low speed, blend in the leavened flour–corn meal mixture in 2 additions, beating just until combined. Scrape down the sides of the mixing bowl with a rubber spatula to keep the batter even-textured. Work in the almonds and cherries.

Turn the dough onto the baking pan and shape into an oval measuring about 12 inches long. Smooth the edges of the dough to neaten it.

Bake the oval of dough in the preheated oven for 35 minutes, or until set and a wooden pick withdraws clean. Cool the solid oval on the baking pan on a rack for 20 minutes.

Reduce the oven temperature to 275 degrees F. Have two cookie sheets or rimmed sheet pans at hand.

Slip an offset spatula underneath the baked oval to loosen it from the parchment paper. Carefully transfer the oval to a cutting board. Using a serrated knife, slice the oval on a slight angle into ¾-inch cookies. Arrange the cookies cut side down on the baking pans. Sprinkle a little sugar on the visible cut surface of each.

Bake the cookies for 20 to 25 minutes, or until they are firm and dry, turning the cookies after 10 minutes. After the turn, the second cut surface of each cookie can be sugared, if you wish. Let the cookies stand on the baking pans for 10 minutes, then carefully transfer them to cooling racks, using a pair of sturdy tongs. Cool completely. Store in an airtight tin.

notes
• bake the sliced cookies until dry, but do not overbake them or the cherries may become leathery and hard

corn meal tea cake

Preheat the oven to 350 degrees F.

Film the inside of a fluted 10-inch false-bottomed tart pan (2 inches deep) with nonstick flour-and-oil spray or softened unsalted butter.

For the batter, sift the all-purpose flour, cake flour, baking powder, and salt into a medium-size mixing bowl. Add the corn meal and whisk it in.

Cream the butter in the large bowl of a freestanding electric mixer on moderate speed for 1 minute. Add the granulated sugar in 2 additions, beating for 45 seconds after each portion is added. Beat in the eggs, one at a time, mixing for 20 to 30 seconds after each addition. Blend in the vanilla extract, *fiori di sicilia,* and orange peel. On low speed, blend in half of the sifted ingredients, the heavy cream, then the balance of the sifted ingredients, beating just until the particles of flour have been absorbed. Scrape down the sides of the mixing bowl frequently with a rubber spatula to keep the batter even-textured.

Spoon the batter into the prepared baking pan. Smooth the top with a rubber spatula.

Bake the tea cake in the preheated oven for 45 minutes, or until risen, set, golden on top, and a wooden pick withdraws clean when tested 1 inch from the center of the cake.

Cool the tea cake in the pan on a cooling rack for 20 minutes. Carefully lift the cake by the bottom, pushing it up and out to unmold, removing the fluted ring. Serve warm or at room temperature, sliced into wedges, enhancing the rounded edge of each slice with a little sifted confectioners' sugar, if you wish. Store in an airtight cake keeper.

notes
- be sure to beat the butter for 1 minute only, as increasing the beating time will affect the overall volume, and thus the texture of the baked cake
- *fiori di sicilia* is available at La Cuisine—The Cook's Resource (see page 501, baking*SelectedSources*); if the essence is unavailable, ¾ teaspoon orange extract and ¾ teaspoon lemon extract may be used in its place (add both along with the vanilla extract)
- using fine corn meal maintains the cake's elegant baked texture; a preferred corn meal for this purpose is Bob's Red Mill Fine Grind Cornmeal (available in 24-ounce packages)

orange, vanilla, and lemon-scented corn meal batter

1¾ cups unsifted bleached all-purpose flour

¼ cup unsifted bleached cake flour

1¼ teaspoons baking powder

½ teaspoon salt

½ cup fine yellow corn meal

½ pound (16 tablespoons or 2 sticks) unsalted butter, softened

1 cup granulated sugar

5 large eggs

1¼ teaspoons vanilla extract

½ teaspoon *fiori di sicilia*

2 teaspoons finely grated orange peel

¼ cup heavy cream

confectioners' sugar, for sifting over the rim of the baked cake (optional)

serving: one 10-inch cake, creating 12 to 14 slices
ahead: 3 days

on the side, but maybe not

In baking, I am totally amazed by the way in which one ingredient, even a small amount of it, can affect the outcome of a recipe.

In this cookie dough, that ingredient is apple cider vinegar. Along with salt, the vinegar accentuates the butter-sugar flavor as the cookie dough mounds caramelize lightly during baking: in this case, the quiet acidity (5 percent) of apple cider vinegar, rather than the more forward-tasting malt or red wine type, fits in nicely with the not-at-all-shy amount of unsalted butter and vanilla extract. Looking back over my research into butter cookies, I can reference that my reason for including the vinegar in the recipe was to tenderize the dough, and give it a crumbly, nearly dissolving texture as you bite into a baked cookie. Old-time recipes of my grandmother's and mother's also included vinegar or lemon juice in butter cake and pound cake batters, as well as some of the plainer cookie doughs. Notice, too, that whole eggs or egg yolks are absent from the ingredient list—this is a pure, undiluted pile of butter

cookies. In the main, the formula is built on a variation of the *butter and sugar cookies* that appear on page 347 of this book—not fancied up with a pastry bag and tip, more everyday, less studied, not at all disciplined. The recipe is also a different take on the *sandy butter dough* in *twice as good cookies, #2 sugar* (page 428) and my mother's drop sugar cookie dough (see notes, page 242). The cookie's texture is fragile and lightly crunchy at the same time.

Although others have repeatedly told me that these are great cookies for serving with mousse, ice cream, vanilla or chocolate pudding, fruit salad, and other sweet endings to a meal, I am set on serving them simply with coffee—they are that good. These may be the ultimate just-for-nibbling, cookie-tin cookies—irresistible with their full throttle of butter. (One suggestion: better find a good hiding place for them.)

the perfect "side-dish" cookie

soft butter dough

2¼ cups unsifted bleached
all-purpose flour

½ teaspoon baking soda

¼ teaspoon baking powder

⅛ teaspoon cream of tartar

½ teaspoon salt

¾ pound (3 sticks) unsalted butter,
softened

1⅓ cups plus 2 tablespoons
granulated sugar

1½ teaspoons vanilla extract

1¼ teaspoons apple cider vinegar

about ⅓ cup granulated sugar, spread
out on a small flat saucer, for coating the
bottom of a juice glass

sprinklings of sea salt (see notes)

serving: about 4 dozen cookies
ahead: 1 week

Preheat the oven to 350 degrees F.

Line several heavy cookie sheets or rimmed sheet pans with lengths of ovenproof parchment paper.

For the dough, sift the flour, baking soda, baking powder, cream of tartar, and salt onto a sheet of waxed paper.

Cream the butter in the large bowl of a freestanding electric mixer on low speed for 3 minutes, or until velvety. Add the 1⅓ cups plus 2 tablespoons sugar in 2 additions, beating for 1 minute after each portion is added. Blend in the vanilla extract and vinegar. On low speed, blend in the sifted ingredients in 2 additions, beating just until the flour particles are absorbed. Scrape down the sides of the mixing bowl with a rubber spatula to keep the dough even-textured.

Place rounded 1-tablespoon-size mounds of dough onto the prepared baking pans, spacing the mounds about 3 inches apart. Smooth the edges of the mounds slightly, rather than leaving them too rough. Lightly grease the bottom of a smooth-surfaced juice glass with a little of the cookie dough, leaving just a residue, then dip the glass in the ⅓ cup granulated sugar. Lightly flatten each mound of dough with the bottom of the dipped glass; be sure to coat the bottom of the glass lightly by dipping it in the sugar before flattening each cookie. The flattened dough mound should measure about 2 inches in diameter. Sprinkle a teeny bit of sea salt in the center of each cookie.

Bake the cookies in the preheated oven for 15 to 17 minutes, or until set and golden. Let the cookies stand on the baking pans for 2 minutes, then transfer them to cooling racks, using a wide offset metal spatula. Cool completely. Store in an airtight tin.

notes
- in hot or humid weather, or in a warm kitchen, refrigerate the dough for 20 minutes before spooning it into mounds
- to build the salty-sweet flavor, the top of each unbaked flattened cookie is flecked with a grain or two of sea salt; for this, I use either Fleur de Sel de Guérande, translated as "flower of salt" (referring to its fresh, infant stage), harvested in the Guérande area of France (Brittany), or Himalania (this pink salt from the Himalayas has a marvelous, gently mineral quality); according to the label, Himalania, available in 8.8-ounce containers, is imported from France by Brandstorm, Inc., Los Angeles, CA (www.himalania.com)
- historical recipe data: my mom's drop sugar cookie recipe used the same quantity of flour, baking soda alone, a lesser amount of granulated sugar and vanilla extract, and, of course, sprinkles of sea salt did not appear as a topping

seriously seeking chewy and plump

Patience. Perseverance. Persistence.

Call it what you will, but I exhibited all of those qualities when faced with the proposition of working out an almond macaroon dough that displays the following characteristics: chewy, rounded and puffed rather than flat when baked, somewhat dense, full of deep almond flavor.

As life would have it, I wasn't really finished buying marzipan (my marzipan escapade in the *almond essence* essay and the accompanying recipe for *a noble marzipan cake* and the *little almond cakes* on pages 39 through 42 will convince you of that), though I thought that I would be giving it a rest for a little while. Oh no. A plump cookie with all of the traits noted perplexed me many nights when, in the peace and quiet, I would stir up yet another dough.

When dozens of cookies came out all wrong (edit to add: "wrong" by my chosen standards, but delicious nonetheless)—over the on-again, off-again time frame of nine months—it appeared as if I were chasing a cookie that would never happen in reality, only in a daydreamlike baking scenario. Not one surfaced as *the cookie*. Yet. There were flat, caramelized almond cookies (interesting) and grainy cookies (swollen, gritty); and cookies far too airy and lightweight of almond flavor, or leaden. Batch after batch made me weary, and my own usual tenacity became annoying. Boxes and cans of almond paste seemed to taunt me as I opened the cabinet door to pull the item for another sweet thing.

Until I baked an almond pound cake.

Making such a cake, using the usual butter cake ingredients, made me rethink texture based on the way sugar and eggs work in a dough or batter. I rearranged the sweetening agents in my cookie recipe to include both granulated and confectioners' sugar so that the cookie dough balls might bake into a chewier texture, and seriously—by that word I mean "assiduously"—measured the egg whites to arrive at just the right moisture content in the dough. I baked off a round of cookies: foiled again. Then, the goddess of the hearth must have felt sorry for me and "caused" an inadvertent stroke of benevolent baking luck. I mixed another round of dough and, distracted by an overflowing gutter in a tropical storm–force rain, I threw the dough into the refrigerator until I returned three hours later to form and bake off the cookies. The rest in the refrigerator gave the dough better structure and allowed the maximum amount of egg and egg white to be used (the measurement ended up to be 1 large egg white plus 1 tablespoon to each 8 ounces of almond paste). Just the right oven temperature maintained the shape of the cookies, allowed a nice puff, and kept the centers moist.

The cookies, delightful with coffee or tea, keep nicely in a tin for several days, as the natural oil present in the nut-based product works in conjunction with the two types of sugar to prevent drying. In fact, cookies that are baked, cooled, and left to "cure" for about five hours or overnight in a container have the loveliest pronounced scent and "chew." The six-year-old great nephew of a friend labeled this technical procedure as "letting the cookies take a nap." Well, most things in the universe seem to profit from a little rest.

almond macaroons in an embrace of flavor and texture

For the dough, crumble the almond paste into the work bowl of a food processor fitted with the steel blade. Cover and process until reduced to moist crumbs.

Turn the almond paste crumbs into a medium-size mixing bowl. Add the granulated sugar, confectioners' sugar, salt, egg whites, vanilla extract, and almond extract. Using a hand-held electric mixer, beat the ingredients on moderately low speed until a smooth, sticky dough is formed, about 2 minutes. Scrape down the sides of the mixing bowl frequently with a rubber spatula to keep the dough even-textured.

Scrape the dough onto a sheet of food-safe plastic wrap, and wrap securely. Refrigerate the dough for 3 hours (or up to 8 hours).

Preheat the oven to 350 degrees F in advance of baking.

Line a large, heavy cookie sheet or rimmed sheet pan with a length of oven-proof parchment paper. Have the sliced almonds at hand in a shallow bowl.

Remove the dough from the refrigerator. Remove and discard the plastic wrap. Divide the dough into 14 even-size pieces. Roll the pieces into balls, then roll the balls in the almonds. Place the balls of dough, 2½ inches apart, on the prepared cookie sheet.

Bake the macaroons for 20 to 25 minutes, or until set, baked through, and light to medium golden on top. The cookies will have puffed gently. Let the cookies stand on the baking pans for 1 minute, then transfer them to a large cooling rack, using a wide offset metal spatula. Cool completely. Store in an airtight tin.

notes
- to use marzipan in place of the almond paste, reduce the amount of granulated sugar by 1 tablespoon
- to maintain the shape of the cookies, bake the cookies as soon as they are rolled and almond-coated (if you cannot bake the cookies straightaway, refrigerate the sheet of cookies rather than holding them on the countertop at room temperature); add about 2 minutes to the baking time for cookies refrigerated up to 45 minutes
- the cookies bake with a rounded puff, not a ballooned one; excessive or uneven oven heat will cause the cookies to flatten, no matter how well you take care with the initial dough, as will an inaccurate measurement of egg whites

almond paste dough

8 ounces almond paste

½ cup granulated sugar

⅓ cup confectioners' sugar

pinch of salt

1 large egg white plus
1 tablespoon egg white

1 teaspoon vanilla extract

¾ teaspoon almond extract

about ⅔ cup sliced almonds, for rolling the unbaked balls of dough

serving: 14 cookies
ahead: 3 days

so tender

In the realm of dough, the identification of "short" indicates, primarily, the amount of fat used to tenderize (and flavor) a leavened or unleavened dough, as well as a discreet amount of leavening (usually baking powder).

An ingredient that is not usually thought of in that description is the sweetening agent—in this case confectioners' sugar—that contributes to the richness and flakiness of a finished product (as does cornstarch when it replaces part of the flour—for that, refer to the recipe for *wildly lush hint-of-salt lavender shortbread, the unrestrained version* on page 303).

Shortbread or any type of cookie dough with a proportion of flour to butter in the neighborhood ratio of 1 cup to 8 tablespoons is, by definition, a good example of a tender, flaky confection. In the *vanilla jewels, just like sandies* and its nutty variation (*pecan gems*) that follow, there is enough butter to relax the dough, making for a wonderfully melting texture that still holds together when molded and baked. When a butter-rich dough is accented with an egg yolk, a somewhat richer, though substantial, composition results; the presence of the fat (butter, and occasionally egg yolks or a whole egg) then necessitates ½ teaspoon of baking powder to be present in order to relax and open the crumb just enough so that the baked cookies are tender rather than hard. Another aspect of tenderness is due to working the dough gently on a cool work surface to smooth it and prevent very large air gaps; smaller gaps are not only evident in the baked cookies, but essential to establishing the exquisite melting texture of the baked cookies (which is why you will see scatterings of small, slightly opened dots scattered throughout their surfaces). After an overnight refrigeration, the to-be-sliced logs are treated to a coating in egg white and a roll in sparkling sugar, creating a lovely sheen and textural surfacing.

Of all the ingredients that make up this kind of recipe, it is the butter that is the most significant. The crop of exemplary butters available at the market allows you to make a great-tasting cookie dough, one that can offer a full taste of the pastureland: creamy and faintly grassy. I have had flavorful results using Celles sur Belle, Beurre Président, Plugrá European Style Unsalted Butter, and Isigny Ste. Mère Beurre Cru de Normandie.

The cookies convey most of the "sweet quotient" through the coating of sparkling sugar, less so from the confectioners' sugar or superfine sugar in the dough itself and, as such, their graceful, understated nature makes them so inviting.

The recipe for *vanilla jewels, just like sandies* is a well-tweaked version of my *chocolate chip sablés* from my previous work *ChocolateChocolate,* and my mother's slice-and-bake sugar cookies. The *vanilla jewels, just like sandies* uses all-purpose flour rather than cake flour, baking powder as the sole leavening agent, and confectioners' sugar rather than superfine; as well, the dough is treated in a different way—it is formed into logs for slicing, rather than rolled into sheets and stamped out with a decorative cutter. The dough for the *chocolate chip sablés* contains more sugar and, of course, a fine cupful of chocolate chips; the sticky dough is rolled out between sheets of waxed paper, chilled well, then frozen before stamping out. The last recipe, for *irene's slice-and-bake sugar cookies,* turns out a beautifully buttery batch; it is the formula on which the recipe for *vanilla jewels, just like sandies* (and further back, the *chocolate chip sablés*) was built.

When my taste memory craves a butter cookie, I turn to these recipes time and time again.

vanilla jewels, just like sandies

vanilla butter dough

4 cups unsifted bleached all-purpose flour

½ teaspoon baking powder

¾ teaspoon salt

1 pound (4 sticks) unsalted butter, softened

1½ cups confectioners' sugar

4 large egg yolks

4 teaspoons vanilla extract

1 large egg white, lightly beaten, for brushing on the logs of dough

about ¾ cup sparkling sugar (plain or a color), for rolling the logs of dough

serving: about 46 cookies
ahead: 3 days

For the dough, sift the flour, baking powder, and salt onto a sheet of waxed paper.

Cream the butter in the large bowl of a freestanding electric mixer on moderately low speed for 4 minutes. Add the confectioners' sugar in 2 additions, beating on moderate speed for 1 minute after each portion is added. Blend in the egg yolks and vanilla extract. On low speed, mix in the sifted ingredients in 3 additions, beating just until the flour particles are absorbed. Scrape down the sides of the mixing bowl frequently with a rubber spatula to keep the dough even-textured. The dough will be soft, but moldable. Work the dough gently on a cool work surface to smooth it and prevent air gaps. Divide the dough in half.

On separate sheets of ovenproof parchment paper, pat-and-press each portion of dough into a log measuring 10 inches long and 2 inches in diameter. Roll up each log into the sheet of parchment paper one full turn to enclose it. Once you have enclosed each parcel of dough in one full turn of the paper, carefully press a ruler or other flat-edge implement (but not a knife) against the long side to tighten the paper. Refrigerate the logs for 2 hours, then enclose in a large, food-safe freezer-weight plastic bag. (For a perfectly round log, repeat the ruler-press and parchment-tightening 4 times, every 30 minutes, for the next 2 hours.) Return the logs to the refrigerator and store overnight.

On baking day, preheat the oven to 350 degrees F.

Line several heavy cookie sheets with lengths of ovenproof parchment paper.

Unroll the chilled logs of dough from the parchment paper. Place the logs on a large sheet of waxed paper. Lightly coat the outside of each log with the beaten egg white, using a soft pastry brush, and let the logs stand for 3 minutes. Scatter the sparkling sugar on a large sheet of waxed paper. Roll and coat each log in the sugar, taking care to cover the outside of the logs completely. Cut each log into generous ¼-inch slices (there should be about 23 cookies cut from each). Place the cookies, 2 to 3 inches apart, on the prepared cookie sheets.

Bake the cookies in the preheated oven for 20 minutes, or until set, baked through, and evenly pale golden in color on the surface, with slightly golden edges. Let the cookies stand on the baking pans for 1 minute, then transfer them to cooling racks, using a wide offset metal spatula. Cool completely. Store in an airtight tin.

notes
- the small amount of cornstarch present in the confectioners' sugar (about 3 percent) contributes to the flaky factor in the baked sandies
- working the dough lightly into an even mass before shaping into logs avoids the formation of large tunnels appearing through the interior of the roll
- a thorough refrigeration of the dough logs sets the shape and makes slicing clean and even
- the cookies should be baked until set as described in the procedure or their centers will be damp and pasty, rather than tender and gently crumbly (that is, assiduously avoid underbaking the cookies)
- when preparing cookie dough for refrigeration or freezing, use organic eggs only

pecan gems

Mix the dough, working in the chopped pecans along with the last third of the sifted flour mixture. Work the dough, shape into logs, refrigerate, coat, and bake as directed in the recipe for the *vanilla jewels, just like sandies.*

notes
- lightly toasting the pecans before adding them to the dough enhances the flavor of the baked cookies

vanilla jewels, just like sandies (page 248)

¾ cups chopped pecans

serving: about 46 cookies
ahead: 3 days

chocolate chip sablés

For the dough, sift the flour, baking powder, cream of tartar, and salt onto a sheet of waxed paper.

Cream the butter in the large bowl of a freestanding electric mixer on moderately low speed for 5 minutes, or until very creamy. Add the superfine sugar in 3 additions, beating on moderate speed for 1 minute after each portion is added. Blend in the vanilla extract. On low speed, mix in the sifted ingredients in 4 additions, beating just until the flour particles are absorbed. Scrape down the sides of the mixing bowl frequently with a rubber spatula to keep the dough even-textured. Blend in the chocolate chips.

Divide the dough into 4 portions. Roll each portion of dough between two sheets of waxed paper to a thickness of ¼ inch. Layer the waxed paper–enclosed sheets of dough on a cookie sheet. Refrigerate the dough overnight. Before cutting out the cookies, place the sheets of dough in the freezer for 1 hour. The dough must be firm.

On baking day, preheat the oven to 350 degrees F.

(continued on the next page)

chocolate chip butter dough

4 cups unsifted bleached cake flour

½ teaspoon baking powder

⅛ teaspoon cream of tartar

½ teaspoon salt

1 pound (4 sticks) unsalted butter, softened

1 cup superfine sugar

3 teaspoons vanilla extract

1 cup miniature semisweet chocolate chips

about ½ cup sparkling sugar (plain or a color), for sprinkling on the unbaked cookies

serving: about 4 dozen cookies
ahead: 5 days

Line several heavy cookie sheets with lengths of ovenproof parchment paper.

Working with one sheet of dough at a time, peel off both sheets of waxed paper and place the dough on a lightly floured work surface. Stamp out cookies with a decorative 2½ to 3-inch cutter. Place the cookies, 2 inches apart, on the prepared baking pans. Top each with a sprinkling of sparkling sugar.

Bake the cookies in the preheated oven for 17 to 20 minutes, or until set. Let the cookies stand on the baking pans for 1 minute, then transfer them to cooling racks, using a wide offset metal spatula. Cool completely. Store in an airtight tin.

notes
• the overnight chilling, plus the 1 hour of freezing time, refine and maintain the shape of the baked cookies—this is important if you are using any kind of cutter, plain or fancy-edged (scalloped or fluted)
• this cookie is, texturally, both delicate and light

irene's slice-and-bake sugar cookies

mild-mannered butter dough

4 cups unsifted bleached all-purpose flour

½ teaspoon baking powder

½ teaspoon salt

1 pound (4 sticks) unsalted butter, softened

1⅓ cups superfine sugar

6 tablespoons confectioners' sugar

2 large eggs

3 teaspoons vanilla extract

1 large egg white, lightly beaten, for brushing on the logs of dough

about ¾ cup sparkling sugar, for rolling the logs of dough

serving: about 46 cookies
ahead: 3 days

For the dough, sift the flour, baking powder, and salt onto a sheet of waxed paper.

Cream the butter in the large bowl of a freestanding electric mixer on moderately low speed for 4 minutes. Add the superfine sugar and beat on moderate speed for 1 minute; add the confectioners' sugar and beat for 1 minute longer. Blend in the eggs and vanilla extract. On low speed, mix in the sifted ingredients in 2 additions, beating just until the flour particles are absorbed. Scrape down the sides of the mixing bowl frequently with a rubber spatula to keep the dough even-textured. The dough will be soft. Work the dough gently on a cool work surface to smooth it and prevent interior air gaps. Divide the dough in half.

Pat and roll each half of the dough into a log measuring 10 inches long and 2 inches in diameter. Place each log of dough on a sheet of ovenproof parchment paper and roll it up. Once you have enclosed the dough in one full turn of the paper, carefully press a ruler or other flat-edge implement (but not a knife) against the long side to tighten the paper. Refrigerate the logs for 2 hours, then enclose in a large, food-safe freezer-weight plastic bag. (For a perfectly round log, repeat the ruler-press and parchment-tightening 4 times, every 30 minutes, for the next 2 hours.) Return the logs to the refrigerator and store overnight (or up to 2 days).

On baking day, preheat the oven to 350 degrees F.

Line several heavy cookie sheets with lengths of ovenproof parchment paper.

Unroll each chilled log of dough from the parchment paper. Place each log on a separate sheet of waxed paper. Lightly coat the outside of one log with the beaten egg white, using a soft pastry brush, and sprinkle over half of the sparkling sugar, rolling and coating all sides in it. Repeat with the second log of dough. Cut each log into generous ¼-inch slices (there should be about 23 cookies cut from each). Place the cookies, 2 to 3 inches apart, on the prepared cookie sheets.

Bake the cookies in the preheated oven for 20 minutes, or until set, baked through, and evenly light golden in color on top and with moderately golden undersides. Let the cookies stand on the baking pans for 1 minute, then transfer them to cooling racks, using a wide offset metal spatula. Cool completely. Store in an airtight tin.

notes
• historical recipe data: the combination of confectioners' sugar and granulated sugar (my mother's ratio has been tweaked, using a lesser amount of confectioners' sugar for stability) creates a dough that bakes into a cookie that is both gently crisp and tender; my mother likely used granulated sugar, but superfine sugar brings a melting—and superior—texture to the baked cookie; the amount of baking powder has been reduced by ¼ teaspoon and granulated sugar was used instead of sparkling sugar for the final sugary exterior finish
• when preparing cookie dough for refrigeration or freezing, use organic eggs only

tender is the bread

This *featherbed bread*, with its silky crumb and substantive butter-and-egg focus, has a captivatingly light, feathery style. You will recognize its briochelike structure by the set of ingredients and the method, though the procedure has been modified in order to create bread that does not require an overnight chill to establish a certain texture and flavor.

However, if your schedule allows (or requires), feel free to turn the prepared dough (after the first lengthy rise at cool room temperature) into a jumbo self-sealing food-safe plastic bag and store it in the refrigerator for 18 to 24 hours, then proceed to form it into rolls, counting on an extra hour or so for the cold dough to elevate to full potential.

The *simple but good hot rolls* happen to be my idea of classic (and fairly upgraded) American dinner rolls—a dough that elevates butter to star status in a way different from the *featherbed bread*. It may be on the rising slope (that is, high end) of roll doughs, but it is my front-runner, go-to roll, so good with meat loaf, roasted chicken, beefy stew—you get the picture. It is also a fine midnight roll, freshly baked and torn open, its surfaces coated all over with jam.

Once the rolls are tucked into a linen cozy or enveloped in a casual paper cone, you will have the scent and taste of homemade on your table—literally. To me, handmade bread is the true symbol of home.

featherbed bread

light and buttery dough

sponge

3 teaspoons active dry yeast

¼ teaspoon granulated sugar

⅓ cup plus 3 tablespoons warm
(105 to 110 degrees F) water

3 tablespoons granulated sugar

⅓ cup plus 3 tablespoons unsifted
bleached all-purpose flour

foundation dough

4 large eggs, lightly beaten

3 cups unsifted bleached all-purpose flour
blended with 1 teaspoon salt

butter and flour
for the finishing dough

½ pound (16 tablespoons or 2 sticks)
cool unsalted butter

½ cup unsifted bleached all-purpose flour

egg yolk and milk glaze

1 large egg yolk

pinch of granulated sugar

pinch of salt

2 tablespoons milk

serving: three 5-inch breads, creating 4
servings each (each bread is composed of
4 rolls that hug one another)
ahead: best on baking day; or freeze for
3 weeks, defrost, bundle in aluminum foil,
and reheat in a preheated 300 degrees F
oven for 10 minutes

For the sponge, stir together the yeast, the ¼ teaspoon sugar, and the warm water in a heatproof measuring cup. Allow the mixture to stand until swollen, 6 to 7 minutes.

Turn the yeast mixture into a small mixing bowl. Stir in the 3 tablespoons sugar and the ⅓ cup plus 3 tablespoons flour. Mix well. Cover the bowl with a sheet of food-safe plastic wrap and set aside at room temperature for 30 to 40 minutes, or until doubled in volume (the surface will be bubbly).

For the foundation dough, scrape the sponge mixture into the bowl of a heavy-duty freestanding electric mixer. Blend in the eggs, mixing with a wooden spoon or flat wooden paddle. Stir in the 3 cups flour-salt blend in 3 additions. The dough will be quite shaggy, with distinct patches of flour that have not been absorbed as yet. Set the bowl in place and attach the flat paddle. Mix to form a dough, beating on moderately low speed for 10 minutes. The dough will be quite smooth and supple at this point.

For the finishing dough, place the butter on a dinner plate and smear it with the heel of your hand. Divide the butter into 8 portions. Mix the butter into the dough, a portion at a time, beating on moderately low to moderate speed until absorbed (about 1 minute) before adding the next amount. The dough will be elastic and very sticky, and will resemble a dense, tacky batter. From time to time in the beating process, stop the mixer and scrape down the sides of the mixing bowl. Turn off the mixer and sprinkle over the ½ cup flour. Beat the dough on moderate speed for 3 minutes. At this point, the dough should be supple and will barely clean the sides of the mixing bowl, leaving a thin, streaky film, and it will not detach from the bottom of the mixing bowl.

Scrape the dough into a bowl heavily coated with softened unsalted butter, lightly turn to coat all sides in a film of butter, make several cuts in the dough with a pair of kitchen scissors, cover tightly with a sheet of food-safe plastic wrap, and let rise at cool room temperature until doubled in bulk, about 2 hours and 30 minutes. Uncover the dough and lightly compress by folding it over on itself 3 or 4 times, using your fingertips. Cover the dough and let stand for 15 minutes.

Film the inside of three 5 by 5 by 3-inch baking pans with nonstick flour-and-oil spray.

To form the rolls, turn out the dough onto a lightly floured work surface and divide it into 12 even-size pieces. Roll each piece of dough into a tight ball.

Place 4 balls of dough in each of the prepared baking pans, assembling them in two rows of 2 each.

Cover each pan of bread loosely with a sheet of food-safe plastic wrap. Let the breads rise at room temperature for 1 hour and 45 minutes to 2 hours, or until almost doubled in bulk (see page 6 to reference this stage). The sections will merge as they rise, filling the gaps in the pans.

Preheat the oven to 375 degrees F in advance of baking.

Remove and discard the sheets of plastic wrap covering the breads about 15 minutes before completely risen.

For the glaze, whisk the egg yolk, sugar, salt, and milk in a small mixing bowl.

Brush the glaze on top of each risen bread. Let stand 2 minutes, then brush on a second coat. Continue to let the breads finish rising, uncovered, for 15 minutes.

Bake the breads in the preheated oven for 30 minutes, or until set and a golden color on top. The baked bread will pull away slightly from the sides of the baking pans. Place the pans on cooling racks and let stand for 10 minutes. Invert the breads onto other cooling racks. Lift off each pan, then invert the breads again to stand right side up. Serve the bread very fresh, pulling apart the sections at their natural seams.

notes
• the best piece of equipment for glazing the tops of the breads is a croissant basting brush—with its long and soft but sturdy bristles—made by Carlisle (#40377)
• the rolls are arranged and baked in three 5 by 5 by 3-inch baking pans; two 8 by 8 by 2-inch baking pans may be substituted, creating smaller rolls and a larger yield (divide the dough into 24 balls and assemble 12 balls in three rows of 4 in each pan), reducing the baking time by 4 to 5 minutes

simple but good hot rolls

gently puffy yeast dough

4½ teaspoons active dry yeast

½ teaspoon granulated sugar

½ cup warm (105 to 110 degrees F) water

1¼ cups milk

⅓ cup granulated sugar

6 tablespoons (¾ stick) unsalted butter, cut into tablespoon-size chunks

3 large egg yolks

4 cups unsifted bleached all-purpose flour, plus an additional 2 tablespoons, as needed for kneading

1 cup unsifted unbleached all-purpose flour

1 teaspoon salt

butter roll

8 tablespoons (1 stick) unsalted butter (preferably clarified, page 1), melted and cooled to tepid

salt finish (optional)

about 1 teaspoon coarse salt, for sprinkling on the risen unbaked rolls

serving: 2 dozen rolls
ahead: best on baking day; or freeze for 3 weeks, defrost, bundle in aluminum foil, and reheat in a preheated 300 degrees F oven for 10 minutes

For the dough, stir together the yeast, the ½ teaspoon sugar, and the warm water in a heatproof measuring cup. Allow the mixture to stand until swollen, 6 to 7 minutes.

In the meantime, place the milk, the ⅓ cup sugar, and the chunks of butter in a small saucepan, set over low heat, and warm until the butter melts. Remove from the heat, whisk well, scrape into a medium-size heatproof bowl, and let stand for 7 to 8 minutes to cool to tepid. Whisk in the egg yolks. Blend in the yeast mixture.

Whisk the 4 cups bleached flour, unbleached flour, and salt in a large mixing bowl. In another large mixing bowl, place 3 cups of the flour mixture, add the milk-butter-egg-yeast mixture, and stir to mix; the mixture will resemble a thick batter at this point. Let the batter stand, uncovered, for 4 minutes. Stir in the remaining 2 cups of the flour mixture, ½ cup at a time. Knead the dough on a lightly floured work surface for 8 to 9 minutes, or until quite smooth, using up to 2 tablespoons extra flour as necessary to keep the dough from sticking. The dough should be moderately firm and slightly bouncy.

Turn the dough into a bowl heavily coated with softened unsalted butter, lightly turn to coat all sides in a film of butter, cover tightly with a sheet of food-safe plastic wrap, and let rise at room temperature for 1 hour and 15 minutes, or until doubled in bulk.

Remove and discard the plastic wrap. Lightly compress the dough with your fingertips or a rubber spatula, and let stand for 5 minutes.

Film the inside of a 13 by 9 by 3-inch baking pan with softened unsalted butter.

To form the rolls, divide the dough into 24 even-size pieces. Roll each piece on the work surface in the cupped palm of your hand into a smooth ball.

For the butter roll, pour the melted butter into a shallow bowl. One at a time, gently roll the dough ball in the butter. The dough balls will be glossy-looking. Arrange the buttered dough balls in the prepared baking pan, assembling them in four rows of 6 each.

Cover the pan of rolls loosely with a sheet of food-safe plastic wrap. Let the rolls rise at room temperature for 1 hour to 1 hour and 15 minutes, or until doubled in bulk and puffy.

Preheat the oven to 350 degrees F in advance of baking.

Remove and discard the sheet of plastic wrap covering the rolls. Sprinkle the tops of the rolls with the coarse salt, if you wish.

Bake the rolls in the preheated oven for 35 to 40 minutes, or until set and quite golden on top. The rolls will rise high, filling the pan completely.

Place the pan on a cooling rack and let stand for 20 minutes. Detach the rolls from the pan in groups of 4 or 6, using two small offset metal spatulas, then lift them out of the pan for serving. Or, invert the pan of rolls onto another cooling rack, then invert again to cool right side up. Serve the rolls warm or at room temperature. Store in an airtight container.

notes
• clarified butter, used for rolling and coating the dough balls, makes for the freshest butter taste and best (non-speckled) appearance on baking
• the rolls are arranged and baked in a 13 by 9 by 3-inch baking pan; two 9 by 9 by 2-inch square baking pans may be substituted

cake for breakfast—oh my!

Pure luxury is cake for breakfast. There, I've said it. Now that confession absolves me—entirely, I hope—for slinking around with a slice of cake in the morning. What a relief it is to come clean, finally.

A slice of this butter-concentrated cake, not too sweet but plenty rich enough, goes down so easily with my morning coffee that I would—almost—be willing to forsake any other form of dough- or batter-baked item in favor of it (with the important exception of any kind of yeasty chocolaty number). The unbaked texture of the dough resembles a very soft, sticky shortbread—with the underscored emphasis on "soft" and "sticky." It is smoothed into a 10-inch, false-bottomed, fluted tart pan and forty minutes later, it bakes up all golden and densely moist, with coy allusions to vanilla and almond drifting about. Though not, strictly speaking, a morning person, I would gather my internal resources and haul myself out from under the covers just to put the recipe together. This praiseworthy note might propel you right into the kitchen in the morning to preheat the oven and get going with the recipe. But don't call me too early, unless you are offering a piece of this cake.

morning butter slice

dense and buttery batter-dough

1½ cups unsifted bleached all-purpose flour

3 tablespoons cornstarch

¼ teaspoon baking powder

¼ teaspoon salt

½ teaspoon freshly grated nutmeg

½ pound (16 tablespoons or 2 sticks) unsalted butter, softened

1 cup plus 2 tablespoons superfine sugar

6 large egg yolks

2 teaspoons vanilla extract

½ teaspoon almond extract

⅓ cup almond flour or almond meal

¼ cup granulated sugar or sanding sugar (fine or coarse, and plain or a color), for sprinkling on the unbaked cake and on the warm baked cake

serving: one 10-inch cake, creating 10 to 12 slices
ahead: 2 days

Preheat the oven to 350 degrees F.

Film the inside of a fluted 10-inch false-bottomed tart pan (2 inches deep) with nonstick flour-and-oil spray or softened unsalted butter.

For the batter-dough, sift the flour, cornstarch, baking powder, salt, and nutmeg onto a sheet of waxed paper.

Cream the butter in the large bowl of a freestanding electric mixer on moderate speed for 1 minute. Continuing on moderate speed, add the superfine sugar in 2 additions, beating for 45 seconds after each portion is added. Blend in the egg yolks, vanilla extract, and almond extract. Blend in the almond flour or almond meal. On low speed, alternately add the sifted mixture in 2 additions, mixing just until the particles of flour are absorbed. Scrape down the sides of the mixing bowl with a rubber spatula to keep the mixture even-textured. The mixture will be thick and dense, resembling a sticky dough more than a proper batter.

Scrape the dough into the prepared baking pan. Spread it evenly in the pan, using a flexible palette knife and light, even strokes. Sprinkle 2 tablespoons (about half) of the granulated or sanding sugar over the surface of the dough.

Bake the cake in the preheated oven for 40 minutes, or until set, golden on top, and a wooden pick inserted into the cake withdraws clean or with stray, moist crumbs attached to it. A few cracks will appear here and there on the top of the baked cake, and this is to be expected. Sprinkle the remaining 2 tablespoons granulated or sanding sugar evenly over the top. Cool the cake in the pan on a cooling rack for 15 minutes. Carefully lift the cake by the bottom, pushing it up and out to unmold and removing the fluted ring. Serve warm or at room temperature, sliced into wedges. Store in an airtight cake keeper.

notes

- butter is a key element in the cake, so you should use one with a well-rounded flavor, such as Beurre Président, Plugrá European Style Unsalted Butter, Lurpak Danish Butter, Isigny Ste. Mère Beurre Cru de Normandie, or Kate's Homemade Butter
- take care to beat the butter and sugar on the mixer speed and for the time directed; overly beaten butter and sugar will create a dough that, on baking, may collapse
- a round 10-inch layer cake pan (2 inches deep) may be substituted for the tart pan
- the dough can also be baked in individual tart pans: for this, film the inside of 8 fluted 4-inch false-bottomed tart pans (1¼ inches deep) with nonstick flour-and-oil spray or softened unsalted butter; divide the dough evenly among the pans, smooth over each top, and assemble on a cookie sheet; bake for 30 minutes, top with sugar as directed, cool, and unmold

cookies that vaporize

Hand-formed butter cookies, very much like shortbread, have considerable appeal, for the dough is enormously manageable and, with their tender baked texture, the crescents and buttons disintegrate in the mouth in the most wonderful way possible.

Almonds (inside the dough and out), ginger, and lemon peel separately embroider each dough and distinguish it along the way.

A dough made with cool melted butter, leavened slightly, sweetened softly, baked, and rolled in more sugar to finish is exactly like adult clay: easily moldable into stubby logs, rounds, quarter-moons, and such. The beautifully malleable dough is handily put together in a mixing bowl; pliable, rich, but mostly dense, it can be refrigerated for a few days or frozen in logs or slabs for up to three weeks.

Presented en masse on a cookie plate, these morsels go so well with a composed fresh (or poached) fruit compote and, simply paired with hot coffee, can be designated as an American-style kind of petit four if made small and dainty. Delectable.

almond crescents

Line several heavy cookie sheets with lengths of ovenproof parchment paper.

For the dough, sift the flour, baking powder, and salt into a medium-size mixing bowl. Scatter over the finely chopped almonds and whisk to combine.

In a large mixing bowl, whisk the melted butter, the ½ cup confectioners' sugar, vanilla extract, and almond extract. Add the flour-almond mixture and stir to form a dough, using a wooden spoon or flat wooden paddle. Chill the dough, wrapped in food-safe plastic wrap or waxed paper, for 45 minutes.

Preheat the oven to 350 degrees F.

Place the slivered or sliced almonds in a small bowl and have at hand.

To form the cookies, scoop up level 1-tablespoon-size pieces of dough and roll into stubby logs. Place each log of dough, 2 inches apart, on the prepared baking pans. Form the logs into crescent shapes, tapering the ends slightly (without creating very pointy ends). Place some of the slivered or sliced almonds on the surface of each crescent. After the nuts have been applied to the tops of the cookies, go back and plump the cookies gently—as necessary—so that they're even-shaped and well-formed.

Bake the cookies in the preheated oven for 15 to 16 minutes, or until set and light golden. Let the cookies stand on the baking pans for 1 minute, then transfer them to cooling racks, using a wide offset metal spatula. Cool completely. Place the 2½ cups confectioners' sugar in a shallow bowl. Carefully—the cookies are quite tender at this point—dredge the cookies in the confectioners' sugar. After 20 minutes, coat them again in a second haze of confectioners' sugar. Cool completely. Store in an airtight tin in no more than two layers, with waxed paper separating each level of cookies.

notes
• when pressing the almonds onto the unbaked cookies, do so firmly but gently; the dough is usually moist enough so that the almonds stick to the surface; if you are working with the cookie dough on a cold, dry day, it may be necessary to use a lightly beaten egg white for painting over the surface in order for the almonds to adhere (to do so, beat an egg white in a clean, dry bowl until light and frothy; use a small pastry brush to film the surface of each crescent, then press on the nuts)
• never consume raw cookie dough

---

almond butter dough

2¼ cups unsifted bleached all-purpose flour

¾ teaspoon baking powder

⅛ teaspoon salt

½ cup very finely chopped almonds

½ pound (16 tablespoons or 2 sticks) unsalted butter, melted and cooled

½ cup confectioners' sugar

1½ teaspoons vanilla extract

½ teaspoon almond extract

about ¾ cup slivered or sliced almonds, for pressing on the unbaked cookies

about 2½ cups confectioners' sugar, for dredging the baked cookies

serving: about 28 cookies
ahead: 2 days

ginger buttons

ginger butter dough

2 cups plus 3 tablespoons unsifted bleached all-purpose flour

¾ teaspoon baking powder

⅛ teaspoon salt

¾ teaspoon ground ginger

⅓ cup very finely chopped walnuts

½ pound (16 tablespoons or 2 sticks) unsalted butter, melted and cooled

½ cup confectioners' sugar

1½ teaspoons vanilla extract

⅓ cup finely chopped crystallized ginger

about 2½ cups confectioners' sugar, for dredging the baked cookies

serving: about 28 cookies
ahead: 2 days

Line several heavy cookie sheets with lengths of ovenproof parchment paper.

Sift the flour, baking powder, salt, and ground ginger into a medium-size mixing bowl. Scatter over the walnuts and whisk to combine.

In a large mixing bowl, whisk the melted butter, the ½ cup confectioners' sugar, and vanilla extract. Using a wooden spoon or flat wooden paddle, stir in half of the flour-walnut mixture. Blend in the crystallized ginger, then the balance of the flour-walnut mixture. Chill the dough, wrapped in food-safe plastic wrap or waxed paper, for 45 minutes.

Preheat the oven to 350 degrees F.

To form the cookies, scoop up level 1-tablespoon-size pieces of dough and roll into balls. Place the balls of dough, 2 inches apart, on the prepared baking pans.

Bake the cookies in the preheated oven for 15 to 16 minutes, or until set and the bottoms are a light golden color. (To check the bottoms, carefully lift up a cookie with a spatula and peek.) Let the cookies stand on the baking pans for 1 minute, then transfer them to cooling racks, using a wide offset metal spatula. Cool completely. Place the 2½ cups confectioners' sugar in a shallow bowl. Handling them thoughtfully—they are very tender when just-baked—dredge the cookies in the confectioners' sugar. After 20 minutes, coat them again in a second haze of confectioners' sugar. Cool completely. Store in an airtight tin in no more than two layers, with waxed paper separating each level of cookies.

notes
• crystallized ginger adds a sweet and spicy edge to the cookie dough; be sure to use the crystallized variety, for ginger preserved in syrup would add undesirable moisture to the dough
• never consume raw cookie dough

lemon melties

Line several heavy cookie sheets with lengths of ovenproof parchment paper.

Combine the lemon peel and lemon extract in a small nonreactive mixing bowl. Set aside to blossom for 3 to 4 minutes.

Sift the flour, baking powder, and salt into a medium-size mixing bowl.

In a large mixing bowl, whisk the melted butter and ⅓ cup plus 2 tablespoons confectioners' sugar. Blend in the lemon peel–lemon extract mixture. Using a wooden spoon or flat wooden paddle, stir in half of the flour mixture, the walnuts, and then the balance of the flour mixture. Chill the dough, wrapped in food-safe plastic wrap or waxed paper, for 45 minutes.

Preheat the oven to 350 degrees F.

To form the cookies, scoop up level 1-tablespoon-size pieces of dough and roll into fat logs. Place the logs of dough, 2 inches apart, on the prepared cookie sheets.

Bake the cookies in the preheated oven for 15 to 16 minutes, or until set and the bottoms are a light golden color. (To check the bottoms, carefully lift up a cookie with a spatula and peek.) Let the cookies stand on the baking pans for 1 minute, then transfer them to cooling racks, using a wide offset metal spatula. Cool the cookies for 35 minutes. Place the 2½ cups confectioners' sugar in a shallow bowl. Dredge the cookies in the confectioners' sugar carefully, as they are fragile. After 20 minutes, coat them in a second haze of confectioners' sugar. Cool completely. Store in an airtight tin in no more than two layers, with waxed paper separating each level of cookies.

notes
• allowing the lemon peel to blossom in the extract for a few minutes develops the intensity of the citrus and builds the flavor of the dough
• never consume raw cookie dough

lemon butter dough

4 teaspoons finely grated lemon peel

1¼ teaspoons lemon extract

2¼ cups unsifted bleached all-purpose flour

¾ teaspoon baking powder

⅛ teaspoon salt

½ pound (16 tablespoons or 2 sticks) unsalted butter, melted and cooled

⅓ cup plus 2 tablespoons confectioners' sugar

¼ cup very finely chopped walnuts

about 2½ cups confectioners' sugar, for dredging the baked cookies

serving: about 28 cookies
ahead: 2 days

Contour

figs in a relaxed envelopment of dough ✳
a big and curvy coffee cake ✳ when a quick
bread bugs out ✳ cinnamon ensnarled ✳
free-form dessert bread and bosomy soup rolls
for a snowy evening ✳ a saucepan dough that
billows ✳ flatbread untamed and wildly good

Fanciful

winter bread

When chilly breezes drift through the air, the winter cook can justifiably think about filling the kitchen with the heady sweetness of a fruit-filled bread.

And when that same cold wind sweeps through, and you have a pot of soup gurgling along to a savory finish, imagine another kind of bread made from a mix of oats and grains to become just the right accompaniment.

But not just any bread.

On the lightly sweetened end of baked things, my bread of choice for the cold, sometimes unforgiving days and nights is a lightly sweetened yeast bread accented with dried fruit. Consider, for the moment, the lode of moist dried fruits that piles up on the market shelves, oftentimes neglected (poor things!), October through December. Collectively, though they speak of deep earthy flavor, dried fruits are just tossed into a random compote or savory stuffing. Yet when the fruits—especially figs, cherries, raisins, prunes, and apricots—get all caught up in a yeast dough, their essence becomes quite animated. The rambling dough for *bread for dessert, bread for cheese: fruit bread* is made with butter and a few eggs and looks like an irregularly plump mattress; it is a prime example of using dried fruits to their flavorful best. The chopped fruits can be added as is to the once-risen dough, or marinated in dribbles of orange liqueur for a few hours while the dough is achieving its first rise. If the fruits are treated in this manner, you could further expand the overall tone by adding a few teaspoons of the liqueur to the final, prebaking wash of melted butter and benevolent shower of turbinado or granulated sugar that caps it. This would make for a very grown-up finish.

Warm from the oven, a platter of rough and irregular tears *is* dessert and, without the final sugar haze, becomes a fantastic accompaniment to cheese, particularly goat or a farmhouse Cheddar, contrasting the savory with the naturally sweet fruit.

On the bread-for-soup end, I love to bake a pan of grainy rolls, the rolls' texture made tweedy and flaky by integrating some cooked 10-grain cereal, rolled oats, a little whole wheat flour, and wheat bran in a raised yeast dough that includes honey and buttermilk. These are exceedingly plump rolls, and their sides and rounded tops meet one another when the formed second rise is complete. At once tender and robust, the dough can be hand-molded into rolls to sit in tight formation and locked into square baking pans, or shaped as fold-overs and arranged—row by row—on one dramatic expanse of a rimmed sheet pan. Personally, having the orderly configuration of the rolls smartly contained in two baking pans appeals to my sense of design, with the following bonus: rolls that are arranged in pans are much more moist and satiny, and then there is that terrific textural contrast of upper crust and soft, bready sides. Irresistible.

I am always mindful of these two recipes at the first forecast of snow, when home—and specifically the kitchen—becomes the destination hideaway for this cook and her baking ingredients.

bread for dessert, bread for cheese: fruit bread

dried fruit yeast dough

2¼ teaspoons active dry yeast

¼ teaspoon granulated sugar

½ cup warm (105 to 110 degrees F) water

¼ cup unsifted unbleached all-purpose flour

⅓ cup milk

3 tablespoons granulated sugar

1¾ teaspoons vanilla extract

2 large eggs

1¾ cups unsifted unbleached all-purpose flour blended with ¼ teaspoon salt

9 tablespoons (1 stick plus 1 tablespoon) unsalted butter, softened

½ cup stemmed and coarsely chopped dried figs

½ cup moist pitted and coarsely chopped prunes

⅓ cup golden raisins

⅓ cup coarsely chopped dried apricots

⅓ cup tart (Montmorency) dried cherries

butter and sugar finish

2 tablespoons unsalted butter (preferably clarified butter, page 1) melted and cooled to tepid

about 3 tablespoons turbinado sugar or granulated sugar (optional)

serving: one flatbread, creating about 15 randomly shaped tears of bread
ahead: best on baking day

For the dough, stir together the yeast, the ¼ teaspoon granulated sugar, and the warm water in a heatproof measuring cup. Allow the mixture to stand until swollen, 6 to 7 minutes. Turn the yeast mixture into a small mixing bowl, stir in the ¼ cup flour, cover with a sheet of food-safe plastic wrap, and let stand at room temperature for 30 to 35 minutes, or until bubbly and expanded by at least half.

Place the milk and the 3 tablespoons granulated sugar in a small saucepan. Set over low heat to warm the milk. Remove from the heat, whisk well, and cool to tepid. Pour the milk mixture into the bowl of a heavy-duty freestanding electric mixer fitted with the flat paddle. Blend in the vanilla extract, eggs, and yeasty flour mixture. Mix on low speed until thoroughly blended. Add the 1¾ cups flour-salt blend in 3 additions, stopping the mixer to scrape down the sides of the bowl after each portion is added. Beat in the butter, 2 tablespoons at a time, then beat in the remaining 1 tablespoon. Stop the machine from time to time to scrape down the sides of the bowl. Beat the dough on moderate speed for 4 minutes. At this point, the dough should be smooth, elastic, shiny, and somewhat moist-sticky. (If the dough seems too unmanageable, you can add up to 2 tablespoons flour, 1 teaspoon at a time.)

Scrape the dough into a bowl heavily coated with softened unsalted butter, lightly turn to coat all sides in a film of butter, make several cuts in the dough with a pair of kitchen scissors, cover tightly with a sheet of food-safe plastic wrap, and let rise at room temperature for 1 hour and 15 minutes, or until doubled in bulk. Remove the sheet of plastic wrap.

Lightly compress the risen dough with a rubber spatula, cover loosely with the plastic wrap, and let stand for 10 minutes. Remove and discard the plastic wrap. Sprinkle over the dried figs, prunes, raisins, apricots, and cherries and knead lightly in the bowl until incorporated. At first the dough will reject the fruits and the fruits will break through the dough, but then it will enclose them (although pieces of fruit will stick here and there to the exposed surfaces).

Film a heavy rimmed sheet pan with softened unsalted butter. Place the dough in the center of the pan and press into a free-form oval, clearing about 4 inches from the four side edges of the pan. Cover loosely with two sheets of food-safe plastic wrap. Let rise at room temperature for 1 hour, or until puffy and almost doubled in bulk (see page 6 to reference this stage).

Preheat the oven to 375 degrees F in advance of baking.

Remove and discard the sheets of plastic wrap covering the bread about 15 minutes before the bread is completely risen.

Using the finish ingredients, lightly brush the melted butter over the surface of the risen bread. Continue to let the bread finish rising, uncovered, for another 15 minutes. Just before baking, sprinkle the turbinado or granulated sugar over the surface of the bread if it is intended as a sweet (omit the sugar sprinkle if serving with cheese).

Bake the bread in the preheated oven for 30 minutes, or until set and a golden color on top. Cool the bread on the pan on a cooling rack for 10 minutes. Serve the bread warm, torn into free-form pieces.

notes
• to lace the dried fruits with orange liqueur, toss them with 5 teaspoons orange liqueur, such as Grand Marnier or Cointreau, before you begin to put together the yeast bread; knead the fruits into the bread as described (the dough will be a little more moist) and continue with shaping and baking

bread for soup: favorite grainy pan rolls

For the cooked cereal, place the 10-grain cereal and water in a medium-size saucepan, set over moderately high heat, and bring to the boil, stirring occasionally. Reduce the heat to low, cover, and simmer the cereal, stirring now and again, for 8 to 10 minutes, or until just cooked through and creamy. Uncover, place on a heatproof trivet, and set aside.

For the dough, stir together the yeast, the ¼ teaspoon granulated sugar, and the warm water in a heatproof measuring cup. Allow the mixture to stand until swollen, 6 to 7 minutes.

In the meantime, place the rolled oats and wheat bran in a medium-size heatproof mixing bowl, pour over the boiling water, stir, and let stand for 10 minutes. Stir in the cooked cereal and set aside.

Place the buttermilk, maple syrup, light brown sugar, honey, butter, and shortening in a medium-size saucepan, set over low heat, and warm until the butter and shortening melt. Remove from the heat, whisk well, scrape into a medium-size heatproof mixing bowl, and let stand for 5 to 7 minutes to cool to tepid. Stir in the cereal mixture and egg, using a wooden spoon or flat wooden paddle. Mix in the baking soda. Blend in the yeast mixture.

(continued on the next page)

cooked 10-grain cereal

⅓ cup 10-grain cereal

1½ cups water

oatmeal, whole wheat, 10-grain cereal, and bran yeast dough

4½ teaspoons active dry yeast

¼ teaspoon granulated sugar

¼ cup warm (105 to 110 degrees F) water

1 cup "old-fashioned" rolled oats

½ cup wheat bran

1 cup boiling water

1½ cups buttermilk

2 tablespoons maple syrup

(continued on the next page)

(continued from the previous page)

3 tablespoons firmly packed
light brown sugar

¼ cup honey (preferably wildflower)

3 tablespoons unsalted butter

3 tablespoons solid shortening

1 large egg

¾ teaspoon baking soda

6 cups unsifted unbleached bread flour,
plus an additional ½ cup, as needed
for kneading

1 teaspoon salt

1 cup unsifted whole wheat flour

serving: 32 rolls

ahead: best on baking day; or freeze for
3 weeks, defrost, bundle in aluminum foil,
and reheat in a preheated 300 degrees F
oven for 15 minutes

Whisk 3 cups of the bread flour, the salt, and whole wheat flour in a large mixing bowl. Add the yeasty, grainy mixture and stir to mix; the yeasty cereal mixture will be thick, moist, and heavy at this point. Let the mixture stand, uncovered, for 5 minutes. Stir in the remaining 3 cups bread flour, 1 cup at a time, waiting 3 minutes between additions. The final cup of bread flour needs to be incorporated by hand and the dough may not receive it all at once. Dust a work surface with a little of the additional ½ cup bread flour. Knead the dough for 8 to 10 minutes, incorporating as much of the additional bread flour to make it manageable, but realize that the finished dough will still be slightly tacky to the touch. Use a pastry scraper at all times to keep the dough moving during the kneading process.

Turn the dough into a bowl heavily coated with softened unsalted butter, lightly turn to coat all sides in a film of butter, make several cuts in the dough with a pair of kitchen scissors, cover tightly with a sheet of food-safe plastic wrap, and let rise in a cozy, slightly warm spot for 1 hour and 20 minutes, or until doubled in bulk.

Film the inside of two 9 by 9 by 3-inch baking pans with nonstick flour-and-oil spray.

To form the rolls, uncover the dough and discard the plastic wrap. Turn the dough out onto a lightly floured work surface, but avoid compressing it. Cut the dough in half, then divide each half into quarters. Further divide each quarter portion into 4 even-size pieces. There should be 32 pieces of dough. Smooth each piece into a plump ball by rolling it on the work surface briskly under the cupped palm of your hand. Place the balls of dough in the prepared baking pans, assembling them in four rows of 4 each.

Cover each pan of rolls loosely with a sheet of food-safe plastic wrap. Let the rolls rise in a cozy place for 1 hour to 1 hour and 15 minutes, or until quite plump and doubled in bulk (see page 6 to reference this stage). The rolls will merge as they rise.

Preheat the oven to 350 degrees F in advance of baking.

Remove and discard the sheets of plastic wrap covering the rolls.

Bake the rolls in the preheated oven for 35 minutes, or until set. Place the pans on cooling racks and let stand for 10 minutes. Carefully invert the rolls onto other cooling racks. Lift off each pan, then invert the rolls again to stand right side up. Serve the rolls warm or at room temperature, by pulling the sections apart at their natural seams. Store in an airtight container.

a fresh fig and pastry jamboree

When fresh Black Mission figs abound at the market, my baking thoughts travel immediately in the direction of this relaxed, country-style tart—it's a baking reflex response. The cookie dough that I use as the wrapper for the fig-rich free-form tart has been in my baking file for more than twenty-five years.

To be honest, it has taken me several figgy seasons to get it just right: more sugar or less of it; banish the ice water!; add leavening—but not too much; include that elusive 1 teaspoon of milk; use a *whole* egg; and on and on. It is a variation of my now-classic (in my baking file's genealogy) rich pie dough. The ice-cold water has been replaced by a whole egg and the amount of sugar is significantly greater: these changes add up to a dough that is a snap to prepare in a food processor and beautifully encompasses—no, embraces—a few more than a dozen lightly sweetened and spiced fresh figs. Really, if any dough can be considered a pushover, then this one is it—not too delicate, beautifully buttery, and leavened a touch to improve its overall texture. Although you will love to make it in a processor, I am offering the by-hand version for those who cherish getting into the "feel" of dough; admittedly, I like to get my fingers into the mix of it all now and then, and I bet that you do, too.

This gala affair of figs and cookie dough takes the form of a somewhat free-handed circle. The round cake of prepared dough is rolled out, keeping its circular form reasonably intact, and is topped with figs. The figs are finished with a discreet amount of sugar that has been seasoned with ground cinnamon and freshly grated nutmeg. The unfettered and unstructured edges of dough are folded over the fruit, leaving a certain amount of it to peek through the center. Those slightly thicker enveloping edges can be treated to a prebaking dusting of granulated sugar or postbaking splash of confectioners' sugar. Once baked, the figs that peek though the center of the rustic edges of pastry can be lightly swabbed with red currant jelly glaze or drizzled with honey. Slices of the tart are even better when offered with lightly sweetened whipped cream or scoops of vanilla ice cream: at once warm, fruity, creamy, and just divine.

As the fresh figs settle into the pastry dough and bake, they get a little jammy as both their flavor and texture concentrate. The bottom finishes tender and flaky, and the wide edges of the pastry dough turn golden. All of this sets the stage for a most alluring slice-of-summer on a dessert plate.

rustic fig tart

buttery dough

2 cups unsifted bleached all-purpose flour

⅛ teaspoon baking powder

¼ teaspoon salt

11 tablespoons (1 stick plus 3 tablespoons) cold unsalted butter, cut into small, rough chunks

5 tablespoons granulated sugar

1 cold large egg

1 teaspoon cold milk

1¼ teaspoons vanilla extract

spiced and sugar-sweetened figs

3 tablespoons granulated sugar whisked with ½ teaspoon ground cinnamon and ¼ teaspoon freshly grated nutmeg

18 fresh figs (about 2½ generous pints), stemmed and left whole

2 tablespoons granulated sugar, for sprinkling on the folded-over edges of the unbaked tart (optional, if you are not using the confectioners' sugar finish)

red currant jelly glaze (optional)

about ⅔ cup best-quality red currant jelly

confectioners' sugar, for sprinkling on the baked tart (optional)

serving: one tart, creating 12 pie-shape wedges
ahead: best on baking day

To make the dough in a food processor, place the flour, baking powder, and salt in the work bowl of a food processor fitted with the steel blade. Cover and process, using quick on-off pulses, to combine the ingredients, 5 to 10 seconds. Add the chunks of butter, cover, and process to reduce the butter to smaller bits. Uncover, sprinkle over the granulated sugar, cover, and pulse once or twice to combine. Whisk the egg, milk, and vanilla extract in a small mixing bowl. Pour the egg mixture over the flour and butter mixture, cover, and process, using 10 to 15 on-off pulses, until the mixture just begins to come together in small clumps. The clumps should look moist. Turn the beginnings of the dough onto a work surface and gather it into one solid mass, smoothing it together lightly with the heel of your hand into a round cake.

To make the dough by hand, whisk the flour, baking powder, and salt in a medium-size mixing bowl. Drop in the chunks of butter and, using a pastry blender or two round-bladed table knives, cut the fat into the flour mixture until reduced to smaller morsels (irregular bits of butter are fine). Sprinkle over the granulated sugar and use a fork to mix it through the butter mixture. With your fingertips, dip into the buttered flour mixture and crumble it to further disperse the fat. Whisk the egg, milk, and vanilla extract in a small mixing bowl. Pour the egg mixture over the flour and butter mixture and mix to form a dough, using a flat wooden paddle or sturdy spatula. It will come together in moist clumps. Turn the rough lumps and pieces of dough onto a work surface. Press, smear, and pat the dough into one solid mass, using the heel of your hand, forming it into a round cake.

Wrap the cake of dough in a sheet of waxed paper and refrigerate for 20 minutes.

Roll the dough between two sheets of waxed paper into a 12 to 13-inch round. It's fine if the edges are slightly ragged and misshapen—this adds to the charm of the overall tart—but be sure to make as even a circle as possible. Place the tart dough round on a cookie sheet or rimmed sheet pan and refrigerate for 2 hours.

Preheat the oven to 375 degrees F in advance of baking.

Line a rimmed sheet pan with a length of ovenproof parchment paper.

To form the tart, carefully peel away the top sheet of waxed paper from the dough. Invert the dough round onto the center of the parchment paper–lined baking pan and peel away the second sheet of waxed paper. Let the dough stand for 15 to 30 minutes, or until just pliable (this will depend upon the ambient temperature of your kitchen). If the dough is too cold, it will crack, splinter, and break when folding it over the figs; if this happens, it is not the end of the world, so just firmly smooth over and press together the cracks with your fingertips to reunite the sections of dough. Rustic is rustic—and pretty.

Sprinkle the surface of the dough with 1 tablespoon of the spiced sugar mixture (taken from the 3-tablespoon quantity), leaving a 2½ to 3-inch outer band of dough clear of sugar. Place the figs in a medium-size mixing bowl, sprinkle over the remaining 2 tablespoons spiced sugar, and toss well (but lightly). Spoon the sugar-spiced figs in one layer onto the center portion of the sugared surface.

Fold over the band of tart dough to create an overlapping border. You can use a flexible palette knife or small offset metal spatula to help lift the dough up slightly and partially over the mound of figs. Make a few pleats in the border as necessary. The center portion of figs will be exposed and a wide circular portion of it will be covered with the pastry dough. Sprinkle the 2 tablespoons sugar on top of the folded-over tart dough border, if you are not planning on dusting the edges of the baked tart with confectioners' sugar.

Bake the tart in the preheated oven for 45 minutes, or until the figs are tender, the natural fruit juices gurgle up here and there, and the pastry is set and golden. Let the tart stand on the baking pan on a cooling rack for 20 minutes. If you are glazing the tart with the red currant jelly, warm the jelly in a small saucepan over low heat until melted down completely and bring to the barest simmer, then paint the figs with the jelly, using a soft pastry brush. Cool the tart to warm or to room temperature. If you have not sugared the folded edges before baking, sift a little confectioners' sugar over the rims' folds before cutting into generous wedges for serving.

notes
• aim for selecting small figs, but small to medium ones will do just fine (leave those whole as well)
• use a serrated knife, preferably an offset one, for slicing the tart; a serrated knife will cut through the baked tart attractively without tearing the tender, yet stable, pastry

inflated and cream-filled, inflated in a savory way

Anything stuffed with cream (whipped, custardy, or a permutation thereof) is a great love of mine. The lightsome collaboration of smooth cream and crackly pastry is heaven-sent.

A cream puff—blown up, boisterous, and boasting a center of stove top–cooked pudding—is so luscious and the perfect union of opposites. Both elements should be prime: the choux puff shells crispy yet submissively tender and the filling thickened to that smoothly limpid state. The two merge beautifully, but cannot sit for hours, only minutes. Bake the bold pastry housings, squirt in the velvety centers, and eat one-two-three. When you crave a light and savory puff, remove the granulated sugar and vanilla extract and add a few shots of liquid hot pepper sauce, such as Tabasco, and generous handfuls of Gruyère cheese. Now you have a toothsome cocktail accessory—serve the puffs just pulled from the oven. Sometimes baking is this ephemeral.

vanilla cream clouds
with soft vanilla center

eggy vanilla dough

1 cup unsifted unbleached all-purpose flour

large pinch of salt

1 cup water

1 tablespoon granulated sugar

1 teaspoon vanilla extract

8 tablespoons (1 stick) unsalted butter,
cut into tablespoon-size chunks

5 large eggs, lightly beaten

soft vanilla center (page 280)

confectioners' sugar, for dredging the
tops of the baked-and-filled sweets

serving: 1 dozen puffs
ahead: baked puffs, 2 hours
(before filling); finished and filled puffs
(immediately after filling)

Preheat the oven to 375 degrees F.

Line two heavy cookie sheets or rimmed sheet pans with lengths of ovenproof parchment paper. Have a 12-inch pastry bag assembled with a ½-inch plain round tip (Ateco #806) at hand. Twist the bottom end of the pastry bag about 2 turns and tuck it into the interior of the tip, then turn down a 2-inch collar on the bag. Set aside.

For the dough, sift the flour and salt onto a sheet of waxed paper.

Place the water, granulated sugar, vanilla extract, and butter in a heavy, medium-size nonreactive saucepan (preferably enameled cast iron). Place over high heat and bring to the boil. As soon as the contents of the saucepan reaches the boil, immediately remove the saucepan from the heat, add the sifted mixture, and mix to form a dough using a flat wooden paddle. This base should be smooth, and the preliminary dough will pull away from the sides of the saucepan. The dough will be somewhat soft at this point. Mix only until the dough comes away from the sides of the saucepan. Reduce the heat to low, return the saucepan to the heat, and let the dough "dry out" for 1 minute, moving it around during this time. Remove the saucepan from the heat. Let the dough stand in the saucepan (still off the heat) for 1 minute. Continuing off the heat, beat in the beaten eggs in 3 or 4 additions, beating until thoroughly incorporated before adding the next portion, and reserving about one-fifth of the beaten eggs. The best device for beating is a flat wooden paddle.

At this point, the dough should be thick. Beat in only enough of the remaining beaten egg mixture, a little at a time, to arrive at a dough that is slightly firm and holds its shape in a spoon. The ambient humidity (or lack thereof) and absorption quality of the flour may have an impact on your results. Note that if the dough is too moist, the resulting baked shape will be flat, squat, or slanted and the pastries may not bake properly; if the dough is too firm, the pastries will not puff or rise as much as they should. Beat the dough for a full 2 to 3 minutes, when it will become very smooth and shiny. Underbeating the dough at this point will result in puny puffs. Holding the pastry bag by the inside of the turned-down collar, fill the bag a little more than half full with the dough (then refill when the contents is depleted). Flip up the collar, undo the twisted bottom end, and carefully press down the mixture with your fingertips. Gently twist the top of the bag to close. The mixture is now ready for piping.

With your fingertips, sprinkle random droplets of water on the baking pans to dampen them slightly. The steam created by the droplets of water will help the large puffs to achieve a better rise and inflation.

Pipe 6 high mounds of dough (about 2 inches in diameter) onto each of the two lined baking pans, spacing the mounds 2 inches apart.

Place the puffs in the preheated oven. Immediately raise the oven temperature to 400 degrees F. Bake the puffs for 30 minutes, or until well-risen, set, and a deep golden brown. Turn off the oven. Remove the puffs from the oven. Quickly and carefully, poke a small hole in the side of each puff to release steam, using the tip of a metal skewer or wooden pick. Return the puffs to the oven for 1 minute, then remove them. Place the baking pans of puffs on cooling racks. Cool for 5 minutes, then transfer the puffs directly to racks to cool completely, using a wide offset metal spatula.

Have the soft vanilla center prepared and refrigerated.

Fit a 12-inch pastry bag with a Bismarck tip (Wilton #230) or a ⅜-inch plain round tip. Twist the bottom end of the pastry bag about 2 turns and tuck it into the interior of the tip and turn down a 2-inch collar on the bag. Holding the pastry bag by the inside of the turned-down collar, fill the bag a little more than one-third full with the soft vanilla center. Flip up the collar, undo the twisted bottom end, and carefully press down the mixture with your fingertips. Gently twist the top of the bag to close. Pipe some of the cream filling into each pastry cloud nudging the tip in through the hole created to allow the steam to escape; refill the bag as it is depleted. Or, simply cut the puff in half, spoon in some of the soft vanilla center, and cover with the top half of the puff.

Dredge the top of the pastries with the confectioners' sugar and serve immediately.

notes
- the baking pans must be heavy or the bottoms of the puffs will darken substantially before the interiors are baked through
- any extra beaten egg can be used to glaze the unbaked puffs before baking, but bear in mind that if you glaze the puffs, they may brown too quickly before their interiors are baked through and, on occasion, the glaze may prohibit maximum rise
- the puffs are baked in what I like to describe as a "rising oven," and this tactic encourages maximum lift
- if the dough is not piped into high mounds, the overall yield of the puffs will be more than a dozen (and nearly 1½ dozen)
- an éclair or Bismarck tip has a long "nose" for inserting into an individual pastry, muffin, or cupcake for filling; in the Wilton tip organizational system, this tip is #230, and it is a handy one to own

soft vanilla center

creamy vanilla filling

⅓ cup plus 1 tablespoon granulated sugar

2 tablespoons cornstarch

large pinch of salt

1½ cups milk

½ cup heavy cream

5 large egg yolks

1¾ teaspoons vanilla extract

1 tablespoon unsalted butter, cut into bits

¼ teaspoon vanilla bean paste (optional)

serving: about 2 cups
ahead: 2 days

Sift the sugar, cornstarch, and salt into a heavy, medium-size nonreactive saucepan (preferably enameled cast iron). Whisk the ingredients together to combine. Slowly pour in the milk, mixing with a wooden spoon or flat wooden paddle as it is added. Blend in the heavy cream.

Set the saucepan over moderately high heat and bring to the boil, stirring slowly all the while with the wooden spoon or flat wooden paddle. Let the mixture bubble until very lightly thickened, about 2 minutes.

In a small heatproof mixing bowl, mix the egg yolks to blend. Remove the saucepan of thickened cream from the heat and stir about ⅔ cup of the cream mixture into the egg yolks a little at a time, mixing well. Continuing with the saucepan off the heat, slowly stir the tempered egg yolk mixture into the cream base. Return the saucepan to moderate heat and cook the pastry cream at a gentle bubble, stirring slowly, until thickened, about 2 minutes. The filling should reach a temperature of 200 degrees F to achieve the appropriate thickness and structure. It will resemble soft pudding.

Place the vanilla extract, bits of butter, and vanilla bean paste (if you are using it) in a medium-size heatproof bowl. Set a fine- or medium-mesh sieve on top of the bowl and scrape the pastry cream into it (if your sieve is small, this will have to be done in batches). Smooth the pastry cream through the sieve, using a heatproof rubber spatula, taking care not to agitate the mixture as you are doing this. Stir to incorporate the butter, vanilla extract, and optional vanilla bean paste. Press a sheet of food-safe plastic wrap directly onto the surface of the vanilla cream.

Cool the vanilla cream for 15 minutes. Remove and discard the plastic wrap. Scrape the filling into a storage container, place a clean sheet of plastic wrap on the surface, cover tightly, and refrigerate for at least 4 hours (or up to 2 days) before using.

notes
- the saucepan must be heavy or the filling will scorch
- when stirring the pastry cream as it cooks—with and without the egg yolks—always use a wooden spoon or flat wooden paddle rather than a whisk (a whisk may shear through the thickened mixture and cause it to break down, thus thinning it out and turning it runny)

Preheat the oven to 375 degrees F.

Line two heavy cookie sheets or rimmed sheet pans with lengths of ovenproof parchment paper. Have a 12-inch pastry bag assembled with a ⅜-inch plain round tip (Ateco #804) at hand. Twist the bottom end of the pastry bag about 2 turns and tuck it into the interior of the tip, then turn down a 2-inch collar on the bag.

Prepare the cream puff dough as directed in the recipe for the *vanilla cream clouds* (page 278), using the ingredient list provided with this recipe (note the omissions of granulated sugar and vanilla extract, the increase in salt, and the addition of Gruyère, paprika, freshly ground black pepper, and liquid hot pepper sauce). The black pepper and liquid hot pepper sauce should be added to the saucepan of water and chunks of butter, and the paprika sifted with the flour and salt. Begin by adding the 4 beaten eggs, adding only enough of the remaining beaten egg, a little at a time, to arrive at a dough that is firm and does not sag when a spoonful is lifted up. The dough will firm up a little more after the cheese is added. After the dough is beaten for the final 2 minutes (after the beaten eggs are incorporated), beat in the Gruyère. Holding the pastry bag by the inside of the turned-down collar, fill the bag a little more than half full with the dough (refill when the contents is depleted). Flip up the collar, undo the twisted bottom end, and carefully press down the mixture with your fingertips. Gently twist the top of the bag to close. The dough is now ready for piping.

Pipe 12 high mounds of dough (about 1 inch in diameter) onto each of the two lined baking pans, spacing the mounds 2 inches apart. Sprinkle the tops of the mounds with the coarse sea salt.

Place the puffs in the preheated oven. Immediately raise the temperature to 400 degrees F. Bake the puffs for 25 minutes, or until well-risen, set, and a deep golden brown. Remove the puffs from the oven. Since the puffs will be served oven-fresh and unfilled, it is unnecessary to poke holes in them. Serve the puffs immediately, presented in a linen- or paper doily–lined basket or on a plate.

notes
• work quickly to incorporate the Gruyère into the warm paste mixture
• if the dough is not piped into high mounds, the overall yield of the puffs will be more than 2 dozen (about 2½ dozen)
• any extra beaten egg can be used to glaze the unbaked puffs before baking, but bear in mind that if you glaze the puffs, they may brown too quickly before their interiors are baked through and, on occasion, the glaze may prohibit maximum rise
• a little extra Gruyère (¼ cup) can be sprinkled on the very tops of the unbaked mounds of dough just before baking, if you wish

cheese cloud dough

1 cup unsifted unbleached all-purpose flour

¼ teaspoon salt

½ teaspoon sweet paprika

1 cup water

6 grinds freshly ground black pepper

½ teaspoon liquid hot pepper sauce (such as Tabasco)

8 tablespoons (1 stick) unsalted butter, cut into tablespoon-size chunks

4 large eggs, beaten, plus 1 large egg, beaten, as needed

1 cup freshly grated Gruyère cheese

coarse sea salt, for sprinkling on the tops of the unbaked puffs

serving: 2 dozen puffs

loopy

Balls of dough—rolled in butter and cinnamon sugar—look rather comical nestled in a big tube pan.

Yet, as they merge and the whole coffee cake rises to magnificent heights, the interconnected orbs form interesting mosaic slices, patterned as they are with dark ripples of spiced sugar. This gentle and supple yeasted coffee cake dough is beautifully manageable; it is enriched with plenty of butter, milk, and whole eggs. Four teaspoons of vanilla extract add a glimmering floral scent. In its plainest version, cinnamon and butter dominate the flavor palette. But you can scatter chopped walnuts or raisins around and about balls of dough as you toss them into the pan, as the extras fill in the little nooks so well.

If you are not slicing this tall sweet-bread-cake into ample slices, do as I do and use it as an interactive centerpiece at brunch, letting each guest have a go at freeing up his or her own cluster of coffee cake.

bubble bread

big-on-butter yeast dough

4½ teaspoons active dry yeast

¼ teaspoon granulated sugar

⅓ cup warm (105 to 110 degrees F) water

1 cup milk

½ cup granulated sugar

4 large eggs

4 teaspoons vanilla extract

6 cups unsifted bleached all-purpose flour, plus an additional ¼ cup, as needed for kneading

2 tablespoons ground cinnamon

1 teaspoon freshly grated nutmeg

1¼ teaspoons salt

½ pound (16 tablespoons or 2 sticks) unsalted butter, cut into tablespoon-size chunks, softened

butter and cinnamon sugar roll

8 tablespoons (1 stick) unsalted butter, melted, cooled to tepid, and whisked with 1 teaspoon vanilla extract

1¼ cups granulated sugar blended with 2 tablespoons ground cinnamon

shimmery finish (optional)

apricot glaze (page 191)

serving: one 10-inch sweet bread, creating about 16 slices
ahead: 2 days

For the dough, stir together the yeast, the ¼ teaspoon sugar, and the warm water in a heatproof measuring cup. Allow the mixture to stand until swollen, 6 to 7 minutes.

Place the milk and the ½ cup sugar in a small saucepan and set over low heat. When the sugar has dissolved, remove the saucepan from the heat. Pour and scrape the mixture into a medium-size heatproof mixing bowl. Let stand for 5 to 6 minutes to cool to tepid, then whisk in the eggs and the vanilla extract. Blend in the yeast mixture.

Place 5 cups of the flour, the cinnamon, nutmeg, and salt in a large mixing bowl. Whisk to combine. Pour over the yeast-egg-milk mixture; mix to combine, using a wooden spoon or flat wooden paddle. Scrape the dough into the bowl of a heavy-duty freestanding electric mixer. Set the bowl in place and attach the dough hook. Add the butter, 4 tablespoons at a time, beating on moderately low to moderate speed until absorbed (about 1 minute) before adding the next amount. The dough will be smooth, elastic, and sticky. Add the remaining 1 cup flour and beat for 1 minute. The dough should be pudgy and somewhat resilient. Throughout the mixing process, stop the machine from time to time to scrape down the sides of the mixing bowl and the dough hook.

Turn the dough out onto a work surface dusted with the additional ¼ cup flour. Knead the dough for 4 minutes, using only enough of the flour to prevent it from sticking too much; the dough should remain somewhat moist.

Turn the dough into a bowl heavily coated with softened unsalted butter, lightly turn to coat all sides in a film of butter, make several cuts in the dough with a pair of kitchen scissors, cover tightly with a sheet of food-safe plastic wrap, and let rise at room temperature for 1 hour and 15 minutes to 1 hour and 30 minutes, or until doubled in bulk.

Remove the plastic wrap. Lightly compress the dough with a rubber spatula, cover loosely with the plastic wrap, and let stand for 5 minutes. Remove and discard the sheet of plastic wrap.

Film the inside of a plain, one-piece 10-inch tube pan (4¼ to 4½ inches deep, with a capacity of 18 cups) with nonstick flour-and-oil spray.

For the butter and cinnamon sugar roll, place the melted butter–vanilla extract blend and cinnamon sugar in separate shallow bowls. Have the bowls at hand at your work surface.

To form the coffee cake, divide the dough into 8 even-size pieces, then divide each piece into 4 portions. There should be 32 balls. Smooth each piece into a plump ball by rolling it on the work surface briskly under the cupped palm of your hand.

Roll each ball first in a film of melted butter, then in the cinnamon sugar. As it is coated, place each ball in the prepared baking pan. Do so in an irregular pattern, filling in the gaps, here and there, as you go. Be sure, however, to arrive at a reasonably even surface area as you finish the final layer, but note that the top will be irregular because the dough balls have rounded surfaces.

Cover the pan of coffee cake loosely with a lightly buttered or nonstick oil spray–filmed sheet of food-safe plastic wrap. Let the coffee cake rise at room temperature for 1 hour, or until almost doubled in bulk (see page 6 to reference this stage). The bread should rise to under ¾ inch of the pan's rim. (If the bread rises too much, you will risk having it collapse in the oven as it bakes; keep in mind that, for this kind of yeast-raised coffee cake, it is better to err on the side of under-rising the formed cake.)

Preheat the oven to 375 degrees F in advance of baking.

Have a rimmed sheet pan at hand.

Remove and discard the sheet of plastic wrap covering the coffee cake. Place the pan of coffee cake on the rimmed sheet pan (to catch any sweet and buttery ooze that bubbles over here and there during baking).

Bake the coffee cake in the preheated oven for 50 minutes, or until set and baked through. The top will be a deep golden brown and the cake will just begin to pull away from the sides of the baking pan. The cake will sound vaguely hollow when the top is lightly tapped with the long handle of a wooden spoon. If the surface of the coffee cake begins to brown too quickly, tent or drape a sheet of aluminum foil loosely over the top of the baking pan (avoid pressing the foil firmly on the top or down the sides of the pan).

Cool the coffee cake in the pan on a rack for 10 to 12 minutes. Carefully invert the coffee cake onto another cooling rack. Lift off the pan. Cool completely. If you are finishing the sweet bread with the apricot glaze, apply it to the top and sides of the coffee cake, using a soft pastry brush. Let the glaze set for at least 1 hour before serving. Store in an airtight cake keeper.

notes
- versions of this sweet bread often call for dividing the dough into smaller balls, but creating jumbo balls seems to make a moister baked coffee cake
- stand by the mixer for the entire beating times referenced in the procedure
- my favorite way to present the coffee cake is upside down, for its geographical surface is the most interesting (you can see the curlicues that the baked dough balls form)

soda "pop"

Lightly crumbly, with the pleasant tang of thick buttermilk and generously dappled with golden raisins or simply darkened with whole wheat flour, soda bread is an easygoing delight—more so when the freshly baked, crusty-edged slices are spread with salted butter.

Double the recipe and the extra becomes a thoughtful neighborly gift or treat to take along if you are a weekend guest. Nearly childlike in its simplicity to create, any form of the dough can be assembled and ready for its oven sojourn in the time it takes to preheat the oven.

The raisin soda bread is moist, spiced with freshly grated nutmeg (plus allspice and cinnamon), leavened with baking powder and baking soda, lightly sweetened, and enriched with several tablespoons of butter and a single egg yolk. The latter two ingredients distinguish the bread, contributing to its overall flavor and textural quality. The whole wheat rendering is not very sweet, but, with its dense yet velvety crumb, it is good paired with any one of the sharp artisanal Cheddars available, or with a smear of ginger or rose petal preserves (if serving with cheese, be sure to include the pecans or walnuts).

The procedure for making the dough resembles biscuit or scone making, as a certain amount of fat (in the form of cold unsalted butter) is reduced to small flakes, flecks, and slightly larger nubbins within the dry ingredients. Following that, a whisked mixture of buttermilk, an egg yolk or whole egg, and vanilla extract in the bread pointed up with raisins, is poured on; any additions (such as fruits or nuts) are scattered over all; and a dough is formed. The dough for either bread is made in its entirety in the mixing bowl, then smoothed into a plump ball on a lightly floured or wheat bran–sprinkled work surface. Once settled on the baking sheet and slashed, it is only a matter of waiting forty to fifty minutes before the aromatic bread can be pulled from the oven. The raisin soda bread is sugared lightly before baking, the wheaty one is left to bake with its clinging overcoat of bran. On baking, both breads spread and pop open at the cross-carved split in an expansive rise. Then the rustic loaves are indeed hard to resist, but do give both at least thirty minutes of resting time before savoring their warm, handmade goodness.

raisin soda bread, sweetly

golden raisin and walnut buttermilk dough

2 cups unsifted bleached all-purpose flour

2 teaspoons baking powder

½ teaspoon baking soda

¼ teaspoon salt

¾ teaspoon freshly grated nutmeg

½ teaspoon ground allspice

¼ teaspoon ground cinnamon

¼ cup granulated sugar

3 tablespoons cold unsalted butter, cut into chunks

¾ cup buttermilk

1 large egg yolk

1¼ teaspoons vanilla extract

1 cup golden raisins

½ cup chopped walnuts or pecans (optional)

about 2 tablespoons sparkling sugar (plain or a color), for sprinkling on the unbaked round of dough

serving: one quick bread, creating about 10 slices
ahead: 2 days

Preheat the oven to 375 degrees F.

Line a heavy cookie sheet or rimmed sheet pan with a length of ovenproof parchment paper.

For the dough, whisk the flour, baking powder, baking soda, salt, nutmeg, allspice, cinnamon, and granulated sugar in a medium-size mixing bowl. Drop in the chunks of butter and, using a pastry blender or two round-bladed table knives, cut the fat into the flour mixture until reduced to pea-size bits.

In a small mixing bowl, whisk the buttermilk, egg yolk, and vanilla extract.

Pour the buttermilk mixture over the flour mixture, sprinkle over the raisins and walnuts or pecans (if you are using either), and stir to form a dough. The dough will be moderately moist. Note that the dough should be mixed only to shape and form, as actual kneading results in a dense-textured crumb.

Transfer the dough to a lightly floured work surface and form into a well-domed ball measuring about 5 inches in diameter. Place the dough ball in the center of the baking pan. With a small sharp knife, cut a cross on top of the bread (about ¼ inch deep) to about 3 inches short of the bottom of the loaf on all four sides. Sprinkle the sparkling sugar over the surface of the dough ball.

Bake the bread in the preheated oven for 40 minutes, or until set and a golden color on top. The baked bread will sound hollow when gently tapped on the bottom with the long handle of a wooden spoon. Let the bread stand on the baking pan for 1 minute, then remove it to a cooling rack, using two wide offset metal spatulas. Serve warm or at room temperature.

notes
• using cold butter controls the texture as you are combining the ingredients and shaping the loaf
• any golden raisins stuck on the surface of the bread will darken somewhat on baking (this is to be expected)
• using a heavy baking pan assures that the bread bakes evenly without scorching
• use a finely serrated knife to cut the bread

lush whole wheat soda bread

Preheat the oven to 375 degrees F.

Line a heavy cookie sheet or rimmed sheet pan with a length of ovenproof parchment paper.

For the dough, sift the whole wheat flour, all-purpose flour, baking soda, baking powder, and salt into a large mixing bowl. Add the sugar and whisk to combine. Drop in the chunks of butter and, using a pastry blender or two round-bladed table knives, cut the fat into the flour mixture until reduced to flakes and pea-size bits.

In a small mixing bowl, whisk the buttermilk, egg, and vanilla extract.

Pour the buttermilk mixture over the flour mixture and stir to form a dough. The dough will be moist and come together in large patches. Collect, gather, and form the dough into a mass that adheres to itself with your hands. Note that the dough should be mixed only to shape and form, as actual kneading results in a dense-textured crumb.

Transfer the dough to a work surface sprinkled with the wheat bran. Gently smooth and roll the dough into a well-domed sphere measuring 5 to 5½ inches in diameter, allowing it to take up a light coating of the bran; the bran will adhere to the dough randomly. Place the dough ball in the center of the baking pan. With a small sharp knife, cut a 4 by 4-inch cross on top of the bread, no more than ¼ inch deep. A deeper, longer cross will allow the loaf to bake out of shape—if this happens, reduce the baking time by about 4 minutes, as the dough will widen a little more during early baking—the bread, however, will still be delicious.

Bake the bread in the preheated oven for 40 minutes, or until set. The baked bread will sound hollow when gently tapped on the bottom with the long handle of a wooden spoon. Since the unbaked dough is somewhat dark to begin with, you will see ruddier patches on all four quadrants created by the cross-slashing. Let the bread stand on the baking pan for 2 minutes, then remove it to a cooling rack, using two wide offset metal spatulas. Serve barely warm or at room temperature. Store in an airtight container.

notes
• the whole wheat flour I use in this bread is King Arthur 100% Organic Whole Wheat Flour
• ¾ cup chopped walnuts can be added with the dry ingredients

earthy whole wheat dough

2 cups unsifted whole wheat flour

1½ cups unsifted bleached all-purpose flour

1¼ teaspoons baking soda

½ teaspoon baking powder

½ teaspoon salt

3 tablespoons granulated sugar

5 tablespoons cold unsalted butter, cut into chunks

1⅓ cups buttermilk

1 large egg

1 teaspoon vanilla extract

2 tablespoons wheat bran, for coating the unbaked round of dough

serving: one quick bread, creating about 13 slices
ahead: 2 days

twisted

The twirly whirl of yeast dough twists, layered with butter and cinnamon sugar, dipped in butter and more cinnamon sugar, and baked to perfection is my idea of splendid.

It's the butter, for sure, that makes the whole yeasty entanglement of dough and cinnamon and sugar taste so good, a dough that bakes up soft, a little stretchy, and really sugar-crunchy on top. The repeated use of cinnamon is the prominent flavoring agent, though a teaspoon of vanilla extract adds an interesting (but not forward-flavored) dimension. The twists of dough, formed singly and placed next to one another in a pan, merge to form a rectangular "cake" that, after baking, is pulled apart, softly, to eat one generous twist at a time. The long edges of each pastry are cushiony, with brushstrokes of butter and cinnamon everywhere. The tops of the twists crackle lightly in a natural kind of way.

This is my desert island pastry: fancier, more complex candidates are not likely to be in the running because they are, well, fancier and more complex. With very little else to carry it except basic baking staples, the yeast dough is easy to manage and sensibly undemanding to put together. The plump dough rises nicely and configures into twists or other shapes without difficulty. You can even make great, imposing cinnamon buns out of the layered and dipped pieces of dough and bake them in jumbo muffin cups (add ⅔ cup chopped walnuts or pecans to the butter filling for these, if you like). But the very essence of buttery, cinnamon-y plainness is what draws me to this recipe—time and time again: I could have a twist every a.m. as the perfect rise-and-shine accompaniment to strong morning coffee.

a yeasty, cinnamon-entwined pastry

a yeasty, cinnamon-entwined pastry

cinnamon yeast dough

2½ teaspoons active dry yeast

¼ teaspoon granulated sugar

¼ cup warm (105 to 110 degrees F) water

½ cup plus 3 tablespoons milk

5 tablespoons granulated sugar

8 tablespoons (1 stick) unsalted butter, cut into chunks

1 teaspoon vanilla extract

1 large egg

3 cups unbleached all-purpose flour blended with ¼ teaspoon ground cinnamon and ¼ teaspoon salt, plus an additional ¼ cup unbleached all-purpose flour, as needed to create a manageable dough

butter and sugar filling

4 tablespoons (½ stick) unsalted butter, softened

½ cup granulated sugar blended with 1 tablespoon ground cinnamon and ⅛ teaspoon freshly grated nutmeg

spiced butter topping

7 tablespoons (1 stick less 1 tablespoon) unsalted butter, melted, cooled to tepid, and poured into a shallow bowl

1¼ cups granulated sugar blended with 4 teaspoons ground cinnamon and placed in a shallow bowl

serving: 10 pastry twists
ahead: best on baking day

For the dough, stir together the yeast, the ¼ teaspoon sugar, and the warm water in a heatproof measuring cup. Allow the mixture to stand until swollen, 6 to 7 minutes.

Warm the milk, the 5 tablespoons sugar, and the chunks of butter in a small saucepan over low heat until the butter melts. Remove from the heat and cool to tepid, then blend in the vanilla extract. Pour the milk mixture into the bowl of a heavy-duty freestanding electric mixer fitted with the flat paddle. Add the egg and mix on low speed until combined. Blend in the yeast mixture. Add two-thirds of the flour-cinnamon-salt mixture; beat for 2 minutes to blend. Add the remaining flour-cinnamon-salt blend and beat for 1 minute to incorporate, stopping the mixer to scrape down the sides of the bowl after each portion is added. Remove the flat paddle and attach the dough hook. Beat the dough on moderate speed for 4 minutes. At this point, it should be smooth, elastic, shiny, and somewhat moist. Add up to ¼ cup additional flour to arrive at a manageable but supple dough and to control any stubborn stickiness as the dough comes together during the beating time. If the day is hot or you are working in a humid or otherwise rainy environment, it may be necessary to use the entire amount of additional flour (or a few teaspoons more) and less flour if it is a cool, cold, or arid day. (In any case, it is best to err on the side of a softer, rather than too-firm dough.)

Turn the dough into a bowl heavily coated with softened unsalted butter, lightly turn to coat all sides in a film of butter, make several cuts in the dough with a pair of kitchen scissors, cover tightly with a sheet of food-safe plastic wrap, and let rise at cool room temperature for 2 hours, or until doubled in bulk.

Remove the sheet of plastic wrap. Lightly compress the dough with a rubber spatula, cover loosely with the sheet of plastic wrap, and let stand for 10 minutes.

Film the inside of a 13 by 9 by 2-inch baking pan with softened unsalted butter.

Remove and discard the sheet of plastic wrap. Place the dough on a lightly floured work surface. Roll the dough into a sheet measuring about 15 by 15 inches. Using the filling ingredients, spread the softened butter on the surface of the dough. Sprinkle the cinnamon-nutmeg-sugar mixture evenly over the buttered dough. Fold the dough in half horizontally. Gently roll the sheet to measure 10 inches in width. Press down on the surface with your fingertips. Cut into 10 even-size strips, using a sharp chef's knife. Let the strips rest, uncovered, for 5 minutes.

Have the spiced butter topping ingredients at hand.

Pick up 1 strip at a time, elongate it, twist it into a corkscrew, and, holding both ends, dip it into the melted butter, then dredge it in the sugar-cinnamon mixture to coat. Place each dipped-and-sugar-coated strip in the prepared baking pan, side by side, in a long row; at this point, the bottom of the pan will show through in random places. Sprinkle over any remaining sugar-cinnamon mixture. Cover the pan loosely with a sheet of food-safe plastic wrap. Let the strips rise at cool room temperature until almost doubled in bulk (see page 6 to reference this stage), about 2 hours (the time will be shorter if it is a warm or damp day); the risen strips will merge into a "cake" that conceals the bottom of the pan.

Preheat the oven to 375 degrees F in advance of baking.

Remove and discard the sheet of plastic wrap covering the twists.

Bake the twists in the preheated oven for 25 to 30 minutes, or until risen and set. The baked pastry will pull away slightly from the sides of the baking pan and its surface will be cinnamon-sugared and butter-encrusted, randomly concealing the top of the pastry. Cool the pastry in the pan on a rack for 20 minutes. Carefully unmold the pastry onto another cooling rack. Lift off the pan, then carefully invert the pastry to stand right side up. Or, you can cool the pastry in the pan on a rack for 30 minutes, then detach the twists from the pan. Serve the twists warm (the ideal) or at room temperature. Store in an airtight container.

notes
- ground China cassia cinnamon is my first choice for this spice, as it has the deepest, most vibrant flavor
- moist dried currants (1/3 lightly packed cup) can be sprinkled over the buttery cinnamon filling ingredients before the dough is folded and rolled

flat *and* puffy

If a yeast dough can be bewitching in both sweet and piquant form, then it must radiate butter and eggs through and through, for this twosome forges an otherworldly bread.

Butter and eggs add structure and richness, supporting a golden crumb and rich flavor. The aroma of a butter-laden chunk of bread, torn away in a shaggy piece, conveys with it such delicious promise.

These two flatbreads, born out of my boredom with the conservative loaf, send their own message: dig in lustfully, savor casually, and enjoy with abandon.

Here's the genesis of one bread (a complicity of cheese in a yeast dough) that brought into being the other (a sweet one dominated by butter, eggs, and sparkly sugar). It happened innocently enough one Thanksgiving many years ago, when I set about to bake bread for the meal. You should know from the outset that I no longer roast a turkey for that holiday, but now I do something like brine and smoke one as part of the December or January festivities. Usually, at my table, I subject guests to a lengthy course-by-course operation that combines bistro French with bistro Italian. Sort of. The meal commonly honors harvest ingredients—chestnuts, sweet potatoes, earthy greens, crunchy roots, and so on—and sometimes you need to look deep within the menu to find my nod to them, but I can assure you that the thought is there somewhere. No one has ever complained straight-out, for they know what they are getting into weeks (and sometimes months) earlier when the invitation is issued: *Please come for Thanksgiving. As you know I won't be making the traditional meal. See you at 2:30. Don't be late.* But they do make sure that the cheese bread is on the menu.

The bread is the celebrity, offered in all its rustic grandness on a big platter positioned in the center of my round table. Guests nibble on it all the way through the meal. I have to wrench it out of their hands before dessert is served. This bread is mighty. Out of a briochelike cocoon comes a big, somewhat inflated, vaguely oval yeasty wonder of four-cheese savoriness, saturated with enough butter, salted just so, and tinged with smoked paprika (see notes, page 297). Although made of yeast, and in two defined stages, it's rather forgiving to make, and the real joy is its free-form lack of construction. You work four kinds of cheese into the once-risen dough, pat it on a baking pan, patiently put it aside again to do its slow but purposeful inflation (for the second time), and bake it. Once baked, a little more butter (or olive oil) is brushed over the top before a final sprinkling with salt, pepper, and a little more cheese. In short order, the bouquet of it all swaddles anyone within sniffing distance.

So, since my baking life continues to be an overarching circle of ideas, each idea bearing some kind of relevance to the next, the cheese version spawned a butter and sugar translation—a sweet sibling of sorts. Built on the same principle of butter and eggs, with a highlight of vanilla extract, the sugar-ornamented version is right at home with a cup of tea or coffee, or on a platter with dried fruits, cheese, and whole, in-the-shell nuts that you crack open yourself.

Far and away removed from any kind of contrived flour-and-yeast invention, carved and chiseled to within inches of their very lives, these two breads are laid-back and genuine. And this notion comes in two flavors, cheese and butter-sugar.

a flatbread busy with cheese

cheese-infiltrated yeast dough

4½ teaspoons active dry yeast

¼ teaspoon granulated sugar

¼ cup warm (105 to 110 degrees F) water

5 large eggs

2 large egg yolks

12 tablespoons (1½ sticks) cool unsalted butter, cut into tablespoon-size chunks

2 cups unsifted bleached all-purpose flour

1½ cups unsifted unbleached all-purpose flour

¾ teaspoon salt

1 cup freshly grated Parmigiano-Reggiano cheese

½ cup freshly grated Gruyère cheese

½ cup freshly grated Pecorino Romano cheese

½ cup grated Provolone cheese

cheese, salt, and pepper finish

2 tablespoons unsalted butter, melted and cooled to tepid, or good fruity olive oil

1 teaspoon coarse sea salt

½ teaspoon black peppercorns, crushed to coarseness (preferably in a mortar and pestle)

¼ cup freshly grated Parmigiano-Reggiano or Pecorino Romano cheese

serving: one large flatbread, creating 12 to 15 randomly shaped tears of bread
ahead: best on baking day

For the dough, stir together the yeast, granulated sugar, and warm water in a heatproof measuring cup. Allow the mixture to stand until swollen, 6 to 7 minutes.

Scrape the yeast mixture into the bowl of a heavy-duty freestanding electric mixer fitted with the flat paddle. Blend in the whole eggs, egg yolks, and chunks of butter; combine on low speed until mixed. Combine the bleached all-purpose flour, 1 cup of the unbleached all-purpose flour, and the salt in a medium-size mixing bowl. Add the mixed flours and salt to the egg and yeast mixture in 3 additions, mixing well after each addition. Beat for 3 minutes on moderate speed. The dough will be dense and sticky. Add the remaining ½ cup unbleached flour and beat for 1 minute. Beat the dough for 4 minutes on moderate speed, or until shiny and smooth. It should clean (or almost clean) the sides of the bowl. (If it does not, and this depends on the absorption quality of the flour and ambient temperature of the day, including any humidity in the air, you can safely beat in an additional 3 tablespoons bleached all-purpose flour.) Stop the machine from time to time during the entire mixing process to scrape down the sides of the mixing bowl.

Scrape the dough into a bowl heavily coated with softened unsalted butter, lightly turn to coat all sides in a film of butter, cover tightly with a sheet of food-safe plastic wrap, and let rise at room temperature for 2 hours and 30 minutes, or until doubled in bulk.

Remove and discard the sheet of plastic wrap. Sprinkle the Parmigiano-Reggiano, Gruyère, Pecorino Romano, and Provolone over the top of the dough. Lightly compress the dough and work in the cheese, kneading it lightly in the bowl. Cover loosely with a sheet of food-safe plastic wrap and let stand for 10 minutes. Remove and discard the plastic wrap.

Film a heavy rimmed sheet pan with softened unsalted butter or line the pan with a length of ovenproof parchment paper. Transfer the dough to the center of the pan and, with your fingertips, lightly press into a wide, free-form oval, leaving a generous border all the way around. The oval should measure 12 to 13 inches long and 9 inches at its widest point. Cover the pan loosely with two sheets of food-safe plastic wrap. Let rise at room temperature for 2 hours to 2 hours and 30 minutes, or until very puffy and almost doubled in bulk (refer to page 6 to reference this stage).

Preheat the oven to 375 degrees F in advance of baking.

Remove and discard the sheets of plastic wrap covering the bread.

Place the bread in the preheated oven, immediately raise the temperature to 400 degrees F, and bake for 30 to 35 minutes, or until set and a medium golden brown color on top.

Remove the bread from the oven and, using the finish ingredients, sweep the melted butter or olive oil over the surface of the bread, using a soft pastry brush. Sprinkle the sea salt, pepper, and Parmigiano-Reggiano or Pecorino Romano on top. Cool the bread on the baking pan on a cooling rack for at least 20 minutes. Slip the bread off the parchment paper, if you have used it to line the pan. Serve the bread warm or at room temperature, hand-torn into big and ragged odd-shaped pieces.

notes
- a variation of this bread that includes sweet (or bittersweet) smoked Spanish paprika (pimentón) is a delight; the paprika, an excellent flavor generator, makes a wonderfully flavored bread for pairing with cheese; for this, blend 1 tablespoon paprika into the 2 cups bleached all-purpose flour and proceed with the recipe
- there are two brands of smoked paprika that I reach for from my cupboard spice shelf: Jose M.ª Hernandez, S.L. Pimentón de la Vera (sweet and bittersweet), and El Rey Pimentón de la Vera (sweet)

a sugared-up flatbread

sweet and eggy yeast dough

2½ teaspoons active dry yeast

¾ teaspoon granulated sugar

½ cup warm (105 to 110 degrees F) water

⅓ cup unsifted unbleached all-purpose flour

5 tablespoons plus 1 teaspoon milk

5 tablespoons granulated sugar

1 tablespoon vanilla extract

2 large eggs

2 large egg yolks

2¼ cups unsifted unbleached all-purpose flour blended with ¼ teaspoon salt

9 tablespoons (1 stick plus 1 tablespoon) unsalted butter, cut into tablespoon-size chunks, softened

butter and sugar finish

3 tablespoons unsalted butter (preferably clarified butter, page 1), melted and cooled to tepid

3 tablespoons sparkling sugar (plain or a color), for sprinkling on the unbaked bread

serving: one flatbread, creating 12 to 15 randomly shaped tears of bread
ahead: best on baking day

For the dough, stir together the yeast, the ¾ teaspoon granulated sugar, and warm water in a heatproof measuring cup. Allow the mixture to stand until swollen, 6 to 7 minutes. Scrape into a small mixing bowl. Stir in the ⅓ cup flour. Cover with a sheet of food-safe plastic wrap, and let stand at room temperature for 35 minutes. By that time, the mixture should be expanded by two-thirds, with medium-size bubbles breaking the surface.

Warm the milk and the 5 tablespoons granulated sugar in a small saucepan over low heat. When the sugar has dissolved, remove the saucepan from the heat, and cool to tepid. Pour the milk mixture into the bowl of a heavy-duty freestanding electric mixer fitted with the flat paddle. Blend in the vanilla extract, whole eggs, and egg yolks; combine on low speed until mixed. Add the yeast mixture and mix to blend. Add the flour-salt blend in 3 additions, stopping the mixer to scrape down the sides of the bowl after each portion is added. Beat in the butter, 1 tablespoon at a time. Stop the machine from time to time to scrape down the sides of the mixing bowl. Beat the dough on moderate speed for 4 to 5 minutes. At this point, the dough should be smooth, elastic, and shiny—and very moist and sticky. If—and only if—the dough seems extremely unmanageable, add up to 3 tablespoons flour.

Scrape the dough into a bowl heavily coated with softened unsalted butter, lightly turn to coat all sides in a film of butter, cover tightly with a sheet of food-safe plastic wrap, and let rise at room temperature for 1 hour and 20 minutes, or until doubled in bulk.

Remove and discard the plastic wrap. Lightly compress the dough with a rubber spatula, cover loosely with a sheet of food-safe plastic wrap, and let stand for 10 minutes. Remove and discard the plastic wrap.

Film a heavy rimmed sheet pan with softened unsalted butter or line the pan with a length of ovenproof parchment paper. Transfer the dough to the center of the pan and, with your fingertips, lightly press into a wide free-form oval; keep the dough somewhat contained, leaving a border of about 3 inches from all four sides of the pan. This is a casual bread without a strictly defined shape. Cover the pan loosely with two sheets of food-safe plastic wrap. Let rise at room temperature for 1 hour to 1 hour and 10 minutes, or until quite puffy and almost doubled in bulk (see page 6 to reference this stage).

Preheat the oven to 375 degrees F in advance of baking.

Remove and discard the sheets of plastic wrap covering the bread about 20 minutes before completely risen.

Using the finish ingredients, brush the melted butter over the surface of the risen bread, taking care not to deflate it. Sprinkle the sparkling sugar over the top. Continue to let the bread finish rising, uncovered.

Bake the bread in the preheated oven for 30 minutes, or until set and a golden color on top. Cool the bread on the baking pan on a cooling rack for 20 minutes. Slip the bread off the parchment paper, if you have used it to line the pan. Serve the bread warm or at room temperature, pulled apart into craggy pieces.

notes
• premium butter—such as Plugrá European Style Unsalted Butter, Celles sur Belle, Isigny Ste. Mère Beurre Cru de Normandie, or Beurre Président Unsalted Butter from France—makes a delectable ingredient in this flatbread

Intense

shortbread to the seriously upper limit, including a lavender sensation ✳ positively cinnamon-y ✳ temptation: a really audacious cupcake ✳ a sweetmeat-type confection layered with flavor ✳ pyramids of coconut ✳ almond-saturated ✳ more-stuff-per-square-inch in a fruitcake batter ✳ cookies that say spicy ✳ swarthychocolate

Bold

a delicious crumble

All bakers take note: when it comes to the contrast of salty and sweet, you can have a field day.

For some time, I had been careful about adding only unsalted nuts to a cookie dough, but one day several years ago, an immediate craving for chocolate chunk cookies with cashews got me thinking otherwise.

In the cupboard, only lightly salted jumbo cashews were to be found. Banish the rules (did I say that?) and full steam ahead to whip together some cookie dough.

The contrast between salty and sweet played out nicely, too, in these butter-substantial cookie dough recipes and, of course, I have long championed—for years and years—the practice of adding salt, if only a small amount, to any chocolate-based dessert. But I usually shied away from adding salt on any level to a shortbread dough.

The usual practice of integrating salt into a batter or dough should have prompted me to think about using salt in a shortbread dough. I was first intrigued, then prompted to examine the interplay of salt, butter, and sugar in shortbread. The absence of salt in shortbread always left me puzzled because it routinely tasted flat, though buttery. I went about adding a pinch of salt to all of the shortbread doughs established in my repertoire. Time passed. One day, while making a plain vanilla shortbread, I spied the container of *fleur de sel* on my countertop (I use *Fleur de Sel de Guérande*) and sprinkled a little of it on top of the unbaked shortbread. The resulting cookie was a fine contrast of sweet with a faintly salty edge. All-chocolate shortbread, plain and minus any embellishments such as chips, would also be a candidate for the lightest dusting of salt. In the next go-around of dough, fine sea salt (the same sea salt I use in all of my doughs and batters for baking) was added to a butter-extreme formula of the *wildly lush hint-of-salt lavender shortbread, the unrestrained version*.

Make no mistake about it. Shortbread is butter-centered. The dough is sweetened enough to add a certain depth and supplied with the proper undertone of extract. In the *hint-of-salt shortbread, the restrained version*, the rounds are baked until golden and lightly caramelized; a whisper of sprinkled-on *fleur de sel* proposes another plane of flavor. In the *wildly lush hint-of-salt lavender shortbread, the unrestrained version*, the salt goes directly into the dough. The latter confection—plush and demurely lavender-scented—is my concept of deluxe and it took me years to get it right: the salt enhances a dough made with all-purpose flour, cornstarch, and white rice flour and it is both the cornstarch and rice flour, along with an extended creaming of the butter, that bring out its delicate texture. The shortbread that follows this one, my *bold, buttery, and basic shortbread,* is the mother of them all, as the formula represents a delicious blueprint for a fundamental dough. The fourth shortbread offering, *a rough-hewn cookie,* is built on rolled oats, given a contrastingly tender shear with white rice flour, sweetened with brown sugar within, and topped with turbinado sugar. It is the bohemian of the lot.

Shortbread is alluring cut into precise, soldierlike squares, batons, or triangles. Or go ahead and crumble it into odd pieces and fragments. Be wrapped up in the flavor package.

hint-of-salt shortbread, the restrained version

butter and *fleur de sel* dough

1⅔ cups unsifted bleached
all-purpose flour

¼ teaspoon baking powder

⅛ teaspoon salt

⅓ cup white rice flour

½ pound (16 tablespoons or 2 sticks)
unsalted butter, softened

⅓ cup plus 2 tablespoons superfine sugar

½ cup confectioners' sugar

2 teaspoons vanilla extract

¼ teaspoon *fleur de sel*

⅓ cup fine sanding sugar (plain or a color)
or granulated sugar, for sprinkling on the
baked shortbread

serving: two 8-inch rounds of shortbread,
creating 8 wedges each
ahead: 2 weeks

Preheat the oven to 325 degrees F.

Have two fluted 8-inch false-bottomed tart pans (1 inch deep) at hand.

For the dough, sift the all-purpose flour, baking powder, and salt into a medium-size bowl. Whisk in the rice flour.

Cream the butter in the large bowl of a freestanding electric mixer on moderately low speed for 4 minutes. Add the superfine sugar and beat on moderately low speed for 45 seconds. Add the confectioners' sugar and beat for 45 seconds longer. Blend in the vanilla extract. On low speed, add the sifted ingredients in 2 additions, mixing just until the particles of flour are absorbed. The dough will be soft.

Divide the dough in half and place each portion in a tart pan. Lightly press the dough into an even layer without packing it down. Sprinkle the top of each shortbread lightly with the *fleur de sel*, dividing it evenly between them.

Bake the shortbread in the preheated oven for 45 minutes, or until set and golden.

Cool the shortbread rounds in their pans on cooling racks for 5 minutes. Sprinkle the sanding sugar or granulated sugar over the top of each shortbread, dividing it evenly between them. Cool for 5 to 7 minutes longer. Carefully unmold each shortbread (leaving it on the round base) and cut each into pie-shape wedges, using a finely serrated knife. Cool completely. Store in an airtight tin.

notes
• white rice flour adds a lovely texture—lightly gritty and flaky at the same time—to the baked shortbread
• pressing, rather than compressing, the dough into the baking pan will keep the baked shortbread crumbly and moist, rather than dense and gummy
• baking the shortbread until golden creates a soft caramel flavor and precludes a pasty core

wildly lush hint-of-salt lavender shortbread, the unrestrained version

Preheat the oven to 325 degrees F.

Film the inside of a 9 by 9 by 2-inch baking pan with nonstick oil spray.

Lengthwise and width-wise, line the inside of the pan with lengths of ovenproof parchment paper, leaving about ¾ inch to extend on all four sides. To prevent the parchment from slipping and sliding when fitting the shortbread dough in the pan, lay in one length of paper, press it against the sides of the pan, spray the paper covering the bottom of the pan in a few strategic places, then lay in the second length of paper and press it against the sprayed bottom and sides.

For the dough, sift the all-purpose flour, cornstarch, rice flour, and cream of tartar onto a sheet of waxed paper. Sprinkle over the *fleur de sel* and whisk it in.

Cream the butter in the large bowl of a freestanding electric mixer on moderate speed for 4 minutes. The butter should be very smooth, exceptionally creamy, and mayonnaise-like. If the butter is not thoroughly softened to start with, wait until it is, otherwise the texture will be dense, rather than melting. However, if the butter is too warm, it will turn greasy on creaming and the resulting dough will be dense and oily-textured, and, on baking, heavy. While the butter is being creamed, place the culinary lavender buds and 1 tablespoon of the superfine sugar in a small mortar and pestle. Grind the mixture until the buds are rendered into fine particles (this will take about 45 seconds). Add the lavender-sugar mixture and the remaining superfine sugar to the creamed butter. Beat on moderately low speed for 2 minutes. Add the vanilla extract and lavender essence and continue beating for 30 seconds longer. On low speed, add the dry ingredients in 2 additions, mixing just until the particles of the flour mixture are absorbed. Throughout each mixing process, scrape down the sides of the bowl with a rubber spatula to keep the dough even-textured. The finished dough will be somewhat soft.

Scrape the dough into the prepared pan. Gently press the dough into an even layer, using a flexible palette knife or the heel of your hand. Finish smoothing the dough with your fingertips.

Bake the shortbread in the preheated oven for 50 minutes to 1 hour, or until set and pale golden on top. The baked shortbread will only begin to pull away from the sides of the baking pan.

(continued on the next page)

lavender butter dough

2¾ cups unsifted bleached all-purpose flour

¾ cup plus 2 tablespoons cornstarch

2 tablespoons white rice flour

¼ teaspoon cream of tartar

½ teaspoon *fleur de sel*

¾ pound plus 3 tablespoons (3 sticks plus 3 tablespoons) unsalted butter, softened

½ teaspoon pesticide-free dried lavender buds (must be food-grade)

¾ cup superfine sugar

1¼ teaspoons vanilla extract

¼ teaspoon pure food-grade lavender essence (or substitute ½ teaspoon food-grade lavender extract)

sugar finish

⅓ cup fine sanding sugar (plain or a color) or granulated sugar, for sprinkling on the baked shortbread

~ or ~

about ⅓ cup confectioners' sugar, for dredging the tops of the baked-and-cut shortbread pieces

serving: one 9-inch square pan of shortbread, creating 18 batons (1½ by 3-inch lengths), 32 triangles (2¼ by 2¼ by 3 inches), or 36 "bites" (1½ by 1½-inch squares)
ahead: 10 days

Cool the shortbread in the pan on a cooling rack for 5 minutes. If you are finishing the shortbread with the sanding or granulated sugar, sprinkle it evenly over the top now. While it is still warm, cut the shortbread into batons, triangles, or bite-size squares, using a small sharp knife. Cool for 15 to 20 minutes. At this point, the shortbread should be tepid. (Refrigerating the shortbread at any time to speed up the cooling or cutting process is undesirable, for the quick chill will spoil its melting texture and may toughen the cookies.) Recut the pieces gently to make sure that they are detached, then remove them from the pan (carefully—the cookies are quite frail when freshly baked), using a small offset metal spatula. Cool completely. Store in an airtight tin. If you are using the confectioners' sugar finish, dredge the tops of the shortbread pieces with the sugar just before serving.

notes

- lavender essence can be obtained from La Cuisine—The Cook's Resource (see page 501, baking*SelectedSources*)
- ¾ teaspoon lavender extract can replace the lavender essence, reducing the vanilla extract to 1¼ teaspoons; Star Kay White Lavender Extract, available in 2-ounce-bottles, is an excellent product
- if you don't own a mortar and a pestle for grinding the lavender buds with the sugar, place the buds on a flat, stable surface, sprinkle with sugar, and crush with the underside of a skillet or the smooth side of a meat pounder
- for the best results, use a straight-sided medium-weight aluminum baking pan; avoid using glass or any baking pan with a dark interior (black or blue steel, or gray/brown release surface) as the oven heat will be drawn in and intensified rather than softly extended, creating a drier, less melting—rather than moist and tender—cookie
- creaming the butter thoroughly is essential to the fine, nearly sandy texture and delicate crumb of the cookie
- this recipe, a result of more than fifteen years' worth of research (and an exhausting but delicious tinker with premium butter), is an elaborated version of the *hint-of-salt shortbread, the restrained version*, substituting a certain amount of cornstarch and white rice flour for the all-purpose flour, adding 1 tablespoon of butter for every 8 tablespoons generally called for (and so using a total of 9 tablespoons for each 1¼ cups of a combined flour and cornstarch mixture), and replacing the combination of superfine and confectioners' sugar with superfine sugar alone (a total of 1 cup cornstarch can replace the white rice flour, if the latter is unavailable or if you prefer an overall smoother, 100 percent melting quality to the cookie)
- the choice of butter, a key element, is pivotal to the character of the baked cookie: being the baking alchemist (and quiet rebel) that I am, I love to mix premium butters in this recipe (much to the delight of butter fanciers; much to the dismay of a few bakers who insist I add unwarranted complexity to their grocery shopping trip); the best commingling to date is one-third each (9 tablespoons) of Plugrá, Beurre Président, and Lurpak, but I can assure you that any one of them alone creates a memorable—if not supernal—dough
- for the holidays or a special occasion—though eating really good shortbread is an occasion in and of itself—use pastel sanding sugar for the topping; consider the very pretty, paler tones of Buttercup, Lavender, or Pink

wildly lush hint-of-salt lavender shortbread, the unrestrained version

bold, buttery, and basic shortbread

butter-forward dough

3 cups unsifted bleached all-purpose flour

1 cup cornstarch

½ teaspoon salt

⅛ teaspoon cream of tartar

1 pound (4 sticks)
unsalted butter, softened

1 cup superfine sugar

3 teaspoons vanilla extract

⅓ cup granulated sugar, for dredging
the top of the baked shortbread

serving: one 10-inch square pan
of shortbread, creating 40 batons
(1 by 2½-inch lengths)
ahead: 10 days

Preheat the oven to 325 degrees F.

Film the inside of a 10 by 10 by 2-inch baking pan with nonstick oil spray.

Lengthwise and width-wise, line the inside of the pan with lengths of ovenproof parchment paper, leaving about ¾ inch to extend on all four sides. To prevent the parchment from slipping and sliding when fitting the shortbread dough in the pan, lay in one length of paper, press it against the sides of the pan, spray the paper covering the bottom of the pan in a few strategic places, then lay in the second length of paper and press it against the sprayed bottom and sides.

For the dough, sift the flour, cornstarch, salt, and cream of tartar onto a sheet of waxed paper.

Cream the butter in the large bowl of a freestanding electric mixer on moderate speed for 4 minutes. The butter should be quite smooth and satiny-creamy; if it is not, continue beating for another minute or two. Add the superfine sugar in 2 additions, beating on moderately low speed for 45 seconds after each portion is added. Blend in the vanilla extract. On low speed, add the sifted mixture in 3 additions, mixing just until the particles of flour and cornstarch are absorbed before adding the next portion. Throughout each mixing process, scrape down the sides of the bowl with a rubber spatula to keep the dough even-textured. The finished dough will be moderately soft.

Scrape the dough into the prepared pan. Gently press the dough into an even layer, using a flexible palette knife or the heel of your hand. Smooth the surface with your fingertips.

Bake the shortbread in the preheated oven for 50 minutes, or until set and very pale golden on top. The baked shortbread will just begin to pull away from the sides of the baking pan.

Cool the shortbread in the pan on a cooling rack for 10 minutes. Dredge the top with the granulated sugar, tilting the pan in all directions to even out the layer of sugar. Cut the shortbread (see notes), using a small sharp knife. Cool for 15 minutes. Recut the shortbread and cool completely. Store in an airtight tin.

notes
- due to the size of the baking pan (10 by 10 by 2 inches), the large block is easiest cut into 5 by 5-inch quarters, with each quarter cut in half horizontally and in 1-inch vertical cuts, yielding 10 batons for each quarter section
- fine sanding sugar (plain or a pastel color) can be used in place of the granulated sugar for dredging the top of the warm shortbread

a rough-hewn cookie

Preheat the oven to 350 degrees F.

Have a fluted 11-inch false-bottomed tart pan (1 inch deep) at hand.

For the dough, sift the all-purpose flour, rice flour, baking powder, and salt into a medium-size bowl.

Cream the butter in the large bowl of a freestanding electric mixer on low speed for 3 minutes. Add the light brown sugar and beat on moderately low speed for 1 minute. Blend in the vanilla extract. On low speed, blend in the rolled oats and the sifted mixture.

Scrape the dough into the tart pan and lightly press in an even layer without compacting or compressing it too much. Be gentle. Sprinkle the turbinado sugar evenly over the top.

Bake the shortbread in the preheated oven for 45 minutes, or until set throughout and evenly medium golden on top.

Cool the shortbread in the pan on a cooling rack for 10 minutes. Carefully unmold the sweet, leaving it on the round base. Cool for 5 minutes. Cut the shortbread into 10 pie-shape wedges, using a finely serrated knife, or cool for 30 minutes and break into uneven pieces. Cool completely. Store in an airtight tin.

notes
• for a fruit-chewy variation, blend ½ cup tart (Montmorency) dried cherries or dark seedless raisins into the dough after the dry ingredients have been added; for a tropical variation, blend ⅔ cup firmly packed sweetened flaked coconut or natural unsweetened short- or medium-flake coconut into the dough after the dry ingredients have been added

oaty buttery dough

¾ cup plus 1 tablespoon unsifted bleached all-purpose flour

3 tablespoons white rice flour

¼ teaspoon baking powder

⅛ teaspoon salt

12 tablespoons (1½ sticks) unsalted butter, softened

½ cup light brown sugar

2½ teaspoons vanilla extract

½ cup plus 2 tablespoons "quick-cooking" (not instant) rolled oats

about ¼ cup turbinado sugar, for sprinkling on the unbaked disk of shortbread

serving: one 11-inch round of shortbread, creating 10 wedges
ahead: 2 weeks

cupcakes, gilded

A crunch of candied popcorn sparked with salt. Velvety, light, and moist cake. Creamy-sweet frosting. Together these announce, if not shout, the word "treat" tidily enclosed in a childlike wrapper.

The meld is a brash one, and joins three of my favorite things—buttercrunch popcorn, good cake, and traditional American frosting. Or is it an excuse to have all three in one deft package?

The cake under it all is quite tender, requiring the support of a paper case: glittery, colorful liners can be festive or quite plain, and my choice for this collaboration of elements is gold, as the metallic shows off the topping and what lurks beneath. The frosting is shaded a pretty pastel color. The tops of the cupcakes are crowned with chunky pieces of *golden popcorn croquant*. (A classic *croquant* is a nut-flecked crunchy caramel brittle. My recipe creates chunks of candied popcorn brittle—a very American-style twist to the confection.)

The coating for the candied popcorn is not so much caramel-flavored alone as it is also buttery, with a firm, crispy-crunchy snap. All by itself, the popcorn makes a great nibble, but when combined with frosted cake, a textural bonanza takes place. (Of course, I'd make the popcorn just to have around for pairing with a flute of champagne for a royally sweet munch, an idea that came from Joe Yonan, the food and travel editor of *The Washington Post*, when I presented him with a few bags of the stuff to test-taste at dinner several years ago.)

Gilded cupcakes are a baking statement, you can be sure.

candy-crunched golden cupcakes: golden cupcakes, golden frosting, golden popcorn croquant

candy-crunched golden cupcakes: golden cupcakes, golden frosting, golden popcorn croquant

golden batter

2½ cups unsifted bleached cake flour

2 teaspoons baking powder

½ teaspoon salt

12 tablespoons (1½ sticks) unsalted butter, softened

1½ cups granulated sugar

2 large eggs

2 large egg yolks

2 teaspoons vanilla extract

¾ cup plus 1 tablespoon milk

golden frosting (page 311)

golden popcorn *croquant* (page 312)

serving: 22 cupcakes (as the capacity of muffin cups can be inconsistent from manufacturer to manufacturer, the exact yield may vary)
ahead: best on baking day

Preheat the oven to 350 degrees F.

Line the inside of 22 muffin/cupcake cups (12 cups to a pan, each cup measuring 2¾ inches in diameter and 1⅜ inches deep, with a capacity of ½ cup) with decorative ovenproof paper baking cup liners.

For the batter, sift the flour, baking powder, and salt onto a sheet of waxed paper.

Cream the butter in the large bowl of a freestanding electric mixer on moderately high speed for 3 minutes. Add the granulated sugar in 3 additions, beating for 1 minute on moderate speed after each portion is added. Beat in the eggs, one at a time, mixing for 45 seconds after each addition, then blend in the egg yolks and vanilla extract. On low speed, alternately add the sifted mixture in 3 additions with the milk in 2 additions, beginning and ending with the sifted mixture. Scrape down the sides of the mixing bowl with a rubber spatula to keep the batter even-textured. The batter will be creamy.

Spoon the batter into the lined muffin cups, dividing it evenly among them (each should be filled a little less than two-thirds full). Mound the batter lightly in the center of each.

Bake the cupcakes in the preheated oven for 20 minutes, or until risen, set, golden on top, and a wooden pick withdraws clean when inserted into the center of a cupcake. Cool the cupcakes in the pans on racks for 10 minutes, then remove them to other cooling racks. Cool completely.

Apply the golden frosting to the tops of the cooled cupcakes by smoothing a thick layer on the top, using a small offset palette knife, and attach odd-shaped pieces of golden popcorn *croquant* to it. Or pipe the frosting decoratively over the frosting-layered surface and tuck one dramatic piece of popcorn *croquant* into the center or onto the side. Garnishing the cupcakes with multiple odd-shaped chunks of the popcorn *croquant* means that you'll have to break the pieces into fragments—the most visually appealing cupcakes look the most whimsical if the pieces of popcorn *croquant* are left craggy. Serve the cupcakes as soon as they are topped with the popcorn *croquant*.

notes

- the cupcake batter can also be divided among about 13 individual straight-sided metal baking pans (each measuring 3 inches in diameter and 2 inches deep, with a capacity of scant ¾ cup); bake the larger cupcakes for 25 minutes
- if you are piping the frosting, swirls made with the Ateco #823 open-star tip look particularly pretty set against the golden popcorn *croquant*
- decorative paper baking cup liners must be food-safe
- any and all ornaments and nonedible embellishments or decorations, including "jewelry" and decorative picks, fastened to the paper baking cup liners or enhancing serving platters, are for decorative use only; otherwise, and without exception, only *décoratifs* or decorations safe for consumption should be eaten
- any ornamental decorations (including chains, golden ropes, strings of pearls, or ribbons) are for decorative use only; decorations should be fastened to the side of the paper baking cup liners or tucked in between the middle of double or triple-layered paper baking cup liners
- frosted cupcakes are perishable and should be consumed within 2 hours of composing them; top the cupcakes with the *golden popcorn croquant* just before serving
- all cupcakes must be served responsibly by an adult

golden frosting

For the frosting, place the butter in the bowl of a heavy-duty freestanding electric mixer fitted with the flat paddle. Beat on moderate speed for 1 minute. Add about half of the confectioners' sugar-salt mixture, the vanilla extract, and the heavy cream. Beat for 1 minute on moderately low speed. Scrape down the sides of the mixing bowl and beat for 15 seconds longer. Add the remaining confectioners' sugar-salt mixture in 2 additions, beating just until smooth. Scrape down the sides of the mixing bowl and beat for 10 seconds longer. Adjust the texture of the frosting as needed to achieve a smooth spreading texture, by adding heavy cream (1 teaspoon at a time) or confectioners' sugar (1 tablespoon at a time).

To tint the frosting, dip a clean wooden pick into the paste food color to bring up a generous dab of the color. Sink the pick into the frosting, remove, and discard. Beat the frosting to integrate the color on low speed for 45 seconds to 1 minute, or until the color is thoroughly dispersed, scraping down the sides of the mixing bowl once or twice. Check for the desired intensity of color, then add more paste color, a little dab at a time, and rebeat until just incorporated. Always use a brand-new, clean wooden pick for each round of coloring.

Use the frosting immediately.

notes
- the food-safe paste food color called Special Pastel Buttercup, made by Cake Craft (Division of Nestelle's, 3540 Brooks Avenue NE, Salem, OR 97303), produces a lovely golden color that is appealingly understated
- this recipe makes a generous amount of frosting to use for topping the cupcakes: if you are concealing the entire surface of the cupcake with the popcorn *croquant*, rather than using one decorative piece and piped frosting, you can safely divide the frosting recipe in half

butter and cream frosting

8 tablespoons (1 stick) unsalted butter, softened

4⅓ cups confectioners' sugar sifted with ⅛ teaspoon salt, plus additional confectioners' sugar, as needed

2 teaspoons vanilla extract

¼ cup plus 2 tablespoons heavy cream, plus 1 to 2 tablespoons additional, as needed

food-safe paste food color (preferably Cake Craft Special Pastel Buttercup color)

serving: about 3½ cups

golden popcorn croquant

candied popcorn

⅓ cup popcorn kernels, air-popped

2 cups granulated sugar

½ cup light corn syrup

⅔ cup water

8 tablespoons (1 stick)
unsalted butter, cut into chunks

¼ teaspoon salt

½ teaspoon baking soda

2½ teaspoons vanilla extract

salty finish

sprinkles of *fleur de sel* (optional)

serving: about 8 cups candied popcorn
(yield is approximate; air gaps between
measured clusters and the overall size of
the broken-up pieces may influence your
own homemade quantity) and lots more
than needed to decorate the cupcakes
(and who would complain about that?)
ahead: 1 week

Preheat the oven to 175 degrees F to 200 degrees F.

Have a large rimmed sheet pan, preferably release-surface, at hand near the work surface.

Wear sturdy, heatproof gloves to protect your hands and forearms at all times when working with the sugar syrup and popcorn.

Place the popped corn in a large heatproof mixing bowl and set in the oven to keep warm.

Sift the sugar into a large, heavy, 4½ to 5-quart casserole (9¾ inches in diameter and 4¼ inches deep; preferably enameled cast iron). Pour in the corn syrup and water. Add the chunks of butter. Cover the casserole, place over moderately low heat, and let the mixture heat thoroughly until the sugar has dissolved. Stir the contents of the pot—slowly, without splashing the sides—with a heatproof spatula (preferably silicone) once or twice. When the sugar has dissolved, uncover the casserole and bring the contents to the boil, whisking once or twice to distribute the milk solids present in the butter throughout the mixture. Cook the syrup at a medium boil until it turns a medium golden color and registers 290 degrees F to 295 degrees F on a candy thermometer. This will take about 10 minutes.

Remove the bowl of popcorn from the oven to a heatproof surface.

Remove the casserole from the heat to a heatproof surface and, using a heatproof spatula, quickly stir in the salt, followed by the baking soda and vanilla extract. The syrup will bubble up furiously when both the baking soda and vanilla extract are added. Carefully—and without delay—pour the hot caramel syrup over the popcorn and quickly stir to coat it well, using the heatproof spatula. (A hot caramel mixture should be handled carefully, using sturdy heatproof gloves to protect your hands and forearms both while it is being made and while being poured onto the popcorn. The caramel mixture, once prepared, must be used while it is fluid, so you need to work both cautiously and efficiently.)

Turn out the candied popcorn—you'll have to move fast now—onto the baking pan, spreading it out as best you can. It is unnecessary (and not really possible) to spread out the confection in an even layer. Craggy is both desirable and perfectly fine. Immediately sprinkle over a little *fleur de sel* (if you are using it). Cool the confection thoroughly before breaking it up into smaller clusters. Store the popcorn in an airtight container (metal, rather than plastic).

notes

• the popcorn kernels must be air-popped as oil-popped corn is too greasy to be properly candied in the way described

• sifting the sugar is all-important in order to rid it of any hard clusters that would mar the syrup as it boils (and thus encourage the dreaded act of crystallization)

• if the syrup is not whisked in the beginning, once the sugar has dissolved, the milk solids will not be integrated into or suspended in the finished caramel and will leave small dark flecks in the mixture

• the popcorn I adore for this confection is the Orchard Blossom premium popcorn available from Fireworks Popcorn (see page 500, baking*SelectedSources*), though most any kind of popcorn can be made into *croquant*

• a full-fat butter, such as Plugrá European Style Unsalted Butter or Kate's Homemade Butter, contributes to a remarkable batch of this confection

• 1½ cups whole roasted peanuts or cashews (50 percent salt-reduced) or ¾ cup natural unsweetened medium-flake coconut (or both) can be tossed with the popcorn before pouring on the hot syrup

• a candy thermometer is essential for accurately taking the temperature of the caramel mixture during the cooking process

• a large casserole is required because the very hot sugar syrup bubbles when boiling, and the foaming bubbles increase exponentially when the baking soda, salt, and vanilla extract are stirred in off the heat; a smaller saucepan or pot should not, under any circumstances, be used

• always protect yourself and your work surface when mixing, stirring, and pouring a hot sugar syrup into other ingredients

sweet finance

Little almondy French pastries called *financiers* are so named to explain their richness: the name is derived from its comparison to a rectangular gold bar or block.

The batter for the sweet is traditionally baked in small, individual rectangular bakeware (called, appropriately, *financier* molds) used specifically for this bakery item. Another corresponding explanation for the name of the cakey/chewy cookie is based on both the kind of individual it references (a wealthy banker or investor type) and the alleged social elegance consistent with this kind of powerful individual, though any slide in economic environment could possibly call for a redefinition of this. These are high-end morsels, deluxe and princely.

The batter is characteristically made of browned butter, sugar, almonds (in the form of the finely chopped nut meal or nut flour), and egg whites. To this I usually add vanilla extract, almond extract, and a pinch of salt, and top the unbaked cakes with sliced or slivered blanched almonds. To upgrade the overall flavor, the just-baked tops can be brushed with a fast glaze of almond liqueur (such as amaretto) and granulated sugar: swiped on the surface, this version and its potency would certainly dovetail nicely with the image of the high-profile power broker—verifiably intense. A stack of rectangular *financier* molds is the sanctioned equipment of choice, but I have also used *barquette* molds with superb results. The only difference is the resulting shape and return, for the *barquette* molds produce a slightly higher yield. The method is identical for both.

Financiers are perfectly wonderful with tea and make an ambrosial plate-mate to a fruit compote, season in, season out.

I have always considered *financiers* an elegant and simple, if not relatively speedy (in the realm of baking, nothing is ever really extremely fast) sweet to make, with the payoff being lots of small treats to have on hand. Yet the texture/flavor combination of these little dainties is what really intrigued me, and I began to think how wonderful it would be if this characteristic could be found in a sweet roll. The *rustic almond macaroon buns* recipe that follows, I can now report to you, is an admirable expression of the almondy motif, different but somehow similar. They are arresting plain or topped with an almond icing and toasty almonds, and are quite the charmers at breakfast or brunch.

financiers

almond batter

8 tablespoons (1 stick) unsalted butter, cut into rough chunks

1½ cups confectioners' sugar

½ cup almond flour or almond meal

6 tablespoons unsifted bleached cake flour

pinch of salt

4 large egg whites

1 teaspoon almond extract

1 teaspoon vanilla extract

almond topping

about ⅓ cup slivered or sliced almonds

almond liqueur glaze (optional)

¼ cup almond liqueur (such as amaretto)

1 tablespoon granulated sugar

~ or ~

about ¼ cup confectioners' sugar, for sifting over the individual baked sweets

serving: 21 *financiers* baked in the rectangular (*financier*) molds, or 26 *financiers* baked in the boat-shape (*barquette*) molds
ahead: 2 days

Place the butter chunks in a small saucepan with a light-colored interior, set over moderate heat, and cook until a nut brown color. Once the butter has melted down entirely, watch the contents carefully so that the butter colors to a tawny brown and does not darken too much (from nut brown to burned can happen in a flash). The butter has a tendency to spurt while cooking, so take care to protect your hands and arms. Remove the saucepan from the heat, pour the contents into a heatproof bowl, and cool to tepid.

For the batter, whisk together the confectioners' sugar, almond flour or almond meal, cake flour, and salt in a medium-size bowl. In another medium-size bowl, combine the egg whites, almond extract, and vanilla extract. Blend in the tepid browned butter. Add the almond flour mixture to the egg white mixture and stir slowly—but completely—to form a batter, using a sturdy whisk, wooden spoon, or flat wooden paddle. You can also use a hand-held electric mixer on low speed to mix the batter. Mix the batter thoroughly to blend in the butter, but avoid overmixing to create a fluffy batter (this will spoil the texture of the baked sweets).

Refrigerate the batter for 20 minutes (uncovered is fine).

Just before preheating the oven, remove the batter from the refrigerator.

Preheat the oven to 375 degrees F.

Film the inside of 21 rectangular *financier* molds (each mold measuring 1⅞ by 2¾ inches, with a capacity of scant 3 tablespoons) or 26 *barquette* molds (each mold measuring 1⅞ by 3¾ inches, with a capacity of 2 tablespoons) with nonstick flour-and-oil spray. Have a rimmed sheet pan at hand.

Fill each mold about two-thirds full of batter, using a teaspoon. Overfilling the molds will cause the batter to creep over and bake against the uppermost edges/lips of the pans, making unmolding difficult and skewing the baking time. Smooth over the tops with a small offset metal spatula. Arrange the molds on the rimmed sheet pan. Sprinkle some slivered or sliced almonds over the center of each batter-filled mold.

Bake the cakes, one sheet at a time (if your baking pans are small and require two rounds of baking), in the preheated oven for 15 to 16 minutes (when baked in *barquette* molds) or 16 to 18 minutes (when baked in *financier* molds), or until risen and golden around the edges. Remove the molds from the baking pan to cooling racks. Cool the cakes in the molds for 5 minutes, then unmold them carefully onto a length of ovenproof parchment paper.

For the optional finish, and if you are glazing the cakes, do so after the cakes have cooled for 5 minutes. Combine the almond liqueur and granulated sugar in a small mixing bowl. Brush the tops of the *financiers* with a little of the glaze, using a soft pastry brush. Serve the *financiers* warm or at room temperature. If you are using the confectioners' sugar finish, cool the cakes completely, then sift the sugar over the edges just before serving. Store in an airtight container.

notes
• using a saucepan with a light-colored interior to cook the butter to the nut brown stage allows you to see the butter's color clearly
• spray a thin, but complete, coating of nonstick flour-and-oil spray or the batter will bubble up here and there on the sides of the mold
• organic butter makes the best-tasting browned butter and, finally, the finest-tasting sweet

rustic almond macaroon buns

sweet almond-scented yeast dough

4½ teaspoons active dry yeast

½ teaspoon granulated sugar

⅓ cup warm (105 to 110 degrees F) water

1½ cups milk

⅓ cup plus 2 tablespoons granulated sugar

2 teaspoons almond extract

2 teaspoons vanilla extract

8 tablespoons (1 stick) unsalted butter, cut into tablespoon-size chunks

2 large eggs

5½ cups unsifted bleached all-purpose flour, plus an additional ⅓ to ½ cup, as needed for kneading

½ cup unsifted unbleached all-purpose flour

1½ teaspoons salt

almond macaroon filling

8 ounces almond paste

1 teaspoon vanilla extract

½ teaspoon almond extract

⅓ cup confectioners' sugar

4 tablespoons (½ stick) unsalted butter, cut into chunks, softened

1 large egg

1 large egg yolk

pinch of salt

(continued on the next page)

For the dough, stir together the yeast, the ½ teaspoon granulated sugar, and the warm water in a heatproof measuring cup. Allow the mixture to stand until swollen, 6 to 7 minutes.

In the meantime, place the milk and the ⅓ cup plus 2 tablespoons granulated sugar in a small saucepan, set over low heat, and warm until the sugar dissolves. Remove from the heat, whisk well, and scrape into a medium-size heatproof mixing bowl. Stir in the almond extract, vanilla extract, and chunks of butter. Cool to tepid, 6 to 7 minutes (the chunks of butter do not need to melt completely), then blend in the eggs and the yeast mixture. Whisk 4½ cups of the bleached flour, the unbleached flour, and salt in a large mixing bowl. Add the yeast-egg-milk-butter mixture and stir well. The consistency of the mixture will be like a loose dough. Let the mixture stand, uncovered, for 5 minutes. Stir in the remaining 1 cup bleached flour; the dough will be shaggy. Dust a work surface with the additional ⅓ to ½ cup flour. Knead the dough for 8 minutes, incorporating as much of the additional flour as necessary to keep the dough moving without sticking too much, though it should remain slightly tacky.

Turn the dough into a bowl heavily coated with softened unsalted butter, lightly turn to coat all sides in a film of butter, make several cuts in the dough with a pair of kitchen scissors, cover tightly with a sheet of food-safe plastic wrap, and let rise at room temperature for 2 hours, or until doubled in bulk.

Compress the dough with your fingertips. Transfer the dough to a lightly buttered double sheet of food-safe plastic wrap, enclose securely, and refrigerate for 2 hours.

For the filling, crumble the almond paste into the work bowl of a food processor fitted with the steel blade. Add the vanilla extract, almond extract, and confectioners' sugar. Cover and process for 10 seconds, using quick on-off pulses. Uncover, add the chunks of butter, cover, and process for 10 seconds. Add the whole egg, egg yolk, and salt; cover, and process for 15 seconds, using quick on-off pulses. Uncover, scrape down the sides of the work bowl, cover, and process for 5 seconds to blend. Scrape the mixture into a small bowl, cover with food-safe plastic wrap, and refrigerate until the buns are ready to be formed (or up to 3 hours). Remove the filling from the refrigerator 20 minutes before you are using it to spread over the chilled dough.

Film the inside of two 9 by 9 by 3-inch baking pans with softened unsalted butter.

To form the buns, remove the dough from the refrigerator, unwrap the package, and gently compress the dough by patting down the top with your fingertips.

Remove and discard the plastic wrap. Lightly flour a work surface. Roll out the dough into a sheet measuring about 15 by 15 inches. Spread the almond filling evenly over the surface of the rolled-out dough, using a medium-size offset metal spatula. Fold in the sides, press them down firmly, and roll the dough tightly into a log. Pinch the long edge to seal. Gently extend the dough to measure 18 inches in length. Cut the dough into 18 even-size slices. Place 9 spirals of dough cut side down in each of the prepared baking pans, assembling them in three rows of 3 each. The spirals will be squishy, the filling will ooze, and everything will look messy now, but all of this is inconsequential, as the buns will rise and contain the filling in the folds of the dough and any ooze will firm up and meld—deliciously—with the dough during baking.

Cover the pans of buns loosely with sheets of food-safe plastic wrap. Let the rolls rise at room temperature for 2 hours, or until doubled in bulk.

Preheat the oven to 350 degrees F in advance of baking.

Remove and discard the sheets of plastic wrap covering the buns.

Bake the buns in the preheated oven for 35 to 40 minutes, or until set and a medium golden color on top. The baked buns will pull away slightly from the sides of each baking pan.

Place the pans on cooling racks and let stand for 10 minutes, if you are icing them. If you are forgoing the almond icing and finish, let the buns cool completely in the pans.

For the optional almond icing and finish, make the icing while the buns are cooling. Sift the confectioners' sugar and salt into a small mixing bowl. Add the milk and almond extract. Using a hand-held electric mixer, beat the ingredients on low speed until smooth, stopping to scrape down the sides of the mixing bowl with a rubber spatula 2 or 3 times.

To ice and finish the buns (and continuing with the optional step), spoon and spread the icing over the surface of the warm buns, letting it flow slightly over the ripply topography that has become the tops of the baked buns. Sprinkle the sliced or slivered almonds randomly over the icing (still freshly applied and wet), dividing it between each pan of buns. Cool completely. Detach the buns from the pan individually or in adhering sections, using two small offset metal spatulas, then lift them out of the pan for serving.

notes
- the confectioners' sugar I use in the filling and icing for the buns is India Tree Fondant & Icing Powdered Sugar (available in ¾-pound bags); it is a very fine rendition of confectioners' sugar
- if you are not icing the buns, dust the tops with confectioners' sugar before serving

almond icing and finish (optional)

2 cups confectioners' sugar

pinch of salt

3 tablespoons milk

¼ teaspoon almond extract

6 tablespoons sliced or slivered almonds, very lightly toasted and cooled completely

serving: 1½ dozen buns
ahead: best on baking day; or freeze for 3 weeks, defrost, bundle in aluminum foil, and reheat in a preheated 300 degrees F oven for 10 minutes, then ice and finish

in the spirit of

Panforte di Siena, or "strong bread" of Siena, can be traced back to medieval times, when this firm and spicy cake became identified as a holiday sweet produced by the bakers in the province of Siena, in the region of Tuscany.

Traditionally, the dark, dense, and chewy round encloses a chain of wintry ingredients, such as nuts, spices, candied fruits, and cocoa powder (for color rather than as a flavoring agent). A honey-based syrup binds the dried fruits and nuts into a sweetmeat-like confection frequently baked directly on a sheet of edible rice paper. The top of the completed disk is then covered in confectioners' sugar or marzipan.

Richly candylike and compelling, this is a sweet that I have made my own.

The recipe you have here uses a mix of ambrosial dried fruits—dates, prunes, nectarines, cherries, red flame raisins, pluots, and such—and one glazed fruit, plus walnuts and pumpkin seeds. Hard, less-than-moist dried fruits have no place in this confection, for on baking, the fruits will turn so tough that the sweet will be difficult to chew; the definition and taste that a combination of walnuts and pumpkin seeds brings about really appeals to me, yet other nuts, such as a pecans, give way unappealingly (that is, soften slightly) and get lost in the translation. A little butter and two tablespoons of a sweet dessert wine have been added to the spiced honeyed syrup; in my kitchen, the trio of spices is boiled directly in the syrup—rather than sifted with the flour—so that the brilliant flavor of each is expressed. A refinement of baking powder is added to improve the dessert's overall baked texture. Unsweetened medium-flake coconut combines with the fruity blend nicely, and contributes a plush element of "chew." I love bites of *moist and chewy fruit slice* along with sips of Essensia.

This *panforte* has a permanent place on my holiday table, and here's hoping that even those who revile fruitcake will embrace it and call it theirs.

moist and chewy fruit slice

honeyed fruit and nut mixture

¾ cup unsifted bleached all-purpose flour

¼ teaspoon baking powder

1 cup granulated sugar

1 cup honey (preferably orange blossom)

5 tablespoons unsalted butter,
cut into chunks

2 tablespoons Essensia (orange muscat
sweet dessert wine)

1 teaspoon freshly grated nutmeg

½ teaspoon ground cardamom

¼ teaspoon ground allspice

¼ teaspoon ground cinnamon

¼ teaspoon salt

1¾ cups firmly packed pitted dates, diced

1 cup firmly packed moist pitted
prunes, diced

¾ cup diced dried pluots

¾ cup firmly packed golden raisins

½ cup diced glazed orange peel

½ cup diced dried papaya spears

½ cup diced dried nectarines
(or dried peaches)

½ cup firmly packed tart (Montmorency)
dried cherries

½ cup firmly packed red flame raisins

1 tablespoon finely grated orange peel

⅔ cup natural unsweetened
medium-flake coconut

(continued on the next page)

Preheat the oven to 325 degrees F.

Film the inside of a 10-inch springform pan (2¼ inches deep) or false-bottomed round 10-inch cake pan (3 inches deep) with nonstick oil spray or softened butter. Line the bottom of either pan with a round of ovenproof parchment paper and film the surface with the spray or softened butter.

For the fruit and nut mixture, sift the flour and baking powder onto a sheet of waxed paper.

Place the granulated sugar, honey, butter, Essensia, nutmeg, cardamom, allspice, cinnamon, and salt in a heavy, medium-size saucepan (preferably enameled cast iron). Cover and set over low heat for 10 to 12 minutes to dissolve the sugar, mixing slowly 2 or 3 times. Uncover the saucepan, raise the heat to moderately high, and bring to the boil. Boil the mixture steadily (at a moderate, but not overly anxious boil) until it reaches 245 degrees F on a candy or instant-read thermometer.

In the meantime, combine the dates, prunes, pluots, golden raisins, glazed orange peel, papaya, nectarines, cherries, red flame raisins, grated orange peel, coconut, walnuts, and pumpkin seeds in a large mixing bowl. Resift the flour mixture over the fruits and toss well. Add the vanilla extract to the hot honey syrup and pour over the fruit-nut-flour mixture; stir to combine well. This must be done very quicky, or the syrup will tighten considerably and firm up before all of the fruits, walnuts, and pumpkin seeds are coated. It is best to use a sturdy heatproof spatula or a lightly buttered flat wooden paddle for mixing.

Immediately turn the mixture into the prepared pan, pressing it lightly to smooth it out into an even layer, using a sturdy heatproof spatula.

Bake the sweet in the preheated oven for 45 minutes, or until set. The top will not look as glossy or moist as it did going in, but it will retain some of its luster; the edges should be bubbly and jammy-looking. The fruits on the surface will have a glazed, caramel-like look—delicious.

Cool the sweet in the pan on a cooling rack for 15 to 20 minutes. Carefully nudge a round-bladed palette knife all the way around between the cake and the edges of the pan. If you are using the springform pan, open the hinge and remove the outer ring, allowing the confection to stand on the circular metal base. Cool for 30 minutes. If you are using the false-bottomed cake pan, gently and carefully lift the confection by the bottom, pushing it up and out to unmold, leaving it on its metal base. Cool completely. Carefully dislodge the sweet from its base, peel away the parchment paper, place on a clean sheet of parchment paper or on a sheet of release-surface aluminum foil, and cool completely.

Sprinkle half of the confectioners' sugar on a sheet of parchment paper, set the sweet on, and shuffle it around to coat the bottom. Sprinkle the remaining confectioners' sugar on the top. Serve the sweet sliced into wedges. Store in an airtight cake keeper.

notes
- the best and most remarkable variety and quality of premium dried fruits comes from Bella Viva Orchards (see page 500, baking*SelectedSources*); not to be missed are the Betty Anne plums, pitted Moyer prunes, Dapple Dandy pluots, Flavor Grenade pluots, tangy apricots, sweet apricots, white peaches, yellow peaches, white figs, pitted Bing cherries, muscat raisins, jumbo golden raisins, nectarines, and pears
- natural unsweetened medium-flake coconut, also known as unsulphured medium shred macaroon coconut, is available at Whole Foods Market and other premium full-scale markets; the *panforte* is just as delicious without the addition of coconut, but you'll need to make up for its absence by adding ⅔ cup nuts or seeds
- Essensia is a sweet wine derived from the orange muscat grape—its bouquet of orange is underpinned by the light, fruity scent that hints of apricot, making it ideal for adding to dried fruit-based batters, pastry cream, icing, and glazes, or for serving with biscotti; Essensia, produced and bottled by Andrew Quady (Madera, CA; www.quadywinery.com), is simply exceptional
- although not essential to do, I prefer to bake the *panforte* in a moist oven environment to encourage the sweet to remain pliable and very chewy even after it has cooled, and do so by placing two 8 by 4 by 3-inch loaf pans half-filled with boiling water on the oven rack on either side of the *panforte*; if your oven is not wide enough to accommodate both the loaf pans and the cake on one level, bake the cake on the middle-level rack and, in place of the two loaf pans, use a 13 by 9 by 2-inch baking pan, half-filled with boiling water, set on the lower-third-level rack
- for longer storage, you can hold the entire *panforte*—uncoated with confectioners' sugar—as soon as it has cooled in an airtight cake keeper for up to 2 weeks; a few hours before serving, slice and lightly coat the triangles with the confectioners' sugar
- use a finely serrated knife to cut the confection

1 cup walnut halves or pieces

¼ cup roasted pumpkin seeds

1½ teaspoons vanilla extract

about ½ cup confectioners' sugar, for dusting the baked sweet

serving: one 10-inch confection, creating about 18 wedges
ahead: freshly baked, within 3 days; for longer storage (up to 3 weeks), and if you are not serving the *panforte* within 2 or 3 days of baking, omit the confectioners' sugar coating and refrigerate the sweet resting on a sheet of parchment paper in the container (enrobe the sweet with confectioners' sugar just before serving)

not dainty

Untamed. Unkempt. Flamboyant.

The coconut in this macaroon mixture gets in a tangle with bumps and clumps of good bittersweet chocolate; vanilla, in the form of extract (and seed scrapings from the bean, if you wish), kicks in its own soft, dreamy scent. This highly moldable mixture is like flaky edible baker's "clay," ready to be configured into impressively moist mounds, looming and plump as they sit in the little tart pans. You could also pack it—lightly and deftly—into other decorative molds, such as baby brioche molds, oval boats, and fluted rectangular bars. All of this bulkiness is held together by four egg whites and some superfine sugar that melts indulgently into the mixture when encountering the other ingredients.

These are rich. And moist. And wonderfully easy.

coconutextreme: macaroons, with chocolate

two coconut-bittersweet chocolate mixture

4 large egg whites

⅛ teaspoon salt

1½ teaspoons vanilla extract

¾ cup superfine sugar

3¼ cups firmly packed sweetened flaked coconut

⅔ cup natural unsweetened medium-flake coconut

6 ounces bittersweet chocolate, hand-cut into small chunks

serving: 16 cookies
ahead: 2 days

Preheat the oven to 350 degrees F.

Film the inside of 16 round tart molds (each mold measuring 2¼ inches in diameter and ½ inch deep, with a capacity of 2 tablespoons) with nonstick flour-and-oil spray. Have a large rimmed sheet pan at hand.

For the coconut-chocolate mixture, whisk the egg whites, salt, vanilla extract, and sugar in a large mixing bowl until combined. Add the sweetened flaked coconut and the unsweetened medium-flake coconut. Mix well to moisten thoroughly. Work in the chunks of chocolate.

Lightly squeeze and form heaping 3-tablespoon-size quantities of dough into rough mounds and place in the prepared tart molds. The macaroons must be formed by pressing the mixture together into a reasonably compact shape that is slightly wider at the base than at the top, each looking like a rounded, contoured hillock, but keep the edges texturally rough and flaky. Set the filled tart molds on the baking pan.

Bake the macaroons in the preheated oven for 21 to 25 minutes, or until set and a golden color. The inside of each macaroon should still be moist. Let the cookies stand in the pans on the baking pan for 5 minutes, then carefully nudge them out of the molds with the tip of a narrow offset metal palette knife. Transfer the macaroons to a length of ovenproof parchment paper and cool completely. Store in an airtight tin.

notes
- the combination of the sweetened flaked coconut and the unsweetened medium-flake coconut makes a texturally interesting macaroon
- seeds from ½ a small vanilla bean, scraped clean, can be added to the mixture along with the vanilla extract
- my favorite bittersweet chocolates to use in the macaroon batter include Scharffen Berger Bittersweet 70% cacao; Valrhona Extra Amer Bittersweet 61% cacao; Lindt Excellence 70% Cocoa Extra Fine Dark Chocolate; Michel Cluizel Chocolat Amer Brut Bitter Chocolate 72% cocoa; Michel Cluizel Ilha Toma 65% cacao; or Valrhona Guanaja Dark Bitter Chocolate 70% cacao
- the macaroons are baked in 16 round tart molds; two miniature muffin pans (12 cups to a pan, each cup measuring 1¾ inches in diameter and ¾ inch deep, with a capacity of 1 tablespoon plus 1 teaspoon) may be substituted, dividing the cookie mixture into 24 mounds and reducing the baking time by 3 to 5 minutes
- on the scale of rich, these are more chocolate-intense and a little less sweet than my *chocolate chip macaroons* in *ChocolateChocolate*

really spicy

Objective described: a spice-laden gingerbread cookie, one with *oomph* and the lingering, gleaming taste of brown sugar, molasses, honey, butter, and an absolute embarrassment of spices. The spices were selected by the level of flavor each contributes, customizing a dough that is high on drama when baked—decorated or not.

For some time, as this gingerbread dough was put under a specialized taste microscope, rigorous testing took place before each holiday season. To be designated a keeper, the formula went through fabled transitions: light on spices, heavy on molasses; heavy on molasses and honey; bold with molasses alone; thoroughly spice-accented and brown sugar–loaded; and on and on. The result? An authoritative presence of ginger, underpinned by cinnamon, nutmeg, cloves, allspice, and cardamom—all supported by the mellowness of molasses and brown sugar—creates a batch of "adult" gingerbread cookies (the spices can be moderated, however, by halving each amount to suit the palates of children). To counteract one of the most disappointing attributes of many gingerbread doughs, that of a cardboardlike texture, I configured the dough to be moister than most; as a result, the rolled-out sheets require refrigeration and freezing to establish their firmness before being cut into shapes.

A flurry of coarse sanding, plain granulated, or crunchy and nubbly turbinado sugar would be a complementary finish for unbaked cookies, or you can veer in the direction of surfacing the cookies with an overlay of royal icing and a deluge of fanciful sprinkles. With or without the sprinkles, the royal icing surface can be painted with food-safe food color powder, using the method outlined on page 331.

Objective met: holiday cookies are the best part of the season. If you need confirmation of this, ask any baker.

For the dough, sift the flour, baking powder, baking soda, salt, ginger, cinnamon, nutmeg, cardamom, allspice, and cloves onto a sheet of waxed paper.

Cream the butter in the large bowl of a freestanding electric mixer on moderately low speed for 3 minutes. Add the light brown sugar and beat on moderate speed for 2 minutes. Add the granulated sugar and beat for 1 minute longer. Add the eggs, one at a time, beating on low speed until incorporated, about 45 seconds. Blend in the vanilla extract and half of the molasses; blend in the remaining molasses. Scrape down the sides of the mixing bowl frequently with a rubber spatula to keep the dough even-textured. On low speed, mix in the sifted ingredients in 3 additions, beating only until the flour particles are absorbed. Divide the dough into 4 portions. Roll each portion of dough between two sheets of waxed paper to a thickness of a generous ¼ inch. Stack the sheets of dough on a cookie sheet. Refrigerate the dough overnight.

On baking day, place the sheets of dough in the freezer for 1½ hours before stamping out the cookies and baking them.

Preheat the oven to 350 degrees F.

Line several heavy cookie sheets with lengths of ovenproof parchment paper.

Remove one sheet of dough at a time from the freezer. Carefully peel off both sheets of waxed paper and place the rolled-out dough on a lightly floured work surface (or, place the rolled-out dough on a sheet of ovenproof parchment paper). Stamp out cookies with a 5-inch cutter or a 3 to 3½-inch cutter. Place the cookies, 2½ to 3 inches apart, on the prepared baking pans. Sprinkle the tops with turbinado sugar, granulated sugar, sparkling sugar, or any shade of sanding sugar desired, or leave the surfaces plain in order to flood them with royal icing and decorate with painted powdered food color.

Bake the cookies in the preheated oven for 11 to 12 minutes, or until set. Let the cookies stand on the baking pans for 1 minute, then transfer them to cooling racks, using a wide offset metal spatula. Cool the cookies completely before decorating with royal icing (see notes) if you wish. Store in an airtight tin.

notes
• to flood the baked cookies with royal icing, use it in its fluid consistency and apply with a ½ to ¾-inch-wide pastry brush, laying the icing on in dabs and coaxing it carefully to the edges; let dry completely if decorating further with various colorations of piped icing, but candies and

(continued on the next page)

gingerbread dough

5¾ cups unsifted bleached all-purpose flour

1¼ teaspoons baking powder

¾ teaspoon baking soda

1 teaspoon salt

4 teaspoons ground ginger

3 teaspoons ground cinnamon

2¼ teaspoons freshly grated nutmeg

¾ teaspoon ground cardamom

½ teaspoon ground allspice

½ teaspoon ground cloves

½ pound (16 tablespoons or 2 sticks) unsalted butter, softened

¾ cup firmly packed light brown sugar

3 tablespoons granulated sugar

2 large eggs

2¾ teaspoons vanilla extract

1 cup unsulphured molasses

turbinado, granulated, sparkling sugar (plain or a color), or fine or coarse sanding sugar, for sprinkling on the unbaked cookies

~ or ~

royal icing (page 331), fanciful food-safe *décoratifs*, and food-safe food color powder for painting (see important ingredient guidelines in notes, page 330)

serving: about 20 cookies (using a 5-inch cutter), or about 30 cookies (using a 3-inch cutter)
ahead: 1 week

other *décoratifs* can be set onto the cookies as soon as the icing is applied (use an impeccably clean pair of tweezers specifically designated and reserved for kitchen work)

• to decorate cookies with royal icing, use a 10-inch pastry bag and royal icing that is firm enough to pipe: secure the tip in the bag, using a coupler if needed; tuck about 1 inch of the bag into the tip, turn down an outward 2-inch collar on the bag; fill the bag one-third full of icing, undo the twisted section of the bag, smooth down the icing, flip up the collar, and twist it closed; squeeze from the uppermost section of the bag to pipe icing onto the surface of each cookie

• regarding *décoratifs*, Elizabeth Parvu of Sugarpaste, a recognized industry expert in a complete range of baking products, recommends that the use of "all purchased *décoratifs*, including pearls, jimmies, and nonpareils be food-grade and food-safe"; further, Ms. Parvu also enjoys "using homemade *décoratifs*, such as pearls, made from a reliable recipe, formed into balls, dried, and enhanced with Pearlesence, which is a glimmery food-grade powdered food color (easiest to find during the winter holiday season)"; refer to Ms. Parvu's Web site recipe—available by clicking on the tab named "edible pearls"—for these formed *décoratifs* made from premade, purchased fondant (see page 502, baking*SelectedSources*, for Web site information)

• I have made and used a range of pearls in different millimeter sizes from fondant and sometimes dust their surfaces with food-safe food color powder (of particular interest to those who enjoy creating handmade projects and, especially, making their own fondant for decorative work); a dependable recipe source for the fondant itself (made primarily from confectioners' sugar, water, gelatin, and glucose) and the method for keeping the shape of the pearls intact can be found on pages 217 and 227 of the excellent instructional and inspirational book *Cakes to Dream On: A Master Class in Decorating* by Colette Peters

• homemade pearls are made by hand-rolling fondant into specific sizes, and it is my preference to use a range of tiny melon ballers to portion out the fondant evenly (a rainy-day project, to be sure, but you can make the pearls weeks in advance); the time-consuming part is not rolling the fondant into pearls, but making sure that the millimeter sizes of the pearls are made of even weight (you may see minute irregularities in the shape of hand-formed pearls from batch to batch)

• never consume raw cookie dough

• important ingredient guidelines: if you purchase any *décoratif* or item for use on baked goods intended for consumption, including and not limited to pearls or food color powder, make sure that it is edible; further, only a *décoratif* specifically considered a food product and safe for consumption should be eaten; otherwise and without exception, the item should be used only as decoration.

royal icing

Place the meringue powder, confectioners' sugar, water, lemon juice, and vanilla extract in the large bowl of a freestanding electric mixer. Beat on low speed for 2 minutes, or until completely combined. Scrape down the sides of the mixing bowl several times. Beat for 1 minute longer, or just until smooth. Use the icing immediately or scrape it into an impeccably clean, glass, food-safe container, cover tightly, and refrigerate.

notes

- meringue powder is a shelf-stable ingredient used to prepare royal icing, in addition to other confectionery items; the main component of the powder is dried egg whites that have been pasteurized
- storing the icing in a glass, rather than plastic, container maintains its integrity and so prevents it from breaking down, staining, or absorbing any lingering surface scents
- as necessary, the icing can be thinned with water to achieve flowing or spreading consistency, or stiffened with additional confectioners' sugar (2 to 3 tablespoons at a time) to reach piping consistency
- to color the icing with food-safe paste food color, place designated amounts of the icing in clean and dry glass bowls; dip the end of a wooden pick in the paste coloring and mix it in; cover and let the icing blossom for 10 to 15 minutes before using

confectioners' sugar–meringue powder icing

5 tablespoons meringue powder (see notes)

6 cups unsifted confectioners' sugar

7 tablespoons water

2 teaspoons freshly squeezed lemon juice

2 teaspoons vanilla extract

serving: about 2½ cups
ahead: 3 days

food color powder application for decorating royal icing–coated cookies

Place a small amount of the chosen food color powder in a ramekin or in the round depression of a decorating palette. Lightly dip the tip of a small pastry brush in a little vodka or gin, then sweep it onto the powder to make a kind of "paint." Paint the dry, royal icing–covered surface of the cookie with the moistened powder, repeating the process and adding more dust to the depression or ramekin as needed. Move quickly in the decorating process as the moistened powder dries fast. In addition, work with only as much "paint" as you can apply in a few strokes. The painted surface usually dries within an hour, though this depends on the atmospheric condition, especially if significant humidity is present in the air.

notes

- Antique Gold Food Powder, available from Sugarpaste, looks beautiful painted on pastel or white royal icing–coated cookies

food-safe decorating materials

food-safe food color powder, in the color(s) of your choice (see important ingredient guidelines in notes, page 330)

food-safe ramekin(s) or other individual container(s), such as a palette with small depressions

a little bowl containing 3 to 4 tablespoons of clear, neutral spirit, such as vodka or gin

to the brim

My definition of fruit*cake*: fruit, nuts, and cake all vying for attention.

The riveting ingredient in this wintry merger of fruits, nuts, and batter is made with plenty of crystallized ginger—extravagant, spicy, opulent (to the brim, indeed). That, plus one attention-getting pound of butter (!), lots of mixed dried fruits, and a punctuating amount of ginger preserves, definitely elevate the cake to holiday status. It also serves as a great cold weather sweet to have at a grand tea. It will cannily divert the culinary mind and palate of fruitcake-haters, as the batter plays up ginger at the forefront of its taste. Once reduced to little chunks, the spicy pieces of ginger become vivid and intense in the brown sugar–sweetened batter. I love to bake the cake in a deep tube pan, for in it the tall slices stay impressively moist and look so pretty mottled with the rum-touched ingredients. For an alluring presentation, consider brushing the top with warm apricot glaze (the *apricot glaze* on page 191 used to coat the surface of the *savarin, well-nourished* would be appropriate in this context) and, before that coating sets, ringing the top with perfect walnut halves, with candied fruits (whole or halves), or with thin cross sections of dried fruit. Or just have it plain. Plainly deluxe, that is.

luxury cake, sparkly and nutty

gingery raisin and walnut batter

3 cups mixed dried fruits (such as apricots, figs, pitted dates, apples, peaches, nectarines, plums, and such), very finely chopped

1 cup golden seedless raisins

1 cup dark seedless raisins

⅔ cup dark rum

2½ cups unsifted bleached all-purpose flour

½ cup unsifted bleached cake flour

1½ teaspoons baking powder

1 teaspoon salt

3 teaspoons ground ginger

1¼ teaspoons ground cinnamon

1¼ teaspoons freshly grated nutmeg

¾ teaspoon ground allspice

1 pound (4 sticks) unsalted butter, softened

2 cups firmly packed dark brown sugar

6 large eggs

3 teaspoons vanilla extract

½ cup best-quality ginger preserves

1 cup crystallized ginger, finely chopped

1½ cups walnut halves or pieces

glaze and fruit finish (optional)

apricot glaze (page 191)

thinly sliced dried or glazed fruit

serving: one 9¾-inch cake, creating about 20 slices
ahead: 5 days

Combine the dried fruits, golden raisins, and dark raisins in a very large nonreactive mixing bowl. Pour over the rum, toss well, and cover loosely with a sheet of food-safe plastic wrap. Let the mixture stand at cool room temperature for 4 hours (or up to 8 hours).

Preheat the oven to 275 degrees F.

Film the inside of a plain, one-piece 9¾-inch tube pan (6 inches deep, with a capacity of 18 cups) with nonstick flour-and-oil spray. Line the bottom of the pan with a circle of ovenproof parchment paper cut to fit and film its surface with the spray. (It is essential to line the bottom of the pan.)

For the batter, sift the all-purpose flour and cake flour with the baking powder, salt, ground ginger, cinnamon, nutmeg, and allspice onto a sheet of waxed paper.

Cream the butter in the large bowl of a freestanding electric mixer on moderately high speed for 3 minutes. Add the dark brown sugar in 3 additions, beating for 1 minute on moderate speed after each portion is added. Beat in the eggs, one at a time, mixing for 30 seconds after each addition. Blend in the vanilla extract and ginger preserves. On low speed, add the sifted mixture in 3 additions. Scrape down the sides of the mixing bowl thoroughly with a rubber spatula after each addition. Scrape the batter over the rum-marinated fruit mixture, add the crystallized ginger and walnuts, and stir to thoroughly mix the fruits and nuts with the batter.

Spoon the batter into the prepared baking pan. Smooth the top with a rubber spatula.

Bake the cake in the preheated oven for 2 hours and 30 minutes, or until set and a wooden pick inserted into the cake withdraws clean. Begin checking the cake at 2 hours and 15 minutes. The baked cake will pull away slightly from the sides of the pan. The surface of the baked cake will be level.

Cool the cake in the pan on a rack for 15 minutes. Carefully invert the cake onto another cooling rack. Lift off the pan, remove the circle of parchment paper if it clings to the cake, and invert the cake to stand right side up. Cool completely. Store in an airtight cake keeper. An hour or two before serving is the ideal time to glaze the top of the cake and apply dried or glazed fruits to it, if you wish. Apply the warm glaze to the top of the cake, using a soft pastry brush. Wait a minute, then carefully place sections or slices of dried or glazed fruit on the surface in a pretty pattern.

one way or the other

The options in baking, meaning the practically unlimited possibilities of how to configure a recipe with regard to taste and texture, are what can keep me going, going, going—relentlessly—on one recipe.

I look at all the angles until a final version declares itself in looks, texture, and taste. This then becomes, for each recipe, a baking moment of truth.

Or not.

What do I mean by "or not"? What if there is no perfectly unilateral recipe for a particular type of cake, cookie, or bread? What if there are two ways to arrive at a recipe's inner essence? I could play a game with you and offer just one of the two versions, secretly keeping the other rendering to myself, or I could fully disclose that there is, verifiably, more than one way to make something delicious. Case in point: the two cakes introduced here.

Each cake is graced with cinnamon and sour cream—two ingredients in a heavenly match. One is made with a mixture of all-purpose flour and cake flour, the other with all-purpose flour alone. One has lots of loose brown sugar and cinnamon crumbs, the other has crumbs moistened with melted butter. Some of the crumb mixture is enclosed in the center of each cake, swirled or left in a single layer. Plain and simple, exceptionally moist, and relaxed in style, either would be an ideal Sunday-morning cake—so good with the richest, boldest cup of coffee.

a delightful brunch cake, two ways:
aroma-of-cinnamon cake, take one; aroma-of-cinnamon cake, take two

aroma-of-cinnamon cake, take one

sugar-cinnamon filling and topping

⅓ cup granulated sugar

⅓ cup firmly packed light brown sugar

4 teaspoons ground cinnamon

sour cream batter

1⅔ cups unsifted bleached
all-purpose flour

⅓ cup unsifted bleached cake flour

1 teaspoon baking powder

¼ teaspoon baking soda

¼ teaspoon salt

10 tablespoons (1 stick plus 2 tablespoons)
unsalted butter, softened

1 cup granulated sugar

2 large eggs

2 teaspoons vanilla extract

1 cup sour cream

confectioners' sugar, for sifting
over the baked cake (optional)

serving: one 9-inch cake,
creating 10 generously-thick slices
ahead: 3 days

Preheat the oven to 350 degrees F.

Film the inside of a 9-inch springform pan (2¾ inches deep) or a round
9-inch cake pan (3 inches deep) with nonstick flour-and-oil spray. If you are
using the 9-inch cake pan, line the bottom of the prepared pan with a circle of
ovenproof parchment paper, then film the surface of the paper and the sides
of the pan with the spray.

For the filling and topping, thoroughly combine the granulated sugar, light
brown sugar, and cinnamon in a bowl. Set aside.

For the batter, sift the all-purpose flour, cake flour, baking powder, baking
soda, and salt onto a sheet of waxed paper.

Cream the butter in the large bowl of a freestanding electric mixer on
moderate speed for 1 minute. Add the granulated sugar in 2 additions,
beating for 1 minute after each portion is added. Beat in the eggs. Blend in
the vanilla extract. On low speed, beat in half of the sifted ingredients, the
sour cream, then the remaining sifted ingredients. Scrape down the sides of
the mixing bowl with a rubber spatula to keep the batter even-textured. The
batter will be thick but creamy-textured.

Spoon a little more than half of the batter into the prepared baking pan.
Sprinkle over half of the sugar-cinnamon filling. Spoon the remaining batter
on top in dollops. If you wish, swirl the batter, using the tip of a rounded
table knife or small offset palette knife. Smooth the top with a palette knife or
rubber spatula. Sprinkle the remaining sugar-cinnamon filling over the top.

Bake the cake in the preheated oven for 45 minutes, or until set and a wooden
pick withdraws clean when tested about 2 inches from the center of the cake,
and the cake pulls away slightly from the rounded edges of the pan. The top
of the baked cake may puff and crack in places—of course, this does not affect
its flavor or wonderfully moist texture—and it will be splintery, with fragments
of the cinnamon sugar forming crunchy sections.

Completely cool the springform-baked cake in the pan on a cooling rack, then
unclasp the outer ring of the pan, leaving the cake on its metal base. Cool the
cake in the round cake pan in the pan on a rack for 10 minutes, then place

a length of ovenproof parchment paper on the top before setting another cooling rack on top. Invert the cake, lift off the pan, peel off the bottom circle of parchment if it has adhered, and invert the cake again to cool right side up. Just before slicing into thick wedges and serving, sift confectioners' sugar over the top of the cake, if you wish. Store in an airtight container.

notes

- to release the cake baked in the round cake pan, you will need to place a sheet of ovenproof parchment paper on top of the cake before setting over a cooling rack, otherwise some of the loose sugar-cinnamon crumbs (the best part!) will drop off
- a false-bottomed round 9-inch cake pan (3 inches deep) may also be used; prepare the pan by filming the inside with nonstick flour-and-oil spray (to unmold the cake after cooling, carefully lift the cake by the bottom, pushing it up and out, and cool completely on its metal base)

aroma-of-cinnamon cake, take two

Preheat the oven to 350 degrees F.

Film the inside of a 9-inch springform pan (2¾ inches deep) or a round 9-inch cake pan (3 inches deep) with nonstick flour-and-oil spray. If you are using the 9-inch cake pan, line the bottom of the prepared pan with a circle of ovenproof parchment paper, then film the surface of the paper and the sides of the pan with the spray.

For the filling and topping, thoroughly combine the brown sugar and cinnamon in a bowl. Turn half of the mixture into another bowl, drizzle over the melted butter and vanilla extract, and combine until the sugar is moistened. The buttered mixture will look like clumpy, damp sand. Set both mixtures aside.

For the batter, sift the flour, baking powder, baking soda, and salt onto a sheet of waxed paper.

Cream the butter in the large bowl of a freestanding electric mixer on moderate speed for 2 minutes. Add the granulated sugar in 2 additions, beating for 1 minute after each portion is added. Beat in the eggs, one at a time, mixing for 45 seconds after each addition. Blend in the vanilla extract. On low speed, beat in half of the sifted ingredients, the sour cream, then the remaining sifted ingredients. Scrape down the sides of the mixing bowl with a rubber spatula to keep the batter even-textured. The batter will be thick but creamy-textured.

(continued on the next page)

half-buttered sugar-cinnamon filling and topping

¾ cup firmly packed light brown sugar

4 teaspoons ground cinnamon

3 tablespoons unsalted butter, melted, cooled to tepid, and blended with ½ teaspoon vanilla extract

sour cream batter

2 cups unsifted bleached all-purpose flour

1 teaspoon baking powder

¼ teaspoon baking soda

¼ teaspoon salt

8 tablespoons (1 stick) unsalted butter, softened

1 cup granulated sugar

2 large eggs

2 teaspoons vanilla extract

1 cup sour cream

(continued on the next page)

(continued from the previous page)

confectioners' sugar, for sifting over the
baked cake (optional)

_____

serving: one 9-inch cake,
creating 10 generously thick slices
ahead: 3 days

Spoon a little more than half of the batter into the prepared baking pan.
Sprinkle over the *unbuttered* sugar-cinnamon mixture. Spoon the remaining
batter on top in dollops and smooth the top with a palette knife or rubber
spatula. If you wish, swirl the batter, using the tip of a rounded table knife
or small offset palette knife. Sprinkle the *buttered* sugar-cinnamon mixture
over the top.

Bake the cake in the preheated oven for 45 minutes, or until set and a
wooden pick withdraws clean when tested about 2 inches from the center
of the cake. The baked cake will pull away slightly from the rounded edges
of the baking pan. It will have a craggy, uneven surface, and this is to be
expected. Completely cool the springform-baked cake in the pan on a
cooling rack, then unclasp the outer ring of the pan, leaving the cake on its
metal base. Cool the cake in the round cake pan in the pan on a cooling rack
for 10 minutes. Invert the cake onto another cooling rack, lift off the pan,
peel off the bottom circle of parchment if it has adhered, and invert again
to cool right side up. Just before slicing into thick wedges and serving, sift
confectioners' sugar over the top of the cake, if you wish.

notes

• the buttered sugar-cinnamon crumbs meld beautifully onto the top of this cake because the
  crumb is a little more substantial than that in the *aroma-of-cinnamon cake, take one*
• a false-bottomed round 9-inch cake pan (3 inches deep) may also be used; prepare the pan by
  filming the inside with nonstick flour-and-oil spray (to unmold the cake after cooling, carefully
  lift the cake by the bottom, pushing it up and out, and cool completely on its metal base)

tipping the scale on chocolate

The following recipe is what happens when chocolate is used to its fullest capacity: dark, rich squares of buttery sweetness, wrapped in underpinnings of vanilla, are interrupted periodically with miniature semisweet chocolate chips.

The batter is dense, and offers some resistance toward the end of mixing in the sifted dry ingredients and, once again, when the chips are integrated for the final blend-in. Basically, it's the commingling of the melted butter, cocoa powder, sugar, and eggs that maintains a certain close-packed texture, with a crumb that is so tight, it can be hard to actually see the little chips, though you will taste their presence (the chips meld into the batter and sometimes form tiny craters within it). It is a jewel of a formula, and will deliver raves greatly out of proportion to the kitchen work involved in its preparation.

dark shadows

buttery cocoa batter

2 cups unsweetened alkalized
cocoa powder

1 cup unsifted bleached all-purpose flour

½ cup unsifted bleached cake flour

½ teaspoon baking powder

½ teaspoon salt

¾ cup miniature semisweet
chocolate chips

1 pound (4 sticks) unsalted butter,
melted and cooled to tepid

2 ounces bittersweet chocolate,
melted and cooled to tepid

8 large eggs

2¼ cups superfine sugar

1¾ cups firmly packed light brown sugar

4 teaspoons vanilla extract

seeds from 1 small vanilla bean,
scraped clean

cocoa and confectioners' sugar topping,
for sifting over the baked bars

¼ cup confectioners' sugar

1 teaspoon unsweetened
alkalized cocoa powder

~ or ~

confectioners' sugar,
for sifting over the baked bars

serving: 20 large squares or 40 bars
ahead: 4 days

Preheat the oven to 325 degrees F.

Film the inside of a 13 by 9 by 2-inch baking pan with nonstick flour-and-oil spray. Or, line the inside of the baking pan, lengthwise and width-wise, with sheets of release-surface aluminum foil, pressing in the foil release side up and leaving 2 to 3 inches of foil to extend on all four sides. Film the inside of the foil-lined pan with nonstick oil spray.

For the batter, sift the cocoa powder, all-purpose flour, cake flour, baking powder, and salt onto a sheet of waxed paper.

Toss the chocolate chips with ¾ teaspoon of the sifted mixture in a small mixing bowl.

In a medium-size mixing bowl, whisk the melted butter and melted chocolate until combined.

In a large mixing bowl, beat the eggs just to mix. Add the superfine sugar and beat for 30 seconds to mix, but not add volume. Blend in the light brown sugar. Blend in the melted chocolate-butter mixture, vanilla extract, and vanilla bean seeds, mixing slowly with a whisk until thoroughly incorporated. Once again, avoid vigorously beating the mixture. Resift the cocoa-flour mixture over the chocolate-butter mixture. Whisk slowly to form a batter, scraping down the sides of the mixing bowl with a rubber spatula to keep the batter even-textured. The batter will be thick. Work in the chocolate chips.

Scrape the batter into the prepared pan. Smooth the top with a flexible palette knife.

Bake the sweet in the preheated oven for 40 to 44 minutes, or until just set. The edges of the baked sweet will puff slightly and there may be a few hairline cracks on the surface; this is to be expected.

Cool the sweet in the pan on a cooling rack. Refrigerate for 1 hour, or until firm enough to cut. If you have used the foil liner, lift the block of bar cookies out of the pan by the edges of the foil. Cut the sweet into 20 squares, or cut each square in half to create bars, using a long, heavy chef's knife. (Peel away the cut squares from the foil.) Remove the squares or bars from the pan, using a small offset metal spatula. Or run amok, and break the big block into odd-shaped pieces and fragments. Store in an airtight tin.

Just before serving, whisk the confectioners' sugar and cocoa powder in a small mixing bowl to combine well, then sift the topping over the tops of the squares or bars. Or, sift plain confectioners' sugar over the tops of the squares or bars.

notes
• make sure that the light brown sugar is sieved to remove any hardened lumps, for these will not melt and will firmly punctuate (in an unattractive way) the baked sweet
• if available, miniature bittersweet chocolate chips can replace the semisweet variety
• in the topping, a combination of confectioners' sugar and cocoa powder adds a finishing flurry to the sweet as well as a secondary level of chocolate flavor; cocoa powder alone would make a simple—but significantly more intense—topping (use about 5 teaspoons to sift over the top in a sheer layer), but confectioners' sugar alone can also be used
• a few of the squares or bars can be reserved and used in the filling for my *"brownie" babka* (page 196)

Polished

besotted-with-butter cookies ❋ pumpkin frames
a batter ❋ an enticement of olive oil (in cake!)
❋ the lure of sour cream ❋ majestic shells
treated to an upgrade ❋ two cakes, two flavors:
loving cardamom *and* loving three extracts ❋
raisins tousled in bread ❋ yeasty breakfast cake

Sophisticated

cookies that cast a butter spell

If you, like me, think that butter is one of nature's prime offerings—the best tasting purely of the pasture—faintly earthy, smooth, and silky in its density, then you possess a true baker's soul.

In this cookie dough, butter, the generously creamy fat, transmits immaculate flavor and, along with sugar and two egg yolks, composes a dough that, when baked, vaporizes lightly into tender crispness between bites. It is the butter that, when you open up the cookie tin, promptly commands all senses, urging you to eat *just one more cookie* because its taste carries with it a long, vanilla-stroked finish.

When softened butter is creamed until pearly and highly malleable, it is ready to welcome a certain amount of sugar, egg yolks, flavoring, and a sifted composite of flour, baking powder, and salt. The meeting of the elements is a fine one: a soft dough is formed—it's not at all right for rolling or hand-molding, sticky as it is—and sits pretty in a pastry bag furnished with an open-star tip.

If the idea of a pastry bag filled with something to be piped seems like some wretched plan for imminent disaster, relax. If you can squeeze and form the capital letter S, then you can make these cookies. Anyone who can write is sure to achieve this with a little practice: in a show-and-tell way, I teach cooks to start just under the top of the S, then swing up slightly and around to form the top, come down to make the long swirly curve, and finish by creating the bottom curl, tucking the end slightly into the lower, inside arch. The dough is supple enough to work in this way, and you may have to rehearse compressing the bag while simultaneously forming the cookie a few times to accelerate the action and load up your sheet with all those graceful cookies. If the first few attempts look misshapen and scrawny, do what I do on occasion—open the bag, plop in the malformed pieces of dough, and start over again. No one will ever know. But for all the truly nervous first-time pastry bag pipers, buy a jar of mayonnaise (the cheaper, the better), fill the bag, and practice on a sheet of waxed paper.

Traditional piped cookies are tight little affairs, with exacting, clearly articulated lines and spirals and, rest assured, they are firmly tough to eat. These are not. The leavening present in this dough opens up the crumb and, on baking, extends it. A pattern is still distinguishable, though, and enough of it is present to capture in its soft folds sprinklings of granulated sugar. That mist of sugar forms a slightly crunchy, luminous coating.

Gorgeous with coffee, the cookies are best hidden and doled out with discrimination. Be prepared, as people will beg you for more. It is for this reason alone that this, my oldest, most-extensively tweaked recipe, finally perfected in its current incarnation and a restructuring of the original (bakers seem to change and refine things relentlessly), yields the quantity it does. The basic spritz cookie recipe (the launching point for this formula) was handed down to me at age seven, just about the time my paternal grandmother gave me her "secret" brownie recipe. Even now—so many years later—I can visualize the cookie dough being squeezed out from her hand-held aluminum cookie press.

butter and sugar cookies

Preheat the oven to 350 degrees F.

Outfit a 14-inch pastry bag with an open-star tip, such as Ateco #823.

Line several heavy cookie sheets or rimmed sheet pans with lengths of ovenproof parchment paper.

For the dough, sift the flour, baking powder, and salt onto a sheet of waxed paper.

Cream the butter in the large bowl of a freestanding electric mixer on moderate speed for 3 minutes. Add the superfine sugar in 3 additions, beating for 1 full minute after each portion is added. Blend in the egg yolks, one at a time. Mix in the vanilla extract. On low speed, beat in the sifted mixture in 3 additions, mixing just until the flour particles are absorbed before adding the next portion. The dough should be quite soft.

Fold back a wide cuff on the pastry bag and fill the bag about one-third full with the dough. Flip up the cuff, smooth down the dough, and twist the top closed.

Pipe swirly S-shape cookies 2 inches apart onto the prepared baking pans, placing 12 swirls on each standard-size pan. Refill the bag as necessary and continue piping. Sprinkle granulated sugar on top of the piped cookies.

Bake the cookies in the preheated oven for 12 to 15 minutes, or until set and golden in color. The raised edges will be a shade darker.

Cool the cookies on the baking pans for 1 minute, then slide a wide offset metal spatula under them and transfer to cooling racks. Or, you can cool the cookies on the parchment paper by carefully easing each paper filled with cookies onto a rack. Cool completely. Store the cookies in an airtight tin.

notes
- this recipe is a composite of my grandmother's cookie-press cookies and my traditional holiday S cookies, and reflects the best attributes of each (as well it should, for I have spent more than 20 years perfecting it)
- before you begin, make sure that the butter has softened thoroughly, for several hours perhaps, otherwise the dough won't be as creamy-textured as it should be and will offer significant resistance to piping; despite everything, if the cookie dough is cranky and unmanageable, all is not lost, as you can form 1-inch balls of dough, roll them heavily in granulated sugar, place them on the cookie sheets, press them down with the tines of a fork

(continued on the next page)

---

butter and sugar dough

3¾ cups unsifted bleached all-purpose flour	
1½ teaspoons baking powder	
¾ teaspoon salt	
1 pound (4 sticks) unsalted butter, softened	
1⅔ cups plus 2 tablespoons superfine sugar	
2 large egg yolks	
4½ teaspoons vanilla extract	
granulated sugar, for sprinkling on the piped cookies before baking	

serving: about 6 dozen cookies (using Ateco tip #823)
ahead: 1 week

to striate, and bake until golden (I had to do this myself once on a brutally cold December evening when, despite 6 hours at room temperature, the butter was not as yielding as it should have been)

- the amount of flour is pivotal to the structure of the dough and its piping consistency; the formula was developed in a room-temperature, low-humidity environment, but you may have to increase the overall amount by 2 to 3 tablespoons in the presence of higher humidity or even on a cold and rainy day
- the value of using superfine sugar cannot be overstated here—the extremely small, sharp granules make a fine, noteworthy dough that bakes the tenderest cookies imaginable
- on baking, an under- or over-leavened butter dough destined for piping, such as this one, creates textural havoc and returns a less-than-delicate cookie, so make sure that you measure the baking powder precisely
- about filling the pastry bag: piping cookies is unwieldy if the bag is overfilled with dough, so filling the bag about one-third full allows you to control the contents and, then, the resulting shape of the cookies
- keep all yet-to-be-piped dough covered with a sheet of food-safe plastic wrap
- baking the cookies until golden makes them tender from the center to the edges; underbaking the cookies (for example, leaving the middle sections light) will create denser, less fine-grained centers
- never consume raw cookie dough
- historical recipe data: first things first—Grandma never piped this cookie dough from a pastry bag; the older formula used cake flour, a larger amount of baking powder, granulated sugar, and a smaller amount of vanilla extract

a cake for twenty-four hours

A round-the-clock cake—at breakfast or brunch, for afternoon tea, or as the sweet closing statement to dinner—is my idea of baking-friendly.

This olive oil–enclosed cake, touched with butter and scented with orange peel, is an obliging mate to coffee in the morning (omit the citrus gloss and dust with confectioners' sugar, if you wish) and to hot or iced tea (pile on the whipped cream spangled with candied orange threads). As dessert, it shines when offered with an orange liqueur–spiked mixed berry salad.

Put this cake on your to-bake list and file it in a sheltered place for those who will be in line to inherit your stash of recipes. This one is a keeper, brought to you after years of discovering how to combine ingredients such as melted butter, olive oil, eggs, sugar, a leavened flour mixture, corn meal, and a flavoring (or two) compatibly. The confluence of two fats, both in a liquid state, can really slant a baking recipe (and not in a good way, may I add), making the integration of the other components difficult or, at the very least, testy. The only way a batter can be formed and baked to a successful conclusion given the set of items is by rapidly beating the whole eggs and egg yolk with superfine sugar until quite swollen. At that point, the extracts and grated orange peel are added, and await the mix-in of both pourable fats, in addition to the flour with its mingled corn meal, baking powder, and salt. The resulting batter is remarkably creamy (for a non-creamed batter, technique-wise) and bakes into a nicely textured cake. The fruitiness of the olive oil adds a certain amount of refined complexity, and a few tablespoons of corn meal, a golden cast (the cake is not that gritty). Once unmolded and while warm, a vivacious citrus blend is brushed over the top and, in addition to that, you can layer on an orange marmalade glaze and tuck in a chunk of candied orange peel (extravagant).

I love to eat this cake before the flush of the oven's heat subsides completely, for then all of the rounded flavors in the olive oil and butter turn up and out, and the tone of the grated orange peel maintains itself—softly.

oily cake

Preheat the oven to 350 degrees F.

Film the inside of a fluted 10-inch false-bottomed tart pan (2 inches deep) with nonstick flour-and-oil spray. Have a rimmed sheet pan at hand.

For the batter, sift the flour, baking powder, and salt into a medium-size mixing bowl. Whisk in the corn meal.

Place the whole eggs and egg yolks in the bowl of a heavy-duty freestanding electric mixer fitted with the whip attachment and beat on moderate speed for 1 minute to blend. Add the superfine sugar in 2 additions, beating for 1 minute on moderate speed after each portion is added. Increase the speed to moderately high and whip for 6 full minutes. Refrain from skimping on the beating time. On moderately low speed, blend in the orange extract, vanilla extract, and grated orange peel. Whisk the melted butter and olive oil in a 2-cup measuring cup. Reduce the mixer speed to low and add the melted butter–olive oil mixture in a thin and continuous stream, mixing just to incorporate. Remove the bowl from the mixer stand. Strain the flour–corn meal mixture over the contents of the mixing bowl in 2 additions, mixing slowly with a whisk (rather than a spoon or spatula) until the particles of flour are absorbed. Scrape down the sides of the mixing bowl with a rubber spatula to keep the batter even-textured. The batter will be buoyant and moderately thick.

Pour and scrape the batter into the prepared baking pan. Smooth the top with a rubber spatula. Place the baking pan on the rimmed sheet pan.

Place the filled cake pan–baking pan assembly in the preheated oven, immediately increase the temperature to 375 degrees F, and bake for 35 to 40 minutes, or until risen, set, and a ruddy golden color on top, with deeper golden edges. The baked cake will pull away gently from the sides of the cake pan. (Testing the center of the cake with a wooden pick may cause the cake to deflate, as this is a sensitive batter.) If, after 25 minutes of baking, the top of the cake is already moderately golden, lightly tent a large sheet of aluminum foil over the top (but avoid folding down the sides of the foil). Cool the cake in the pan on a cooling rack for 5 minutes.

While the cake is cooling in the pan, make the citrus gloss. Combine the lemon juice, orange juice concentrate, and granulated sugar in a small mixing bowl. The mixture will not dissolve entirely—and should be used in that state.

(continued on the next page)

orange olive oil batter

2 cups unsifted bleached all-purpose flour

1 teaspoon baking powder

½ teaspoon salt

3 tablespoons fine yellow corn meal

3 large eggs

3 large egg yolks

1 cup plus 2 tablespoons superfine sugar

1¼ teaspoons orange extract

¾ teaspoon vanilla extract

1 tablespoon plus 2 teaspoons finely grated orange peel

6 tablespoons (¾ stick) unsalted butter, melted and cooled to tepid

½ cup plus 1 tablespoon blood orange olive oil (see notes)

citrus gloss

3 tablespoons freshly squeezed lemon juice

1 tablespoon best-quality orange juice concentrate

2 tablespoons granulated sugar

~ or (or both) ~

finish

orange marmalade glaze (see notes)

candied orange peel (page 353), to garnish the slices of cake (optional)

confectioners' sugar, for sifting over the edges of the baked cake (optional)

serving: one 10-inch cake, creating 12 slices
ahead: best on baking day

Using a soft pastry brush, sweep the citrus gloss over the top of the cake, doing so in 2 or 3 stages, layering brushstroke upon brushstroke to do so. Cool for at least 20 minutes.

Carefully lift the cake by the bottom, pushing it up and out to unmold, and removing the fluted ring. Serve the cake warm or cool completely, cut into pie-shape wedges and finish with a piece of candied orange peel and a little confectioners' sugar sifted on the edges, if you wish. Store in an airtight cake keeper.

notes

- this recipe is loosely based on my recipe for *corn meal tea cake* (page 239), but departs from it in the set of ingredients and method for establishing the batter; though some of the elements appear similar, the introduction of the olive oil and treatment of the sugar and eggs set this cake apart from the tea cake
- the best olive oil to use in this recipe is Stonehouse Extra-Virgin Blood Orange California Olive Oil, produced by Stonehouse California Olive Oil
- make sure that both sugars are free of any small, hardened particles before preparing the batter and the citrus gloss
- whipping the eggs and egg yolks with the sugar until quite thick gives the cake volume and structure, and adds to its enriched, detailed crumb and moist baked texture; take care not to underbeat the mixture
- initially, the batter was created as entirely olive oil–based, but the replacement of melted butter for part of the oil seemed preferable to arrive at a texturally consistent cake with the rich flavor of olive oil and butter; the fat is used in the liquid state and, as such, requires a specific mixing procedure—that of whipping the sugar and egg yolks to a creamy, cloud-like thickness before a whisked mixture of melted butter and olive oil is added, followed by the dry ingredients
- in addition to the citrus gloss, the baked cake can be finished with an orange marmalade glaze (the best marmalade to use for the glaze is Dundee marmalade made with Seville oranges by James Keiller & Son, and is available in 1-pound jars): cool the cake for 20 minutes after unmolding it, and while it rests, simmer 1 cup orange marmalade with 1 tablespoon water and 2 teaspoons freshly squeezed lemon juice in a small nonreactive saucepan until bubbly; apply the glaze over the top of the cake, using a soft pastry brush, and let the cake stand until the glaze has set before slicing (about 1 hour)
- the cake is baked in a fluted 10-inch false-bottomed tart pan (2 inches deep); a round 10-inch layer cake pan (2 inches deep) may be substituted
- use a finely serrated knife to cut the cake

candied orange peel

Cut each orange in half horizontally, then cut each half into 4 sections to create triangles. A part of each orange section will be slightly rounded; you can leave it this way or trim it to create straight-sided triangles. Peel away the flesh and use it for another purpose.

Place the peel in a medium-size nonreactive saucepan. Cover with cold water and bring to the boil over moderately high heat. Drain the peel, pouring out the water. Return the peel to the saucepan, cover with more cold water, and bring to the boil over moderately high heat once again. Drain the peel, pouring out the water, and cover again with cold water. Bring the peel to a boil over moderately high heat, reduce the heat to moderately low, and simmer the peel for 20 minutes.

Drain the peel, pouring out the water, and set aside.

Clean and dry the saucepan thoroughly. Place the sugar, corn syrup, and the 1½ cups water in the saucepan. Cover and set over low heat to dissolve the sugar, stirring the contents of the pan a few times with a wooden spoon or heatproof rubber spatula. When the granules of sugar have dissolved, uncover the pan, bring the contents to a rapid simmer, add the orange peels, and reduce the heat so that the peels simmer slowly. Simmer in the syrup, uncovered, for 45 minutes to 1 hour, or until the peels are tender and fairly translucent-looking.

Line a rimmed sheet pan with a length of ovenproof parchment paper. Set a cooling rack large enough to accommodate all of the peel in a single layer on the parchment paper. Using a pair of heatproof tongs, transfer the peel to the cooling rack, arranging the pieces so that they stay separate, without overlapping or touching in any way. Let the peel stand on the rack, uncovered, until dry, for 24 hours (overnight) or up to 2 days, depending on the temperature of your kitchen and atmospheric climate of the day (on a spate of rainy or humid days, or in a warm kitchen, the peel may take up to 2 days to dry).

The peel is now ready to be enrobed in sugar, if you wish. Place the 1 cup sugar in a wide bowl and, a few pieces at a time, coat the peel lightly in the sugar. Store the peel (sugared or not), arranged in layers, in an airtight tin, with parchment paper protecting each layer.

notes
- select firm, bright-colored organic navel oranges; navel oranges are preferred for candying as they are thick-skinned
- between the plain and sugar-dusted peels, I prefer the plain, unsugared peels for their glimmery appearance and smoother texture

orange peel and simmering syrup

3 navel oranges

cold water for boiling the orange peel

1½ cups granulated sugar

3 tablespoons light corn syrup

1½ cups water

about ½ cup granulated sugar, for dusting the glazed peel (optional)

serving: 2 dozen large triangles
ahead: 1 week

sweet bread tart

Lingering at the table on a late, lazy weekend morning is a fine circumstance for placing this yeasty, supremely light and buttery breakfast bread on the menu. Just for fun, the dough, simplistic and direct, is baked in a deep tart pan.

The resulting sweetened bread can be sliced into pie-shape wedges and offered as pastry or as an accompaniment to smoky protein (thick bacon or ham) and eggs.

The key to making a distinguished bread tart is twofold—to establish a decent rise of the dough to develop flavor and to fashion just the right butter and sugar finish. In this case, the finish is a generous topping of light or dark muscovado sugar and butter that forms crusty, irresistible flavor pools on the top. The focus is, at once, on sweet, soft, and tenderly crusty, but know that bits of dried fruit (such as a generous ¾ cup of cranberries, cherries, and apricots—alone or in combination) or chopped crystallized ginger (3 tablespoons) can be kneaded into the dough after the first rise. The bread is an inviting canvas for a baker's imagination, but the plain version is just fine with me.

a regal breakfast bread

sponge

2¼ teaspoons active dry yeast

¼ teaspoon granulated sugar

¼ cup warm (105 to 110 degrees F) water

¼ cup unsifted unbleached all-purpose flour

1 tablespoon warm
(105 to 110 degrees F) water

butter dough

¼ cup milk

3 tablespoons granulated sugar

2 teaspoons vanilla extract

2 large eggs, lightly beaten

seeds from ⅓ small vanilla bean,
scraped clean (optional)

2 cups unsifted unbleached
all-purpose flour

⅛ teaspoon salt

8 tablespoons (1 stick) unsalted butter,
cut into tablespoon-size chunks, softened

butter and muscovado sugar finish

3 tablespoons cool unsalted butter
(preferably clarified butter, page 1), diced

3 tablespoons firmly packed light or dark
muscovado sugar, or a combination of both

serving: one 10-inch sweet bread,
creating about 10 slices
ahead: 2 days

For the sponge, stir together the yeast, the ¼ teaspoon granulated sugar, and the ¼ cup warm water in a heatproof measuring cup. Allow the mixture to stand until swollen, 6 to 7 minutes.

Scrape the swollen yeast mixture into a small mixing bowl. Blend in the flour and the 1 tablespoon warm water. Cover with a sheet of food-safe plastic wrap, and let rise in a warm place for 30 minutes, or until foamy or almost doubled in bulk. Remove and discard the plastic wrap.

To complete the butter dough, combine the milk and the granulated sugar in a small saucepan and set over low heat; when the sugar has partially dissolved (after 3 to 4 minutes), remove from the heat and scrape into a medium-size heatproof mixing bowl. Cool for 5 minutes, or until lukewarm, then blend in the vanilla extract, beaten eggs, vanilla bean seeds (if you are using them), and sponge mixture. Whisk the flour and salt in a large mixing bowl. Add the egg-sponge-milk mixture to the flour and stir to form a sticky, dense mixture, using a wooden spoon or flat wooden paddle. By hand, beat in the softened butter, 2 tablespoons at a time. The dough mixture will be sticky and dense, and offer resistance during the mixing. Persevere! Continue to beat the dough for 4 to 5 minutes, when it will turn quite elastic (it will still be quite sticky); this step establishes its texture.

Turn the dough into a bowl heavily coated with softened unsalted butter and, with your buttered fingertips, lightly turn to coat all sides in a film of butter (it will turn into a sticky mass, not a tight cohesive "ball" as some other yeast doughs do), make several cuts with a pair of kitchen scissors, cover tightly with a sheet of food-safe plastic wrap, and let rise at cool room temperature for 1 hour and 30 minutes to 1 hour and 45 minutes, or until doubled in bulk. Rushing the rise in an environment warmer than room temperature will cause the butter to ooze out and the resulting dough (and baked cakelike bread) to turn out heavy, dense, and coarse-textured, rather than light and eggy; if this happens, lightly work an additional 4 teaspoons bleached all-purpose flour into the dough, enclose the dough in waxed paper, and refrigerate for 1 hour before continuing with the recipe. If the dough is refrigerated for the hour, increase the next rise of the formed dough, before it is topped with the butter and sugar, up to 30 minutes.

Film the inside of a fluted 10-inch false-bottomed tart pan (2 inches deep) with softened unsalted butter.

Remove and discard the sheet of plastic wrap covering the dough. With your buttered fingertips, lightly compress the risen dough, turn it into the prepared pan, and tap it lightly into an even layer. The dough will be sticky, and if it resists tapping into an even layer, let it rest for 5 to 10 minutes, then resume. Cover the pan loosely with a sheet of food-safe plastic wrap. Let rise at room temperature for 30 minutes.

Remove and discard the plastic wrap covering the dough. Scatter the diced pieces of butter over the surface, then crumble on the muscovado sugar, taking care to avoid sprinkling it too close to the rim of the tart pan (to avoid sticking problems after baking). Let rise for an additional 25 minutes, uncovered, or until nicely puffy and just doubled in bulk (the edges will rise to about ⅓ inch below the top of the pan). On a dry day, or in a cold kitchen, the additional rise (after the topping has been applied) could be as long as 30 to 35 minutes.

Preheat the oven to 375 degrees F in advance of baking.

Place a rimmed sheet pan in the oven 5 minutes before baking the bread.

Place the dough-filled tart pan on the sheet pan.

Bake the bread in the preheated oven for 25 minutes, or until set, a deep golden color on top, and baked through. The surface of the baked bread will be uneven (slightly higher and slightly lower in various places), depending on how the butter and sugar have melted down into large and small pools— very natural, deliciously rustic, and texturally interesting. Cool the bread in the pan on a cooling rack for 5 minutes. Unmold the bread, leaving it on the round base, then return to the cooling rack. Cool for 30 to 45 minutes. Serve tepid (to prevent biting into a too-hot sugar topping) or at room temperature, cut into wedges. Or tear the bread into irregular pieces. Store in an airtight container.

notes
- muscovado sugar has a rich and prominent molasses flavor (the dark more so than the light) and can be used in spice cake or gingerbread as well as in toppings and fillings; light brown sugar or dark brown sugar can be substituted, but the flavor of the topping will be less intense and molasses-y
- the sweet bread is baked in a fluted 10-inch false-bottomed tart pan (2 inches deep); a round 10-inch layer cake pan (2 inches deep) may be substituted for the tart pan (in which case, you will need to line it first with a circle of ovenproof parchment paper)
- the bread must be served tepid, as the butter and sugar finish retains significant heat
- use a finely serrated knife to cut the bread if you are not hand-tearing it into irregular pieces

chocolate dressed for autumn

For some, autumn inspires stocking the wardrobe with woolly sweaters and thick socks in anticipation of snowy ski slopes and slick ice-skating rinks. Not being the outdoorsy type, except for a long late-afternoon walk followed by a good and lusty meal, I retreat into the kitchen (plus, all that wool makes me terribly itchy).

For it is in the kitchen that the tawny colors and flavors of fall, and all the earthiness that accompanies the season, appear in my mixing bowls and on my table.

When the air takes an annual swerving turn from September-warm to October-crisp, I blend pumpkin puree and chocolate chips into a butter cake batter rich in eggs. The puree essentially ensures moistness while coloring the batter a demure, dusky orange with a tinge of yellow ochre. The only seasoning agent present is vanilla extract—spices are absent here as they would conflict with the chocolate—and its vaguely perfumelike quality becomes the natural link between the vegetable and the sweet batter. The pumpkin entrenches itself in the batter, but does not overtake it, and cushions all of those chocolate chips in gentle softness, qualities that make the cake a prime candidate for adding to the Thanksgiving roundup of sweets.

pumpkin cake, with chips

pumpkin cake, with chips

pumpkin–chocolate chip batter

2¼ cups unsifted bleached
all-purpose flour

¾ cup unsifted bleached cake flour

2¼ teaspoons baking powder

¼ teaspoon baking soda

1 teaspoon salt

2 cups miniature semisweet
chocolate chips

½ pound (16 tablespoons or 2 sticks)
unsalted butter, softened

2¼ cups granulated sugar

5 large eggs

2½ teaspoons vanilla extract

one 15-ounce can plain,
solid-pack 100% pumpkin

confectioners' sugar,
for sifting over the baked cake

serving: one 10-inch cake,
creating about 16 slices
ahead: best on baking day

Preheat the oven to 350 degrees F.

Film the inside of a 10-inch Bundt pan (generous 3¾ inches deep, with a capacity of 14 cups) or a 10-inch Bundt pan (4½ inches deep, with a capacity of 15 cups) with nonstick flour-and-oil spray.

For the batter, sift the all-purpose flour, cake flour, baking powder, baking soda, and salt onto a sheet of waxed paper.

Thoroughly toss the chocolate chips with 2 tablespoons of the sifted mixture in a medium-size mixing bowl.

Cream the butter in the large bowl of a freestanding electric mixer on moderate speed for 3 minutes. Add the granulated sugar in 4 additions, beating thoroughly after each portion is added. Beat in the eggs one at a time, beating for 30 seconds after each addition. Blend in the vanilla extract. On low speed, add the pumpkin puree and blend until combined. The mixture will look slightly curdled at this point, but will smooth out during the next step. On low speed, add the sifted mixture in 3 additions, beating just until the particles of flour are absorbed. Scrape down the sides of the mixing bowl frequently with a rubber spatula to keep the batter even-textured. Stir in the chocolate chips.

Spoon the batter into the prepared baking pan. Smooth the top with a rubber spatula.

Bake the cake in the preheated oven for 1 hour, if you are using the 10-inch Bundt pan (generous 3¾ inches deep, with a capacity of 14 cups), or 1 hour and 5 minutes to 1 hour and 10 minutes, if you are using the 10-inch Bundt pan (4½ inches deep, with a capacity of 15 cups), or until risen, set, and a wooden pick withdraws clean or with a few moist crumbs attached.

Cool the cake in the pan on a rack for 10 minutes. Invert the cake onto another cooling rack. Lift off the pan. Cool the cake completely. Store in an airtight cake keeper. Just before serving, sift confectioners' sugar over the top.

notes
• the combination of all-purpose flour and cake flour builds a well-structured cake with a supple texture
• tossing the chocolate chips with the sifted flour mixture keeps them suspended in the batter
• use a finely serrated knife to cut the cake

cultured

If a cake could be described as urbane, this one would qualify, for its batter is genteel and polished—an exquisite mixture if there ever was one.

Interestingly enough, I think of this cake mostly in the summertime. The golden-topped cake, svelte of crumb and beautifully moist within, becomes the perfect warm-weather dessert when served with handfuls of ripe berries and vanilla- or almond-flavored whipped cream. The berries can be sweetened lightly and left to stand, creating a stream of flavorful, natural juice for the weave of the cake's crumb to take in. To do this, carefully spoon 2 tablespoons of superfine sugar into each 2½ cups of berries or sliced stone fruit (such as peaches, plums, or nectarines) you have on hand and let them linger in the bowl until you see a natural welling up of juice—at cool room temperature this will take about 45 minutes. The amount of sugar should be adjusted to the tartness of the fruit, remembering that the natural flavor present should be highlighted, not obscured. Once you have that flow of juice, the fruit can be sprinkled with a few teaspoons of a highlighting liqueur (such as amaretto or Cointreau), for that would add depth to the composed sweet.

This is the sour cream cake I have loved for years. It is a classic, and I'm thinking of renaming it my cloud-nine cake.

all-praise-the-virtues-of-sour-cream cake

Preheat the oven to 325 degrees F.

Film the inside of a plain, one-piece 10-inch tube pan (4¼ to 4½ inches deep, with a capacity of 18 cups) or a 10-inch Bundt pan (4½ inches deep, with a capacity of 15 cups) with nonstick flour-and-oil spray (including the entire rise of the selected pan's tube that will be exposed to the batter).

For the batter, sift the flour, baking soda, and salt onto a sheet of waxed paper.

Cream the butter in the large bowl of a freestanding electric mixer on moderate speed until creamy, about 4 minutes. Add the superfine sugar in 4 additions, beating for 1 minute after each portion is added. Beat in the eggs, one at a time, mixing for 30 seconds after each addition. Scrape down the sides of the mixing bowl with a rubber spatula to keep the batter even-textured. Blend in the vanilla extract and almond extract. On low speed, alternately add the sifted mixture in 3 additions with the sour cream–heavy cream blend in 2 additions, beginning and ending with the sifted mixture. Scrape down the sides of the mixing bowl thoroughly with a rubber spatula after each addition.

Spoon the batter into the prepared baking pan. Smooth the top with a rubber spatula.

Bake the cake in the preheated oven for 1 hour to 1 hour and 5 minutes, or until nicely risen, set, golden on top, and a wooden pick inserted into the cake withdraws clean. If, after 45 minutes of baking, the top of the cake is already moderately golden, quickly and carefully tent a large sheet of aluminum foil over the top (avoid folding down the sides).

Cool the cake in the pan on a rack for 10 minutes. Carefully invert the cake onto another cooling rack. Lift off the pan, then invert again to stand right side up. Cool completely. Store in an airtight cake keeper. Just before slicing and serving, sift confectioners' sugar over the top of the cake.

notes
- use the thickest sour cream available, preferably organic; thick, full-fat yogurt (such as any of the Greek yogurts, and especially the brand Fage Total All Natural Greek Strained Yogurt) would be a good exchange for the sour cream
- use a finely serrated knife to cut the cake

buttery sour cream batter

3 cups unsifted bleached all-purpose flour

¼ teaspoon baking soda

1 teaspoon salt

½ pound (16 tablespoons or 2 sticks) unsalted butter, softened

2½ cups superfine sugar

6 large eggs

3 teaspoons vanilla extract

1¼ teaspoons almond extract

1 cup sour cream blended with 2 tablespoons heavy cream

confectioners' sugar, for sifting on top of the baked cake

serving: one 10-inch cake, creating about 16 slices
ahead: 2 days

the butter cake challenge

A tubby pound* cake, more pound (read: weight) than cake, can be shaky business. Generations have baked them into big, hulking doorstops, bereft of flavor, and largely lacking nuance. And where is all that buttery taste, anyway?

In an effort to right those wrongs, I've taken on pound* cake baking as my personal project, with a view toward settling on a set of ingredients that can compose a cake to have at hand for serving with berries and cream or with poached dried fruit (such as my *syrupy red wine prunes*), or toasting and cramming onto the saucer that holds the cup of my morning coffee. The objective, as you can probably tell, is purely self-serving: I love pound* cake.

No dinky loaf cake would make me happy, nor would a cake that involves too many extracts, too rough a texture, not enough butter, or too few eggs. It should be *momentous* and *attention-getting*—as in large, moist, and golden—and cut cleanly and decisively into blessedly thick slices. "Skimpy" is not the operative word here. Rather, I am going for impressive yet delicate, and have determined that the proportions of 4 cups of cake flour to 1 full pound of butter, leavened with ¾ teaspoon baking powder, and enriched with 10 (!) eggs is the way to go. About the baking powder: before you quibble with it, remember my warning about overly dense and heavy cakes. The baking powder, as well as the judicious creaming of the butter and sugar, advances and broadens the nap of the cake just so and makes it as tender as can be. For seasoning, the batter is shaded with freshly grated nutmeg and mellowed with two extracts: vanilla and almond. The addition of nutmeg is a nod to old-timey cakes that employed mace, the overlay of the nutmeg

seed, dried and ground. Mace or nutmeg—the choice is yours, and it would be a subjective one.

Moving and dignified, this cake is ravishing. (Even stale, then sliced, dipped in a lightly sweetened, whisked cream and egg batter, and panfried as for French toast, the cake is so good.)

However….

When my baking kitchen makes great mercurial swings from old-fashioned to new-fashioned and back again, I begin to play around. The last time I enacted such baking drama with an accenting agent for pound* cake, the nutmeg was replaced with the seeds cracked open from green cardamom pods. The seeds, subsequently crushed in a mortar, were introduced into the creamed butter and sugar mixture for maximum flavor effect. Initially, the spice's shadowy aroma in the baked cake disturbed me because my own baking heritage dictated the use of a more dulcet scent. But the cardamom contributed a serene and rounded edge to the taste of the cake. And the act of cracking the little pods and pounding the seeds became an intensely fragrant, aggressively pacifying baking step. The blueprint for a cardamon version of butter cake, the *cake with maximum heft—and the delicacy of cardamom*, comes directly from the *center stage butter cake* recipe. In the end, just-baked, released from the pan, sliced, and eaten barely warm and out of hand, the cake's lingering flavor will enwrap you.

---

*Classicists take note: I am aware that traditional pound cake is without chemical leavening, and technically what follows is a butter cake. So, if you don't mind, I am using my own elastic definition of the phrase "pound cake." Thank you.

center stage butter cake ✳ syrupy red wine prunes

center stage butter cake

buttery scented batter

4 cups sifted bleached cake flour

¾ teaspoon baking powder

1 teaspoon salt

1 teaspoon freshly grated nutmeg

1 pound (4 sticks) unsalted butter, softened

2¾ cups superfine sugar

10 large eggs

3 teaspoons vanilla extract

1½ teaspoons almond extract

confectioners' sugar,
for sifting on top of the baked cake

serving: one 9¾-inch cake,
creating about 16 slices
ahead: 2 days

Preheat the oven to 350 degrees F.

Film the inside of a plain, one-piece 9¾-inch tube pan (6 inches deep, with a capacity of 18 cups) with nonstick flour-and-oil spray.

For the batter, resift the flour with the baking powder, salt, and nutmeg onto a sheet of waxed paper.

Cream the butter in the large bowl of a freestanding electric mixer on moderate speed for 5 minutes. Add the superfine sugar in 3 additions, beating for 1 minute after each portion is added. Beat in the eggs, one at a time, mixing for about 30 seconds after each addition. Scrape down the sides of the mixing bowl with a rubber spatula to keep the batter even-textured. Blend in the vanilla extract and almond extract. On low speed, add the sifted mixture in 3 additions, beating just until the particles of flour are absorbed. Scrape down the sides of the mixing bowl thoroughly with a rubber spatula after each addition.

Spoon the batter into the prepared baking pan. Smooth the top with a rubber spatula.

Bake the cake in the preheated oven for 1 hour and 5 minutes to 1 hour and 15 minutes, or until risen, golden, and a wooden pick inserted into the cake withdraws clean. If, after 55 minutes of baking, the top of the cake is already moderately golden, tent a large sheet of aluminum foil on the top (avoid folding down the sides). The baked cake will pull away slightly from the sides of the pan.

Cool the cake in the pan on a rack for 10 to 15 minutes. Invert the cake onto another cooling rack. Lift off the pan, then invert the cake again to stand right side up. Cool completely. Store in an airtight cake keeper. Just before slicing and serving, sift confectioners' sugar over the top of the cake. Serve with spoonfuls of *syrupy red wine prunes* (page 368), if you wish.

notes

- the mingling of two extracts lightly flavors the batter, with the emphasis on vanilla and a hint of almond
- the cake is baked in a plain, one-piece 9¾-inch tube pan (6 inches deep, with a capacity of 18 cups); a plain, one-piece 10-inch tube pan (4¼ to 4½ inches deep, with a capacity of 18 cups) may be substituted, reducing the baking time by 5 to 6 minutes
- use a finely serrated knife to cut the cake

cake with maximum heft— and the delicacy of cardamom

Preheat the oven to 350 degrees F.

Film the inside of a plain, one-piece 10-inch tube pan (4¼ to 4½ inches deep, with a capacity of 18 cups) with nonstick flour-and-oil spray (including the entire rise of the tube that will be exposed to the batter). Line the bottom of the pan with a circle of waxed paper or ovenproof parchment paper cut to fit and film its surface with the spray.

For the batter, resift the flour, baking powder, and salt onto a sheet of waxed paper.

Cream the butter in the large bowl of a freestanding electric mixer on moderate speed until creamy, about 4 minutes. Add the superfine sugar in 4 additions, beating for 1 minute after each portion is added. The creamed mixture should be light. Blend in the cardamom seeds and beat for 45 seconds. Beat in the eggs, 2 at a time, mixing for about 30 seconds after each addition. Scrape down the sides of the mixing bowl with a rubber spatula to keep the batter even-textured. Blend in the vanilla extract. The mixture may look somewhat curdled at this point, but will stabilize and smooth out after the entire quantity of flour is added. On low speed, add the sifted mixture in 4 additions, beating just until the particles of flour are absorbed. Scrape down the sides of the mixing bowl with a rubber spatula thoroughly after each addition. Beat for 45 seconds longer.

Spoon the batter into the prepared baking pan. Smooth the top with a rubber spatula.

Bake the cake in the preheated oven for 1 hour, or until nicely risen, set, golden on top, and a wooden pick inserted into the cake withdraws clean. The baked cake will pull away ever-so-slightly from the sides of the pan.

Cool the cake in the pan on a rack for 10 to 12 minutes. Carefully invert the cake onto another cooling rack. Lift off the pan, peel away the paper if it is adhering to the cake, then invert the cake again to stand right side up. Cool completely. Store in an airtight cake keeper. Just before slicing and serving, sift confectioners' sugar over the top of the cake. Serve with spoonfuls of *syrupy red wine prunes* (page 368), if you wish.

(continued on the next page)

buttery cardamom batter

4 cups sifted bleached cake flour

1½ teaspoons baking powder

1 teaspoon salt

1 pound (4 sticks) unsalted butter, softened

2⅔ cups superfine sugar

crushed and pounded seeds from 1 tablespoon plus 1 teaspoon whole, lightly cracked cardamom pods (see notes)

10 large eggs

1 teaspoon vanilla extract

confectioners' sugar, for sifting on top of the baked cake

serving: one 10-inch cake, creating about 16 slices
ahead: 2 days

notes
- for the cardamom, it is preferable to use green, rather than black, cardamom (the white variety is the bleached version of the green)
- to crack open the cardamon, crush the pods lightly with a beef or veal pounder, or the bottom of a small, heavy skillet, sort out the seeds, and pound them in a mortar and pestle; using the spice in this, the authentic, fully aromatic form, contributes the finest fragrance—and taste— to the batter
- reducing the amount of vanilla extract in the batter when crushed and pounded cardamom seeds flavor it allows the flavor-and-essence profile of the spice to fully expand in the finished cake
- use a finely serrated knife to cut the cake

syrupy red wine prunes

prune compote

2 cups fruity red wine

1½ cups water

1 cup granulated sugar

1 pound prunes (see notes)

1 tablespoon orange liqueur
(such as Cointreau)

about 3 cups prunes and syrup
ahead: 6 weeks (refrigerated)

Place the red wine, water, and sugar in a heavy, medium-size saucepan or casserole (preferably enameled cast iron). Set over moderately low heat to dissolve the sugar, stirring the contents from time to time with a wooden spoon. When the sugar has dissolved, raise the heat to high and boil for 1 minute. Add the prunes and simmer, covered, for 30 to 35 minutes, or until they are tender (but maintain their figures, and avoid cooking to mushy— this would make them so forlorn!). Let the prunes stand, covered, with the heat turned off, for 1 minute.

Carefully remove the prunes from the syrup with a slotted spoon to a medium-size nonreactive heatproof mixing bowl. Stir the orange liqueur into the red wine poaching liquid, bring to the simmer, then simmer briskly for 5 minutes. At this point, the liquid should be slightly syrupy. Remove the pan from the heat. Cool for 10 minutes.

Strain the syrup through a fine- to medium-mesh sieve directly over the prunes. Cool completely. Turn the syrupy prunes into a storage container, cover them tightly, and refrigerate. If you are using prunes with the pits intact, pit the prunes before serving.

notes
- the timing of the prunes as they soften to tenderness (once they are placed in the red wine syrup) depends on their quality and age
- the prunes are simmered uncovered to intensify their flavor
- I use Moyer plums (prunes), with the pits intact, for the best flavor, though the pits should be removed just before serving; the dried plums are available from Bella Viva Orchards (see page 500, baking*SelectedSources*)
- the red wine I consistently use in this fruity stew is a merlot (preferably one with a defined black cherry/cranberry edge with hints of raspberry and plum, and a wispy vanilla finish)

the royal treatment

Curvaceous cakes—soft, buttery, lightly perfumed madeleines: this is the dreamy kind of easy baking I love to do.

Once you have the molds in your *batterie de cuisine,* it is just a matter of mixing up a fine and simple batter, and flavoring it according to mood—chocolate (no surprise there!) and lemon are my current delights. For the madeleines, I take each flavor in a different direction: the chocolate version is paired with a dunking sauce and the lemon interpretation is brushed (while still hot) with a sweet-tart glaze. Each resulting confection is dessert: casual and, most certainly, best right out of the oven. A big bowl or individual ramekins of fresh berries (raspberries for the chocolate cakes or blueberries for the lemon cakes come to mind) wouldn't be out of order either.

two kinds of madeleines: lemon soakers, chocolate dunkers, and liquid chocolate

lemon soakers

lemon batter

1 cup plus 1 tablespoon unsifted bleached cake flour

¼ teaspoon baking powder

⅛ teaspoon salt

8 tablespoons (1 stick) unsalted butter, softened

½ cup superfine sugar

3 large eggs

1 large egg yolk

2½ teaspoons finely grated lemon peel

½ teaspoon lemon extract

brushing glaze

¼ cup freshly squeezed lemon juice

¼ cup granulated sugar

serving: 2 dozen madeleines
ahead: best on baking day

Preheat the oven to 375 degrees F.

Film the inside of 24 shells in the *plaques à coques* (3 shell-shaped madeleine molds; each *plaque* contains 8 shells, each shell measuring 2½ inches long and 2½ inches at the widest point, with a capacity of 1 tablespoon plus 2¾ teaspoons each) with melted clarified butter (page 1), using a soft pastry brush. When the film of butter has set, dust the insides with all-purpose flour.

For the batter, sift the flour, baking powder, and salt onto a sheet of waxed paper.

Cream the butter in the small bowl of a freestanding electric mixer on moderate speed for 1 minute. Add the superfine sugar and beat for 45 seconds. Beat in the whole eggs, one at a time, mixing for 15 seconds after each is added. Blend in the egg yolk, lemon peel, and lemon extract. On low speed, blend in the sifted mixture. Scrape down the sides of the mixing bowl with a rubber spatula to keep the batter even-textured. The batter will be moderately thick and creamy. Let the batter stand for 2 minutes.

Divide the batter among the prepared molds, mounding it slightly in the center of each shell. Lightly rap each tray on the countertop.

Bake the cakes in the preheated oven for 14 minutes, or until plump, set, and a wooden pick withdraws clean or with a few crumbs attached. The baked madeleines will be golden around the edges.

Cool the cakes in the pans on racks for 1 minute, then unmold them, ridged side up, onto other cooling racks. Lift off the pans.

For the glaze, combine the lemon juice and granulated sugar in a small nonreactive mixing bowl. (There is no need to wait for the sugar to dissolve, so use the glaze as soon as it is mixed.) Sweep the glaze over the ridges of the warm madeleines, using a soft pastry brush, and serve.

notes
• using superfine sugar contributes to the light and creamy-delicate texture of the madeleines
• the batter will bake up fairly close-textured, so the little cakes do not fall apart when brushed with the glaze

chocolate dunkers

Preheat the oven to 350 degrees F.

Film the inside of 24 shell-shaped madeleine molds (2 shell-shaped madeleine molds; each *plaque à madeleine* contains 12 shells, each shell measuring 3 inches long and 1¾ inches at its widest point, with a capacity of a scant 2 tablespoons each) or 24 shells in the *plaques à coques* (3 shell-shaped madeleine molds; each *plaque* contains 8 shells, each shell measuring 2½ inches long and 2½ inches at the widest point, with a capacity of 1 tablespoon plus 2¾ teaspoons each) with melted clarified butter (page 1), using a soft pastry brush. When the film of butter has set, dust the insides with all-purpose flour.

For the batter, sift the flour, cocoa powder, baking powder, and salt onto a sheet of waxed paper.

Toss the chocolate chips with ½ teaspoon of the sifted mixture in a small mixing bowl.

Cream the butter in the small bowl of a freestanding electric mixer on moderate speed for 1 minute. Add the sugar and beat for 1 minute. Beat in the eggs, one at a time, mixing for 15 to 20 seconds after each addition. Blend in the vanilla extract. On low speed, blend in the sifted mixture. Scrape down the sides of the mixing bowl with a rubber spatula to keep the batter even-textured. The batter will be moderately thick and creamy. Blend in the chocolate chips, using a flexible spatula. Let the batter stand for 2 minutes.

Divide the batter among the prepared molds, mounding it down the middle of each *plaque à madeleine* shell or in the center of each *plaques à coques* shell. Lightly rap each tray on the countertop.

Bake the cakes in the preheated oven for 14 to 16 minutes, or until plump, set, and a wooden pick withdraws clean or with a few moist crumbs attached.

Cool the cakes in the pans on racks for 1 minute, then unmold them, ridged side up, onto other cooling racks, lifting off the pans. Serve the freshly baked madeleines, lightly dusted with confectioners' sugar (if you wish), alongside small bowls of the warm dunking sauce.

notes
- the chocolate chips bolster the taste of chocolate throughout the batter, adding little pools of flavor

fudgy chocolate batter

½ cup unsifted bleached cake flour

½ cup unsweetened alkalized cocoa powder

¼ teaspoon baking powder

⅛ teaspoon salt

⅓ cup miniature semisweet chocolate chips

8 tablespoons (1 stick) unsalted butter, softened

½ cup plus 2 tablespoons superfine sugar

4 large eggs

1¾ teaspoons vanilla extract

dunking sauce

liquid chocolate (page 372)

serving: 2 dozen madeleines
ahead: best on baking day

liquid chocolate

flowing chocolate cream

1 cup heavy cream

1 tablespoon plus 2 teaspoons superfine sugar blended with 1 teaspoon unsweetened alkalized cocoa powder

pinch of salt

8 ounces bittersweet chocolate, finely chopped

3 tablespoons unsalted butter

¾ teaspoon vanilla extract

serving: about 1²/₃ cups
ahead: 4 days

Place the heavy cream, sugar-cocoa powder blend, and salt in a medium-size saucepan (preferably enameled cast iron), set over moderate heat, and scald, whisking from time to time. Turn off the heat but leave the saucepan on the burner. Add the chocolate and butter. Let stand for 1 minute, then stir slowly to blend the mixture thoroughly. Turn the heat to low and let the mixture warm for 4 to 5 minutes, or until well-amalgamated. Stir the sauce continually, and slowly, as it warms, using a wooden spoon. Strain the sauce into a heatproof bowl, stir in the vanilla extract, and use straightaway, or cool, cover, and refrigerate.

notes
• to rewarm the sauce, do so slowly in a small heavy saucepan over low heat

whirly and twirly

The deep and wide flutes of a classic swirled baking pan provide a beautiful house for a cakelike yeast bread filled with fruit—the raisin bread of my dreams, if there ever was one.

The bread is eggy and buttery, soft of crumb, and dotted with both the golden and red flame variety of the dried grape. The sticky, silky dough rises to great heights in the pan and, in an aristocratic way, bakes into a golden crown, deep with sideswiping whirlpool-like twists. As soon as the bread composes itself after baking (certainly way earlier than most expert bread bakers instruct—who can wait *that long*?—and, OK, I hear the collective groans of a few experts), I smear thick, supernally light slices with softened salted butter and apricot jam. A day or two later, the bread is prime material for toast, or for a dip into a whisked egg, milk, and vanilla extract mixture, then a quick fry on a buttered griddle, French toast style. The pleasure of the bread is not in the eating alone, for putting together the dough, in all its sultry, satiny elasticity, is a way to engage in hands-on art—and have something delicious to show for it.

an aristocratic raisin bread

raisin-flecked yeast dough

4¼ teaspoons active dry yeast

¼ teaspoon granulated sugar

¼ cup warm (105 to 110 degrees F) water

½ cup milk

½ cup granulated sugar

5 large eggs

2 teaspoons vanilla extract

3¼ cups unsifted bleached all-purpose flour

1 cup unsifted unbleached all-purpose flour

1 teaspoon salt

11 tablespoons (1 stick plus 3 tablespoons) unsalted butter, cut into tablespoon-size chunks, softened

1¼ cups combined jumbo golden, red flame, and dark seedless raisins (or substitute ¾ cup golden seedless raisins and ¾ cup red flame raisins)

2 tablespoons brandy

serving: one 10-inch fluted bread, creating about 16 slices
ahead: best on baking day; or freeze for 3 weeks, defrost, bundle in aluminum foil, and reheat in a preheated 325 degrees F oven for 15 to 20 minutes

For the dough, stir together the yeast, the ¼ teaspoon sugar, and the warm water in a heatproof measuring cup. Allow the mixture to stand until swollen, 6 to 7 minutes.

In the meantime, place the milk and the ½ cup sugar in a small saucepan and set over moderate heat. When the sugar has dissolved, remove from the heat, pour into a medium-size heatproof mixing bowl, and cool to tepid. Whisk in the eggs and vanilla extract. Blend in the yeast mixture.

Place 2 cups of the bleached flour, the unbleached flour, and the salt in a large mixing bowl. Whisk to integrate the salt. Beat in the milk-eggs-yeast mixture, using a wooden spoon or flat wooden paddle. Mix well to form a very dense mixture; it will resemble a thick batter. Stir in 1 cup of the remaining bleached flour; the dough will be quite shaggy and resist absorbing all of the flour.

Turn the dough into the bowl of a heavy-duty freestanding electric mixer and let stand for 2 minutes. Set the bowl in place and attach the flat paddle. Mix to form a dough, beating on moderately low speed for 3 minutes. The dough will be smooth and very sticky at this point. Beat in the softened butter in 3 additions, mixing on moderate speed for 1 minute after each portion is added. Add the remaining ¼ cup bleached flour and beat for 3 minutes on moderate speed, stopping the mixer once or twice during this time to scrape down the sides of the mixing bowl and the paddle. The dough will be smooth, elastic, pull-y, and soft/sticky. It will ball up on the paddle and leave a thick film on the sides of the mixing bowl.

Scrape the dough into a bowl heavily coated with softened unsalted butter, lightly turn the dough around and about with a spatula to coat all sides in a film of butter, make several cuts in the dough with a pair of kitchen scissors, cover tightly with a sheet of food-safe plastic wrap, and let rise at cool room temperature for 2 hours and 30 minutes to 3 hours, or until doubled in bulk.

While the dough is rising, place the raisins in a medium-size nonreactive mixing bowl. Add the brandy and stir to mix well. Let stand, uncovered, while the dough is rising.

Remove and discard the sheet of plastic wrap covering the dough. Scatter the marinated raisins over the dough and, using a buttered flat wooden paddle or sturdy spatula, work the raisins into the dough. Let stand for 5 minutes.

Film the inside of a deeply swirled 10-inch tube pan (4¼ inches deep, with a capacity of 12 to 13 cups) with nonstick flour-and-oil spray or softened unsalted butter.

To form the bread, create an opening in the center of the ball of dough with your fingertips. The opening of the dough ball should be large enough to fit around and down the center tube of the pan. Turn the dough into the prepared baking pan, fitting the opening over the center rise of the pan. Using your fingertips once again, pat the dough into an even layer.

Cover the pan loosely with a buttered sheet of food-safe plastic wrap. Let the bread rise at cool room temperature for 1 hour and 30 minutes, or until it reaches to ½ inch of the top of the pan, or until almost doubled in bulk (see page 6 to reference this stage).

Preheat the oven to 375 degrees F in advance of baking.

Remove and discard the sheet of plastic wrap covering the bread.

Bake the bread in the preheated oven for 45 minutes, or until set and a deep golden brown on top. If, after 30 minutes of baking, the top of the bread is already a moderately golden color, tent a large sheet of aluminum foil on the top (avoid folding down the sides). Place the pan on a cooling rack and let stand for 10 minutes. Invert the bread onto another cooling rack to stand fluted side up. Lift off the pan. Serve the bread very fresh—it has a wonderfully cozy flavor a few hours after the intensity of the oven's heat has subsided. Store any remaining bread for slicing and toasting in an airtight container.

notes
• for the best integration and dough development, the temperature of the softened butter should be about 60 degrees F
• the dough can be scented with 1 teaspoon freshly grated nutmeg and ½ teaspoon ground allspice, in addition to the vanilla extract; whisk the spices into the 2 cups bleached and the unbleached flour at the stage when it is combined with the salt
• the deeply swirled 10-inch tube pan (4¼ inches deep, with a capacity of 12 to 13 cups), with wide-angled flutes is known as a kugelhopf pan; a 10-inch Bundt pan (generous 3¾ inches deep, with a capacity of 14 cups) may be substituted, reducing the baking time by 5 to 7 minutes
• use a finely serrated knife to cut the bread

Comfy

creating a cookie "larder" ✳ morphing that breakfast bowl of oatmeal ✳ oh, how sweet: a lightly perfumed version of the baba ✳ brunch*waffles* ✳ liftoff for potato dough ✳ reclaiming the crêpe ✳ a batter goes blond and nutty ✳ a bread batter turns up the vanilla volume

Cozy

a sweet soaking

Doused in a sweet-scented syrup flavored with rose flower water, cakey yeast-raised babas (given their cylindrical shape by letting portions of the soft dough rise in individual molds) are softly tender and moist.

While kirschwasser (cherry brandy) or rum represents the spirit frequently used in the syrup or for brushing the warm cakes, it's always interesting to turn the tables and create another beaming flavor enhancement, and so I have chosen distilled rose water and rose petal preserves to refresh the dessert.

The dough for the individual cakes is buttery and eggy, and it, too, is uplifted with rose flower water essence; it bakes into jaunty cakes that crest and balloon at the top. The advantage to the dough is its laid-back nature, as it can be used immediately for forming after the first rise or refrigerated to use the next day; or the fully-baked babas can be frozen for a period of time, defrosted, and revived in a warm oven before spooning over the soaking solution.

These babas taste of spring and summer, and they are gently bright. When small, intense strawberries, with their delicate stems and hulls peeking up in pint baskets, are offered at the market, think of them as a perfect complement to the cakes. Further along throughout the summer, pair the babas with lush blueberries, golden or red raspberries, or quartered ripe figs. When the cakes are warm, a simple syrup thoroughly moistens them, then the tops can be glazed with warm rose petal preserves. This completes the flavor profile. Dollops of whipped cream—never out of place (or out of character)—would finish the plate nicely.

rose water babas, rose water syrup

For the dough, stir together the yeast, the ¼ teaspoon sugar, and the warm water in a heatproof measuring cup. Allow the mixture to stand until swollen, 6 to 7 minutes.

Whisk the flour and salt in the bowl of a heavy-duty freestanding electric mixer. Whisk the whole eggs, egg yolk, the 3 tablespoons sugar, the rose flower water essence, and vanilla extract in a medium-size mixing bowl. Blend in the yeast mixture. Pour the eggs-yeast mixture over the flour-salt blend and stir to form a craggy mass (the dough will not come together at this point). Add the butter. Set the bowl in place and attach the flat paddle. Beat the dough on low speed until just combined, then increase the speed to moderate and beat for 4 to 5 minutes longer, or until shiny, silky, and very smooth. Stop the machine from time to time to scrape down the sides of the mixing bowl and the paddle. Remove the flat paddle and scrape down any dough that clings to it.

Turn the dough into a bowl heavily coated with softened unsalted butter, lightly turn to coat all sides in a film of butter, make several cuts in the dough with a pair of kitchen scissors, cover tightly with a sheet of food-safe plastic wrap, and let rise at room temperature for 1 hour and 30 minutes, or until doubled in bulk.

Film the inside of 12 (or 9; see notes) individual baba molds (each mold measuring 2¼ inches high and 2½ inches in diameter [measured across the top], with a capacity of ⅔ cup) with softened butter or nonstick oil spray. Have a rimmed sheet pan at hand.

Uncover the dough and discard the plastic wrap. Turn the dough out onto a work surface and divide it into 12 even-size pieces.

To form the babas, smooth each piece of dough into a plump ball by rolling it briskly on the work surface in the cupped palm of your hand. Place a ball of dough in each of the prepared molds; each mold should be filled about one-third full by the ball of dough. Arrange the molds on the rimmed sheet pan.

Cover the babas with a sheet of food-safe plastic wrap. Let them rise at room temperature for 1 hour and 15 minutes, or until just about tripled in bulk.

Preheat the oven to 350 degrees F in advance of baking.

Remove and discard the sheet of plastic wrap covering the babas.

Bake the babas, still on the rimmed sheet pan, in the preheated oven for 15 to 18 minutes, until set and a golden color on top.

(continued on the next page)

rose water yeast dough

2½ teaspoons active dry yeast

¼ teaspoon granulated sugar

2 tablespoons warm
(105 to 110 degrees F) water

1¾ cups plus 1 tablespoon unsifted bleached all-purpose flour

⅛ teaspoon salt

2 large eggs

1 large egg yolk

3 tablespoons granulated sugar

½ teaspoon rose flower water essence

1 teaspoon vanilla extract

6 tablespoons (¾ stick) unsalted butter, softened

rose water syrup (page 382)

rose petal preserves glaze (optional)

⅓ cup rose petal preserves

1 teaspoon water

serving: 12 babas
ahead: best on baking day; or freeze for 1 month, defrost, bundle in aluminum foil, and reheat in a preheated 300 degrees F oven for 10 minutes before soaking in syrup

Transfer the baba molds to cooling racks and let stand for 15 minutes. Carefully unmold the babas onto other cooling racks, lifting off the molds. Place the warm rose water syrup in a large heatproof mixing bowl. Add the babas to the syrup, a few at a time, and let them soak up the syrup, turning and rolling them over and about, then remove them to a cooling rack set over a large sheet of waxed paper to catch any drips. If you are using the glaze finish, blend the rose petal preserves with the water in a small saucepan, set over low heat to warm, then brush only the tops of the syrup-soaked babas with the glaze. Set the babas on their sides on a serving dish. Serve the babas with softly whipped cream and fresh berries or a dried fruit compote, if you wish.

notes
- dividing the dough into 12 pieces makes ladylike babas; one afternoon, I divided the same quantity of dough into 9 baba molds, and the result was startling—mushroomed babas with great big dramatic crowns (you can do the same, reducing the baking time by a minute, or until set and golden on top)
- any seasonal collection of berries that accompanies the babas can first be tossed in a little organic rose syrup (available in limited quantities at La Cuisine—The Cook's Resource; see page 501, baking*SelectedSources*)
- a crystallized violet (must be designated as food-safe) can be set in place on top of each freshly glazed baba, if you wish

rose water syrup

scented syrup

1½ cups water

1¼ cups granulated sugar

¼ cup rose flower water (see notes)

⅛ teaspoon rose flower water essence

serving: about 1¾ cups plus 1 tablespoon
ahead: 2 weeks; reheat in a saucepan for 5 minutes to warm

Place the water and sugar in a medium-size saucepan, cover, and place over moderately low heat. Stir the contents of the pan from time to time, using a wooden spoon. When the sugar has dissolved, uncover the pan, raise the heat to high, and boil the sugar water for 6 minutes. Add the rose flower water and simmer for 3 minutes. Remove the syrup from the heat and stir in the rose flower water essence. Turn the syrup into a small nonreactive mixing bowl and cool to warm.

Use the syrup warm for soaking the babas, or chilled for folding through and sweetening seasonal fruits. Store in an airtight container.

notes
- the light and gently fragrant rose flower water I use in this syrup is Lebanese, labeled Mymouné Rose Water (Eau de Roses), produced by Mymouné Ain el Kabou-Lebanon, and it can be used in the quantity stated above; if the rose flower water you have on hand is stronger and thus more pungent, reduce the amount to 2 to 3 teaspoons (depending on strength)
- depending on the absorbency of the babas, the entire quantity of syrup may not be used; the remaining syrup, strained of any crumbs or particles, stores beautifully, refrigerated in a tightly covered container for up to 2 weeks (splash spoonfuls on berries or sliced fresh peaches or nectarines; sprinkle on a freshly baked butter cake to moisten and scent; or use to flavor-sweeten hot or iced tea)
- the rose flower water essence I use in this syrup and in the baba dough recipe is quite aromatic, and is sold in stoppered bottles at La Cuisine—The Cook's Resource (see page 501, baking*SelectedSources*); it is a highly concentrated essence and should be used in a discreet quantity

fresh-ahead

I crumble for a moist, freshly baked cookie.

Although I admire the foresight industrious cooks have as they load up, seal, and stack cookie tins for those (inevitable) weeks of storage, I've never been particularly tempted by the contents, which tend to fade—in both taste and texture—over time. There are distinguished exceptions, of course, such as some rolled cookies, anything styled as shortbread or shortbreadlike, and biscotti, and these keepers certainly maintain their goodness. In a flawless world, a cookie that I bite into, with its melty little dots and dashes of chocolate chips (or, for that matter, rich textural contrast of rolled oats and coconut, or complex flavor of peanut butter, or candy-laden mound) is just-baked. And it is, by far, the best cookie imaginable. With this ideal in mind, we can take a cue from pastry chefs who prepare substantial quantities of dough in advance, then bake off what is needed as the situation requires.

A firm chill in the refrigerator or firmer hold in the freezer can convert a range of cookie doughs into baking capital. What a friendly assist this is for the weeknight or weekend cook who enjoys pulling out trays of soft, crisp, or crisp-chewy cookies as the mood (or need) requires. I say "requires" here because the necessity for a freshly baked cookie can really take over. One night, after a late trip to the market to stock up on some pantry essentials, I looked longingly at the promise of deliciousness broadcasted on the front of the boxes and bags of all those prefabricated cookies on the shelf. Of course, my mind jumped in directions way beyond reaching for a box and instead quickly skipped over to picturing a buttery, chunky batter sitting all content in a mixer bowl, ready to be spooned up. It was 10:00 p.m. How I wished that I had one of these doughs at hand. Now I do, thanks to some honest manipulation of ingredients to arrive at the correct texture and consistency of cookie doughs bound for storage longer than just a few hours.

Imagine your own stash of dough ready and waiting: logs to cut into chunks, thick "cakes" of dough ready to break off into rugged-edged morsels and bake right up—this is home, this is inviting. Your spirit will rise incrementally as each sheet of sweetness is baked. Let others make gallons of chicken stock. I'll make dough for the following goodies: *oatmeal cookies— bundled up; toffee, dried cherry, and bittersweet chocolate gems; coconut butter balls;* and *minties.* Oh yes, I have many more varieties of dough based on beloved recipes and refined over the years nested on shelves, so at any point in time there could be about ten types present, solidified in cold and loving firmness. It is so much fun to make the doughs, pick out a flavor, and bake away.

On the sensory level, the promise of good baking always soothes.

a quartet of cookie doughs that survives cold storage:
oatmeal cookies—bundled up; toffee, dried cherry, and
bittersweet chocolate gems; coconut butter balls; minties

oatmeal cookies—bundled up

For the dough, whisk the flour, baking soda, salt, and nutmeg in a small mixing bowl.

Cream the butter in the large bowl of a freestanding electric mixer on moderate speed for 3 minutes. Add the dark brown sugar in 2 additions, beating on moderate speed for 1 minute after each portion is added. Add the granulated sugar and beat for 2 minutes longer. Blend in the egg and vanilla extract. On low speed, mix in the whisked ingredients until just blended, followed by the rolled oats. Work in the raisins and walnuts or pecans. Scrape down the sides of the mixing bowl frequently with a rubber spatula to keep the dough even-textured. If you are preparing the dough ahead, refrigerate or freeze it now.

Up to 1 day in advance of baking, defrost the frozen dough by placing it in the refrigerator.

Preheat the oven to 325 degrees F.

Line several cookie sheets or rimmed sheet pans with lengths of ovenproof parchment paper.

Place heaping 2-tablespoon-size mounds of dough on the prepared baking pans, spacing the mounds about 2½ inches apart.

Bake the cookies in the preheated oven for 16 to 17 minutes, or until just set and golden in random spots. Let the cookies stand on the baking pans for 1 minute, then transfer them to cooling racks, using a wide offset metal spatula. Cool completely. Store in an airtight tin.

notes
- when preparing cookie dough for refrigeration or freezing, use organic eggs only
- baking the cookies until set and little patches of golden color appear on their surfaces now and then keeps them moist and chewy-textured
- if you want to form and bake the cookies immediately, preheat the oven and prepare the baking pans before you make the dough
- never consume raw cookie dough

oatmeal butter dough

⅔ cup plus 2 tablespoons unsifted bleached all-purpose flour

⅛ teaspoon baking soda

¼ teaspoon salt

¼ teaspoon freshly grated nutmeg

13 tablespoons (1 stick plus 5 tablespoons) unsalted butter, softened

⅔ cup firmly packed dark brown sugar

½ cup granulated sugar

1 large egg

2½ teaspoons vanilla extract

1¼ cups "quick-cooking" (not instant) rolled oats

1 cup dark seedless raisins

1 cup walnut or pecan halves or pieces

serving: about 1½ dozen cookies
ahead: best on baking day; refrigerate cookie dough for 2 days or freeze for 1 month

toffee, dried cherry, and bittersweet chocolate gems

bulky butter dough

1½ cups unsifted bleached
all-purpose flour

⅛ teaspoon baking soda

¼ teaspoon salt

12 tablespoons (1½ sticks) unsalted butter,
softened

1 cup firmly packed light brown sugar

2 tablespoons granulated sugar

1 large egg

1 tablespoon vanilla extract

7 ounces bittersweet chocolate,
hand-cut into chunks

1 cup chopped toffee (such as Heath bars)

¾ cup walnut or pecan halves or pieces

⅔ cup tart (Montmorency) dried cherries

½ cup firmly packed sweetened
flaked coconut

serving: about 2 dozen cookies
ahead: best on baking day;
refrigerate cookie dough for 2 days
or freeze for 1 month

For the dough, sift the flour, baking soda, and salt onto a sheet of waxed paper.

Cream the butter in the large bowl of a freestanding electric mixer on moderate speed for 3 minutes. Add the light brown sugar in 2 additions, beating on moderate speed for 1 minute after each portion is added. Add the granulated sugar and beat for 1 minute longer. Blend in the egg and vanilla extract. Scrape down the sides of the mixing bowl frequently with a rubber spatula to keep the dough even-textured. On low speed, add the sifted ingredients and beat just until the particles of flour are absorbed. Blend in the bittersweet chocolate, toffee, walnuts or pecans, cherries, and coconut. If you are preparing the dough ahead, refrigerate or freeze it now.

Up to 1 day in advance of baking, defrost the frozen dough by placing it in the refrigerator.

Preheat the oven to 325 degrees F.

Line several cookie sheets or rimmed sheet pans with lengths of ovenproof parchment paper.

Place heaping 2-tablespoon-size mounds of dough onto the prepared baking pans, spacing the mounds about 3 inches apart.

Bake the cookies in the preheated oven for 16 to 17 minutes, or until just set and golden in random spots. Let the cookies stand on the baking pans for 1 minute, then transfer them to cooling racks, using a wide offset metal spatula. Cool completely. Store in an airtight tin.

notes
- when preparing cookie dough for refrigeration or freezing, use organic eggs only
- when cutting up blocks or bars of bittersweet chocolate, aim for ⅓ to ½-inch pieces; be sure to add the smaller bits and shards that inevitably result from chopping the chocolate because they will deliciously enrich the dough
- if you want to form and bake the cookies immediately, preheat the oven and prepare the baking pans before you make the dough
- never consume raw cookie dough

coconut butter balls

For the dough, sift the flour, baking powder, and salt onto a sheet of waxed paper.

Cream the butter in the large bowl of a freestanding electric mixer on moderate speed for 3 minutes. Add the confectioners' sugar and beat for 1 minute. Blend in the vanilla extract. On low speed, blend in half of the sifted ingredients, the coconut, and, finally, the balance of the sifted ingredients. Scrape down the sides of the mixing bowl frequently with a rubber spatula to keep the dough even-textured. If you are preparing the dough ahead, refrigerate or freeze it now.

Up to 1 day in advance of baking, defrost the dough by placing it in the refrigerator.

Preheat the oven to 350 degrees F.

Line several cookie sheets or rimmed sheet pans with lengths of ovenproof parchment paper.

Scoop up level 1-tablespoon-size pieces of dough and roll into balls. Place the balls of dough on the prepared baking pans, spacing the balls 1½ to 2 inches apart.

Bake the cookies in the preheated oven for 12 to 14 minutes, or until set and the bottoms are a light brown (carefully lift up a cookie with a small offset metal spatula to check the color). Let the cookies stand on the baking pans for 1 minute, then transfer them to cooling racks, using a small offset metal spatula. After 5 minutes, dredge the cookies in the 3 cups confectioners' sugar. Cool the cookies completely, then coat them again in the remaining confectioners' sugar. Cool completely. Store in an airtight tin in 2 layers, with waxed paper separating each tier.

notes
• if you want to form and bake the cookies immediately, preheat the oven and prepare the baking pans before you make the dough
• for a change, you can roll the orbs of dough in additional coconut just before baking; place about 1½ cups of coconut in a shallow bowl for enrobing them; if you are preparing the dough in advance and plan to do this additional flavoring and textural step, use the dough chilled rather than frozen
• natural unsweetened short-flake coconut is available in bulk or packaged at natural food markets
• never consume raw cookie dough

snowy butter dough

2¼ cups unsifted bleached all-purpose flour

¾ teaspoon baking powder

⅛ teaspoon salt

½ pound (16 tablespoons or 2 sticks) unsalted butter, softened

⅓ cup confectioners' sugar

2 teaspoons vanilla extract

⅔ cup natural unsweetened short-flake coconut

about 3 cups confectioners' sugar, for dredging the baked cookies

serving: about 3½ dozen cookies
ahead: best on baking day; refrigerate cookie dough for 1 day or freeze for 1 month

minties

mint chocolate butter dough

1⅓ cups unsifted bleached
all-purpose flour

2 tablespoons plus 2 teaspoons
unsweetened alkalized cocoa powder

⅛ teaspoon baking soda

¼ teaspoon salt

13 tablespoons (1 stick plus 5 tablespoons)
unsalted butter, softened

1 cup granulated sugar

1 large egg

1¼ teaspoons vanilla extract

¾ teaspoon peppermint extract
(or ¼ teaspoon peppermint essence)

2 ounces unsweetened chocolate,
melted and cooled

1¼ cups roughly chopped or diced
chocolate-covered peppermint patties

¾ cup semisweet or bittersweet
chocolate chips

serving: about 1½ dozen cookies
ahead: best on baking day;
refrigerate cookie dough for 2 days
or freeze for 1 month

For the dough, sift the flour, cocoa powder, baking soda, and salt onto a sheet of waxed paper.

Cream the butter in the large bowl of a freestanding electric mixer on moderate speed for 3 minutes. Add the sugar in 2 additions, beating on moderate speed for 1 minute after each portion is added. Blend in the egg, vanilla extract, and peppermint extract. Blend in the melted chocolate. On low speed, mix in the sifted ingredients until just blended. Scrape down the sides of the mixing bowl frequently with a rubber spatula to keep the dough even-textured. Work in the chopped peppermint patties and chocolate chips. If you are preparing the dough ahead, refrigerate or freeze it now.

Up to 1 day in advance of baking, defrost the frozen dough by placing it in the refrigerator.

Preheat the oven to 325 degrees F.

Line several cookie sheets or rimmed sheet pans with lengths of ovenproof parchment paper.

Place heaping 2-tablespoon-size mounds of dough onto the prepared baking pans, spacing the mounds about 2½ inches apart.

Bake the cookies in the preheated oven for 16 to 17 minutes, or until just set. Let the cookies stand on the baking pans for 1 minute, then transfer them to cooling racks, using a wide offset metal spatula. Cool completely. Store in an airtight tin.

notes
- when preparing cookie dough for refrigeration or freezing, use organic eggs only
- peppermint essence is available from La Cuisine—The Cook's Resource (see page 501, baking*SelectedSources*)
- using chocolate-covered peppermint patties with tinted peppermint centers is a fun contrast with the dark chocolate dough; orange-colored filled patties are generally available seasonally in the fall, and if you use those, consider adding 1½ teaspoons finely grated orange peel to the dough, along with the peppermint extract (and omit the vanilla extract) for a nice contrast of chocolate and orange
- if you want to form and bake the cookies immediately, preheat the oven and prepare the baking pans before you make the dough
- never consume raw cookie dough

not a bowl of hot oatmeal

Devotion to the oatmeal cookie, in all its old-fashioned splendor, swayed me to translate that taste to a scone dough and supple yeast dough. And so you have a quick bread wrapping rolled oats and raisins in a buttery brown sugar–flavored backdrop, and a sweet roll that is soft and lightly husky.

Both are, far and away, not your basic morning bowl of gruel. (Oatmeal-lovers, don't hate me, for I am one of you. But how much porridge can you eat before it gets repetitive?)

Wonderfully textural, a bunch of scones or rolls will richly fill the morning breadbasket and encourage the sleepy-eyed to surface and glow—or at the very least, make it to the table without too much grumbling. I should know. I mutter and croak like crazy, and usually wouldn't win the award for

"bright and cheery" before 10:00 a.m. Traditionally, an icing or glaze is absent from oatmeal cookies, but this kind of gilding would not be out of order as a topping for either delight that follows. (Likewise vanilla confectioners' sugar.) I adore the kind of slick, sweet overcoating that a vanilla icing furnishes, for it adds a dash of luxury, and you have my best recipe for it here. Well, it's possible that I'd be a little more pleasant *before* 10:00 a.m. if either goodie awaited me that morning.

"oatmeal raisin cookie" scones

oatmeal raisin cream dough

4¼ cups unsifted bleached
all-purpose flour

4 teaspoons baking powder

¾ teaspoon baking soda

1¼ teaspoons salt

1½ teaspoons ground cinnamon

1¼ teaspoons freshly grated nutmeg

½ teaspoon ground allspice

½ teaspoon ground cloves

¾ cup firmly packed
light brown sugar, sieved

1½ cups "quick-cooking" (not instant)
rolled oats

12 tablespoons (1½ sticks) cold
unsalted butter, cut into small chunks

4 large eggs

1 cup plus 2 tablespoons heavy cream

4 teaspoons vanilla extract

1 cup golden raisins

vanilla icing (page 392),
for spreading on the warm scones

serving: 1 dozen large scones
ahead: best on baking day; or freeze for
3 weeks, defrost, bundle in aluminum foil,
and reheat in a preheated 300 degrees F
oven for 10 minutes, reserving the frosting
finish for after reheating

For the dough, place the flour, baking powder, baking soda, salt, cinnamon, nutmeg, allspice, and cloves in a large mixing bowl and whisk well to combine. Add the light brown sugar and rolled oats, and mix thoroughly, using a wooden spoon or flat wooden paddle. Drop in the chunks of butter and, using a pastry blender or two round-bladed table knives, cut the fat into the flour and oat mixture until reduced to irregular bits the size of large peas.

In a medium-size mixing bowl, whisk together the eggs, heavy cream, and vanilla extract.

Pour the whisked egg mixture over the oat mixture, scatter over the raisins, and stir to form a moist, cohesive dough. Mixing the dough until it comes together may take a little arm power, but, in the end, the dough will come together nicely—slightly moist, but firm. Knead the dough lightly in the bowl, 5 or 6 turns, for about 30 seconds. Divide the dough into two 6½-inch disks. The disks should be nicely rounded and plump, or the baked scones will slump. Wrap each disk in waxed paper. Transfer to a cookie sheet and refrigerate for 45 minutes.

Preheat the oven to 400 degrees F.

Line two cookie sheets or heavy rimmed sheet pans with lengths of ovenproof parchment paper.

Place the disks on a lightly floured work surface. Cut each into 6 wedges. Place the scones on the prepared baking pans, 6 scones to a pan, spacing them 3 to 3½ inches apart.

Bake the scones in the preheated oven for 20 minutes, or until set.

While the scones are baking, prepare the vanilla icing.

Cool the baked scones on the baking pans for 2 minutes, then remove them to cooling racks, using a wide offset metal spatula. Let stand for 3 minutes. Place a sheet of waxed paper underneath each cooling rack holding the scones.

Spread the icing over the hot scones, using a flexible palette knife. As the icing melts down, it will randomly meld with the surface while flowing here and there. Cool completely. Serve the scones freshly baked.

notes
- sieving the brown sugar is important to the creation of the dough, as this act eliminates those dreaded nubby clumps that could wander through the baked scones
- refrigerating the disks of dough sets the texture before baking
- in place of the icing, sprinkle a little turbinado sugar (⅓ cup total amount) on top of each scone just before baking

"oatmeal raisin cookie" morning rolls

For the dough, stir together the yeast, the ¼ teaspoon granulated sugar, and the warm water in a heatproof measuring cup. Allow the mixture to stand until swollen, 6 to 7 minutes.

In the meantime, place the buttermilk, dark brown sugar, and the chunks of butter in a small saucepan, set over low heat, and warm until the butter has melted. Remove from the heat, whisk well, and scrape into a medium-size heatproof mixing bowl. Blend in the vanilla extract and rolled oats. Let the mixture stand for 10 to 15 minutes to cool to tepid, stirring once or twice. Whisk in the whole egg and egg yolks. Blend in the yeast mixture. Whisk the unbleached flour, 1 cup bleached flour, cinnamon, and salt in a large mixing bowl. Add the oat-yeast mixture and stir to mix well, using a wooden spoon or flat wooden paddle. The dough will be shaggy, with sections of moist dough and fragments of flaky dough. Let the dough stand, uncovered, for 5 minutes.

Turn the dough out onto a work surface sprinkled with the additional bleached flour. Knead the dough for 8 minutes, or until resilient, moderately firm, and supple.

Turn the dough into a bowl heavily coated with softened unsalted butter and lightly turn to coat all sides in a film of butter, make several deep cuts in the dough with kitchen scissors, cover tightly with a sheet of food-safe plastic wrap, and let rise at room temperature for 2 hours, or until doubled in bulk.

Remove and discard the plastic wrap. Sprinkle the raisins on top of the risen dough. Lightly knead the dough in the bowl to incorporate the raisins. This will take 2 to 3 minutes.

Film the inside of a 12 by 8 by 3-inch baking pan with softened unsalted butter.

To form the rolls, roll out the dough into a sheet measuring 12 by 12 inches. Using the filling ingredients, spread on the butter and sprinkle evenly with the

(continued on the next page)

oatmeal raisin yeast dough

2¼ teaspoons active dry yeast

¼ teaspoon granulated sugar

¼ cup warm (105 to 110 degrees F) water

⅔ cup buttermilk

¼ cup firmly packed dark brown sugar

5 tablespoons unsalted butter, cut into tablespoon-size chunks

1 tablespoon vanilla extract

⅔ cup "old-fashioned" rolled oats

1 large egg

2 large egg yolks

2 cups unsifted unbleached all-purpose flour

1 cup unsifted bleached all-purpose flour, plus an additional 2 tablespoons, for kneading

1 tablespoon ground cinnamon

½ teaspoon salt

raisins knead-in

¾ cup moist dark seedless raisins

(continued on the next page)

(continued from the previous page)

butter and cinnamon sugar filling

6 tablespoons (¾ stick) unsalted butter, softened

½ cup granulated sugar blended with 2 tablespoons ground cinnamon

sweet vanilla finish

vanilla icing (below), for spreading on the warm rolls

~ or ~

vanilla sugar (page 2), made with confectioners' sugar, or plain confectioners' sugar, for sprinkling on the baked rolls

serving: 10 rolls
ahead: best on baking day; or freeze for 3 weeks, defrost, bundle in aluminum foil, and reheat in a preheated 325 degrees F oven for 10 minutes, then ice or sprinkle with confectioners' sugar (vanilla-scented or plain)

creamy icing

1½ cups confectioners' sugar

pinch of salt

2 tablespoons unsalted butter, softened but cool

3 tablespoons cold heavy cream blended with ¼ teaspoon vanilla extract

serving: a generous ¾ cup
ahead: 1 hour

---

cinnamon sugar. Fold in the sides, press them down firmly, and roll the dough tightly into a log. Cut the dough into 10 even-size slices. Place the spirals of dough in the prepared baking pan, assembling them in two rows of 5 each.

Cover the pan of rolls loosely with a sheet of food-safe plastic wrap. Let the rolls rise at room temperature for 2 hours to 2 hours and 30 minutes, or until doubled in bulk.

Preheat the oven to 350 degrees F in advance of baking.

Remove and discard the sheet of plastic wrap covering the rolls.

Bake the rolls in the preheated oven for 35 minutes, or until set and golden.

Place the pan on a cooling rack and let stand for 5 to 7 minutes. Spoon and sweep the vanilla icing over the surface of the warm rolls, spreading it carefully as it melts down over the irregular surfaces. Cool the rolls completely in the pan. Or, cool the buns in the pan and, just before serving, sift the vanilla or plain sugar over the tops. Detach the rolls from one another and lift out of the pan for serving.

notes
- the dough will be moderately firm when assembled, but it will surprise you once it is risen (both the first and second time) as it puffs into a soft, cozy, and highly workable mass
- though the rising times are somewhat extended, note that allowing the dough to rise in a very warm spot to hasten the rising time will cause it to destabilize and bake into denser, smaller rolls

vanilla icing

Sift the confectioners' sugar and salt into a medium-size mixing bowl. Add the butter and heavy cream–vanilla extract blend. Using a hand-held electric mixer, beat the ingredients on low speed until smooth, stopping to scrape down the sides of the mixing bowl with a rubber spatula 2 or 3 times. The icing will be thick, creamy, and dense. The icing is wonderful spread over just-baked, still-warm scones or sweet biscuits, as well as sweet yeast rolls and buns. Use the icing immediately or place a sheet of food-safe plastic directly on the surface of the icing and set aside at cool room temperature for up to 1 hour.

notes
- the butter must be soft—but still cool—for the smoothest finished consistency
- challenging the full amount of confectioners' sugar (that is, using less of it) will yield an icing that looks vaguely separated (as the butter and cream will not be fully amalgamated in a lesser amount of confectioners' sugar)
- mix the ingredients on low speed to combine them without introducing too much air; the icing should be smooth and dense rather than fluffy

sticks, rounds, and hearts

Full-fledged waffle makers, bored with squares, can travel into the land of sticks and hearts.

Thick batons, long and not very wide, or interconnected hearts, are really fun shapes to ease out of a hot iron, for they look whimsical on the plate. The batons appear like tubby, rounded pegs, yet they are golden on the exterior and tender within. The link of five hearts looks just like a waffle doily.

The batter presented here (my favorite all-purpose mixture, and just buttery enough) is simple to master and so easy to flavor in a number of directions—with baby chocolate chips or ground spices or droplets of essence. While most cooks present waffles with warm maple syrup, I prefer the likes of maple butter (maple syrup whipped into unsalted butter), a confit of simmered and sweetened dried fruit (especially apricots), or berry syrup. In the winter, I am prodded by the lushness of the many varieties of pears and apples and prepare them roasted, baked, or pan-sautéed in butter to serve with the waffles. A full shower of confectioners' sugar adds just the right distinction of sweetness and does not obscure the waffles' inherent goodness.

Pancake fans will be delighted with the puffed-up rounds baked in a traditional *aebleskiver* pan: cakelike and buttery, these confectioners' sugar–sprinkled balls are made from a creamed batter, not the usual melted butter-milk-egg yolks batter. Whipped egg whites and baking powder buoy up the mixture, making for tender, yet substantial, three-bite morsels. These appear on my table with apricot or peach jam—that is, a spoonful of jam on the outside, but many cooks I know like to drop a teeny dollop of jam in the middle of each round (as soon as the indentations are filled with batter), letting it sink slightly into the middle as the mixture firms up. I really don't care for the interior surprise of hot jam, and besides, it can make the mid-griddle become a bit of a sticky situation. Roly-poly pancakes are too deliciously playful to make and eat only once and a while, which is why I keep the pan (with its rather cherubic depressions) close to my working equipment in the vicinity of the stove top as a reminder that a plate of the warm, puffy treats would make a delicious end-of-the-week reward on Sunday morning.

waffle batons and hearts

plain vanilla batter

3 cups unsifted bleached all-purpose flour

5 teaspoons baking powder

¼ teaspoon salt

⅓ cup granulated sugar

4 large eggs

2 cups half-and-half

8 tablespoons (1 stick) unsalted butter, melted and cooled to tepid

4 teaspoons vanilla extract

confectioners' sugar, for sprinkling on the griddled waffles

serving: about 8 trays/turns of 3 double-stick double-connected waffle sticks each (creating 24 double sticks; 3 double-stick double-connected waffles makes a good single serving, creating 8 servings) or about eight 5-heart waffles (each composed of 5 small interconnected hearts)

Preheat a 6-stick (3 double sticks) waffle iron (each single grid measuring 5 by 1½ inches) or a 5-interconnected-heart waffler (see notes).

For the batter, sift the flour, baking powder, salt, and granulated sugar into a medium-size mixing bowl. In another medium-size mixing bowl, whisk the eggs, half-and-half, melted butter, and vanilla extract. Pour the whisked egg mixture over the sifted ingredients and stir to form a batter, using a wooden spoon or flat wooden paddle. The batter will be moderately thick and slightly lumpy. Avoid mixing the batter to smooth it out.

Spoon about ⅓ cup of the batter into each of the 3 double-grid sections of the 6-stick waffle iron (note that the ⅓ cup batter is to be spooned directly over each double grid; it is not necessary to divide it between the two single grids as the lid of the waffler will compress the batter when you close it). Spoon about ⅔ cup of batter into the center of the interconnected 5-heart waffler. Cover the waffler by closing the lid and griddle until golden (at setting #5 or #6, if you are using the Uno Stick Waffler described in the notes) or until golden and cooked through, if you are using the 5-heart waffler (this waffler does not have adjustable settings). The griddled waffles will be crusty on the outside and tender within. Carefully lift the waffles off the grids, dust with confectioners' sugar, and serve immediately.

notes
• for this waffle batter, I use the Uno Stick Waffler (Model V2008) by VillaWare; the grid is composed of 6 sticks measuring 5 by 1½ inches), or the Vitantonio Danish Waffler, composed of 5 interconnected hearts (the diameter of the grid is 7 inches)

pancake rounds, griddled

For the batter, sift the all-purpose flour, cake flour, baking powder, and salt onto a sheet of waxed paper.

Cream the butter in the large bowl of a freestanding electric mixer on moderate speed until smooth, about 2 minutes. Add the granulated sugar and beat for 1 minute. Add the egg yolks and beat for 1 minute. Blend in the milk, vanilla extract, and vanilla bean seeds (if you are using them). On low speed, add the sifted mixture in 2 additions, beating until the particles of flour are absorbed. Scrape down the sides of the mixing bowl with a rubber spatula after each addition. At this point, the batter will be reasonably thick.

In a small mixing bowl, whip the egg whites until firm. Stir a large spoonful of the whipped egg whites into the batter, then fold in the remaining whites, making sure that all flecks and filaments of the whipped whites are dispersed.

Set a 7-half-round indentation *aebleskiver* pan (each indentation measuring 2⅛ inches in diameter, with a capacity of 3 tablespoons) over moderate heat to preheat it.

Spoon a heaping tablespoon of batter into each indentation. Let the rounds griddle for 3 to 4 minutes, then turn them, and finish griddling for 2 to 3 minutes longer, or until golden and cooked through. Remove the pancake rounds from the pan and griddle the next batch. Serve the pancake orbs immediately, dusted with confectioners' sugar, with fruit preserves alongside.

notes
- the batter can take 3 egg whites, whipped, but my preference is for the texture resulting from using just 2 of the whites (the batter is more stable and less difficult to maneuver in the pan)
- my *aebleskiver* pan is made of cast iron, and I always film the surface of the circular indentations with nonstick oil spray before spooning in the first round of batter, even if the pan is well-seasoned
- at first, turning the pancakes to cook the second side is tricky, but it gets easier as you go along; the simplest way to turn the pancakes is to nudge them loose to one side, using the rounded tip of a thin offset metal spatula, then easing it over to reverse the side (another way to turn them is to lift them slightly to one side with the offset spatula, then use a thin wooden skewer to snag each and roll it over)
- for a sweeter pancake, increase the amount of granulated sugar to 6 tablespoons

butter-vanilla batter

1 cup plus 1 tablespoon unsifted bleached all-purpose flour

½ cup unsifted bleached cake flour

1¾ teaspoons baking powder

⅛ teaspoon salt

8 tablespoons (1 stick) unsalted butter, softened

¼ cup granulated sugar

3 large egg yolks

¾ cup plus 2 tablespoons milk

2½ teaspoons vanilla extract

seeds from ½ small vanilla bean, scraped clean (optional, but wonderful)

2 large egg whites

confectioners' sugar, for sprinkling on the griddled pancakes

best-quality apricot, peach, raspberry, or strawberry preserves, to accompany

serving: about 2 dozen pancakes

thin and jam-packed

The griddle-and-eat process of serving freshly made crêpes keeps you at the stove, but I've always thought of this as a friendly, communal way to connect the cook with guests.

The crêpe batter is basic and foolproof, requiring only a brief mix in the blender and some time to "cure" in the refrigerator. During the chilling time, the flour absorbs the fat and liquid, creating tender pancakes. The surprise ingredient in the crêpe batter is water: it helps to make pancakes that are delicate, not tough, as an excess of milk or the presence of soft dairy, such as sour cream, would produce a thicker, denser (and sometimes rubbery-textured) pancake. Don't think that you are making a better batter by using milk entirely in place of the milk and water.

A crêpe pan, made of carbon steel, is a classic, enduring piece of equipment. Both its figure—a flat bottom and sides that open outward on an angle—and physical composition allow the pan to conduct heat quickly and efficiently, and turn out crêpes with the right texture and a beautiful color. A new crêpe pan must be seasoned in order to keep the pancakes from sticking. To do so, preheat the oven to 275 degrees F and, using an abrasive pad, scour away the protective coating on the inside and outside of the pan. Rinse and dry the pan well, thickly coat the inside with solid shortening, place the pan in the oven, and let it "cure" for 2 hours; remove it to a heatproof surface (using padded oven mitts to protect your hands at all times), cool completely, then mop up the shortening with a thick wad of paper towels. A crêpe pan may need to be seasoned once again from time to time, especially if the pan has not been in use for more than six months; to do this, follow the basic procedure, but reduce the oven-curing time to 1 hour. Always store the seasoned crêpe pan in a dry place, away from moisture or humidity.

The size crêpe pan I love to use for this recipe makes small, vanilla-scented "handkerchief" pancakes, a genteel snack if there ever was one. A larger pan makes impressive pancakes as well, but for endearing appeal, you can't improve on the adorable-factor of the petite size. An instant, speedy finish to a crêpe is to spoon and spread preserves or jam onto its second-sided griddled surface (it's the one that looks haphazardly spotty) and fold it in half or into quarters. That's it, and few things are more delicious.

crêpes, slathered

vanilla batter

⅔ cup plus 2 tablespoons milk

⅔ cup plus 2 tablespoons water

3 large egg yolks (see notes)

2 tablespoons superfine sugar

6 tablespoons (¾ stick) unsalted butter, melted and cooled to tepid

2 teaspoons vanilla extract

1⅓ cups plus 2 tablespoons unsifted bleached all-purpose flour

⅛ teaspoon salt

about 2 tablespoons melted clarified butter (page 1)

about 1 cup best-quality apricot preserves, for spreading on the finished crêpes

confectioners' sugar, for sprinkling over the filled and folded crêpes

serving: about 26 crêpes

For the batter, whisk the milk, water, egg yolks, superfine sugar, melted butter, and vanilla extract in a medium-size mixing bowl. Place the flour and salt in the container of a 40-ounce-capacity blender. Add the whisked milk mixture. Cover securely and blend on low speed for 30 seconds. Uncover the blender, scrape down the sides with a rubber spatula to distribute the flour evenly and to break up any lingering clumps of flour. Cover tightly and blend on moderate speed to form a smooth batter, about 1 minute. The batter should resemble moderately thick, liquidy cream. Strain the batter through a large fine-mesh sieve into a bowl, cover with a sheet of food-safe plastic wrap, and refrigerate for 2 hours before using it. The batter can be stored in the refrigerator overnight, but must be used within 18 hours of mixing.

Remove the batter from the refrigerator about 15 minutes before cooking the crêpes. Whisk well.

Heat a seasoned crêpe pan 6¾ inches in diameter across the top (the base will measure 4¾ inches) over moderately high heat. Dip a double thickness of folded-over paper towels into a little clarified butter. Using a comfortable pot holder and lifting the pan off the heat at a slight tilt, quickly and carefully coat the bottom of the pan with the butter. Return the pan to the heat and let it sit on the burner for 45 seconds. Lift the pan away from the heat, add a scant 2 tablespoons of the batter to the hot pan, and quickly circulate the batter around by tilting the pan slightly in a circular movement to coat the bottom evenly. You want to cover the entire bottom of the pan with the batter quickly before it has the chance to set in one area. (If the batter misses a few very small, sliver-y sections, don't worry; a few lacy areas in a finished pancake are fine, and even quite pretty.) Return the pan to the heat and cook for about 45 seconds, or until the crêpe is a netlike golden color underneath. Using a slender wooden crêpe spatula (specifically designed for this purpose), or other thin wooden spatula, lift the crêpe away from the edges of the pan and turn it over. Cook the crêpe on the second side (this side will turn a mottled brown) for about 20 seconds longer, then lift it off. Continue to make crêpes in this way, buttering the pan as necessary.

Spread a little of the jam on the mottled side of each crêpe, fold the crêpe in half, then in half again (creating a triangular quarter), dust the top with confectioners' sugar, and serve immediately.

notes
• when preparing the batter for refrigeration longer than 2 hours, use organic egg yolks only

zoom!

Soaring but not out of control, a bread baker's dream dough is made of cooked and riced potatoes, though you would never figure that out by its flavor. The moist, nearly fluffy texture of the baked rolls is the giveaway.

Once either of the doughs (the *gossamer potato rolls* or the *butter-striated potato rolls*) is formed into linked pan rolls, the rolls really take off, sailing high to plumpness due to the addition of silky riced mashed potatoes, a little of the potato cooking water (in one of the recipes), buttermilk or evaporated milk, and enough butter to enrich it all. The creamy-textured potatoes generate a fine, silky grain and, at the same time, lightness. Butter appears in the two recipes, but the recipe for *butter-striated potato rolls* has you layering the once-risen, rolled-out dough with more butter and a good sprinkle of sea salt. (Sea salt is a natural enhancement for potato bread.) The result? Another wallop of flavor.

A puffy, high-rise potato dough turns into wonderfully curvaceous rolls that fill up deep baking pans—so very generously—becoming a perfect addition to that fine, plump chicken you'll have to roast in their honor.

gossamer potato rolls

For the dough, stir together the yeast, the ½ teaspoon sugar, and the warm water in a heatproof measuring cup. Allow the mixture to stand until swollen, 6 to 7 minutes.

Place the buttermilk and the ½ cup sugar in a medium-size saucepan and set over moderate heat to warm the buttermilk and begin to dissolve the sugar, 6 to 7 minutes. The buttermilk will appear slightly separated, and this is to be expected. Pour and scrape the buttermilk mixture into a medium-size heatproof mixing bowl. Stir in the chunks of butter and the riced potatoes. Let stand until lukewarm, 8 to 10 minutes. Add the yeast mixture, the beaten eggs, and baking soda, and mix well.

In a large mixing bowl, whisk 6 cups of the flour and salt. Add the potato-yeast-buttermilk mixture and stir to combine, using a wooden spoon or flat wooden paddle. The dough will be moist in sections and scraggly in other parts, and will smooth out during the kneading process. Flour a work surface with the additional ⅔ cup flour. Knead the dough on the work surface, incorporating the flour to create a soft, cushy dough. The dough should be bouncy and resilient.

Turn the dough into a bowl heavily coated with softened unsalted butter, lightly turn to coat all sides in a film of butter, make several cuts in the dough with a pair of kitchen scissors, cover tightly with a sheet of food-safe plastic wrap, and let rise at cool room temperature for 2 hours, or until doubled in bulk.

Uncover the dough and discard the plastic wrap.

Butter the inside of two round 10-inch cake pans (3 inches deep).

To form the rolls, place the dough on a lightly floured work surface. Divide the dough in half, then cut each half into 16 even-size pieces, creating 32 pieces in total. Smooth each piece into a plump ball by rolling it on the work surface briskly under the cupped palm of your hand. Place 16 balls of dough in each of the prepared baking pans, assembling them in an outer round of 10 balls, in an inner ring of 5 balls, and, finally, 1 in the center.

Cover each pan of rolls loosely with a sheet of food-safe plastic wrap. Let the rolls rise at cool room temperature for 1 hour and 30 minutes, or until doubled in bulk. The rolls will merge as they rise.

(continued on the next page)

buttermilk potato dough

4½ teaspoons active dry yeast

½ teaspoon granulated sugar

6 tablespoons warm (105 to 110 degrees F) water

1½ cups buttermilk

½ cup granulated sugar

12 tablespoons (1½ sticks) unsalted butter, cut into tablespoon-size chunks

two 6-ounce russet potatoes (peeled, chunked, boiled until fork-tender, drained, and riced), to yield about 1¼ cups riced potatoes

2 large eggs, lightly beaten

¼ teaspoon baking soda

6 cups unsifted unbleached all-purpose flour, plus an additional ⅔ cup, for kneading

1¼ teaspoons salt

butter and salt finish

about 3 tablespoons butter (preferably clarified butter, page 1), melted and still warm

coarse sea salt, for sprinkling

serving: 32 rolls
ahead: best on baking day; or freeze for 3 weeks, defrost, bundle in aluminum foil, and reheat in a preheated 300 degrees F oven for 10 minutes

Preheat the oven to 375 degrees F in advance of baking.

Remove and discard the sheets of plastic wrap covering the rolls.

Bake the rolls in the preheated oven for 25 to 30 minutes, or until set and a golden color on top. The rolls will rise nicely, filling the pan completely.

Place the pans on cooling racks and let stand for 15 minutes. Carefully and gently (the rolls are quite tender now), invert the breads onto other cooling racks. Lift off each pan, then invert the breads again to stand right side up. For the butter and salt finish, brush the tops of the breads with the melted butter and top with a few sprinklings of coarse sea salt. Detach the rolls at their natural seams and serve warm or at room temperature. Store in an airtight container.

notes
- a few (and no more than 2 or 3) unpeeled sections from one potato can be boiled with their skin on, then riced as usual; if you use organic russet potatoes (well-scrubbed, in any case), flecks of the skin will add great flavor and mottle the tops of the rolls here and there—lovely
- the dough can be made with whole milk in place of the buttermilk, and to do so, simply omit the baking soda from the list of ingredients
- the secret to the great, fine-grained crumb of the baked rolls is allowing the dough to rise (both times) at cool room temperature; hastening the rise in a warmer location will cause the rolls to be denser and more compressed in texture
- this fine, soft dough can also be divided, formed, and baked as individual rolls, yielding a big batch, suitable for the holidays; butter the inside of 4 dozen muffin/cupcake cups (12 cups to a pan, each cup measuring 2¾ inches in diameter and 1⅜ inches deep, with a capacity of ½ cup) and place a plump ball in each cup, cover each pan with a sheet of food-safe plastic wrap, let rise for 1 hour and 20 minutes or until doubled in bulk, remove and discard the sheets of plastic wrap covering the rolls, and bake in a preheated 375 degrees F oven for 15 minutes, or until set and a golden color on top

butter-striated potato rolls

For the dough, peel the potato and cut it into large chunks. Place the potato chunks in a large saucepan, cover with cold water by 2 inches, and bring to the boil. Boil at a moderate pace until the chunks of potato are fork-tender and falling apart, about 15 minutes. Drain the chunks well, reserving ⅓ cup of the potato cooking water. Put the potato chunks through a ricer fitted with the fine-hole disk. There should be a scant 1 cup of riced potatoes.

Stir together the yeast, the ½ teaspoon of sugar, and the warm water in a heat-proof measuring cup. Allow the mixture to stand until swollen, 6 to 7 minutes.

In the meantime, place the evaporated milk, the ½ cup sugar, and the potato cooking water in a small-to-medium-size saucepan. Place over moderate heat to warm the milk, about 5 minutes (the sugar will not dissolve completely). Pour and scrape the milk mixture into a medium-size heatproof mixing bowl. Stir in the chunks of butter and the riced potatoes. Let stand until lukewarm, 8 to 10 minutes. Blend in the yeast mixture and the eggs, mixing well.

Place 2 cups of the unbleached flour, 1 cup of the bleached flour, and the salt in the bowl of a heavy-duty freestanding electric mixer; whisk well to combine. Pour in the potato-yeast mixture and mix well, using a wooden spoon or flat wooden paddle. The dough will be wet, like a very thick batter. Stir in another 1 cup of the unbleached flour; the dough will be slightly shaggy at this point. Let stand for 10 minutes. Sprinkle over the remaining ¼ cup unbleached flour. Set the bowl in place and attach the dough hook. Mix on moderately low speed until the mixture is combined and smooth, about 3 minutes. Add another 1 cup of the bleached flour, ¼ cup at a time, mixing on moderately low speed to combine. Stop the machine from time to time to scrape down the sides of the mixing bowl and the dough hook. Add the remaining ⅔ cup bleached flour and beat on moderately low speed for 5 minutes. The dough should be plush, smooth, resilient, and almost clean the sides of the mixing bowl, leaving a slight film.

Scrape the dough into a bowl heavily coated with softened unsalted butter, lightly turn to coat all sides in a film of butter, cover tightly with a sheet of food-safe plastic wrap, and let rise at room temperature for 1 hour and 20 minutes, or until doubled in bulk.

Remove the plastic wrap. Lightly compress the dough with your fingertips or a rubber spatula, cover with the plastic wrap, and let stand for 10 minutes.

(continued on the next page)

potato yeast dough

one 9 to 10-ounce russet potato

4½ teaspoons active dry yeast

½ teaspoon granulated sugar

¼ cup warm (105 to 110 degrees F) water

⅔ cup evaporated milk

½ cup granulated sugar

⅓ cup potato cooking water

8 tablespoons (1 stick) unsalted butter, cut into tablespoon-size chunks

2 large eggs

3¼ cups unsifted unbleached all-purpose flour

2⅔ cups unsifted bleached all-purpose flour

1 teaspoon salt

butter and salt filling

8 tablespoons (1 stick) unsalted butter, softened

1 teaspoon coarse sea salt

cream wash

3 tablespoons heavy cream

serving: 1½ dozen rolls
ahead: best on baking day; or freeze for 3 weeks, defrost, bundle in aluminum foil, and reheat in a preheated 300 degrees F oven for 10 minutes

Film the inside of two 9 by 9 by 3-inch baking pans with nonstick flour-and-oil spray.

To form the rolls, remove and discard the plastic wrap. Roll out the dough on a work surface to a sheet measuring 15 by 17 inches. Using the filling ingredients, dot the surface with the softened butter and spread it evenly over the dough, using an offset palette knife and light, agile strokes. Sprinkle on the sea salt. Fold the dough into thirds as you would a business letter, then extend the dough into a thick slab about 18 inches long, using a heavy rolling pin. Beginning at the short end, roll up the dough into a thick and plump jellyroll. Divide the roll in half, then cut each half into 9 even-size pieces; these will end up to be big, bosomy rolls. Form the pieces into smooth balls and assemble them in the prepared baking pans, arranging three rows of 3 dough balls each.

Cover each pan of rolls loosely with a buttered sheet of food-safe plastic wrap. Let the rolls rise at cool room temperature for 2 hours, or until almost doubled in bulk (see page 6 to reference this stage).

Preheat the oven to 375 degrees F in advance of baking.

Remove and discard the plastic wrap covering the rolls.

Brush the tops of the rolls with the heavy cream, using a soft pastry brush and light, sensitive strokes.

Bake the rolls in the preheated oven for 30 to 35 minutes, or until set and a golden brown color on top. The baked rolls will pull away slightly from the sides of the baking pan. Place the pans on cooling racks and let stand for 10 minutes. Invert each block of rolls onto another cooling rack, remove the pan, then invert again to cool right side up. Serve the rolls very fresh, gently and casually detaching them from one another where they have joined during rising and baking.

notes
- for the most supple dough, the well-cooked potato chunks should be riced, not merely mashed
- the rolls are assembled and baked in two 9 by 9 by 3-inch baking pans; one 13 by 9 by 2-inch baking pan may be substituted, creating smaller rolls and a larger yield (divide the dough into 24 pieces, form into smooth rolls, and assemble in four rows of 6 rolls each), reducing the baking time by 5 to 7 minutes

blond, beautiful (of texture), and brown sugary

Simple ingredients. Simple luxury. Easy and opulent, not always compatible attributes in one recipe, are characteristics materialized in the formula below.

Don't you just love that? (And I *mean* easy: the batter is put together by hand.)

A flood of milk chocolate–covered peanut butter cups, a smattering of semisweet chocolate chips, a few spoonfuls of peanut butter, a suggestion of caramel in the sweetening package of light brown sugar, and a significant pour of vanilla extract frame the flavor and texture of this batter, traditionally baked as bar cookies. I like to turn the dense and creamy batter—lightly leavened with baking soda—into a pretty fluted tart pan. This builds a thicker, chewier confection, with a concentrated taste.

Now, it seems, this recipe has become my all-purpose blondie-styled cake. It is liberating to know that you can substitute chopped nuts (pecans, walnuts, macadamias, and so on) for the peanuts, and likewise another coordinating nut butter, or replace the semisweet chocolate chips with chopped bittersweet bar chocolate (figure on 3 ounces, or a little more, of chocolate in the 60% to 65% cacao category). For a deeper caramel effect, use dark brown sugar or even dark muscovado sugar instead of the light brown variety.

This cake is rich, substantial in a playful, candylike way, and wonderfully moist. Is there anything else you could wish for in such a relaxed recipe?

blondie cake

Preheat the oven to 350 degrees F.

Film the inside of a fluted 8½ to 9-inch false-bottomed tart pan (2 inches deep) with softened unsalted butter.

For the batter, sift the flour, baking soda, and salt onto a sheet of waxed paper.

Whisk the eggs in a medium-size mixing bowl to blend. Add the light brown sugar and whisk for 45 seconds. Add the granulated sugar and whisk just to combine, about 30 seconds. Blend in the melted butter, peanut butter, and vanilla extract. Resift the flour mixture over the butter and sugar mixture. Whisk slowly to form a batter, scraping down the sides of the mixing bowl with a rubber spatula to keep the batter even-textured. Stir in the chunks of peanut butter cups, the peanuts, and chocolate chips. The batter will be fairly thick and heavy.

Scrape the batter into the prepared pan. Smooth the top with a flexible palette knife.

Bake the sweet in the preheated oven for 30 to 35 minutes, or until just set. The top will puff slightly, then retreat a little on cooling. The top will be golden in between the nubbins of chocolate chips, candy chunks, and peanuts. Avoid overbaking or the cake will be dry instead of moist. Cool the sweet in the pan on a cooling rack for 20 minutes. Carefully lift the cake by the bottom, pushing it up and out to unmold, and remove the fluted ring. Cool completely. Cut the cake into pie-shape wedges and remove from the pan, using a small offset metal spatula. Store in an airtight tin.

notes
- in addition to guarding against overbaking, the key to the moistest cake is to use very fresh brown sugar and the melted butter while it is still warm
- firmly packed light muscovado sugar would provide a focused caramel-like flavor to the sweet and can be substituted for the light brown sugar
- a handful of each addition—the milk chocolate-covered peanut butter cup chunks, peanuts, and semisweet chocolate chips—can be reserved and sprinkled over the top of the cake after 25 minutes of baking
- this cake, conceived in honor of my photographer, Ben Fink, is affectionately known as "Ben's blondie" (he ate the whole thing himself)
- use a finely serrated knife to cut the cake

peanut butter candy and chocolate chip batter

1 cup unsifted bleached all-purpose flour

¼ teaspoon baking soda

⅛ teaspoon salt

2 large eggs

⅔ cup plus 1 tablespoon firmly packed light brown sugar

5 tablespoons granulated sugar

10 tablespoons (1 stick plus 2 tablespoons) unsalted butter, melted and cooled to warm

3 tablespoons smooth (creamy) peanut butter

2 teaspoons vanilla extract

1¼ cups milk chocolate-covered peanut butter cup chunks

⅔ cup lightly salted roasted and skinned peanuts

⅓ cup semisweet chocolate chips

serving: one 8½ to 9-inch cake, creating 8 to 10 slices
ahead: 2 days

alluring

When the "nose" of vanilla winds through a butter- and egg-rich yeast dough (in the form of a powerful combination of extract and seed scrapings from the bean), you can just about expect to be enfolded in what I call "the scent of home."

This phrase is difficult to describe, but, if bottled and let into the air in several trailing wafts, it would be the symbolically aromatic equivalent of sweet baking, pure and simple.

Here is a yeast dough that performs very well, and well it should as it is boosted by whole eggs (four of them) and enough butter to keep the crumb moist and urbane. The surface of the swirly-looking, freshly baked bread gets a final supercharge of melted butter and sugar, sending a message that bread plus butter plus sugar equals an arresting something to slice and serve at a weekend brunch or coffee hour. The bread is special enough to star on its own, but in all likelihood you'll have it, sliced, alongside good smoky bacon and a golden scramble of eggs. Or with a platter of fresh fruit, roasted nuts, and yogurt. But most of all, the bread is, for me, a stellar model of how well a few elementary baking ingredients, plus one that is eminently floral, translate and compose themselves into an exceedingly light yeast bread dough: it is exactly this synergy of elements that continues to draw me into the baking process, and, yes, it is that alluring.

a very vanilla bread

vanilla-scented yeast dough

4½ teaspoons active dry yeast

¼ teaspoon granulated sugar

¼ cup warm (105 to 110 degrees F) water

¾ cup milk

½ cup granulated sugar

8 tablespoons (1 stick) unsalted butter, cut into tablespoon-size chunks

4 large eggs

1 tablespoon vanilla extract

seeds from 2 small vanilla beans, scraped clean

5 cups unsifted bleached all-purpose flour, plus an additional ⅓ cup, for kneading

1 teaspoon salt

butter and sugar finish

about 3 tablespoons butter (preferably clarified butter, page 1), melted and still warm

sparkling sugar (plain or a color), vanilla sugar (see notes), or homemade vanilla sugar (page 2) for sprinkling on the baked bread

serving: one 10-inch fluted bread, creating 16 ample slices
ahead: best on baking day; slice and toast up to 3 days thereafter, or freeze for 1 month, defrost, bundle in aluminum foil, and reheat in a preheated 325 degrees F oven for 15 minutes, reserving the butter and sugar finish for after reheating

For the dough, stir together the yeast, the ¼ teaspoon granulated sugar, and the warm water in a heatproof measuring cup. Allow the mixture to stand until swollen, 6 to 7 minutes.

In the meantime, place the milk and the ½ cup granulated sugar in a small saucepan and set over moderate heat. When the milk has warmed and the sugar has almost dissolved (about 4 minutes), remove the saucepan from the heat, pour the mixture into a medium-size heatproof mixing bowl, stir in the chunks of butter, and cool to tepid. Whisk in the eggs, vanilla extract, and vanilla bean seeds. Blend in the yeast mixture.

Place 4 cups of the flour and the salt in a large mixing bowl. Whisk to integrate the salt. Beat in the butter-milk-eggs-yeast mixture, using a wooden spoon or flat wooden paddle. Mix well. The dough will be quite dense, like a stiff batter, at this point. Let the dough stand, uncovered, for 5 minutes, then work in the remaining 1 cup flour. The dough will be moderately moist. Flour a work surface with the additional ⅓ cup of flour. Knead the dough on the work surface for a full 8 minutes, incorporating as much of the flour as necessary to create a smooth and only moderately firm dough (usually, it will take all of the ⅓ cup flour). Even with the knead-in of the additional flour, the dough will still be slightly sticky. The total amount of flour is, of course, dependent on the atmospheric conditions of the day and the age and absorption quality of the flour used.

Turn the dough into a bowl heavily coated with softened unsalted butter, lightly turn to coat all sides in a film of butter, make several cuts in the dough with a pair of kitchen scissors, cover tightly with a sheet of food-safe plastic wrap, and let rise at cool room temperature for 1 hour and 45 minutes, or until doubled in bulk. It is important that the dough rise in a cool atmosphere, unrushed, as the eggs and butter add richness that is temperature-sensitive.

To form the bread, remove and discard the sheet of plastic wrap covering the dough. Compress the dough lightly with your fingertips and let stand for 5 minutes. With your fingertips, form an opening in the center of the ball of dough and let the dough stand for 3 minutes longer.

Film the inside of a 10-inch Bundt pan (4½ inches deep, with a capacity of 15 cups) with nonstick flour-and-oil spray or softened unsalted butter.

Transfer the dough to the prepared baking pan, fitting the opening over the center rise of the pan. Using your fingertips, lightly pat the dough into an even layer. Cover the pan loosely with a buttered sheet of food-safe plastic wrap. Let the bread rise at cool room temperature for 1 hour and 30 minutes, or until doubled in bulk. It should rise to ¾ inch under the rim of the pan and crown gently in the middle. Make sure to monitor the dough at this point to achieve the best oven-rise and stability.

Preheat the oven to 375 degrees F in advance of baking.

Remove and discard the sheet of plastic wrap covering the bread.

Bake the bread in the preheated oven for 40 minutes, or until set and a deep golden brown color on top. Place the pan on a cooling rack and let stand for 10 minutes. Invert the bread onto another cooling rack to stand fluted side up. Lift off the pan. Brush the top of the bread with the melted butter and top with sprinklings of sugar. Serve the bread cut into thick slices.

notes
• the bread dough balloons in the oven, as it has great oven-spring
• if you are using vanilla sugar in the butter and sugar finish, consider using India Tree Vanilla Sugar Turbinado Style (available in 7-ounce jars), for this brand has a delicious flavor and beautiful texture
• the bread is baked in a fluted 10-inch Bundt pan (4½ inches deep, with a capacity of 15 cups); a plain, one-piece 10-inch tube pan (4¼ to 4½ inches deep, with a capacity of 18 cups) may be substituted
• use a finely serrated knife to cut the bread

Lush

revved up with oodles of bittersweet chocolate in cake and cookies ✳ once upon a sugar cookie ✳ lovingly perfecting a high-intensity sweet roll ✳ the toffee candy effect ✳ holiday*style*: a delicious tangle of fruit-in-dough makes a courtly bread ✳ a savory something for the cocktail hour

Exuberant

a liberal use of toffee

In the best possible way, the thought of toffee—in bits, pieces, and shards—is completely distracting to my baking mind. When present in batters and doughs, buttercrunch candy has long been a flavoring obsession of mine, satisfied in the cake you have here. Two full cups of chopped-up Heath bars congest the buttery, buttermilk-reinforced batter.

It doesn't need any other flavor enhancement. Have thick slices of the cake with scoops of caramel ice cream, butterscotch sauce, or just plain-in-the-buff.

Besides stirring the toffee into a buttery cake batter, remember to add it to the following mixtures just before turning them into the pan: brownies and blondies profit from delicious pockets of flavor that the pieces create; drop cookie dough (especially brown sugar, oatmeal, or butter-and-sugar cookie dough) is made richer by the candy; and dessert waffles rise to another level entirely with toffee speckling them. If you want to be devilishly exuberant, work a coarsely chopped ¾ cup of the candy into a brioche dough for a very American twist on a French classic—and an unforgettable mixed-baking-culture combination of dough and ingredient.

Quite simply, toffee transports a batter or dough into the realm of a confection. This is one sweet orbit of a cake.

brown sugar toffee cake

Preheat the oven to 350 degrees F.

Film the inside of a 10-inch Bundt pan (4½ inches deep, with a capacity of 15 cups) with nonstick flour-and-oil spray. The preparation of the pan must be thorough or the pieces of chopped toffee that land against the sides and central rise of the pan will stick, making unmolding tricky.

Sift the flour, baking powder, baking soda, and salt onto a sheet of waxed paper.

Toss the toffee with 2 tablespoons of the sifted mixture in a medium-size mixing bowl.

Cream the butter in the large bowl of a freestanding electric mixer on moderate speed for 4 minutes. Add the granulated sugar in 2 additions, beating for 1 minute after each portion is added. Add the dark brown sugar and beat for 1 minute longer. Beat in the eggs, one at a time, mixing for about 20 seconds after each addition to combine. Blend in the vanilla extract. On low speed, alternately add the sifted mixture in 3 additions with the buttermilk in 2 additions, beginning and ending with the sifted mixture. Scrape down the sides of the mixing bowl thoroughly with a rubber spatula after each addition. Stir in the toffee, making sure to fully incorporate the candy.

Spoon the batter into the prepared baking pan. Smooth the top with a rubber spatula.

Bake the cake in the preheated oven for 55 minutes to 1 hour, or until risen, set, and a wooden pick inserted into the cake withdraws clean or with a few moist crumbs attached. The baked cake will begin to pull away from the sides of the baking pan.

Cool the cake in the pan on a rack for 10 minutes. Invert the cake onto another cooling rack. Lift off the pan. Cool completely. Store in an airtight cake keeper. Just before slicing and serving, sift confectioners' sugar over the top of the cake, if you wish.

notes
• Heath bars (Heath Milk Chocolate English Toffee Bar) make the best-tasting candy addition to the cake batter; hand-chop the bars into rough-cut ¼-inch pieces
• use a finely serrated knife to cut the cake, doing so in a slightly exaggerated sawing motion

---

toffee butter batter

3 cups unsifted bleached all-purpose flour

2 teaspoons baking powder

½ teaspoon baking soda

¾ teaspoon salt

2 cups chopped toffee (such as Heath bars)

½ pound (16 tablespoons or 2 sticks) unsalted butter, softened

1 cup granulated sugar

½ cup firmly packed dark brown sugar

4 large eggs

2¾ teaspoons vanilla extract

1 cup buttermilk

confectioners' sugar, for sifting over the baked cake (optional)

serving: one 10-inch cake, creating about 16 slices
ahead: 2 days

formula for excess

Oatmeal cookies that are elegant and beam with bittersweet chocolate chips or chunks and bumps of bittersweet chocolate are at once textural and full of flavor. If oatmeal cookies can be described as supercharged, then a batch made from the recipe on page 420 would measure up to that description.

A bolt of bittersweet chocolate—a highly noticeable twelve ounces—becomes a galvanizing addition to a simplistic butter dough built on the customary baking staples that include a nuance of leavening, all-purpose flour, two types of sugar (granulated and light brown), two egg yolks, and a slurp of vanilla extract. One-quarter teaspoon of salt is the cunning factor in the recipe, for it is the salt that unites the rustically styled oats with the regal chocolate.

A distinguishing characteristic of the recipe is that the formed mounds bake at a lower temperature, comparatively speaking, than do other oatmeal cookie doughs. At 325 degrees F, the cookies set into gentle tenderness and retain a certain amount of moisture, resulting in a sweet that is softly chewy. The baked cookies settle into a relaxed richness on the sheets.

In this cookie, you have your all-inclusive, not-to-be-spared amount of per diem chocolate in a down-to-earth setting of burly, but kindly, rolled oats. Even though I think nuts would get in the way of all this lusciousness, a walnut- or pecan-laden variation also follows, breaking the boundaries with a crunchy texture.

sweet-surplus-of-chocolate cookies

bittersweet chocolate and oatmeal butter dough

⅔ cup plus 1 tablespoon plus 1 teaspoon unsifted bleached all-purpose flour

⅛ teaspoon baking soda

¼ teaspoon salt

11 tablespoons (1 stick plus 3 tablespoons) unsalted butter, softened

¾ cup firmly packed light brown sugar

3 tablespoons granulated sugar

2 large egg yolks

2½ teaspoons vanilla extract

1 cup plus 3 tablespoons "quick-cooking" (not instant) rolled oats

12 ounces bittersweet chocolate chips, bittersweet chocolate chunks, or bittersweet bar chocolate, hand-cut into small chunks (see notes)

⅔ cup firmly packed sweetened flaked coconut

serving: about 21 cookies
ahead: best on baking day; refrigerate cookie dough for 2 days or freeze for 1 month

Preheat the oven to 325 degrees F.

Line two heavy cookie sheets or rimmed sheet pans with lengths of ovenproof parchment paper.

For the dough, sift the flour, baking soda, and salt onto a sheet of waxed paper.

Cream the butter in the large bowl of a freestanding electric mixer on low speed for 3 to 4 minutes. Add the light brown sugar and beat on moderate speed for 1 minute. Add the granulated sugar and beat for 1 minute longer. Add the egg yolks, beating on low speed until just incorporated. Blend in the vanilla extract. On low speed, blend in the sifted ingredients, beating just until the flour particles are absorbed. Scrape down the sides of the mixing bowl frequently with a rubber spatula to keep the dough even-textured. Blend in the rolled oats. Work in the chocolate chips or chunks and coconut.

Place level 3-tablespoon-size mounds of dough onto the prepared baking pans, spacing the mounds about 3 inches apart and arranging 9 mounds on each standard-size sheet. Keep the mounds of dough chunky, with craggy edges.

Bake the cookies in the preheated oven for 16 to 17 minutes, or until just set. The edges of the baked cookies will be a little darker than the centers; the tops will no longer look shiny. Let the cookies stand on the baking pans for 1 minute, then transfer them to cooling racks, using a wide offset metal spatula. Cool completely. Store in an airtight tin.

notes
- in place of the sweetened flaked coconut, nuts can be added to the cookie dough along with the chips or chunks of bittersweet chocolate; use ¾ cup coarsely chopped walnuts or pecans (or 1 cup halves and pieces)
- of the many choices for the chocolate quotient in this cookie dough, consider Ghirardelli 60% cacao Bittersweet Chocolate Baking Chips (available in 11.5-ounce bags) or Scharffen Berger Bittersweet Baking Chunks ("Fine Artisan Dark Chocolate," 70% cacao, available in 6-ounce bags); and for bar chocolate to be hand-cut into chunks, choose from Valrhona Extra Amer Bittersweet 61% cacao, Valrhona Caraïbe Dark Chocolate 66% cacao, El Rey Bucare Bittersweet Chocolate (Carenero Superior) 58.5% cacao, Lindt Chocolate Créé à Berne Swiss Bittersweet Chocolate, Lindt Excellence Swiss Bittersweet Chocolate, or Lindt Excellence 70% Cocoa Extra Fine Dark Chocolate
- when preparing cookie dough for refrigeration or freezing, use organic eggs only
- never consume raw cookie dough

high-volume chocolate

A raging amount of bittersweet chocolate flavors this (wonderfully creamy) one-layer marvel, upended only by butter, whole eggs, egg yolks, and a jot each of cake flour, cocoa powder, superfine sugar, and vanilla extract.

If I am in an expansive mood, I'll add the seed scrapings from a small vanilla bean and forsake the extract in place of the same amount of cognac (this, in an elusively rounded way, builds the chocolate taste), my current favorites being Jules Lormin Cognac X.O. (Grande Champagne Premier Cru de Cognac; Thénac, France) or Navan, a cognac with Madagascar vanilla (Vanille Noire Naturelle de Madagascar Cognacs de France) that hails from the House of Grand Marnier.

The batter, a slightly viscous and ropy mess, bakes into a sublime thickness of chocolate goodness. Don't let this trait deter you, as it is consistent with the type of batter it is. If you try to disguise the cake's original nature, that of a slightly irregular top, you will only confound the dessert—so enjoy it as is, simply with sifted confectioners' sugar rained over the surface or a mixture of confectioners' sugar and cocoa powder, with an undercoating of *chocolate darkness,* with whipped cream, or sincerely and totally plain stark-naked.

The cake is, in one exact word, "sybaritic." Joseph Campbell, the renowned mythologist and author of *The Power of Myth,* coined one of the most persuasive statements ever: "Follow your bliss." For me, this directive would logically and directly lead to this recipe.

a what-you-can-do-with-a-pound-of-good-chocolate cake, chocolate darkness

Preheat the oven to 350 degrees F.

Film the inside of an 8½-inch springform pan (2½ inches deep) with nonstick flour-and-oil spray.

For the batter, sift the superfine sugar, cocoa powder, flour, and salt onto a sheet of waxed paper.

Scrape the warm melted chocolate into a large mixing bowl. Blend in the butter, 2 tablespoons at a time, using a heatproof rubber spatula. At this point, the mixture should look like a creamy chocolate "mayonnaise." Blend in the beaten whole eggs, beaten egg yolks, and vanilla extract. Move quickly when adding the eggs and egg yolks or the mixture may set up too soon. Resift the flour-cocoa powder mixture over the melted chocolate-butter mixture and blend well. In a small mixing bowl, whip the egg whites until soft peaks are formed, add the cream of tartar, and continue whipping until moderately firm peaks are formed. Scrape the whipped whites into the chocolate mixture and stir them in, using light strokes and a flexible spatula. The mixture should be evenly chocolate-colored, without any veins of whipped egg whites swirling through it. The batter will be moderately dense.

Pour and scrape the batter into the prepared baking pan. Gently smooth the top with a rubber spatula.

Place the cake in the preheated oven and immediately reduce the oven temperature to 300 degrees F. Bake the cake for 30 minutes, or until just set around the edges—the center will be softly set. The edges of the baked cake will be firm and stable, with a fudgier center portion—a terrific contrast of textures.

Cool the cake in the pan on a cooling rack for 45 minutes. Open and close the hinge on the side of the pan; at this time, you may notice that the sides are wrinkled here and there, and this is to be expected. On cooling, the cake will pull together and descend about ⅛ inch. Refrigerate the cake for 3 hours. Open the hinge on the side of the pan and remove the outer ring, allowing the cake to stand on its circular metal base. For the topping, and just before serving, whisk the confectioners' sugar and cocoa powder in a small mixing bowl to combine well, then sift the topping over the cake.

(continued on the next page)

buzzing-with-bittersweet chocolate batter

3 tablespoons superfine sugar

2 tablespoons unsweetened alkalized cocoa powder

2 tablespoons unsifted bleached cake flour

⅛ teaspoon salt

1 pound bittersweet chocolate, melted and cooled to warm (see notes)

10 tablespoons (1 stick plus 2 tablespoons) unsalted butter, cut into tablespoon-size chunks, softened

4 large eggs, lightly beaten

2 large egg yolks, lightly beaten

2 teaspoons vanilla extract

2 large egg whites

pinch of cream of tartar

cocoa and confectioners' sugar topping, for sifting over the baked cake

¼ cup confectioners' sugar

1 teaspoon unsweetened alkalized cocoa powder

chocolate darkness (page 424)

serving: one 8½-inch cake, creating 8 slices
ahead: 3 days

Serve the cake, cut into thick slices, using a long, thin knife. Spoon a little of the warm chocolate sauce to the side of each helping, if you wish. Refrigerate any remaining cake in an airtight cake keeper.

notes
• delicious results can be had with these bittersweet chocolates: Scharffen Berger Bittersweet 70% cacao; Michel Cluizel Ilha Toma 65% cacao; Weiss Ebene Bittersweet Chocolate 72% cocoa; Lindt Excellence 70% Cocoa Extra Fine Dark Chocolate; Domori Caranero Superior Cocoa Estate Couverture 75% cocoa; Valrhona Guanaja Dark Bitter Chocolate 70% cacao; Michel Cluizel Chocolat Amer Brut Bitter Chocolate 72% cacao; or Valrhona Caraïbe Dark Chocolate 66% cacao

 chocolate darkness

dark chocolate sauce

4 ounces best-quality unsweetened chocolate, coarsely chopped

1 ounce bittersweet chocolate, coarsely chopped

4 tablespoons (½ stick) unsalted butter, cut into tablespoon-size chunks

¾ cup heavy cream

pinch of salt

2 cups granulated sugar, sieved

1¼ teaspoons vanilla extract

serving: about 2 cups
ahead: 1 week; or freeze for 1 month

Place the unsweetened chocolate and bittersweet chocolate in a medium-size heavy saucepan or casserole (preferably enameled cast iron and about 2 quarts). Set over very low heat to initiate melting the chocolate. When the chocolate is three-fourths melted, add the chunks of butter, the heavy cream, and salt. Add the sugar, pouring it widely in the middle of the pan so as to avoid sloshing it around the sides. Cover the pan and place it over low heat to dissolve the sugar, stirring gently now and again. Uncover, raise the heat to moderate, and bring the contents to a simmer, stirring or whisking all the while. Simmer for 5 minutes, or until lightly thickened. Turn off the heat and, with the pan still on the burner, blend in the vanilla extract. Let the mixture stand in the pan on the heat for 45 seconds longer. The sauce should be smooth and shiny at this point. Remove the pan from the heat.

Strain the sauce through a fine- or medium-mesh sieve into a large heatproof bowl. Use immediately. Or, drape a sheet of food-safe plastic wrap over the bowl, but do not let it touch the sauce. Cool completely. Parcel out the sauce into two individual containers, cover, and refrigerate or freeze until needed.

notes
• high-quality unsweetened chocolate, such as Valrhona, makes the best-tasting and smoothest sauce
• the sauce thickens after a sojourn in the refrigerator or freezer; rewarm slowly in a heavy saucepan and adjust the consistency—as desired—with a few tablespoons of milk or heavy cream
• it is possible to double the recipe with excellent results, as I often do (use a larger pan, about 3½ quarts), for it is a sweet asset to have in the freezer

hundreds of cookies later

My Christmas cookie assortment is never complete without, at the very least, one big tin of sugar cookies—the bake-a-thon that takes place during the month of December requires these buttery, textural wonders.

Christmas aside, the cookies—both kinds—make a regular appearance in my kitchen, filling up jars and tins or stacked in a cascade on a platter or on footed stands. Collectively, both varieties have been baked in the hundreds and, by now, I have lost track of the sheer number of dozens rolled out, hand-formed, baked, cooled, and lifted into storage containers.

Two varieties of cookies are represented by the recipes that follow: *#1 sugar* is exactingly rolled and cut into natural, uncomplicated shapes or fancy shapes (the choice is yours); the other, *#2 sugar,* sandy-textured and mellow, is formed into pillows. The shear of the rolled kind is crunchy-crisp-buttery; the texture of the hand-rolled is "short" and fairly brittle. Both cookies convey a good sense of eggs and magnify butter, so they are sure to please the purist with classic tastes.

#1 sugar

For the dough, sift the flour, baking powder, and salt onto a sheet of waxed paper.

Cream the butter in the large bowl of a freestanding electric mixer on moderately low speed for 4 minutes. Add the granulated sugar in 3 additions, beating on moderate speed for 1 minute after each portion is added. Add the eggs, one at a time, beating on low speed until incorporated, about 45 seconds. Blend in the vanilla extract and heavy cream. On low speed, mix in the sifted ingredients in 3 additions, beating just until the flour particles are absorbed. Scrape down the sides of the mixing bowl frequently with a rubber spatula to keep the dough even-textured.

Divide the dough into 2 portions. Roll each portion of dough between two sheets of waxed paper to a thickness of a scant ¼ inch. Stack the sheets of dough on a cookie sheet and refrigerate overnight.

On baking day, place the sheets of dough in the freezer for 1 hour before stamping out the cookies with a cutter.

Preheat the oven to 375 degrees F.

Line several cookie sheets with lengths of ovenproof parchment paper.

Remove one sheet of dough at a time from the freezer. Carefully peel off both sheets of paper and place the length of rolled-out dough on a lightly floured work surface (or, place the rolled-out dough on a sheet of ovenproof parchment paper). Stamp out cookies with a 4 to 4½-inch cutter. Place the cookies, 3½ inches apart, on the prepared cookie sheets, arranging a maximum of 6 cookies to a pan. Sprinkle the tops with the sparkling sugar or the granulated sugar.

Bake the cookies in the preheated oven for 12 to 13 minutes, or until set, baked through, and light golden in color on the edges. Let the cookies stand on the baking pans for 1 minute, then immediately sprinkle the tops with additional granulated sugar, if you have used the granulated sugar to top the cookies before baking; if you have used sparkling sugar, leave them as is. Transfer the cookies to cooling racks, using a wide offset metal spatula. Cool completely. Store in an airtight tin.

notes
- these are crisp cookies, best formed big and impressive
- when preparing cookie dough for refrigeration or freezing, use organic eggs only
- never consume raw cookie dough

classic butter dough

3 cups unsifted bleached all-purpose flour

½ teaspoon baking powder

¼ teaspoon salt

½ pound (16 tablespoons or 2 sticks) unsalted butter, softened

1½ cups granulated sugar

2 large eggs

1½ teaspoons vanilla extract

2 tablespoons heavy cream

sugar finish

sparkling sugar (plain or a color), for sprinkling on the unbaked cookies

~ or ~

granulated sugar, for sprinkling on the cookies before and after baking

serving: about 14 large cookies
ahead: 5 days

#2 sugar

sandy butter dough

4 cups unsifted bleached all-purpose flour

1 teaspoon baking soda

1 teaspoon cream of tartar

1 teaspoon salt

½ pound (16 tablespoons or 2 sticks)
unsalted butter, softened

1 cup neutral vegetable oil
(such as soybean or canola)

1 cup superfine sugar

1 cup confectioners' sugar

1 large egg

2 large egg yolks

4 teaspoons vanilla extract

seeds from 1 small vanilla bean,
scraped clean

about 2 cups granulated sugar, for
dredging the cookie dough balls
before baking

serving: about 4 dozen cookies
ahead: 5 days

For the dough, sift the flour, baking soda, cream of tartar, and salt onto a sheet of waxed paper.

Cream the butter in the large bowl of a freestanding electric mixer on moderately low speed for 4 minutes. Blend in the oil, beating it in in a thin, steady stream. At this point, the mixture will look somewhat soupy. Add the superfine sugar in 2 additions, beating on moderately low speed for 45 seconds after each portion is added. Add the confectioners' sugar and beat for 1 minute longer. Add the whole egg and beat on low speed until just incorporated, about 30 seconds. Add the egg yolks and beat for 30 seconds longer. Blend in the vanilla extract and vanilla bean seeds. On low speed, mix in the sifted ingredients in 3 additions, beating just until the flour particles are absorbed. Scrape down the sides of the mixing bowl frequently to keep the dough even-textured. The mixture will be quite soft and sticky at this point—which is natural for this type of dough.

Refrigerate the dough, covered with a sheet of food-safe plastic wrap, for 3 hours, or until firm enough to handle (or overnight, if you wish).

Preheat the oven to 375 degrees F in advance of baking.

Line several cookie sheets or rimmed sheet pans with lengths of ovenproof parchment paper.

Place the granulated sugar in a wide, shallow bowl.

Scoop up heaping 2-tablespoon-size mounds of dough and roll into balls. Roll each ball in the granulated sugar, and place on the prepared baking pans, spacing them about 3 inches apart, and arranging 9 cookies to a pan. Gently flatten the cookies in a crisscross or one-way striated (corrugated) style with the tines of a table fork; if you are using the striated look, corrugate the cookies decisively to give the baked surfaces an interesting texture.

Bake the cookies in the preheated oven for 13 to 15 minutes, or until set and light golden. Let the cookies stand on the baking pans for 1 minute, then transfer them to cooling racks, using a wide offset metal spatula. Cool completely. Store in an airtight tin.

notes
• for a lovely hint of citrus, omit the vanilla bean seeds, reduce the vanilla extract to 2 teaspoons, and add 1 teaspoon each of orange extract and lemon extract
• when preparing cookie dough for refrigeration or freezing, use organic eggs only
• never consume raw cookie dough

rolled and folded

Of all the doughs in the cosmos of pastry and bread baking, not one of them gives me more pleasure to put together than those that come under the category of "laminated."

By definition, "lamination" refers to the method by which a block of butter is rolled and folded into a primary (or base) dough, leavened with yeast or lacking any leavening agent, creating such specialties as puff pastry, Danish pastry, or croissants; as well, a richer variation of brioche dough can be established by using this technique, adding multiple striations of butter to this eggy dough. (*Webster*'s defines "to laminate" as "to cause to separate into thin plates or layers; to divide into thin plates.") Of the four kinds of dough mentioned that will readily accept the layering of butter, creating thin, multiple layers, two contain whole eggs and/ or egg yolks (variations of Danish and brioche), and eggs in any form are absent from the third and fourth varieties (croissant and puff pastry), though maverick pastry chefs are always in the process of rearranging the boundaries. The resulting baked texture is a crisp (nearly brittle), shattering exterior, because the surface areas exposed to the oven heat create a firm flakiness. As the butter melts between the layers of dough, steam is discharged and expands the layers; the interiors, by contrast, become richly moist. The way that the ingredients are handled and the layering method establish the texture of the resulting bread or pastry.

Let me introduce you to a version of Danish pastry that has been tweaked in my kitchen for two decades: an enriched, lightly sweetened buttermilk dough is mixed, left to rise for 45 minutes, then refrigerated for 45 minutes. Cool, slightly pliable butter is lightly pounded with some flour, formed into a cake, and refrigerated for 30 minutes. The butter, which should be as close as possible to the temperature of the chilled dough at this point, is enclosed in the rolled-out dough, then the package is rolled out and folded into thirds. Between rollings and foldings (there are three more), the dough is refrigerated for 35 minutes at each juncture; this rest firms up the butter and relaxes the dough so that it is easy to roll and does not fight back on subsequent go-arounds. When all is said and done, the dough is refrigerated for 2 hours (or overnight) to prepare for rolling and shaping. Though the sweet rolls can be formed after that 2-hour refrigerator rest, the best flavor and texture are created when the dough develops during an overnight chill. This admirable dough is rolled out once again; its surface is spread with butter and topped with granulated sugar before it is treated to another fold-and-roll to enclose the sugar. Then—and finally—the dough is ready for cutting and configuring into individual shapes.

Pockets of dough can receive a range of wonderful fillings, of course, but to really appreciate its flavor and buttery complexity, I tend to do very simple pastries, like these *sugar love knots*. That easy combination of butter and sugar becomes the filling for the knots. On baking, the outer surfaces turn into a crunchy, flaky crust—a real delight.

The reason for having these around is elementary: love knots make dazzling breakfast or brunch pastries. But who wouldn't love a glistening one midafternoon, when accompanied by good strong coffee?

For the dough, stir together the yeast, the ¼ teaspoon sugar, and the warm water in a heatproof measuring cup. Allow the mixture to stand until swollen, 6 to 7 minutes.

Place the buttermilk and the 5 tablespoons sugar in a small saucepan and set over low heat. When the mixture is warm (the buttermilk may look slightly separated at this point), after about 4 minutes, remove the saucepan from the heat and pour and scrape the mixture into a medium-size heatproof mixing bowl (the sugar will not have dissolved completely). Cool to tepid. Whisk in the vanilla extract, egg yolks, baking soda, and yeast mixture.

Whisk the flour and salt together in a large mixing bowl. Add the buttermilk-yeast mixture and mix, using a wooden spoon or flat wooden paddle, until it comes together into a rough dough; patchy flour segments will remain. Turn the dough out onto a work surface, along with any unincorporated flour, and knead lightly for 1 minute; the dough will be sticky, but persevere, using a pastry scraper to move it along. Sprinkle on the additional 2 tablespoons flour and knead for 5 minutes. The dough will be soft.

Turn the dough into a bowl heavily coated with softened unsalted butter, lightly turn to coat all sides in a film of butter, make several cuts in the dough with a pair of kitchen scissors, cover tightly with a sheet of food-safe plastic wrap, and let rise at room temperature for 45 minutes. The dough will have expanded by about one-third its original size at this point.

Remove and discard the sheet of plastic wrap covering the dough. Lightly compress the dough, turn onto a lightly buttered sheet of plastic wrap, wrap tightly, and refrigerate for 45 minutes.

In the meantime, make the butter fold-in. Place a large sheet of ovenproof parchment paper on a stable work surface. Line up the 3 sticks of butter right next to one another (touching) in the middle of the paper. Sprinkle half (1½ tablespoons) of the flour on top of the butter and beat it in with a rolling pin. When most of the flour has been absorbed, scrape up the mass of butter, turn it over, sprinkle on the remaining 1½ tablespoons flour, and beat it in with the rolling pin. The butter will take in the flour. Shape the butter into a smooth block of even thickness measuring 5½ by 7 inches; make sure that the top and sides are smooth. Enclose the butter in the parchment paper and refrigerate for 30 minutes.

(continued on the next page)

buttermilk yeast dough

4½ teaspoons active dry yeast

¼ teaspoon granulated sugar

¼ cup warm (105 to 110 degrees F) water

⅔ cup plus 2 tablespoons buttermilk

5 tablespoons granulated sugar

2 teaspoons vanilla extract

3 large egg yolks

¼ teaspoon baking soda

3⅓ cups unsifted bleached all-purpose flour, plus an additional 2 tablespoons, for kneading

½ teaspoon salt

butter fold-in

¾ pound (3 sticks) cool unsalted butter

3 tablespoons unsifted bleached all-purpose flour

butter and sugar filling

4 tablespoons (½ stick) unsalted butter, softened

¾ cup granulated sugar

serving: 1 dozen large and luxurious sweet rolls

ahead: best on baking day; or freeze for 3 weeks, defrost, bundle in aluminum foil, and reheat in a preheated 325 degrees F oven for 10 minutes

To enclose the butter block in the dough, remove the dough from the refrigerator. It will have risen into a lightly puffy pillow. On a lightly floured work surface and with a lightly floured rolling pin, roll out the dough to a sheet measuring 13 by 13 inches. Take the butter block from the refrigerator, remove and discard the paper, and place it in the center of the rolled-out dough. Fold the top and bottom edges onto the butter block, then fold over the left and right sides of the dough onto the butter block. Press down the folds with your fingertips to seal the butter in the surrounding dough. Turn over the dough-wrapped butter block. Gently roll out the dough to a sheet measuring 10 by 17 inches. Fold the dough package into thirds, as you would a business letter: the bottom third up to the middle third and the top third over the middle. Press down the edges with your fingertips. In addition, seal the dough by gently bearing down on the surface in three or four evenly spaced places with the rolling pin, avoiding the short edges where you can see the folds. This rolling and folding constitutes one full roll-and-fold.

Refrigerate the dough, wrapped in waxed paper, for 35 minutes. When wrapping the dough, make sure that all sides are sheltered by the paper. Protecting the dough in this fashion prevents the edges from becoming crusty and, later on, the butter layer from breaking through the dough. This is a small, but important, technique to remember when preparing the rolled-out dough and butter block for refrigeration, and is especially helpful to remember when producing any other kind of laminated dough.

Repeat the rolling, folding, and refrigerating 3 additional times. (It may be necessary to use a fresh sheet of waxed paper after two rounds of rolling-and-folding.) After the last roll-and-fold, enclose the dough in a sheet of lightly oiled food-safe plastic wrap, place in a jumbo self-sealing food-safe freezer-weight plastic bag, and seal. Refrigerate the dough for 2 hours. The dough will be puffed and cushion-like. At this point, the dough can be formed into sweet rolls, or refrigerated overnight (or up to 24 hours). If you are refrigerating the dough overnight, it must be compressed lightly twice, once after a total of 3 hours (the initial refrigeration time of 2 hours plus another 1 hour) and again 2 hours later. The next day, the dough will have expanded to a puffy pillow—this is an active dough—despite the compressions.

Film the inside of 12 jumbo muffin/cupcake cups (6 cups to a pan, each cup measuring 4 inches in diameter and 1¾ inches deep, with a capacity of 1⅛ cups) with nonstick flour-and-oil spray.

For the filling, have the softened butter and sugar at hand on the work surface.

To form the pastry knots, remove the dough from the refrigerator. Remove and discard the wrappings. Using a lightly floured rolling pin, roll out the dough on a lightly floured work surface to a sheet measuring 13 by 17 inches. Using the filling ingredients, spread the butter on the surface and sprinkle evenly with the sugar. Fold the dough in half, bringing up the 17-inch side, and give it 2 or 3 firm presses with a rolling pin to seal. Dust off any extra flour. Carefully roll the dough to increase the depth to 10 inches. Cut the dough into 12 even-size strips. Picking up 1 strip at a time, twirl the strip into a corkscrew, form into a knot, and place it in a prepared muffin cup. Sprinkle the tops of the knots with any sugar that has fallen out of the pastries as you are twisting them (this is inevitable).

Cover each pan of sweet rolls loosely with a sheet of food-safe plastic wrap. Let the sweet rolls rise until swollen and puffy, about 1 hour and 45 minutes. The risen knots will look puffy, but not completely doubled in bulk. If the formed sweet rolls are over-risen, they will have a tendency to disconnect, breaking out of their twisty figures, and bake out of shape.

Preheat the oven to 375 degrees F in advance of baking.

Remove and discard the sheets of plastic wrap covering the knots.

Bake the sweet rolls in the preheated oven for 30 minutes, or until set and a golden color on top. Place the baking pans on cooling racks and let stand for 15 minutes. Carefully nudge out the sweet rolls from the baking pans, then stand them right side up on the cooling racks. Serve the knots warm or at room temperature.

notes
- an equal amount of whole milk (²⁄₃ cup plus 2 tablespoons) may be used in place of the buttermilk for a less-complex-tasting sweet roll; if you are using whole milk, omit the baking soda from the ingredient list
- use the freshest, highest-quality unsalted butter available; luscious pastries evolve from the use of Lurpak Danish Butter Unsalted, Plugrá European Style Unsalted Butter, and Kate's Homemade Butter Unsalted
- use a neutral vegetable oil, such as canola, to coat the sheets of food-safe plastic wrap before enclosing the dough; lightly oiling the plastic wrap that comes in contact with the dough allows it to be freely removed after refrigeration without any dough adhering in patches to the wrapping
- instead of filming the cups with nonstick flour-and-oil spray, the muffin/cupcake cups may be lined with jumbo ovenproof paper baking cup liners
- use a rounded palette knife to nudge out each sweet roll from the inside of its muffin/cupcake cup

stand tall

A plate of towering slices of panettone, accented with fruit, in all their full-length glory is a *particular* joy of the holiday baking kitchen—though I doubt anyone would turn down a slice in, say, April or May.

In the double sense of the word "particular," I mean it as "special" *and* "choosy." "Choosy" because I am really interested in enclosing in a dough only the dried fruits that appeal to me. In this, my-way-with-panettone, an eye-catching pastiche of dark Monukka raisins, dried cherries, dried cranberries, dried apricots, and crystallized ginger, becomes the chosen mosaic, but certainly others will do, and do very well. Notably, for this recipe, think about using glazed Australian apricots, golden raisins, or diced dried papayas, mangoes, or dates. The congenial, firm but moist, and lightly sweetened bread houses enough butter, whole eggs, and egg yolks to enrich it all. And as it is rather rich, the dough would invite chunks of bittersweet chocolate or bittersweet chocolate chips to be kneaded into it instead of the mix of dried fruits.

Serve one of the breads, as I do, freshly baked, the top glistening with a painting of warm ginger preserves. Or liberally top the bread with confectioners' sugar, slice it thickly, and have softened salted butter and a contrasting jam, such as apricot (or drizzles of honey), nearby. You can also, quite purposely, allow the second—and deliberately plain—bread to stale, cut it up, dip it in eggs whisked with a pour of cream (light or heavy) and a swig of vanilla extract, sauté it in butter until golden on each side, and serve it at breakfast or brunch as a kind of transcultural French toast. This will indulge everyone at the table for sure.

fruit bread, ginger preserve glaze

fruity dough

½ cup dark seedless raisins
(preferably Monukkas)

½ cup tart (Montmorency) dried cherries

½ cup dried sweetened cranberries

½ cup diced crystallized ginger

½ cup diced dried apricots (preferably
the Blenheim variety)

3 tablespoons dark rum

4¼ teaspoons active dry yeast

¼ teaspoon granulated sugar

⅓ cup warm (105 to 110 degrees F) water

½ cup milk

12 tablespoons (1½ sticks) unsalted butter,
cut into chunks

⅓ cup plus 2 tablespoons granulated
sugar

3 large eggs

2 large egg yolks

2 tablespoons vanilla extract

1 tablespoon mild honey (such as clover)

3¼ cups unsifted bleached
all-purpose flour

2 cups unsifted unbleached
all-purpose flour

1 teaspoon salt

(continued on the next page)

For the rum-marinated fruits, toss the raisins, cherries, cranberries, crystallized ginger, and apricots in a medium-size nonreactive bowl. Sprinkle over the rum, toss well, cover loosely with a sheet of food-safe plastic wrap, and let stand until needed (the fruit will be incorporated once the dough completes its first rise).

For the dough, stir together the yeast, the ¼ teaspoon sugar, and the water in a heatproof measuring cup. Allow the mixture to stand until swollen, 6 to 7 minutes.

Place the milk, the chunks of butter, and the ⅓ cup plus 2 tablespoons granulated sugar in a small saucepan and set over low heat to melt the butter (the sugar does not need to dissolve entirely). Remove from the heat, pour into a medium-size heatproof mixing bowl, and cool to tepid. Whisk in the whole eggs, egg yolks, vanilla extract, and honey. Blend in the yeast mixture.

Combine 3 cups of the bleached flour, the unbleached flour, and salt in a large mixing bowl. Pour over the eggy yeast mixture and mix to create a moist and shaggy dough, using a wooden spoon. Work in 2 tablespoons of the remaining ¼ cup bleached flour. Knead the dough on a work surface dusted with the remaining 2 tablespoons bleached flour for 7 to 8 minutes, or until quite smooth and satiny. The dough will be resilient, but moderately firm.

Scrape the dough into a bowl heavily coated with softened unsalted butter, lightly turn to coat all sides in a film of butter, cover tightly with a sheet of food-safe plastic wrap, and let rise at cool room temperature for 2 hours to 2 hours and 30 minutes, or until doubled in bulk. Remove and discard the plastic wrap.

Scatter the rum-marinated fruits over the surface of the dough. Fold the dough over itself 10 times. Knead the dough gently in the bowl to incorporate the fruits. This will take about 5 minutes; at first, the fruits will resist integration into the dough, but soldier on! Cover the bowl with the sheet of food-safe plastic wrap and let stand for 10 minutes.

Film the inside of two fluted panettone molds (each mold measuring 6 inches in diameter and 5½ inches deep, with a capacity of about 8 cups) with nonstick flour-and-oil spray.

Remove and discard the sheet of plastic wrap covering the dough. Cut the dough in half. Form each piece into a rounded plump ball, compressing the dough ball lightly to form a small pinched seam at the bottom. Place each dough ball seam side down in a prepared baking pan. Cover the top of each pan loosely with a buttered sheet of food-safe plastic wrap. Let the sweet breads rise at cool room temperature for 2 hours to 2 hours and 20 minutes, or until the dough rises in the center of each in a softly rounded crown (like a mound) that creeps up ½ to ¾ inch above each pan's edge. However, the edges of each should rise only just short of ⅓ inch under the rim of the pan. The formed dough should at least double in bulk.

Preheat the oven to 350 degrees F in advance of baking.

Remove and discard the sheet of plastic wrap covering each sweet bread.

Bake the sweet breads in the preheated oven for 45 minutes, or until set and deeply golden brown on top. If, after 30 minutes, the breads already look beautifully browned, lightly cover the top of each bread (avoid folding down the sides) with a tent of aluminum foil. Cool the breads in the pans on cooling racks for 15 minutes. Carefully unmold the breads, lifting off each pan, and set them right side up on cooling racks. Cool for 20 minutes.

For the glaze (if you are using it), combine the ginger preserves and water in a small heavy saucepan (preferably enameled cast iron), and bring to a gentle simmer. Remove the saucepan from the heat and stir in the vanilla extract. Paint the top of the sweet breads with a veneer of the hot preserves mixture, using a sturdy pastry brush. Cool completely. If you are not using the glaze, sift confectioners' sugar over the top of the breads just before slicing and serving. Store in an airtight container.

notes
• confectioners' sugar, lavishly sifted over the top of each bread, makes a quick and fine finish for the sweet breads, to use in place of the ginger preserve glaze—no apologies here
• a favorite, and lovely, ginger preserve, Dundee Ginger Preserve, is made by James Keiller & Son and is available in 1-pound jars
• use a finely serrated knife to cut the bread, using a slightly exaggerated sawing motion

ginger preserve glaze

⅔ cup best-quality ginger preserves

1 tablespoon water

¼ teaspoon vanilla extract

~ or ~

confectioners' sugar,
for sifting over the baked bread

serving: two 8½ to 9 inches tall sweet breads, creating 8 slices each
ahead: 2 days

a savory nibble

On its own or with a glass of wine, this briochelike bread that snags two kinds of cheese and diced salami (or pepperoni) in its tantalizing web is a particularly good change from a more formal offering of dainty cocktail bites.

Instead of serving little manicured tidbits made from oddly combined ingredients, I am encouraging you to go rustic, and to bake something bold and friendly. The mission of this dough is to catch the savory elements of cheese and spicy meat (the other additions you'll think of beyond my ingredient list will be numerous and varied, I'm sure) in a richly textured bread. Bake it in a fluted form, then cut it into wedges or pull it into shaggy pieces. The form—a fluted tart pan that is two inches deep—limits and frames the enriched bread dough as it bakes. The dough takes

off into soft and puffy directions, its surface swaying from lower points to higher points, with dots of cheese and meat hitched to it in random places during the initial oven-spring, becoming an unstudied surface. Once you understand how the dough behaves, the playfulness can begin: experiment with different types of cured meats, other types of cheese, fresh leafy herbs added with a light hand, and so on. This recipe is a formula that will enlarge your repertoire while delighting guests who arrive on your doorstep with those familiar, well-timed appetites.

appetizer bread

savory yeast dough

2½ teaspoons active dry yeast

¼ teaspoon granulated sugar

¼ cup warm (105 to 110 degrees F) water

2¼ cups plus 2 tablespoons unsifted bleached all-purpose flour

1 teaspoon sweet or hot paprika (optional)

¼ teaspoon salt

¼ teaspoon coarsely ground black pepper

3 large eggs

8 tablespoons (1 stick) unsalted butter, cut into tablespoon-size chunks, softened

1 cup diced Provolone cheese

⅔ cup diced salami or pepperoni

⅓ cup freshly grated Pecorino Romano cheese

glaze and salt topping (optional)

1 large egg, lightly beaten

¼ teaspoon flaky sea salt (such as Maldon)

oil and cheese finish

2 tablespoons good fruity olive oil

3 to 4 tablespoons freshly grated Parmigiano-Reggiano cheese

serving: one 10-inch bread, creating about 10 slices
ahead: best on baking day

For the dough, stir together the yeast, sugar, and warm water in a heatproof measuring cup. Allow the mixture to stand until swollen, 6 to 7 minutes.

Whisk 2¼ cups of the flour, the paprika (if you are using it), salt, and pepper in a large mixing bowl. In a medium-size mixing bowl, whisk the eggs, then blend in the butter and the yeast mixture. Pour and scrape the egg-butter-yeast mixture onto the flour mixture. Stir the mixture, using a wooden spoon or flat wooden paddle, until a rough, but moist dough is formed. Place the dough in the bowl of a heavy-duty freestanding electric mixer. Set the bowl in place and attach the dough hook. Mix on moderately low speed until the dough is combined and smooth, about 2 minutes. Add the remaining 2 tablespoons flour and beat on moderately low speed for 5 minutes. The dough will be smooth, springy, and slightly sticky; it will film the sides of the bowl, in addition to adhering to the bottom of the bowl.

Scrape the dough into a bowl heavily coated with softened unsalted butter, lightly turn to coat all sides in a film of butter, make several cuts in the dough with a pair of kitchen scissors, cover tightly with a sheet of food-safe plastic wrap, and let rise at cool room temperature for 1 hour and 30 minutes, or until doubled in bulk. Remove the sheet of plastic wrap.

Sprinkle over the Provolone, salami or pepperoni, and Pecorino Romano. Lightly press the savory additions into the dough. Turn the dough out onto a work surface and knead in the cheeses and salami (this will take about 2 minutes); inevitably, some pieces will surface here and there, but the majority will be integrated into the dough. Let the dough stand, uncovered, for 5 minutes.

Film a fluted 10-inch false-bottomed tart pan (2 inches deep) with softened unsalted butter. Place the dough in the center and lightly press it into the pan in an even layer. Cover loosely with a sheet of food-safe plastic wrap. Let rise at cool room temperature for 1 hour and 45 minutes to 2 hours, or until puffy and doubled in bulk (the edges will rise to about ¼ inch below the top of the pan). In cold weather, the rising time could take as long as 2 hours and 30 minutes, and in warmer, humid weather, as little as 1 hour and 30 minutes; the point is to avoid rushing the second rise. The bread will rise in puffy sections because the additions of cheese and salami or pepperoni will irregularly punctuate the dough here and there—charming (and to be expected).

Preheat the oven to 375 degrees F in advance of baking.

Remove and discard the sheet of plastic wrap covering the bread.

For the glaze and salt topping (if you are using it), sweep the beaten egg over the top of the bread, using a soft pastry brush (only a small amount of the beaten egg will be needed). Sprinkle the flaky sea salt on top of the bread.

Bake the bread in the preheated oven for 35 to 40 minutes, or until a light golden color on top, if the bread is unglazed, or until a medium golden color on top, if the bread is glazed with the beaten egg, and set. The bread must be baked through for the crumb's texture to develop. Cool the bread in the pan on a cooling rack for 5 minutes. Lightly brush the top of the bread with the olive oil and sprinkle the top with the Parmigiano-Reggiano. Let the bread stand for 5 minutes. Gently and carefully lift the bread by the bottom, pushing it up and out to unmold. Cool the bread on its metal base on the rack for 20 minutes before carefully lifting the bread from its base to a work surface for slicing. The interior of the bread will be dotted—here and there— with the pockets of cheese and salami or pepperoni—lovely. Refrigerate any bread not enjoyed within 2 hours on baking day.

notes
• the glaze adds a certain luster to the top of the baked bread and the bread bakes a shade more golden in color than if baked without it; however, the dough, which is rich and delicate, should not be encouraged to color any deeper than a medium golden color
• on baking, the bread's oven-spring at the beginning of the bake session is impressive
• the bread is baked in a fluted 10-inch false-bottomed tart pan (2 inches deep); a round 10-inch layer cake pan (2 inches deep) may be substituted for the tart pan (butter the pan, line the bottom with a round of ovenproof parchment paper, and butter the paper); once the bread has cooled in the pan for 10 minutes, invert it onto another cooling rack, peel off the parchment paper if it has adhered to the bread, invert again to stand right side up, then brush the top with olive oil and sprinkle with Parmigiano-Reggiano

Down

cinnamon buns go way back in time and are fast-forwarded to the present ✳ bring back the biscuit in every delightful way ✳ the lure of gingerbread ✳ streusel crumbles deliciously ✳ chocolate chip cookie alert ✳ a sweet vanilla turn on a soft pretzel ✳ bread baking for friends ✳ baking rolls as the groundwork for a custom

Home

nothing fancy

The following image of my paternal grandmother comes to mind every time I make *the cinnamon-raisin buns of my childhood, #1*: seeing her stuff a bunch of paper napkin–swathed rum buns into her purse, purloined from the Sunday-dinner breadbasket of a neighborhood restaurant, scanning the scene to make sure that no one in charge knew what was going on.

That was decades ago, long before the "formal" doggie bag was created for a diner to take home whatever leftovers from a meal were desired. She never actually asked for the buns "to-go," but simply expected someone to replace those that we ate along with our fried chicken or seafood dinner, so she could subsequently pilfer as many of them as she could fit into her fairly large pocketbook. My mother and I always thought that she chose a specific purse based on the restaurant selected—the place with the warm, soft rum buns usually got a mini luggage-size version brought along as the efficient delivery-to-home system. It was effective, for this purse was nearly big enough to qualify as an overnight bag. As the rolls were transferred, we looked the other way (and likewise hoped everyone else did) and rolled our eyes, a conceding gesture that meant, "That's just Grandma."

The pull and tug of nostalgia has prompted the development of these two head-on basic cinnamon-raisin bun recipes: the *buttermilk yeast dough* makes a resplendent sweet roll, as does the *ring of golden yeast dough*. I date the development of each formula back to the time when, about twenty-five years ago, I began to search for culinary connections that would somehow keep the memory of those who departed close by my side, if only to be linked through recipes. The #1 buns are cushy, reasonably plain, and far and away less complex than the madly delicious *rich, richer, richest sticky buns* (page 231). A small change in the icing, that of replacing some of the half-and-half with a little light or dark rum and marinating the raisins in 2 tablespoons of light or dark rum while the yeast dough is rising, will closely approximate the buns of my childhood, the very ones that, so fresh and plush, usually sag under their own weight when stacked. *The cinnamon-raisin buns of my childhood, #2* are set into a ring mold, each right up against the next, and rise to form a circle of pull-apart rolls. This version would have been difficult for Grandma to put in her purse, but charms nonetheless.

The two recipes are, in their own singular ways, home-style, nothing fancy, and to-the-moon wonderful.

For the dough, stir together the yeast, the ½ teaspoon granulated sugar, and the warm water in a heatproof measuring cup. Allow the mixture to stand until swollen, 6 to 7 minutes.

In the meantime, place the buttermilk and the ½ cup granulated sugar in a small saucepan, set over low heat, and warm until the sugar just begins to dissolve. The buttermilk is likely to separate slightly, and this is fine. Remove from the heat, whisk well, scrape into a medium-size heatproof mixing bowl, and let stand for 5 to 6 minutes to cool to tepid. Whisk in the vanilla extract and eggs. Blend in the yeast mixture.

Whisk 3 cups of the unbleached flour, the bleached flour, and the salt in the bowl of a heavy-duty electric mixer. Add the yeast-egg-buttermilk mixture and stir to mix; the dough will be rough and shaggy and not come together entirely at this point. Set the bowl in place and attach the dough hook. Beat the dough on low speed until smooth (it will be sticky), about 3 minutes. From the remaining 1¼ cups unbleached flour, add ¼ cup flour and beat for 1 minute. Add the butter, 1 tablespoon at a time, beating on low speed to blend; after all of the butter has been incorporated, the dough will look silky, shiny, and moist, and still be sticky/pull-y. Add the remaining 1 cup unbleached flour, ¼ cup at a time, beating for 1 minute on low speed after each portion is added. Increase the speed to moderately low and beat the dough for 3 minutes. During the entire mixing process, stop the machine from time to time to scrape down the sides of the mixing bowl and the dough hook. After the final beating, the dough will clean the sides of the mixing bowl.

Scrape the dough into a bowl heavily coated with softened unsalted butter, lightly turn to coat all sides in a film of butter, make several cuts in the dough with a pair of kitchen scissors, cover tightly with a sheet of food-safe plastic wrap, and let rise at room temperature for 2 hours, or until doubled in bulk.

Remove and discard the plastic wrap. Lightly compress the dough with your fingertips or a rubber spatula, and let stand for 10 minutes. Sprinkle the raisins on the dough and fold the dough over on itself about 8 turns. Knead the dough in the bowl until the raisins are integrated.

Film the inside of a 12 by 8 by 3-inch baking pan with softened unsalted butter.

(continued on the next page)

buttermilk yeast dough

4½ teaspoons active dry yeast

½ teaspoon granulated sugar

½ cup warm (105 to 110 degrees F) water

½ cup buttermilk

½ cup granulated sugar

2 teaspoons vanilla extract

3 large eggs

4¼ cups unsifted unbleached all-purpose flour

1 cup unsifted bleached all-purpose flour

1 teaspoon salt

8 tablespoons (1 stick) unsalted butter, cut into tablespoon-size chunks, softened

1 cup dark seedless raisins

butter and cinnamon sugar filling

5 tablespoons unsalted butter, softened

⅔ cup superfine sugar blended with 2 tablespoons ground cinnamon

a simple sweet roll icing (page 448)

serving: 15 sweet buns
ahead: best on baking day; or freeze for 3 weeks, defrost, bundle in aluminum foil, and reheat in a preheated 325 degrees F oven for 10 minutes, then ice

To form the buns, roll out the dough on a lightly floured work surface to a sheet measuring 15 by 15 inches. Using the filling ingredients, spread the softened butter on the surface of the rolled-out dough and sprinkle over the cinnamon sugar. Fold over about ½ inch of each side and pinch to seal. Roll the dough into a tight, thick jellyroll. Seal the long seam end by pinching it lightly between your thumb and forefinger. Gently roll-and-pull the roll lengthwise to elongate it to a length of 15 inches if it has contracted slightly during the rolling process. Cut the roll into 15 even-size slices, using a sharp chef's knife. Let the slices stand for 10 minutes, then plump them into rounded mounds, making sure that the outer circle of dough is pinched taut: this step will allow the risen mounds to bake evenly. Place the spirals of dough in the prepared baking pan, assembling them in three rows of 5 each.

Cover the pan of buns loosely with a buttered sheet of food-safe plastic wrap. Let the buns rise at cool room temperature for 2 hours, or until doubled in bulk and beautifully swollen.

Preheat the oven to 375 degrees F in advance of baking.

Remove and discard the sheet of plastic wrap covering the buns.

Bake the buns in the preheated oven for 30 to 35 minutes, or until set and a golden color on top. The buns will be lofty.

Place the pan on a cooling rack and let stand for 5 minutes. Spoon and sweep the icing over the surface of the warm buns, spreading it carefully as it melts down. As soon as the icing sets (about 1 hour, more or less, depending on the temperature of your kitchen), you can detach the buns from one another and lift them out of the pan, using an offset spatula, for serving.

notes
- to complement the scent of cinnamon in the filling, I sometimes add 1 teaspoon freshly grated nutmeg to the flour mixture
- for a rummy scent to the sweet, toss the dark raisins in 2 tablespoons light or dark rum and let stand for 2 hours, uncovered, at room temperature while the dough is undergoing its first rise
- when assembling the spirals of dough in the pan, make sure that the edges of each sits up level against the neighboring ones; this will encourage an even rise and prevent a section of one bun from creeping under the side of another (and baking unevenly)
- the buns are arranged and baked in a 12 by 8 by 3-inch baking pan; a 13 by 9 by 2-inch baking pan may be substituted, creating smaller buns and a larger yield (elongate the roll to 20 inches in length, cut into 20 slices, form into tight and plump spirals, and assemble four rows of 5 buns each), reducing the baking time by about 5 minutes

the cinnamon-raisin buns of my childhood, #2

For the dough, stir together the yeast, the ¼ teaspoon granulated sugar, and the warm water in a heatproof measuring cup. Allow the mixture to stand until swollen, 6 to 7 minutes.

In the meantime, place the buttermilk and the ⅓ cup granulated sugar in a small saucepan, set over low heat, and warm until the sugar just begins to dissolve. The buttermilk is likely to separate slightly, and this is fine. Remove from the heat, whisk well, scrape into a medium-size heatproof mixing bowl, and let stand for 5 to 6 minutes to cool to tepid. Whisk in the vanilla extract, whole eggs, egg yolks, and chunks of butter (the butter will stay in pieces at this time, but will be absorbed in a moment when the mixture, with the yeast blend, is introduced and mixed into the flour). Blend in the yeast mixture. Whisk the flour and salt in a large mixing bowl. Add the yeast-egg-buttermilk mixture and stir to mix; the dough will be shaggy and in big, scraggly pieces at this point. Dump out the dough mixture onto a work surface and, with your hands, combine to create a dough. Knead the dough for 6 minutes. At this point, the dough should be smooth and resilient.

Scrape the dough into a bowl heavily coated with softened unsalted butter, lightly turn to coat all sides in a film of butter, make several cuts in the dough with a pair of kitchen scissors, cover tightly with a sheet of food-safe plastic wrap, and let rise at cool room temperature for 1 hour and 30 minutes to 2 hours, or until doubled in bulk.

Remove and discard the plastic wrap. Lightly compress the dough with your fingertips or a rubber spatula. Lightly oil a large sheet of food-safe plastic wrap and wrap up the dough in it. Refrigerate the dough overnight, compressing it lightly after 2 hours.

Film the inside of a 10-inch ring mold (measuring 3 inches deep, with a capacity of 12 cups) with softened unsalted butter.

To form the sweet bun ring, remove the dough from the refrigerator. Remove and discard the plastic wrap. Roll out the dough on a lightly floured work surface to a sheet measuring 16 by 15 inches. Using the filling ingredients, spread the softened butter on the surface of the rolled-out dough and dot with the raisins. Sprinkle over the cinnamon sugar. Fold over about ½ inch of each side and pinch to seal. Roll the dough into a tight, thick jellyroll. Seal the long

(continued on the next page)

ring of golden yeast dough

2½ teaspoons active dry yeast

¼ teaspoon granulated sugar

¼ cup warm (105 to 110 degrees F) water

¾ cup buttermilk

⅓ cup granulated sugar

2 teaspoons vanilla extract

2 large eggs

2 large egg yolks

8 tablespoons (1 stick) unsalted butter, cut into tablespoon-size chunks, softened

4 cups unsifted bleached all-purpose flour

¾ teaspoon salt

butter, raisin, and cinnamon sugar filling

8 tablespoons (1 stick) unsalted butter, softened

¾ cup dark seedless raisins

1 cup superfine sugar blended with 3 tablespoons ground cinnamon

a simple sweet roll icing (page 448)

serving: one ring of interconnected sweet buns, creating 12 pull-apart buns
ahead: best on baking day

seam end by pinching it lightly between your thumb and forefinger. Gently roll-and-pull the roll lengthwise to elongate it to 18 inches. Cut the roll into 12 even-size slices, using a sharp chef's knife. Place the sliced spirals side by side, with one side of the spiral facing up, in the prepared baking pan, making them fit snugly without overlapping the slices. You should see the circles of dough and filling, even if they fit tightly in the pan.

Cover the pan of buns loosely with a buttered sheet of food-safe plastic wrap. Let the buns rise at cool room temperature for 2 hours, or until almost doubled in bulk (see page 6 to reference this stage).

Preheat the oven to 375 degrees F in advance of baking.

Remove and discard the sheet of plastic wrap covering the buns.

Bake the buns in the preheated oven for 35 minutes, or until set. The fully baked ring of buns will have pulled away slightly from the rounded edges of the baking pan.

Place the pan on a cooling rack and let stand for 7 to 10 minutes. Invert the pan onto another cooling rack, then invert again onto a heatproof serving dish to stand right side up (if you are icing and serving the sweet bread within 30 minutes). Spoon-and-sweep the icing over the surface of the warm buns, spreading it carefully as it melts down. Or, cool the ring for 30 minutes on a cooling rack, then drizzle a slightly thinner version of the icing (see notes) over the ring of buns, letting it form casual zigzags. Lovely! As soon as the icing sets, you can detach the buns from one another for serving.

notes
• to make a *simple sweet roll icing* for drizzling, increase the amount of half-and-half in the recipe by 1 to 2 tablespoons to create an icing that flows thickly from the tip of a teaspoon

a simple sweet roll icing

creamy icing

2 cups confectioners' sugar

pinch of salt

2 tablespoons unsalted butter, cut into teaspoon-size chunks, softened

¼ cup half-and-half

½ teaspoon vanilla extract

serving: scant 1 cup

Sift the confectioners' sugar and salt into a medium-size mixing bowl. Add the chunks of butter, the half-and-half, and vanilla extract. Using a hand-held electric mixer, beat the ingredients on low speed until smooth. Adjust the consistency, adding extra teaspoons of confectioners' sugar or half teaspoons of half-and-half to arrive at an icing that is smooth and spreadable. Use the icing immediately on the freshly baked rolls.

notes
• for a rum-flavored icing, reduce the amount of half-and-half to 3 tablespoons and add 1 tablespoon light or dark rum along with it and the vanilla extract

biscuits without apology

Without apology? Do I have to justify or rationalize my mania for biscuits? Probably, depending on your point of view.

As far as I am concerned, biscuits are not stuck in any time period, for their permanence and goodness are a steady reminder that such a respected quick bread endures. To some, this is not fashionable bread—it does not possess the shaggy tear of a big bold crust, a feisty and holey crumb, or an insinuating flavor compound. Too bad. Some biscuits are tender, some flaky; some high-rising, some low-level. But every kind is a good kind, good and home-style. Well, on second thought, a tray of biscuits looks (and tastes) high-style on my dining room table. It's a warming sight to see buttermilk biscuits especially, beaming with a last-minute brush of melted butter.

Of the many interpretations and iterations that a biscuit dough can go through—leavened by baking powder or baking soda (or both); with baking powder and cream of tartar; or raised with yeast—the plainest of each variety is the most enchanting to me. A basic buttermilk biscuit, with its slight tang and creamy crumb; a heavy cream–endowed biscuit; and a biscuit inflated with yeast, baking powder, and baking soda—somewhat fine-textured and really tender—all appeal. Pulled from the oven rack, filling the air with the fragrance of good baking, a tray full of biscuits requires having a block of salted butter ready to smear on, appropriately blurring the broken-apart surfaces. Preserves, honey, or fruit butter are always inviting,

too, as their sweet intensity is a fitting contrast to the demure makeup of a biscuit's internal composition. A biscuit half also becomes a comfortable surface for thin slices of country ham—a cushion for the smoky and the salty.

Yet, when a biscuit becomes shortcake, something fantastically different happens: three elements converge and become, as far as the last course is concerned, a dessert that trumps any other summer confection. A cascade of juicy and gently sweetened peach slices or blueberries, a cream biscuit, and a fluff of good whipped cream all mingle together naturally—joining, at once, the buttery, the fruity, and the creamy. The rich biscuits emerge from the oven with a soft crackle to the crust, generous sprinkles of sugar having dusted their unbaked tops. Split in half, a biscuit greets either one of my favorite toppings— warm buttered peaches or a blueberry compote— though three cups of lightly sugared raspberries or blackberries could stand in nicely. The thickest heavy cream you can find, whipped into substantial clouds, is not only the accepted accompaniment, it is the most delicious one.

Yet, I have to warn you that biscuits have the power of blurring other elements of the menu. They are just that mighty.

thistledown biscuits

For the dough, stir together the yeast, the ½ teaspoon sugar, and the warm water in a heatproof measuring cup. Allow the mixture to stand until swollen, 6 to 7 minutes.

Whisk the flour, baking powder, baking soda, the 6 tablespoons sugar, and salt in a large mixing bowl. Scatter over the chunks of shortening and lard and, using a pastry blender or two round-bladed table knives, cut the fat into the flour mixture until reduced to irregular bits about the size of large peas. In a medium-size mixing bowl, combine the yeast mixture and buttermilk. Pour over the flour mixture and stir to form a dough, using a wooden spoon or flat wooden paddle. With floured hands, knead the dough lightly in the bowl for about 1 minute, or until it comes together smoothly. The dough will be soft. At this point, the dough can be patted into a thick cake, enclosed in several sheets of food-safe plastic wrap, and refrigerated overnight. (If the dough is stored overnight, it will balloon into a fat pillow.) Or, cover the bowl with a sheet of food-safe plastic wrap and let stand at room temperature for 30 minutes.

Film the bottom of a large heavy rimmed sheet pan with nonstick oil spray. Or, line the pan with ovenproof parchment paper.

To form the biscuits, on a lightly floured work surface, with a lightly-floured rolling pin, roll out the dough to a thickness of a scant ¾ inch. Stamp out biscuits, using a 2½ by 2½ inch cookie or biscuit cutter. Avoid twisting the cutter or the biscuits may not rise evenly. Place the biscuits on the prepared baking pan, spacing them about ¼ inch apart. Cover the pan with food-safe plastic wrap and let the biscuits rise at room temperature for 1 hour and 15 minutes, if the dough has just completed the 30-minute room temperature rise, or for 2 hours to 2 hours and 15 minutes, if the dough has been stored overnight in the refrigerator, or until puffy. The biscuits will not have doubled in bulk.

Preheat the oven to 400 degrees F in advance of baking.

Remove and discard the sheet of plastic wrap covering the biscuits.

Bake the biscuits in the preheated oven for 15 minutes, or until set and a golden color on top. Cool the biscuits on the baking pan on a rack for 2 to 3 minutes, then remove them to other cooling racks in sections, using a wide offset metal spatula. Carefully pull the biscuits apart for serving.

(continued on the next page)

yeast-leavened buttermilk dough

5½ teaspoons active dry yeast

½ teaspoon granulated sugar

¼ cup warm (105 to 110 degrees F) water

5⅓ cups plus 1 tablespoon unsifted bleached all-purpose flour

3 teaspoons baking powder

1 teaspoon baking soda

6 tablespoons granulated sugar

1½ teaspoons salt

8 tablespoons (½ cup) cool solid shortening, cut into tablespoon-size chunks

8 tablespoons (½ cup) cool lard, cut into tablespoon-size chunks

2 cups buttermilk

serving: about 2 dozen biscuits
ahead: best on baking day; or freeze for 3 weeks, defrost, bundle in aluminum foil, and reheat in a preheated 300 degrees F oven for 10 minutes

notes
• the combination of shortening and lard yields biscuits that are both tender and flavorful; all shortening (1 cup) or ½ cup solid shortening and 8 tablespoons unsalted butter can replace the shortening-lard combination
• the shortening and lard should be at cool room temperature in order to produce biscuits with a tender, feathery texture
• if the baking pan you are using is not large enough, use two sheet pans

enduring buttermilk biscuits

buttermilk dough

2¾ cups unsifted bleached all-purpose flour

¼ cup unsifted bleached cake flour

3 teaspoons baking powder

¾ teaspoon baking soda

⅛ teaspoon cream of tartar

¾ teaspoon salt

2 tablespoons granulated sugar

6 tablespoons (¾ stick) cold unsalted butter, cut into chunks

6 tablespoons cold solid shortening, cut into chunks

1 cup buttermilk whisked with ½ teaspoon freshly squeezed lemon juice

butter swipe (optional)

3 tablespoons butter, melted and warm

serving: about 1½ dozen biscuits
ahead: best on baking day

Preheat the oven to 400 degrees F.

Have a large rimmed sheet pan or heavy cookie sheet at hand.

For the dough, whisk the all-purpose flour, cake flour, baking powder, baking soda, cream of tartar, salt, and sugar in a large mixing bowl. Scatter over the chunks of butter and shortening and, using a pastry blender or two round-bladed table knives, cut the fat into the flour mixture until reduced to irregular bits about the size of large peas. With your fingertips, further reduce the fat to smaller flakes. Stir in the buttermilk-lemon juice blend to form a dough, using a wooden spoon or flat wooden paddle. Knead the dough lightly in the bowl for 20 seconds, about 6 turns.

To form the biscuits, on a lightly floured work surface, with a lightly floured rolling pin, roll out the dough to a thickness of a scant 1 inch. Stamp out biscuits, using a 2 or 2½-inch square or round cutter. Avoid twisting the cutter or the biscuits may not rise evenly. Place the biscuits on the baking pan, spacing them about 2½ inches apart.

Place the pan of biscuits in the preheated oven, immediately raise the oven temperature to 425 degrees F, and bake for 15 minutes, or until risen, set, and a golden color on top. Cool the biscuits on the baking pan on a cooling rack for 5 to 10 minutes, then brush the tops with the melted butter, if you wish. Remove the biscuits to a pretty, cloth-lined dish, using a medium-width offset metal spatula. Serve warm.

notes
• use the thickest buttermilk you can find
• adding a little lemon juice to the buttermilk creates a whisked mixture that contributes to a very tender batch of biscuits
• if cake flour is unavailable, use a total of 3 cups unsifted bleached all-purpose flour; the texture of these biscuits will be a little tighter than those made with the small amount of cake flour, but just as delicious
• if the baking pan you are using is not large enough, use two sheet pans or cookie sheets

• the biscuits can also be baked in an 8 by 8 by 2-inch baking pan: to do this, roll out the dough to a 7 by 7-inch square, cut into 9 squares, transfer the squares to the lightly buttered pan (leaving a hairline space between them), brush the tops of the biscuits with heavy cream, and bake for 20 minutes, or until set and golden on top; cool the biscuits in the pan on a rack for 5 minutes, then remove them with a small offset metal spatula

 enduring pan biscuits

Preheat the oven to 400 degrees F.

Film the inside of an 8 by 8 by 2-inch baking pan with nonstick flour-and-oil spray. Or, film the inside of the pan with softened unsalted butter.

For the dough, whisk the flour, baking powder, cream of tartar, salt, and sugar in a medium-size mixing bowl. Scatter over the chunks of butter and shortening and, using a pastry blender or two round-bladed table knives, cut the fat into the flour mixture until reduced to irregular bits about the size of large peas. With your fingertips, further reduce the fat to smaller flakes. Stir in the heavy cream and blend to form a dough, using a wooden spoon or flat wooden paddle. Knead the dough lightly in the bowl for 20 seconds, about 6 turns. The dough should be moist and slightly sticky.

On a lightly floured work surface, quickly pat the dough into as even a 7-inch square as possible, but feel free to keep it relatively rough (that is, the square does not have to be perfect). Cut the cake of dough into 9 squares. Transfer the squares to the prepared baking pan, lifting them carefully into the pan, using a small offset metal spatula.

Place the pan of biscuits in the preheated oven, immediately raise the oven temperature to 425 degrees F, and bake for 20 to 25 minutes, or until risen, set, and a golden color on top. Cool the biscuits in the baking pan on a cooling rack for 10 minutes, then brush the tops with the melted butter, if you wish. Remove the biscuits to a breadbasket, using a small offset metal spatula. Serve warm.

notes
• this is a pan version of my *buttery cream drop biscuits* (page 486)

heavy cream-wonderful dough

2 cups unsifted bleached all-purpose flour

4 teaspoons baking powder

½ teaspoon cream of tartar

½ teaspoon salt

1 tablespoon plus 2 teaspoons granulated sugar

4 tablespoons (½ stick) cold unsalted butter, cut into chunks

4 tablespoons cold solid shortening, cut into chunks

1 cup plus 2 tablespoons cold heavy cream

butter swipe (optional)

2 tablespoons butter, melted and warm

serving: 9 biscuits
ahead: best on baking day

biscuits and a pile of fruit: summer shortcakes—as in rich cream dough, buttered peaches, blueberry compote, vanilla cream topping

rich cream dough

2 cups plus 2 tablespoons unsifted bleached all-purpose flour

2¾ teaspoons baking powder

⅛ teaspoon salt

¼ cup granulated sugar

6 tablespoons (¾ stick) cool unsalted butter, cut into ½-inch-size cubes

2 large eggs

½ cup cold heavy cream

1¾ teaspoons vanilla extract

2 tablespoons plain sparkling sugar or sanding sugar, for sprinkling on the unbaked triangles of dough

buttered peaches (page 455)

~ or ~

blueberry compote (page 455)

vanilla cream topping (page 456)

serving: 6 large dessert biscuits, for splitting and topping
ahead: best on baking day; or freeze for 3 weeks, defrost, bundle in aluminum foil, and reheat in a preheated 300 degrees F oven for 10 minutes, then assemble

For the dough, whisk the flour, baking powder, salt, and the ¼ cup granulated sugar in a large mixing bowl. Scatter over the cubes of butter and, using a pastry blender or two round-bladed table knives, cut the fat into the flour mixture until reduced to pearl-size bits. With your fingertips, lightly crumble the fat into the flour for 45 seconds (reducing the butter to smaller flakes of varying sizes).

In a small mixing bowl, whisk the eggs, heavy cream, and vanilla extract until well-combined. Pour the egg and cream mixture over the butter-enhanced dry ingredients and stir to form a dough. Knead the dough lightly in the bowl for 20 seconds, about 6 turns. Pat the dough into a 5 to 6-inch round on a sheet of waxed paper or ovenproof parchment paper, wrap up to enclose, and refrigerate for 2 hours.

Preheat the oven to 400 degrees F in advance of baking.

Have a heavy cookie sheet or rimmed sheet pan at hand.

Cut the dough into 6 pie-shape wedges. Arrange the biscuits on the baking pan, placing them 3 inches apart. Sprinkle the tops with the sparkling or sanding sugar.

Bake the biscuits in the preheated oven for 17 to 18 minutes, or until firm, set, and a golden color on top. Lift off the biscuits to a cooling rack, using a wide offset metal spatula.

While the biscuits are baking, prepare the buttered peaches or blueberry compote.

To assemble the shortcakes, split the warm biscuits in half horizontally, using a finely serrated knife, and set the bottom half of each on a dessert plate. Spoon over the buttered peaches or blueberry compote (dividing the fruit evenly among the 6 biscuits), then cover each shortcake with a biscuit top. Place a dollop of vanilla cream topping over or to the side of each shortcake. Serve immediately.

notes
• if sparkling sugar or sanding sugar is unavailable, granulated sugar can be used for sprinkling on
   top of the unbaked triangles of dough

buttered peaches

Toss the peach slices with the lemon juice in a medium-size nonreactive mixing bowl.

Heat the butter in a wide skillet over low heat until melted. Slide in the peaches. Increase the heat to moderate, turn the peaches in the butter for 1 minute, sprinkle over the sugar, stir lightly, and continue lightly sautéeing the peaches for 1 minute longer. Remove the skillet from the heat to a heatproof surface. Let the peaches stand in the skillet, off the heat, for 2 minutes, at which time the sugar should be dissolved. Turn the peach mixture into a nonreactive heatproof bowl and let stand for 10 minutes for the fruit and juices to meld, then spoon over the bottom half of each freshly baked biscuit.

notes
• to peel the peaches, dip them, 2 at a time, into a pot of boiling water for 45 seconds to 1 minute, then transfer them to a bowl of ice water for 1 minute; slip off each peel, using a small, sharp nonreactive paring knife
• ripe nectarines, plums, or pluots (halved, pitted, and thickly sliced) may be substituted for the peaches (only the peaches need to be peeled)

buttery peach sauté

6 juicy ripe peaches, peeled, halved, pitted, and thickly sliced

1 tablespoon freshly squeezed lemon juice

2 tablespoons unsalted butter

2 tablespoons superfine sugar

serving: about 2⅔ cups, depending on the size of the individual pieces of fruit
ahead: within 20 to 25 minutes of turning the peach mixture into the bowl

blueberry compote

Sift the sugar, cornstarch, and salt together into a heavy, medium-size saucepan (preferably enameled cast iron). Whisk the ingredients together to blend well. Slowly stir in the pomegranate-blueberry juice.

Set the saucepan over moderately high heat and bring the juice mixture to the boil, stirring slowly and thoroughly with a wooden spoon or flat wooden paddle. Boil the sauce base slowly until clear and lightly thickened, about 1 minute, stirring slowly but constantly. Avoid whisking or rapidly beating the mixture or it may thin out at this point or later, as it cools. Off the heat, carefully add the blueberries and stir gently. The berries should glisten in the thickened sauce. Return the saucepan to low heat and let the berries warm through—they should just begin to lose their firmness, but not collapse or burst—about 1 minute.

Remove the saucepan from the heat, stir in the vanilla extract, and carefully spoon the blueberry compote into a nonreactive heatproof mixing bowl.

(continued on the next page)

lightly cooked blueberry sauce

¼ cup granulated sugar

3 teaspoons cornstarch

pinch of salt

1 cup pomegranate-blueberry juice

2 cups blueberries, picked over

½ teaspoon vanilla extract

serving: about 2½ cups
ahead: within 45 minutes of turning the blueberry mixture into the bowl

Place a piece of ovenproof parchment paper directly on the surface of the blueberry mixture. Use the compote warm or tepid, spooned over the bottom half of each freshly baked biscuit.

notes

• pomegranate-blueberry juice, used as the liquid component, creates the best- and most-complex-tasting compote and is worth searching out for this recipe, but pure blueberry juice or pomegranate juice alone may be substituted

vanilla cream topping

vanilla cream

1 cup cold heavy cream

1 tablespoon plus 2 teaspoons superfine sugar

¾ teaspoon vanilla extract

serves: about 2 cups
ahead: use the cream immediately, when it will be at its smoothest, finest best

Chill a set of beaters and a medium-size mixing bowl for at least 45 minutes.

Pour the heavy cream into the bowl and whip until just beginning to mound.

Sprinkle over the sugar and continue whipping for 2 minutes longer, or until the cream holds its shape in soft mounds in the bowl of a spoon. Stir in the vanilla extract.

notes

• superfine sugar, rather than confectioners' sugar, is ideal for sweetening the cream, as it will produce a topping with a clean, clear (rather than chalky) taste

ginger, front and center

Can a tea cake be cuddly? In a soothing kind of way, yes.

The mingling of five warm spices, the balmy flavor of molasses, a spark of freshly grated gingerroot, and its inviting moistness make it so. The pumpkin squares, a lightly sweetened cake/bread containing flickers of ginger, are equally delicious. My favorite way to serve the former is as a homespun dessert beefed up with two amiable dollops—of whipped cream laced with ginger preserves and of sunshiny lemon butter. At my table, the pumpkin squares get loaded onto a plate and passed, in place of rolls, during autumn and winter to enjoy with a robust stew or main-course soup.

a snuggly gingerbread tea cake, lemon butter, gingered cream

Preheat the oven to 350 degrees F.

Film the inside of a round 9-inch cake pan (3 inches deep) with nonstick flour-and-oil spray. Line the bottom with a round of ovenproof parchment paper and film the surface with the spray.

For the batter, sift the flour, baking soda, salt, ginger, cinnamon, allspice, cloves, and cardamom (if you are using it) onto a sheet of waxed paper.

Place the oil and granulated sugar in the large bowl of a freestanding electric mixer. Beat on moderate speed for 1 minute. Add the egg, vanilla extract, and molasses and beat for 1 minute longer. Blend in the gingerroot. On low speed, add half of the sifted mixture, followed by the boiling water, and the balance of the sifted mixture. Blend well after each addition to create a smooth batter, scraping down the sides of the mixing bowl with a rubber spatula to keep the batter even-textured, but avoid protracted beating. The batter should be creamy and pourable.

Pour and scrape the batter into the prepared baking pan.

Bake the tea cake in the preheated oven for 45 to 50 minutes or until risen, set, and the cake withdraws slightly from the circular edges of the baking pan. (An ultra-thin band just below the surface of the cake will remain moist—it is the section that begins the crumb of the cake—so testing the cake with a wooden pick is a less-advantageous way to test the cake and could result in an overbaked cake.) Cool the cake in the pan on a rack for 10 minutes. Invert the cake onto another cooling rack. Lift off the pan, peel away the parchment paper, and invert again onto another rack. Serve the cake warm or cool completely. Sift confectioners' sugar over the top of the cake just before slicing into triangular-shaped wedges and serving. Spoon a little of the lemon butter and gingered cream to the side of each slice. Store in an airtight cake keeper.

notes
- the batter for this tea cake has been finely tuned over a period of years to arrive at a cake that bakes into a plump layer without sinking; oftentimes, a high proportion of liquid (including a liquid sweetening agent, such as molasses) to an inappropriate amount of flour and leavening agent contributes to an unstable batter that collapses, and for this reason be very meticulous when measuring the molasses, boiling water, flour, and baking soda
- protracted beating of the batter at any stage of the procedure may cause the cake to bake somewhat concave in the center

---

spiced fresh ginger batter

2⅓ cups plus 3 tablespoons unsifted bleached all-purpose flour

1 teaspoon baking soda

¼ teaspoon salt

2 teaspoons ground ginger

1 teaspoon ground cinnamon

½ teaspoon ground allspice

¼ teaspoon ground cloves

¼ teaspoon ground cardamom (optional)

½ cup neutral vegetable oil (such as soybean or canola)

⅔ cup granulated sugar

1 large egg

1 teaspoon vanilla extract

¾ cup plus 1 tablespoon light unsulphured molasses

2 tablespoons peeled and grated fresh gingerroot

¾ cup boiling water

confectioners' sugar,
for sifting over the baked tea cake

lemon butter (page 460)

gingered cream (page 461)

serving: one 9-inch cake, creating 8 to 10 slices
ahead: best on baking day

lemon butter

lemon curd "spread"

7 large egg yolks

1¼ cups superfine sugar

pinch of salt

½ cup plus 2 tablespoons freshly squeezed lemon juice

7 tablespoons (1 stick less 1 tablespoon) cold unsalted butter, cut into small chunks

lemon juice and lemon peel for finishing the butter

1 tablespoon freshly squeezed lemon juice

3 teaspoons finely grated lemon peel

serving: about 1¾ cups lemon butter
ahead: 2 days

Whisk the egg yolks and sugar together in a medium-size nonreactive mixing bowl for 1 minute. At first, the mixture will resemble heavy wet sand, but it will begin to liquefy and loosen up after about 45 seconds. Whisk in the salt.

Pour and scrape the egg yolks-sugar mixture into a heavy, medium-size nonreactive saucepan (preferably enameled cast iron). Blend in the lemon juice. Mix in the chunks of butter. Set the saucepan over moderate heat and cook, stirring continuously with a wooden spoon, flat wooden paddle, or heatproof rubber spatula, for 10 minutes. At the end of the 10 minutes, a good portion of the foamy surface should disappear, the butter will be melted entirely, and it will register 190 degrees F on an instant-read thermometer. Continue cooking for 3 minutes longer, stirring continuously, or until lightly thickened, all of the foam has disappeared, and the mixture registers 198 degrees F on an instant-read thermometer. Avoid allowing the mixture to even approach the simmer; using a heavy pan for this step is important because it moderates the heat. The suave, smooth mixture should just lightly coat a wooden spoon, flat wooden paddle, or heatproof rubber spatula at this point. Using cold butter initially helps to keep the lemon mixture creamy-textured, rather than dense or oily. Overcooking the curd will give it a final texture that is slightly gummy or rubbery.

Set a fine-mesh sieve over a medium-size nonreactive mixing bowl. Pour and scrape the lemon butter into the sieve and press it through, using a heatproof rubber spatula. Set this bowl into a larger bowl filled with enough ice cubes and cold water to fill it by one-third. Stir the 1 tablespoon finishing lemon juice and the lemon peel into the butter. Let the lemon butter chill for 10 minutes, stirring it now and again. At this point, the temperature will drop to 78 degrees F and the mixture will resemble soft pudding.

Remove the bowl containing the lemon mixture from the water bath and thoroughly dry the outside of the bowl. Scrape the lemon butter into a sturdy, impeccably clean, nonreactive storage container and press a sheet of food-safe plastic wrap directly onto the surface. Cover and refrigerate for at least 2 hours or overnight.

notes
- organic egg yolks, with their yellow-orange hue, produce the best-tasting and most beautifully colored lemon butter
- be sure to refrigerate the lemon butter in an airtight container, as lemon butter is infamous for absorbing any lingering savory scents in the refrigerator

gingered cream

Chill a set of beaters and a small mixing bowl for at least 45 minutes.

Pour the heavy cream into the bowl and whip until just beginning to mound.

Sprinkle over the sugar and continue whipping for 2 minutes longer, or until the cream holds its shape softly in the bowl of a spoon. By hand, blend in the ginger preserves and vanilla extract, using a rubber spatula and a few swift, sweeping stirs. Use immediately.

notes
• once the ginger preserves are added, the cream will begin to firm up, so it is important to use the accompaniment as soon as it is prepared

spiced cream

1 cup cold heavy cream

1 tablespoon superfine sugar

2 tablespoons best-quality ginger preserves

½ teaspoon vanilla extract

serving: about 2 cups

gingered pumpkin squares for the breadbasket

gingery pumpkin batter

2⅓ cups plus 3 tablespoons unsifted bleached all-purpose flour

1 teaspoon baking soda

½ teaspoon salt

2 teaspoons ground ginger

½ teaspoon ground cinnamon

½ teaspoon freshly grated nutmeg

¼ teaspoon ground cloves

8 tablespoons (1 stick) unsalted butter, softened

⅓ cup firmly packed light brown sugar

¼ cup granulated sugar

2 large eggs

2 teaspoons vanilla extract

½ cup light unsulphured molasses

½ cup plain, solid-pack 100% pumpkin

2 tablespoons peeled and grated fresh gingerroot

¾ cup plus 1 tablespoon sour cream

serves: one 9-inch quick bread, creating 12 squares
ahead: 2 days

Preheat the oven to 350 degrees F.

Film the inside of a 9 by 9 by 2-inch baking pan with nonstick flour-and-oil spray.

For the batter, sift the flour, baking soda, salt, ginger, cinnamon, nutmeg, and cloves onto a sheet of waxed paper.

Cream the butter in the large bowl of a freestanding electric mixer on moderate speed for 2 minutes. Add the light brown sugar and continue beating for 2 minutes. Add the granulated sugar and beat for 1 minute longer. Beat in the eggs, one at a time. Blend in the vanilla extract and molasses, followed by the pumpkin. Blend in the gingerroot. The mixture will look curdled. On low speed, blend in half of the sifted mixture, the sour cream, then the balance of the sifted mixture. Scrape down the sides of the mixing bowl frequently with a rubber spatula to keep the batter even-textured. The batter will be dense, but soft.

Spoon and scrape the batter into the prepared baking pan.

Bake the quick bread in the preheated oven for 30 to 35 minutes, or until set and a wooden pick withdraws clean when inserted 2 inches from the center. The baked quick bread will pull away from the sides of the baking pan. Cool the quick bread completely in the pan on a cooling rack. Cut the bread into squares directly from the pan and remove them, using a small offset metal spatula, to a breadbasket. Store any remaining squares not served on baking day in an airtight cake keeper.

notes
• the bread is wonderfully downy and moist
• squares of this pleasing and not overly sweet autumnal quick bread would be a fine addition to the Thanksgiving table breadbasket

streusel overload

"Wow! Those are scones-to-the-max."

That is a direct quote from one very scone-obsessed friend.

As my pal looked at the tray of scones being pulled right out of the oven, glowing and broadcasting the scent of cinnamon and butter all over the place, the phrase—meant as a genuine compliment—was uttered. (Oddly enough, others have offered the same phrase.) The next step was, of course, to pull a still-warm scone from the cooling rack and take it away to eat with a milky cup of strong coffee. It was a stealthy, catlike move on the part of my friend, sneaking an irresistible scone an hour before brunch guests were to arrive. I pretended, nevertheless, that the event did not occur, for I know that a freshly baked scone is a toothsome thing. These mimic coffee cake. (He concurred—on all counts.)

Now, if you would like a moist, ultra-buttery, cakey associate to the scones, the coffee cake that follows is just that. The engaging scent of vanilla is softly front and center in the butter and buttermilk-structured cake batter and the extract mellows out the crumbly surface of the topping. Four eggs, along with the buttermilk, define and establish the cake's crumb. Together, the cake and streusel topping fill a 13 by 9 by 2-inch baking pan nicely, offering one grand cake for cutting into stocky fingers or squares. The firmly tender streusel that hugs the surface of the silky cake creates something wonderful, a cake that has a certain deliciously trustworthy, heirloomlike quality to it.

I'll take either (or both) and, please, don't hold back on the streusel.

scones-to-the-max

cream and egg dough

4¼ cups unsifted bleached
all-purpose flour

5¼ teaspoons baking powder

1 teaspoon salt

2 teaspoons ground cinnamon

¼ teaspoon freshly grated nutmeg

¾ cup granulated sugar

½ cup natural unsweetened medium-flake
coconut or very finely chopped walnuts

12 tablespoons (1½ sticks) cold unsalted
butter, cut into small chunks

4 large eggs

1 cup heavy cream

3 teaspoons vanilla extract

cinnamon streusel topping

⅔ cup unsifted bleached all-purpose flour

¼ teaspoon ground cinnamon

pinch of salt

¼ cup firmly packed light brown sugar

¼ cup granulated sugar

¼ cup natural unsweetened medium-flake
coconut or chopped walnuts

6 tablespoons (¾ stick) cold unsalted
butter, cut into small chunks

1 teaspoon vanilla extract

(continued on the next page)

For the dough, whisk the flour, baking powder, salt, cinnamon, nutmeg, granulated sugar, and coconut or walnuts in a large mixing bowl. Drop in the chunks of butter and, using a pastry blender or two round-bladed table knives, cut the fat into the flour mixture until reduced to irregular pea-size bits.

In a medium-size mixing bowl, whisk together the eggs, heavy cream, and vanilla extract. Pour the whisked egg mixture over the flour mixture and stir to form a dough. Knead the dough lightly in the bowl for about 30 seconds, 5 or 6 turns. The dough will be firmly moist. Divide the dough in half and, on a lightly floured work surface, form into two 6-inch disks. Make sure that the disks are tightly formed, or the scones may bake unevenly or break open. The scones will bake with an irregular surface and the top and sides may splinter at various places, but this is to be expected and is part of their tender/flaky/buttery nature (and what makes them so visually interesting and so good to eat). Wrap the disks in waxed paper and refrigerate for 2 hours.

For the topping, sift the flour, cinnamon, and salt into a medium-size mixing bowl. Thoroughly mix in the light brown sugar, granulated sugar, and coconut or walnuts. Scatter over the chunks of butter and, using a pastry blender or two round-bladed table knives, reduce the fat to small bits. Sprinkle over the vanilla extract. Using your fingertips, firmly crumble the mixture until large and small lumps are formed, making sure that you end up with a bowl of irregular lumps. (It is virtually impossible to overwork the mixture.) The lumps will be moist.

Preheat the oven to 400 degrees F.

Line two heavy cookie sheets or rimmed sheet pans with lengths of ovenproof parchment paper.

Place the dough disks on a lightly floured work surface, and cut each into 5 wedges. Place the scones on the prepared baking pans, 5 scones to a pan, spacing them 3 to 3½ inches apart.

Using a soft pastry brush, film the top of each scone with a little of the heavy cream–vanilla extract blend, making sure that it stays on top and does not drip down the sides (or the scones will not rise as high as they would otherwise). Firmly but carefully, press some of the streusel mixture on top; if the streusel sits loosely on top, it will fall over during baking, so make sure you have pressed it down securely. Inevitably, the triangular shapes of dough will compress slightly as the streusel is pressed on, but just plump them up with your fingertips to restore their figures.

Bake the scones in the preheated oven for 22 minutes, or until firm and set. Cool the scones on the baking sheets for 2 minutes, then remove them to cooling racks, using a wide offset metal spatula. Serve the scones freshly baked. Just before serving, lightly sift confectioners' sugar over the tops of the scones, highlighting the streusel mixture, if you wish.

notes
- natural unsweetened medium-flake coconut is also known as unsulphured medium-shred macaroon coconut
- the streusel topping can be made up to 2 days in advance and refrigerated in a tightly sealed container; remove the refrigerated topping as soon as you preheat the oven to bake the scones

brushing mixture

3 tablespoons heavy cream blended with ¼ teaspoon vanilla extract

confectioners' sugar, for sifting over the baked scones (optional)

serving: 10 large scones
ahead: best on baking day; or freeze for 3 weeks, defrost, bundle in aluminum foil, and reheat in a preheated 300 degrees F oven for 10 minutes

a decadent streusel coffee cake

Preheat the oven to 350 degrees F.

Film the inside of a 13 by 9 by 2-inch baking pan with nonstick flour-and-oil spray.

For the topping, whisk the flour and salt in a medium-size mixing bowl. Blend in the granulated sugar and light brown sugar. Scatter over the chunks of butter and, using a pastry blender or two round-bladed table knives, reduce the fat to small bits. Sprinkle over the vanilla extract. Using your fingertips, firmly gather and press the mixture together until moist, small and medium-size clumps are formed.

For the batter, sift the flour, baking powder, baking soda, and salt onto a sheet of waxed paper.

Cream the butter in the large bowl of a freestanding electric mixer on moderate speed for 3 minutes. Add the granulated sugar in 3 additions, beating for 1 minute after each portion is added. Beat in the eggs, one at a time, mixing for 30 seconds after each addition. Blend in the vanilla extract. On low speed, alternately add the sifted mixture in 3 additions with the buttermilk in 2 additions, beginning and ending with the sifted mixture. Scrape down the sides of the mixing bowl with a rubber spatula to keep the batter even-textured. The batter will be moderately dense and creamy-textured.

Spoon the batter into the prepared baking pan. Smooth the top with a rubber spatula. Sprinkle the streusel mixture evenly over the top, using all of it.

Bake the cake in the preheated oven for 1 hour, or until risen, set, and a wooden pick withdraws clean when tested about 2 inches from the center of the cake. The top of the cake will be golden brown and the streusel mixture will have melded into it. The baked cake will pull away from the sides of the baking pan. Cool the cake in the pan on a cooling rack. Serve the cake cut into squares or fingers directly from the pan. Lift out the pieces of cake, using a small offset metal spatula. Sift a haze of confectioners' sugar over the top of the pieces just before serving. Store in an airtight cake keeper.

notes
• for an abundant topping, using the following amounts: 1½ cups unsifted bleached all-purpose flour, large pinch of salt, 1 cup granulated sugar, ¼ cup firmly packed light brown sugar, 12 tablespoons (1½ sticks) cool unsalted butter (cut into small chunks), and 2½ teaspoons vanilla extract; this is a significant amount of streusel, so sprinkle it evenly in order to avoid irregular pools of butter surfacing as the cake bakes (there is no need to panic if small, random pools of butter appear, as the butter will reabsorb as the cake cools)
• for the silkiest batter, use organic buttermilk

---

vanilla streusel topping

1 cup unsifted bleached all-purpose flour

pinch of salt

⅔ cup granulated sugar

2 tablespoons firmly packed light brown sugar

8 tablespoons (1 stick) cool unsalted butter, cut into small chunks

1½ teaspoons vanilla extract

vanilla butter batter

3 cups unsifted bleached all-purpose flour

1¼ teaspoons baking powder

¾ teaspoon baking soda

¾ teaspoon salt

½ pound (16 tablespoons or 2 sticks) unsalted butter, softened

1⅔ cups plus 3 tablespoons granulated sugar

4 large eggs

3 teaspoons vanilla extract

1 cup buttermilk

confectioners' sugar, for sprinkling over the baked cake

serving: one 13 by 9-inch cake, creating 20 squares or 24 fingers
ahead: 2 days

friendship baking

These oaten, lightly wheaty rolls—the little ones and the big ones—are, by design, the breads I make with and for friends and, by extension, serve as a friendly accompaniment to soup and such things.

The "friendship baking experience" all started many years ago—rather by happy accident—when a reunion of my nearest and dearest converged in the kitchen one cool day in early autumn to celebrate nothing more than the fact that time and circumstance brought us all together, despite the demands that crazy schedules tend to inflict. I happened to have had a yeast dough on the rise, and a little time after the guests arrived, it was ready to form—so I pressed them into service, teaching the art of hand-forming rolls. We ate the bread with a beef ragout that included a savory dried fruit compote. Ever since then, I think of this dough, which has undergone several delicate and not-so-delicate changes to polish it into the form you have here, as friendship bread.

The baking of bread is both a quiet, one-person act that you sneak in to your weekend (perhaps making the dough one day and baking it off into a loaf or batch of rolls the next) and the collective work of good friends assembled around a mixing bowl. This one is a casual kind of yeast-risen bread dough, nubby with oats, stepped up with whole wheat flour, and moistened with buttermilk. A modulated richness comes from butter and eggs. Initially, the recipe contained only oats and unbleached all-purpose flour, but I enlarged it to bring a kind of wintry depth to the bread. The buttermilk, butter, and eggs create a silky crumb usually uncharacteristic of earthier bread doughs. This is also a dough that takes nicely to swirling with sugar and spice, and along with it, expansively accepts additions such as raisins, dried tart (or sweet) cherries, diced dried apricots, or dried pluots in its rippling, sugar-filled eddies.

The dough itself is an amiable one, for it can be formed into small cloverleaf rolls, king-size cloverleaf rolls, or two small but plump loaves. If any bread says "friendship," this one does.

a gift of bread

oaty, lightly wheaty yeast dough

1¼ cups buttermilk

¼ cup granulated sugar

1½ cups "old-fashioned" rolled oats

4 tablespoons (½ stick) unsalted butter,
cut into tablespoon-size chunks

3 teaspoons active dry yeast

¼ teaspoon granulated sugar

¼ cup warm (105 to 110 degrees F) water

2 large eggs, lightly beaten

½ teaspoon baking soda

2½ cups unsifted unbleached all-purpose
flour, plus an additional ¼ cup, as needed
for kneading

¾ cup whole wheat flour

1 teaspoon salt

serving: 2 dozen standard-size cloverleaf
rolls or 8 king-size individual cloverleaf
breads
ahead: best on baking day; or freeze for
1 month, defrost, bundle in aluminum foil,
and reheat in a preheated 325 degrees F
oven for 10 to 15 minutes

For the dough, place the buttermilk and the ¼ cup sugar in a medium-size saucepan, set over moderate heat, and let the buttermilk reach a moderately hot temperature, about 6 minutes (the sugar does not need to dissolve completely). Place the oats in a medium-size heatproof mixing bowl. Pour and scrape the buttermilk mixture over the oats, drop in the chunks of butter, and stir to mix. Let the oat mixture stand for 20 minutes.

Stir together the yeast, the ¼ teaspoon sugar, and the warm water in a heatproof measuring cup. Allow the mixture to stand until swollen, 6 to 7 minutes.

Blend the eggs, baking soda, and the yeast mixture into the oat mixture. Combine 2 cups of the all-purpose flour, the whole wheat flour, and the salt in a large mixing bowl. Add the oat-yeast mixture and mix to combine, using a wooden spoon or flat wooden paddle. Work in the remaining ½ cup all-purpose flour. Place the additional ¼ cup flour on a work surface. Turn the dough out onto the surface and knead it, incorporating as much of the flour as needed to create a soft, resilient, but slightly sticky dough. Knead the dough for 6 minutes.

Turn the dough into a bowl heavily coated with softened unsalted butter, lightly turn to coat all sides in a film of butter, make several cuts in the dough with a pair of kitchen scissors, cover tightly with a sheet of food-safe plastic wrap, and let rise at room temperature for 1 hour, or until doubled in bulk.

Remove the plastic wrap. Lightly compress the dough with a rubber spatula, cover loosely with the plastic wrap, and let stand for 10 minutes. Remove and discard the plastic wrap.

In the meantime, film the inside of 24 muffin/cupcake cups (12 cups to a pan, each cup measuring 2¾ inches in diameter and 1⅜ inches deep, with a capacity of ½ cup) with softened unsalted butter. Or, film the inside of 8 king-size muffin cups (6 cups to a pan, each cup measuring 3½ inches in diameter and 3 inches deep, with a capacity of 1¼ cups) with softened unsalted butter.

To form the standard-size rolls, divide the dough in half. Cut each half into 12 even-size pieces. Cut each of the 12 pieces into 3 even-size pieces. Roll the pieces into smooth balls. Place 3 balls in the bottom of each prepared muffin cup, forming a cloverleaf.

To form the king-size rolls, divide the dough into 8 even-size pieces. Cut each piece into 4 even-size pieces. Roll the pieces into smooth balls. For each roll, place 1 of the 4 balls in the bottom of the prepared cup as the base, press down lightly, then arrange the remaining 3 balls on top, forming a cloverleaf.

Cover each pan of rolls loosely with a sheet of food-safe plastic wrap. Let the standard-size rolls rise at room temperature for 45 minutes. Let the king-size rolls rise at room temperature for 1 hour, or until doubled in bulk. They should look puffy, but stable.

Preheat the oven to 375 degrees F in advance of baking.

Remove and discard the sheets of plastic wrap covering the rolls.

Bake the standard-size rolls in the preheated oven for 12 to 15 minutes, or until set and a medium brown color on top. Bake the king-size rolls in the preheated oven for 20 to 22 minutes, or until set and a medium brown color on top. Cool the standard-size rolls in the pans on cooling racks for 5 minutes and the king-size rolls for 10 minutes. Carefully release the rolls onto cooling racks and let stand for at least 30 minutes before serving.

notes
- king-size muffin cups, made by Wilton (see page 502, baking*SelectedSources*), make great-looking and generously sized individual breads
- the rolls are arranged and baked in muffin tins; two 8 by 4 by 3-inch loaf pans may be substituted, creating 2 loaves (divide the dough in half, form into 2 loaves, assemble in the buttered pans, and let rise for 1 hour to 1 hour and 10 minutes or until doubled in bulk), increasing the baking time to a total of 40 minutes, or until set

bundles of joy

On my memory board of fragrances, deep within my baking consciousness, nothing is more firmly embedded than the scent of chocolate chip (or chunk) cookies while they are baking.

Biting into a warm cookie that highlights the demure seepage of chocolate, the light taste of caramel, and the echoing flavor of butter returns me to my childhood, when I presided over a baking sheet filled with chunks of dough. (Is anything new? I still hover over baking sheets of chocolate chip cookie dough.)

The triumph of the ingredients, melding as they do into one parcel of dough, is what good baking is all about. When life hands me the inevitable dilemma, I head into the kitchen and mix up a few dozen of any one of these charmers—their presence does not change the course of an event (would that a cookie had such power), but it does lighten the way.

The potency of a chocolate chip cookie is all-encompassing. Hand over a cookie to a cranky person and it weakens his or her ornery resolve. Scent your kitchen with the alluring aroma of dough baking into golden, crisp-and-chewy rounds, and anyone nearby will become an instant friend.

I am terribly particular about chocolate chip cookie dough. Emotional even. The constant tweaking of the *melting for chocolate chip cookies* recipe has made it dearer to me, more sensory-involving, more of an intellectual tangle to be reckoned with. The current recipe for CCC (as it is known in my private shorthand) has a different complexion from other cookies in my life, unveiling a slightly altered ratio of flours and sugars and a little more salt. Chocolate chips dominate. The aroma is pure. And the baking? Both simple and sublime.

But…

When you are a dogged baker, there is always a "but." Just when a nipped-and-tucked recipe for CCC is put together and baked, another concept comes to mind—a little more caramel-y, a little more butterscotch-y—and the fiddle results in this spin: *when chocolate chip cookies go butterscotch.*

No sooner is the second play-on-the-traditional over than along comes *melty, lush: empowered-with-bittersweet-chocolate,* a third incarnation of the CCC. As these cookies bake, they puddle into relaxed saucers. With globs of bittersweet chocolate poking through, and crisply tender edges. Loosely based on the preceding two recipes, this cookie dough contains a little more butter and sugar for the amount of flour used and places bittersweet chocolate at the forefront. When baked at a higher temperature, the less-structured dough mounds collapse gently, giving the baked cookies a tenderly snappy edge and chewy middle. As the dough pools around the irregular pieces of chocolate while baking, the butter and sugar caramelize—not in a brilliantly dark way, but in a dusky and shadowy fashion. A batch is of-the-moment, to be eaten—preferably depleted—within hours of baking, though the dough does hold up well in the refrigerator for two days. In a butter frenzy, the CCC odyssey finishes with *wild ones,* a fairly profound version of a chocolate chip cookie dough.

So much for all the talk-y descriptions. The pleasure is in the baking (and in the eating). And, well, one day a batch of cookies might, in fact, change the course of events.

melting for chocolate chip cookies ✳ *when chocolate chip cookies go butterscotch*
melty, lush: empowered-with-bittersweet-chocolate ✳ *wild ones*

melting for chocolate chip cookies

buttery sugar-smacked dough

1⅔ cups unsifted bleached
all-purpose flour

⅓ cup unsifted bleached cake flour

1 teaspoon baking soda

¾ teaspoon coarse sea salt

½ pound (16 tablespoons or 2 sticks)
unsalted butter, softened

¾ cup firmly packed light brown sugar

¾ cup granulated sugar

2 large eggs

1 tablespoon vanilla extract

2⅓ cups semisweet chocolate chips

serving: about 3 dozen cookies
ahead: best on baking day;
refrigerate cookie dough for 2 days
or freeze for 1 month

Preheat the oven to 350 degrees F.

Line several heavy cookie sheets or rimmed sheet pans with lengths of
ovenproof parchment paper.

For the dough, sift the all-purpose flour, cake flour, and baking soda into a
medium-size mixing bowl. Sprinkle over the salt and whisk it in.

Cream the butter in the large bowl of a freestanding electric mixer on
moderately low speed for 2 minutes. Add the light brown sugar and beat on
moderate speed for 1 minute. Add the granulated sugar and beat for 1 minute
longer. Add both eggs at once and beat on low speed until just incorporated.
Blend in the vanilla extract. On low speed, mix in the sifted ingredients in
2 additions, beating just until the flour particles are absorbed. Scrape down
the sides of the mixing bowl frequently with a rubber spatula to keep the
dough even-textured. Blend in the chocolate chips.

Place generous 2-tablespoon-size mounds of dough on the prepared baking
pans, spacing the mounds about 3 inches apart, and arranging 9 mounds on
each standard-size sheet.

Bake the cookies in the preheated oven for 13 to 15 minutes, or until set and
golden. Let the cookies stand on the baking pans for 1 minute, then transfer
them to cooling racks, using a wide offset metal spatula. Cool completely. Store
in an airtight tin.

notes
• ½ teaspoon fine sea salt can be substituted for the ¾ teaspoon of coarse sea salt
• the bumper amount of chocolate chips makes a lavish cookie, but you can reserve ½ cup (or
   use an additional ¼ cup chocolate chips) to sprinkle over the cookie mounds just before baking
   or halfway through the baking time—very pretty, very chocolaty
• the cookie dough can be formed into a thick cake or several logs, wrapped securely, and frozen
   for up to 1 month; defrost the dough in the refrigerator before forming and baking, adding 1 to 2
   minutes to the total baking time to accommodate for the chilled dough
• when preparing cookie dough for refrigeration or freezing, use organic eggs only
• never consume raw cookie dough

when chocolate chip cookies go butterscotch

For the dough, sift the all-purpose flour, cake flour, baking soda, baking powder, cream of tartar, and salt onto a sheet of waxed paper.

Cream the butter in the large bowl of a freestanding electric mixer on moderately low speed for 4 minutes. Add the light brown sugar in 2 additions, beating on moderate speed for 1 minute after each portion is added. Add the granulated sugar and beat for 1 minute. Add the dark brown sugar and beat for 1 minute longer. Add the eggs, one at a time, beating for 30 seconds after each addition. Blend in the vanilla extract and caramel essence (if you are using it).

On low speed, blend in the sifted ingredients in 3 additions, beating just until the flour particles are absorbed. Scrape down the sides of the mixing bowl frequently with a rubber spatula to keep the dough even-textured. Blend in the chocolate chips. Cover the bowl of dough with a sheet of food-safe plastic wrap and refrigerate for 3 hours, or until firm enough to handle.

Preheat the oven to 350 degrees F.

Line several heavy cookie sheets or rimmed sheet pans with lengths of ovenproof parchment paper.

Place heaping 2-tablespoon-size mounds of dough on the prepared baking pans, spacing the mounds about 3½ inches apart, and arranging 6 mounds on each standard-size sheet.

Bake the cookies in the preheated oven for 13 to 14 minutes, or until set. The cookies should be evenly baked through, without any paler centers. Let the cookies stand on the baking pans for 1 minute, then transfer them to cooling racks, using a wide offset metal spatula. Cool completely. Store in an airtight tin.

notes
- the mating of organic butter and organic eggs (especially in this recipe) returns a dreamy batch of cookies
- caramel essence is available in stoppered bottles at La Cuisine—The Cook's Resource (see page 501, baking*SelectedSources*)
- the cookie dough can be formed into a thick cake or several logs, wrapped securely, and frozen for up to 1 month; defrost the dough in the refrigerator before forming and baking, adding 1 to 2 minutes to the total baking time to accommodate for the chilled dough
- when preparing cookie dough for refrigeration or freezing, use organic eggs only
- never consume raw cookie dough

butterscotch–chocolate chip dough

2¾ cups unsifted bleached all-purpose flour

¼ cup unsifted bleached cake flour

1¼ teaspoons baking soda

¼ teaspoon baking powder

⅛ teaspoon cream of tartar

¾ teaspoon salt

¾ pound (3 sticks) unsalted butter, softened

1 cup firmly packed light brown sugar

¾ cup granulated sugar

½ cup firmly packed dark brown sugar

3 large eggs

4 teaspoons vanilla extract

½ teaspoon caramel essence (optional; see note)

3 cups semisweet chocolate chips

serving: about 4 dozen cookies
ahead: best on baking day; refrigerate cookie dough for 2 days or freeze for 1 month

melty, lush: empowered-with-bittersweet-chocolate

buttery and chunky dough

1¾ cups unsifted bleached all-purpose flour

⅛ teaspoon cream of tartar

½ teaspoon salt

½ pound (16 tablespoons or 2 sticks) unsalted butter, softened

1 cup firmly packed light brown sugar

¼ cup firmly packed dark brown sugar

1 large egg

2 teaspoons vanilla extract

12 ounces bittersweet chocolate, cut into ½-inch chunks (or substitute bittersweet chocolate chips)

serving: about 3½ dozen cookies
ahead: best on baking day; refrigerate cookie dough for 2 days or freeze for 1 month

For the dough, sift the flour, cream of tartar, and salt onto a sheet of waxed paper.

Cream the butter in the large bowl of a freestanding electric mixer on moderate speed for 2 minutes. Add the light brown sugar in 2 additions, beating on moderate speed for 1 minute after each portion is added. Add the dark brown sugar and beat for 30 seconds longer. Blend in the egg and vanilla extract. On low speed, blend in the sifted ingredients in 2 additions, beating just until the flour particles are absorbed. Scrape down the sides of the mixing bowl frequently with a rubber spatula to keep the dough even-textured. Work in the chocolate chunks. Cover the bowl of dough with a sheet of food-safe plastic wrap and refrigerate for 3 hours, or until firm enough to handle.

Preheat the oven to 375 degrees F in advance of baking.

Line several heavy cookie sheets or rimmed sheet pans with lengths of ovenproof parchment paper.

Place heaping 2-tablespoon-size mounds of dough on the prepared baking pans, spacing the mounds 3 inches apart, and arranging 8 mounds on each standard-size sheet.

Bake the cookies in the preheated oven for 11 to 12 minutes, or until the centers are just set and the edges are golden. Let the cookies stand on the baking pans for 1 minute to firm up slightly, then transfer them to cooling racks, still on the parchment liners. Cool completely. Slip a wide offset metal spatula underneath the cookies and serve. Store in an airtight tin.

notes
• for cookies with an outstanding butter flavor, use Plugrá European Style Unsalted Butter
• if the butter is not fully softened, the cookies will be thicker and not puddle enough as they bake
• although you may be tempted, make sure that the amount of salt is not reduced
• for bittersweet chocolate to hand-cut into chunks, consider Lindt Excellence 70% Cocoa Extra Fine Dark Chocolate; Scharffen Berger Bittersweet 70% cacao; or Michel Cluizel Chocolat Amer Brut Bitter Chocolate 72% cacao
• the cookie dough can be formed into a thick cake or several logs, wrapped securely, and frozen for up to 1 month; defrost the dough in the refrigerator before forming and baking, adding about 2 minutes to the total baking time to accommodate for the chilled dough
• when preparing cookie dough for refrigeration or freezing, use organic eggs only
• never consume raw cookie dough

For the dough, sift the flour, baking soda, and salt onto a sheet of waxed paper.

Cream the butter in the large bowl of a freestanding electric mixer on moderate speed for 1 minute, or until just smooth. Add the dark brown sugar and beat for 45 seconds; add the light brown sugar and beat for 45 seconds longer. Add the granulated sugar and beat for 45 seconds longer. Blend in the eggs and beat on low speed for 1 minute, or just until incorporated. Blend in the vanilla extract. On low speed, blend in the sifted ingredients in 2 additions, beating just until the flour particles are absorbed. Scrape down the sides of the mixing bowl frequently with a rubber spatula to keep the dough even-textured. Remove the bowl from the mixer. Add the chocolate chips and work them in, using a sturdy rubber spatula or wooden spoon. The dough will be creamy, moderately dense, and packed with chips.

Divide the dough into thirds and turn each portion onto a sheet of food-safe plastic wrap, seal completely, and refrigerate overnight (or for at least 8 hours).

On baking day, remove the packets of chilled dough from the refrigerator.

Preheat the oven to 375 degrees F.

Line several cookie sheets or rimmed sheet pans with lengths of ovenproof parchment paper.

Place level 3-tablespoon-size mounds of dough on the prepared baking pans, spacing the mounds about 3 inches apart, and arranging 6 mounds on each standard-size sheet. Keep the top and edges of the mounds rough-textured.

Bake the cookies in the preheated oven for 13 to 14 minutes, or until just firm. The edges will be slightly darker (a medium golden color) than the centers; the centers should be just set and not wet-looking. Let the cookies stand on the baking pans for 1 minute, then transfer them to cooling racks, using a wide offset metal spatula. Cool completely. Store in an airtight tin.

notes
• the cookies are deeply buttery and an interesting contrast of dense/cakey centers and crisp/chewy edges
• the cookie dough can be formed into a thick cake or several logs, wrapped securely, and frozen for up to 1 month; defrost the dough in the refrigerator before forming and baking, adding about 2 minutes to the total baking time to accommodate for the chilled dough
• when preparing cookie dough for refrigeration or freezing, use organic eggs only
• never consume raw cookie dough

raging, buttery chocolate chip dough

3 cups unsifted bleached all-purpose flour

¼ teaspoon baking soda

1 teaspoon salt

¾ pound plus 6 tablespoons (3 sticks plus 6 tablespoons) unsalted butter, softened

⅔ cup firmly packed dark brown sugar

⅔ cup firmly packed light brown sugar

½ cup granulated sugar

2 large eggs

2 tablespoons vanilla extract

3 cups semisweet chocolate chips

serving: about 32 cookies
ahead: best on baking day; refrigerate cookie dough for 2 days or freeze for 1 month

just for fun

A simple and relaxed kind of dough, perfect for sweet yeasted pretzels, is one of those crafty (craft-like, handmade, a delight of a weekend-afternoon project—not tricky or dodgy by any means) bread-styled sweets that is nifty to have in your baking file.

After a reasonably short rise, a nice, pull-y puff of dough is divided into a dozen pieces, rolled into ropes, tied in random places, set to rise for a brief thirty minutes, then glazed, sugared, and baked. Soft, lightly crunchy, and with a vanilla "nose," the pretzels will enchant anyone within their presence.

Sweet pretzel sticks are fun to make, and a bang-up way to bring working with yeast into your baking life. Warm from the oven, the pretzels make people smile and, you can be sure, will engage conversation about the way they are created. Small children, who make great kitchen helpers, will want to try their hands at twisting and tying the dough, and even the malformed, slightly distorted specimens will bake into delicious treats. You'd be surprised how fanciful imperfect pretzel sticks can look once they are baked.

My own foray into pretzel-dom has moved way forward from the classic variety to the lighter, sweeter version represented in this recipe. It is my interpretation of how a scented, vanilla-caressed, yeast-raised pretzel dough should be, and I love its informality. You will not get into a flap with it, for the dough behaves well, and even a somewhat mishandled dough will provide you with a good batch, so you just know that I am in love with this trait. In addition to its seasoning with vanilla, the dough can be swept up with ground spice (cinnamon-sugar pretzels—*mmm*) or dotted with miniature semisweet chocolate chips (well, I had to offer this), and even topped with a light icing while still warm (in that case, cancel the final sugar glaze). And if you take out the vanilla and ¼ cup granulated sugar (plus the glaze), the dough segues into a savory mode—add finely (and freshly) grated Parmigiano-Reggiano, whisk a little smoked paprika into the flour, and sprinkle with an interesting coarse sea salt—you get the idea.

The pretzel sticks can be fat and pudgy, curvy, long, or short, with little knots or big knots at the top or bottom or in the middle—any way you pull and maneuver the dough, the architecture of the pretzel will amuse you.

sweet vanilla pretzel ties

vanilla sweet dough

2¼ teaspoons active dry yeast

¼ teaspoon granulated sugar

¼ cup warm (105 to 110 degrees F) water

¾ cup milk

¼ cup granulated sugar

5 tablespoons unsalted butter, cut into tablespoon-size chunks

2 teaspoons vanilla extract

1 large egg

1 large egg yolk

2 cups unsifted bleached all-purpose flour

½ teaspoon salt

1⅓ cups unsifted unbleached all-purpose flour, plus an additional 2 tablespoons, for kneading

sugar glaze

1 large egg white

about 5 tablespoons sugar (preferably Tur-binado Style Vanilla Sugar; see notes) or vanilla-scented granulated sugar (page 2), or sparkling sugar (plain or a color), for sprinkling on the unbaked pretzels

serving: 1 dozen pretzels
ahead: best on baking day

For the dough, stir together the yeast, the ¼ teaspoon granulated sugar, and the warm water in a heatproof measuring cup. Allow the mixture to stand until swollen, 6 to 7 minutes.

Place the milk and the ¼ cup granulated sugar in a small saucepan and set over moderate heat to warm the milk and begin to dissolve the sugar, about 5 minutes. Pour and scrape the milk mixture into a medium-size heatproof mixing bowl; stir in the chunks of butter and the vanilla extract. Let stand until lukewarm, about 6 minutes. Add the yeast mixture, the whole egg, and egg yolk, and mix well.

In a large mixing bowl, whisk the bleached flour and salt. Add the yeast-milk-butter-vanilla mixture and stir to combine, using a wooden spoon or flat wooden paddle. At this point, the dough will be thick and sticky. Blend in the unbleached flour and mix to combine most of the flour; The dough will be scraggly. Turn the mixture out onto a work surface and knead lightly to create a smooth dough. Dust the work surface with the additional 2 tablespoons unbleached flour. Knead the dough for 5 minutes. After 5 minutes, the dough will be bouncy and moderately soft.

Turn the dough into a bowl heavily coated with softened unsalted butter, lightly turn to coat all sides in a film of butter, make several cuts in the dough with a pair of kitchen scissors, cover tightly with a sheet of food-safe plastic wrap, and let rise at room temperature for 1 hour, or until doubled in bulk.

Uncover the dough and discard the plastic wrap.

Line several cookie sheets or rimmed sheet pans with lengths of ovenproof parchment paper.

To form the pretzels, place the dough on a lightly floured work surface. Divide it in half, then cut each half into 6 even-size pieces, creating 12 pieces in total. Roll each piece into a 6, 7, 8, or 10-inch rope; the length depends on the overall size you wish to create—pudgier pretzels or longer, more slender pretzels. The size of the pretzel ropes in the image on page 479 began as 7 inches. Tie the ropes into knots, either in the middle or at one end (or vary the knots). Place the pretzels on the prepared baking pans, spacing them at least 3 inches apart, and arranging 4 pretzels on each pan.

Cover the pans of pretzels loosely with sheets of food-safe plastic wrap. Let the pretzels rise at room temperature for 30 minutes, or until just puffy.

Preheat the oven to 400 degrees F in advance of baking.

Remove and discard the sheets of plastic wrap covering the pretzels.

For the glaze, whip the egg white until frothy in a small mixing bowl. Film the top of each pretzel with the whipped egg white, using a soft pastry brush and gentle strokes. Sprinkle a little of the vanilla sugar or sparkling sugar on top of each egg white–glazed pretzel.

Bake the pretzels in the preheated oven for 15 minutes, or until set and golden. Place the pans on cooling racks and let the pretzels stand in the pans for 5 minutes. Remove the pretzels to other cooling racks, using a wide offset metal spatula. Serve the pretzels warm or at room temperature.

notes
• a dip into a side dish of apricot or peach preserve sauce (heat 1 cup best-quality preserves with ⅓ cup unsweetened apple juice, bring to the simmer, then flavor with ¼ teaspoon vanilla extract) is a smashing accompaniment to the freshly baked sweet pretzels
• India Tree Vanilla Sugar Turbinado Style is a lightly crunchy, vanilla-imbued sugar that, when sprinkled on sweet yeast-risen breads, returns sweetly scented surfaces

flavored, dropped

One of the best-tempered—and the fastest—ways to have a tray full of small breads ready to pile into a basket is to become an accomplished drop biscuit maker.

Moving into the land of the hot biscuit means that, for one dinner or another, you will forsake serving the omnipresent "crusty loaf" of bread. Wise thinking.

A rustic drop biscuit is really a simple side step from its rolled-and-cut biscuit cousin, made by integrating fat into the standard leavened flour mixture and binding this into a moist dough with a liquid—usually whole milk, heavy cream, or buttermilk. On occasion, however, a soft dairy item such as sour cream or yogurt is utilized for its tanginess. The defining element is the possible range of additions that distinguish the dough, lending a fine aroma and texture—dried fruits, spices, nuts, and like things all blend nicely against the dough's efficient blank canvas. The dough can be neatly plopped onto a baking sheet or enclosed in baby-size individual molds (the latter, I admit, really appeals to me)—

miniature loaf or brioche pans are ideal. Even the most well-crafted baked drop biscuits look something like moon rocks—rugged all the way around—and this is not a baking mistake, so have no fear. Another switchover from dropping the dough onto a baking sheet is to mound it into standard-size or miniature muffin pans: this is a handy, favorite way to create another shape and retain the biscuits' primal moisture content as well. I love to do this with the *buttery cream drop biscuits* on page 486.

With biscuits, salted butter is the ideal accompaniment—it is simply the most tantalizing of all spreads, for its creamy, well-rounded dairy essence lushly sinks into the flaky highs and lows of the bread. The sight and scent of a warm biscuit, lifted right from the baking pan, split open, and smeared with butter, points to some good country-style baking.

corn meal and cranberry drop biscuits ✳ *buttery cream drop biscuits* ✳ *minature cream drop biscuit muffinettes*

corn meal and cranberry drop biscuits

cranberry buttermilk dough

1½ cups unsifted bleached all-purpose flour

½ cup plus 1 tablespoon stone-ground yellow corn meal

2 teaspoons baking powder

½ teaspoon baking soda

⅛ teaspoon cream of tartar

½ teaspoon salt

2 tablespoons granulated sugar

8 tablespoons (1 stick) cold unsalted butter, cut into chunks

⅔ cup dried sweetened cranberries

1 cup buttermilk, plus an additional 1 to 2 tablespoons, as needed

serving: about 21 biscuits
ahead: best on baking day

Preheat the oven to 400 degrees F.

Have several heavy cookie sheets or rimmed sheet pans at hand.

For the dough, whisk the flour, corn meal, baking powder, baking soda, cream of tartar, salt, and sugar in a large mixing bowl. Scatter over the chunks of butter and, using a pastry blender or two round-bladed table knives, cut the fat into the flour until reduced to pearl-size bits. With your fingertips, lightly crumble the fat into the flour for 45 seconds (reducing the butter to smaller flakes of varying sizes). Scatter over the cranberries and toss lightly to disperse them. Pour the 1 cup buttermilk over the fruit and butter–enhanced dry ingredients and quickly stir to form a dough, using a wooden spoon or flat wooden paddle. The dough should be moderately soft and hold its shape in a spoon; add 1 or 2 extra tablespoons of buttermilk, a little at a time, if needed, to achieve this state. Give the dough 4 or 5 quick kneading turns in the bowl, using a rubber spatula. Let the dough stand in the bowl for 1 minute.

Drop heaping 2-tablespoon-size mounds of dough onto the baking pans, spacing the mounds about 3 inches apart, and arranging 9 mounds on each standard-size sheet. Keep the mounds tall and plump.

Bake the biscuits in the preheated oven for 15 minutes, or until set and a spotty golden color on top. The undersides of the baked biscuits will be a medium golden color. Lift off the biscuits to a cooling rack, using a wide offset metal spatula. Serve warm.

notes
- stone-ground yellow corn meal contributes to a wonderfully textural biscuit; avoid substituting fine corn meal as the structure, flavor, and crumb of the biscuits will be compromised (fine corn meal will cause the biscuits to flatten somewhat); a favorite meal to use in this recipe is Arrowhead Mills Organic Yellow Corn Meal, available in 2-pound bags
- the final amount of buttermilk needed to bring the dough together will depend on the absorption quality of the flour and the humidity present in the atmosphere on baking day
- the dough can also be divided among 12 small fluted brioche molds (each mold measuring 3¼ inches in diameter across the top, from end of flute to end of flute, and 1⅝ inches deep, with a capacity of ⅓ cup plus 1 tablespoon plus 2½ teaspoons); bake the breads until set and a spotty golden color on top, about 20 minutes

drop biscuits, spice cake-style

Preheat the oven to 400 degrees F.

Have several heavy cookie sheets or rimmed sheet pans at hand.

For the dough, whisk the flour, baking powder, cream of tartar, salt, cinnamon, nutmeg, allspice, ginger, cloves, and sugar in a large mixing bowl. Scatter over the chunks of butter and, using a pastry blender or two round-bladed table knives, cut the fat into the flour until reduced to pearl-size bits. With your fingertips, lightly crumble the fat into the flour for 45 seconds (reducing the butter to smaller flakes of varying sizes). Scatter over the raisins and toss lightly to disperse them. Pour the 1 cup milk-vanilla extract blend over the fruit and butter–enhanced dry ingredients and quickly stir to form a dough, using a wooden spoon or flat wooden paddle. Give the dough 4 or 5 quick kneading turns in the bowl, using a rubber spatula. Let the dough stand in the bowl for 1 minute. (Note that the dough should be dense, but moist; add additional tablespoons of milk as needed to bring it to this state; the dough should hold its shape in a spoon.)

Drop heaping 2-tablespoon-size mounds of dough onto the baking pans, spacing the mounds about 3 inches apart, and arranging 9 mounds on each standard-size sheet. Keep the mounds tall and plump.

Bake the biscuits in the preheated oven for 15 minutes, or until firm and set. Lift off the biscuits to a cooling rack, using a wide offset metal spatula. Serve warm.

notes
- the final amount of milk needed to bring the dough together will depend on the absorption quality of the flour and the humidity present in the atmosphere on baking day
- as soon as the baked biscuits are pulled from the oven, you can raise the flavor and sweetness quotient by sprinkling cinnamon sugar over them (use ¼ cup granulated sugar blended with ½ teaspoon ground cinnamon), or the tops of the hot biscuits can be spread with *vanilla icing* (page 392)

spiced dough

2 cups unsifted bleached all-purpose flour

4 teaspoons baking powder

½ teaspoon cream of tartar

¼ teaspoon salt

1 teaspoon ground cinnamon

½ teaspoon freshly grated nutmeg

¼ teaspoon ground allspice

¼ teaspoon ground ginger

⅛ teaspoon ground cloves

¼ cup granulated sugar

8 tablespoons (1 stick) cold unsalted butter, cut into chunks

⅔ cup dark seedless or golden raisins

1 cup milk whisked with ¾ teaspoon vanilla extract, plus an additional 1 to 2 tablespoons milk, as needed

serving: about 21 biscuits
ahead: best on baking day

buttery cream drop biscuits

cream dough

2 cups unsifted bleached all-purpose flour

4 teaspoons baking powder

½ teaspoon cream of tartar

¼ teaspoon salt

2 tablespoons granulated sugar

8 tablespoons (1 stick) cold unsalted butter, cut into tablespoon-size chunks

1¼ cups heavy cream, blended with ¼ teaspoon vanilla extract

3 tablespoons unsalted butter, melted, for brushing over the baked biscuits

pinches of *fleur de sel,* for sprinkling (optional)

serving: about 23 biscuits
ahead: best on baking day

Preheat the oven to 400 degrees F.

Have several heavy cookie sheets or rimmed sheet pans at hand.

For the dough, whisk the flour, baking powder, cream of tartar, salt, and sugar in a large mixing bowl. Scatter over the chunks of butter and, using a pastry blender or two round-bladed table knives, cut the fat into the flour until reduced to pearl-size bits. With your fingertips, lightly crumble the fat into the flour for 45 seconds (reducing the butter to smaller flakes of varying sizes). Pour the heavy cream-vanilla extract blend over the butter-enhanced dry ingredients and quickly stir to form a dense and slightly sticky dough, using a wooden spoon or flat wooden paddle. Give the dough 4 or 5 quick kneading turns in the bowl, using a rubber spatula. Let the dough stand in the bowl for 1 minute.

Drop heaping 2-tablespoon-size mounds of dough onto the baking pans, spacing the mounds about 3 inches apart, and arranging 9 mounds on each standard-size sheet. Keep the mounds tall and plump.

Bake the biscuits in the preheated oven for 15 minutes, or until set and a spotty golden color on top, with medium golden undersides. Immediately gloss over the tops with the melted butter, using a soft pastry brush, and sprinkle lightly with *fleur de sel,* if you wish. Lift off the biscuits to cooling racks, using a wide offset metal spatula. Serve warm.

notes

• the combination of heavy cream and butter establishes a drop biscuit with a denser, richer texture and exceptional dairy flavor
• the vanilla extract, though not overtly noticeable, builds on the flavor of the heavy cream
• the final amount of heavy cream needed to bring the dough together will depend on the absorption quality of the flour and the humidity present in the atmosphere on baking day
• the dough can also be divided among 12 miniature loaf pans (each pan measuring 3¼ by 2 inches and 1¼ inches deep, with a capacity of a scant ½ cup), lightly buttered or filmed with nonstick flour-and-oil spray; mound the dough in the center of each, and the biscuits baked for 17 minutes

miniature cream drop biscuit muffinettes

Preheat the oven to 400 degrees F.

Film the inside of 33 miniature muffin cups (12 cups to a pan, each cup measuring 1¾ inches in diameter and ¾ inch deep, with a capacity of 1 tablespoon plus 2 teaspoons) with softened unsalted butter. Or, line the cups with miniature ovenproof paper baking cup liners.

For the dough, whisk the flour, baking powder, cream of tartar, salt, and sugar in a large mixing bowl. Scatter over the chunks of butter and the shortening and, using a pastry blender or two round-bladed table knives, cut the fat into the flour until reduced to pearl-size bits. With your fingertips, lightly crumble the fat into the flour for 45 seconds (reducing the fat to smaller flakes of varying sizes), then pour over the heavy cream. Quickly stir to form a firmly moist but slightly sticky dough, using a wooden spoon or flat wooden paddle. Give the dough 4 or 5 quick kneading turns in the bowl, using a rubber spatula.

Scoop the dough into the prepared muffin cups, dividing it evenly among them and mounding the dough toward the center. Keep the dough rough-textured. Sprinkle tiny flakes of *fleur de sel* on top of each muffinette, if you wish.

Bake the muffinettes in the preheated oven for 13 to 14 minutes, or until risen, set, and a spotty golden color on top. Cool the muffinettes in the pans on racks for 5 to 7 minutes, remove them from the pans, and serve warm.

notes
• White Lily flour, a softer winter wheat flour with a lower protein content (9 grams of protein in 1 cup), is available in 2-pound bags at many specialty food markets
• the dough can also be divided among 18 baby fluted brioche molds (each mold measuring 2¼ inches in diameter across the top, from end of flute to end of flute, and 1 inch deep, with a capacity of 2 tablespoons); if you are using these molds for baking, bake the breads at 375 degrees F for 20 minutes, or until set and a spotty golden color on top

moist and creamy dough

2 cups unsifted bleached soft winter wheat, low-protein all-purpose flour (preferably White Lily flour; see notes)

4 teaspoons baking powder

½ teaspoon cream of tartar

¼ teaspoon salt

2 tablespoons granulated sugar

4 tablespoons (½ stick) cold unsalted butter, cut into chunks

4 tablespoons solid shortening, at room temperature

1¼ cups heavy cream

pinches of *fleur de sel*, for sprinkling (optional)

serving: 33 muffinettes
ahead: best on baking day

establishing a tradition

This is my world: I am a homebody whose life revolves around orchestrating an environment that beckons and calms.

It is also a life that revolves around a mixing bowl or, more precisely, around a mixing bowl filled with dough or batter. Once in my own kitchen, and after a slew of life experiences tossed me about, I decided that certain traditions needed to be created for the purpose of grounding myself. The custom turned into baking a series of sweet and savory things (no surprise) to be served to invitees, or to have around just for me—for filling a cookie jar, an antique bread box, or one of my many cake keepers of various sizes and depths.

One of the first—and now permanent—customs was to bake rolls on the weekend. Simple rolls, tender and moist, that are assembled in a baking pan and placed closely enough so that they eventually kiss when risen and baked, became a fixture almost every time a chicken was sent into the oven to roast. The rolls were such a staple that I named the bread, quite affectionately, *"roasted chicken" rolls*. Once in a while, someone actually thought that roasted chicken was an ingredient in the dough, never quite making the leap from its place in the menu to the name. Eventually, there would be a few rolls called by that name, including sweet potato rolls, cheese rolls, oatmeal rolls, and so on, then each and every one of them was called a "roasted chicken" roll, even if the steamy bundle of

them was served with roasted turkey, braised short ribs, you name it. (The never-ending questions "Are *these* the roasted chicken rolls?" followed by "May I have the recipe?" are answered below. Finally!)

The twenty rolls, plump and glossy with a last-minute brush of butter, routinely disappeared in short order, and once I was challenged by someone to turn this into a sweet breakfast roll. How bad could that be? The sweeter version may have been good, but my recipe (now considered the "classic") never quite achieved the status of its plainer forerunner. (In short, and in my opinion, the two concepts never met.) I have them at hand right now, and I can assure you that they make a seamless transition to each season. The sweet potato version, with its pale golden crumb, is equally winning; the rolls are welcome on the table during fall and throughout the winter, for they pair pleasantly with any kind of soup or stew. The #1 rolls are a year-round basic bread.

Do you have a bedrock recipe that has become a baking tradition? If not, begin with this one, and consider adding *"roasted chicken" rolls, #1* to the roster. And let me know if you've modified them somehow, changing the dough this way and that, thus making them a part of your own culinary history.

"roasted chicken" rolls, #1

fluffy dough

2¼ teaspoons active dry yeast

¼ teaspoon granulated sugar

¼ cup warm (105 to 110 degrees F) water

¾ cup milk

3 tablespoons granulated sugar

5 tablespoons unsalted butter, cut into tablespoon-size chunks

one 6-ounce russet potato (peeled, chunked, boiled, drained [reserving 1 tablespoon of the cooking water], and riced), to yield about ⅔ cup riced potato

2 large egg yolks, lightly beaten

3 cups unsifted bleached all-purpose flour

½ teaspoon salt

butter and salt finish (optional)

about 3 tablespoons butter (preferably clarified butter, page 1), melted and still warm

coarse salt, for sprinkling

serving: 20 rolls
ahead: best on baking day; or freeze for 1 month, defrost, bundle in aluminum foil, and reheat in a preheated 325 degrees F oven for 10 to 15 minutes, then apply the butter and salt finish

For the dough, stir together the yeast, the ¼ teaspoon sugar, and the warm water in a heatproof measuring cup. Allow the mixture to stand until swollen, 6 to 7 minutes.

Place the milk and the 3 tablespoons sugar in a small saucepan and set over moderate heat to warm the milk and begin to dissolve the sugar, about 5 minutes. Pour and scrape the milk mixture into a medium-size heatproof mixing bowl. Stir in the chunks of butter and the riced potato. Let stand until lukewarm, about 6 minutes. Add in the yeast mixture, the egg yolks, and the 1 tablespoon potato cooking water. Mix well.

In a large mixing bowl, whisk the flour and the salt. Add the potato-yeast-milk mixture and stir to combine, using a wooden spoon or flat wooden paddle. The dough will be dry in sections and softer-moister in other patchy sections. Turn the mixture out onto a work surface and combine to create a cohesive dough. Knead the dough for 7 minutes, at which point it should be smooth, supple, and moderately soft.

Turn the dough into a bowl heavily coated with softened unsalted butter, lightly turn to coat all sides in a film of butter, make several cuts in the dough with a pair of kitchen scissors, cover tightly with a sheet of food-safe plastic wrap, and let rise at cool room temperature for 1 hour and 30 minutes, or until doubled in bulk.

Uncover the dough and discard the plastic wrap.

Film the inside of a 13 by 9 by 2-inch baking pan with softened unsalted butter.

To form the rolls, place the dough on a lightly floured work surface. Divide the dough in half, then cut each half into 10 even-size pieces, creating 20 pieces in total. Smooth each piece into a plump ball by rolling it on the work surface briskly under the cupped palm of your hand. Place the balls of dough in the prepared baking pan, assembling them in five rows of 4 each.

Cover the pan of rolls loosely with a sheet of food-safe plastic wrap. Let the rolls rise at cool room temperature for 1 hour to 1 hour and 15 minutes, or until doubled in bulk. The rolls will merge as they rise. At doubled in bulk, the rolls will rise to about ¾ inch short of the rim of the baking pan (the dough rises into fine, light rolls and may collapse if over-risen—so take care to monitor the second rise).

Preheat the oven to 375 degrees F in advance of baking.

Remove and discard the sheet of plastic wrap covering the rolls.

Bake the rolls in the preheated oven for 25 to 30 minutes, or until set and a medium golden color on top.

Place the pan on a cooling rack and let the rolls stand for 10 minutes. Carefully and gently (the rolls are fragile), invert the pan of rolls onto another cooling rack, then invert again to stand right side up. If you are using the butter and salt finish, brush the surface of the rolls with the melted butter and top with a few sprinklings of coarse salt. Serve the rolls warm or at room temperature, by detaching them at their natural seams. Store in an airtight container.

notes
• in this recipe, the emphasis is less on the potato (as opposed to the recipes in the *zoom!* essay, pages 401 through 406) than it is on the overall butter-milk-egg yolk fluffiness of the dough, as the riced potatoes become a "background" ingredient

"roasted chicken" rolls, #2

For the dough, stir together the yeast, the ¼ teaspoon sugar, and the warm water in a heatproof measuring cup. Allow the mixture to stand until swollen, 6 to 7 minutes.

Place the milk and the ¼ cup sugar in a small saucepan and set over moderate heat to warm the milk and begin to dissolve the sugar, about 5 minutes. Pour and scrape the milk mixture into a medium-size heatproof mixing bowl. Stir in the chunks of butter and the riced potato. Let stand until lukewarm, about 6 minutes. Add the yeast mixture and the egg. Mix well.

In a large mixing bowl, whisk the unbleached flour, salt, and 1 cup of the bleached flour. Add the potato-yeast-milk mixture and stir to combine, using a wooden spoon or flat wooden paddle. Let the mixture stand, uncovered, for 5 minutes. Stir in the remaining ½ cup bleached flour. The dough will have both dry and moist patches at this point. Turn the mixture onto a work surface and combine to create a cohesive dough. Sprinkle the additional 5 tablespoons bleached flour on the work surface and knead the dough for 5 to 7 minutes, using as much of the flour as necessary to create a moderately firm dough; most times, the dough will take all of the flour, but this will

(continued on the next page)

sweet potato dough

2¼ teaspoons active dry yeast

¼ teaspoon granulated sugar

¼ cup warm (105 to 110 degrees F) water

¾ cup milk

¼ cup granulated sugar

6 tablespoons (¾ stick) unsalted butter, cut into tablespoon-size chunks

one 8-ounce sweet potato (peeled, chunked, boiled, drained, and riced), to yield about ¾ cup riced potato

1 large egg

2 cups unsifted unbleached all-purpose flour

(continued on the next page)

(continued from the previous page)

¾ teaspoon salt

1½ cups unsifted bleached all-purpose flour, plus an additional 5 tablespoons, as needed for kneading

serving: 20 rolls
ahead: best on baking day; or freeze for 1 month, defrost, bundle in aluminum foil, and reheat in a preheated 325 degrees F oven for 10 to 15 minutes

depend on the atmospheric conditions and absorption quality/age of the flour. The dough should be supple and bouncy after kneading.

Turn the dough into a bowl heavily coated with softened unsalted butter, lightly turn to coat all sides in a film of butter, make several cuts in the dough with a pair of kitchen scissors, cover tightly with a sheet of food-safe plastic wrap, and let rise at cool room temperature for 1 hour and 30 minutes, or until doubled in bulk.

Uncover the dough and discard the plastic wrap.

Film the inside of a 13 by 9 by 2-inch baking pan with softened unsalted butter.

To form the rolls, place the dough on a lightly floured work surface. Divide the dough in half, then cut each half into 10 even-size pieces, creating 20 pieces in total. Smooth each piece into a plump ball by rolling it on the work surface briskly under the cupped palm of your hand. Place the balls of dough in the prepared baking pan, assembling them in five rows of 4 each.

Cover the pan of rolls loosely with a sheet of food-safe plastic wrap. Let the rolls rise at cool room temperature for 1 hour to 1 hour and 15 minutes, or until doubled in bulk. The rolls will merge as they rise. At doubled in bulk, the rolls will rise to about ½ inch short of the rim of the baking pan.

Preheat the oven to 375 degrees F in advance of baking.

Remove and discard the sheet of plastic wrap covering the rolls.

Bake the rolls in the preheated oven for 30 minutes, or until set and a deep golden color on top.

Place the pan on a cooling rack and let the rolls stand for 10 minutes. Carefully invert the pan of rolls onto another cooling rack, then invert again to stand right side up. Serve the rolls warm or at room temperature, by detaching them at their natural seams. Store in an airtight container.

notes
• even when riced, the sweet potatoes will contain some threadlike filaments that will show up in the kneaded dough and finished rolls—very pretty

Baking Storybook Epilogue

every last crumb

I unearthed my long-forgotten recipe for homemade crackers. Starters, in all strengths of sour and in varying degrees of quantity, are nurtured only to take over an entire refrigerator shelf or countertop, depending on which day what sludgy, pasty, or sticky mass demands my attention. The innards of a lonely clump of country bread are turned into a tasty bread salad. Chewy rectangles of packed-with-energy bars loaded with organic dried fruits, nuts, seeds in a range of complexions, and sweeteners formerly unknown to the mainstream supermarket shelf, continue to be lifted tidily from a nine-inch baking pan.

A large, slightly stale hunk of my newest iteration of *pain de mie* has been chunked up, soaked, and layered in a suave coconut custard mixture and baked. A gorgeous block of rich white cornbread was resuscitated into a grand stuffing for Cornish hens. And then there was the morning that I whipped up four varieties of cookie dough, lovingly formed them into paper-wrapped logs, tied the ends with twine, lined a freezer shelf with the largess, and sat back to admire my diligence and foresight.

Let me tell you what has been happening in the kitchen over the last few years: I have morphed into my own resource for whatever baked sweet or savory my needs require.

Depending on having everything—and I do mean everything—homemade is my new religion. Let me refine that: entirely homemade. And refine that further: faith is what you really need here in order to keep up this strategy. Even for someone who is entirely passionate about baking and the baking process (that is me!), the very notion of "entirely homemade" had turned into an ongoing test of sorts. Since reliability does have its slippery side, occasional backslides of adherence have occurred over time.

My attempt, based on the urge for self-sufficiency for every last crumb emanating from my kitchen and my kitchen alone, has me baking wildly in all directions—tender breakfast breads, crusty dinner breads (and, with a good quick turn of a serrated knife, *croûtes* and *croûtons*), teatime cookies, biscotti and shortbread for the coffee break and as take-along sustenance for car trips, chewy-crispy-crunchy granolalike sweetmeats, and so much more. Need a snack? No problem. There is a tin of something already baked lurking somewhere on two if not three floors of my home. Blocks of fudgy brownies lounge in the freezer next to swirls of pastry created from a dough that takes—on and off—three days to complete. At any given time, I may have a minimum of, say, three to five kinds of dinner rolls, one or two coffee cakes, unbaked spirals of cream cheese–centered dough expecting to be assembled on a baking sheet to—presto!—become *rugelach,* a date-nut bread waiting to be sliced, or a parade of sticky buns, in addition to random toppings and sauces. My freezer is a riot of stage-ready things.

The perilous conditions of a damaging ice storm many years ago that turned most of the streets in Washington, D.C., into a premier citywide ice skating rink tested my resourcefulness, as seven guests were a day away from congregating around my dining room table for a casual supper. You couldn't drive to a store for a loaf of bread, and even walking was touch and go. The hungry eaters were coming anyway and, to this day, I can't figure out how they made it safely, as the streets were lined with what seemed like one continuous carpet of packed snow overlaid with ice. Luckily, all of the provisions for dinner were in-house, except for the bread, so I decided to put together an overnight dough for a rambling, savory cheese bread to rip apart and serve with the main course. The next day, as I pressed out the dough onto a big baking sheet while the lamb shanks and white beans were bubbling slowly on a back burner, I realized that my inability to buy bread a few blocks away at a neighborhood bakery had upended my usual can-do attitude. The scenario was unnerving, but it did teach me that I could depend on my own initiative.

Yet the path to baking self-sustainability is not without its rough patches—the bad, messy ones.

If you are on the outside peering in, my catalog of mishaps reads like a kitchen comedy of sorts. However, if you are the one trying to manage a new, self-imposed infrastructure of all-homemade-all-the-time, there is that moment in time when it seems more appealing to run out, cash tucked into a pocket, for the nearest *boule*. Here is a recount of several episodes that stand out, testing the patience of mind, body and, might I add, my cleanup skills:

Episode A: I stored a batch of soupy pre-ferment (the basis for several holey and crusty flatbreads) in what seemed like a roomy container. The active mixture broke through the lid and danced out onto the refrigerator shelf, worked its way between the frame of the door and the rubber seal that usually secures the door, and forced the unit open by about 1 inch. The goo puddled in a nice pattern on the floor.

The exuberance of the mixture—and it was a randy one—exceeded my expectations. But not in a good way. Postscript: I was away for eight hours when this event occurred. (Ugh.)

Episode B: The most expensive loaves of bread I ever "purchased," about $500-worth, were "bought" during the weekend I cranked up the oven to 500 degrees F during a summer heat wave to bake several breads for a picnic. The air-conditioning promptly failed and I lingered in my own sauna for a dreadful day until the unit was repaired. The bread was delicious, but not $500-delicious.

Episode C: In the Midnight-Baking-Can-Be-Fun department, let me recount for you the time that I miscalculated the bake-off schedule for a previously refrigerated dough. Four dozen butter rolls of some delicacy were timed to be loaded into the oven for a bake at the agreeable hour of 12:00 noon. Wrong. Make that 1:30 a.m. A mathematical error thus created my longest babysitting session ever on record. (It even exceeded the leisurely wait for a multigrain dough destined to be sandwich bread; eventually, I gave up and made rolls out of the massive glob that would have been a well-constructed loaf—if patience had allowed—and so trimmed the waiting time by five hours, or more.)

The rhythm of baking, flowing from one philosophically serendipitous moment to another, does have its charm—if you take the long view, with a certain relaxed mentality (which I am still attempting to accomplish). The "Look, Ma, I Made Everything Dinner Party (or Brunch, or Lunch, or Tea)" perspective captivates friends who now expect the whole deal to come from my girl-powered hands. This is now my lot and it is always rewarding, if not occasionally challenging. I hope that I can keep it up. I'd tell you more, but I have to put this bittersweet chocolate tea bread into the oven.

a snazzy bittersweet chocolate tea bread

Preheat the oven to 375 degrees F.

Line a heavy rimmed sheet pan or cookie sheet with a length of ovenproof parchment paper. (The baking pan must be heavy or the bottom of the bread will darken considerably before the interior is entirely baked.)

For the dough, sift the flour, baking powder, salt, and granulated sugar into a medium-size mixing bowl. Drop in the chunks of butter and, using a pastry blender or two round-bladed table knives, cut the fat into the flour mixture until reduced to small bits.

In a small mixing bowl, whisk the heavy cream, egg, and vanilla extract.

Pour the heavy cream–egg-vanilla extract mixture over the flour mixture, sprinkle over the chopped chocolate, and stir to form a crumbly dough, using a wooden spoon or flat wooden paddle. With your fingertips, bring the mixture together until a cohesive dough is formed. The mixing and forming of the dough should not take longer than about 1 minute. Note that the dough is mixed only to shape and form, as light kneading frequently results in a dense-textured crumb.

Transfer the dough to a lightly floured work surface and form into a well-domed ball measuring about 5 inches in diameter, keeping the dough ball as plump as possible. Place the dough ball in the center of the baking pan. With a small sharp knife, cut a cross on the surface of the bread (about ¼ inch deep). Sprinkle the sparkling sugar over the surface of the bread.

Bake the bread in the preheated oven for 40 minutes, or until set and golden. Let the bread stand on the baking pan for 2 minutes, then remove to a cooling rack, using two wide offset metal spatulas. Serve at room temperature.

notes
• the amount of heavy cream needed to bring the dough together depends on the density of the cream (thicker is better), the absorption quality of the flour, and the atmospheric conditions of the day; you can safely add 1 to 2 tablespoons heavy cream in order to create a cohesive dough, but realize that a too-slack dough may bake out of shape—in other words, aim for a dough ball that holds its shape, but is not *too* moist (if you are unsure, begin with ½ cup and go from there), keeping in mind, however, that the overall moistness of the dough contributes to the bread's rich, silky quality and enticing crumb.
• use a finely serrated knife to cut the bread

vanilla and chocolate chunk dough

2 cups unsifted all-purpose flour

2¾ teaspoons baking powder

¼ teaspoon salt

3 tablespoons granulated sugar

6 tablespoons (¾ stick) cold unsalted butter, cut into tablespoon-size chunks

⅔ cup heavy cream

1 large egg

2 teaspoons vanilla extract

7 ounces bittersweet chocolate (in the cacao range of 60% to 70%), chopped into small nuggets

about 2 tablespoons sparkling sugar, for sprinkling on the unbaked round of dough

serving: one tea bread, creating about 10 slices
ahead: best on baking day

baking*Diary*

scrapbooking your baking memories

Like a patchwork quilt of many stitched-together pieces that, taken as a whole, presents a larger, more complex pattern, a baking diary reveals the personal baking history of its author, recipe by recipe. The experience of detailing your favorite recipes, including the intimately historical elements that contribute to them, is a way of scrapbooking food memories.

Annotating a recipe with observations and stories will bring your favorite baked goods to life long after they are devoured, for the journal itself becomes a personal dialogue of your baking.

Creating a journal is straightforward once you have a working template for expanding on a recipe. A recipe is the foundation, but the entry should include a dated chronicle of it, plus notes on particulars or peculiarities. Think of this as a sort of an expanded recipe card, one that has a certain background and a recollection or two.

Following is the simple model I use to form a framework for each individual entry in a culinary-style daybook. Your very own cookbook—for sharing and for teaching—will then be filled with many pages of personal recipes and baking memorabilia, becoming an important touchstone for the next generation of cooks to follow.

recipe title

ingredients

_____

_____

_____

_____

_____

_____

_____

_____

yield

_____

_____

prepared on

_____

procedure

_____

_____

_____

_____

_____

_____

_____

_____

_____

_____

thoughts and observations

_____

_____

_____

_____

_____

baking*SelectedSources*

The following references for purchasing products are dependable sources for cooks and bakers of all experience levels and needs and, over time, they have distinguished themselves from the standpoint of quality and customer service. Be sure to check and verify items for availability, as changes in stock are possible as the months progress or various inventories shift with regard to their offerings.

August Thomsen Corporation (Ateco)

www.atecousa.net

August Thomsen Corporation is the source for Ateco products, which include a high-quality, selected range of specialty baking tools (including molds and pans), cake decorating tools, and other baking-related supplies.

Bella Viva Orchards

www.bellaviva.com

Bella Viva Orchards sells gorgeous dried fruits (and nuts) of exceptional quality. The range includes yellow nectarines and white nectarines; white peaches and yellow peaches; Dapple Dandy pluots; Betty Anne plums, Moyer prunes, and French prunes; Bing cherries and Rainier cherries; red flame raisins, Thompson raisins, and Golden Thompson raisins; sweet apricots, tangy apricots, and slab apricots; cranberries; and pears. It is well worth it to stock up for fall and winter baking when the flavors and textures of dried fruits are so appealing when added to cake, bread, and cookie batters and doughs.

Bob's Red Mill Natural Foods, Inc.

www.bobsredmill.com

Bob's Red Mill is a premium source for an extensive and high-quality range of whole grain cereals, grains, flours, seeds, and meals; cornstarch; leavenings; and sugars, among other baking items. Both the quality and variety of the goods are stunning. The full catalog list may be viewed on the Web site, but I love having the actual mail-order catalog booklet in my hands.

Bridge Kitchenware Corporation

www.bridgekitchenware.com

Bridge Kitchenware is a destination shopping place for fine baking tools, including sifters and dredgers, knives, pastry blenders, all kinds of bakeware (muffin pans, cake pans, and tart pans), spoons and spatulas, baking sheets, rolling pins, pastry decorating equipment, and other items for the avocational and professional cook.

Fireworks Popcorn

www.popcornlovers.com

Fireworks Popcorn offers twelve varieties of beautiful popcorn (non-genetically modified). Of particular interest for creating caramel popcorn is the Orchard Blossom variety (it is actually pink, but pops large and white). All varieties are quite flavorful, with a genuine (and most delicious) corn flavor. The sampler of all twelve types is a great way to experience the range of textures and flavors that the company sells.

Fran's Cake and Candy Supplies

www.franscakeandcandysupplies.com

Sallee McCarthy, the owner of Fran's Cake and Candy Supplies, maintains the quality of the business, a respected resource for cake decorators, sugar artists, and bakers of all levels of proficiency. The store carries a range of cake decorating supplies, including food-safe paste colors; all types of baking pans (both traditional and whimsical); piping gel; sprinkles and sanding sugar; decorative cupcake picks and ovenproof paper baking cup liners; icing and offset spatulas; pastry bags, brushes, and tips; materials for wedding cake specialists and showpiece work; and all types and sizes of bakery boxes for presentation, among other items. Fran's Cake and Candy Supplies also holds cake and cookie decorating classes, as well as classes on the art of sugar work and candy making (for details, check in with the store for a calendar of events). Ms. McCarthy, highly knowledgeable in the area of cake decorating and cake craft, is responsive to even the most detailed questions, and generously offers solutions to decorating concerns and queries.

India Tree

www.indiatree.com

Consult the store locator on the India Tree Web site to find a business that stocks India Tree products, which include sparkling sugars, light and dark muscovado sugars, golden baker's sugar, demerara sugar, and maple sugar.

JB Prince Company, Inc.

www.jbprince.com

JB Prince sells a high-end selection of bakeware and cutlery. Not to be missed is the superb array of serrated knives and pastry equipment, which inlcudes cutters, cooling racks, cake pans, whisks, tongs, strainers, and other specialty tools.

King Arthur Flour

www.kingarthurflour.com

King Arthur Flour stocks baking supplies and ingredients, tools, and equipment, including decorating sugars, flours, yeasts, extracts, leaveners, thickeners, and spices; measuring equipment; baking pans; processors and mixers; and bread-crafting equipment and the like for bakers of all proficiency levels.

La Cuisine—The Cook's Resource

www.lacuisineus.com

In its perfectly edited space, La Cuisine offers a range of French pastry essences; gorgeous copper of all shapes and descriptions; essential baking molds and tins; woodenware; cast iron; a wonderful French fryer assembly (basket and fry pot); cutters and decorating equipment; all this in addition to seasonal supplies and edibles. The small staff takes pride in kitchen-testing the goods on the shelves and, as such, can extend valuable information to any consumer—this is especially helpful for the esoterica.

La Cuisine is also an important reference point for some of the items used in the recipes contained in this volume and offers an availability list of chosen bakeware and baking-related products that dovetail with my recommendations for equipment, flavoring agents, and like goods. For your consideration, connect with the store's Web site and its informative newsletter to view what's currently available. As well, La Cuisine takes pride in securing, when available, specialty items for customers through telephone or e-mail contact. La Cuisine ships worldwide.

New York Cake and Baking Distributor

www.nycake.com

New York Cake and Baking Distributor is a destination location for all goods related to baking. The store stocks a complete range of bakeware in many types and styles, including cake pans, tart pans, and muffin pans; cookie sheets and cookie cutters; cooling racks; molds of all sizes and shapes; strainers; measuring equipment; whisks and spatulas; and a detailed range of pastry bags, pastry tips, and food-safe paste food colors. The staff is knowledgeable and committed to the art, craft, and execution of baking.

Rose Levy Bakeware

Rose Levy Beranbaum, author of *The Cake Bible* and *Rose's Heavenly Cakes* (among other notable books), is, to say the least, cake-savvy and baking-eloquent. Two bakeware items that you will be proud to have and use in your *batterie de cuisine* have been perfected by Rose and are available at www.amazon.com: a band that hugs a cake pan and a pie dish. Rose's Heavenly Cake Strip, a silicone band that fits around the sides of a 9-inch layer cake pan or an 8-inch square pan, allows the batter to rise evenly, creating moist edges, and virtually eliminates any annoying peaking or cresting. (Avid layer cake bakers should consider owning two cake bands.) Rose's Perfect Pie Plate, with its deeply fluted edge (9 inches in diameter, with a capacity of 4 cups), is a natural for baking pies, of course, but it also works for snuggling hand-formed yeast rolls and brownie or blondie batters destined to become crustless "pies."

Sugarpaste, LLC

www.sugarpaste.com

Sugarpaste's Crystal Colors are U.S. Certified Food Colors: dried food-safe food color powders perfect for applying with a neutral spirit (vodka is recommended) for "painting" on royal icing–coated cookies, kneading into fondant icing, mixing into buttercream frostings or royal icing, or for dusting on gum paste flowers; there is a beautiful color range available (view the color chart online). Sugarpaste also carries flower cutters, veiners, and molds for decorative gum paste work. The owner of Sugarpaste, Elizabeth Parvu, is an accomplished sugar artist and instructor, and welcomes professional queries through her Web site. Ms. Parvu also teaches classes in the art of gum paste worldwide. Be sure to consult her Web site for a calendar of appearances and the special recipe for handmade pearls to enhance royal icing–coated cookies, fondant-covered cakes, and buttercream-decorated cakes. Ms. Parvu has posted this recipe especially for the readers of *Baking Style*. Regarding a source for fondant (a component for creating the handmade pearls), Ms. Parvu recommends the fondant ingredient, Satin Ice, available at www.satinfinefoods.com.

Sur la Table

www.surlatable.com

Sur La Table is a resource for cookware, bakeware, and a range of food- and baking-related products. Of particular interest to bakers is the extensive range of decorating tools, baking pans (including bread molds), baking sheets, and mixing bowls.

Ultimate Baker

www.cooksdream.com

Ultimate Baker carries a wide range of Ateco products (view the online catalog on the Web site) for baking plain and fancy.

Whole Foods Market

www.wholefoodsmarket.com

The following, available at regional Whole Foods Market locations, are of particular interest to bakers: dried fruits, chocolates, crystallized ginger, honey and maple syrup, nuts and seeds, whole grains and whole grain flours, extracts, whole and ground spices, oils, organic eggs, premium butters and other organic dairy products, organic all-vegetable shortening (nonhydrogenated), sugars (including natural turbinado sugar, organic turbinado raw cane sugar, evaporated cane juice sugar, pure cane rough-cut cubes, organic ground cane sugar, raw cane sugar, and demerara sugar cubes), and unsulphured medium-shred macaroon coconut and natural unsweetened medium-flake coconut.

Williams-Sonoma

www.williams-sonoma.com

Williams-Sonoma stocks bakeware and cookware, including cake and muffin/cupcake pans, cookie sheets and sheet pans, bread pans, mixing bowls, measuring equipment, and various seasonal pastry tools, among other items.

Wilton Industries, Inc.

www.wilton.com

Wilton is a reliable source for cake decorating supplies, and the Wilton *Cake Decorating!* yearbook is an essential guide to cake decorating products and how-to information. Wilton stocks a range of pastry tips and pastry bags; baking pans and molds; ingredients for icing and frostings (including meringue powder); and many cake decorating-specific supplies, such as levelers, doilies, corrugated cake boards, stencils, and packaging materials.

baking*Bibliography*

Lovely confections of all sorts are contained in the volumes listed here—individually and collectively, they speak to the great and ever-growing expanse of what you can do with butter, sugar, flour, eggs, leavening, and other baking-centered ingredients. This literature makes sweet reading and many offer remarkably precise and definitive technical information on subjects narrow and wide. Best of all, even armchair bakers will be drawn to the kitchen by the captivating way the authors relate the tale of a batch of cookies, a towering layer cake, or bounteous loaf of bread. Dig in.

Books

Alston, Elizabeth. *Biscuits and Scones: 62 Recipes from Breakfast Biscuits to Homey Desserts.* New York: Clarkson N. Potter, 1988.

Amendola, Joseph, and Donald Lundberg. *Understanding Baking: The Art and Science of Baking.* New York: Van Nostrand Reinhold, 1992.

Appel, Jennifer. *Buttercup Bakes at Home: More Than 75 New Recipes from Manhattan's Premier Bake Shop for Tempting Homemade Sweets.* New York: Simon & Schuster, 2006.

The Baker's Dozen, Inc. *The Baker's Dozen Cookbook: Become a Better Baker with 135 Foolproof Recipes and Tried-and-True Techniques.* Edited by Rick Rodgers. New York: William Morrow, 2001.

Beard, James. *Beard on Bread.* New York: Alfred A. Knopf, 1973.

Beranbaum, Rose Levy. *The Bread Bible.* New York: W. W. Norton, 2003.

——. *The Cake Bible.* New York: William Morrow, 1988.

——. *The Pie and Pastry Bible.* New York: Scribner, 1998.

——. *Rose's Christmas Cookies.* New York: William Morrow, 1998.

——. *Rose's Heavenly Cakes.* Hoboken, NJ: John Wiley & Sons, 2009.

Bilheux, Roland, and Alain Escoffier. *Petits Fours, Chocolate, Frozen Desserts, and Sugar Work.* Vol. 3 of French Professional Pastry Series. Under the direction of Pierre Michalet; translated by Rhona Lauvand and James Peterson. Paris: Compagnie Internationale de Consultation Education et Media. New York: John Wiley & Sons, 1998.

Bloom, Carole. *All About Chocolate: The Ultimate Resource for the World's Favorite Food.* New York: Macmillan, 1998.

——. *The Essential Baker: The Comprehensive Guide to Baking with Chocolate, Fruit, Nuts, Spices, and Other Ingredients.* Hoboken, NJ: John Wiley & Sons, 2007.

Boyle, Tish. *The Cake Book.* Hoboken, NJ: John Wiley & Sons, 2006.

Bradshaw, Lindsay John. *The Ultimate Book of Royal Icing.* London: Merehurst, 1992.

Braker, Flo. *Baking for All Occasions: A Treasury of Recipes for Everyday Celebrations.* San Francisco: Chronicle Books, 2008.

——. *The Simple Art of Perfect Baking.* Updated and revised. Shelburne, VT: Chapters Publishing, 1992.

——. *Sweet Miniatures: The Art of Making Bite-Size Desserts.* New York: William Morrow, 1991.

Braun, Margaret. *Cakewalk: Adventures in Sugar.* New York: Rizzoli, 2001.

Brown, Edward Espe. *The Tassajara Bread Book.* Boston & London: Shambala Publications, 1995.

Buys, Alain, and Jean-Luc Decluzeau. *Decorating with a Paper Cone.* Translated by Anne Sterling. Paris: Cicem S.A. and New York: John Wiley & Sons, 1996.

Clayton, Bernard, Jr. *Bernard Clayton's New Complete Book of Breads.* New York: Simon & Schuster, 1973, 1987.

——. *The Breads of France and How to Bake Them in Your Own Kitchen.* Indianapolis: Bobbs-Merrill, 1978.

Corriher, Shirley O. *BakeWise: The Hows and Whys of Successful Baking with Over 200 Magnificent Recipes*. New York: Scribner, 2008.

——. *CookWise: The Secrets of Cooking Revealed*. New York: William Morrow , 1997.

Crocker, Betty. *Betty Crocker's Cooky Book*. Facsimile edition. New York: Hungry Minds, 2002.

Dannenberg, Linda. *French Tarts: 50 Savory and Sweet Recipes*. New York: Artisan, 1997.

Desaulniers, Marcel. *Death by Chocolate: The Last Word on a Consuming Passion*. New York: Rizzoli, 1992.

Dodge, Jim, with Elaine Ratner. *The American Baker: Exquisite Desserts from the Pastry Chef of the Stanford Court*. New York: Simon & Schuster, 1987.

Field, Carol. *Focaccia: Simple Breads From the Italian Oven*. San Francisco: Chronicle Books, 1994.

Fleming, Claudia, with Melissa Clark. *The Last Course: The Desserts of Gramercy Tavern*. New York: Random House, 2001.

French Culinary Institute, and Judith Choate. *The Fundamental Techniques of Classic Pastry Arts*. New York: Stewart, Tabori & Chang, 2009.

Gisslen, Wayne. *Professional Baking*. New York: John Wiley & Sons, 1985.

——. *Professional Baking*. Fourth Edition. Hoboken, NJ: John Wiley & Sons, 2005.

Glezer, Maggie. *Artisan Baking Across America: The Breads, the Bakers, the Best Recipes*. New York: Artisan, 2000.

——. *A Blessing of Bread: Recipes and Rituals, Memories and Mitzvahs*. New York: Artisan, 2004.

Gourmet, editors of. *Gourmet's Best Desserts*. New York: Condé Nast Books, 1987.

Greenspan, Dorie. *Baking: From My Home to Yours*. Boston and New York: Houghton Mifflin, 2006.

——. *Baking with Julia: Savor the Joys of Baking with America's Best Bakers*. New York: William Morrow, 1996.

Greenstein, George. *Secrets of a Jewish Baker: Recipes for 125 Breads from Around the World*. Freedom, CA: Crossing Press, 1993.

Greweling, Peter P., CMB, and The Culinary Institute of America. *Chocolates and Confections: Formula, Theory, and Technique for the Artisan Confectioner*. Hoboken, NJ: John Wiley & Sons, 2007.

Hadda, Ceri. *Coffee Cakes: Crumb Cakes, Tea Breads, Pound Cakes, and Fresh Fruit Tortes—Simple Recipes for All Occasions*. New York: Simon & Schuster, 1992.

Hammelman, Jeffrey. *Bread: A Baker's Book of Techniques and Recipes*. Hoboken, NJ: John Wiley & Sons, 2004.

Hansen, Kaye, and Liv Hansen. *Christmas Cookies from the Whimsical Bakehouse*. New York: Clarkson Potter, 2005.

——. *Whimsical Bakehouse*. New York: Clarkson Potter, 2002.

Healy, Bruce, and Paul Bugat. *The Art of the Cake: Modern French Baking and Decorating*. New York: William Morrow, 1999.

Heatter, Maida. *Maida Heatter's Book of Great American Desserts*. New York: Alfred A. Knopf, 1983.

——. *Maida Heatter's Book of Great Desserts*. New York: Alfred A. Knopf, 1974.

Hermé, Pierre, and Dorie Greenspan. *Chocolate Desserts by Pierre Hermé*. Boston: Little, Brown, 2001.

——. *Desserts by Pierre Hermé*. Boston: Little, Brown, 1998.

Klivans, Elinor. *Bake and Freeze Chocolate Desserts*. New York: Broadway Books, 1997.

Laver, Norma. *The Art of Sugarcraft: Piping*. London: Merehurst Press, 1986.

Leader, Daniel, and Judith Blahnik. *Bread Alone: Bold Fresh Loaves from Your Own Hands*. New York: William Morrow, 1993.

——. with Lauren Chattman. *Local Breads: Sourdough and Whole-Grain Recipes from Europe's Best Artisan Bakers*. New York: W. W. Norton, 2007.

Lebovitz, David. *The Perfect Scoop: Ice Creams, Sorbets, Granitas, and Sweet Accompaniments*. Berkeley, CA: Ten Speed Press, 2007.

——. *Ripe for Dessert: 100 Outstanding Desserts with Fruit—Inside, Outside, Alongside*. New York: HarperCollins, 2003.

Lepard, Dan. *The Art of Handmade Bread: Contemporary European Recipes for the Home Baker*. London: Mitchell Beazley, 2007.

Levy, Faye. *Dessert Sensations: Fresh from France*. New York: Dutton, 1990.

Luchetti, Emily. *Classic Stars Desserts: Favorite Recipes by Emily Luchetti*. San Francisco: Chronicle Books, 2007.

McGee, Harold. *On Food and Cooking: The Science and Lure of the Kitchen*. New York: Charles Scribner's Sons, 1984.

Malgieri, Nick. *A Baker's Tour: Nick Malgieri's Favorite Baking Recipes from Around the World*. New York: HarperCollins, 2005.

——. *How to Bake: The Complete Guide to Perfect Cakes, Cookies, Pies, Tarts, Breads, Pizzas, Muffins, Sweet and Savory*. New York: HarperCollins, 1995.

——. *Perfect Cakes*. New York: HarperCollins, 2002.

Medrich, Alice. *Alice Medrich's Cookies and Brownies.* New York: Warner Books, 1999.

———. *Bittersweet: Recipes and Tales from a Life in Chocolate.* New York: Artisan, 2003.

———. *Pure Dessert: True Flavors, Inspiring Ingredients, and Simple Recipes.* New York: Artisan, 2007.

Ortiz, Gayle, and Joe Ortiz, with Louisa Beers. *The Village Baker's Wife: The Desserts and Pastries That Made Gayle's Famous.* Berkeley, CA: Ten Speed Press, 1997.

Ortiz, Joe. *The Village Baker: Classic Regional Breads from Europe and America.* Berkeley, CA: Ten Speed Press, 1993.

Patent, Greg. *A Baker's Odyssey: Celebrating Time-Honored Recipes from America's Rich Immigrant Heritage.* Hoboken, NJ: John Wiley & Sons, 2007.

———. *Baking in America.* Boston and New York: Houghton Mifflin, 2002.

Peck, Paula. *The Art of Fine Baking: Cakes and Pastries, Coffeecakes, Breads with a Continental Flavor.* New York: Simon & Schuster, 1961.

Pépin, Jacques. *La Methode.* New York: Times Books, 1979.

———. *La Technique.* New York: Pocket Books, 1976.

Peters, Colette. *Cakes to Dream On: A Master Class in Decorating.* Hoboken, NJ: John Wiley & Sons, 2005.

Peterson, James. *Baking.* Berkeley, CA: Ten Speed Press, 2009.

Purdy, Susan G. *A Piece of Cake.* New York: Atheneum, 1989.

Reinhart, Peter. *The Bread Baker's Apprentice: Mastering the Art of Extraordinary Bread.* Berkeley, CA: Ten Speed Press, 2001.

———. *Crust and Crumb: Master Formulas for Serious Bread Bakers.* Berkeley, CA: Ten Speed Press, 1998.

Rosenberg, Judy, with Nan Levinson. *Rosie's Bakery All-Butter, Fresh Cream, Sugar-Packed, No-Holds-Barred Baking Book.* New York: Workman Publishing, 1991.

Rubin, Maury. *Book of Tarts: Form, Function, and Flavor at the City Bakery.* New York: William Morrow, 1995.

Sanchez, Maria Bruscino. *Sweet Maria's Cake Kitchen: Classic and Casual Recipes for Cookies, Cakes, Pastry, and Other Favorites.* New York: St. Martin's Griffin, 1998.

Scherber, Amy, and Toy Kim Dupree. *Amy's Bread: Artisan-Style Breads, Sandwiches, Pizzas, and More from New York City's Favorite Bakery.* New York: William Morrow, 1996.

Shere, Lindsey Remolif. *Chez Panisse Desserts.* New York: Random House, 1985.

Silverton, Nancy, with Heidi Yorkshire. *Desserts by Nancy Silverton.* New York: Harper & Row, 1986.

———. *Nancy Silverton's Breads from the La Brea Bakery.* New York: Villard Books, 1996.

Sutton, Judith. *Sweet Gratitude: Bake a Thank-You for the Really Important People in Your Life.* New York: Artisan, 2005.

Thompson, Sylvia. *The Birthday Cake Book.* San Francisco: Chronicle Books, 1993.

Villas, James. *Biscuit Bliss: 101 Foolproof Recipes for Fresh and Fluffy Biscuits in Just Minutes.* Boston: Harvard Common Press, 2004.

Walter, Carole. *Great Cakes.* New York: Ballantine Books, 1991.

———. *Great Coffee Cakes, Sticky Buns, Muffins & More: 200 Anytime Treats and Special Sweets for Morning to Midnight.* New York: Clarkson Potter, 2007.

Welch, Adrienne. *Sweet Seduction: Chocolate Truffles.* New York: Harper & Row, 1984.

Willan, Anne. *Anne Willan's Look and Cook: Chocolate Desserts.* London and New York: Dorling Kindersley, 1992.

Wilson, Dede. *A Baker's Field Guide to Chocolate Chip Cookies.* Boston: Harvard Common Press, 2004.

Wolke, Robert L. *What Einstein Told His Cook: Kitchen Science Explained.* Reprint edition. New York: W. W. Norton, 2008.

Yockelson, Lisa. *Baking by Flavor.* New York: John Wiley & Sons, 2002.

———. *ChocolateChocolate.* Hoboken, NJ: John Wiley & Sons, 2005.

Periodicals

Yockelson, Lisa. "Brownies: A Memoir." *Gastronomica: The Journal of Food and Culture.* Berkeley: University of California Press, Winter 2002, Volume 2, Number 1, 84–88.

———. "Fruitcake Without Remorse." *Gastronomica: The Journal of Food and Culture.* Berkeley: University of California Press, Fall 2007, Volume 7, Number 4, 61–63.

———. "The Gentle Rise of (Real) Cake." *Gastronomica: The Journal of Food and Culture.* Berkeley: University of California Press, Summer 2004, Volume 4, Number 3, 75–77.

———. "In Pursuit of the Cream Waffle." *Gastronomica: The Journal of Food and Culture.* Berkeley: University of California Press, Winter 2006, Volume 6, Number 1, 60–61.

bakingStyleIndex

*Page numbers in italics indicate photographs;
n indicates notes section*